Marketing in Management

Basic Principles

Mike Worsam
D Berkeley Wright

PITMAN
PUBLISHING

PITMAN PUBLISHING
128 Long Acre, London WC2E 9AN

A Division of Pearson Professional Limited

First published in Great Britain in 1995

British Library Cataloguing in Publication Data
A CIP catalogue record for this book can be obtained from the British Library

ISBN 0 273 60736 7

10 9 8 7 6 5 4 3 2 1

Illustrations on pages 5, 6, 10, 44, 51, 69, 121, 153, 265 and 442 by Colin E Swan.

Typeset by 🅐 Tek-Art, Croydon, Surrey
Printed and bound in Singapore

The Publishers' policy is to use paper manufactured from sustainable forests.

CONTENTS

SCENARIOS

LIST OF FIGURES

AN INTRODUCTION FOR STUDENTS

Welcome to this book. You are probably wondering whether it is going to be of value to you, so try asking yourself these questions:

- Do I need to know about marketing management?
- Do I want to enjoy finding out about management?
- Do I need the maximum of practical help?
- Do I like plenty of illustrations?
- Do I value chapter summaries?
- Do I value a helpful index?
- Do I like self-checks that give answers?

If you answered yes to all or most of these questions then you will learn from this book – and enjoy and value it at the same time.

TEXTBOOKS NEED NOT BE DIFFICULT

Something as exciting as management should not be difficult. There is no need for management textbooks to be boring, or use difficult language – learning should be enjoyable. To some extent everybody has to manage – it is a part of life that should be as normal as breathing. We have people to relate to, decisions to make, responsibilities to welcome, challenges to overcome. So do managers. To be a good manager – of anything – requires certain skills, understanding and practice.

To an extent we all have management capability – but management is a learned skill which improves with understanding and practice. It is necessary to learn how to manage effectively.

LEARNING

Managers need to learn in order to improve their understanding and skills. This learning can be 'on the job' (where you learn by your own mistakes), or away from the job. Obviously it is better to learn where mistakes do not affect your work or harm other people.

In this book you will meet over 30 managers who will help you to master the practical skills of management. The skills you will need to be a good manager are covered one by one, and you will see why each is needed and how it is used. Learning must be worthwhile, clear in purpose and enjoyable. In this way learning is not hard work; and who wants to work harder than they need?

Many people struggle to cope with facts and information and then find that they can only remember part of what they have learned. However, we all remember what is important to us and what we can *use*. Understanding and Use (The 'Double U' principle) are the two keys to effective learning. If you fail to understand you will not be able to remember (why should you?). If you do not find a use for learning you will automatically treat it as unimportant.

The Double U principle of Understanding and Use underpins effective learning. This book will help you to understand and to use the skills employed by a successful manager.

BENEFITS

In more formal language, we can say that the major benefits you will gain from this book are:

- an insight into marketing management at work
- an appreciation of the benefits that management techniques offer to marketers
- an introduction to the key management tools
- an understanding of key management theories
- the ability to pass your examination.

SCENARIOS

Each new topic covered in this book opens with a *scenario* that describes a situation faced by a manager at work and as you read you will be able to picture the management situation. You will learn faster and more completely if you pretend that you are actually a part of the scenario – in management education this is called 'putting yourself into role'. Doing this will enable you to see why action is needed, and how a manager thinks and works to achieve objectives and planned results.

In the first scenario Charles and Joshua find that it isn't quite as easy to operate a mobile shop as they thought; later in the book you will help Bob James set up an airline. You will become involved in a desperate effort to get an injured rugby player to hospital. You will work alongside a brand manager in a global company, and discover why Mrs Long received a brand new electric oven, and why the managing director was furious. From these and 31 other scenarios you will come to understand the principles of marketing in management.

SELF-CHECKS

As self-checks you will find both work- and school or college- based assignments at the end of each Chapter. Suggested answers are at the end of each Part. You decide which assignments to tackle – both will help you to prepare for your examinations:

- Work-based assignments
  These are designed for those who are already working – not necessarily in marketing, but who are able to apply newly learned skills at work.
- School or college-based assignments
  For students who intend to get a job in marketing at some future date.

YOUR CAREER

Marketing is an excellent place to start a career in management. All marketers are managers – even the most junior marketing person has responsibilities and takes decisions, and marketers are often involved with every aspect of an organisation's activities. Success in marketing opens major career opportunities. Success in marketing plus a formal qualification opens senior management career opportunities.

Membership of professional bodies is very helpful, especially to younger managers and those just starting out on their careers. The benefits are considerable in terms of getting formal and informal help from senior people who have made their way along exactly the same route as you are taking, and have faced the same problems and taken advantage of similar opportunities.

For many, the London Chamber of Commerce and Industry Examination Board's examinations open the way into professional bodies such as the Chartered Institute of Marketing and/or the Institute of Management. Others are able to make a direct entry to professional examinations. No matter which route you choose, this book provides the necessary foundation in management.

In the interests of clear communication, the masculine pronoun is used unless there is clear reason to do otherwise. This stems solely from a desire for clarity and to avoid ugly and cumbersome language. No discrimination, prejudice or bias is intended.

Enjoy this book, benefit from the immediate improvements you will notice in your everyday relationships, and profit from the career opportunities that your studies will open up for you.

MW
September 1994

ACKNOWLEDGEMENTS

Writing a book such as this occupies many months, and one experiences the peaks of success when a section goes well, and the depths of frustration when the words won't come.

The immediate family suffers most when an author struggles, but we both enjoyed such unstinting support from our families – and notably from our wives – that their major contribution must be gratefully acknowledged above all others. Thank you.

The words must be generated from somewhere and we have drawn extensively from the published and unpublished work of many others. Due acknowledgement is given, as appropriate, for copyright material . . . but much has been developed from close association with other authors, tutors, students and publishers. These contacts have ranged from a flash of insight when working with a student to an ongoing relationship which has endured for many years. It is not possible to tie down the specific assistance, pointers, criticisms and encouragements, but we are very grateful for them.

Most of the scenarios in this book are 'faction' (fact-based fiction) and have been created to be enjoyable, instructive in themselves and to lead into each Chapter. We are particularly grateful to Captain Graham Brown and Paul Lockwood for sharing their expertise, to the staff of Havant Borough Council for research data and advice and to over a thousand entrepreneurs in new business start-ups.

Colin Swan deserves a special mention. This is the first book he has illustrated and he immediately demonstrated the classic responses so necessary to marketing success . . . he accepted the job, quibbled about the fee, complained about the deadline . . . and then met his deadlines, accepted the need for minor corrections, handled authors' requests for changes, and has now gone freelance. Thanks, Colin. Thanks, also, to Michael Hobson, BSc, for his original artwork on the carpenter's toolbox.

Pitman Publishing have shown their faith in the concept, and trusted us to get it done. We are grateful in particular to Simon Lake for his overall support, to Keith Stanley for publishing and contractual issues and to Lisa Howard who has put it all together and produced the final result.

Every effort has been made to trace and acknowledge ownership of copyright. The publishers will be glad to hear from any copyright holders whom it has not been possible to contact.

Despite all the support, we probably have allowed some errors to get through. If so, we are sorry and we hope everyone will understand. Above all, though, we hope that we have provided a focused effort which brings a wide range of knowledge and skills together to the benefit of students – who are the future marketers and managers upon whom we shall all depend.

MW, DBW
September 1994

GLOSSARY OF ACRONYMS

3As	Awareness, Attitude, Action
4Ps	Product, Place, Price, Promotion
ACD	Automatic Call Distribution
ACORN	A Classification of Residential Neighbourhoods
AIDA	Attention, Interest, Desire, Action
ANA	Article Number Association
ASEAN	Association of South East Asian Nations
BARB	British Audience Research Board
BCG	Boston Consulting Group
BFA	British Franchise Association
BIFA	British International Freight Association
BM	Brand Manager
BMRB	British Marketing Research Bureau
BOTB	British Overseas Trade Board
BSI	British Standards Institute
CATS	Cost, Accuracy, Time, Security
CE	Chief Executive
CEO	Chief Executive Officer
CIF	Carriage Insurance and Freight
CIM	Chartered Institute of Marketing
CIVR	Computer Integrated Voice Response
CLI	Calling Line Identification
CoD	Channel of Distribution
CSF	Critical Success Factor
CTN	Confectioner, Tobacconist, Newsagent
DAGMAR	Defining Advertising Goals for Measured Advertising Results
DDI	Direct Dial Identification
DMP	Decision-Making Process
DMU	Decision-Making Unit (See SPADE/F)
DP	Decision Process
DTI	Department of Trade and Industry
EC	European Commission (*not* European Community)
ECGD	Export Credit Guarantee Department
ECU	European Currency Unit
EDI	Electronic Data Interchange

EDIFACT	Electronic Data Interchange for Administration and Transport
EEA	European Economic Area
EFTA	European Free Trade Association
EFTPOS	Electronic Funds Transfer at Point of Sale
EMC	Export Management Company
EPOS	Electronic Point of Sale
ERM	Exchange Rate Mechanism
EU	European Union
FAS	Free Alongside Ship
FIFO	First In, First Out
FMCG	Fast Moving Consumer Goods
FOB	Free on Board
FOR	Free on Rail
GATS	General Agreement on Trade in Services
GATT	General Agreement on Tariffs and Trade
GBM	Group Brand Manager
GIGO	Garbage In, Garbage Out
GP	Gross Profit
HLRS	Higher Level Response Set
ICR	Intelligent Call Routing
IFA	International Franchise Association
IFF	Identification Friend or Foe
IT	Information Technology
JIT	Just in Time
LCCI	London Chamber of Commerce and Industry
LILO	Last In, Last Out
MBE	Management by Exception
MBO	Management by Objectives
MD	Managing Director
MFN	Most Favoured Nation
MIS	Management Information System
MkIS	Marketing Information System
MNC	Multinational Company
MOST	Mission, Objectives, Strategies, Tactics
MR	Marketing Research
MTT	Minimum Total Transactions
NPD	New Product Development
OECD	Organisation for Economic Co-operation and Development
PAT	Profit after tax
PBT	Profit before tax

PDM	Physical Distribution Management
PEST	Political, Economic, Social and Technological (See STEEPLE)
PIMS	Profit Impact of Management Strategy
PLC	Product Life Cycle
PoP	Point of Purchase
PoS	Point of Sale
PoU	Point of Use
PR	Public Relations
R & D	Research & Development
ROCE	Return on Capital Employed (same as ROI)
ROI	Return on Investment (same as ROCE)
SBU	Strategic Business Unit
SCM	Supply Chain Management
SEM	Single European Market
SITPRO	Simpler Trades Procedures Board
SLEPT	Social, Legal, Economic, Political, Technological (See STEEPLE)
SPADE/F	Starter, Purchaser, Adviser, Decider, End-User/Financier
STEEPLE	Social/Cultural; Technological; Economic and Market; Education, Training, Employment; Political; Legal; Environmental (see PEST and SLEPT)
SWOT	Strengths, Weaknesses, Opportunities, Threats
TEDIS	Trade Electronic Data Interchange System
TGI	Target Group Index
TQM	Total Quality Management
USFTA	United States Free Trade Association
VAT	Value Added Tax

PART 1

Marketing management –
the focus

In this part you will discover that marketing is a very important part of any organisation. Whatever the aim, from cash profit to health care, marketing has an important job to do.

Marketing has a major role to play in contact with customers, clients and consumers, just as production has a major role in actually making goods and purchasing has in negotiating for the best terms when buying for the organisation. Each of the 'functions' of an organisation – finance, personnel, production, distribution, purchasing, marketing – has a 'tactical' job to do.

Management involves 'strategic' as well as 'tactical' issues. It has to provide a direction for the organisation, a long-term plan. It has to co-ordinate everybody's efforts so that all pull in the same direction. It has to measure results against plan so it knows what has been achieved, and what is left to do. Managers have to provide leadership.

Each of the functions in an organisation has to continually justify its existence because our environment is constantly changing. Before marketing proved its worth most organisations had an advertising and a sales department. Now public relations, a part of marketing, is important enough for some

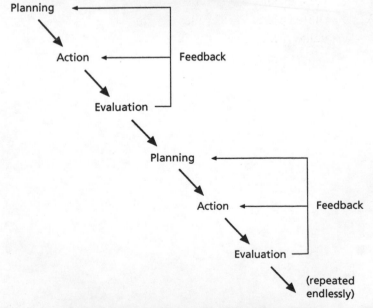

Fig. 0.1 Management is a never-ending series of planning action and evaluation

organisations to set it up as a separate department. As managers we have to be alert to provide what is actually needed rather than what we have always provided.

Change is natural. To stay competitive, whatever the organisation, requires alert management who are not afraid to take stock of a situation, carefully evaluate the options and then take firm decisions. They have to communicate their strategic decisions to those who will implement them. They must also ensure that there is motivation to succeed.

Tactical action follows the strategic guidelines and management must monitor results, praise those doing well, support those having problems, co-ordinate the activity. Finally, in the next planning session, management must take into account how results have worked out compared with the plan.

CHAPTER 1

What marketing does

Charles and Joshua had worked very hard for over three years without any time off except for national holidays. Even then they were careful not to go far, and to cut back on luxuries. Everything they could save went into a special bank account.

Two years ago they had enough to buy a second-hand van and equip it as a mobile shop. They cut a serving hatch in the side, put in shelves, a counter, a cash register and had it professionally painted in pale blue with a dark blue motif. They decided to wear black trainers, dark blue slacks with black leather belts, and pale blue open necked shirts with short sleeves. The whole outfit looked very smart.

On day one they were at the market by 04.00 a.m. and selected a whole range of prime stock; vegetables picked that morning, local fruits that were in season and a small quantity of imported fruits. They also bought a case of fresh eggs that were on special offer. Then they went to the cash and carry wholesaler to stock up with their dry goods. Cans of milk, jars of coffee, bottles of sauces – everything that a household should need.

A quick breakfast and they were ready to start trading . . . they were so excited . . . three years of effort was about to pay off.

Unfortunately by the end of their first day they were not so excited. They had served only 21 customers, despite covering over 70 miles and knocking on more doors than they could count. Still, they figured, it was the first day. it would be better tomorrow.

It wasn't.

On day two they tried to cover their route again, but found that a street market slowed them down, and prevented them reaching many of the streets they had visited the day before. Tired at the end of the day they found that their takings covered the costs of their petrol, but that they had to throw away almost a quarter of their fresh stock!

Day three saw them at the market again and they set off re-stocked and with fresh confidence. Again they managed to cover their petrol costs, but lost more stock through deterioration. The rest of the week was much the same and after six days they found that they were losing money so fast that they could not survive more than another two weeks! Something had to be done, and quickly.

They took action and two years later each has his own van, with an assistant, and they are expecting to add two more vans within 3 months.

What do you think they did to turn a potential disaster into a triumph?

Table 1.1 What they did and why they did it

What they did	Why they did it
1 Thought about the situation. What was happening, what was good, what bad	To be able to make decisions based on facts before their money ran out.
2 Stopped trading.	To gain time to rethink their plans, and to prevent further losses in the meantime.
3 Took all their fresh stock off the van. Kept what they could use themselves and sold the rest at give-away prices.	It was better to salvage what they could from the fresh stock, which goes bad. Cans and bottles hold their value.
4 Analysed where their trade had come from. Which areas and which type of customer.	To help them plan their daily journey so that they only visited areas where their type of customer lived.
5 Analysed what had been bought – and what had been commented on as good or bad about their service. Also, what people had said they actually wanted from them.	To help them buy goods that meet the needs of their customers.
6 Plotted on a map the locations of shops within the area they intended to serve, and matched shop location with customer area.	To see that they avoided areas well served already.
7 Discovered what goods were carried by shops – and at what prices – in areas similar to the areas in which they had done well.	To see what must be carried, and which items were unlikely to be popular.
8 Prepared a detailed stock list of items they should carry.	So that they had a balanced stock, at the right quality and price.
9 Set their prices.	To meet needs of customers, and to make it simple for themselves. They pre-bagged fruit and vegetables at standard prices for simplicity, speed and to indicate value.
10 Worked out a route, with target times to arrive and leave each major location.	So they could be regular and customers would learn to trust them to arrive each day.
11 Designed simple leaflets, had them professionally printed and sent their younger brothers and sisters out to deliver them at homes one day before they were scheduled to be in the area.	So potential customers would know what they were offering, and when to expect them to arrive.
12 Re-stocked with fresh goods at minimum level.	To minimise potential loss. (They accepted they would sell out, but that they would quickly gain experience and not to lose money was the priority.)
13 Followed their plans.	Because a plan is made to be followed, not ignored!
14 Visited a selection of their customers to ask how good they thought the service was, and what could be done to improve.	To confirm that they had understood and were providing what was wanted. To get ideas for improvement.

Fig. 1.1 Marketing – the bridge to the customer

What Charles and Joshua did was to adopt the marketing concept. They thought about what customers were available, and what they wanted. Then they set about providing for the actual needs of their 'target' customers. They were successful because they found out what was needed, and then supplied those needs.

As we progress through the book we shall take a careful look at exactly how to manage marketing to earn profits. For now let us think about what we actually mean by 'marketing'.

Marketing has been described as the bridge with the customer and consumer – the bridge over which information and cash flows in and communications and products flow out.

Markham, a British advertising executive, says that marketing's job is to discover, create, arouse and satisfy consumer needs.

DISCOVER   Social

A marketer has to check exactly what people want and what they will pay for. There is no point in offering something that is not wanted. So a marketer has to research to find what people want, and if there are enough people to justify satisfying the demand. He also has to find a way to communicate with the people who have the need, and a way to get the goods through to them.

He has to do all this, in outline, first. (Charles and Joshua learned this the hard way.)

CREATE

Whatever is needed has to be created – perhaps from a totally new design, perhaps by adapting an existing product. Charles and Joshua as retailers could choose what to buy, and they had to choose the type of goods and the quality of goods that their 'target' customers wanted.

AROUSE

Knowing where the customers are, and having the right goods is not enough! The customer's interest and desire have to be aroused. This means some form of 'promotion' – advertising, special prices and good salesmanship in Charles and Joshua's case. Their mobile shop was already attractive, and their uniforms neat and clean, and so they had understood the importance of presentation. Now they had to price their goods at the correct level and let their potential customers know they were good people to shop with.

SATISFY

Customer requirements have to be satisfied. Therefore there is need to check after supply as well as before. Researching market needs is an on-going activity.

Charles learned a valuable lesson on their second day. A little lad had come out with a message from his mother. He was to buy a tin of peas for their dinner. Unfortunately Charles had sold out of peas and offered the boy a tin of beans instead.

The mother came storming out after him down the road and demanded her money back: 'When I want beans I'll say so. Don't you ever take advantage of my child again!' The mother was the 'decider'; the one who controlled the purchase. The boy was simply the purchaser, without the power to change a decision.

What Charles learned was that behind every purchase is a decision-making unit.

The decision-making unit (DMU) is made up of six factors which can easily be remembered as a 'SPADE in a FERTILIZER':

Fig. 1.2 'SPADE in Fertilizer'

S	Starter	A person, or thing, which triggers a purchase decision. It might be Charles and Joshua's van appearing in the street, an advert on TV, a nearly empty jar in the larder.
P	Purchaser	The person who actually buys the product.
A	Adviser	A person, or anything else, which gives advice or recommendation. A neighbour, perhaps; or past experience 'that's a good brand'. Charles and Joshua can be advisers to their customers and if honest will come to be trusted.
D	Decider	The person who decides to purchase. There will always be only one who decides. On a huge purchase there may be one or several committees, but the final decision will always be made by one person.
E	End-user	The person who uses the product.
F	Finance	The money, or credit, that allows a purchase to be made.

Obviously a single person can start a purchase decision, Advise himself, Decide to buy, Purchase using his own Finance and then be the End-user. Whenever you make a purchase all six roles are carried out by someone – this is inevitable.

A professional manager of marketing researches the DMU for every purchase and plans to trigger a Start, encourage a Decision through Advice and encouragement, make it easy to Purchase by having the goods close to the purchaser and satisfy the Financial need by setting an acceptable price and/or offering credit. End-use is encouraged through devices such as easy opening packs and special promotions inside the packs. Finance enables sales.

CUSTOMERS AND CONSUMERS

A customer is one who buy; a consumer is one who consumes. A problem is that many careless marketers use either customer or consumer to mean both! We have to be very careful to say what we mean because the difference is important.

A customer is motivated by simplicity and by profit. A customer is concerned to move goods down the 'channel of distribution' as easily as possible so that profits are earned. Obviously he will be concerned to sell goods that are of an acceptable quality but he will tend to regard products as 'boxes on the shelf' that contain goods that others want to buy. Provided they are legal, safe, fast moving and profitable he has little other direct interest.

A consumer is concerned with the product in use. He relies on the purchase to do what he bought it for and so is motivated by the value in use. (We shall look at the difference between value and price in Chapter 30).

In many cases a consumer has only advisory involvement in a purchase:

1 A young child eats what his mother gives him. If he doesn't like it the mother may find it easier to change brands, but it is her decision.

Manufacturer	Customer
Wholesaler	Customer
Retailer	Customer
Housewife	Customer
Child	Consumer

Fig. 1.3 Channel of distribution

2 A workman uses the tools bought by his company. He may prefer a different make or model, but can only ask that it be provided. He does not have the power of decision.

In some cases, of course, a consumer is also a customer. When you buy a hamburger for your lunch you are both a customer and a consumer.

You will sometimes see 'final consumer' or 'ultimate consumer' used to describe the person who uses up the product. This is not necessary if you are careful in your use of language.

The marketing manager has a range of tools to help him do his job, just as any other professional. The only difference is that a marketing manager's tools are intellectual rather than physical.

Tools can always be grouped, subgrouped and subsubgrouped:

1 *A carpenter's tools* group and subgroup as shown in Fig. 1.4. Each tool group has a specific purpose, and the tools within the group enable specialised work to be done efficiently.

2 *The marketing toolbox.* A marketer has six major tool categories. Each of these subgroups into fine detail, as we shall see later:

Topic	Covered in Chapter
Planning	4
Research	8–11
Product	23
Price	29
Place	25
Promotion	30, 31.

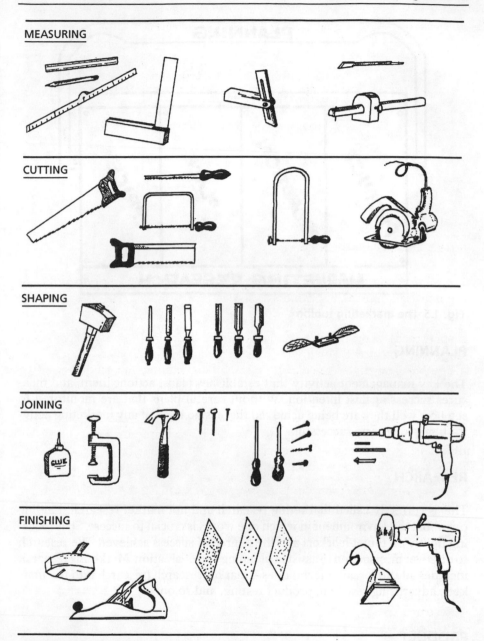

Fig. 1.4 A carpenter's tools
Artist: M. Hobson

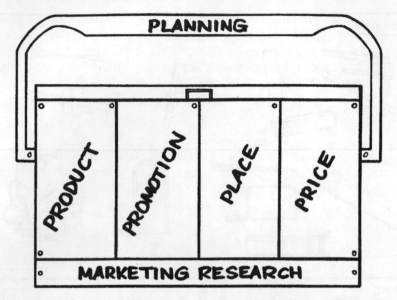

Fig. 1.5 The marketing toolbox

PLANNING

The key management activity that establishes plans, actions them, and measures success against intention. Without careful plans that are monitored to see how well they are being achieved there is no hope of any marketing activity being long-term successful.

RESEARCH

This is correctly called marketing research and not market research. Finding out about the environment in which one works is crucial to success. So is focusing tightly on target markets and the degree of success achieved. We research to discover information to assist in planning and evaluation. Marketing research includes all the research techniques – market research (research into the market), advertising research, product testing, and so on.

PRODUCT

Everything to do with what an organisation offers to its clients is known as a product. It is made up of three elements:

- *Physical* – the tangibility. For example, molten glass is formed into a glass tumbler. In time the tumbler is re-cycled, perhaps into a bottle.
- *Functional* – the use(s) for the product. For example, a tumbler can be drunk from, it can hold pens and pencils on a desk, be used as a makeshift sugar bowl.

- *Symbolic* – the emotional or psychological meaning carried by the product. For example, glasses may be given in a set as a wedding present, or they may carry a favourite drink's logo (Coca-Cola, Pepsi, Stella Artois, Guinness, etc.). We shall see that the symbolic aspect is by far the most important factor in most purchase decisions.

Note: A service differs from a product because it has no physical presence. It is intangible, e.g. a haircut, a fax bureau, classified advertisements in a local newspaper.

There is a 'grey area' between product and service when a tangible product is offered but the quality of the offer differs. The same can of motor oil (a product) acquires a different degree of 'added value' service when it is:

- bought off the shelf in a supermarket;
- bought in a filling station;
- put into your engine by a forecourt attendant;
- selected for you, and put into the engine, by a smiling and helpful forecourt attendant.

We shall follow marketing convention and use product and 'product offering', to include services. Thus, when you see 'product' in this book read it to mean 'product or service', unless we specifically refer to a service.

PROMOTION

Persuasive communication with customers and/or consumers. The main tools are public relations, advertising, sales promotion and the sales force. We must always remember that our promotional messages must reach our target customers and consumers and so media availability must be taken into account before selecting distribution channels.

PLACE

The routes, 'channels of distribution', through which the product moves to reach its customers and consumers.

PRICE

The sum total of what is actually paid for the product after allowances and discounts have been deducted and taxes and credit charges added. Price and value are different, as has been said. We shall explain in Chapter 29.

THE MARKETING MIX

The marketing mix is made up of the four Ps (product, price, place and promotion). The four Ps allow day-to-day 'operational' or 'tactical' plans to be made. Some authors have developed as many as 22 elements within the marketing mix, but we feel these are better subgrouped under the four Ps, as you will see in Parts 7 and 8.

PACKAGING

The way that a product is packed is becoming a very important element of product, and of promotion. This is partly because of the impact of self-service stores, where each product has to sell itself off the shelf; partly because of legal and security requirements to protect the contents and partly because consumers are demanding ever higher standards of environmental friendliness.

A package is physically part of the P of product but also provides a valuable asset to the P of promotion. (Products carry promotional messages, whether they are on a shelf in the supermarket or at home, in use by professional workmen in the street, or seen being used by characters in a film or on TV.)

KEY POINT SUMMARY

- Marketing management is a continual process of planning, action and evaluation.
- The main function is to bridge between producer and customer or consumer.
- Marketing activities discover, create, arouse and satisfy needs.
- Definitions of marketing :

  Marketing is the management process responsible for identifying, anticipating and satisfying customer requirements profitably. (The Chartered Institute of Marketing)

  The key to achieving organisational goals consists in determining the needs and wants of target markets and delivering the desired satisfactions more efficiently and effectively than competitors. (Kotler, P)

  The aim of marketing is to know and understand the customer so well that the product or service fits him and sells itself. (Drucker, Peter F.)

- Marketing is a management function founded on research and analysis of customer needs.
- Marketing is used to forecast and predict change.
- It brings to market goods in demand at the right price and place for the ultimate benefit of the consumer and profit to the company.
- The core concept for Kotler is 'societal'. This covers the satisfying of needs and wants, providing satisfaction through value and yielding utility through competitive exchange transactions.
- Marketing is a set of customer- and consumer-driven functions.
- The nature of marketing is the exchange process between buyers and sellers. This includes goods, services, technologies, business systems, informa-

tion, concepts and ideas, plus the interchange of skilled professional managers.

- The DMU has six factors – "SPADE-F" – starter, purchaser, adviser, decider, end-user and the essential factor, finance.
- A customer is one motivated by profit and concerned with quality, safety and the availability of goods through the channels of distribution.
- A consumer is concerned with value and the use of a product.
- The marketing manager uses a set of tools consisting of planning, research, product, promotion, place and price.
- The combination and application of these tools to short-term tactical marketing situations is the four Ps, or marketing mix.

WORK-BASED SELF-ASSESSMENT QUESTIONS

1 Using practical examples and illustrations from your working environment, define and explain marketing.

2 Briefly explain the marketing concept with reference to your workplace.

SCHOOL- OR COLLEGE-BASED SELF-ASSESSMENT QUESTIONS

1 Define the main role and functions of a marketing manager.

2 Distinguish the differences between serving a customer and marketing products to consumers.

See the end of Chapter 4 for answer guidelines.

CHAPTER 2

What management does

John, Jean and Jacqueline all report to the same manager, Christine. John is responsible for sales in the southern region, Jean for the midlands and Jacqueline for the north. Each has five sales people reporting to them. Each visits Christine in turn as plans for the next sales promotional budget are being finalised:

- John asks for 45% of the budget on the grounds that his team have 45% of company sales revenue.
- Jean asks for 50% because her region has the greatest potential to increase sales and John, in particular, is well established and needs less support.
- Jacqueline wants 35% of the budget because she produces 30% of profits and has potential to increase this.

Christine has a limited budget, and wants to hold 10% as a contingency reserve. The basis problem, therefore, is in allocating the budget,

$$45 + 50 + 35 + 10 = 140\%!$$

Secondary problems are in motivating the team to accept the decision and in their motivation of the salespeople to achieve the needed results.

Christine knows that management's primary job is to take decisions. Of all the possible management traits the ability and willingness to take decisions rates highest in the opinion of senior managers. It is also necessary to hold the team together, because total sales results have to reach budget. One demotivated sales area will have disastrous effects on results and on morale in the other areas.

How Christine decides to allocate budget between the claims we shall come to later in the book. For now let us see what happens when the decision is made.

The decision

Region	Budget (%)
South	30
Midlands	35
North	30
Reserve	5
	100%

Christine ponders the figures. How does she communicate the decision to the team?

It is important to achieve the following:

- acceptance of the decision;
- commitment to achieve budgeted results;
- confidence to subdivide the budget across the salespeople's area;
- firmness, without rigidity, in dealing with individual salespeople.

The basic tasks of a manager are as follows:

- to make decisions to achieve results, keep team commitment, involve staff and make the future happen;
- to structure through corporate, strategic and operational objectives, around which decisions focus;
- to delegate authority for others to act, but not responsibility which resides with the manager;
- to motivate the team;
- to plan and set clear objectives for each member of the team;
- to analyse results and take appropriate action;
- to inform the team of situational problems;
- to take risks and hunt for alternative solutions;
- to select and implement action;
- finally, to control activities so that objectives are achieved to time, in terms of sales or results, quality and overall effectiveness.

These principles were put forward in 1911 by Frederick Winslow Taylor, an American engineer in the Midvale Steel Works, Philadelphia in his famous publication, *The Principles of Scientific Movement*. It was republished together with other works in 1947, as *Scientific Management*, by Harper & Brothers, New York. His key concepts were:

- use scientific methods rather than subjective guess-work;
- create an atmosphere of co-operation among workers;
- enable successful harmonisation of activities within groups;
- work for maximised output;
- develop worker potential for the benefit of the individual and the organisation.

Taylor, generally regarded as the father of scientific management, led a field of writers loosely termed 'management classicists', pioneering traditional management theory. He advocated harmony in the work place, planning responsibility and designing work systems to help workers achieve their potential.

Henry Fayol, a French industrial owner manager, is the originator of modern management theory. His monograph focused on six management activities:

1 technical – production
2 commercial – buying/selling
3 financial – optimum use of capital
4 security – property, persons
5 accounting – including statistics
6 managerial – planning, organising, command, co-ordination and control.

Henry Gantt, working with Taylor on incentive schemes, developed the charting system or bar charts known as Gantt charts, which ensure that programme goals are interlinked and allow company plans to be communicated in simple terms to all staff. The Gilbreths (husband and wife), he being a building contractor, worked on Taylor's ideas and studied the motions of work, reducing, for example, bricklayer's movements from 18 to 5 only.

Mary Parker Follett studied co-ordination and put forward four principles for cross-relations between departments, suggesting that the head should 'subordinate the good of his department to the good of the whole undertaking' and establishing the need for collective effort for future organisational effectiveness.

In the post-1930s human relations study developed with Hawthorne, Mayo and Roethlisberger. More recently sociologists and psychologists contributed several critical studies of human behaviour: Likert, Maslow, McGregor, Argyris, Tannenbaum and Herzberg.

In the 1970s and 1980s the training boards, polytechnics and universities assisted companies to develop systems of appraisal, analysis and quality circles, helping people to contribute with more commitment to the activities of management, and to benefit from a clearer understanding of their role, responsibility and value to the organisation.

We shall return to issues of organisational structure in Chapter 5.

John Adair has shown that a manager has three major areas of concern:

- to achieve the task.
- to keep the team together.
- to involve individuals to form the team (see Figure 2.1).

The task is important because that is the purpose for which all are employed, towards which all are striving. But task must never become more important than people, because the people make it happen. No people, no results!

Individual people make up a team and a team is stronger than a group of individuals. The term 'synergy' describes how strength comes from group efforts.

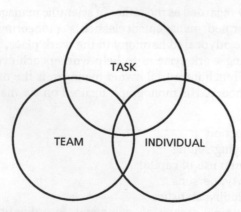

Fig. 2.1 Adair's model of leadership

Source: Reproduced, with permission, from Effective Team Building (1986), Gower Publishing Limited.

> Synergy: combined effects are greater than individual efforts. (A bundle of
> sticks is far stronger than the total strength of each individual stick.)

Therefore each individual must be made to feel important, that their contribution is useful and valued. Christine knows that the three Js are a good team, that they know a decision has to be made and, providing it is seen to be fair, it will be accepted.

Rosemary Stewart writes that a manager 'decides what should be done, and then gets other people to do it'. Falk says that management is 'getting things done through other people'.

Christine also knows that responsibility for achievement cannot be passed on to others. The full responsibility for success rests with the chief executive (CE), who will answer for all successes and any failures to the shareholders. The CE cannot do everything personally and so delegates to managers. In turn each manager knows that the task must be subdivided further and delegated to others.

Managers, therefore, accept delegation and then delegate in their turn. There is a clear line of responsibility running from the very top to the very bottom of every organisation. Every action taken at operational level combines with others to ensure that strategic and corporate objectives are met.

What can Christine delegate given that responsibility remains with the CE? What has been delegated to Christine?

- *Authority – power to act.* Christine is given the power to act on behalf of the person who delegated the authority. In turn this power can be delegated. Thus any person can be given authority to act, but the responsibility for

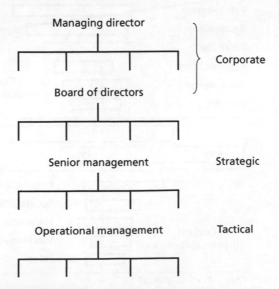

Fig. 2.2 Management hierarchy

action rests with the person who delegates the authority.
- *Accountability – an obligation to achieve.* Acceptance of delegation means that one accepts that results will be measured and that one is expected to achieve what has been delegated.

Christine knows that the three Js have accepted delegation. They are account-able for the results achieved in their regions. As their part of the deal they have said how much budget they need to achieve their plans. Christine can-not given them the budget for which they asked. It is necessary to help them understand why the decision has been made, and to help them achieve the necessary results with less than they asked for.

Christine knows that her manager will in turn hold him accountable for over-all sales results and so it is very good sense for her to help his team to achieve. Mutual self-interest is a great team motivator.

- *Motives* come from within. Motivation is a mental state which is particular to each individual.
- *Incentives* are external to individuals. They offer inducements to achieve. The best incentives link to motives. Thus the best managers discover what motivates team members and then tailor incentives to link to identified moti-vation.
- *Money* is not a direct motivator! People use money in different ways and so it is what people can do with money that motivates. (One may buy a ten-

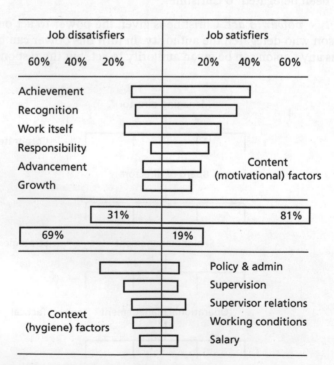

Fig. 2.3 Herzberg's motivation – hygiene theory

nis racket, another a CD player, a third may save towards a holiday, a fourth may pay the rent.) A good manager targets incentives to match motive. 'Achieve your budget, Bill, and you can have that new CD player.'

Often the best incentives are not financial! Praise is a great motivator, and so is pleasure in a job well done. Herzberg investigated the motivators and hygiene factors that impact upon people in work. His studies show that people are highly motivated by intangibles. Salary increases are soon absorbed and forgotten. Work conditions are taken for granted – they are necessary and must be provided.

Christine knows that it is not her job to go out and get the sales, nor is it her job to manage the sales teams on a daily basis. Her task is to unite her three managers into an effective team and to ensure that each is equipped to support and motivate the sales team as a whole. This does not mean she has no opinion! It does not mean she cannot go out to meet salespeople!

But she must route control through the regional managers so that they deal directly with their team. She would dislike her boss giving direct orders to any one of the three Js and must not fall into the leap-frog trap herself.

The *leap-frog trap* awaits all managers. Often an employee and a senior manager will have worked together for some time and built a relationship. Perhaps the manager worked alongside the employee for a time before being promoted. The friends may well meet socially, but both must be very careful that the relationship does not result in the employee seeming to leap-frog his immediate manager and talking business with the senior. This can only reduce the authority of the junior manager in the eyes of the team.

PLANNING THE MEETING

Christine has decided that she will bring the team together to announce her decision, explain the rationale and lead a planning session on how to achieve the expected results. She will not justify her decision.

She knows that each of the team will have asked for more than they actually expect to get. That is human nature. She also knows that they will not willingly admit this and so won't attempt to get them to do so. She believes, from experience, that there is scope for improved teamwork in each region and that the planned results can be achieved within the budgets. Finally she wants to achieve greater synergy across the country by taking the best practices from each region and introducing them to the others. The shortfall in budget expectation gives a perfect opportunity to introduce this as a mutually beneficial development.

She sets clear objectives for the meeting:

- It will start and finish on time – 10.00–12.30.
- The tone of discussion will be positive throughout.
- The three Js will individually and collectively accept the budget figures.
- Three specific areas for cross-region exchange will have been identified and the expected results quantified.

- Each cross-exchange area will have been delegated to a specific person for action within an agreed time scale.
- Individual planning and developmental sessions will have been set up with each of the three Js.

THE RESULTS

The three Js had indeed asked for more than they needed on the basis that their request was bound to be reduced. All were disappointed with the size of the reductions, but meeting as a team did ensure that all heard exactly the same explanation. There could be no concern that individuals meeting with Christine were given different explanations. The positive suggestion of sharing the best from each region at first met resistance, because none wanted to give away secrets of their success. Christine had an overview, however, and was able to give examples from each regions. When each J found that they would receive two ideas in exchange for one they came round quickly to the proposal.

The meeting quickly moved on to detailed planning for implementation, and a sales meeting was planned, with specific objectives, for each region.

All four went off at 12.30 for a team lunch, and were back at their desks working on implementation plans by 14.00.

MANAGEMENT

The organ of society specifically charged with making resources productive (Drucker).

Managers are the skeleton that holds an organisation together and give it shape and purpose. Just as different animals have purpose-built skeletons, so do organisations. The major difference is that an animal cannot change its shape from a dog to an ape, but an organisation can change over time. Whatever change is needed the basic need for a management 'skeleton" or structure remains.

A skeleton links all parts of an organisation and provides a structure along which nerves, muscles and blood vessels flow within the flesh protected by a tough skin. Very little of any animal is without a skeletal support, but some items needed temporarily can be altered in shape by muscular contraction and/or engorgement with blood. In just the same way an organisation can establish a short-term activity, but for long-term existence a management structure is needed.

Non-vertebrate animals are held together by a hard shell or tough outer skin. Ants have the potential to take over the world – there is little that humans could do against their determined and overwhelming power. They are prevented not by intelligence but by size. They have no skeleton and so cannot grow beyond a certain size. Thank goodness!

A major problem faced by an owner–entrepreneur with 'helpers' is to grow. Managers are needed and yet they may be too expensive in the short-term. If they can be afforded, a self-made businessman may experience difficulty in truly delegating. Yet without delegation no manager can operate effectively.

THE HIERARCHY

Structure is commonly shown as a hierarchy, with the chief executive at the top and the junior staff at the bottom. This is very helpful in expressing the 'chain of command' and it clearly shows where responsibility lies. Figure 2.4 shows a typical hierarchy today. Compare it with a Roman legion's table of organisation (Fig. 2.5). Can a military structure dating back to Roman times be right for today's management?

There is a need to move very fast today as technology, in particular, is forcing change on all aspects of society. In many organisations this need for rapid response has brought about a radical re-think of structure. No longer is it possible to take the time to communicate up and down a hierarchy. It is necessary to cut across directly, to bring teams together to handle projects, manage everyday affairs.

The hierarchy is still needed because it provides a structure that ensures

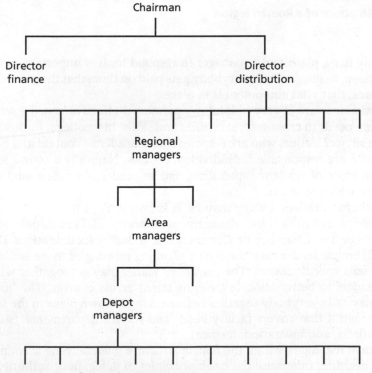

Fig. 2.4 Structure of a modern company

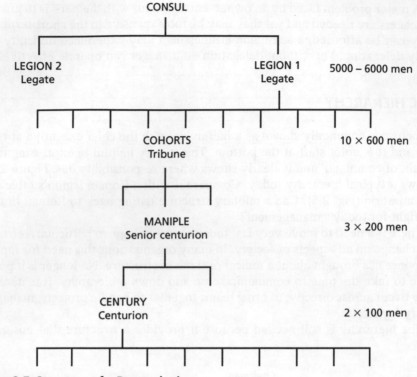

Fig. 2.5 Structure of a Roman legion

everybody has a place and a manager to respond to. It is important as a service function, to ensure that everybody gets paid on time, that there is enough office space, that vital equipment is in place.

A matrix structure is very helpful to operational effectiveness. To set up a matrix one needs to cross-reference roles and skills. In a college, for instance, there are subject leaders who are responsible for academic content and course leaders who are responsible for individual courses. Naturally a course leader needs a mixture of academic specialists, and an academic needs a mixture of courses on which to teach.

A matrix for a college faculty may be as shown in Fig 2.6.

Each designated person has management authority, and can initiate action. Thus the London Chamber of Commerce & Industry Examinations Board (LCCIEB) course leader may convene a planning meeting of those academics teaching on a specific course. The marketing leader may get together with all course leaders to better allocate teaching talent across courses. The head of faculty may call everybody together before taking his own place in the senior manager matrix that covers faculty heads and service departments, (such as student affairs, administration, finance).

Individual managers within the matrix structure must become accountable for each decision, otherwise the basic principles of delegation, authority and accountability are not followed.

Course Leaders	Subject leaders				
	Marketing	Management	Finance	Legal	. . .
LCCIEB					
CIM					
NVQ					
. . .					

Fig. 2.6 A college matrix management structure

DECISIONS

Decisions are the key to management success, yet many managers are afraid to make decisions in case they are wrong. The problem is that deciding to take no decision can be even more 'harmful' or 'wrong' than any other decision! Consider Table 2.1, which shows management ratings in terms of decision-making (Hatton, Roberts and Worsam).

Table 2.1

% correct decisions	Manager's performance
55	Reasonable
60–65	Good
65–70	Excellent
70–80	Superb
80+	Untruthful!

When tempted to do nothing remember that it takes a decision to take no decision!

Wrong decisions have to be accepted without shame, but corrected as quickly as possible. Information is vital and it must come to management very quickly so that results can be judged against intention. When results are not as expected, remedial action can be taken. (One reason why Christine kept a contingency reserve was so that she could provide additional funds, if and where needed.) We look at Management Information Systems in Chapter 7.)

THE DECISION-MAKING PROCESS (DMP)

The decision-making process consists of five basic steps:

1 define the problem;
2 analyse the situation;
3 identify possible courses of action;
4 establish decision criterion;
5 select a specific course of action.

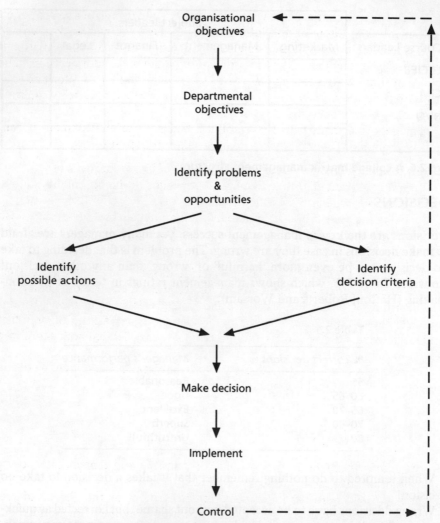

Fig. 2.7 The decision-making process

This is then followed by implementation of the decision and control of out-comes with feedback and corrective action to achieve targets.

You will find the SWOT tool to be extremely effective in the DMP process, as we shall see in Chapter 6.

PROBLEM DEFINITION

Information, not data, is required.

Information is extracted from data, because data is a set of facts which may or may not contain any useful information. A telephone directory is made up of data. We go through the data to find the actual numbers we need. Well structured data, like a telephone book, helps us to find the information we require.

Too many people confuse data with information – and drown in a sea of paper!

Your job is to discover the 'information gap' between what is known and what is needed in order to take an effective decision. Sufficient information is needed. Just enough to allow the problem to be defined and a decision to be made, in time, with a known degree of risk. Gathering extra information is costly in time and money and delays the decision. Rarely does delay improve the quality of any decision.

Managers can never wait for 'certainty' because the environment is constantly changing. The aim, therefore, is to take calculated risks.

* *Risk:* to take a chance where the probability of loss is known.
* *Gamble:* to take a chance with no pre-knowledge of the probability of loss. For example, when diving into a swimming pool
  Checking the pool-side markings reduces risk, going in feet first reduces risk further. Diving in head first, without pre-checking, assumes too much and is a major gamble.

As managers know they are taking calculated risks, they, and their bosses, should expect a degree of error. With practice and experience the good manager learns how to calculate risk more and more precisely, which is why junior managers have limited authority. The top managers blend intuition with fact and learn to trust their instincts, but this is not a recommended policy for those new into management!

The true test of management effectiveness is overall achievement – not the percentage of right and wrong decisions.

SITUATION ANALYSIS

Ensure that a problem has been defined accurately and that its satisfactory solution provides a means to a desired end.

There is need here for judgement, for assessment of the degree of risk involved. The costs must be calculated in terms of money, time and other resources. The degree of urgency must be determined.

ALTERNATIVE SOLUTIONS

Imagination and creativity are at a premium since as many solutions as possible need to be identified. It is dangerous to blindly follow established custom because this is predictable. By all means follow custom, especially when marketing a long-established product with an established market presence, but never do it without consideration of the options. True success comes from originality of thought. For an established product the originality may be in the promotion or the channels of distribution, rather than in the benefits package, but originality has a part to play.

It is essential to:

* establish decision criteria;

- identify alternatives;
- quantify each short-listed alternative.

DECISION CRITERIA

Management has to know what is within the organisational policy and what lies outside. Therefore, before developing alternative solutions it is necessary to exclude all those options that are not acceptable. Thus a manager will establish criteria such as the following:

A new product must:

- complement the existing products;
- use existing productive capacity;
- sell through existing channels of distribution;
- produce a profit (return on capital employed) of XX%

SELECT ACTION

Possible alternatives have to be examined so that the best are selected. There is seldom any clear cut obvious answer. The need is to select between a range of alternatives with good potential. Therefore it is certain that some decisions will be wrong. It is important to recognise that a 'wrong' decision only becomes obvious at a later date. At the time the decision was taken it best reflected all known facts.

The Beatles were refused by record companies, as was Barbra Streisand!

Key questions that help a manager at this stage are:

- Does the decision contribute toward achievement of stated objectives?
- Does it represent the maximum degree of economic effectiveness?
- Is it capable of execution?
- Are the results capable of measurement?

IMPLEMENTATION

It is crucial that the selected alternatives are expressed in decisions that are implemented in the spirit as well as the letter of the intention.

There is danger of:

- Bureaucratic institutions taking decisions, but failing to action them;
- Misinterpretation.

Unintentional misinterpretation can come from many sources. The most common is a simple failure in communication.

Intentional misinterpretation is usually based on arrogance, a distrust of the manager, or self-interest. Arrogant people feel they know best, whatever the situation. Those who distrust (or dislike) their manager may want to cause trouble for him. Self-interest ranges from sheer laziness through to a calculation that a failure may damage the organisation but provide kudos for the individual.

If a junior manager can achieve excellent short-term sales by intentionally misinterpreting a pricing decision, he may go ahead if he believes that he can use the immediate results to boost his promotional prospects. His successor can take responsibility for the losses that the organisation will incur!

Other dangers are:

- Non-acceptance by subordinates: for rational reasons.
- Irrational resistance.

We have to be careful when we use terms such as rational and irrational because rationality is subjective. What is rational to one person may appear totally irrational to another. What is clear logic to one may be confused thinking to another. Irrational resistance comes about, often unconsciously, when a person feels threatened, perhaps because of failure to understand the full implications of the plan.

To achieve wholehearted support it is essential to show individuals why it is beneficial to take required actions. People are reluctant to step blindly into the future. There is usually no requirement for a detailed explanation, but the key issues need to be brought out and dealt with effectively. If they are not, they will fester under the surface, sour relationships and endanger the implementation of the plan and the building of the team.

Managers have to ensure that decisions are communicated effectively, and that they are followed through to ensure that what was expected is actually happening. If it is not, they have to find out why and then take corrective action.

CONTROL

Unless managers monitor progress they will not know whether anything is happening at all! Control is a term which includes the tasks of monitoring and reporting process as well as the evaluation of results.

Control has to be systematised so that:

- the right amount of information reaches
- the right manager(s)
- in time for the right action to be taken.

Control is a major factor in the on-going decision process because it provides information to trigger the next decisions that need to be taken.

OBJECTIVES

Clarity of purpose is essential. Without clarity there can be no shared understanding and it is unlikely that a range of people will achieve what the manager intended.

Objectives must be established, in writing, and used:

- to brief all involved in their achievement;
- as the control factor against which to measure achievement.

Objectives must:

- be set against time;
- state the quantity and/or the quality to be achieved;
- be an effective and efficient guide to future activities.

It is not easy as first to write specific and unambiguous objectives, but the skill comes with practice. You will have plenty of opportunity to practice writing management objectives as we progress through the book and you will probably find that if you write down what you want to happen, you will be able to see exactly what you mean to achieve:

What I want to achieve

I want the sales team to achieve their budgets for sales revenue next period and I want all the important customers seen once a month. Less important customers can be seen every two months. Customers must pay their invoices on time or else we don't make a profit, so there is no point getting orders from insolvent traders.

OBJECTIVES:

Before the start of the next sales period we must:

1 identify all key customers who merit a sales call each month;
2 establish sales targets for each key customer;
3 identify all customers who have a bad credit record;
4 establish control on sales reports to identify each customer called on by date, revenue, outstanding debt.

Within the next sales period our objectives are to:

1 visit all key customers once a month;
2 visit all other customers every two months;
3 achieve planned sales targets;
4 achieve planned sales budget;
5 reduce days of debt to agreed terms of trade in good credit customers;
6 obtain specific commitment for settlement from bad credit customers;
7 identify for management decision any customers with whom no further trade should take place.

EFFECTIVE OR EFFICIENT?

Management objectives should cover both effectiveness or efficiency in addition to being quantified against time.

- Doing the wrong things right . . .   is . . . efficient without being effective.
- Getting the result, at what cost: . . . is . . . effective without being efficient.
- Doing the right things right . . .   is . . . both effective and efficient.

This objective covers all the requirements:

- Defective vehicles shall be restored to full roadworthy condition within 24 hours of being reported to the maintenance manager.

It is not a realistic objective to say 'We intend to repair defective vehicles promptly'.

Note that the modern and very common practice of saying that something will be done 'as soon as possible' is not an indication of urgency! Who determines the degree of priority? Who says when something is possible? It is vital to press for a definite commitment, a definite time and/or date otherwise the job will be done when it suits and not before!

KEY POINT SUMMARY

The manager's prime task is to take decisions. The basic tasks are to

- make decisions to achieve results, keep team commitment, involve staff and make the future happen;
- structure through corporate, strategic and operational objectives, around which decisions focus;
- delegate authority for others to act, but not responsibility which resides with the manager;
- motivate the team;
- plan and set clear objectives for each member of the team;
- analyse results and take appropriate action;
- inform the team of situational problems;
- hunt for alternative solutions;
- take risks;
- select and implement action;
- control activities so that objectives are achieved in time.

Frederick Winslow Taylor identified five management principles:

- Use scientific methods rather than subjective guess-work.
- Create an atmosphere of co-operation among workers.
- Enable successful harmonisation of activities within groups.
- Work for maximised output;
- Develop worker potential for the benefit of the individual and the organisation.

- Henry Gantt developed incentive schemes, bar charts and simplified internal company communications.
- The Gilbreths introduced the measurement of work.
- Human relations in management developed during the Hawthorne experiments, conducted by Mayo and Roethlisberger.
- Herzberg suggested how hygiene factors and motivators impact on people at work.
- Motivators are internal inducements to achieve.
- Incentives are external inducements to act.
- Money is not directly a prime motivator.
- Later systems of analysis, appraisal, motivation and incentives led to the involvement of employees in managing the organisation.
- John Adair identified three areas of leadership: task, team and the individual.
- Authority is the delegation of power to act.
- Responsibility cannot be delegated.
- Delegation is part of a mutually supportive system.
- Hierarchies operate through a chain of command.
- Decision-making is a core skill of a manager.
- The decision-making process sets objectives from which activities are generated.
- Information = facts which are of value at this time.
- Data = facts which may be of value, now or later.
- Managers take risks based on information that can never be complete.
- Decisions require the skill to select from alternatives.
- Decisions are measurable only after implementation.
- Control is the process of monitoring the results of decisions.
- Objectives are quantified, set against a time scale and guide future activities.
- Objectives should be efficient and effective.

WORK-BASED SELF-ASSESSMENT QUESTIONS

1 How are decisions made and what control procedures operate in your organisation?

2 Review the structure and draw an organisational chart of your own company.

SCHOOL- OR COLLEGE-BASED SELF-ASSESSMENT QUESTIONS

1 Consider what the marketing objectives may be for a librarian appointed to a new library to be built in your educational establishment. (Think through what you mean by 'library'. We shall examine a librarian's marketing in Module 3.)

2 Chart the lines of authority from your headmaster or principal to include all departments, both teaching and non-teaching.

See end of Chapter 4 for answer guidelines.

CHAPTER 3

Why marketing is necessary

Alisa Montgomery is thrilled by her new job. She has been selected from over 250 applicants to be the librarian in Avenue Park Library. The library, of which she is to take charge, is the newest of eight sub-libraries in the suburbs of a large town which has its mains reading and reference library next to the Town Hall.

Avenue Park Library is newly opened. It has been built as part of a 'green field' development which extends the suburbs into what has previously been agricultural land. The development comprises a major public authority housing estate, a substantial number of privately owned homes, a new primary school and a small industrial estate. The local college is only two miles away and a major industrial area is on the other side of the college.

The library is a single structure building with parking space for 25 cars and access for the infirm and the elderly. Toilets are in the entrance hall. Opening from this area are the library, the stockroom and a large meetings and exhibition room. The building was designed for flexibility and so Alisa can arrange internal partitions and shelves as she wishes. She will also be able to rearrange the layout, as and if needed, with a minimum of difficulty.

The head librarian has drawn up a suggested list of library contents and this is causing Alisa come concern. She notices that the suggestions are heavily biased towards the provision of books, with a fairly even mixture across the topics from light romance to science fiction. A small reference section is proposed and a newspaper and periodical reading area. For the young, a small children's library, a reading and a play area are proposed.

Alisa has been asked to allocate her budget across specific purchases – but she is far from certain that she is equipped with sufficient information on which to base her decisions.

> What should she do?
> How she should do it?
> Why should she do it?

Alisa's problem is that her head librarian is working from a product orientation. His view is centred on the product that he is used to supplying, on the service he is accustomed to give.

This is a very common approach – which very seldom is justified. De Beers have this approach, but they have control of the bulk of the world's diamond supplies. Together with the Russian producers they control the quantity of diamonds reaching the world's markets and so they exercise power.

Table 3.1 What should be done and why

What she should do	Why she should do it.
1 Define a library in the context of the people living locally.	Because a library can be an information source, an entertainment centre, a social focus, a place to study, ... Book provision may be only part of what is needed.
2 To achieve (1) she must research the needs, opinions, attitudes of those who are in her area.	If the local people don't want what she provides they will not visit. Without clients her library will fail.
3 Define the groups from which clients will come and count the number of people in each.	Student needs differ as they move from primary to secondary school – and then on to college. Similarly other groupings will sub-divide into specific interest clusters.
4 Establish exact need for each group and, from this understanding, prepare an overall statement of what the library must be and what it must provide.	Without a clear definition of purpose she cannot provide the best balance of stocks. Nor will she be able to evaluate achievement against plan.
5 Prepare a detailed proposal of the library she wants to manage starting from a definition of 'library' as understood by the people she will serve.	So that she has a clearly thought-through strategic plan which she can present to the head librarian for approval.
6 Implement tactical decisions to action the approved strategy.	So that there is a logical sequence to ordering materials; putting the physical structure in place; engaging, briefing and training her staff; promoting the new library; opening it to the public.
7 Monitor the actual uptake of the library services by each of the groups identified and provided for. Discover who else is attracted into the library, and for what purpose.	So that plans can be amended in the light of achievement.
8 Continuously monitor the consistency of the quality of the service against changing client population and needs.	To ensure that the service does not become dated . . . that it remains a valuable and valued asset within the community.

It is only from power that a 'product- or production-centred approach' will work. As soon as monopoly power is broken, as soon as competition enters the market, a product-centred approach is no longer possible. In many cases it can actually be very damaging long-term because if it is abused – by overcharging perhaps – a deep resentment can form that will come out in a rapid switch to a rival product as soon as one comes available.

Examples of monopoly power are common, and so is government action to break the monopolies. In the UK the General Post Office had a monopoly on post, parcels and telecoms. The GPO was split up and replaced by Royal Mail and British Telecom. These two monopolies have been further broken down by the allowance of free competition for post and packets costing over £1.00 to send, government approval of private postal networks (the legal profession have greatly benefited) and the awarding of licences to private telecom suppliers, e.g. Mercury.

Some monopolies are rewards for innovation and expire naturally. For example, Nestlé had a 25-year monopoly on instant coffee because they patented the invention. Thus Nescafé had a head start on competition. Whilst they had a monopoly they had market power, but were competing alone against all other beverages. Once the patent expired, Maxwell House entered the market with a high profile promotional campaign and their market size grew rapidly. Other producers entered the market and instant coffee as a 'generic product' competed against ground coffee, tea and all other beverages.

Because of consumer demand, and with the stimulus of competition, Nestlé now have eight Nescafé brands each in a range of sizes and each with a specific market target. Naturally their market share has declined – from 100% when they had monopoly power, to 57.1% in 1992. But the total market has increased dramatically in size and value. Many more people now drink coffee. The result is that in 1992 retail Nescafé sales were £288.3m – over £50m more than the second placed hot beverage brand!

It is possible to give up a potential monopoly. For example, Philips invented the audio cassette and could have held exclusive rights to it while under patent. They released their rights (for a fee), and it became the world standard. The video tape situation was quite different. Only after a major and expensive world-wide battle did the VHS system win out over Betamax for domestic use.

Obviously a sub-library has no power in the marketplace and so Alisa is right to take a marketing view and to centre on her clients and their needs.

Only if client needs are satisfied will there be satisfaction. Only if there is satisfaction will clients return. Only from regular trade will long-term profits be generated.

There is an old saying that advertising can sell anything – once! After that it is for the product to 'sell' itself. If it is liked it will be re-bought. The same principle applies across the whole of the marketing scene – profits come from the return of satisfied clients. So it is essential to find out what will satisfy clients and to provide it if you can.

This 'conceptual' approach to marketing management must be understood because the marketing concept is not a definition of marketing. The marketing concept is a deeply held belief that the focus must be on the consumer, and that there is little point trying to sell what the consumer does not want. Therefore the organisation must be 'consumer driven'.

To be clear:

- A *concept* is an underpinning philosophy, a way of thinking.
- A *definition* is a precise description of an activity, made possible by the concept.

Thus a concept is wider than a definition and the marketing concept supports all forms of marketing, whether of product or of service. The difference will be in the exchange. In some cases goods will be exchanged for cash. In others time is exchanged for pleasure. The marketing concept is operating whenever there is an exchange that is of benefit to both sides.

The main areas where marketing will operate strongly are:

1 commercial organisations: suppliers of products, or of services;
2 industrial, business-to-business, consumer durables, fast moving consumer goods:
   — objective: cash profits for owners;
3 commercial/social organisations (e.g. charities):
   • fund-raising activities (commercial);
     — benefit(s) to society (social) or (societal, i.e. customs and lifestyle of a community or nation);
     — objectives: Cash to make 'good works' possible (commercial);
     — benefits to targeted members of society (social);
   • social-service organisations;
   • fund-raising activities (state supported);
     — objectives: cash to make 'good works' possible and to meet the declared social objectives of the organisation.
   • voluntary services (social).
     — objectives: attract and retain sufficient volunteers to run the organisation and to meet the declared social objectives of the organisation.

Note that income is always required, and usually in cash. Thus a major objective of every organisation is to raise enough income for it to function effectively. A commercial organisation attempts to make profits on sales. A social organisation may have a small income from sales but will secure its major funding from donation and/or grant or subsidy.

Organisations which depend on donations and grants have to be skilled marketers on two fronts. They have to convince donors that they are a worthwhile charity, and they have to attract calls for aid from people who qualify for their help. There is little point generating funds if nobody applies for them and it is distressing to generate demand from people who do not qualify (see Figure 3.1).

Alisa listed the major marketing targets for the new library. They were:

• the elderly/senior citizens;
• young mothers – home, baby-care, hobbies;
• fathers – hobbies/sport;
• students – college, university – by subjects;
• pupils – school set books for examination subjects;
• special interest groups;
• reference works;
• newspapers, magazines and journals;
• tapes, records and discs;
• a new section to be considered

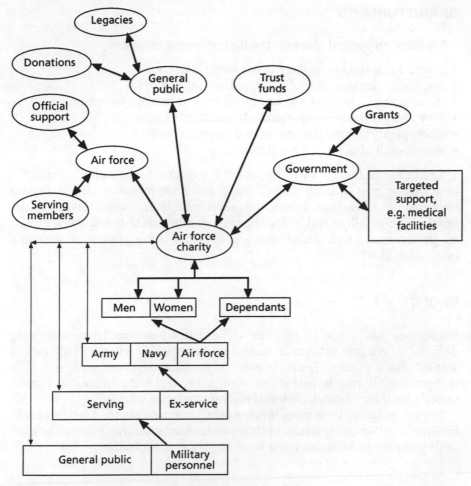

Fig. 3.1 Major marketing targets for an airforce charity

— videos;
— interactive videos – lectures, natural history and sciences, drama and theatre.

Alisa now defined her market targets and began to assemble a strategy for the new library. First she devised a plan for researching opinions, attitudes and demand for library services and activities likely to be in demand for the next six months. This required several brainstorming sessions with teams of local groups. Try taking a sheet of paper and expanding the main marketing targets that Alisa listed above.

BRAINSTORMING

Alisa drew up general ideas for the brainstorming sessions:

- create a relaxed atmosphere in the committee room;
- encourage the free flow of ideas, old, recent and new;
- avoid critical comment and any evaluation or priority for action;
- give everyone equal opportunity to contribute ideas;
- allow plenty of time for people to think and confer;
- record each idea for future reference.

She balanced this for each segment of the market listed under 'strengths' – new studies from LCCIEB, BTEC, C & G and RSA; invitations to local sports organisations to visit and demonstrate skills in football, cricket, tennis, squash, bowls, fishing, sailing and hiking. Hobbies exhibitions to help generate interest in developing new skills. Alisa was now in a better position to present a plan to her chief.

PROFIT

Remember that 'profit' is the same as 'benefit' when considering marketing definitions. We gain substantial self-esteem as a benefit when we help people weaker than ourselves. The Red Cross and the United Nations, each with their distinctive uniforms, impart status – but many feel self-fulfilment is reward enough for their medical, custodial and humanitarian efforts.

People exchange their time, involvement, support, cash for a return of self-fulfilment, self-esteem, status. Mutual satisfaction is the true measure of marketing success and this can come from any form of exchange.

INTERNAL AND EXTERNAL

Marketing must operate both internally and externally.

- Internal marketing is needed to inform, persuade, convince, win on-going support for marketing plans and then for the decisions and activities that must follow.
- External marketing is needed to achieve the declared 'profit' objectives.

Regrettably it is easy to be brilliant at external marketing, but to forget that individuals throughout the whole organisation need to be:

- committed to the marketing concept and
- aware of their part in the marketing plan.

Some examples of failed internal marketing:

- The UK Government set up a 'cones hot line' so that drivers could telephone in and report those motorways where stretches were coned of for too long and where little work was being done. Unfortunately, nobody informed the switchboard, nor the person whose internal extension had been chosen. The first callers told the operator what was happening, but all he could do was take names and addresses. An answerphone had been installed by the time the press rang! The resultant publicity was extremely damaging!

- An advertising agency was commissioned to repeat a campaign that was designed to generate enquiries, so that the sales force could follow up each enquiry. 'How did you do last time?', they asked. It was found that all the enquiries from the last campaign were still in a cardboard box under a secretary's desk, because no one had remembered to inform her of what procedure to adopt, nor noticed that enquiry forms had not been sent out!
- A large college commissioned 2000 ring binders for its students, and had them delivered a week before the start of term. Delivery was refused because there was no room to store them. A major refurbishment was in progress and nobody had checked with maintenance!

EVOLUTION

Marketing is relatively new in the form that we understand it today, but the concept and philosophy had always strongly influenced the actions of all successful organisations.

Before today's marketing, with its integrated range of tools, advertising and sales were supreme. With a strong outward focus these together are very powerful tools for pushing products or services through the system to consumers. They are not as effective in generating demand pull for products through the channel of distribution.

Marketing's strength is such that it senses the need to generate 'demand-pull', and this became especially important when self-service stores began to replace retail counter service. As counter hands were displaced, so the last link in the sales chain vanished and the product was forced to compete alone. It was quickly found that advertising alone was insufficient – promotional tactics become an important factor within the marketing toolbox.

There is no need for marketing:

1 *Where there is a monopoly of essential goods.* By definition people must have essential goods. Whilst governments in a free society require the application of marketing principles, supplier's only apply these tools to long-term strategies or short-term tactics, i.e. if they wish to boost the number of people using the product, or the number of occasions on which it is used.

2 *Where there is a cartel controlling the market.* A cartel is an agreement between suppliers that has the effect of creating conditions similar to a monopoly. Cartels are usually illegal because they are in restraint of trade but some, e.g. the diamond cartel of De Beers and the Russian diamond producers, transcend national boundaries and are difficult to police.

De Beers are highly skilled marketers. The slogan 'A Diamond is Forever' dates only from 1948. In the United States diamond sales were $23 million in 1939 and \$2.1 billion in 1979! In 1968 fewer than 5% of Japanese women received a diamond engagement ring. By 1981 some 60% of Japanese brides wore engagements rings to the altar. Thus 1500 years of tradition was revised in only 15! Faced with a glut of small diamonds De Beers created the concept of the eternity ring in the mid-1960s. How many people today realise how far their 'traditional' expectations have been affected by skilful marketing during the last 50 years?

Another example of cartel operations is the cross-channel ferry service between the UK, France and Belgium. There are various different competing companies, prices and services, but all result in very similar total invoices for a family and car crossing at similar seasons and times of the day.

3 *Where demand exceeds supply.* Consider the absence of marketing in the Russian retail industry. Only when supply catches up with demand will there be need to apply marketing principles.

Marketing is needed when:

1 *There is an open market.* In an open market suppliers will compete for trade and customers and consumers have freedom of choice. Reasons for choice must be built into the product offering, and it is best to build in consumer preference, style and taste. Hence a marketing 'consumer-centred, consumer-driven' approach is needed.
2 *When supply exceeds demand.* For the last several years airline capacity has exceeded market demand. In efforts to survive, the airlines have stepped up their already highly geared, competitive marketing operations. Better service levels are being provided as standard – Continental have merged their Business and First Class into a new class called Business First; British Airways have opened superb lounges in the major airports, Virgin are offering high-quality in-seat entertainment.

In addition to these long-term structural changes there are many short-term incentives to fly. Two-for-the-price-of-one offers; 40% discount on a flight when spending £250 in Sainsbury; half-price 'Air miles' flights if one full price flight is taken.

In 1993 Hoover made many enemies by failing to provide free flights for those who purchased specific products in the late 1992 pre-Christmas period. The offer was a disaster when the company was unable to meet every flight request from irate customers, who felt cheated.

THE ALTERNATIVES TO MARKETING

The production concept

Focus is on the product (or the service). The impression is that the supplier decides that 'We know what is best for the customer'. This rather arrogant and self-centred view is resented by customers and consumers alike.

In organisations adopting this approach there is no incentive to improve the offering, and little concern with the realities of the marketplace. Thus a competitor who tailors products to meet real or actual need will have an easy route into the market. As an example, Japanese radios quickly dominated the American market because of the benefits to be derived from the American invented transistor. American production-centred manufacturers ignored the transistor until it was too late.

- Once tooled up to produce a product it is a very hard decision to make a change before the full value has been extracted from the investment. Thus British car manufacturers in the 1980s persisted with less efficient drum brakes even though their competitors were fitting disc brakes and moving on to ABS.

The predictable results of a product-centred approach are:

- antagonistic customers who willingly switch to a competitor as soon as possible;
- a stagnant organisation, staffed by personnel who cannot cope with market demands.

The sales concept

Focus is on selling what is made. This results from the production concept as non-direct competition is detected. The efforts are directed to pushing the product down the channel of distribution. There is often little concern for the consumer, since it is the customer who controls the purchases.

In organisations with this approach there is high enthusiasm and hard selling. Concern is to make the sale, not for the use to which the product is put, nor with the true needs of the customer or consumer in mind.

- Double glazing organisations have acquired a reputation for hard selling. Commonly they buy-in their product and sell it on, through sales people who are paid low salaries but high commission. The result is that householders are subjected to long sales presentations and many find it difficult to say 'no'! It is easier to sign the contract just to get rid of the salesman! This approach became so serious that in the UK legislation now protects the potential purchaser.

Time share sales teams are recruited to hard sell the product, holiday studios and apartments in the main. Devices such as free gift offers are used to persuade people to attend their presentations, which turn out to be hard sales pitches. There is no genuine concern for the client's long-term needs.

The predictable results of a sales-centred approach are:

- customers actively search for alternative suppliers;
- consumers lobby for protection;
- power switches to those who have both contact with consumers and control over the route to them;
- pricing policies are affected by the customers because of their power;
- customers may take over the suppliers because the product is needed, but the approach is unsuitable.

The financial concept

Focus is on the return on investment. All decisions are made with a view to achieving financial objectives. This is a short-term concept since it focuses on maximum rather than optimum return (optimum meaning 'best'). It also tends to ignore the major factors of what the consumer wants and what is the optimum price-to-volume combination for the long-term. There is a tendency to extract profits from a market too soon, with the results that a product loses its marketing support and suffers at the hands of competitor's tactics. Market share is usually more valuable than short-term profitability, but long-term investment is needed to secure it.

- Western organisations have tended to look for short-term profits, and Western banks have traditionally been cautious in protecting their loan capital. Thus many smaller firms constantly struggle to balance the conflicting needs to invest in the market, and to pay interest on debt. Japanese industry is far better supported by their financial community with an acceptance that market entry is a long-term activity and that long-term returns justify short-term risk.
- The Mars bar has for over 70 years been established in a clear market position, consistently generating planned profits. Would it have reached its position of dominance if funds had been withdrawn as profits in its early days?

The predictable results of a finance-centred approach are:

- alienation of customers and consumers if they are unable to afford the product, especially if it is vital to health;
- alienation of customers by an over-rigorous concern with credit control;
- market dominance by rivals who invest with a view to long-term market presence.

There are occasions when a product, sales or finance concept is in the best interests of the organisation. Perhaps it has been set up to take advantage of a short-term market opportunity? In this case a long-term view would be quite wrong. When productive capacity is limited it is tempting to adopt a product-centred approach – but this will damage long-term prospects if it is planned that in time capacity will exceed demand. Each situation must be judged on its merits, but usually a marketing approach offers the best prospects of long-term profitable survival.

ADOPTION OF MARKETING

The marketing concept must be adopted at 'corporate' level if it is to be influential throughout the organisation. Those who take corporate decisions – the directors and very senior managers – must thoroughly understand the full implications of adopting the marketing concept.

Whatever the size of the organisation it is only possible to work effectively within the marketing concept if all top managers accept it wholeheartedly.

- Barnsley Co-Op, one of the largest in the UK, showed that they had no understanding of marketing when they decided to keep national brands at the back of the store and to feature their own Wheatsheaf brand at the front. Their assumption was that customers would see promotion for national products such as Carnation, Libby and Ideal milk, but then buy the Wheatsheaf alternative. (Barnsley Co-Op was run by an elected committee who lacked corporate and commercial skills, and would not delegate to their employed managers.)
- When marketing came in to the UK, in the early 1960s, it was first adopted by the fast-moving consumer goods (FMCG) manufacturers because they were the firms making the major shift from counter to self-service. From FMCG the concept has spread to the point where it is now adopted by business professionals (lawyers and accountants), educationists (colleges and schools), charities and government agencies. All experienced similar problems at the beginning – it is easy to change titles, but very hard to fully comprehend and accept the marketing concept.

Sales directors can easily change their title to marketing director. What is crucial is that they change attitudes and also adapt their skills base. This takes determination, dedication, time, training and resources. The transition is not easy, but it is very worth while in the long run.

Only when marketing has been established at corporate level can corporate objectives be set. We shall see in Chapter 4 that corporate decisions must be taken first, because corporate acceptance of marketing has implications for the objectives of every aspect of the organisation.

KEY POINT SUMMARY

- It is crucial to identify exactly what people want, what they understand by concepts such as 'library'.
- A production-centred approach can work only from a position of producer power.
- Monopoly situations are common, but so is government action to break them.
- Some monopolies are rewards for innovation and expire naturally.
- Advertising may sell anything – once.
- A product has to be liked to be re-purchased.
- A concept = an underpinning philosophy.
- A definition = a precise description.
- Marketing operates in all types of organisation.
- Both internal and external marketing are needed.
- Marketing has evolved from advertising and selling.
- Monopolies and cartels have little use for marketing.
- Marketing is needed when there is an open market and/or where supply exceeds demand.
- Alternative concepts are: production, sales and financial.
- Marketing must be adopted at corporate level.

- Marketing establishes:
  — target consumer's need;
  — channels of distribution;
  — promotional contact;
  — the base from which other functions operate.

WORK-BASED SELF-ASSESSMENT QUESTIONS

1 Examine and explain any recent changes in your company or organisation made in order to focus more on customers and to promote a more vigorous marketing policy.

2 Identify recent marketing procedures adopted by your company or organisation to determine consumer demand.

(*Note:* In both questions identify what should be done if it hasn't been done or isn't being done.)

SCHOOL- OR COLLEGE-BASED SELF-ASSESSMENT QUESTIONS

1 Focusing on three areas only, books, tapes and videos, determine how you would persuade the Head Librarian to modify stocks.

2 How could you generate demand for the new, improved, library service?

See the end of Chapter 4 for answer guidelines.

CHAPTER 4

Marketing management planning

Mohammed Hsaini is the marketing manager of Midi Fabri-electrique SA, who manufacture electrical equipment ranging from switchgear through consumer units to light switches. Their major interest is in the domestic market, for which they are the leading suppliers in the south of France. Their head office and factory is in Arles, at the southern end of the Rhone valley. Thus they are able to deliver north up the Rhone valley, as well as east to the urban areas of Toulon, Cannes and Nice, and west to Montpellier, Narbonne and the Spanish border.

The formation of the European Union (EU) has opened the borders of the 12 EU countries and Mohammed has been examining his company's options. The EU standardisation policy has created a major marketing opportunity as common standards for electrical equipment and installation are to be introduced across the EU. No longer will it be possible for national states to impose their own standards. Equipment that meets EU standard will be legal in each country. There has been much resistance from countries, notably the UK, who have traditionally set the highest standards of the 12 EU countries (particularly in electric plugs – three-pin earthed and not two-pin, as in the EU generally), but standards for electrical goods have been agreed and it is now possible to plan for a trans-EU operation because Midi Fabri-electrique's equipment already matches the new EU standards.

This is of major benefit because competitors who currently manufacture to standards that are above EU requirement will be forced either to price their products at a premium, or restructure their manufacture of produce to the less expensive EU standard.

The major question is 'should Mohammed recommend that Midi Fabri-electrique SA become a trans-EU company?'

At first he was very excited by the prospect, but once the initial enthusiasm had passed he took a long and careful look at the opportunity:

- Could Midi Fabri-electrique produce enough to meet an EU-wide demand?
- If they could, could they handle the sales effort?
- Could they distribute?
- Could they provide after-sales support?
- Could they manage the EU exchange rate problems?

In theory they could, given time to gear up their operation and providing the necessary finance was available.

Mohammed felt that this marketing opportunity had to be seized – this was

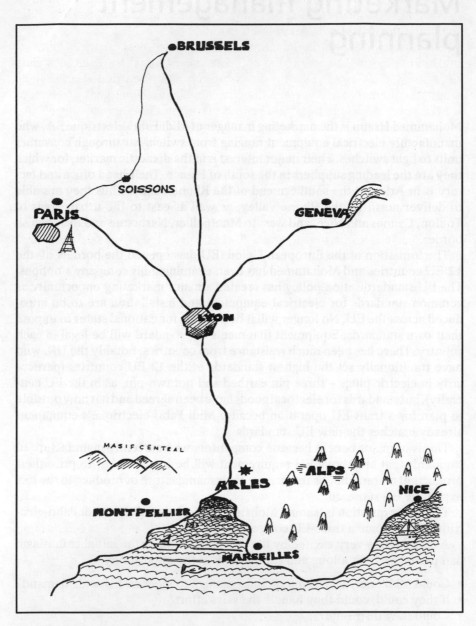

Fig. 4.1 Midi Fabri-electrique SA sales area

a unique opportunity for Midi Fabri-electrique to establish themselves as a European company, to spread their opportunities and take greater risks outside France, to move into mass marketing. It was necessary to move positively and quickly to secure the initiative ahead of other manufacturers. He decided to discuss the matter with his marketing director.

Yves Durand, the Marketing Director, was an electrical engineer by training, but had learned his marketing during ten years with the French subsidiary of Siemens, the German electric and electronic giant. He listened carefully to what Mohammed had to say and then explained what would have to happen if Midi Fabri-electrique became a serious player on the European stage.

'We shall have to make a major shift in policy. Currently we are a specialist manufacturer with a strong local base where we are well known. We are financed to provide for the needs of our region, and we can protect our market because our manufacturing base is very close to our target customers.

'Our service is excellent because we have short lines of distribution and because we are still small enough to retain a sense of family. This sense of family extends to our major customers and is much valued within French culture.

'Our financial results match the needs of our current shareholders – and funding the type of expansion you propose would carry an unacceptable degree of risk. We just can't leap in one bound from a successful smaller supplier to a player in the major European league.

'What we can do, however, is target for gradual expansion. I accept that the traditional values within national states and regions will gradually change, and that we will be unwise to think we can continue for too long as we are. I will therefore consider proposing a policy change and, if it is accepted, this will open the way for you to begin a gradual shift of strategy.

'Before I can do any more, however, I need some hard information. Think through what I have said and come back at 08.00 tomorrow with some ideas of the information we need, so that we can begin the process of establishing clear research proposals.'

Whatever the size of organisation – a single entrepreneur or a multinational giant corporation – the management and planning processes are the same. Obviously the scale of the process changes but, just as an individual passes through every stage of the DMU when buying even a bar of chocolate, so an organisation must pass through every stage of the planning process.

Before you can select from a menu in a restaurant you have to run through your own personal planning process:

- Policies, assumptions and objectives:
  — health – what allergies do you have?
  — alcohol – is it prohibited?
  — diet – are you counting calories?
- Strategy:
  — Two courses from the á la carte menu, or for the same price the four-course table d'hôte menu?
- Tactics:
  — salad before or with the main course?

— butter, margarine or plain bread?
— coffee with or after the last course?

After your meal you will run through your control measures:

- Meal well cooked? Well served?
- Staff friendly?
- Environment good? (Not too warm or too cold, no kitchen smells, etc.)
- Value for money?
- Overall: would I return?

In just the same way an organisation has to establish policies for each key issue, develop these into strategies and then into tactics and, finally, ensure that results are controlled.

Midi Fabri-electrique SA has a typical structure, as indicated in Fig. 4.2.

- The board of directors sets policies.
- Senior managers establish strategies.
- Operational managers carry out the tactics needed to achieve the strategies.

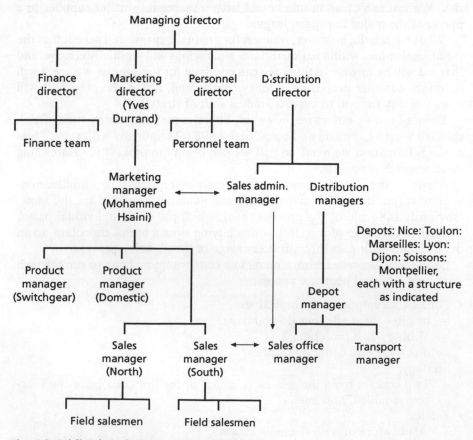

Fig. 4.2 Midi Fabri-electrique SA structure

Marketing is a management activity – it gets things done through people. Yves relies upon the marketing team lead by Mohammed who, in turn relies on the product and sales managers. They are also dependent upon people – perhaps not directly under their authority, but who have a major influence on their success.

There is crucial need for product managers to have excellent relationships with personnel in other departments. Willing co-operation achieves far more than formal communication through an official hierarchy. Note that formal confirmation of actions is always needed – but action can often be taken to prevent rather than solve problems if there is mutual respect and mutual trust.

Strategic marketing is concerned with the overall achievement of consumer and customer satisfaction. At operational level it is concerned with achieving tactical objectives to help with the overall task.

In the same way every functional element of the organisation has a dual role:

- concern with corporate achievement, longer-term;
- concern with detailed achievement and results within the area of expertise.

Left to themselves managers may apply different methods of solving the same problem. If it is known that profits are falling, the functional responses may vary considerably:

- Marketing may press for higher sales through wider distribution. The sales force may therefore actively search for new accounts.
- Production may decide to trim back on reserve stocks to release capital and thus reduce interest changes. This may lead to a cut in overtime until the new lower stock levels have been achieved.
- Purchasing may select raw materials of marginal quality, and may hold back on commitment to future purchases against the hope that prices will fall.
- Distribution may amalgamate depots and accept the slower delivery times that follow.
- Personnel may freeze wages, even freeze recruitment for a time.
- Accounts may decide to close unproductive accounts, and to vigorously pursue all overdue invoices. They may also extend the time they take to settle invoices owing to their suppliers.

The results can be catastrophic! The sales force meet with complaints from existing customers because they are receiving firm letters from credit control. Their new account proposals may be refused in the light of the new tighter credit guidelines.

Product availability will fall, so that customers find they have empty shelves and turn to competitors. Product quality may fall so that consumer complaints rise and some consumers switch to rival products. Morale within the company may fall – not only are wages frozen, but departing staff are not replaced and work pressure builds. Also there is additional work in dealing with the rise in customer and consumer complaints and queries.

This could all have been avoided if a clear policy had been established at corporate level – and if it had been communicated effectively throughout the organisation. Each manager's action was right in itself – but by striking out with the best of intentions each hindered rather that helped.

Top management's prime task is to set policy so that senior managers can establish strategies to achieve that policy. Only if strategies are set within a common policy is it likely that they will be in harmony. Tactical plans are developed from strategic decisions.

Management's task at all levels is to ensure co-ordination between tactical, strategic and corporate objectives. A control system which feeds back results against objectives allows for measurement of achievement in time for revisions to be planned, if needed. With an efficient and effective control system a cut back in production would be immediately noticed and questions asked. If this happened at the same time as the marketing department were stepping up their sales efforts, both functions would be held to account. We shall return to the important element of control in Chapter 17.

FOCUS AND CO-ORDINATION

A major task for top management is to provide a clear focus that allows co-ordination of effort. The prime focus is expressed in a mission statement.

MISSION STATEMENT

The mission statement is a short statement that clearly and precisely sets out the underlying philosophy and purpose of the organisation. It takes a considerable time to draft, discuss, revise and agree, because it is fundamental to every other aspect of planning.

A mission statement can only be prepared at board level, but it must be widely communicated so that all staff know exactly what is the prime focus of their organisation. Avis car rental have one of the best, and shortest, mission statements:

We are in the business of renting cars without drivers.

With this mission statement it is absolutely clear to everybody that if a manager wants to recommend the renting of any other type of vehicle, say commercial trucks, he has to go to the main board for consideration. It is not a policy option, not a strategic opportunity, not a tactical possibility.

Marks and Spencer have a longer mission statement, but it gives explicit guidance to the formulation of policies. From it we can deduce the strategic, tactics and controls that are most likely to be used.

POLICIES OF MARKS AND SPENCER

- To sell merchandise of the highest quality and outstanding value.
- To offer the highest standard of customer care in an attractive shopping environment.

- To improve quality standards continually throughout our operation by investment in modern technology.
- To support British industry.
- To pursue mutually rewarding long-term partnerships with suppliers.
- To ensure staff and shareholders share in our success.
- To nurture good human relations with staff, customers and the community.
- To minimise the environmental impact of our operations and merchandise.

These are the company principles of Marks & Spencer.

When presented with such clear statements of policy, senior managers have little difficulty in setting strategies because they understand exactly what top management require. Tactics follow from strategy and so the day-to-day activities of even junior managers are greatly influenced.

To comply with M & S policy management has to:

- Discover who the customers and consumers are, and what they require.
- Determine how to continually keep in the forefront of design.
- Find out what the customers consider to be an attractive offer.
- What are the reasonable prices in the context of product quality and customer expectations of value.
- Become involved with the suppliers' techniques of production and quality control.
- Keep up to date with the latest discoveries in science and technology.
- Initiate and maintain high standards of quality control.
- Be active in store location and design.
- Constantly seek better ways to streamline procedures.
- Develop and maintain excellent personal relations.

This is a formidable list, which for many firms would exist on paper as intentions – but be neglected in the urgency to deal with everyday matters. To ensure that policies are complied with there is need for strict controls.

CONTROL TECHNIQUES

Control is only effective if it deals with the detailed issues. If each detail is correct then it follows that the whole will be correct. Some errors of detail cancel themselves out – such as when one store oversells a line and another falls short. These are not critical, except to the next round of sales forecasting. Other errors are of crucial importance – such as when there is variation in the quality of an ingredient used, or when a customer does not receive prompt and courteous treatment in store.

Managers need to see for themselves and not take a supplier's statements of intention on trust. Marks and Spencer's even insist on monitoring factories of blue chip suppliers who are jealous of their reputation for quality! No supplier should be taken on trust. Checks are carried out on the warp and weft counts of each material supplied to ensure that these are as contracted with suppliers, e.g. Marks & Spencer's shirts, dresses and night-gowns, etc., are produced to a quality standard that M & S control.

Staff must be highly qualified in production and quality control techniques and be alert to world wide developments so that they are able to deal with suppliers as equals and, on occasion, be ahead of the supplier's staff. This requires an investment in training which has no obvious payback – it is justified by the need to comply with policy requirements.

Similarly all policy issues translate through strategies to tactical involvement and to the vital area of human skills, expertise and attitude.

You will see that no mention has been made of budget. This is because the overall budget implications can be deduced from the mission statement. If management are demanding very high standards, they are aware that those high standards have to be paid for. If they specify 'high-quality, well-designed and attractive merchandise at reasonable prices' and their customers are clearly coming from the affluent levels of society it follows that 'reasonable' does not mean 'cheap'.

A budget will be needed, of course, it is a vital part of management planning and control as we shall see in Chapter 16. The issue at this stage is that each individual making a bid for funds knows the expected level of activity. He or she can make budget proposals that are set at a level for which management will already have made provision.

VALUE-LOADED TERMS

Be very careful not to use value-loaded terms such as 'cheap', 'expensive', 'reasonable', 'long', 'short'. These are all relative to the experience of those using the terms. What is 'expensive' to an 18-year-old in their first job may be 'cheap' to a 55-year-old company director.

The same person is 'tall' when with a woman netball player and 'tiny' next to a Harlem Globetrotter!

Always specify exactly what you mean, otherwise you leave your intentions open to misinterpretation. Use quantification as routine. Practice turning your intentions into quantifiable terms.

Not	But
This is expensive.	The price is £25.00
It will take a long time.	Allow two weeks.
As soon as possible.	I'll do it next: come back in 3 hours.
He's very tall.	He's over 6ft 6 in, around 2 metres!

You develop the use of non-quantifiable terms when dealing with qualities such as attitude, or personality, but as we shall see in Chapter 10, there are several ways of expressing attitudes in numerical terms.

Fig. 4.3 Tall or tiny?

PLANNING TERMINOLOGY

These key terms must be understood:

- *Mission*. We have seen that the mission is a short statement that provides a focus for all decisions. It expresses the underlying philosophy and purpose of the organisation and takes considerable time to draft, discuss, and agree. It should remain constant over a considerable period.
- *Policies*. Policies are derived from the mission. Each functional area is guided by one or more policies, they need to be consistent with the agreed mission statement and to be consistent with each other.

Policies are long-term statements of intention, expressed as corporate objectives.

Thus a policy for a retail store group might be:

- To open 10 new stores in England each year to the end of the century.

This gives a specific and measurable intention from which strategies can be derived. It does not attempt to narrow the options any further than is necessary, e.g. it specifies England, and so excludes the rest of the United Kingdom (Northern Ireland, Scotland and Wales), but it does not specify which English region(s) should be targeted.

A personnel policy might be:

- To recruit only staff who can show evidence of relevant experience in our industry and who can be security bonded.

A security policy is commonly phrased as:

- We always prosecute.

AIMS

These are general statements and have no direct value in the planning process. They are a convenient way of expressing a general intention, e.g. it is our aim to be the best employer in town. This aim can only be achieved if it flows from a mission and is expressed as one or more policies from which strategies are derived.

GOALS

A goal is a quantified objective. The term is sometimes used in place of corporate objective.

CORPORATE OBJECTIVE

This is a more meaningful term to use than 'goal' because it reminds you that an objective is required and objectives are always quantified.

Corporate objectives come directly from policies and are the way in which policies are expressed. Therefore, to all intents and purposes there is very little difference between a policy and a corporate objective. Both terms are in common use, but there is no agreement on which is better.

STRATEGIES

Strategies break down corporate objectives into specific individual achievement requirements. They are expressed in objective terms. We have seen how the Marks & Spencer mission statement is expressed in areas of policy and how it is easily possible to deduce from this the exact areas in which activity is required.

The necessary activity is first expressed as corporate objectives, and then broken down into the key elements, which are expressed as strategic objectives.

Thus the security policy, 'we always prosecute', leads to the following strategic objectives:

In the design of all new stores:
- State-of-the-art security cameras and mirrors will be provided.
- Cash points will be equipped with one-way safes protected by time locks.
- All existing stores will, by 1 December next, be brought up to the standards requisite of new stores.
- Security manuals will be on managers' desks at all times.
- Telephone numbers for company security and the local police will be prominently displayed on the staff notice board and alongside all telephones.
- Sales staff will receive security training:
  as part of initial training   –   one day;
  in store, within first 2 days   –   3 hours;
  refresher, in store   –   3 hours each month.
- Management will receive security training:
  on appointment   –   three days;
  refresher   –   3 hours each quarter;
  They will also carry out the in-store refresher training for the sales staff.

TACTICS

Tactical objectives derive from strategic objectives. Sometimes called operational, sometimes functional, they are concerned with the day-to-day actions needed to get the job done. As objectives they are always expressed in quantified terms, within a time factor. Usually they are the easiest to prepare since they are each tightly focused. Great care is needed, however, to separate each single objective. It is too easy to use an 'and' and join two separate objectives.

Not
All security equipment
will be in place and the staff trained.

But
By 31 July:
1. All security
   equipment will be in place.
2. All staff will be trained in
   its use.

You will achieve, an average call rate
of 9 per day, an order-to-call ratio
of 60% and an average order size of
£4000.

In Sales Period 6
you will achieve:
1. An average call rate of 9 per
   day.
2. An order-to-call ratio of 60%
3. An average order size of
   £4000.

This structure may not seem important at first – but if each objective is not separated, it cannot be separately controlled. It is unlikely that all will be achieved to exactly the same degree, therefore each must be taken separately to allow effective follow-up action.

CONTROL

This is the active means by which achievement against objective is measured. A control system must be fast enough to report progress to the appropriate managers, in time for them to take whatever action is appropriate.

A system which reports on history is not a system of control! Thus financial accounts, such as the profit and loss account and the balance sheet, are records of achievement but they are not control documents. Management needs the same financial information – but whilst it is current, not after it has passed into history.

Organisations maintain financial and management accounts to meet this exact need. The management accounts are of everyday use and are highly confidential because they contain current information of extreme value to competitors. Financial accounts are produced from the same data, and are produced in full versions for internal management use and usually only in the minimum form required by law for publication.

Control is sometimes incorrectly called evaluation. This is incorrect because evaluation is the passive use of control information, i.e. results are evaluated once they have been produced by control.

SIMPLIFY THE TASK!

You can make it very much easier for others to understand if you make a habit of always prefixing your objectives to show their level, e.g. write 'corporate objective' or 'tactical objective':

- To achieve the corporate objective of achieving a market share of 55% by

31 December 199X, our key strategic objectives are:
— To increase the size of the sales force by 15% before 30 April next.
— To widen distribution from 50 to 65% by 31 August.

Unfortunately there is one last issue which sometimes causes students a problem when they first meet it. It is the fact that each manager operates his own structure within the overall corporate construction.

Thus each manager can set policies for the area he controls provided they fit within corporate policy. From his policy he can product 'corporate' and 'strategic' objectives. You thus sometimes find a statement such as you will have noticed within the security strategic objectives quoted above. One of them read 'Security manuals will be on managers desks at all times.' this is a clear statement of security policy, but it is expressed here as a strategy!

If you feel confused, don't worry! Just remember always to prefix your policies and objectives, and your exact meaning will be clear.

A consolation is that in business there is no problem in understanding what a good manager means. It is when these processes have to be explained in theory that some overlap in terminology becomes noticeable.

TIME

Objectives must, as we know, always be expressed against a time frame. In planning it is common to see the terms: long-, medium- and short-term used in connection with plans. Compare these statements of long-term aim:

• Our long-term plan is to have a new source of energy on line by the year 2050.
• Our long-term plan is to be established in every British city within 10 years.

It should be obvious that long, medium and short are all terms that need to be quantified. That the length one needs to plan forward depends on circumstance. Energy suppliers such as Shell and Esso plan well into the next century, whilst consumer durable manufacturers need look only 10 years forward. A retailer may have a three- to five-year horizon.

It is important, therefore, so specify what is meant by each term when it is used for the first time. This is easy, so please remember to do it. Simply run the time alongside the term, i.e. 'Our main short-term (6 month) plan is to get our new depot functional.'

BUDGETS

The whole planning process is made effective by a budget. We shall cover budgets and budgeting in Chapter 16. For now it is enough to say that the budgetary process exists to ensure that an organisation's plans have consistency across functions. Under budgetary control individual managers cannot go off on their own initiative without its being noticed.

More importantly, a budgetary control system allows variations in achievement against objective to be quickly communicated to all who need to know. Thus there should be no embarrassments caused by one function proceeding in ignorance of a support function's collapse.

KEY POINT SUMMARY

- Mohammed Hsaini was asked for plans to allow gradual expansion.
- Policy would need to be changed to allow strategy to shift.
- Information was needed to justify a policy-change recommendation.
- Policies are set by directors so that senior managers can establish strategic objectives.
- Strategic objectives allow tactical objectives to be set.
- Communication and timing are factors to be given priority.
- Top management sets policy and focus.
- The mission statement clearly and precisely defines policy.
- Aims are general statements and are not quantified for control purposes.
- Goals are quantified objectives.
- Strategies translate corporate objectives into activities.
- Tactics derive from strategic plans and are formed from operational objectives.
- Control is the measurement of activities and the comparison of results against objectives.
- Time is an important factor in planning control and should always be carefully quantified.
- Avoid value-loaded terms.

WORK-BASED SELF-ASSESSMENT QUESTIONS

1 Analyse the objectives and tactics for your unit and describe the methods of communicating these to staff.

2 Explain why objectives must be set in terms of quantity against time.

SCHOOL- OR COLLEGE-BASED SELF-ASSESSMENT QUESTIONS

1 Show how clear objectives would allow a headmaster or college principal to manage better.

2 Explain why objectives must be set in terms of quantity against time.

See the end of this Part for answer guidelines.

SUGGESTED ASSISTANCE TO SELF-ASSESSMENT QUESTIONS FOR CHAPTERS 1–4

WORK-BASED QUESTIONS

Chapter 1

1 This question of 'using practical examples' and 'illustrations' allows you to use select-ed and well-prepared diagrams of your company organisation. Definitions of mar-keting require you to quote accurately from the CIM, Kotler, or other well-known and accepted sources. Remember to always quote the name of the author or the source of any definition or quotation.

2 The marketing 'concept' refers to general ideals about marketing within your own organisation. How does the organisation relate to customers and consumers? How does it plan its marketing overall? How is research used to obtain information that helps to produce products or services and to establish details of price, promotion and place? How does it select appropriate strategic and tactical 'mixes'? How far is all of this activity centred on customer and consumer needs?

Chapter 2

1 Is there a clear DMP which management follow? Is there a regular report on the results of each decision in time for action? Give illustrations from your experience.

2 The structure of the company needs to be drawn so that delegation is possible and communication both up and down the company is maintained. The organisation chart should to be top to bottom and unique to your organisation.

Chapter 3

1 Customer service is the area you need to explore in detail here. Using diagrams con-trast the organisational approach of several years ago with today. Emphasise the pro-motional techniques used to make customers aware and the methods of creating demand for your products or services.

2 Research will include questionnaires, group meetings, all the methods of meeting and talking to customers, including handling customer complaints.

Chapter 4

1 This requires a detailed analysis of the marketing objectives, tactics and communi-cation systems operating in your department.

2 If objectives are not set in terms of quantity there is no way to assess if they have been achieved. If they are not set against time it is impossible to evaluate when suc-cess is expected, and to initiate action if it is late.

SCHOOL- OR COLLEGE-BASED QUESTIONS

Chapter 1

1 The role and functions of the marketing manager will vary depending on the type and size of the organisation. He will be expected to link all marketing functions with corporate policies and company objectives, communicate to all company managers, represent the department. In finer focus his responsibilities are for customer and consumer satisfaction. Products and services must be designed for this purpose, and tactical objectives set in pricing, promotion, packaging, selling and distribution.

2 In serving customers we are analysing short-term tactics of product and service, price and value, benefits and promotional aspects; why it is wise to buy here and not from competitors. Consumers seek benefits and value and is concerned with the product in use.

Chapter 2

1 Marketing objectives for the librarian shape the nature of the service offered. The services are focused on what the borrowers require.

2 The chart starts with the head or principal and includes line functions such as teaching, administration, student services, maintenance. Each of these should subdivide until individual members of staff are shown.

Chapter 3

1 As the role of the library changes, so marketing research is needed to set future objectives from which new strategies and ranges of services can be planned. Research consumer need and compare what is available. The need to fill the resultant gap is what has to be 'sold' to the head librarian. He or she has to be helped to see the need to provide for consumer need/demand if the library is to continue to be successful.

2 Consumers have to know that the library has improved. Word-of-mouth comment will spread the word, but more positive action in the form of leaflets and posters will get the message out more efficiently and more effectively.

Chapter 4

1 Clear objectives, set against time of course, enable a senior manager to delegate effectively – in any organisation. Schools and colleges are not different! Once a manager can delegate he can spread the load, develop his subordinates, concentrate on his role as a leader.

2 If objectives are not set in terms of quantity there will be no way to assess if they have been achieved. If they are not set against time it is impossible to evaluate when success is expected, nor to initiate action if it is late.

PART 2

Market forces and the environment –
the way forward

In this Part you will discover that a marketing-oriented organisation has a crucial need to interact with the environment as a whole; not simply with customers and consumers.

Once an organisation adopts the marketing concept every activity is adapted to the common focus of consumer satisfaction. This belief and supporting policies should motivate every person in the organisation, so that even the newest recruit in despatch is cheerfully aware of how to do his job, so that the total effort will have a combined effect on those served by the organisation. The willingness to 'go the extra mile' – to make every effort to supply on time, to keep customers informed, to follow through after delivery, then flows totally, naturally and becomes routine.

Every organisation has to exist within a global environment. With the increasing pace of technological and communication systems, even small operations cannot for long focus simply within their national frontiers. It is obviously impossible to monitor the mass of data that exists, and in which essential information is hidden. Therefore it is necessary to systematise the process of information gathering and circulation.

Information is the life blood of management – for decisions based on inadequate information are far more likely to be a gamble rather than a quantified risk. It is essential, therefore, to supply managers with the information they need at the time that they need it. A management information system is structured to achieve just this objective.

Once information is flowing it must be processed in the light of need. SWOT analysis takes the raw information and sorts it into factors that reveal the strengths and weaknesses of the organisation and the opportunities and threats it encounters.

Without a thorough auditing process a manager is forced to work blindly. Thus the effective marketing manager is alert to the necessity of gathering relevant information, to process it appropriately, and then use it as a basis for decision-making and control.

Management should make only informed decisions.

Market forces and the environment – the way forward

CHAPTER 5

Organisation and the environment

Patricia Long was most surprised when she answered a knock on her door. On the step was a cheerful young man in overalls and carrying a clipboard. 'Mrs Long?' 'Yes'. 'I'm from CookCo Cookers and I've brought your new electric stove. Can I bring it in?'

Patricia was delighted, but somewhat puzzled. Why was she receiving a new stove? She had only just taken delivery of a brand new cooker! True that she had reported teething problems with it, but they had settled down now and it was working well. She had written to CookCo with some adverse comments – in fact she had been quite annoyed when she wrote – but the problems were really not too serious. However, she stood back and watched with growing incredulity as the young man and his mate disconnected her stove and then carried in a new top of the range model. The very one she had wanted, but couldn't afford!

Had they made an error? She hardly dared ask, but felt she had to: 'No mistake, Mrs Long, the delivery note is very clear. The replacement has been authorised by the Managing Director.'

Leaving a bemused but delighted Mrs Long the delivery van pulled away and the phone rang. It was the service manager from the local depot. 'I just wanted to check that you have had delivery of your new stove?' . . . 'Thank you, yes.' . . . 'Any further problem, anything at all, just call me. Call me personally – the number is on the delivery note, can you see it? Good.'

Patricia made herself a cup of coffee on her new stove and took her phone onto her lap to call around her friends to tell them what had happened. It was wonderful – and all it took was a simple letter of complaint addressed to the managing director! What a wonderful company!

Back in CookCo's head office the product manager (stoves) happily put his phone down and picked up his dictaphone.

'Memo to the Group Product Manager.

Subject: Mrs Long.

In accordance with instructions we have today delivered and installed a DeLuxe Model K. The Service Manager has made personal contact and I have made a diary note to follow up with Mrs Long directly on Friday next. The replaced Model B is being returned to the factory for inspection.'

In due course the group product manager reported to the marketing manager, who informed the marketing director so that he could update the managing director.

The managing director was furious!

'It was a simple installation problem, nothing wrong with the stove at all – why on earth have we replaced the product? And why with our best model?' An investigation showed that:

1 Mrs Long had written directly to the managing director with a complaint – that the stove had not been installed properly and therefore she couldn't cook for her family.
2 The managing director had scribbled a note to the marketing director – 'Tom, get this dealt with, please.'
3 The marketing director had written a memo to the marketing manager – 'We have had a complaint from a Mrs Long (see attached copy). The managing director has asked for action. Please deal with this urgently and advise me of the outcome soonest.'
4 The marketing manager had written to the group product manager – 'We need urgent action on this – customer must be satisfied – that is central to our image.'
5 The group product manager had sent a memo to the product manager (stoves) and also rung him: 'Jack, this shouldn't happen, and we need to rectify the situation very quickly. Please take immediate action to satisfy the customer and let me know the outcome.'
6 The product manager had rung the service manager: 'We have an urgent problem that's come all the way from the managing director. He wants it fixed, fast. Can you replace the stove for Mrs Long? Only got a Model K available? OK, let's do that then – I want to get this settled quickly.'

CookCo had, for the best of reasons, over-reacted. In marketing, the 'customer is king' – but even kings appreciate that not every one of their wishes is a Royal Command! Fortunately the managing director accepted responsibility for the time, effort and expense of this over-reaction, but determined that it would not happen again.

The key changes demanded were:

1 A reduction in the levels of management. 'Do we really need five tiers of management? Can we flatten the structure by combining mid-management roles? Prove why we need both a marketing manager and a group product manager.
2 Effective delegation so that issues went directly to the appropriate manager. In Mrs Long's case her letter should have gone directly from the managing director to the product manager for action.
3 Attitude change so that managers felt empowered to act as they thought best and not in fear of their managers' reaction.

SPAN OF MANAGEMENT

A major problem with a long management chain structure is that top management loses touch because it is so far away from day-to-day activities. Viewed from below, a senior manager can appear godlike – only visible when very important things are happening. It follows that even a simple instruction from on high acquires an importance and urgency because of its source.

Effective delegation ensures that issues are put into perspective by the manager charged with their effective management. It does not mean that the managing director loses interest, simply that the best way to respond is to give the job to the person best qualified. The CookCo managing director intended the complaint to go down the line, but each subsequent manager felt the need to add something to the message. When it arrived on the product manager's desk he naturally gave it priority treatment; because of top management involvement, not because it justified priority.

Note that when bypassing levels of management it is important to keep each informed of important issues. The risk is that junior staff are given instructions without the knowledge of their seniors, which causes embarrassment at best and destroys effective management and morale at worst. This requires a compromise between the efficiency of getting matters dealt with and the effectiveness of doing them thoroughly.

Just when a senior manager needs to be involved because of the contribution he can make is a matter of judgement. The need falls between always and never: both extremes are wrong! Usually a senior manager wants more involvement with a newly appointed junior's actions than with an experienced and trusted subordinate. An insecure manager demands more involvement, an over-confident one may ask for too little. Management is all about achieving results through people, and solving the 'people equation' is a constant and always fascinating challenge.

Letters of complaint to the managing director are a routine matter, however, and an alert organisation will provide a system to deal with them.

A typical system would be for the managing director's secretary to:

- sort complaints from the post;
- enter them in a complaints log;
- draft an appropriate response promising action;
- take the complaints over as soon as the MD has signed the letters;
- route them to the appropriate manager(s) for action;
- follow through if necessary;
- receive a response from the manager(s);
- draft a letter to the customer for the MD to sign;
- update the log;
- ensure that the logged details are included in the regular reports on complaints received by the organisation.

SPAN OF MANAGEMENT CONTROL

How many departments, managers, people should be placed under the management of a single individual? A manager performs the functions of planning, organising, leading and controlling, and so there must be a limit to the number of subordinates he can handle effectively. The span of management control therefore has a direct bearing on the number of levels of management in an organisation, and that in turn establishes the length of the organisation's lines of communication.

The flatter the structure the fewer levels of management, and the current trend is towards the flattening of structures that grew too tall during the growth periods of the 1970s and early 1980s. Hence the large numbers of early retirements, voluntary and forced redundancies that affected white collar staff in the late 1980s an early 1990s.

ORGANISED STRUCTURES

Structure is needed if an organisation is to operate effectively. As was shown in Chapter 2, managers form the skeleton that provides the foundation of the organisation. Just as a skeleton must be composed of specialist bones, each designed for a purpose and each interconnected, so an organisational structure must have a logical base. An organisation has the major benefit of being able to form and revise its structure – to adapt to need. Organisational structures should take advantage of this ability – structure should be built of glass, never stone nor elastic!

- A glass structure has form, strength and rigidity, but it shatters when stretched.
- A stone structure endures despite the elements, until it either wears away or is destroyed by a gale or earthquake.
- An elastic structure is all things to all people. It stretches and reshapes itself to accommodate with no regard for consistency of purpose.

DEPARTMENTS

Most of the time 'organisation' is actually reorganisation, because as soon as the organisation is formed it has structure. Change to this structure is reorganisation, a process of changing and refining the present structure and personnel.

The need for departments comes from the need to delegate as an organisation grows. A single entrepreneur must in time split off part of his job and delegate it to others. In turn they need assistants, and so an organisation grows. If this process is not managed, the result is an elastic structure which disguises a hodgepodge of departments often with overlapping areas of authority and little accountability.

The most usual bases for departmentalisation are:

- *Function.* Logically simple because functions are easy to distinguish. Finance, marketing, personnel, production, procurement, distribution – all are functionally independent, and all are composed of specialist functions, so subdivision is straightforward.
- *Product.* Where diversified product lines exit it is possible to create depart-

ments based on them. Other functions such as sales and finance are likely to retain their integrity since they service all product-based departments.

- *Customer.* Where special needs exist a structure can provide for them, e.g. sales can divide into specialist departments to sell soap to the retail, catering and industrial markets.
- *Geography.* The requirement to organise geographically dates from the time when communication was poor, and distance factors required local management with authority to act independently. Geographic organisation is less important now that good communication exists and the time taken to cover distances has shortened dramatically.
- *Process.* Process or equipment used in production may dictate the structure. Manufacture may be separated from Canning within the same factory unit.
- *Sequence.* Departments sometimes follow alphanumeric or time sequences. Customers with surnames from A to M may be handled by one department, from N to Z by another. Separate shifts, each of 8 hours, are a natural basis for departmentalisation.

Note that the term 'span of control' is old-fashioned but still occasionally used to designate span of management. In this sense 'control' means to direct and command. Control is better kept for use to describe the routine monitoring and reporting of progress against objectives – as we do consistently.

Structure is best illustrated with an example.

THE CITY STORE

Linda Congdon is the managing director of City Store. She runs the company with an assistant managing director and marketing, purchasing, and personnel directors. The company secretary is responsible for all legal matters, and is also finance director. The store has 40 departments, approximately 500 staff, of whom 350 are full- and 150 part-time.

If you were to ask Linda to describe the structure of the company she might draw a chart like Figure 5.1.

This shows that the line authority goes directly through David, the assistant managing director, to all other staff except for Linda's private secretary, who has a *staff* relationship. The display manager is in line to the marketing director, but both have staff relationships within the organisation.

- Line authority and responsibility joins those directly responsible for achieving an organisation's mission.
- Staff authority and responsibility links those in support of line staff.

The assistant managing director is shown in line. If the same person were assistant to the managing director he would be shown as staff, as in Figure 5.2.

The organisation chart expresses the formal lines of authority which enable activities to take place under a manager or supervisor. So Linda's private secretary can send memos to staff in her own right, but under the *derived authority* of her boss. She has no line authority of her own. In the same way the

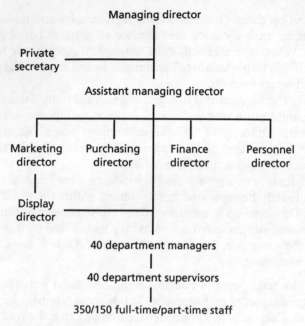

Fig. 5.1 City Store structure

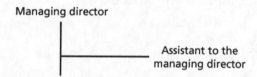

Fig. 5.2 Assistant to the Managing Director

marketing director can instruct the display manager, but has to advise the department managers.

In practice, of course, if the marketing director wants something done it will happen – but he will rely upon the next senior in line management for his derived authority to give instructions.

Koontz and O'Donnell say that staff roles 'create an environment for individual performance' because they allow individuals to act as though they have direct responsibility.

Traditionally structures have been very 'tall', with many layers of management. This has proved to be unwieldy, and unnecessary, and so we are currently seeing a 'flattening' of structure as layers of management are removed.

Flat structures, where fewer first line and middle rank managers are employed, means that those managers left have to spread their control over more staff. This, in turn, means that staff are individually acquiring greater personal responsibility and control over their actions.

Within City Store Bill Samuels is a furniture salesman. He specialised in selling dining room furniture, knows the supply companies and their specialist products, their representatives come to him with their new lines and special

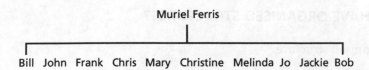

Muriel Ferris

Bill John Frank Chris Mary Christine Melinda Jo Jackie Bob

Fig. 5.3 Flat structure

promotions. Customers rely on him for his detailed and extensive knowledge. His nine colleagues each have their own specialities and together they make up a team that is lead by Muriel Ferris.

Bill sees his part of City Store as a flat structure (Fig. 5.3). He is also acutely aware that the 40 department managers and 40 supervisors are likely to be slashed . . . possibly by combining the two posts into one. This will mean major reorganisation, and reduce by half Bill's expectations of achieving a managerial appointment!

He has, therefore, raised the matter with Ishmail, the personnel director, since it directly affects his future.

'What we may very well do,' Ishmail explained, 'is to move to a matrix structure. This would open far greater opportunities for individuals to contribute, and put the old-fashioned line and staff roles into perspective.' Between them he and Bill sketched a possible matrix for City Store (see Figure 5.4).

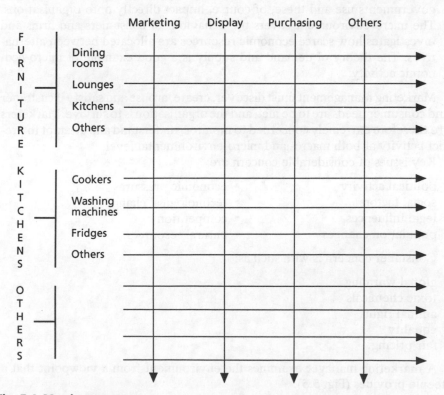

Fig. 5.4 Matrix structure

WHY HAVE ORGANISED STRUCTURES?

An organised structure:

- allows delegation of authority and accountability;
- defines who owns any problems that need to be solved;
- clarifies where (by whom) decisions have to be made;
- focuses professional expertise;
- indicates information sources and information need;
- targets managers for internal marketing.

NEED TO INTERACT WITH THE GREATER ENVIRONMENT

Economists distinguish macro- and micro-environments and this is helpful to marketing management, who must be aware of what is happening in the world in which the organisation earns its living.

- The macro-environment is the setting of objectives by governments and their actions in attempting to meet them. Typical macro-environmental objectives cover the need for full employment, avoidance of inflation, economic growth and balance-of-payments. Fiscal and monetary policy are the main tools that governments use and these, of course, impact directly onto organisations.
- The micro-environment covers the behaviour of consumers and firms and investigates how scarce economic resources are allocated between alternatives. The theory of demand and supply is a good example of micro-economic activity.

Marketing management must discover, create, arouse and satisfy if customer and consumer needs are to be met, and the organisation is to survive. Marketers are therefore extremely concerned to monitor, understand and attempt to predict activity at both macro- and micro-environmental level.

Key issues of considerable concern are:

- political activity
- social factors
- legal influences
- population changes

- economic pressures
- technological change
- competition
- natural resources.

Consumer concern is with such as:

- global warming
- toxic chemicals
- animal rights
- equality
- fair pricing.

A marketing manager examines the environment from a viewpoint that a steeple provides (Fig. 5.5).

Fig. 5.5 A marketing manager's viewpoint

We shall examine the STEEPLE factors in detail in Chapter 6. For now, note that the key issues of concern have been structured into the seven categories covered by the STEEPLE acronym.

S   Social/cultural
T   Technological/product innovation
E   Economic/market competition
E   Education/training/employment
P   Political
L   Legal
E   Environmental protection

(*Note:* The acronym PEST has been very well known for decades. It is no longer comprehensive enough, however, and has therefore been extended to STEEPLE.)

ORGANISATIONS IN THE ENVIRONMENT

At one time the only exterior organisations that were of concern to an organisation were government and government agencies, large individual customers, and competitors. Many customers were small, and without organisation they lacked effective power. Those days are long gone, however, and today's environment is composed of powerful groupings who are able to achieve results. Most of the environmental organisations are skilled marketers of their own particular cause – and all of the biggest and most powerful have marketing teams that rival the very best commercial trading organisations.

Organisations are constrained by statute as well as by common law and in all countries a number of statutes are being added each year to ensure fair trading of goods that are fit for their purpose and which are environmentally friendly in manufacture, supply and use.

We shall examine the key UK consumer protection laws in Chapter 6.

Common law is the body of law that has built up over the years as a result of previous court decisions. These establish legal precedents which have to be followed in subsequent court actions.

Statute law is laid down by government legislation, and is entered into the Statute Book in the Houses of Parliament after it receives the Royal Assent. Ministers of the Crown, if authorised by parliament, have the power to impose statutory instruments and to make orders which have the force of law even though they do not specifically pass through a vote in parliament.

Typical non-commercial organisations which exist to protect and promote the interests of their member or of the public at large include:

- trade unions, and the Trades Union Congress;
- employer associations and the Confederation of British Industries;
- chambers of trade, and of commerce and industry;
- trade associations such as the Cocoa & Chocolate Alliance;
- product organisations such as the Tea Council;

- protection organisations such as the Advertising Standards Authority;
- self-regulatory bodies such as the Health and Safety Executive.

CONSUMERISM

An organised movement to protect the interests of consumers, consumerism has been officially incorporated into British monopoly policy since the 1973 Fair Trading Act.

The rights of consumers were very badly protected under common law where the guiding principle was caveat emptor, i.e. let the buyer beware. The consumerism movement started in America in the early 1960s. Ralph Nader formed the most successful early consumer group, Public Citizen, and lifted consumerism into a major social force by attacking unsafe automobiles and forcing control legislation through Congress in 1962.

Also in 1962 President Kennedy published his Consumer Bill of Rights. This did not become law but greatly influenced thinking on the subject and provided a foundation upon which consumer legislation has been built. The key points of the 'Kennedy Bill' are:

- *The right to safety*. To be protected against the marketing of goods which are hazardous to health and life.
- *The right to be informed*. To be given the facts needed to make an informed choice.
- *The right to choose*. To be assured, whenever possible, of access to a variety of goods and services.
- *The right to be heard*. To be assured that consumer interests will receive full and sympathetic consideration in the formulation of government policy and fair and expeditious treatment in its administrative tribunals.

The 'green' movement

A concerted effort to prevent further damage to the environment has worldwide support from activist groups drawing on the experience gained by the consumerism movement. Skilful use of marketing tactics has harnessed public opinion to bring pressure to bear on governments and organisations of all types. The aim of the movement is to preserve the quality of life on our planet and activities range from parliamentary lobbying, through the formation of local groups to the strong actions taken by the crew of the Rainbow Warrior to prevent nuclear testing. Of great concern are the terrorist tactics of a group that has splintered from the Animal Liberation Front. This group has planted explosives and used sabotage to draw attention to manufacturers who have allegedly tested their products on live animals.

The issue has been recognised as so important that virtually all major organisations have a declared 'green' policy. It must also be recognised that 'green' sells products and so there is good commercial sense in supporting what is obviously a worthwhile cause. Typical changes that have been brought about by the efforts of the green movement are:

- natural food production with no additives nor colourings added in manufacture;
- replacement of CFC gases in refrigerators and aerosols to protect the ozone layer;
- action to reduce deforestation – in particular of the Amazonian rain forest;
- action to reduce acid rain and the subsequent loss of vegetation;
- protection of water supplies coupled with higher quality standards for drinking water, coastal waters and the high seas.
- energy savings through such as extraction of methane gas from waste and landfill sites;
- major efforts to recycle waste products, and to use biodegradable materials in packaging;
- efforts to reduce the quantity of wrapping and packaging.

Marketing planning and corporate decisions on product development and promotion must take green and consumer issues very seriously into account. It is not enough to be a green organisation; it is necessary to tell everyone – to show that 'green consciousness' is genuine and not simply a promotional gimmick.

Products need to have safety, durability and high quality designed into them. Consumers need to be encouraged to demand environmentally friendly products and to reject the resource-wasteful 'throw-away' society. These key concerns must be achieved whilst holding prices at affordable levels. Consumer demands are putting organisations under pressures that they have never before had to face, but many are succeeding in transforming what was routine but is now unacceptable.

Two examples of successful green activities are:

- Body Shop have a strict corporate policy against animal testing and will not stock any product that is not environmentally safe. Their sales are booming, even through the recession.
- Volkswagen have introduced their new Audi with an aluminium body that can be completely recycled.

CORPORATE IDENTITY

Organisations have a presence in the environment but until the late 1970s many failed to recognise the need to check consumer perceptions, or to take any actions to improve their image. Many were extremely effective in building the images of their brands, but found that their corporate identity was completely hidden by their brands.

This became important when the drive to consolidate took hold and major companies suddenly found themselves subject to hostile take-over bids. Even the giant Ranks Hovis McDougall found that as an organisation they were virtually unknown and so had little power when communicating in the money market. They had developed very popular cartoon characters – the Flour Graders – to sell their self-raising flour brand, and they even brought these into play on behalf of the company! To no avail. They lost the battle, and their independence with it.

Suddenly it became obvious that organisations had a personality, and that shy and retiring were not qualities that ensured success! It also dawned on senior managers that global communications were opening up, and that they needed to be visible across national borders. A great deal of creative effort was devoted to applying marketing skills to the branding of organisations.

- Nestlé continue trading through their subsidiary companies such as Crosse and Blackwell, Findus and Maggi – but have added their name to all products. Thus one now buys a Nestlé/Rowntree Kit-Kat.
- ICI spent many million of pounds on an apparently simple change to their famous 'ICI' logo. They explained that it had to be updated for the 90s and also become totally acceptable wherever ICI products were sold, which was everywhere!
- BP totally revised their image and adopted bright green as their corporate colour. All filling stations, every vehicle, all BP exposure had to be repainted and/or reprinted. The vast cost was justified in terms of the need for a strong corporate identity that expressed the company's commitment to the environment.

MARKETING PLANNING

Marketing planning is now no longer confined to products; it has to take corporate presence into account. Thus whatever corporate communication objectives are decided upon, these will affect the overall marketing functions. In BP for example, whatever a product manager has done, or wants to do, the new corporate policy on colour now has to be complied with.

There is now more corporate discussion concerning the role of public relations. Traditionally it has been a part of the marketing promotional mix, but now it is operating at corporate level. There it is helping to set corporate communication objectives which marketing has to follow. This may show that PR is growing into a major force which is separate from marketing. If so, will it reduce the importance of marketing at corporate level? Probably. But it will only be continuing the process of change which saw marketing's creation from 'advertising' and 'sales'.

KEY POINT SUMMARY

- Do not take unnecessarily urgent action simply because the order comes from top management.
- Ensure that a system to handle complaints is in place and effective.
- Span of management control describes the number of subordinates answering to a manager.

- Structures are becoming 'flatter'.
- Structure is needed to operate effectively.
- Structure should be of 'glass' so it shatters when changed.
- Departments are created by the need for growth.
- The most usual bases for departmentalism are: function, product, customer, geography, process and sequence.
- Line authority joins those directly responsible for achieving an organisation's mission.
- Staff authority links those in support of line staff.
- Derived authority allows action to be initiated on the authority of the next senior line manager.
- 'Assistants' are line appointments.
- 'Assistants to . . .' are staff appoints.
- A matrix structure allows individuals greater freedom to exert influence and to take responsibility.
- An organised structure is needed to:
  — Allow delegation.
  — Define who owns problems.
  — Clarify where (by whom) decisions must be made.
  — Focus professional expertise.
  — Indicate information sources and need.
  — Target managers for internal marketing.
- The macro-environment is governmental level concerns.
- The micro-environment is the behaviour of consumers and firms.
- Marketers are very concerned with both macro- and micro-environmental issues.
- The STEEPLE acronym guides a structured information search.
- Common law has built up over the years and is based on precedent.
- Statute law is laid down by government legislation.
- Non-commercial organisations exist to protect and promote the interests of their members and of the public at large.
- Consumerism is an organised movement to protect the interests of consumers.
- Consumerism was founded by Ralph Nader in the 1960s.
- President Kennedy published his 'Consumer Bill of Rights' in 1962.
- The green movement is a concerted effort to prevent further damage to the environment.
- Products need to have safety, durability and high quality designed into them.
- Corporate identity must be marketed to ensure that organisations, as well as their products, have an identity.
- Marketing planning must now take corporate presence into account.
- Public relations has a major role in corporate marketing.

WORK-BASED SELF-ASSESSMENT QUESTIONS

1 Using the organisation chart you drew for your organisation (Chapter 2), define the duties and responsibilities of your marketing manager.

2 What effect will the green movement have on future marketing planning in your department/organisation?

SCHOOL- OR COLLEGE-BASED SELF-ASSESSMENT QUESTIONS

1 Using the organisation chart for your school or college (Chapter 2), define the duties and responsibilities of each department and section head.

2 Describe the effect of consumerism on your school or college. Explain what changes you expect to see implemented within the next 5 years.

See the end of Chapter 7 for answer guidelines.

CHAPTER 6

Environmental factors and SWOT

Bob James faced a crisis. Aged 48 he had been a qualified pilot since he was 18 years old. He flew Vulcans in RAF Bomber command, then transferred to Jaguar strike aircraft. He retired from the RAF in 1985 and after extensive re-training qualified for his commercial pilot's licence. He then joined Air Europe as a command pilot flying into the major European airports. Air Europe was a substantial British charter airline, with interests in building scheduled flights, and expanding into the provision of reliable transportation for British holiday-makers taking package tours to Europe – notably to Mediterranean destinations.

The combination of the recession of 1990–92 and the effects of the Gulf War forced Air Europe out of business and in due course Bob's jetliner pilot's licence was revoked because he was unable to log sufficient flying hours. He was then only licensed to fly small aircraft commercially. Medically fit to fly, but with only a limited licence, Bob had to decide what to do. He could opt for retirement, but that was against his nature. As a fit and active man he needed to be occupied. Flying was the focus of Bob's life as he had no family – surely there were opportunities waiting to be exploited?

As a first step he checked through his assets:

- a private four-seater Cherokee plane based at Exeter, in the South West of England;
- a business interest in a school of flying instructors at Newcastle airport in the North East;
- savings and investments worth about £100 000;
- a small summer cottage 10 miles from Exeter airport at Exmouth;
- a flat in Whitley Bay, some 6 miles from Newcastle airport;
- a current pilot's licence;
- extensive experience of commercial flying in Europe;
- personal experience of flying into the major European airports;
- many personal contacts in the world of flying;
- management and leadership skills – from his RAF days particularly;
- strength of character and determination – which had led to his selection as an RAF command pilot in the first place.

Should he start his own business? If so, should this be based on his vast knowledge of flying? It was certainly his main instinct. Was it possible to make it work? Perhaps a limited freight service operating from Exeter, Newcastle, or both airports? A link with London City Airport might be a possibility?

He needed hard information to help him decide; his RAF training had implanted the need for reconnaissance and planning before commitment to action – surely these planning skills would be applicable to the commercial world?

He knew what he had to discover:

- Was it possible, at acceptable risk, to start a small air freight business based in the UK? If so:
- What form should it take?
- Where should it be based?
- What routes should it fly?

Bob drew on his RAF experience and decided to copy the intelligence officers who had briefed him before missions. They drew key information from the mass of data that was available, and they provided just enough detail to allow the mission to go ahead safely. Conditions on route to the target were important, but information became more detailed as they drew nearer to the target. The actual attack was planned with precision, and in great detail.

Bob would follow the same structure in his information gathering and then in his planning. He needed general details to determine if the 'mission' were possible. Only if it was feasible would he plan an actual route and then determine the equipment and personnel needed to carry through the mission satisfactorily.

Bob was not surprised to discover that businessmen came to similar conclusions long ago and that a methodology existed to help him obtain the information he needed.

Marketing management, he discovered, identify a market from an understanding of the major influences within the macro- and micro-environments. They proceed to audit the environments, to locate and extract information to help them decide appropriate action. This matched the model with which Bob was familiar. It was what he had been trained to do in the RAF (although different terms were used).

PEST was the auditing framework he first found, but he soon discarded it because it divided the environment into only four factors (Political, Economic, Social and Technological). This did not seem to be detailed enough and Bob happily abandoned it for the STEEPLE approach to auditing.

The STEEPLE factors necessary for successful environmental auditing are:

S   Social/Cultural
T   Technological/Product Innovation
E_1 Economic/Market Competition
E_2 Education/Training/Employment
P   Political
L   Legal
E_3 Environmental protection

S – SOCIAL AND CULTURAL INFLUENCES

Language, culture, attitudes and behaviour follow separate patterns in each society – these in turn influence buying behaviour and studies of societal influences can aid the development of marketing plans and strategies and lead to the markets of tomorrow.

T – TECHNOLOGICAL AND PRODUCT INNOVATION

Management must be active in searching for details of advanced research if it is not to be relegated to yesterday's technology. Electronics, in particular, are revolutionising the world's products and services and are having dramatic effects on communication in particular. 'Communication' includes everything from satellite TV and radio, through global security clearance for credit card sales, to personal communicators that will do away with hard wired telephones. New technology is allowing draft contracts to be agreed in writing by fax, interactive retailing via TV, the detailed and immediate monitoring of stocks and of sales, commercial aircraft to be flown by voice to wire command.

E – ECONOMIC AND MARKET COMPETITION (E,)

Economic activity and market competition are closely linked. When economic conditions are weak there is competitive pressure as the less efficient and simply unlucky businesses are forced to close. The improvement in economic conditions encourages consumer confidence and willingness to spend and therefore stimulates business expansion. Issues such as the business cycle, inflation rates, patterns of energy costs, investment and exchange rate fluctuations, make differences to economic levels of activity in each country.

Of particular concern are the:

- *Demographic profile and consumer buying habits.* How is the human population changing in terms of hard facts such as age and sex distribution, the geographical and occupational distributions? What is being bought, from where, and how is it being paid for?
- *Currency value and inflation rate.* The value of any one currency in relation to others will have a major effect on international competitiveness and, coupled with inflation rate, will be important to organisations, whether trading internationally or protecting their home market against competition from overseas.
- *Business cycle.* Nothing is static, and business tends to move in a cycle that has four phases. *Depression* is a period of rapidly falling demand that leads to very low levels of output and heavy unemployment. *Recovery* shows an upturn in demand, with rising output and a reduction in unemployment. *Boom* conditions are when demand reaches and then exceeds sustainable output levels, full employment is reached and excess demand causes infla-

tion. *Recession* follows a boom. Demand falls, small falls in output and employment follow – and depression can follow. A major concern of government is to stabilise an economy to avoid, or minimise the effects of, the worst phases of the business cycle.

- *Unemployment, levels of training and of retraining.* Where there is high unemployment there is likely to be cheaper labour, but severely limited demand. Trained workers command more wages, but produce to a higher quality and at a greater level of technological skill. Under good management a trained workforce, properly supported with capital investment, will be highly productive: the man hours taken to produce the same product may vary from 100 in a less developed area to only 5 or 6 where a trained and supported workforce is operating.
- *Income levels, disposable income, savings.* Income alone is not a valuable measure since individuals have some degree of choice in how it is spent. In good times the tendency is to spend because of confidence that the next pay cheque is secure, and confidence breeds confidence. With insecurity there is need to secure the future and savings levels increase, thus removing cash from the economy and making trading conditions worse.

  Disposable income is a measure of the moneys left available when all essential payments have been made. Taxes and National Insurance have to be paid, as do rent and service charges for water, electricity and gas. Food has to be bought, as does clothing. There is some degree of choice in how much heating to have in a house, what food to eat, what to wear, but the higher the basic income the larger the amount of disposable income and the wider the choice of how it is spent.
- *Availability of resources.* Natural resources are in limited supply, and their availability can be crucial to long-term success. Production resources require continual reinvestment if plant and machinery are not to become outdated. This has serious implications for the financing of an organisation since maximum benefit has to be extracted from capital investment before it becomes redundant. Redundancy occurs in times of fast technological change before the full worth has been extracted from the investment – equipment that still has many years of service has to be replaced if an organisation is to remain competitive, and this waste has to be financed.
- *Resources and competitive forces within an economy.* Economies typically have a wide variation in their resources, and in their competitiveness. What they need to import and what they can offer in export has a crucial effect on their ability to sustain a standard of living. Economies that are dependent upon imported supplies are particularly vulnerable.

E – EDUCATION, TRAINING AND EMPLOYMENT (E₂)

The levels of achievement by school pupils, college and university students, early learners and trainees in industry, are important to the long-term capability of the economy. In many countries there is a widening of the achievement level between the school leavers and those who go on to achieve master's degrees. Lower levels of literacy and shorter attention spans are beginning to have an effect on the quality of service. Organisations are actively seeking older employees in preference to school leavers. This 'E2' factor has possibly the most important long-term effect on an economy's long-term survival.

P – POLITICAL

Government, legal and voluntary frameworks control and may influence the way we behave, the things we do, what we buy and how we make decisions. National and local government have a direct effect on our lives. In the EU there is an ever-growing range of standardisation, measures of harmonisation agreed by the member nation states and then brought into force within nations as directives. Other bodies such as the Institute of Management use self-regulation and codes of conduct to influence the way their members behave.

L – LEGAL

Legislation to control such issues as competition and unfair trading practices, consumer protection and consumer legislation exist in most countries. How effective they are is dependent upon national attitude and the degree of control and its efficiency. There is an increasing need to know, understand and comply with all relevant legal control measures, for ignorance of the law is no defence. A wise marketing manager relies upon an experienced lawyer, or legal department to ensure that actions taken are within EU regulations. Key legal and voluntary controls within the UK are covered below.

E – ENVIRONMENTAL PROTECTION (E₃)

Each country has evolved uniquely different environmental control regulations. These range from zoning regions for specific purposes, to detailed planning permissions for modification to individual buildings. There is growing international concern with global environmental protection, air, water and land usage, but considerable difficulty in securing agreement on detailed action from individual governments. The green movement (see Chapter 5) is extremely active, on an international basis, to encourage governments, organisations and individuals to introduce and enforce strict measures to protect the environment.

KEY LEGAL AND VOLUNTARY CONTROLS WITHIN THE UK

In setting up his new airline Bob needs to understand the basic legislation protecting customers. The most important legislation includes:

- *Trades Descriptions Act 1968.* This act makes it a criminal offence in the UK to apply a false description to any goods, or supply of goods. Trading Standards Officers are empowered to enter premises and to inspect goods and/or records, and to seize goods if necessary.
- *Fair Trading Act 1973.* This act regulates monopolies and mergers, not of particular interest to Tim, but it affects larger airlines. The Secretary of State can refer a business merger to the Monopolies and Mergers Commission if 25% of goods and/or services will be supplied by a single company.
- *Consumer Credit Act 1974.* This act controls the granting of consumer credit and provides protection to consumers through the licensing of credit firms. When the debtor has paid a third of the value of the property the creditor is unable to re-possess the goods without a court order, since they are deemed to be 'protected'.
- *Weights and Measures Act 1985.* This updates the acts of 1963 and 1979 to ensure that the customer is given accurate measure, by whatever means, weight, quantity, or numerical count.
- *Consumer Protection Act 1987.* This enforces protection for consumers in the UK through trading laws giving powers to local authorities to set up, under the national umbrella of a Minister of State, the Office of Fair Trading, local Consumer Advice Centres, publications and advisory services for the protection of consumer rights and procedures when goods or services are not of merchantable quality.
- *The Consumer Credit (Advertisement) Act 1989.* This act strengthened the laws protecting consumers against wrongful descriptions of credit facilities.

The key bodies empowered to protect consumers include:

- *Trading Standards Department (Government and Local Government).* Larger towns and cities in the UK have local walk-in Consumer Advice Centres, providing consumers with detailed information on the procedures for complaint against suppliers, i.e. cases of under-weight, wrongly described, or deficient goods of less than merchantable quality. Officers will represent consumers and bring pressure to bear on suppliers. The centres are operated by local authorities under the Minister of State for Consumer Affairs.
- *Environmental Health Departments.* Local government provides protection against unclean premises (food, restaurants, etc.) and safeguards food and drinks through a system of inspectors acting mainly on information received from the public.
- *Trade and Users' Associations.* Trade and Users' Associations protect consumers within their group of suppliers through codes of practice by which each supplier will operate to a quality standard agreed by Association members. Associations work closely with the Office of Fair Trading and discipline any member who fails to observe agreed standards. The most influential are for cars and car repairs, electrical goods and companies providing holidays.
- There are also various bodies involved in regulation and consultation, with consumer protection, price limitation and competition as their main objectives, such as:
  — OFTEL – the telephone consumer protection group, deals with complaints from telephone users and is instrumental in reducing the price of

telephone calls.
— OFFER – The Office of Electrical Regulation insist on accountability in the £50 billion industry, and competition in the generation of electricity.
— OFGAS – The Office of Gas Supply is the British Gas watchdog protecting against price rises and maintaining quality of service to users.
— OFWAT – The Office of Water Services is the Water Boards' user committee with powers similar to OFFER and OFGAS.
— MOPS – Mail Order Protection Scheme, handles any consumer problems arising from the purchase of goods through newspaper or magazine advertisements.
— POUNC – Post Office User's protection committee.

Each watchdog committee is empowered to protect the consumer against the power of monopoly suppliers and 'regulates the regulators'.

CITIZEN'S CHARTERS

By 1994 there were 32 Citizen's Charters, which are statements of time, quality and service a consumer might expect. They are designed to protect the quality and levels of pubic service provided, e.g. British Rail, Royal Mail, and financial services. In education, health and service industries the aim to be leaner, fitter and more competitive must focus on the consumer, rather than work against consumer interest. The term 'Citizen's Charter' was therefore developed to describe the basic and fundamental levels to be accepted from each particular service.

The Citizen's Charter for Health explains the plans and policies for improving health care, improving quality of NHS provision, choice, rising standards and value for money:

1 The levels of service from the National Health Service.
2 The rights to be registered with a family doctor, access to records, referral and emergency care.
3 The rights of the patient to dentist treatment.
4 Hospital treatment – arrival of the ambulance in emergency:
   (a) within 14 minutes living in an urban area;
   (b) within 18 minutes in a rural area;
   (c) within 21 minutes in a sparsely populated area.
5 Treatment and waiting times:
   (a) admission within 2 years on a waiting list;
   (b) no cancellation on the day of an operation;
   (c) if the operation is postponed twice, admission within one month of the planned date of the second operation;
   (d) discharge from hospital only after nursing care is arranged;
   (e) out-patients to be seen within 30 minutes of their appointment.

Information is then given concerning the patient's rights when treatment goes wrong, where to get additional information and useful addresses. The charter gives quality levels in time and qualified statements to help those in sickness to understand the NHS and for those supplying care to understand the level of provision expected.

MARKETING AUDITS

As used in management the term auditing means to carry out a detailed check of a particular subject around a specified focus. The idea is to obtain answers to the key questions:

* Where is the organisation now?
* What are the alternative options available?

An audit is a detailed study which provides management with information. An audit is not a tool of decision. It helps managers to make decisions, because it provides the vital information needed. Major decisions are always made by managers, never by the juniors they employ.

Who paints a picture?	The brush and oils	or the artist?
What makes a table?	Saws, hammers, nails	or the joiner?
Who makes a decision?	Research	or the manager?

Management audits are made regularly to give management an overview of the current position of an organisation. Key audits include financial, resources, marketing, personnel skills and training, production methods and results, customer accounts and administration.

A marketing audit is designed to provide the information needed in order that plan(s) of action can be recommended. A regular, comprehensive and systematic review of an organisation's marketing environment is set against the corporate policies, strategies and tactics, so that problem and opportunity areas are identified.

Marketing audits are especially concerned with the marketing environment, customers, consumers and competitors, organisational, systems, productivity and functions (Wilson, Gilligan with Pearson, 1993). Each of these main classifications breaks down into sub-issues that relate to the items within the extended marketing mix. Every issue of current and potential importance must be identified and researched.

They must be:

* *regular*, because the environment is constantly changing and current information is needed. It is normal to carry through a full audit before each budget period, usually annually, but limited audits are a valuable aid to any strategic decision.
* *comprehensive*, because it is necessary to have all the relevant facts. Beware of the danger of too deep a research which provides too much information. This is better, however, than shallow research which is lower in price but of limited value. A major problem with shallow research is that you have no

idea of what you do not know! Therefore it is better to err on the deeper side, and cut back in the light of experience.

- *Systematic*: only a logical and orderly sequence of steps which cover the marketing environment, internal marketing system and actual marketing activities will provide the necessary detail.

The audits must deal with:

- *Problems*: these must be identified because they have to be faced. Unwelcome they may be, but they will not go away without specific action, and it is better to tackle a problem whilst it is still small – even better to prevent it ever starting.
- *Opportunities*: there are always opportunities, usually a very wide range to choose from. They must be identified if they are to be evaluated – remember that competitors will also be auditing and they are likely to discover the same opportunities. Thus one which is rejected may surface later as a problem if a competitor decides to pursue it.

A marketing audit normally covers these major areas:

- macro-environment – using the STEEPLE headings;
- task environment – covering immediate issues such as market, customers, consumers, distribution and suppliers;
- strategies – re-examination of the mission, objectives and strategies;
- organisation – effective and efficient?
- systems – is the organisation operating to optimum effect?
- productivity – relative profitability and cost-effectiveness;
- mix tactics – each of the four Ps examined in detail to consider such issues as age and likely future of each product, effectiveness of the pricing policy, structure of the distribution channels, appropriateness of the promotional activity.

Each major area will be subdivided into considerable detail and a full audit will occupy months, rather than weeks for a major organisation. Once the auditing process has become established, however, it is far easier to repeat. Initial set-up is likely to be time consuming and the results will not be fully detailed. Smoothness and completeness both improve with practice, and the 'learning curve' has to be experienced if long-term benefits are to be obtained.

SWOT ANALYSIS

The tool of SWOT analysis is absolutely essential to all managers and individuals find that it becomes second nature to 'SWOT' their way through to decisions in private, as well as organisational, life. As with all tools it becomes easier to use, and more effective, with practice. A major strength is that it is simple to understand and easy to use.

SWOT stands for strengths, weaknesses, opportunities and threats:

- Strengths and weaknesses are internal.
- Opportunities and threats are external.

SWOT principles

1 Divide a sheet of paper into four quadrants and label them S, W, O, T.
2 Brainstorm – never try to SWOT by logically completing one quadrant at a time.
3 Work in rough at first. Polish the SWOT later, when you are evaluating the importance of each issue.
4 Expect strengths to be matched by weaknesses and opportunities by threats. They are not always matched, but very often they are, e.g. a city office location can be a strength, but its costs can be a weakness. Does the strength outweigh the weakness?

The easiest way to understand how to carry out a SWOT analysis is to relate it to an actual situation. Think back to Alisa and her need to audit her library. She carried through a SWOT which looked as shown in Table 6.1.

Table 6.1 SWOT of Avenue Park Library

Strengths	*Weaknesses*
Support by local population	Book provision – mainly novels
A study centre for students	No reference section
A focal point for families	No reading area
Entertainment centre/exhibitions	No research into demand
New buildings in new site	No segmentation
Adjacent to new housing/school	No balance of stock
Industrial centre close	Delays in requisitions
Car park space – 25 cars	No monitoring/control
To raise quality of service	Video – and cable companies
Cater for each segment:	Apathy of youngsters – youth's short attention span
	New interactive video
• school pupils	Video games
• college/university students	Computer-aided learning
• families	Book shops (competition from)
• sports enthusiasts	Competing activities
• hobbies	Apathy to learning
• reading room for the elderly	All other providers
• creche facilities for mothers	
Opportunities	*Threats*

Bob James listed all the features that applied to his situation and set about constructing a SWOT. These are the features he listed. Practise the technique by constructing a SWOT from Bob's features. When you have finished compare your SWOT with Bob's result (Table 6.2).

- inner strength and determination;
- flying skills;
- current pilot's licence;
- skills of managing:
  — aircrews,
  — maintenance crews,
  — airport systems,
  — aircraft spares,
  — radar systems;
- wide administrative experience;
- financial security;
- no family commitments;
- contacts across the world of flying;
- personal experience of the main European airports;
- living accommodation at both potential sites;
- no single base for flying operations;
- no airport facilities or contacts;
- no contact with other larger flying operations in:
  — freight services,
  — passenger services,
  — overseas operations in the EU,
  — travel companies;
- no links with finance houses, banks, or financial backers;
- no knowledge of:
  — marketing research,
  — potential customers,
  — knowledge of competitors;
- no first-hand experience of business;
- no understanding of market developments;
- EU opening routes across Europe – to fly:
  — freight, passengers – or both,
  — in UK, or across Europe;
- flight benefits:
  — cost and time savings,
  — convenience and comfort;
- trade into the EU and Europe actively supported by the UK government;
- London City Airport only 6 miles from the City of London;
- aircraft available for lease;
- demand for global air travel expanding rapidly and the UK export drive requiring managers to travel in order to sell;
- boredom, leading to the potential loss of enthusiasm and drive;
- many smaller companies, potential competitors, successfully expanding;
- alternative travel, notably the new Channel Tunnel;
- overseas based airlines operating into the UK;
- larger airlines opening smaller, feeder routes;
- insufficient capital to become established.

Notes on the SWOT

- Cabotage is the legal right of aircraft or trucks of one EU country to ply for hire in another. Full cabotage will become EU law in 1997, and so help reduce freight costs because return loads will become legal. An EU 'open skies' policy will then be in place under which there will be freedom for airlines to open routes without specific government approval.
- London City Airport is only 20 minutes by taxi from the City of London. It has a short runway which will only take small aircraft. A suitable aircraft, with a 300 mile range, can reach many key EU cities, including Paris, Brussels and Amsterdam. It does not look like an opportunity for a major airline, but for a small operator could be a significant opportunity.
- Aircraft can be leased rather than bought outright. Older, slower aircraft, that no other airline require, might prove to be economic for Bob. He might even lease them on an 'as needed', rather than an annual basis.

Table 6.2 Bob James' SWOT

Strengths	Weaknesses
Inner strength/determination	No airport facilities
Bob's flying skills	No airport contacts
Current pilots licence	No freight/air taxi/ overseas operations
Bob's management skills	contacts
Financial security	No financial links – no bankers/backers
No family commitments	No marketing research
Contacts across the flying world	No knowledge of customers nor
Experience of EU airports	competitors
Exeter/Newcastle living accommodation	No understanding of market development
	No business experience
	Boredom – possible loss of drive
Free to choose base	Competitors' plans unknown
EU open skies policy opening new	New Channel Tunnel
routes for freight and passengers	Overseas competitors – EU open skies
Passenger cost and time savings	works into UK as well as out from it!
Passenger convenience and comfort	New feeder routes
Government supported trading policy	Larger airlines possibly going into
London City Airport open to him	smaller airfields and routes
Aircraft available on lease	Insufficient capital?
Global air travel demand expanding	
UK export drive into Europe.	
Opportunities	Threats

Bob James' SWOT shows him to be highly aware of his own strengths and weaknesses, and shows how little hard information he actually has about the market he is considering entering. It shows what he has to achieve even before he can start the serious business of management decision-making. He has to learn about marketing research, for example – also to discover something about sources of finance, and the requirements of financiers, before they will consider a loan.

Bob James was highly motivated and so very quickly learned enough basic marketing and management skills to move ahead in his auditing – which we shall return to in Chapter 7.

KEY POINT SUMMARY

- STEEPLE factors are a framework for environmental auditing.
- The STEEPLE factors are: Social & Cultural; Technological and Innovation; Economics and Market Competition; Unemployment, Levels of training; Education Training & Employment; Political; Legal; Environmental Protection.
- The key acts in consumer protection are:
  — The Trades Description Act 1968
  — Fair Trading Act 1973
  — Consumer Credit Act 1974
  — Weights & Measures Act 1985
  — Consumer Protection Act 1987
  — The Consumer Credit (Advertisement) 1989.
- Key bodies that represent consumer interests and reinforce legislation are:
  — Environmental Health Departments
  — Trade and Users Associations
  — Regulatory bodies such as: OFTEL, OFFER, OFGAS, OFWAT, MOPS and POUNC.
- Citizen's Charters state the levels of consumer quality of service to be expected.
- Management and marketing audits are detailed checks of a particular subject around a specified focus.
- An audit is a detailed study which provides management with information.
- Audits must be: regular, comprehensive, systematic. They must identify problems and opportunities.
- SWOT analysis is an excellent way to clarify a situation.
- Strengths and Weaknesses are internal factors.
- Opportunities and Threats are external factors.

WORK-BASED SELF-ASSESSMENT QUESTION AND SCHOOL- OR COLLEGE-BASED SELF-ASSESSMENT QUESTION

All to complete:

Draw a quadrant and produce a personal SWOT analysis of your own position. Audit your own strengths, weaknesses, opportunities and threats. Use your SWOT to identify key areas of activity that you should be undertaking to exploit opportunities and capitalise on strengths. Carefully note threats and weaknesses and plan your actions accordingly.

See the end of Chapter 7 for answer guidelines.

CHAPTER 7

The business plan

A business has to be developed from an initial idea into a commercial reality. Bob James had to progress from his SWOT analysis, consolidate his strengths, minimise his weaknesses, quantify the opportunities and threats, and take clear decisions.

Bob had to produce a business plan which would itemise his intentions and, most importantly, show the revenue he expected to generate and the costs he would incur. Only if there was an acceptable surplus of revenue over costs, i.e. profit! – would it be possible to go forward.

To start up any business somebody has to advance sufficient money to establish the office, the factory, the equipment – everything needed to make trade possible. Money is also needed to support the new business whilst it builds up revenue.

- *Fixed capital* is the moneys tied up in tangible assets. If Bob invested in aircraft that turned out to be too small, or too large, it would be a serious matter to replace them. If he located in the wrong place this could add additional and unnecessary costs over a long-term period. Every fixed capital decision is crucial because of its long-term implications.
- *Working capital* consists of funds that are held liquid, e.g. cash at bank, to meet on-going expenses such as salaries, insurance and fuel for the aircraft. Some expenses are fixed because they are incurred whether or not the business has any income (e.g. insurance and standing charges for telephones, gas and electricity). Other are variable because they vary with use (e.g. fuel is only consumed when the aircraft are working).
- *Cash and cash flow* are the two most important considerations for all managers. Many profitable companies have been forced out of business because their customers took too long to pay their bills, or did not pay them at all! The amount of cash to meet daily commitments ran out.
- *Leasing of capital equipment* allows a business to equip itself without committing capital. It also can add considerable flexibility as equipment can be upgraded as needed. The downside is the commitment to the lease, the absence of fixed assets within the organisation and the long-term higher costs (because the leasing company must make a profit in return for the service it provides). On the other hand Bob needed to examine the tax implications of owning as against leasing equipment – a very complex area for which he wisely took advice from an experienced accountant.

When Bob began to discuss his potential financial needs he found that financiers have prepared guides to help entrepreneurs devise an acceptable business plan. The National Westminster Bank, for example, produces a *Small*

Business Finance Guide which 'aims to explain, in plain English, the bare minimum that you need to know to understand and help to control the finances of your business.'

The NatWest *Small Business Finance Guide* is packaged in an outer folder which contains three clearly written Guides and three sets of Worksheets:

• Break-even Guide	How to understand how much trade is needed to at least cover costs. What gross margin is and how to calculate fixed costs.
• Cash Guide	Control of cash and of working capital. Debtors, creditors and stock management.
• Growth Guide	How to control growth.
• Cash Worksheets	Pro formas set out ready for the user to fill in his own figures, and to use as a basis when setting up a firm's books.
• Growth Worksheets	
• Break-even Worksheets	

Funding the healthy growth of any business requires care. The Growth Worksheet provides a format to ensure that no major element is missed (see Figure 7.1). It also contains (as do all the documents) the formulae needed to calculate the key figures that a manager needs.

PURPOSE OF TRADE

Drucker states that 'a clear definition of the mission and purpose of the business makes possible clear and realistic business objectives'. The clear purpose of trade is to achieve an acceptable profit – acceptable for business survival, acceptable by customers. The first stage of planning, therefore, is to determine what is an acceptable level of profit.

There is no point investing in a project with any degree of commercial risk unless the return is expected to be comfortably above what is safely available in interest from the finance houses. If an investment in a bank or building society brings in a safe return of, say, 5%, it follows that acceptable profit has to be at least 10% to justify the risk of the investment . . . as interest rates in an economy rise and fall, so do the profits needed to justify continued investment in industry. Hence the concern of businessmen when interest rates rise, and their relief when they fall.

Interest rates have a much greater impact on business and profits, however. As they risk the amount to be repaid on loans increases. Thus a business has to achieve a higher level of profits just to meet the increased interest on its debt – and it has to do this at the same time as customers are squeezed because trade is depressed by the rise in interest! Managers are therefore always extremely aware of their cash position, and are anxious to minimise outgoings, whilst maximising income.

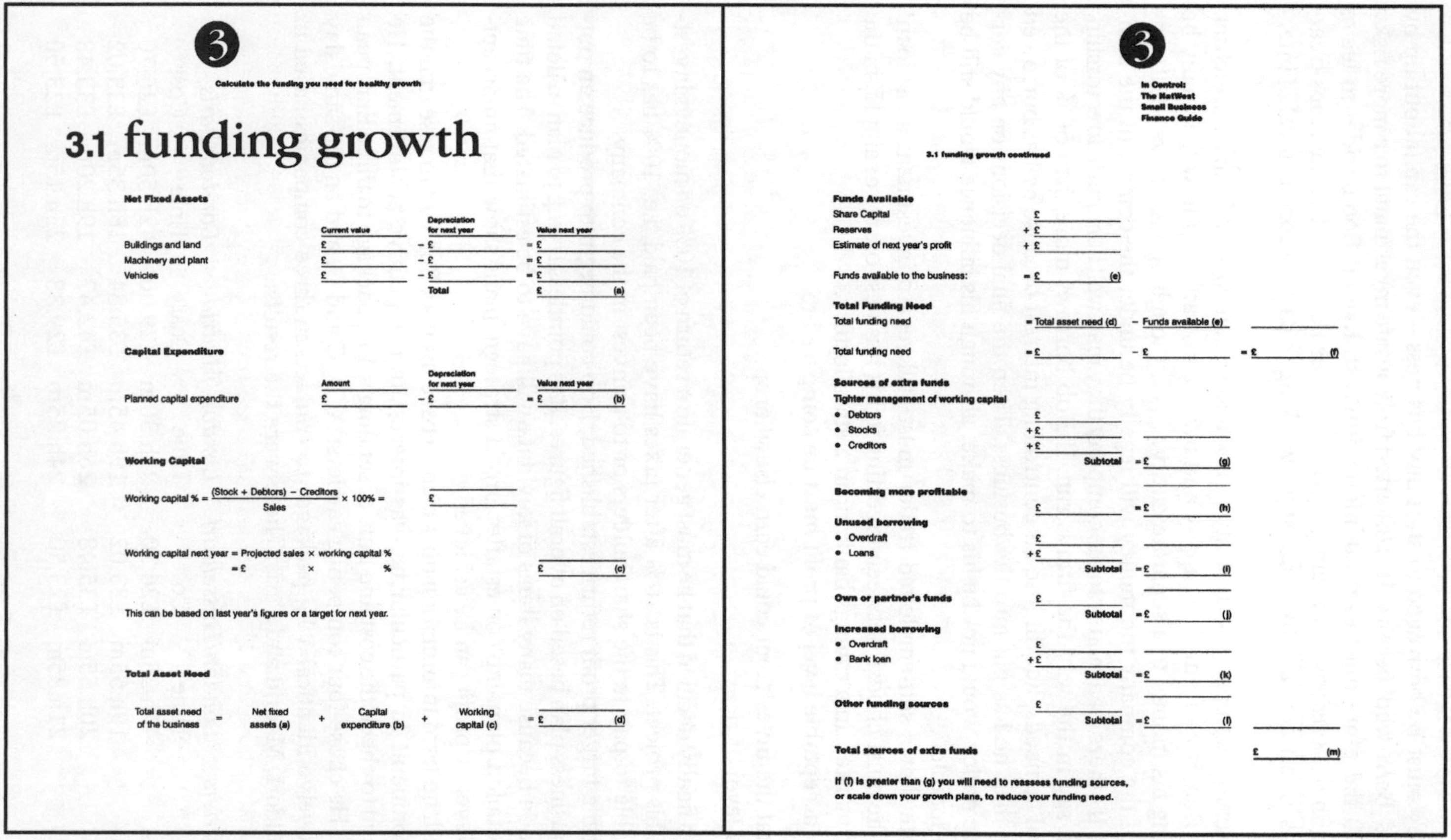

3

Calculate the funding you need for healthy growth

3.1 funding growth

Net Fixed Assets

	Current value		Depreciation for next year		Value next year	
Buildings and land	£	–	£	=	£	
Machinery and plant	£	–	£	=	£	
Vehicles	£	–	£	=	£	
			Total		£	(a)

Capital Expenditure

	Amount		Depreciation for next year		Value next year	
Planned capital expenditure	£	–	£	=	£	(b)

Working Capital

Working capital % = $\frac{\text{(Stock + Debtors) – Creditors}}{\text{Sales}}$ × 100% = £

Working capital next year = Projected sales × working capital %
= £ × % £ (c)

This can be based on last year's figures or a target for next year.

Total Asset Need

Total asset need of the business = Net fixed assets (a) + Capital expenditure (b) + Working capital (c) = £ (d)

3

In Control:
The NatWest
Small Business
Finance Guide

3.1 funding growth continued

Funds Available

Share Capital	£	
Reserves	+ £	
Estimate of next year's profit	+ £	
Funds available to the business:	= £	(e)

Total Funding Need

Total funding need = Total asset need (d) – Funds available (e)

Total funding need = £ – £ = £ (f)

Sources of extra funds

Tighter management of working capital

- Debtors £
- Stocks + £
- Creditors + £

Subtotal = £ (g)

Becoming more profitable £ = £ (h)

Unused borrowing

- Overdraft £
- Loans + £

Subtotal = £ (i)

Own or partner's funds £

Subtotal = £ (j)

Increased borrowing

- Overdraft £
- Bank loan + £

Subtotal = £ (k)

Other funding sources £

Subtotal = £ (l)

Total sources of extra funds £ (m)

If (f) is greater than (g) you will need to reassess funding sources, or scale down your growth plans, to reduce your funding need.

Fig. 7.1 Growth worksheets

Source: Reproduced from *In Control* (Guide to Small Businesses), February 1994, published by National Westminster Bank Plc in conjunction with the Small Business Centre of Durham University Business School.

LOAN CAPITAL

Money must be borrowed to start any business – even the capital put up by Bob is 'borrowed' because it is diverted from a safe investment to a more risky one. It therefore must earn additional interest. Even if Bob decides to leave profit in the business – to reinvest it – this does not mean that he stops treating his investment as a loan, nor stops working to pay the correct level of interest.

A limited company is an entity in law and so can borrow from its directors. Thus Bob, if he forms a company and invests his capital in it, will actually be loaning his money to a separate entity. Even though he may have total control of the company the money will legally be under the control of the company. If others loan money to the company they may well demand a directorship, and a say in the way the firm is run. If Bob borrows more than 50% of the capital he needs, he will lose his controlling interest because he has borrowed more than he has put into the business. Then the final decisions on any corporate policy would not be his to make, although his influence would still be considerable.

Note that a self-employed trader must still regard investment as a 'loan' since he must choose between investing in his business or, for example, in the stock market, in a savings bank, or in a state lottery.

An acceptable level of profit must be compared to:

• what the investment could earn elsewhere;
• the level of risk.

Bob finally decided that he must generate a return of 10% on moneys invested in his project. This is 10% after taxes have been paid, i.e. 10% has to be available to pay to the shareholders or to reinvest in the company.

With a target profit return established, Bob could begin to produce an outline business plan based on overall figures. It is pointless trying to plan in detail too soon because many items of key data will have to be estimated. The time for detailed planning comes after broad strategic plans show that an acceptable level of profit can be achieved.

With no hard information on which to base his plan Bob had to research the environment. In particular he was interest in competitive achievement. He decided to check the cost and time of sending a 1 kg package to three European cities. He chose four competing carriers: A, B, C and D, and on the same day sent twelve identical 1 kg packages to contacts in three companies based in Düsseldorf, Madrid and Paris. These were the results:

Carriers	London/Düsseldorf		London/Madrid		London/Paris	
	Time	Cost	Time	Cost	Time	Cost
1 A	41h.35m	£26.70	21h.30m	£29.00	42h.50m	£26.70
2 B	19h.55m	£33.02	19h.45m	£35.84	18h.35m	£33.02
3 C	20h.55m	£35.48	26h.05m	£42.47	19h.20m	£35.48
4 D	21h.35m	£23.50	24h.25m	£29.38	23h.15m	£23.50

These results surprised Bob. The shortest distance, London to Paris, took much longer in the case of carrier A than the packages to Madrid, which was the furthest. The packages to Paris cost exactly the same as those to Düsseldorf, yet the distance to Paris is shorter. The fastest was not always the most expensive.

Questions
- What did Bob really learn from these timings and pricings?
- How could he use this information in his business plan?

Answers
- *Timings and pricings.* Bob questioned several potential customers and found that distance, time and price are less critical than quality of service and arrival without loss, theft, or damage. Bob could either undercut competitors by charging, say, £22 to any destination he flies to, or offer a premium service and charge £40 into European destinations for a 1 kg package.

Quality of service is more important to customers than speed of delivery. Safety is more important than price, or speed. This made him consider also the possibility of a joint venture with a European carrier for onward delivery from the airfields he selects for regular flights. Bob therefore needs to consider selecting a high, medium, or low pricing strategy with a direct bearing on volume and his target sales for the year.

Next Bob checked the cost of aircraft hire. He found that the lowest hire charges for aircraft, pilot, fuel, insurance and landing fees were:

Passengers	Per hour	Per 8 hour day
Up to 3	£60.00	£450.00
4–6	£250.00	£1900.00
7–10	£350.00	£2500.00

Typically three managers could, within a single working day, visit Europe, land close to final destination, hold a two hour meeting and return to London at a cost of £450.

Using a scheduled airline would require a flight from a British 'gateway' airport (e.g. London) to another gateway (e.g. Paris). There would be need to travel to and from both gateways. Bob found that 34 hours was the average time needed for the same two hour meeting, using scheduled flights, and including travel from final gateway to the meeting.

Bob also checked the cost per mile of European travel. He felt that many companies might be paying more than they need for transporting personnel to destinations within the European Union. The costs he discovered are shown in Table 7.1

Table 7.1

London to:	Average cost (pence/mile)
Paris	0.71
Amsterdam	0.57
Copenhagen	0.36
New York	0.31
Tokyo	0.24
Hong Kong	0.16

Bob found many discrepancies between price over distance and that the number of competitors on each route was the main price determinant. Where competition was fierce the price per mile, particularly for scheduled flights, fell quite sharply.

The savings he could offer were in 'time away from desk' – savings in time, rather than in the fares paid. He also found that the comfort, prestige and convenience of a flying taxi were factors to consider, but these he found difficult to quantify for inclusion in comparative costings.

Question
- How does this give Bob a basis for planning an air taxi service giving quality service for managers and executives meeting in Europe?

Answers
Bob found that:

- The major airlines – British Airways, Lufthansa, Malaysia Airways, Quantas, Singapore Airways and Virgin – were all targeting business travellers. 'Frequent flier programmes' were designed to give preferential treatment, exclusive lounges, free flights and other gifts to businessmen who show loyalty to one airline.
- He also found that the Business Travel Liaison Group (BTLG) was formed in 1988 to give advice to companies spending millions of pounds every year on flight tickets.
- British Airways claim they derive two main advantages from their frequent flyer programmes: loyalty of regular customers and a sound database for their strategic planning.
- Lufthansa offered one return trip free for every seven Business Class round trips taken `– a powerful incentive to stay loyal to that airline.
- Organisations prefer their employees to take the lowest cost fares, whilst the employees prefer the incentives.
- A survey of American travel habits showed that some executives were deliberately planning the longest route to build up personal mileage.

Question
- How does this information help Bob plan his business?

Answer
- He has identified key issues that are of importance to managers who, like himself, have businesses to run at a profit and are interested in cash flow and value for money. He could use his unique knowledge and skills to build an advisory service for small to medium-sized companies, arranging travel that yields fewer perks for staff, and lower travelling costs to the company.

Since the beginning of open skies legislation in January 1993 European carriers have the right to fly anywhere in the EU. Unfortunately many of the largest European airports are fully loaded. All flying 'slots' are then allocated to national airlines. Smaller airfields such as Exeter, Newcastle and Stansted still have available slots and charge lower landing fees. (Stansted is London's third airport and is located 40 miles north-east of the city. It is not a popular airport, nor can it be easily reached.)

Bob considered selecting a niche segment of the market where large airlines charge a high price per mile, but where deregulation by the EU will lower these prices in future. He did think that a link between Exeter, London and Newcastle, with Amsterdam, Brussels, Luxembourg and Paris, might be a set of possible entry points to consider for a new service – but by charter or by schedule?

Questions
- What are Bob's alternative marketing strategies?
- Is there a marketing niche to be opened up, given the research data now in Bob's possession?
- Should he concentrate on flying freight, or passengers, or both?

Answers
- Bob did not have the experience to judge the potential market.
- He lacked finely tuned marketing research on customer demand from UK into Europe.
- He did not have sufficient information on the freight market.
- He needed details of patterns of freight movements through UK.

The Department of Trade and Industry statistics showed the flow to be:

Table 7.2 Goods moved in UK (thousand million tonnes per kilometre)

Year	Moved by road	Moved by rail
1969	83.4	25.3
1974	89.9	24.2
1979	102.3	19.9
1984	99.9	12.7
1989	137.4	17.3

Reductions in government rail subsidies in the 1980s had caused rises in rail pricing. Rail freight in volume is in decline. More goods are being trucked by road. The fluctuations also suggest changes to be in response to economic activity. In boom times the demand, for freight carriers increases sharply (1979, 1989). In recession demand falls away (1984).

Just-in-time management (JIT), introduced by the more efficient UK factories, created a growing demand for flexibility and dependability in the delivery of freight. Delays cost dearly. This led to increasing use of road haulage and to a decline in rail.

Increase in road haulage coincided with increases in the use of cross-channel ferries and, after January 1993, the open frontier policy in the EU altered the patterns of imports and exports. Cross-border trade is bound to increase and to open new opportunities for Bob. He needed to know the competitive strength of the cross-channel ferry operators, P & O, Stenna Sealink and Hoverspeed. He also needed to know what effect the Channel Tunnel might have on cross-channel passengers and freight when fully opened in 1994.

Whilst he was gathering this data Bob felt it would be helpful to talk seriously with others in the business. A typical visit was to Nigel Harris, the managing director of UK's smallest scheduled airline.

Nigel Harris' company, London Flight Centre (LFC), was formed in 1982 and is based at Stansted Airport. It had steadily increased to 28 aircraft, mainly 10-seater Chieftains. Nigel Harris not only ran three small subsidiaries of LFC, but was an active company pilot.

LFC's scheduled services were from Biggin Hill, 12 miles south of London, and Lydd in Kent, to Le Touquet on the French coast, a flight of some 15 minutes. Named 'Love Air', this scheduled serviced is marketed by Harris to newlyweds and offers short weekend breaks. The peak season is June to October.

In October Harris moves his total operation to the West Indies, where his airline, Air St Kitts and Nevis, operates a medical evacuation service for elderly and affluent visitors and residents requiring transport to airports or hospital in the Windward Islands. This service has a high season from November to April. He then moves the operation back to UK.

Meanwhile he leases out and charters some of LFC's planes through his UK company, London Flight Centre Charters. Many of his pilots were trained in his pilot training school near to Carcassonne, in the south of France. Income from the school helped Harris to purchase, rather than lease, his 28 aircraft. Total staff had reached 65 by 1993 and they were highly flexible within an expanding and successful company, but the recession of 1990/92 had reduced profits quite substantially.

Bob, in talking to Nigel, became increasingly convinced that the concept of niche flying depended on small aircraft, carrying small numbers of passengers, at high frequency, on scheduled flights and at low cost. Hence the need for Harris and Love Air to operate basic, regular, no frills, scheduled flights from UK to France. These were regarded as 'international' flights in the 1980s, but with the EU open sky policy were now 'domestic' flights within Europe. Harris was developing further services to Pontois, an airport within easy travelling distance of the centre of Paris.

BOB'S PLANS

Aims

Bob decided that his corporate aims should be to start a flying business from the UK into Europe. He should operate at low cost, yet ensure high-quality customer relations, feature safety consciousness, promote passenger care 'with the personal touch'.

Bob decided that he had to feature his intentions in his company's name and after great care, and with the help of targeted research, selected 'EuroFlying Services Ltd'. This did not tie him to a particular form of air service – instead it left his options wide open! To form the company he had to produce Articles of Association which set out exactly the limits within which a company will trade. It is important to phrase these with care, since they must be designed to cover all aspects of his potential future business opportunities so far as they can be anticipated.

Potential strategies

Bob listed his possible strategic marketing options as:

1 to start regular scheduled passenger services between Exeter and small airports adjacent to: Amsterdam, Brussels, Düsseldorf, Paris;
2 to start regular scheduled passenger services between Newcastle and small airports in (1);
3 to start regular freight services between Exeter and the small airports in (1);
4 to start regular freight services between Newcastle and the four main centres in (1);
5 to start regular passenger/freight services from Exeter and Newcastle, to London City Airport;
6 to start a flying school for pilot training in Exeter;
7 to start a flying school for pilot training in Newcastle;
8 to provide a passenger taxi service as and when required into Europe;
9 to provide an advisory service to companies saving cost on travel.

Bob used a strategic options matrix to help evaluate in his decision-taking, as shown in Figure 7.2. (*Note:* This is an Ansoff matrix, as discussed in Chapter 13.)

Segmentation

Bob identified business passengers as the segment of the market he could best serve by setting up scheduled services. He approached the Chambers of Commerce in Exeter and Newcastle and discussed with business people the problems of commuting to and from European meetings. A distinct need for early morning flights to London, from both centres, with return flights in the evening of the same day, headed a long list. To identify the travel needs of businesses managers he visited several top Travel Agencies in Exeter and

		PRODUCTS/SERVICES	
		Existing	New
M **A** **R**	Existing	No scheduled flights from Exeter.	Internal flights: Exeter – Newcastle Freight only to EU Scheduled services: Exeter/London/Newcastle
K **E** **T** **S**	New	New scheduled flights UK to EU. Exeter flying school. Newcastle flying school. Passenger taxi service on request. Company travel services.	Regular schedules from Exeter/London/Newcastle to four EU centres.

Fig. 7.2 Strategic Options matrix – EuroFlying Services Ltd

Newcastle and found the greatest demand for overseas flights was from Newcastle to Amsterdam, Brussels and Düsseldorf. From Exeter it was for flights to London and Brussels. There were two major market niches – business executives and holidaymakers.

Study of this twin section segmentation suggested that businessmen, as a priority, would provide Bob with a regular annual demand. He therefore concentrated on this segment of the market. Holidaymakers represent segments to be developed in future expansion plans.

Identifying customers and market niches available

The focus and positioning now induced Bob to evaluate the short-listed possibilities and make key decisions:

1 He would develop the route in most demand – Exeter to London and to Brussels.
2 Scheduled flights between London or Newcastle and Brussels could not be developed with current resources, but he could start these routes by charter flights at irregular intervals, on an 'as and when needed' basis.
3 Newcastle to London City Airport and return was a strong possibility for future development when a planned new underground railway line opens to give a 15 minutes access time from the City to the airport.

The business plan

The research enabled Bob to put together an estimate for the first three years. He decided that he needed to raise start-up capital of £500 000. He anticipated that he would generate sufficient income to break even in his second year and show a profit in year three. His estimated ESL Business Plan, assembled for his own use for control and a meeting with the bank, was extensive and detailed. The key financial estimates are shown in Table 7.3.

Table 7.3 EuroFlying Services Ltd: outline financial forecasts

Estimates (£)	Year 1	Year 2	Year 3
Revenue	500 000	850 000	1 200 000
Cost of operations	300 000	510 000	740 000
Gross Profit	200 000	340 000	460 000
Support costs	100 000	160 000	225 000
Interest charges	180 000	180 000	180 000
Profit before tax	–80 000	0	55 000
Profit after tax	–80 000	0	38 000

Note: These are outline figures simply to give Bob a perspective for the first three years. They are, of course, supported by highly detailed calculations and the exact content of each main heading is defined. Doubtless this initial forecast will need major revisions in the light of experience – another reason why an effective and efficient management information system (see the section on this, which follows) is vitally important.

Eventually Bob secured the needed financial support. There had been long and detailed discussions, which necessitated ever more detailed planning, and the use of specific information to justify the plans. Bob had been supported by his accountant in the discussions with the bank, and took specialist legal advice before going firm on his detailed plans. It was time well spent, however, because when he was able to make a start it was on a solid, well-planned foundation.

THREE YEARS LATER

Bob operates his airline from his office at Exeter Airport. He rarely flies because he is too busy developing and controlling the business. He is set to delegate many of the routine tasks as ESL grows and develops so that he is free to plan new services.

He started, as planned, with short scheduled flights. As demand increased he added more flights and now has a daily service from Exeter to Amsterdam and Brussels, via London. He is currently talking to many small to medium-sized companies in the area from Bristol to the south-west of England and South Wales and will be starting a regular freight-only schedule, shared with two large international carriers on a joint venture basis.

His aircraft are leased and his pilots are all ex-RAF. He offers personal comfort, safety, reliability and connections with international airlines. These he believes are the key benefits. Customers come first.

Prices for both business and holiday passengers are kept about 10% below equivalent prices for railway tickets.

His main promotional tactics are the use of public relations and TV advertising, supported by close links with travel agencies. Speed and safety are the main communication messages in all advertising and sales promotions. Free tickets are donated as prizes for local radio quiz games.

Bob keeps a close personal contact with his market. He goes out to visit actual and potential clients, is an active member of the Chamber of Commerce and makes a point of meeting his passengers at the Exeter terminal at 08.00 on weekdays so that he can talk to them about their needs and his services.

Bob sees his main task as the development of new services within the budgets and strategies he sets for the company. His key role, he believes, is as a strategic and tactical *manager of marketing*, creating a sustained increase in business whilst continuing to return 10% on capital invested.

MANAGEMENT INFORMATION SYSTEMS

The success of Bob's first three years in the flying business was in part due to his investment in a sound computing system. His management information system (MIS), was designed to give him a continual flow of key information on such issues as cash flow, revenue, costs; the work rate of planes and of pilots; marketing efforts and results; administration; legal and contractual obligations. Bob was very satisfied with his system and he felt able to control the operation from the information generated.

All files within the four main directories – reports, marketing research, personnel and finance – were integrated to give Bob information to monitor and control the company. He attributes much of his success to the flexibility of his MIS. The system allows him to identify critical success factors (CSFs) and call up on screen any information he needs. A typical CSF is the need to build up competitive intelligence on costs of travel, new services, and competitor activity. Bob's MIS allows him to make policy decisions, change objectives speedily and rearrange schedules for customers, freight, planes, pilots and crews.

MIS AND MkIS

A **marketing** information system will be found within the **management** information system. Known as an MkIS, it provides all the key information that marketing requires to be both effective and efficient. An MkIS exists to provide for the information needs of marketing, an MIS for the information to all management. Thus an MkIS can exist without an MIS, but an MIS must have an MkIS within it.

Much information is routinely generated by an organisation – payroll, orders received, processed, invoiced, credit control, orders placed, good received, debtor control, etc. This is all *targeted information*, of value to specific man-

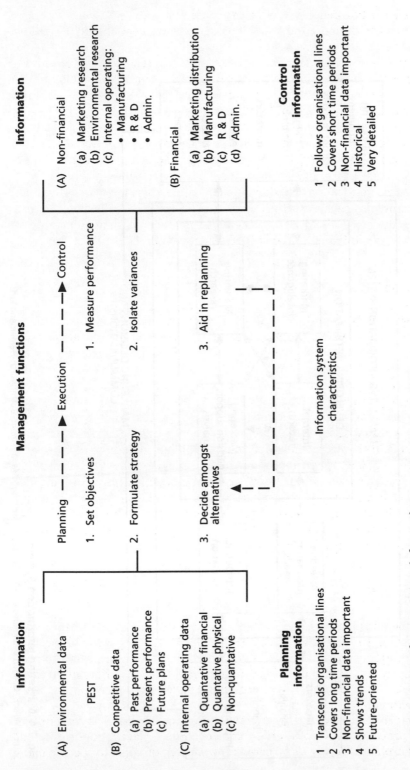

Fig. 7.3 Anatomy of management information

Source: Wilson, Gilligan and Pearson (1992), *Strategic Marketing Management*, Butterworth-Heinemann Ltd.

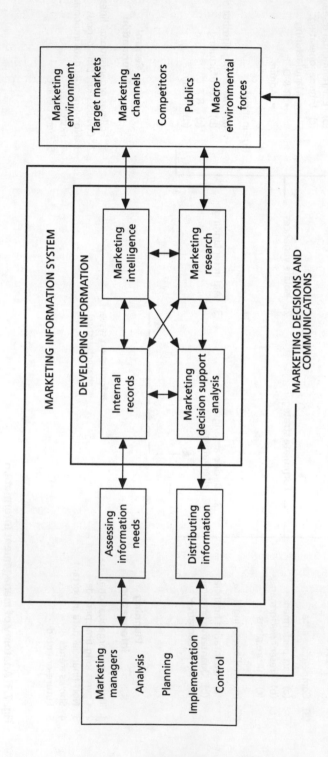

Fig. 7.4 Marketing Information System
Source: Wilson, Gilligan and Pearson (1992), *Strategic Marketing Management*, Butterworth-Heinemann Ltd.

agers. Only when it is cross-referenced within an MIS (or MkIS) will all the management information be combined, e.g. the relationships between order size, production efficiency, distribution effectiveness, payment reliability and sales force effort can be combined to inform strategic decisions.

Data is researched from the macro- and micro-environments and processed into information that reaches the desks of interested managers *in time to help them in decision and control*. The anatomy of management information is shown in Figure 7.3.

The MkIS is vitally important to marketing managers and today it is difficult to see how any organisation can operate without a computerised database which provides relevant information both accurately and when needed. Marketing managers have to take decisions that directly impact into the marketplace and that information has to be developed. Without a computer it can either take too long or be prohibitively expensive in staff time.

KEY POINT SUMMARY

- A business plan is an itemised summary of cash flow, profit, and capital requirement giving the purpose of the enterprise in a quantified plan.
- Fixed capital is money tied up in tangible assets.
- Working capital is funds that are held liquid (e.g. cash).
- Cash and cash flow are the two most important management considerations.
- Leasing of capital equipment allows equipping without commitment of capital.
- Major banks provide detailed guidance to new business start-ups.
- The clear purpose of trade is profit.
- Loan capital is often crucial to an organisation.
- Control can be lost if an entrepreneur seeks too high a level of financial support.
- Information must be gathered to enable the business planning process.
- Outline an then detailed research is needed into the macro- and micro-environments.
- Outline plans are made before detailed planning is commenced.
- Critical success factors (CSFs) must be identified and then considered in the planning process.
- Market niches matched to customer need must be located.
- Segmentation divides a market into target groups.
- The Management Information System combines data from a range of sources and provides relevant information to managers in time for action.
- The Marketing Information System combines data of marketing interest, and informs marketing management.

SELF-ASSESSMENT QUESTIONS FOR ALL

1 Analyse and comment on the marketing planning and control problems Bob faced when setting up ESL as a new airline.

2 Bob's first step in setting up ESL as a new airline was to complete a mission statement. Draft a mission statement for ESL and show how this would help Bob decide on key marketing objectives and strategies.

See the end of this Chapter for answer guidelines.

SUGGESTED ASSISTANCE TO SELF-ASSESSMENT QUESTIONS FOR CHAPTERS 5–7

WORK-BASED QUESTIONS

Chapter 5

1 The main duties and responsibilities will centre upon the tasks of managing the marketing department, deciding organisation objectives, strategies and tactics. The tasks of organising will decide the purpose, roles an functions of staff, and will structure the marketing functions, the staff contribution, career development and individual responsibility.

2 The effect of the green movement on marketing planning begins at strategic level with the consumer the focal point of marketing activities. Mercedes-Benz, BMW and VW are featuring recycling strongly in their new car advertising. Food products are labelled and promoted with natural goodness a main feature. Customer satisfaction must be fully accepted as a basic operational objective for the marketing-oriented organisation.

Chapter 6

1 Your SWOT will be highly personal and will reflect how you see your priorities and will reflect how you interpret the signals you are receiving from the environment. Why not test its accuracy by sharing it with somebody who knows you personally – your manager or a parent perhaps?

Chapter 7

1 The strategic marketing decision to start ESL will depend on the identification of market opportunities on the ability to attract sufficient passengers and/or freight; on the likelihood that the macro-environmental factors will at least remain stable – not worsen. Information in needed on which to base decisions. At first this must be generalised – only as outline thinking is proven to be correct will more detailed planning be carried through to verify.

  Excellent control can be maintained through an MkIS. Bob has no requirement for a full MIS since his operation is small enough to be totally marketing centred.

2 The mission statement will focus on the long-term business of ESL flying passengers with safety, courtesy and on time. It will be good only if it leads to objectives that are clear and precise and understood by all who need to know – customers, staff, freight handlers, suppliers, and lenders of capital to ESL.

SCHOOL- OR COLLEGE-BASED QUESTIONS

Chapter 5

1 The organisation chart of the school will show the line authority from the Head or Principal, through deputies, heads of department and sections to senior staff and their sections. Remember to identify the staff relationships: secretarial, maintenance,

support technicians, etc. Duties and responsibilities include curriculum planning, staff allocation, resource procurement. Control factors will be such as attendance, continuing assessment, examination results. Many organisations will carry out marketing research in classes since education is such a subjective issue.

2 Consumers of school services not only include pupils, students and parents, but also employers and the community in general. The government through Her Majesty's Inspectorate will also influence control through curriculum and examination systems. Consumerism is encouraging education to regard pupils as clients and to design 'learning environments' rather than old-fashioned 'chalk and talk' classrooms.

Chapter 6

1 This question was given to all – see under Work-based Questions.

Chapter 7

1 Both questions given to all – see under Work-based Questions.

PART 3

Marketing research –
an information base

Marketing research describes all types of research that is used by marketing managers. In this chapter you will learn why it is of fundamental importance.

There is a major difference between *data*, which is a collection of facts and figures, and *information* which is contained within the data. In many cases it is possible to obtain the information that a manager needs from data that already exists, either because the data is regularly supplied to meet on-going needs, or because somebody else has researched the area of interest for their own purposes.

The word 'data' is a Latin noun, and means 'the given facts'. Note that it never appears with an 's' added (datas is wrong!). Information is also never used in the plural (informations is wrong!). Both of these misspellings are very common in examination answers, so do take care.

Information may be extracted from *secondary data*, which is far quicker and cheaper to obtain. Therefore a manager should *always* turn to secondary data first.

Primary data is obtained from research that is specially commissioned for a purpose. It must be commissioned with care since its costs, and the time taken to secure it, must be taken into account in judging its value. Primary data should fill the gaps in the secondary data.

In many cases managers have a tendency to drown in a sea of data – usually because they have not thought through their exact needs and therefore failed to approach their research task with a clear plan.

Research findings exist to *help managers take decisions*. Research *never* replaces a manager's decision-making role.

The most effective managers understand that they need only enough information to take a decision – that too much information can confuse, just as too little can conceal. Marketing research data is an essential element of the MIS and MkIS, which should ensure that the relevant information reaches the appropriate managers in time for their decision-making needs.

CHAPTER 8

Types of research

Rashid Indrani had though that being 16 would be great, but it wasn't turning out that way. Life was suddenly extremely complex . . . people seemed to be turning against him!

Where he has simply asked for information he now had to find it for himself . . . even his mother had taken to pointing to the timetable when he asked the time of the next bus to town!

Needing a phone number for a Zubrenski was no handicap, but without an initial he was frustrated in his search for a Patel or a Smith.

He had problems with the filing system. He had been told to file by the first letter of correspondents' names . . . and then got into trouble because the T section of the filing cabinet was over-full. It had seemed logical to file The Abbey Company before The Baker Company. How was he to know they should have been filed under 'A' and 'B' instead of 'T'?

When a customer phoned he forgot to ask for their reference number, and it took a long time to locate their credit rating.

He was lost in the building for over 30 minutes when looking for Room 372. How could he know that the third floor was divided and that rooms above 350 were in the annex and not the main building?

The sales director was very cross with him – when asked for an update on sales figures Rashid called for a printout of all 3500 customer accounts and very quickly supplied the director with 60 sheets of computer printout. Apparently a single page summary was required!

Rashid's problem was partly in distinguishing data from information, partly in the way he was approaching each situation.

- Timetables and telephone directories are full of data. A key piece of information such as the time of the next bus is within the data – if you know where and how to look.
- A logical structure, such as filing alphabetically or numbering rooms by floor, is fine – but only if everybody understands the logic.
- Presenting information so that it is immediately available to those who need it is a skill that eases a manager's workload.

The first principle of effective research is to start by assuming that at least some of the needed information is available. The problem then reduces to deciding what questions need to be asked, and who to ask.

PROBLEM

Your boss has a vintage motor car which he is restoring. He asks you to find where he can buy paint of a specific make and colour to match the maker's original specification. He needs the paint within a week. The makers of the car have long since vanished from the market, and none of the easily available modern paints is suitable.

Assumption

The paint can either be obtained, or mixed specially.

Where to look? Who to ask?

The potential sources of information include:

- paint manufacturers;
- car repairers;
- vintage car associations;
- specialists in vintage car restoration;
- other owners of the make and/or model;
- insurance assessors.

Objectives

An information search must be taken step by step, with a clear understanding of the objectives at each step. The prime objective is:

- to locate a source of the required paint within a week.

Secondary objectives

- to locate potential routes to the needed information;
- to follow the routes in order of the highest probability of success;
- at each step to either secure the information or to find at least one other potential source.

The approach

- Rank the potential sources of information:
  — specialists in vintage car restoration;
  — vintage car associations;
  — other owners of the make/or model;
  — car repairers;
  — paint manufacturers;
  — insurance assessors.
- Determine a primary contact:
  — Yellow Pages under 'Cars', 'Vintage cars', 'Automobiles', 'Restoration';

— specialist magazines – at a good newsagents, or from a trade directory.
- Phone a potential contact . . .
  'I wonder if you can help me with a problem, I'd be most grateful . . .'
  Conclude the call with . . .
  'Thank you very much for your time. I wonder if you could suggest somebody else that I could contact?'
- Phone the most likely secondary contact and follow exactly the same method. You are building a *network* of contacts.

Experienced *networkers* can secure almost any piece of information from anywhere in the world with a maximum of six levels of contact. They treasure their network contacts, and as trust develops the power of their network increases dramatically. If ever you have contact with a research librarian, perhaps in a large advertising agency, you will be astonished by the speed and thoroughness of response to even the most complex and perplexing questions.

Good managers ask for information they need to help in their decision-making. Researchers decide the questions that have to be asked to secure the information they need. It is not for a manager to formulate questions nor to determine methodology because the skills of a line manager are unlikely to match those of an experienced researcher.

MARKETING RESEARCH

Marketing research is defined as:

The systematic gathering, recording and analysing of data about problems relating to the marketing of goods and services. (The American Marketing Association).

- *Systematic* research is carefully planned and managed at every stage to ensure that the results are statistically valid.
- *Gathering* of data that is directly of value. The temptation to ask additional questions adds cost, but not value.
- *Recording* data must be recorded accurately.
- *Analysing* analysis and cross-referencing translates data into information.

Note that the marketing researcher is skilled in research; he is not a line manager. Hence any recommendations made should be about the research and its validity, not about the decisions that the manager must take.

Marketing research includes every aspect of research of value to a marketing manager. It therefore *includes* market research which is research into the market. It also includes research to assist in such areas as:

- new product development
- promotion
- pricing
- packaging
- distribution
- competitive action.

The role of the marketing researcher is to design the best ways to collect the data required by a manager who is facing the need to make a specific decision. When a manager is faced with a series of similar decisions – e.g. regarding market share of a particular product – a programme of continuous research may be needed. This constantly updates key information so that the on-going decision need is met.

The role of the manager is to clearly state what information he must have to take a decision. It is helpful to test a list of information needs against a three-stage priority list:

- what must be known?
- what would be nice to know?
- what could be useful?

Only the information that *must be known* should be researched. It is astonishing how easy it is to ask for 'nice to know' information, and how hard to justify each piece of information as 'must be known'. The key questions are 'Why?' – 'What?' – and 'How?':

- why do I need that information?
- what am I going to do with it?
- how will it help me take a better decision?

MARKET RESEARCH

Market research is the systematic analysis of the character of a single market, e.g. a market for a new computer, or a new children's toy. The data gathered, recorded and analysed by market research includes:

- estimated size of the total market, estimates of new potential markets, their location and size;
- growth rates, type and location of new markets;
- identification of specific market characteristics;
- market trends and changes expected;
- sales forecasts for each market segment, with total aggregated sales forecasts;
- names, age, location by area, gender and social classification of known and potential customers.

COMPETITOR RESEARCH

Competitors can be *direct* or *indirect*.

For a supplier of pre-recorded video tapes the direct competition is other pre-recorded tape suppliers. The indirect competitors include everything that can occupy target consumers in place of pre-recorded video. This includes:

- telecasters providing a live service;

- blank video tapes used to record TV for time-shift viewing;
- camcorders and the subsequent viewing of their results;
- radio, CDs, audio cassettes, records;
- cinema and theatre;
- even alternative activities such as sports clubs are competitive in the sense that they reduce the time consumers spend watching pre-recorded video.

It is very important to define exactly who the key competitors are and to determine where, when, how and why each will compete in the market place. Competitor activity is examined before any strategic marketing decisions are taken, and monitored throughout tactical activity.

Key information needed includes:

- strengths and weaknesses of competitive products and services;
- pricing strategies for new and existing products and services;
- distribution strategies;
- promotional strategies;
- strengths and weaknesses of competitor resources;
- competitors' ability to build and maintain supplier relations;
- the speed, timing and reliability of deliveries for just-in-time management.

Marketing success requires offensive or defensive strategies and tactics:

- Market leaders protect and defend their leading market share.
- Market challengers compete aggressively and often attempt to enlarge their resources through the acquisition of smaller companies.
- Market followers defend their market share by concentrating on segments or on market niches. They tend towards specialisation, quality of service and customer services.

Each company must decide on the marketing strategy and tactics best suited to their corporate objectives of survival, expansion, entry to specific markets. For this they require information on current actions – and they need to make intelligent forecasts of the likely reaction of competitors.

- When Rowntree-Mackintosh launched their Yorkie bar on to the UK market they were prepared for an immediate and powerful reaction from Cadbury, the market leader. None came for 18 months, when Cadbury launched their own chunky bar of milk chocolate.
- It seems that Cadbury misread the potential of the Yorkie bar and so allowed it to secure a market presence that was too strong to challenge.
- Managers given the information have the task of evaluation before decision. In Cadbury's case the management knew exactly what Rowntree-Mackintosh were doing, and could have mounted an aggressive defensive campaign. They chose not to – which is not the fault of the research.

DISTRIBUTOR RESEARCH

Essential details of distributor strengths and weaknesses are required. The distributive system must be analysed. The most effective channels from manufacturer or producer, through to agent or broker, to wholesaler, retailer and on to the ultimate consumer can then be selected.

The logistics of transporting goods by truck, train, ferry, barge, ship or aircraft need careful examination in order to make the most cost-effective decisions.

SUPPLIERS AND AGENCIES

Strengths and weaknesses of available suppliers and their purchasing agencies are of great benefit to producers. The locations, costs, delivery dates and quality of product and service are of great consequence. Managers need to discover when, why and how individual companies might be open to a suggestion that they change or add to their suppliers list.

PROMOTIONAL RESEARCH

Marketing as the bridge to the consumer is primarily a communicator. Under the heading of *Promotion* fall all the communication tools. (We shall examine promotion in Part 8.)

A marketing manager is concerned with the effectiveness of his promotion. To be effective promotion has to:

- be targeted on to the correct audience(s);
- reach the designated target(s);
- achieve the intended result(s).

Promotional research is therefore concerned with such matters as:

- target audience identification;
- how to get a message across to the target audience;
- the number of times to repeat the advertisement;
- media cost and effectiveness;
- the results achieved;
- competitive activity.

Communication tools are used in a *mix* to achieve optimum results. The effectiveness of the mix as a whole must be evaluated as well as the effectiveness of each element in the mix.

TRACKING STUDIES

Continuous research is referred to as *tracking* because it keeps track of developments in the area of research. It is used where there is need to monitor a situation before, during and after research. Some tracking studies have a long history – the effectiveness of Persil advertising, for example, is said to have been tracked for close on 80 years.

Continuous monitoring can be carried out by linking an organisation's MkIS system to electronic point-of-sale (PoS) equipment. The large retailers, such as Safeway, have now realised the value of the information which they collect at PoS and sell it to interested organisations such as suppliers.

Typical uses for continuous monitoring are in the tracking of:

* promotional effectiveness;
* new products from pre- to post-launch;
* price variations in specific regions;
* the trail of products passing through several channels of distribution – wholesalers, agents, stores, supermarkets, shops, or direct to consumers.

Tracking results before, during and after action aids fine-tuning adjustments to make the action more effective. Future actions will be designed using information from previous tracking studies. Tracking studies enable researchers to supply managers with constantly updated results.

PoS usage of tracking studies

Goods received in stores and supermarkets are checked in using bar codes from the outers or cases. Electronic cash points record each sale by bar code. Sales and stock levels can then be tracked through the store computer to regional or national computers. The company MkIS can be programmed to track immediate changes, variations in patterns of sales and pockets of sales resistance, so that local tactical changes in product, packaging, promotion, pricing or positioning can be based on actual achievement. Such tracking enables decisions to be taken which are based on current information. Global marketing decisions can be made from central offices using tracking studies because today's technology allows virtually instant contact with any part of the world.

OMNIBUS SURVEYS

Everybody can travel by omnibus if they can pay their fare. Everybody can join an omnibus survey if they can pay the fee.

Omnibus surveys are mounted at regular intervals by reputable marketing research companies to provide research data to clients whose needs do not justify a dedicated survey. Thus an omnibus survey contains questions from a range of sponsors. The results are separately analysed for each sponsor, and complete confidentiality is guaranteed.

An omnibus survey is of great value to a small organisation, but also to a large one that is concerned to discover only a limited amount of information about a specific topic.

ACCESS is an omnibus survey operated by the British Market Research Bureau (BMRB). Over 2000 adults are interviewed at home, each week. Sponsors add questions to the survey and the answers are collated within days to yield in-depth analysis. This aids participating companies speedily and at lower costs to individual companies than single surveys.

A C Nielsen use the omnibus technique to support their in-store survey of product sales and stock levels. Researchers visit a sample cross-section of retailers and wholesalers to carry out shelf- and stock-checks from which market share can be calculated. Nielsen reports have become the industry standard and are used by suppliers, wholesaler and retailers for tactical marketing purposes. They make information available at reasonable cost that otherwise would be prohibitively expensive to obtain.

Telephone surveys are increasingly omnibus in nature. The tele-omnibus survey mounted by TMRB contacts 500 adults and gives next-day results.

The common feature of omnibus surveys is speed of results and lower costs. Data obtained is classified on grounds such as household composition, age, gender, social grouping and TV viewing preferences to provide information.

PIGGY-BACKING

Joining with others to lower cost is referred to as *piggy-backing*. Piggy-back surveys are combined surveys. They are particularly useful in researching international markets where there is common interest in securing basic facts.

Wherever there are non-competing interests the opportunity for piggy-backing occurs. It makes sense to spread the set-up costs across a research project where possible and often a marketing research organisation takes the initiative in suggesting to their clients that an opportunity to piggy-back exists.

An omnibus survey allows an organisation to piggy-back cost-effectively since the total costs of the survey are shared in proportion across the sponsors.

RESEARCH NEED

If a manager has all the information he needs there is no requirement for research. If not, he must identify exactly what is needed to take a quality decision with a high probability of being correct.

The information gap

• It is necessary to decide that you need to commission research!
• If you don't need it, don't commission it!
• You have to discover if there is an information gap.

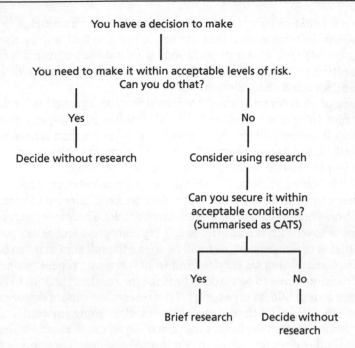

You have a decision to make

You need to make it within acceptable levels of risk.
Can you do that?

Yes — Decide without research

No — Consider using research

Can you secure it within
acceptable conditions?
(Summarised as CATS)

Yes — Brief research

No — Decide without
research

Fig. 8.1 Is there an information gap?

THE RESEARCH PROCESS

Chisnell shows that there are five steps in the research process:

- the research brief;
- the research proposal;
- data collection;
- data analysis and evaluation;
- the research report.

The research brief

Sets out exactly the questions to which the manager needs answers. It is designed to give only the information that the researcher needs to know in order to carry out the research effectively. There are a minimum of six headings in a research brief:

- *Security*. Inform the researcher what level of security is required. Research into a new product proposal needs to be highly secret because of the need to keep it from competitors. Research into attitude change after a promotional campaign need not be kept secret – but the results are highly confidential. 'Confidentiality is like virginity, once it's gone it's gone for ever.' Evan Hendricks, Privacy Times, Washington.
- *Objectives*. The objectives of the research must be concise, clear and unambiguous. In marketing research we are usually concerned to prove or

disprove a belief or an opinion, not to investigate from scratch.

Managers determine what they expect, or hope, to find, and then set about proving or disproving their expectations. This is done because it is far more cost-effective to target research than to go into the process with an open mind, and an open cheque book!

- *Background.* A researcher must have sufficient background information to enable him to operate effectively. A full briefing on company policy and objectives is not necessary – just enough and no more than is needed to fulfil the task. It is generally better to provide too little background, and then to fill it out in the oral briefing in response to questions.
- *Budget.* Marketing research is often a compromise between what is needed and what can be afforded. It is a pointless waste of money to commission research on a budget that prohibits effective results. Therefore the researcher must know how much can be afforded. A reputable researcher will not accept a brief that is under-funded, nor will he spend the full sum that can be available. (He is marketing his services and wants on-going repeat business too.)
- *Time.* Decisions have to be made in time for the resultant actions to be effective. Thus a time budget is necessary. If a researcher cannot deliver reliable information within the time budget it is pointless going forward.
- *Other factors.* Any other factors that are of significance should be included. Perhaps similar research has been conducted by a sister company, or another research organisation may have carried out preliminary research earlier. Anything that can help the researcher must be included; it is stupid to keep facts from the researcher because if they are needed he will research them and bill you anyway!

The research proposal

The researcher will examine the data needs of the client and devise a method of securing what is needed within the conditions of the brief. If necessary he will return to the manager with questions so that his proposal is as complete and accurate as possible.

When presented to the client the proposal will:

- define the research problems to be solved;
- match the research objectives to the manager's information needs;
- state:
  — the methods of research to be used;
  — the data collection methods;
  — the methods of collation and reporting;
  — the level of confidence that can be placed in the results. (Research cannot be wholly accurate, but it is possible to calculate how confident one can be in the results . . . how much error might be in the final figures. Commonly this is ± 5% in marketing research.)
- confirm the timing, deadlines and date for presentation of the final report, and of any stage reports;
- recommend a budget for the overall project.

Commissioning

If the client agrees with the proposal – perhaps after discussion and modification – he will commission the research. That is, he will enter into a formal contract that authorises the researcher to go ahead in line with the proposal.

Data collection

The researcher proceeds with the collection of the data, as established in the research proposal. We shall come back to this point in Chapter 9.

Data analysis and evaluation

The researcher is equipped to carry out all the manipulation of the data so that it is presented as information to the client. Using highly developed data bases it is very simple for a skilled researcher to cross-reference data so that it is presented in a helpful way, e.g. instead of a list of numbers and percentages a researcher may take a suitable base – a typical customer, perhaps, and then relate the other data to him. Thus the manager will receive his information in charts, diagrams, graphs and tables that are easy to understand.

The research process from the perspective of the research agency

1 Receive brief from client.
2 Develop the brief, fully understand the requirements – discuss and clear queries with the client.
3 Agree the research objectives and outline budget with client.
4 Decide types and sources of information.
5 Determine methodologies.
6 Formulate research proposals.
7 Present proposals and detailed budget to the client.
8 Accept commission.
9 Design the pilot survey.
10 Conduct the pilot survey – collate results – design the main survey.
11 If appropriate make an interim report to the client.
12 Complete the main survey and collate results.
13 Analyse and interpret survey results – ensure the objectives have been met.
14 Prepare and rehearse presentation to client.
15 Present and take questions.
16 Submit invoice.
17 Receive payment.

The research report

Normally a researcher presents the findings to the client manager – perhaps to a team from marketing and senior management. Researchers are highly

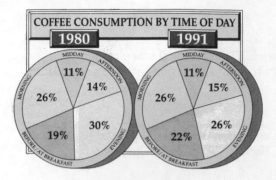

INSTANT COFFEE SALES BY SECTOR				
(% VALUE)	1988	1989	1990	1991
GRANULES	60%	59%	59%	58%
FREEZE DRIED	24%	27%	29%	30%
POWDERS/ MIXTURES	16%	14%	12%	10%
SPECIALITIES	–	–	–	2%

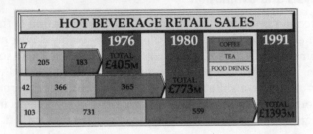

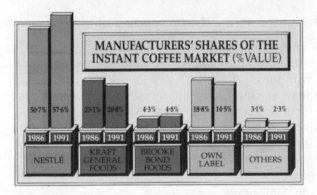

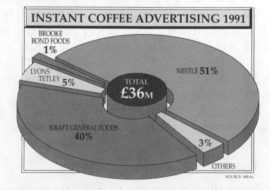

Fig. 8.2 Examples of marketing research presentation

Source: The Hot Beverages Report, 1992, published by Nestlé UK Ltd

trained presenters and cover the key material using multimedia suitable to the purpose – anything from video to a flip chart.

The researcher takes questions from the audience, and summarises what the research team see as the key points. He will be sure to point out any inconsistencies, and any areas where there are less than agreed levels of confidence.

(*Note*: The researcher's task is to provide answers to management's questions. It is for management to decide. *Never* allow the researcher to make the decision. Listen to their report, to their evaluation, then make your decision. For the researcher the figures are data – for you they are information.)

CONSTRAINTS ON MARKET RESEARCH

In all research there is need to trade off benefits across the four major constraints on the manager who is considering the research. The four constraints can be remembered as CATS.

Fig. 8.3 The constraints on market research – cost-effectiveness, accuracy, time and security

C   *Cost-effectiveness*. Research has to be cost-effective. Thus a research budget must be justified against the benefits it brings. Potential loss must be quantified taking the cost of research into account. Potential loss must be set against research cost (Table 8.1).

Table 8.1

Potential loss without research	Cost of research	Likely decision
£100 000	£80 000	No research
	£60 000	No research
	£40 000	Commission the research
	£20 000	Confirm the briefing was accurate!

A Accuracy. Research that is not accurate cannot be relied upon. It is for the researcher to ensure accuracy, and to show the client the steps taken to ensure accuracy.

Bias in questions must be removed through running pilot tests of the survey. Interviewers must be well trained, motivated and managed. Their results must be audited by repeat calling on interviewees and by cross-checks within the survey. The input and manipulation of data must be monitored, and statistical models and techniques must be managed by well-qualified and experienced personnel.

Researchers are anxious to ensure that they achieve and retain a reputation for excellence as this is their major selling point. Clients should, nevertheless, always confirm that accuracy is both built-in and managed effectively.

The best researchers are always booked ahead, but substitutes will often be offered. If these are acceptable, well and good. If they are junior staff, inexperienced in the field, it may be better to wait for a researcher of experience.

Beware of the research agency that passes your brief from the experienced person who took it to a junior who carries out the work. If you are paying for a top researcher you are entitled to their work.

T Time. Results must come through in time for them to be of value. The researcher must have time to to the job effectively. The results must be as current as possible to avoid *decay factors* in the survey results. (All data decays, changes, over time.)

The manager must provide the longest possible lead time so that the researcher can organise the work to provide optimum results. Late commissioned research is typical of the *fire-fighting* manager who fails to plan ahead. It also leads to the work being carried through by researchers who are available, and these are not normally the most appropriate.

S Security. Secrecy and/or confidentially are crucial in any research. A reputable researcher routinely maintains the necessary degree of security, but has to be briefed since it is the client who determines the sensitivity of the research.

High security needs restrict the researcher and may limit the effectiveness of the research, so never brief a higher level than is absolutely required.

KEY POINT SUMMARY

- Always assume that information needed can be obtained.
- Set clear research objectives for the information search.
- Approach the problem logically.
- Build and treasure a network of contacts.
- Marketing research is the systematic gathering, recording and analysing of data.
- Marketing research provides information to aid management decision-taking.
- The marketing researcher's task is to design surveys and obtain the needed information – not to make management decisions.

- Marketing research includes every aspect of research of interest to a marketer.
- Key questions are Why? What? and How?
- 'Tracking studies' constitute continuous research which gives information before, during and after.
- Omnibus surveys allow several marketers to piggy-back within one survey.
- Define the information need when considering research.
- The five steps in the research process are: brief, proposal, data collection, data analysis and evaluation, the report.
- The brief is given by the client.
- The proposal is made by the researcher.
- The constraints on marketing research are CATS: cost, accuracy, time and security.

WORK-BASED SELF-ASSESSMENT QUESTIONS

1 When a company decides to become more marketing oriented, what information does it need and what criteria may be used to decide whether to brief a research agency?

2 How can marketing research contribute to a better understanding of a specific market? Outline the areas of research that can be useful.

SCHOOL- OR COLLEGE-BASED SELF-ASSESSMENT QUESTIONS

1 Map the steps you would take to research the insurance market to locate a provider of European motor insurance cover.

2 List and explain the marketing research techniques you might employ to identify a new market for marketing textbooks.

See the end of Chapter 11 for answer guidelines.

CHAPTER 9

Secondary and primary research

THE HAMPSHIRE HOTEL

The English Channel separates the City of Portsmouth from Europe and by approximately 80 miles (128 km). Several car ferry routes cross this, the most congested seaway in the world. Portsmouth harbour is home to the Royal Navy, which has major depots and docking facilities in and around Portsmouth. The harbour is huge, with plenty of room for commercial and pleasure craft, yacht clubs and cross-channel ferries. The ferry port is in the upper reaches of the harbour, well sheltered from the sea and enjoying only small tidal changes.

The opening of the Channel Tunnel, between Folkestone and Calais, provides rail links between major cities in UK and continental Europe. It is felt that this competitive cross-channel link will not kill off the traffic generated through the ferry port, due to the distance of 140 miles (225 km) between the cross-channel rail tunnel at Folkestone and the passenger and car ferries at Portsmouth.

Jim Burns was a successful businessman in Portsmouth with a computer and communications company. On the death of his father he inherited a large house and grounds on Hayling Island, some 10 miles by road from the Ferry Port. Jim's father had owned and operated several large farms in Hampshire and West Sussex and left Jim the house, the grounds and over £500 000 in securities and investments. It took Jim two years to clear up his father's financial affairs and to turn the investments into cash at the bank.

Two plans seemed possible at that stage:

1 to convert the house and grounds into a country hotel, with a sporting emphasis, or
2 to convert the house and grounds into a residential management centre, offering it for hire to the 290 university and college management departments in the UK.

In either case a major benefit was the ease of access to France and the Channel Islands because of its proximity to the ferries into Cherbourg, Caen, Le Havre, St Malo, Jersey, and Guernsey.

Jim decided to start forming his strategic plans with a detailed secondary data search of the holiday market. He received help from the Southern Tourist Board and his Borough District Council and put together a profile of visitor characteristics, using surveys of 2000 visitors.

The results (%) were:

1

Age of visitors	1980	1985	1990	Conclusions
16–25	12.3	13.4	13.7	rising slowly
26–40	42.7	43.3	44.4	rising
41–60	32.4	29.8	28.9	falling
60+	12.6	12.5	13.0	stable

2 The average size of each holiday group was 3.7 persons.

3 Foreign visitors had almost doubled from 1.5% in 1980 to 2.9% in 1990.

4 Residence: 84% of visitors lived within a radius of 100 miles (162 km) of Portsmouth.

5 Means of travel for holidays (%):
Car   88.5
Train   2.5
Bus/coach   6.5
Other   2.5

6 Length of stay (%):
1–3 days   22.0
4–6 days   10.9
1 week   44.2
8–13 days   3.9
2 weeks   16.5
2 weeks +   2.5

7 The reasons for visiting the area in priority order were:
   7.1 pleasant environment/familiarity/good atmosphere/Royal Navy historic sites;
   7.2 convenient and accessible;
   7.3 visiting relatives and friends;
   7.4 water-sports, boating and fishing;
   7.5 beach facilities and swimming;
   7.6 wanted a change of venue for holiday.

8 Use of facilities in the area in order of popularity:
   8.1 restaurants available;
   8.2 local shopping facilities;
   8.3 funfair and amusements;
   8.4 sailing;
   8.5 clubs – sporting/entertainment;
   8.6 fishing and sporting facilities.

9 Visitor-nights and expenditure per head:

Type of accommodation	Visitor-nights	Expenditure/head (£)
9.1 Caravan sites (static)	729 882	8.95
9.2 Relatives & Friends	539 220	9.04
9.3 Holiday Camps	325 080	9.37
9.4 Touring Caravans/Tents	313 212	7.91
9.5 Hotel/Gust Houses	117 776	21.99
9.6 Bed & Breakfast	87 720	13.40

10 Visitors for the whole season (including night and day visitors):
    Total: 2 946 680 visitors.

Jim plotted these research findings on graphs and pie-charts (see Figures 9.1–9.5) so that the trends in visitor behaviour patterns became easier to understand.

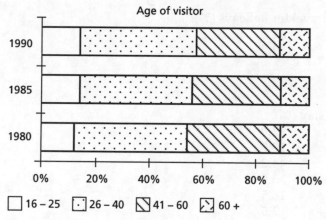

Fig. 9.1 Age of visitors

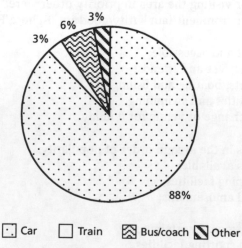

Fig. 9.2 Means of travel for holidays

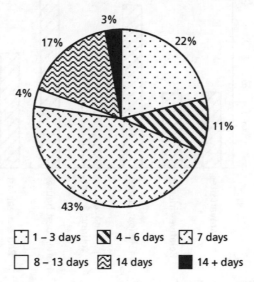

Fig. 9.3 Length of stay

1 – 3 days   4 – 6 days   7 days

8 – 13 days   14 days   14 + days

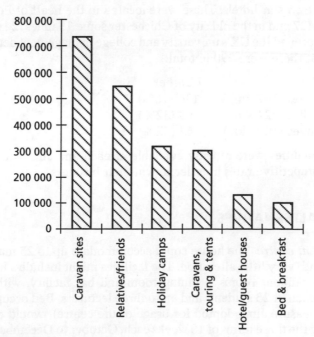

Fig. 9.4 Visitor-nights

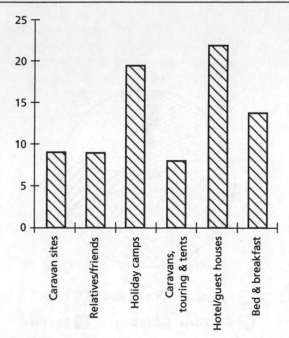

Fig. 9.5 Expenditure per head

Investigation of the area within 20 miles (32 km) showed that there were only three 4 or 5 star hotels. These were located in the heart of Portsmouth, close to the M27 and in the old city of Chichester some 15 miles (24 km) away.

Next he surveyed the UK's university and college management departments. He found that there were 290 in total:

Location	Number
Within 100 miles (162 km)	134 (46%)
Within 200 miles (324 km)	93 (32%)
Within 650 miles (1050 km)	63 (22%)

Residential facilities were already available at each and Jim would need to offer very competitive rates in order to win their business.

PRODUCT ALTERNATIVES

- *Management centre*. The house could accommodate up to 25 management students with very little alteration. The facilities might include a lecture theatre, three seminar rooms, a dining room and bar facility, with separate rooms for each of 25 students and up to three lecturers. Bed occupancy (the standard measure Jim adopted for usage of the centre), would need to be high during the three terms of 10 weeks each, October to December, January to March, and May to July.

The estimate of conversion costs for a residential management centre was £250 000. This conversion included 4 teaching and seminar rooms, 32 double rooms, accommodating up to 64 staff and students, closed circuit TV, interactive videos, monitors for language translation, overhead projectors, computing facilities and software, screens and flip charts.

* *Hotel.* To develop a full hotel facility for 100 guests, with 45 double rooms an 10 single rooms, would require an extension costing £750 000, and sporting facilities would also need to be extended. The £750 000 would provide a separate block connected to the main house. It would house 13 double an 10 single rooms with full en suite facilities. The price would also cover the refurbishing and equipment of the bar and restaurant areas.

From the secondary data already obtained it seemed apparent that the major opportunities lay in the establishment of a hotel. Perhaps there were other services that could be offered to make a hotel more attractive?

Jim listed the existing facilities and their most likely development:

Existing facilities	*Possible development*
1 10 hectares of gardens. (1 hectare = 2.147 acres)	9-hole golf course.
2 A cultivated garden, of 4 hectares.	2 grass tennis courts, 1 croquet lawn.
3 2 hectares of orchard.	Car parks/heated greenhouses.
4 4 reception rooms.	1 dining room and bar, 1 lecture theatre, 3 seminar rooms.
5 12 large bedrooms.	24 double bedrooms with en suite facilities.
6 2 large attics.	8 double bedrooms with en suite facilities.
7 Basement area.	Indoor swimming pool, jacuzzi, sauna and changing rooms.
8 Stable buildings	6 squash courts, showers and changing rooms.

It really began to seem that the hotel alternative was likely to be the best option:

1 The market potential was much wider.
2 Hotel demand was likely to grow as more travel to and from the Continent was fostered by the combined efforts of the channel tunnel and car ferry operators.
3 Hotel users were more 'elastic' in the prices they could afford – especially the corporate users.
4 The hotel could be open and active 52 weeks a year. (A management centre was tied to academic terms.)
5 There were no rival hotels positioned up market.

Jim decided it was necessary to carry out some primary research to see if other segments could be identified for targeting in the Southern Tourist Board's area. He drafted an outline of what he thought should be attractive and then approached a representative sample of potential users to discover their reactions.

He made contact with managements of:

- large companies and service providers;
- public utilities;
- management consultants;
- local authorities;
- magistrates/courts;
- chambers of commerce;
- media and TV companies;
- management trainers;
- tour operators;
- sports councils;
- sports organisations;
- large football clubs;
- church organisations;
- youth clubs;
- yacht clubs;
- marketing departments of local authorities in the south of England.

From the results of his secondary and primary research Jim was able to decide that there was a market for a hotel offering high-quality accommodation, excellent food and wines, conference, meetings and sports facilities. He could move on to the stage of strategic planning.

SECONDARY AND PRIMARY DATA

- *Secondary data* is data which has been researched for another purpose. It is therefore available much quicker and far more cheaply than by doing the research for the first time.

It may seem contradictory, but a manager must always look for secondary data first! Only when secondary data sources are exhausted should primary data be commissioned.

You will understand that the secondary data did not provide enough information for Jim to make hard and detailed decisions about the form the hotel should take. It did, however, show very clearly that one of his two alternatives, hotel rather than management centre, was a much better strategic choice. It saved him from an expensive and time-consuming investigation of the university and college market.

Once he could see that there was a strong probability that the hotel was the best choice he carried out a minimum amount of primary research.

- *Primary research* is the gathering of data for the first time, for a specific purpose:

— Primary data immediately becomes available as secondary data.
— Sales invoices are primary data for accounts management, but the details they contain of sales by product line and geographic area are valuable secondary data to the marketing manager.

Jim's main task was not to find out exactly who would use his hotel. That would have been highly impractical since nobody can forecast with any accuracy what they will do in the future. What seems like a good idea today may look very different in only a few weeks time. Therefore Jim was interested in finding out the type of services that certain types of people and groups of consumers wanted. He then had to make a decision about whether enough customers would want what he offered when he was able to offer it. Management, remember, is about taking calculated risks on the basis of less than perfect information.

DATA CONTAINS INFORMATION

- Data is a range of facts and figures having many possible uses.
- Information is fact and figures appropriate to a particular use.
- A manager is always concerned to turn data into information.
- Secondary data is held in databases (Table 9.1).

Table 9.1

Type	Coverage
Reference databases	Specific topics
Full databases	Complete data on an area
Source database	Detailed listings of full and reference databases

Thus a source database such as the population statistics held in the Central Statistical Office and collated by the UK government through census figures will direct a researcher to a range of detailed statistics. Information referring to population, employment, incomes and expenditure is readily available. Jim defined his catchment area as a radius of 100 miles (160 km) of Hayling Island. Within this he decided to use county boundaries to define each of the age categories used in his secondary data search.

SOURCES OF DATA

Data is available from many sources. A problem for management in the 1990s is that far too much data is being produced on a regular basis for active managers to be able to read it, let alone isolate the pertinent information within it. Hence the need for an efficient MIS and specific MkIS systems for data collection.

SECONDARY RESEARCH DATA SOURCES

Secondary data searches are done at a desk, and so are also called desk research.

Secondary data is comparatively low cost to gather and to store in the MkIS. Two problems arise with this data:

- *date and relevance*: it can age very quickly, and may not be totally relevant to your actual needs;
- *accuracy and appropriateness*: only trust data that is shown to come from a reliable source and that is appropriate to your need.

The rule is to first complete desk research and then fill gaps with primary research. This is because:

- Secondary data searches can be done quickly.
- Qualified market researchers are usually not needed.
- The process can be managed in-house, and costs absorbed in normal operations.

The most reliable data banks are those of the government, of universities, chambers of commerce, research organisations, big advertising agencies and the media, e.g. the *Financial Times* has a superb reference service.

International research must be conducted very carefully. The data available from many markets may be dated, inaccurate and unreliable.

Check sources and reliability thoroughly before use.

STATISTICAL INTELLIGENCE

Kotler states that 'No firm can conduct its business successfully without trying to measure the actual size of markets, present and future.' Statistical intelligence is available for markets, customers and competitors from many sources. Statistical data is presented in many forms – to meet the needs of those who commissioned it as primary research. It therefore has to be interpreted and presented in clear, precise reports which can be easily understood by managers. To make this translation there is a strong case of hiring a statistically competent manager, rather than a mathematician who is not a manager.

A major flow of intelligence is internal and will include:

- sales analysis of each unit, product, or brand despatched;
- cost analysis from each department in the form of materials, labour, packaging, transportation, selling, etc;
- Financial analysis: cash flow, income/expenditure statement, etc.

Any data produced internally has potential to become secondary data for other departments if they are aware that it exists. Again a need for an effective MIS and/or MkIS.

Major sources of external data

- *Government*: the Central Statistical Office provides data on agriculture, balance of payments, education, employment, foreign trade, geographical regions, incomes, national accounts, population, prices, transport.
- *Local Authorities* can provide data on amenities and community services, the arts, local employment, child care and education, environmental services, health, finance and grants, housing and planning, land utilisation, licensing, the mentally ill, public libraries, roads and traffic control, social services, youth services and welfare.
- *Trade associations* are concerned with representation to government, provision of services to members and the regulation of trading practices. Whilst some data is trade confidential most is freely released as part of the trade association's public relations and/or lobbying activities.
- *Employers' organisations* can provide data on wages, salaries and categories of individual occupational groups. Data on wage levels and negotiations on wages and conditions of work can be compared with that produced by the trade unions.

   Both employers organisations and the trade unions are concerned with national issues on behalf of their members, and both support active research teams. A wide range of information is available on a surprising number if issues.

- *Trade unions* represent their members and have a wealth of data on employment issues. They are also, as has been said above, very interested in national issues and are active in lobbying for action to improve living and environmental standards as well as conditions of employment.
- *Trade directories* are especially useful to obtain named contacts. Typical directories are:
  — *UK Kompass Management Register*: seven volumes of detailed company information.
  — *Kelly's Trade Directory*: data on manager identification within each company.

MARKETING RESEARCH AGENCIES

The use of specialist agencies to conduct specific primary marketing research projects is advisable. An independent agency uses specialist, trained and experienced staff. Many advertising agencies provide independent data search facilities, but this is often subcontracted.

THE MANAGER'S ROLE

A marketing manager cannot be an expert in each of the highly detailed areas of marketing skills. It is very important, however, to have sufficient information and knowledge to be able to understand what each specialist does and can offer, and to be able to evaluate their level of effectiveness.

To put it bluntly, it is important that a manager knows when a specialist is throwing up a smoke screen, waffling, or avoiding an issue. It is not necessary to be able to do each job. But it is vital to know what must be done. Therefore a basic understanding of the key marketing research issues is very important for managers.

INFORMATION REQUIREMENTS

The three essential requirements for information are that it must be:

- *Reliable*. Measurement must be repeatable and consistent, i.e. it must show the same results if repeated. It must be free from random errors, and be as precise as is necessary.
- *Valid*. Research must provide relevant information for each specific issue the manager wishes to measure, i.e. when researching the raincoat market a survey into 'rainware' it not likely to be of use since it will cover everything from galoshes to plastic hoods.
- *Accurate*. Research must be unbiased and described what is supposed to; e.g. the accuracy of a clock may be to within a second per year, but if it is set either fast or slow by an unknown amount the validity of its information is destroyed.

Baker suggests that a manager needs to confirm that a researcher has statistically validated the report that he is submitting.

DATA COLLECTION

The three basic methods for gathering data are:

- *Observation*, where one watches what happens. This produces accurate data because there is no intervention by a researcher. Included in 'observation' are the physical counts such as grocery items going over a bar code reader, or the number of people buying tickets for a particular film.
- *Experimentation*, where a situation is created and the results measured. A new product can be test marketed in an area typical of the whole market. This is an experiment to enable results to be evaluated before a national launch is approved.

    Checking which biscuits are the most popular can be done by offering respondents a plate with several biscuits whilst they have a cup of tea at mid-morning. Noting which biscuits are eaten is more reliable than asking the respondents which they prefer.
- *Questioning*, do not confuse questioning with questionnaires! All research uses a questionnaire because research exists to find answers to specific

questions. Questioning means actually asking questions directly of a respondent. This may be face-to-face, by telephone, or in the post.

Chisnell says 'Questionnaires are the backbone of most surveys and require careful planning and execution.' Time must be taken to pilot every questionnaire so that survey errors are eliminated. The major survey errors occur through:

- Wrong interpretation:
  — of questions by the respondents.
  — of answers by interviewers.
- Wrong answers given deliberately by the respondent:
  — giving an answer that makes them look good.
  — answering what they think the researcher wants to hear.

SAMPLING

A survey is a representation of the total population, or of people within a specific market. It is not necessary to question everybody because it has been found that if a sample is taken statistically from the universe the results of the survey based on that sample provides sufficiently accurate data for most marketing needs.

The Census of Population is taken every 10 years (in the first year of each decade). The Census is unusual because respondents are legally compelled to answer on behalf of everybody under their roof on the appointed date of the Census. Every 5th year the Census is updated by a 10% sample representative of the whole.

Samples can be decided upon in several ways:

- *Probability or random sample.* Where every person has an equal opportunity of being selected. To make this possible every individual has to be identified on a sampling frame and then each must be drawn totally at random in the same way that national lottery prize winners are selected. Thus a random nationwide survey of every tenth car own might require 100 persons to be interviewed in Glasgow, 40 in Edinburgh, 35 in Leeds, 1 each in half of the tiny villages in the Welsh hills, and so on.

  Think how expensive it would be!

  Also we have to be sure that every person selected is interviewed. What about those who are out? Who have moved away? Who have died? Who refuse? The enormous cost and complexity rule this method out for anything other than government-sponsored research such as the Sample Census.

- *Quota sample.* This is the preferred method and is done by selecting a sample that represents the make-up of the whole.

If the universe for the survey is made up 48/52% male/female, and the social classification split is also known, the quota may be a total of 100 interviews made up as shown in Table 9.2.

Table 9.2

Social classification	Male	Female
AB	5	5
C1	20	13
C2	5	13
D	18	21
E	0	0

Qualification for the quota is determined first by the interviewer who uses personal judgement to pick likely people, and secondly by a series of introductory questions to confirm that the person meets the quota criteria. As soon as 5 AB men have been interviewed there is no point in interviewing a sixth. Instead one has to hunt for people to complete the missing slots in the quota.

Quota samples operate throughout marketing research because of their cost-effectiveness. A risk is that they will produce biased results because the individuals that the interviewer will meet on the street, or in a shopping centre are of a certain type.

During the day it is unlikely that workers will be found for interview. Those who are housebound will also be ignored – but those at work and at home make up a significant part of the population. There is a greater probability of locating them at home in the evenings, which is why so many marketing research surveys are conducted at that time.

- *Multi-stage samples.* Researchers work within the statistical laws of probability to use true random selection to locate areas within which to research and then to pin-point specific targets for research. By selecting an appropriate sampling universe where every unit can be identified a multi-stage sample can be produced with almost total reliability.

If using Parliamentary boundaries the stages will be as shown in Table 9.3.

Table 9.3

Stage	Number	Total research selected	areas selected
Parliamentary constituencies	5	5	
From each constituency:			
Polling districts	2	10	(5 × 2)
From each polling district:			
Streets	6	60	(10 × 6)
From each street:			
Houses	2	120	(60 × 2)

The result is that researchers have to visit 120 identified houses in 60 streets within 10 polling districts. If a target house is vacant, or the occupants are out, a strict rule will send the researcher to an alternative – perhaps the next highest number or the house next door to the left.

The detailed work in constructing sample universes and devising quota and/or multi-stage surveys, is a task for the expert researcher. It is foolish for the marketer to intervene unless he comes from a research background, but he must know what he wants, and he has to be confident that the researchers are delivering it cost-effectively.

Don't hire a master painter to paint you a masterpiece and then hang over his shoulder making suggestions.

Primary research data sources

Key sources are:

- interviews face-to-face or by telephone;
- postal questionnaires;
- panel research;
- group interviews;
- retail audits;
- TV and video monitoring;
- attitude surveys.

COLLECTING INFORMATION

- *Interviews*. These can easily be conducted nationwide. A highly structured questionnaire is used and the interviewers are trained in its use. Speedy and flexible, and with high response rates, personal interviewing is a most favoured technique. There is a tendency for them to be urban-biased due to the cost of reaching rural areas.
- *Telephone surveys*. Used extensively in the USA (computer assisted telephone interviewing CATI), but with only a slow take-up in the UK. There is some resentment to these in the UK because high-pressure telephone selling has tended to use imitation research interviews to secure appointments to visit.
- *Postal*. Rural as well as urban participants can be included but the response rate is often low, which of course destroys the statistical validity of the survey. They are less important in consumer survey work than in industrial data collection, where individual respondents can be identified and followed up if necessary.

  A recent omnibus postal survey by the Consumer Research Bureau contained about 1000 questions on holidays, interests, motoring, health, finance, the home, shopping, and general interests. The participants were offered a free prize draw as compensation for completing this mighty piggy-back survey.
- *Panels*. Consumer panels are established and respondents are usually supplied with a diary in which to record their purchases and their views. Mostly conducted through the mail, once established, it is nevertheless possible to

convene panels for discussions chaired by experienced researchers. A vital part of the panel process is to record conversational feedback, but refrain from paraphrasing, or altering precisely what was said – i.e. do not introduce bias.

- *Group interviews.* Often called discussion groups, a group interview is a gathering of 6–10 respondents who share one or more characteristics such as age, gender, financial status. They are encouraged to talk about their attitudes towards the subject of the research and usually the researcher will begin by introducing a wide ranging discussion which will gradually focus on specific areas of key interest.

- *Retail* — Auditing of retail activities includes on-going audits of stocks and sales to determine brand share. These are very similar to omnibus surveys because the research is made possible only because the researcher is able to divide the cost between a number of clients.

  — *Specialised primary research.* This includes 'mystery shoppers' who shop in retailers who have commissioned their services and then report back on the standards of service they received. Harris International carry out detailed research into shopping habits – in particular they have expertise in discovering what goes on at point of sale. Many shoppers go into a store intending to buy one brand, and come out with an alternative. It is important to discover why.

- *TV and video monitoring.* The British Audience Research Board (BARB) have their People-Meters installed in homes across the UK. These are used to monitor TV and video use. All TV and video equipment (up to 10 units per home) is wired into the People-Meter and every use is monitored and recorded. Even time-shift viewing ,where recorded tapes are played back at a later time, is monitored. Data is captured electronically and automatically, and fed back by telephone each night to a central computer.

  This marks the beginning of Interactive Interviewing via the TV screen. People-Meters are interactive with equipment, but as cable TV networks are developed, so interactive interviewing will become more practical with questions and responses flowing electronically to and from computers.

  Certainly the TV networks and competing Cable TV companies will speedily introduce telemarketing linked to research on sales.

- *Attitude surveys.* Attitude is of crucial importance and is extremely difficult to research. Specialist researchers evaluate attitude, often within tracking studies, which monitor attitude change over a period of time. Some important brands have tracking studies that have continued for over 50 years. This is qualitative research which we shall come to in Chapter 10.

KEY POINT SUMMARY

- Secondary data has been researched for another purpose.
- Secondary data is always researched first.
- Desk research and secondary data research are different names for the same activity.

- Primary data is researched only to fill any gaps left after secondary sources are exhausted.
- Primary data, once collected, immediately becomes secondary data available for another use.
- Reference databases = specific topics.
- Full databases = complete data on an area.
- Source database = detailed listing of sources.
- Secondary data sources include: government, local authorities, trade associations, employers' association, trade unions, trade directories.
- Marketing research agencies are advisable for primary research work.
- The manager must know what can be done – not necessarily how to do it.
- Information should be reliable, valid, accurate.
- Data can be gathered by observation, experimentation, questioning.
- Probability or random samples are too expensive for marketing research.
- Quota sampling is the preferred method.
- Multi-stage sampling uses true random selection to locate research areas.
- Primary research sources include interviews, postal surveys, panel research, group interviews, retail audits, TV and video monitoring, attitude surveys.

WORK-BASED SELF-ASSESSMENT QUESTIONS

1 How can marketing research contribute to better marketing plan?

2 What problems would you expect to encounter when drawing up plans for marketing research to help in strategic planning for the Hampshire Hotel?

SCHOOL- OR COLLEGE-BASED SELF-ASSESSMENT QUESTIONS

1 Advise Jim on the marketing research approach you feel is most appropriate when planning the facilities for his hotel.

2 Comment on the reasons why Jim Burns began with secondary data before selecting primary research.

See the end of Chapter 11 for answer guidelines.

CHAPTER 10

Qualitative research

One day in early Spring Mary MacDonald was staying at the Hampshire Hotel. She had been most impressed with the brochure, and with the swift and friendly response when she phoned to make her booking. She had been expected, and a small fresh flower arrangement was in her room.

Dinner had been superb and she had made friends with a young woman who had arrived to take part in a conference starting the next morning. Over coffee in the lounge they began to chat and the conversation naturally turned to what each did for a living.

Mary had a successful boutique, selling high-quality and premium-priced china and glassware in the heart of a major city. Much of her trade came from high-spending tourists who had only a short time to spend in the UK. Many of these expressed regret that time prevented them from visiting Mary's native Edinburgh. This led Mary to a thought, if they couldn't visit Edinburgh, could she bring at least a taste of Edinburgh to them?

There was a vacant shop next door to her boutique – could she open it as a Scottish Heritage Centre and serve traditional Scottish snacks, sell typical Scottish artefacts and generally create a genuine Scottish experience that was neither tacky nor touristy?

Mary's companion, Alisa, was very interested. 'I had much the same problem', she said. 'When asked to create a new library from scratch I knew that there were sufficient people to make it a success – but I didn't know what they wanted.'

Jim Burns was passing and overheard the comment. 'I hope you don't mind my interrupting,' he said, 'but I had the same situation a couple of years ago when planning this hotel. I felt sure there were enough people to make it a success; but I didn't know what it was they really wanted, nor how to promote what I decided to provide.'

Mary was fascinated. Two very different marketing situations – but a common problem. 'What did you do?' she asked.

Alisa answered first. 'I had to count the number of different types of people who were within reach of the library, those in its catchment area. That was quite easy because I had detailed secondary research available from the Town Hall in particular. But I didn't know why they should come to the library. I also didn't know how I should set about telling them that we existed.' Jim agreed: 'That exactly describes my problem – and it is not one that really goes away. Not one you can solve once and forget. Decor, style, things like that, can be determined and you can then refurbish. But people's attitudes change over time, and people also grow more demanding with experience. Then, of course, competitors come into the market and try to out-do you, so you have to keep on your toes and in touch with your customers.'

QUANTITATIVE AND QUALITATIVE RESEARCH

* Quantitative research deals with 'quantifiable' elements. It can provide answers to Who? Where? When? and How? questions.
* Qualitative research deals with 'qualitative', or subjective factors. It is concerned with What happens? and How? and Why does it happen?

AWARENESS

Logically it would seem that all we have to do is ask people what they are doing, or what they prefer. Then listen to their answers, sort the answers into groups of similar types, and then decide on a line of action to meet the needs we discover. Unfortunately it doesn't often happen that way. For many reasons we cannot take what people say at face value.

This is not necessarily because they are lying, or not deliberately so. It is more that we all regard certain things as private and others as slightly shameful (adults avoid appearing to be 'childish'). Deep inside we all have feelings and emotions of which we are not aware. This unconscious or repressed central focus has a very strong influence on our actions, but generally we are unaware of the source of the influence.

'Give me a child until he is seven and he is mine for life' – this Jesuit understanding of the importance of forming attitudes, beliefs and convictions early in life holds true whether we individually come under deliberate or random influences. It is impossible, of course, to grow up without being influenced by the culture in which one develops.

Cultural values learned early are a consistent influence on actions in later life – but for the most part they are followed unconsciously.

Therefore a respondent may feel he is giving a totally honest answer to an interviewer. Logically he probably is. But will he act as he says he will? If not, why not? Qualitative research exists to attempt to penetrate the causes of certain behaviours.

BUYER AWARENESS

Kotler examined buyer behaviour and buyer awareness of products. He was able to show that buyers have a degree of awareness of product offerings which may not be complete. They can choose only from the products of which they are aware. Some are immediately excluded – for a range of reasons from the logical (e.g. too expensive) to the emotional (e.g. I will *not* buy from that

Table 10.1 Successive sets involved in Consumer Decision-Making

Total set	Awareness set	Consideration set	Choice set	Decision
Peugeot	Peugeot	Peugeot	Peugeot	?
Mazda	Mazda	Ford	Ford	
Renault	Renault	Vauxhall		
Volvo	Ford	Toyota		
Mercedes-Benz	Vauxhall			
Ford	Toyota			
Vauxhall				
BMW				
Opel				
Toyota				
Subaru				
Hyundai				

firm/country!). The number of products from which the actual choice is made has to be reduced to a size that makes choice possible. Finally a decision is taken (see Table 10.1).

This shows the process through which purchasers can be observed to move, but it does not explain what happens at each stage, why some are excluded, why the eventual decision is made.

Engel, Kollat and Blackwell are only one team of many interested in helping to determine the stages of behaviour through which a purchaser moves. They suggest that there are five decision process stages, each following one from the other:

- *Problem recognition* means that activity is stimulated by a consumer's awareness that he has a problem. 'Problem' is used to describe any situation when a decision is needed. It may be external – such as a puncture requiring the purchase of a repair kit. It may be internal – such as feeling hungry. It may be how to obtain a necessity – such as food. It may be complex – such as the choice of somewhere to eat.
- *Information search* is the process of obtaining information. From the memory, at first, but then extending outwards as far as is needed to achieve an acceptable solution. An information search may not be complete – not every make and model of car may be identified, only those of which the individual can most easily become aware, provided that one or more of them can solve his 'problem'.
- *Alternative evaluation* is the cross-comparing of the benefits offered by each alternative solution. The ideal solution is a perfect match between problems and benefits, but often there is need for compromise . . . Product #1 does A & B, but not C. Product #2 does B & C, not A, but offers D as well (which I didn't really want).
- *Choice* is often a complex process of weighing up the alternatives and selecting the closest fit – in all respects. Sometimes, when a 'problem' is not pressing, a decision is postponed because a clear choice cannot be made. At other

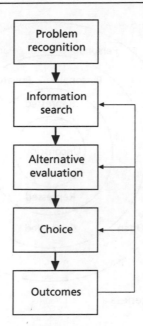

Fig. 10.1 The sequential decision process

times the wrong choice may be made because the problem has to be solved *now*.

- *Outcomes* are results of the solution in use. Does the new car perform as expected? Is the puncture repair kit complete and easy to use as it said on the box? Is the restaurant good value for money? The feedback from the usage of the product has major implications on future purchasing since it becomes part of the individual's memory and influences future information searches. The marketer's ideal is to have such good feedback that his product offering becomes an automatic repurchase. There is no need for the individual to go through the whole process: Problem: Box empty . . . Solution: Buy another.

(*Note:* The issue of value for money is complex. It is measured in the subjective opinion of each individual and takes into account every aspect – logical and emotional. It is far more significant than price, which is one element of value. We return to value in Chapter 29.)

The marketing researcher meets individuals who are each at different points in the process of purchase decision, but it will not be easy to discover where they are, nor why they act as they do. Responses are conditioned by unconscious factors such as attitudes, cultural background and education.

We all have a central core of which we are unconscious. This very deeply held set of values and beliefs is built up over the years and, because individuals are not aware of their innermost thoughts and reactions, they are also not aware that they are being self-influenced.

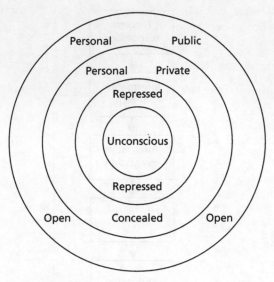

Fig. 10.2 Levels of awareness

Around this central core is another which contains personal experiences, attitudes, values, etc., which individuals choose to repress. These can be tapped into at will, but there has to be strong motivation to encourage this to happen.

The outer layers contain the personal and private, and the personal and public value systems. We all know that how one behaves in public is not necessarily the same as in private. It is necessary to evaluate what people actually do, rather than what they say they will do. Determining why they have done it is far more difficult!

In the outer layers people are able to communicate their true feelings (if they want to). As one progresses inwards the ability to directly express what one feels or believes becomes increasingly difficult. Pride in one's country is far deeper in most of us than we can ever express. We 'know what we mean', and we can give examples of why we are proud – but we cannot actually express the underpinning beliefs that stem from our very core.

USE THE CORRECT TOOLS

In all trades we must use the correct tools if we are able to get the job done effectively. In research it seemed for years that quantitative research was the research tool, especially as it appeals to our desire to have clean, hard, observable facts on which to base our decisions. Unfortunately life isn't like that; much of human behaviour is shaped by concealed and personal motivations.

Traditionally there has been a view that the two forms of research are mutually exclusive. That one turns to qualitative research only after quantitative research has failed. Probably this is due to the battle that the first qualitative researchers had in the 1930s to secure acceptance of their methods. But is also due to a reluctance to accept so-called soft data.

Qualitative versus quantitative

Typical descriptions of the two forms of research are shown in Table 10.2.

Table 10.2

Quantitative	Qualitative
Hard	Soft
Dry	Wet
Fixed	Flexible
Explains	Describes
Scientific	Non-scientific
Numerical	Non-numerical

This view shows the two forms of research as competitive. It seems to suggest that one is firm and clear, the other vague. This is not so, it is necessary to take the two forms of research as complementary, since we need to know not only 'what?' but also 'why?' Consider this example:

Raffia Products Limited

A customer may buy one of our raffia waste baskets. We may sell 100 000 of them and be very happy to have met our budget and to have made a good profit. We know what has happened. We have made 100 000 waste baskets, and sold them at a profit. Good!

But is that what has happened? Why have the baskets been bought? What are they used for?

Researching the actual use of the baskets may show the results in Table 10.3.

Table 10.3

Uses of the 'basket'	Percentage used
As a light shade	55
As a point-of-sale dump bin	25
As a waste basket	15
Other uses	5

We discover that it is easy to cut a hole in the bottom so that the 'basket' can be upended and used as a shade – we may also discover that this is a passing fad to do with the general use of raffia products in the home. The benefits of the 'basket' at point of sale should have been obvious, but we didn't think of it. Only 15% actually use our product as a waste bin!

This research tells us several things:

- Our original market for waste bins is still there. We have penetrated only 15% of it. Why, therefore, was our promotion so ineffective? We were selling baskets but people were buying light shades and point-of-sale aids.

  What must we do to reach our original market, and still keep the ones we found by accident?
- The raffia fashion will come to an end. Possibly it is tailing off already. When it stops we lose 55% of our sales!

  What action must we take to replace this business, and when is the decline likely to happen?
- PoS opportunities must be ripe for exploitation. If we have sold 25 000 units without trying how can we discover what else might be needed? By whom will they be needed? And how best can we promote our PoS products when they are ready?

  It is surely obvious that we have to use quantitative and qualitative research as full partners.

THE QUALITATIVE–QUANTITATIVE PARTNERSHIP

Table 10.4

Quantitative	Qualitative
Factual information as a framework	Framework validity
Counts numbers	Evaluates purpose
Records events	Predicts behaviour
Scientific – mathematical	Scientific – social sciences
Numeric – scalar	Numeric – evaluative

Baker says that in very broad terms one should use qualitative research to:

- define the parameters of the market.
- understand the nature of the decision-making process.
- elicit attitudinal and motivational factors which influence behaviour.
- help understand why people behave as they do.

SCALAR AND NON-SCALAR

These terms are used to indicate what type of numbers we are working with.

Scalar

A ruler is a scale. Measurements taken with it are scalar. A ruler has fixed zero point and every step away is of equal length. Thus measurement of scalar data can be related. Three is half of six, a third of nine, and twelve times three are always thirty-six. Minus quantities are always on the same scale. So –1 is as far below 0 as + 1 is above.

Scalar measurements apply to length, weight, volume – to the physical universe in which we live. They can be interrelated if one knows the correct formula:

- 1 inch   = 25.40 millimetres
- 1 mile   = 1.609 kilometres
- 1 square yard   = 0.8361 square metres
- 1 gallon   = 4.546 litres
- 1 ounce   = 28.35 grams
- 98.6 degrees Fahrenheit   = 37 degrees Centigrade
- Barometric pressure decreases with altitude.
- Water boils at sea level at 212 degrees F (100 degrees C) but as one climbs higher the boiling point decreases in direct proportion to the pressure.

We live with these interrelationships so normally that they only give us problems when, as happened in the UK, the door manufacturers changed to metric measurements while the architraves (the door surrounds) were still only available in imperial measurements. Doors fitted nearly, but not quite – most frustrating!

Non-scalar

Non-scalar numbers measure a ranking, not a place. They allow subjective factors to be expressed in numbers. If asked to evaluate five different skirts, a woman will combine a range of factors in making her decision. She may reach the opinions given in Table 10.5.

Table 10.5

Skirt	Opinion	Ranking
A	Excellent	1
B	Very good	2
C	Adequate, about the same as D	3
D	About the same as C	4
E	Poor	5

This ranking opens up a lot of questions? The two key ones from which others flow are:

- What does she mean by her terms? Is her 'excellent' typical of what others feel; of how others use the word?
  Similarly will 'very good', 'adequate' and 'poor' be terms agreed and understood by everybody?
- If C and D are about the same how did she select C for the higher rank?

It becomes important to find out exactly what people mean when they use terms we ordinarily take for granted. Also to find out if terms mean the same when applied to different items. Does 'excellent' have the same shade of meaning when applied to describe a skirt, a motor car, a bank, a meal? Or do we have to define terms within the context in which they are used?

Non-scalar numbers give us only the rank order. They can be processed statistically, but as there is no mathematical distinction between the scale of the numbers, they cannot have a scale distinction after they have been processed. It does not matter how powerful the computer, or how complex the software. If the base data is non-scalar the processed data is non-scalar also.

Non-scalar data is extremely useful – but always remember that its numbers provide convenient 'handles' by which it can be manipulated. They do not measure precisely.

OPINIONS AND ATTITUDE SURVEYS

Thurstone and Chave published a series of scales in 1929 which attempted to overcome the non-scalar nature of subjective evaluation. They attempted to produce an equal-interval scale from a large number of statements relating to the subject matter of the research. These are assessed by a panel of judges and about 25 are selected. These are then presented in random order to respondents who indicate those with which they agree. Total scores are calculated by taking the mean or the median of the value of all the statements confirmed.

If this sounds complicated don't worry – it is! So complicated, in fact, that Thurstone scaling is seldom used. The approach is valuable to understand, however, for it led to Likert scaling, which is in regular use today.

LIKERT SCALING

Likert's scaling technique was published in 1932, and has led to modern techniques of measuring feelings, perceptions and attitudes.

The researcher gathers a large number of statements relating to the object being surveyed. Respondents then react to each question individually. Each is asked to say for each statement whether they:

(a) strongly agree;
(b) agree;
(c) are uncertain;
(d) disagree;
(e) strongly disagree.

The five categories are then scored from 5 to 1 and individual scores can be calculated and compared to the maximum possible score. Thus a set of 10 statements has a maximum value of 50 (10×5) and a minimum of 10 (1×5). Note that the minimum is not zero.

Results from the whole survey can, of course, be combined so that each question in a survey of 200 respondents will have a maximum value of 10 000 and a minimum of 2000 (200×50 and 200×10).

The nearer the score is to the maximum, the more favourable the attitude. The statements can be expressed as negatives, in which case the scoring is reversed,

e.g. advertising is good for the consumer, (scored 5–1.)
advertising is bad for the consumer, (scored 1–5).

Some researchers feel it is best to mix positive and negative statements so that respondents are encouraged to think about each and avoid a habit of responding 'agree' to everything. Others feel that this asks too much, and recommend that only positive statements are used.

SEMANTIC DIFFERENTIAL

Osgood developed his 20 rating scales which have been proved to have a very wide application. Semantic differential is an extremely powerful tool of qualitative research because it is very flexible, easy to use and reasonably reliable. It takes a similar approach to Likert scaling, but allows more flexibility because the rating scales are more open.

Osgood's 20 rating scales, which have been found to have universal understanding are:

active/passive	unsuccessful/successful
cruel/kind	important/unimportant
curved/straight	angular/rounded
masculine/feminine	calm/excitable
untimely/timely	false/true
savoury/tasteless	usual/unusual
hard/soft	colourless/colourful
new/old	slow/fast
good/bad	beautiful/ugly
weak/strong	wise/foolish

Respondents must understand exactly what each term means, and that understanding must be shared. Osgood's adjectives have very strong and consistent recognition and have been proved in use over many years.

A major strength of this technique is that individual researchers are able to devise other scales to meet specific needs. It is this ease of adjustment which makes the technique so popular and valuable.

Semantic differential scales usually extend from 1 to 7, but 1 to 6 is quite often used. The argument for an even number of alternatives is that it forces the respondents to judge either positively or negatively. There is no mid-point of 'neutral opinion' in a 1–6 scaling.

Results are simple to evaluate and simple to understand. They can be presented in visual form, as the following example indicates.

Bolt Building Products

Wishing to research aspects of pre-purchase behaviour the marketing manager commissioned a qualitative survey using semantic differential scaling. The results of part of the response are in Figure 10.3. You will see that the views of installers/contractors, builder's merchants, architects and all customers are graphed. Obviously Bolt Building Products have a higher rating from installers/contractors, and don't do so well with architects. The marketing manager now has a basis for more detailed research to discover why these ratings are as they are, and what to do about the situation.

STANDARD DEVIATION

When means (averages) are calculated they do not show how much agreement there was between individual respondents. Individual scores are simply tabulated and cross-added, then the result is divided by the number who responded.

For a survey of 100 respondents the first five questions may score as shown in Table 10.6.

Table 10.6

Question	Total scores	Number of respondents*	Average (mean)
1	400	100	4.0
2	525	100	5.25
3	620	95	6.53
4	430	100	4.3
5	480	86	5.58

*Some may not answer every question.

It is important not to simply take the arithmetic mean average score for each question because for question 1 the mean of 4.0 could have come from a range of different answers. The technique of standard deviation, which measures the amount of agreement, is easily calculated (there is no need to go into the mathematics!). When this is done we can easily see how much agreement there was between respondents. Three ways of achieving a mean of 4.0 are shown, together with the standard deviation. You will see that full agreement shows no deviation – a score of zero. The larger the SD score, the wider the range of answers, the less reliable the data.

Possible responses to question 1 are shown in Table 10.7.

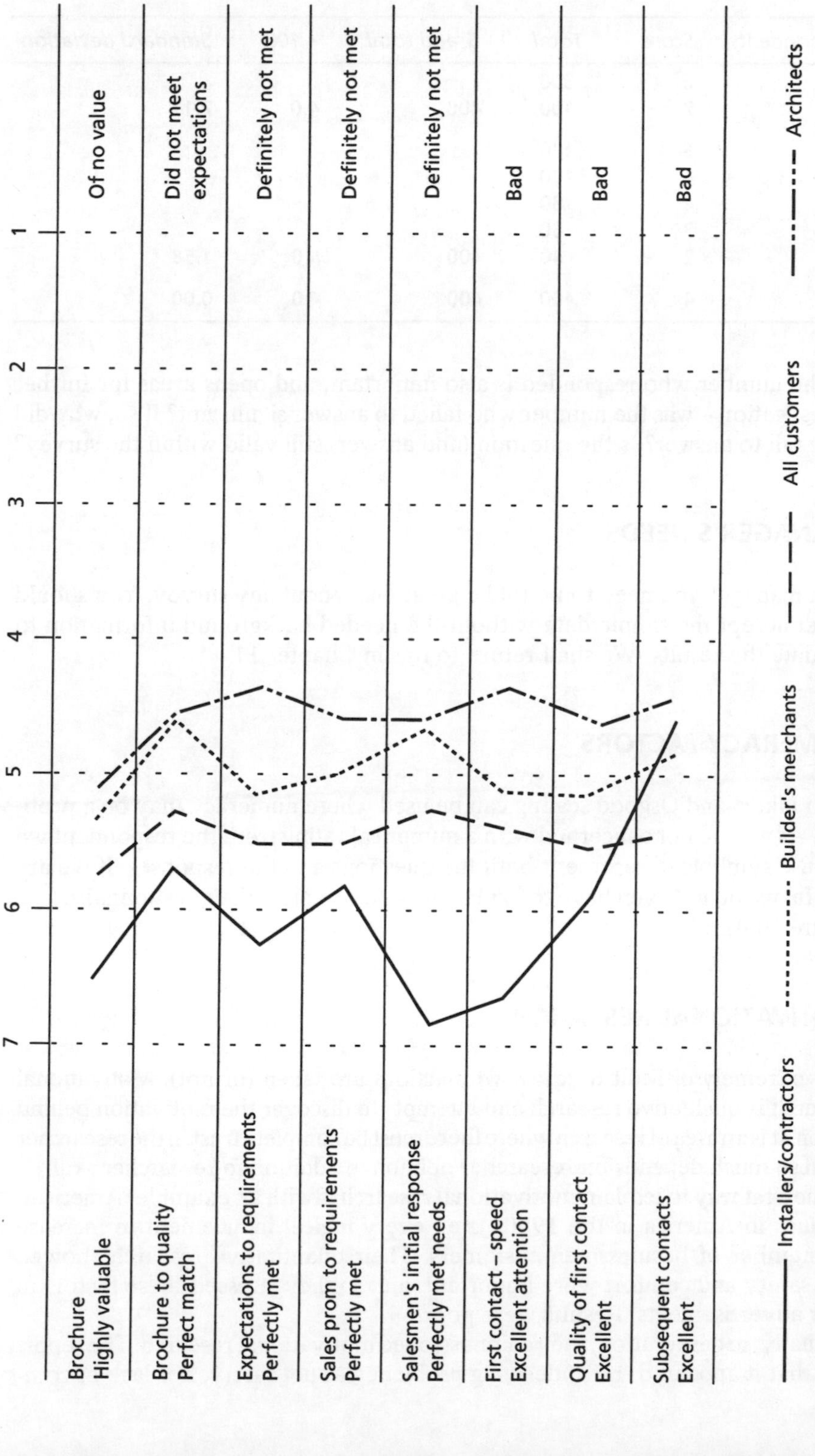

Fig. 10.3 Semantic differential scaling – Bolt Building Products (Quality audit – Product pre-purchase).

Table 10.7

Respondents	Score	Total	Grand total	÷ 100	Standard deviation
50	6	300			
50	2	100	400	4.0	2.11
20	6	120			
20	5	100			
20	4	80			
20	3	60			
20	2	40	400	4.0	1.58
100	4	400	400	4.0	0.00

The number who responded is also important, and opens areas for further investigation – was the number who failed to answer significant? If so, why did they fail to answer? Is the question (and answer) still valid within the survey?

MANAGER'S NEEDS

As a manager you need to be told a great deal about any survey. You should never accept the simple data without the needed background information to validate the results. We shall return to this in Chapter 11.

NUMERACY FACTORS

Both Likert and Osgood scaling can be used where numeracy may be a problem. As we are not concerned with a numerical rating from the respondent we can use symbols to represent both the questions and the responses. If we are careful we do not even have to explain how to complete the questionnaire (see Figure 10.4).

MOTIVATIONAL RESEARCH

It is extremely difficult to know why actions are taken (or not). Motivational research is qualitative research and attempts to discover the motivation behind action. It is an area of research where there must be complete trust in the researcher because much depends on researcher opinion in addition to researcher skill.

The best way to explain motivational research is with an example. American Airlines in America in the 1950s tried every logical inducement to increase the number of businessmen customers. Their quantitative research showed that safety and comfort were important, and so they stressed these factors in their advertisements. Results were poor.

Finally, in desperation, they commissioned motivational research. The report said that it appeared the underlying problem was not safety, nor lack of com-

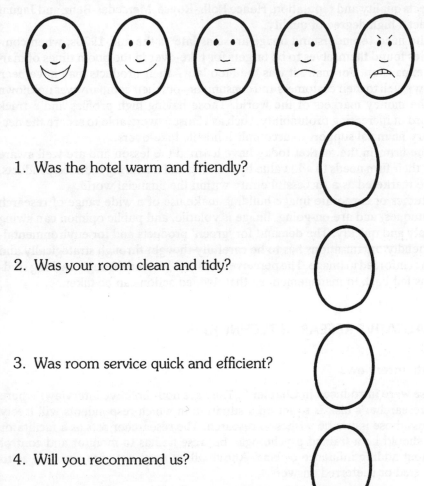

SEASIDE HOLIDAYS

We hope that you have had an excellent holiday and are sorry that you have to leave.

Before you go, we shall be grateful if you will please take a few minutes to tell us what you feel about your holiday and our services.

Against each of the questions is a blank face. Please fill it in to show us your opinion:

1. Was the hotel warm and friendly?

2. Was your room clean and tidy?

3. Was room service quick and efficient?

4. Will you recommend us?

Fig. 10.4 Non-numerate questionniare – SeaSide Holidays

fort. It was fear that if the aircraft crashed and they were killed, their widow would say 'Silly fellow, I told him he should go by train!'

This may sound odd in the extreme – but business picked up when American Airlines switched their campaign to the wives, and promoted the fact that the husbands would be home sooner if they flew.

Obviously this approach could have been tried without motivational research, but it was only when the motivational researchers made their report that understanding developed and action was taken.

IMAGE STUDIES

The image of an organisation in the minds of the clientele is crucial. Image reflects quality and reputation. Hence Rolls-Royce, Mercedes-Benz and Jaguar reflect a high degree of quality.

The need to understand image arose as late as the mid-1970s, when companies found themselves to be targets for take-over in the boom times of market expansion. For many it was then too late – their products may have been known well to their customers and consumers – but their company was unknown to the money markets of the world. Those having high profiles and a track record of increasing profitability, such as Hanson, were able to secure the necessary financial support to accomplish hostile take-overs.

The firms in the market today have learned the lesson and are well aware that their firm needs to add value by creating and nurturing branded products, to be marketed as a successful entity within the financial world.

Studies of corporate image building make use of a wide range of research techniques, and are on-going. Image is volatile, and public opinion can swing widely and quickly. The demand for 'green' products and for environmentally friendly organisations has to be carefully thought through strategically and then reinforced in image. The perceived image, obtained through tracking studies, is fed back to management so that needed action can be taken.

QUALITATIVE RESEARCH TECHNIQUES

Depth interviews

These were introduced in Chapter 9. They are non-directive interviews where the researcher's task is to set up a situation in which respondents will freely discuss those issues he wishes to research. The researcher acts as a facilitator and should be a trained psychologist because he has to monitor and control without adding influence or bias. Above all he must not give any clue as to expected or preferred answers.

Projective techniques

Indirect methods of obtaining information are often best since they allow the respondent to answer without expressing a personal opinion and without personal commitment. Usually what is projected is a direct reflection of personal opinion, but it is not directly attributable and so is easier to express.

Oppenheim listed the major benefits of projective techniques:

- They help to penetrate the barriers of awareness and reach the areas where people are unaware of their own motives and attitudes.
- The barriers of rationality can be breached, i.e. some people do not have a 'rational motivation' during the research process, even though each may feel that their own purchase behaviour is rational.
- Non-ideal behaviour can be tested through projective techniques.
- Self-incrimination is avoided.
- The politeness barrier is breached. People can project impolite behaviour which would otherwise be in breach of social convention.

Ernest Dichter, one of the major influences in the creation of motivation research, said that projective techniques provide verbal or visual stimuli which, through their indirection and concealed intent, encourage respondents to reveal their unconscious feelings and attitudes without being aware that they are doing so.

There are eight techniques in common use, but these have been extended and adapted by many research organisations. The basic principles are presented here, but these tests should only be used in practice under the guidance and supervision of qualified psychologists, particularly for the final stage of interpreting the outcomes.

- *Third person test.* By encouraging a respondent to discuss a 'pretend' person's buying behaviour he is likely to project his thoughts on buyer preference whist believing that he is hiding his personal feelings.
- *Word association test.* Responses to 'free association' with words given can often be revealing. Typical responses may be as shown in Table 10.8.

Table 10.8

Stimulus	Response
Soap	Clean
Mud	Dirty
Sunset	Beautiful
Puppy	Cuddly
Computer	Frightening

- *Sentence completion test.* Developed from word association. Respondents are asked to complete a short sentence: 'I like to shop in Jackson's because . . .' Responses, when classified, reveal in-depth attitudes and feelings which many people find great difficulty in expressing during direct questioning.
- *Story completion test.* Respondents are asked to go beyond the sentence completion test, and complete a short story. This helps experts to unravel complex attitudes.

- *Cartoons.* Cartoons are provided by the researcher, but with the speech bubbles left blank, or perhaps one person in the cartoon has said something. The respondents usually enjoy completing the bubbles and in doing so reveal something about their attitudes to the subject of the cartoon. It is very important that cartoons are produced with great care since otherwise the response may not be to the focus that was intended, e.g. respondents may relate to the character's clothes rather than to his situation.
- *Thematic apperception test (TAT).* A series of pictures, a little like cartoons, are used to focus the research. These are usually incomplete, with each feature left deliberately open for the respondent to relate to. The incompleteness is subtle – and respondents actually draw on their own perceptions to see what they believe to be a complete picture. Sometimes it is hard for individuals to perceive the actual pictures – what is physically present on the page – once they have 'completed' them for themselves.
- *Rorschach ink-blot test.* Rorschach found that ten carefully developed 'ink blots' could help respondents to reveal inner thoughts and facets of personality. These tests are mainly used in clinical psychology but are occasionally used in marketing research.
- *Psychodrama.* Respondents are asked to act out imaginary buying situations and behavioural reactions are interpreted. Again this is a technique mostly used in clinical psychology and psychiatry.

(*Note carefully* that qualitative research techniques and results can appear very simple to carry out, and to understand. This is almost always a false impression. Qualitative research is used to try to discover why things happen – or do not. Many people do not actually know why they do things and so it is very important to move carefully, one step at a time, and to test and validate as the research and subsequent action progresses.)

KEY POINT SUMMARY

- Buyers select from products known to them.
- Buyers move through stages from problem recognition to evaluation of outcome.
- Levels of awareness are built up around a central unconscious core.
- Quantitative and qualitative research should be partners.
- Qualitative research attempts to answer questions of What happens? How? and Why?
- Scalar measurements have a zero point.
- Non-scalar measurement has no zero, and is relative.
- Opinions and attitudes can be researched using Thurstone, Osgood or Likert scaling.
- Semantic differential is an easy to use non-scalar technique.
- Semantic differential measures the range of respondent's views.
- Motivation research is concerned to discover underlying motivations.
- Depth interviews and projective techniques are tools which must be used by trained researchers.

- A qualitative researcher is valuable for his opinions – perhaps even more so than for the facts he presents.

WORK-BASED SELF-ASSESSMENT QUESTIONS

1 What contribution might marketing research take to planning a new product or service?

2 What behavioural problems might a marketing researcher encounter and how can they be resolved?

SCHOOL- OR COLLEGE-BASED SELF-ASSESSMENT QUESTIONS

1 What are the main advantages of quantitative and qualitative marketing research?

2 How might you use qualitative research to help you present a case for a different teaching style to be introduced?

See the end of Chapter 11 for answer guidelines.

CHAPTER 11

Research budgeting

Alistair Macintyre of Kintyre Raincoats was a very unhappy marketing director. On his desk was a marketing research report from the American agency that his predecessor had commissioned. Alistair had been told at his selection interview that his most important activity was to be a new product launch. The company, well established in the UK and northern Europe, intended to introduce its range of high-quality raincoats to America. A research report had been commissioned, and it would be available within a week of his taking up his post.

Well, the report had been delivered as promised. Alistair's problem was that it was virtually useless!

The report, from MBA Associates of New York, ran to over 90 pages. It was professionally presented and full of impressive tables and graphs. Superficially it looked good value for money. It was a combination of secondary data taken from official sources and primary data obtained from a postal survey sent out to 2000 respondents.

Unfortunately the report did nothing to help Alistair – rather the contrary in fact because he was facing the difficult task of convincing his managing director that the report was useless, and that the work would have to be done over again. Managing directors don't like to be told that their money and time have been wasted, but it was a task that Alistair had to take on. He pondered the report and decided to extract seven of the tables to use as illustration. Taking the tables one by one Alistair made notes to show why they could not be relied upon.

Table 11.1. The average amount of rainfall over 14 years is an interesting statistic – but what relevance does it have to the sale of high-quality raincoats? Is there a correlation between rainfall and raincoat purchase? Certainly the people in the hotter states would not want one of Alistair's coats because they would be too heavy. In Florida and Louisiana the need would be for lightweight, perhaps plastic, mackintoshes.

Table 11.2. Retail sales of apparel includes everything that is worn – it is not exclusive to raincoats. It is hardly surprising that apparel (clothes) sales equate to the population and to the disposable income . . . that data took him nowhere.

It was impossible, anyway, to relate geographic areas to the states shown in Table 11.1. The researchers should have been consistent in their geographic divisions, and this applied to many tables in the report.

Table 11.1 20 metropolitan areas in six rainfall categories (year –14 to –1, averages)

Annual amount of rainfall (inches)	Area
0–10	Phoenix, Arizona
11–20	Los Angeles, California
	San Francisco, California
	Denver, Colorado
21–30	Minnesota-St Paul, Minnesota
	Detroit, Michigan
31–40	Chicago, Illinois
	Pittsburgh, Pennsylvania
	Cleveland, Ohio
	St Louis, Missouri
	Kansas City, Missouri
	Seattle, Washington
41–50	New York, New York
	Philadelphia, Pennsylvania
	Boston, Massachusetts
	Washington, D.C.
	Houston, Texas
	Atlanta, Georgia
51–60	Miami, Florida
	New Orleans, Louisiana

Source: Weather Bureau

Table 11.2 Retail sales of apparel, population, and income by region (as percentage of total United States)

Area	Apparel sales	Population	Disposable income
New England	7%	6%	6%
Middle Atlantic	22	18	20
South Atlantic	14	15	14
East North Central	19	20	21
West North Central	7	8	8
East South Central	5	6	5
West South Central	9	10	8
Mountain	4	4	4
Pacific	13	13	14

Source: Adapted from Sales Management, Survey of Buying Power.

Table 11.3 Rainwear distribution by type of outlet

	Men		Women	
Store	Last purchase	Next purchase	Last purchase	Next purchase
Department	47%	55%	59%	72%
Speciality	30	30	19	15
Chain clothing	8	8	7	7
Discount	6	4	7	6
Other	9	3	9	4

Source: MBA Consumer Survey.

Table 11.4 Retail raincoat prices paid by consumers

	Men		Women	
Price	Last purchase	Next purchase	Last purchase	Next purchase
Under $20	8%	3%	9%	2%
20–39.99	17	8	28	13
40–59.99	40	37	38	44
60–89.99	31	46	22	38
90 and over	4	7	2	3
	100%	100%	100%	100%

Source: MBA Consumer Survey.

Table 11.5 Multiple ownership of raincoats, by rainfall areas

Areas by rainfall inches	Total respondents	Total with at least one coat	Those with second coat	Those with third coat
0–10	39	34*	4*	1*
11–20	136	84	44	4
21–30	122	60	49	7
31–40	301	149	109	35
41–50	331	183	110	27
51–60	56	37*	13*	3*

* The numbers of respondents in these categories is too small to be significant.
Source: MBA Consumer Survey.

Table 11.3. Raincoat distribution was needed, not rainwear!

'Last purchase' is meaningless without quantification since some will have bought a raincoat yesterday, others last month, some last year and a few many years ago.

'Next purchase' is also meaningless because we don't know when that might be, and it is only a prediction of expected intention.

Table 11.6 Ranking of brands

	Actual price	Appraised price*	Appraised qualityt
Protector	1	4	5
AquaWear	2	3	3
Raincatcher	3	2	2
Dickins	4	1	1
Arid	5	6	4
MACKintosh	6	5	6
Dropulet	7	7	7

*1 for the highest price, 2 for next highest, and so on.
tAppraised: that is, as ranked by consumers on returned questionnaires.
Source: MBA Consumer Survey.

Table 11.7 Brand preference (percentage of those responding)

	Raincatcher	Dickins	Other brands	Don't care
Total respond	10	44	8	26
By age:				
Under 20	5	58	13	16
20–35	5	50	8	24
36–55	15	42	6	26
55+	12	36	8	32
By income:				
High	13	43	9	23
Medium	11	46	5	27
Low	8	41	3	37
Students	1	53	16	20
By education:				
High school	12	44	4	28
College	9	47	9	24
Graduate school	10	41	9	27
By sex:				
Male	12	45	6	25
Female	4	43	10	30

*Some 12% did not answer the question.
Source: MBA Consumer Survey.
Note: Tables 11.1–11.7 and their sources are fictitious.

Table 11.4. Raincoat prices should be interesting – but again we don't know when the last purchase was. We certainly can't rely on a prediction of what will be paid for the next purchase, whenever that may be.

Table 11.5. Multiple ownership of raincoats is interesting . . . can it be correlated with the rainfall data in Table 11.1? Not really, because Table 11.1 refers to all raincoats, including plastic, and the rainfall areas are State wide. A US State is bigger than many nation states. We wouldn't accept a rainfall-figure for the whole of the UK as valid data; no more can we accept data for a single US State.

This table does, however, give a clue as to value of the survey. We know that 2000 questionnaires were mailed out. In this table we are told that a total of 985 respondents replied to this question. That is a very high response to a postal survey.

Table 11.6. Ranking of brands is an extremely subjective matter . Research into it has to be conducted with care, certainly not as a simple question within a postal survey. In any case, to ask respondents to appraise price and quality of seven brands makes major assumptions about their awareness of the brands, their experience with them, their ability to appraise price and quality.

Table 11.7. Brand preference is shown as 'a percentage of those responding'. Responding to the survey? Or to this question? How many answered question? How many questionnaires were returned? How many of these could be used?

This is a typical gee whiz table. 'Gee whiz, look at that!' It appears impressive but the underpinning requirements of detailed brand awareness are suspect. Subjective values are used: what is a 'high' income? Why not quantify, especially as it would have been easy to do? e.g. Above $100 000, $80–99 999, $60–79 999, etc.

Some 12% did not answer the question. 12% of all responding we presume(?). That should mean that the answers represent 88% of the respondents. But when we try to understand the figures there is no way to equate them with Table 11.5, where we were told that there were 985 respondents. It would have been far better to have shown both the actual numbers and the percentages in the table.

Inaccurate or unclear mathematics anywhere in a marketing research report raises doubts about its overall accuracy and reliability. Gee whiz tables and graphs open serious questions about the skills and/or integrity of the researchers!

General points

1 Alistair was forced to wonder about the calibre of his predecessor who commissioned the research. Had he not briefed MBA thoroughly? Surely if they had known about the quality of the raincoats, and who were typical customers in the UK and northern Europe, they would not have researched the southern States? How was MBA selected? If they were a quality agency they should have sought clarification before making their proposal.
   He would certainly not use them again!
2 MBA should have made it clear how the respondents were selected, and where they were located. Response levels, overall and for each question, should have been quoted.
3 Inaccuracies and imprecision reduce the value of what is submitted.
4 The report is unstructured, and provides data in a confused way.
5 Unfortunately the research will have to be rebriefed – to another agency – and this report will have to be written off.

Having reached his conclusions Alistair called in his personal assistant: 'Norman, this report has come in from MBA. It's rubbish! There are three things I want you to do. I've made some notes to get you started.

'1 Please go through the report and satisfy yourself that I'm right. Then draft a memo from me to the managing director. I intend to see her first thing in the morning, and so I need a crisp summery of my views that we have bad data and need to consider radical action. That will 'soften her up' for the detail of what I have to tell her.

'2 When you've done that please make detailed notes on the report overall. Notes that I can use to show the MD why we can't use this report, and incidentally, that I can also use when I refuse to pay MBA's account.

'3 Finally, get started on a proper briefing document for the new agency that I intend to locate later this week.'

COST AND VALUE OF INFORMATION

The key question is 'Are we getting value for money?' Is the total cost of marketing research viable and sustainable for the level of sales revenue? Is the cost of new product research acceptable within long-term profit objectives? Qualitative information is usually more difficult to budget for, whereas quantitative data may be costed with more accuracy.

A fine balance needs to be decided between the cost of marketing research and its value to marketing decision-making.

Managers must determine and establish a budget for all marketing research activities. The budget will depend on the type of products, size of organisation and the capabilities of the marketing department. The budget is not a set of marketing research plans. It is an expression of research plans in money terms – of how much is set aside to spend on marketing research.

The overall marketing budget within which we will find the research budget we come to in Chapter 16. It comprises:

1 revenue (sales);
2 costs of goods sold;
3 costs of distribution, freight and warehousing;
4 marketing research costs;
5 promotional expenses;
6 cost of customer services;
7 administration costs.

The separate budget items to be considered in planning marketing research are:

1 an estimate of sales;
2 an estimate of marketing research costs;
3 an estimate of profits.

A marketing research plan needs to draw information from all pertinent sources. Clear objectives are set. Strategies and tactics are planned. Specific timing and activities are budgeted to meet marketing targets.

BUDGETING OF RESEARCH

The marketing research budget requires great care in preparation. Secondary data can be relatively inexpensive, but the temptation is to secure much more than is needed on the arguments that:

- It is available, we might as well have it.
- It's not expensive so we can afford it.

Neither argument can be justified!

Much secondary data can be researched by an organisation's own staff. It is an inexcusable waste of funds to hire an expensive specialist research agency to gather routine background data.

Primary data is the field of the specialist researcher, and organisations usually do not have the need to justify the expense of an in-house research department.

There are several approaches to the budgeting of research. Which to use will depend on the exact needs of the organisation.

1 *Fixed annual budget*. A fixed amount is spent each year for research. Often, unfortunately, based on 'what we spent last year'. This historical approach makes no allowance for what is needed. Therefore it will be either too high, because last year was busy, or too low, because last year was slow. It is unlikely to be the actual amount needed to achieve the marketing objectives.

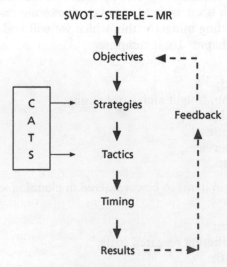

Fig. 11.1 Marketing research budget process

2 *Percentage of sales.* A fixed percentage of sales revenue is spent on research. This is also a false basis for allocating the budget. In a good year the budget will be high. In times of decline, when research may be urgently needed, the funds may not be available. (NB this approach also applies to promotion with organisations cutting back on their promotional budget as sales fall, and increasing it when they rise.)

3 *Match the competition.* When competitors raise research budgets the firm matches the increase. How can this make sense? Just because a competitor needs information does it follow that you do also? Who is running the organisation anyway!

4 *What is left?* All costs, including return on capital investment, are calculated and deducted from sales revenue, leaving a sum for the research budget. Again, no individual justification for research, simply a feeling that 'we ought to have it and if we can afford it we will'.

5 *Market expenditure model.* Marketing models are used to test what level of budget is needed to achieve the desired result. This is a complex process, but one that is very powerful – especially as experience is gained and the models become more reliable.

6 *Problem and task.* The research needed is costed against the strategies to be selected and the budget will provide the actual amount required.

PROBLEM AND TASK BUDGETING

In problem and task budgeting it is necessary to itemise exactly what is required within each area of marketing interest.

- *Single item MR budget.* Cost analysis is made of existing and potential markets. Forecasts of demand for present and new products give an estimate of total sales revenue. Decisions are made to determine the need for market intelligence – e.g. the types of market surveys, trend analysis, models, characteristics of the market – are decided and this analysis is costed item by item. The overall research budget then sets itemised costs against overall sales revenue, normally in percentages.

- *Product research.* Usually budgeted by category, and then by each individual requirement. Analysis of consumer attitudes is normally on-going and a regular item in the budget. Comparative shopping surveys, consumer panels, package and design evaluation, test marketing, etc., can all be provided for separately.

- *Pricing research.* Analysis of buyer behaviour at varying price levels through large wholesalers and selling organisations includes elasticity of demand, costs, profit margins required, changes in buying due to changes in credit facilities available, pricing, quality and branding. Research need is for personal interviews and in-depth analysis of buyer behaviour. It must therefore be budgeted especially carefully since too low a spend will be wasted.

- *Promotional research.* The external budget for promotional research will analyse costs for surveys by interview, mail and telephone to test the effectiveness of such as advertising messages and media coverage. The costs of measuring the effectiveness of direct marketing must be included in this budget since it is marketing research conducted internally.

- *Distribution research*. The costs of reaching each location, centre, or sales point, must be researched and costed. Channel of distribution decisions affecting such as the use of direct delivery from factory to customer, store, or warehouse will hinge on the analysis of these costs.

MR BUDGETING SEQUENCE

The budgeting for marketing research follows a logical sequence:

1 Define the research data needed.
2 Determine the alternative methods available and cost each.
3 Place alternative plans in the MkIS system to determine costs against revenues – using models and forecasting statistics.
4 Make an effective research plan.
5 Check and control the research activities.
6 Appraise the results and ensure they flow through the MkIS.
7 Feed back results to improve future budgeting.

Frain states that 'no model exists which demonstrates a clear relationship between communication expenditure and sales volume.' It is suspected that this statement is also true for product, pricing, and distributive research.

KEY POINT SUMMARY

- Inaccurate or unclear mathematics anywhere in an MR report raises doubt about the whole report.
- Researchers should show how respondents are selected, how many responded overall and to each question.
- Agencies should not accept unclear briefs.
- Never compare like with unlike!
- Gee whiz graphs are impressive but carry useless information.
- 'Are we getting value for money?' is the key question always to be asked.
- Check the cost-to-value ratio of collecting information.
- Much secondary data can be researched by internal staff.
- MR agencies should be used, when needed, for primary data research.
- Budgets for MR can be associated with last year, sales revenue, the competition – but with no justification.
- MR budgets should be problem and task defined.
- The budgeting sequence is clear: define the need – examine alternative methods – cost these – make an effective plan – check and control activities – appraise results – feed back to improve.

WORK-BASED SELF-ASSESSMENT QUESTIONS

1 How can budgeting help the manager to select marketing research when planning a promotional campaign?

2 What are the main budgeting factors to be considered with commissioning new marketing research?

SCHOOL- OR COLLEGE-BASED SELF-ASSESSMENT QUESTIONS:

1 As Alistair's personal assistant, make notes of the key points you will put into the draft of Alistair's memo to the managing director.

2 When producing a marketing research budget for a small newly formed airline what types of research would you expect to provide for?

SUGGESTED ASSISTANCE TO SELF-ASSESSMENT QUESTIONS FOR CHAPTERS 8–11

WORK-BASED QUESTIONS

Chapter 8

1 Key information need is focused on the consumer and the customer. First step is to determine what information is needed, then to ascertain what is already available. Secondary data first! When (if) there is an information gap it can be filled by the marketer himself – or by an agency. CATS establishes the criteria of whether to brief an agency.

2 Marketing research contributes by providing management information in time for action to be taken. The areas of research range from market to promotional – as listed and explained in the chapter.

Chapter 9

1 Planning depends on objectives and decisions – both must be founded on accurate information. Generally speaking, the better the research – within CATS criteria – the better the planning.

2 The main problems are likely to be identification of data sources and the CATS considerations of obtaining sufficient information within what must be a modest budget. Identifying the catchment areas, problems of promotion and communication, resources available and development costs will require very careful management of the research.

Chapter 10

1 Quantitative research provides hard data about the potential market. Qualitative research provides detailed guidance about actual consumer need and suggests factors to take into account in design, packaging and promotion.

2 The main problem is of obtaining opinions and attitudes. If you ask respondents 'Do you think this is strong?' the main problem is in the interpretation of the descriptive noun 'strong'. Interpretation requires great skill. Likert scaling is possibly indicated, but other techniques are needed to help decide why customers actually buy, as opposed to why they say they will or do buy. Projective techniques encourage respondents to, unconsciously, reveal part at least of their hidden motivations.

Chapter 11

1 Budget considerations drive a manager to select essential rather than non-essential information. Information which would be nice to know cannot be justified and, in fact, every aspect of information requirement and research methodology is put under scrutiny. This is less likely to happen without the management discipline of the budget.

2 When commissioning new marketing research you need quick, reliable and usable intelligence. Brief the agency thoroughly, clearly and precisely in terms of informa-

tion need and budgets for cash and time. Balance the CATS factors against 'need to know' and 'must have' considerations.

SCHOOL- OR COLLEGE-BASED QUESTIONS

Chapter 8

1 Duplicate the steps shown for the paint research. Prime sources are the AA, the RAC and Insurance Brokers. Secondary sources will include the motoring press and the Yellow Pages.

2 A two-dimensional matrix helps to tease out the market segments you need to analyse. The textbook readers and users will follow specialist subject lines, business, engineering, catering etc., the user groups within each subject will form the second side of your matrix – degree, sub-degree, diploma, certificate and special groups.

  Where each subject and user group meet is a potential niche market that must be evaluated for its potential – i.e. size, growth, ability to access. Information will also be needed on how to persuade customers to purchase.

Chapter 9

1 The problem is to choose management training or sporting hotel. What information gaps need to be filled by research? Is the data available sufficient, accurate, valid and relevant? What other secondary sources, and then primary, can be targeted?

2 Cost and budget plus a readily available and supportive Tourist Board made secondary data a first consideration. He needs to decide on the basis of hard facts whether to concentrate on management or sporting activities. Resources would not allow both. He will only use primary data to fill any essential gaps left after an exhaustive secondary data search.

Chapter 10

1		*Advantages*	*Disadvantages*
Quantitative		Numeric	Numbers do not tell the whole story
		Accurate	Only if proper systems and controls are in place
		Quick	May be superficial
		Answers logical questions	Logic isn't everything!
		Relatively cheap	
Qualitative		Ranks data	No scalar relationships
		Subjective	Dependent on opinion of skilled researcher
		Takes time	Can you wait?
		Suggests motivations	Relatively expensive

(*Note*: All research is dependent for its value on accuracy, reliability and validity. They are harder to prove with subjective research, however.)

2 A semantic differential questionnaire is fast to construct, pilot and carry through. Therefore you could collect the opinions of all members of the class and present them

as weighted average opinions (with standard deviations to indicate the degree of agreement on each question). It would be very easy to transfer your data to graph, as in the case of Bolt Building Products, to show the styles of each of your individual teachers.

Chapter 11

1 The MD needs to know why the report is useless – not what is in it. (That will come later.) She needs to be told that it contains irrelevant information, is inaccurate, imprecise and unstructured. That the agency have produced a non-professional report which does not answer the brief given them. She also needs a clear recommendation that (a) they are not paid and (b) that a new agency be located and briefed as a matter of urgency.

2 A small airline has the advantage of being able to know its major customers individually. Therefore user research should not be prohibitively expensive, nor need a marketing research agency. The major use for the budget is likely to be in locating new market niches – mostly secondary research, and in research into promotional effectiveness – primary research. Given the limited budget it would be better to concentrate and do fewer jobs properly than spread the money and do more jobs less well.

PART 4

Market understanding –
the key to success

Segmentation is a major key to marketing success. Markets may seem to be huge, and based on a common need – but when looked at in the right way they can be seen to be made up of many segments. Each segment has different characteristics and can be treated as a separate marketing opportunity.

A distinct marketing mix is tailored for each target segment, with the product positioned and packaged to appeal to the customers and consumers within the target segment.

Social class has only recently been superseded by techniques such as geodemographic segmentation which is made possible by the postcode system and the power of modern computers. Major new marketing opportunities have opened as individual consumers who make up segments of the market can now be accessed with both information and product.

Databases allow ever more detailed profiles of target markets to be developed and extended. They provide a foundation which the marketers of the next decade will take for granted.

Vectors are segments that have direction as well as size. A vector is likely to remain reasonably consistent whilst the segments within it may vary over time. Thus vectoring is strategic whilst segmentation is tactical.

Positioning is the creation of a mental image of the product offered in the minds of the target customers and consumers. Products are not positioned – it is the concept that makes up the whole package of benefits which has to be seen as unique by its target DMU.

Forecasts give advance warning in time to take beneficial action. Control provides information on the results of action. Whilst forecasts can never be totally accurate they are necessary because without them there can be no direction. Forecasts turn guesses into quantified risks.

Scenario and What-if? planning allows alternative futures to be identified, quantified, evaluated and planned. Without contingency plans a management is likely to be slow in response to change – perhaps too slow for survival!

CHAPTER 12

Segmentation

Jan Ericson is a new product development manager within Sports Shoes plc. The days are long over when sports shoes meant heavy leather boots for football and rugby, spiked shoes for athletes and canvas and rubber plimsolls in black or white for everyone else. Specialist shoes are now available for virtually every sport.

Jan's continual problem is to devise a way to satisfy newly identified needs – perhaps needs that even the consumers don't know exist. Here is how he identified an opportunity, and how it is being brought to the market.

The first step was mental – he had to throw away prejudice – if something has not been done it means there is opportunity. Whether the opportunity can yet be taken up is a matter to check, but the opportunity must be seen to exist. Only from this positive, some might think wildly optimistic viewpoint, can innovation happen and be recognised.

Jan first identified the main sporting activities and roughly categorised them from a shoes 'need perspective' as shown in Table 12.1.

Table 12.1

Broad category	Examples
Athletics	Track and field
Field	Cricket, hockey and baseball
Stability	Tennis and squash
Mobility	Boxing and judo
Contact	Football and rugby

After much thought, and considerably detailed analysis, he came across a short article in the sports pages of his newspaper. It told how the game of billiards had been transformed from an interesting pastime to a skilful game. The secret was deceptively simple.

Billards had been played with straight sticks, called cues. These enabled the players to strike a billiard ball and send it across a green baize table top – but without much accuracy and with no control. The breakthrough came when a nobleman in prison for debt became bored. To fill his time he experimented and eventually found that by sticking a circular piece of leather to the end of the cue he could exert control over the billiard ball.

This was a revelation! When he was released from gaol he toured Europe with his invention and was hailed as a miracle player!

If the addition of a gripping surface had so revolutionised billiards could the principle be applied elsewhere?

Where in sport was physical contact important, not yet developed and shoe related?

- Athletics   Shoes were for support, for grip. Not for contact.
- Field   Cricket, hockey and baseball needed a lot of contact between bat/stick and ball, but not between footwear and anything other than the ground.
- Stability   Tennis and squash players needed mobility to get around the court, and stability before making their shots, but contact was with the racquet.
- Mobility   Boxing and judo have plenty of physical contact, but it is glove and hand, not shoe related.
- Contact   Both football and rugby players need to play the ball with their feet. But football is by far the biggest shoe contact sport.

Could anything be done to improve the interface between football boot and ball?

It is now possible to approach a specific problem. The aim: To devise a method for improving footballer's control of the ball. By when should it be done? Obviously 'as quickly as possible', but what real time scale is appropriate?

When is the next major marketing opportunity? A moment's thought showed that the premier football showplace is the World Cup. The next was scheduled for 1998.

The new product objectives could therefore be written as:

- to create a football boot that will allow players to control the ball;
- to have the boot available for play in the World Cup, June 1998.

Marketing objectives, of course, needed to be produced to ensure that the launch at the World Cup would be powerful, and that the new boots would be available to the public at an acceptable price.

Many types of surface were devised and tested before it was possible to test some prototypes. In conditions of great secrecy three world class players were selected and invited to test the boots. They were enthusiastic from the first, and as the quality of the contact improved following each successive test they became anxious to put the boots to use in their regular league matches. Not surprising when top-quality strikers improved their goal targeting by 40%!

All tests were completed in good time and the marketing strategy could confidently be planned. The company signed up their contracted players and teams to exclusive use of the new boot. In January 1998 they announced that it would be launched at the World Cup, and predicted that it would revolutionise the game of football.

SEGMENTATION

By definition segmentation is:

The act of dividing the market into specific groups of consumers/buyers who share common needs and who might require separate products and/or marketing mixes (adapted from Kotler).

Three key terms which a marketing manager must have at his fingertips are:

- *Market segmentation.*   The act of dividing the market into specific groups of consumers who share common needs.
- *Market targeting.*   The act of evaluating and selecting one or more of the groups (segments) to enter.
- *Product positioning.*   Establishing the package clearly in the minds of the consumers.

We discuss targeting and positioning in more depth in Chapter 13.

Segmentation is the foundation of successful marketing. It must be accurate, valid and up to date. In the scenario the approach by Jan is to address the needs of players in a variety of sports. As many consumer perspectives exist as there are consumers to hold them. Thus the ultimate position in segmentation must include every individual – some 56 million 'segments' in the UK alone.

Obviously segmentation by individual is impossible for most products – but not by all. Those who market yachts needing a crew of 20 and complete with a gold embossed dinner service and crystal glasses can identify the relatively few individuals in the world who would want and could afford such a product.

For all but a very few products, however, the need is to segment to a grouping of consumers and potential consumers who have needs that your offering can satisfy.

In the scenario very broad segments were defined. In reality these would have been broken down into considerable detail, as two examples will confirm.

Levi Straus

When planning the introduction of Tailored Classics – a new range of ready-to-wear wool blended men's suits – Levi Straus produced the product concept first, and then investigated how best to market it.

They found that they could divide the American male clothes buying market into five segments. They labelled them Q1–Q5 (Table 12.2).

The two major potential markets for Tailored Classics were the Q3 and Q5 segments. With the Q5 consumer most closely matching Levi's product it was decided to 'go after this guy tooth and nail'.

Unfortunately Levi's distribution was through departmental stores – they had no distribution through speciality stores. Their promotion was 'Our top

Table 12.2

Segment	% of market	Description
Q1	26	Utilitarian jeans wearer. No interest in suits.
Q2	19	Trendy casual. Highly fashionable wanting to be noticed.
Q3	20	Main stream traditionalist, loves polyester, is over 45, married, conservative, shops with his wife in department stores.
Q4	12	Price shopper. Looks for bargains, looks and style are not important.
Q5	21	Classic independent. A 'clothes horse' spending more than the others shoppers. Wants wool blended suits, but they must be tailored to fit. 'Looking right' is important, knows what he wants, shops alone in speciality stores.

fits your top, our bottom fits your bottom' – but the Q5s wanted to individualise their purchases.

The launch failed. Department store buyers had no need for a new product range – they already had a long standing competitor to Levi doing well in their stores. There was no channel to those stores where the Q5s shopped, and no facility to tailor the Levi product. The product was good. The research was excellent. Problem – the marketing decision-making was poor.

THE PARETO PRINCIPLE

Also known as the 80:20 Rule, the Pareto Principle is that 80% of activity is generated by 20% of those taking part. Thus 80% of business is done with 20% of the customer base and 80% of complaints come from 20% of customers. The 80:20 rule will be found to hold throughout life. (It will not always be exactly 80:20 of course, but the majority of action will tend to come from a minority of those acting.)

The UK alcoholic drinks market

Much of the marketing activity goes into chasing 'heavy users'. To discover who were the heavy users, and where they may be located, an overview survey of the market was taken using secondary data sources. This found that the market divided into 14 segments (see Table 12.3).

It can be seen that just over 1% of the UK adult population accounts for 42% of the vodka drunk. Just under 1% for 34% of the bottled lager – and so on.

Much more detailed descriptions of each segment are available from the same secondary data sources.

Table 12.3 The UK alcoholic drinks market

Type	% of adults	Main market importance (%)	Others
1 The Dinner Party Set	8.1	Gin 49 Scotch 44 Wine 28 Port 25	Many
2 The Bittermen	6.4	Ale 44	Rum, Whisky
3 Glasnost in Glasgow	1.2	Vodka 42	Lager (premium), 'new' spirits
4 Rum Nights	0.3	White Rum 29	Lager, 'new' spirits
5 Boppers	0.7	'New' spirits 35	Draught lager, cider
6 Lager Garglers	6.1	Lager 40	White rum
7 The Bottle Party	0.8	Bottled lager 34	Lager, vodka
8 Tropic of Ruislip	1.7	Vermouth 41	Gin, port, wine and sherry
9 Rosy with Cider	1.1	Cider 39	Vodka, bitter
10 My Sherry Amour	2.9	Sherry 40	Port, gin, table wine
11 Heavy to Port	0.1	Port 11	Many
12 The Brandy Brigade	0.5	Brandy 22	Bottled beer, wine, sherry, scotch
13 Jolly Rogers	0.2	Dark rum 23	Canned ale/lager, white rum, ports and brandy
14 The Light Majority	69.9	Wine 40	Many

Source: 'Glass Distinctions' in Marketing Week, Jan 20, 1989. Reproduced with permission from Centaur Communications.

'My Sherry Amour' is described as:

A group of mostly elderly housewives (mainly 65+) ABC1 account for two out of every five glasses of sherry consumed. They are found in upmarket, suburban and rural areas and high-status, non-family areas in town. Home and car ownership is well above average and their leisure activities include bridge, rambling and theatre-going. They like entertaining at home and also drink plenty of orange juice and Perrier. Le Piat D'Or, Teachers, Gordons and bottled Guinness also appear in a repertoire that is, frankly, very surprising. Will demographic changes to the drinking population result in an upsurge of Malibu for this segment?

SEGMENTATION CRITERIA

- *Identification.* Segments must be identified in terms of distinctive needs that are applicable to the organisation's purpose. There is no set way to segment, and new methods are constantly being devised.
- *Responsiveness.* Segment members must show positive reaction to the offering. Unless the individuals who make up the segment are interested, or can be made interested, the segment exists only in theory.
- *Market potential.* Segments must be large enough to be profitable.
- *Accessibility.* Customers and consumers must know about a product, and be able to obtain it, if the segment is to be viable.

- *Promotion* must be able to cost-effectively access the members of the segment.
- *Distribution*. Product must have a channel of distribution that takes it to the targeted customers.
- *Stability/growth*. Segments must at least replace themselves or, preferably, be able to grow in size. Age profiles are constantly changing, with a swing in the UK towards a greater proportion of older people. This will have a natural effect on such factors as childbirth as fewer younger women are available to have children, but the effects of demographic change are far wider reaching than the simply physical.

Segmental attitudes change, for example, as new members join an age-based segment and the older ones leave. Will the 'My Sherry Amour' segment become the 'Malibu Marvels' as those who are now 55 replace those who now occupy the segment? Is it, in fact right to segment by age in this case? Would it be better to segment by consumption habits and attitudes?

SEGMENT IDENTIFICATION

Early segmentation was based on social class – now only a useful shorthand description.

Social classification

Social class groupings have been used for years, in the absence of anything better. Their diminished value is obvious when one appreciates that:

- They are based on the occupation of the 'head of the household'.
- The head of the household is presumed to be a man.

Thus a high earning professional woman is categorised by her husband's position – and he may be a poorly paid, blue collar worker.

Social classification divides the population into six groups:

A Upper Middle Class   (Bishops, Surgeons, Directors of large firms, etc.)
B Middle Class   (Vicars, College Lecturers, Police Inspectors, etc.)
C1 Lower Middle Class   (Curates, Student Nurses, Police Sergeants, etc.)
C2 Skilled Working Class   (Foremen, Craftsmen, Police Constables, etc.)
D Manual Workers   (Most semi-skilled and unskilled workers.)
E Those at the lowest level of subsistence.

To demonstrate how clumsy the data is – and remember that it is distorted out of all recognition by the use of the man as the determining factor – examine the % split (Table 12.4).

Trying to work with a single classifier that can account for 27% of the population (and that inaccurately!) is obviously not viable, especially when alternatives exist which offer accurate and reliable splits of between 0.3 and 4.5% of the population.

Table 12.4

	1971	1981	1991	
A/B	13%	16%	18%	(A = 3%, approx.)
C1	24%	23%	24%	
C2	30%	31%	27%	
D	25%	19%	18%	
E	8%	11%	13%	

The only remaining use for the social classification is as a form of shorthand when one wants to indicate a particular overall type and when one is talking very broadly. (As in the description of the individuals who make up the 'My Sherry Amour' segment.)

For serious segmentation a tool which gives precise results is needed.

> Sometimes in real life, and often within an examination, you will have to work with social class data because that is specified, or because better tools are not available. Small budget operations and organisations in countries where the newer techniques are not yet possible, for example. Where you can you should make it clear that you would prefer to use a better technique, and build it into your plans, and budget.

Age and life cycle

Where certain needs and/or patterns of behaviour can be identified it makes overall segmentation appear to be very easy. A bank targeting school leavers must take into account the background, experience and expectations of school leavers from different types of schools and from differing social backgrounds as well as age and gender. Thus within the overall target market are several specific individualised niches. This principle holds throughout this type of general segmentation, but does not invalidate its major benefit – simplicity.

The National Westminster Bank sets out the stages of the life cycle, and the financial implications, in a leaflet focused on savings and pension plans.

- You're born   And are reliant on somebody else for everything.
- You go to school   With 11 years to look forward to. It costs about £139 000 to educate a child at a boarding school and £5500 at a day school. Paying out of income is almost impossible – take out a regular savings plan early.
- You get a job   The last thing you think about is life assurance and pensions – but remember if you start a personal pension at 20 instead of 30 you could pay 9% less of your salary each year and still secure the same pension.
- You start a family   A real need for protection. 1 in 5 men die before they are 65. Take out insurance!
- You buy a house   You can choose between term assurance or an endowment plan.

- You plan time off   You will need money to live on. NatWest can help with saving and investment plans.
- You run your own business   You may need to borrow, to arrange life assurance, a tax efficient way to save for the future.
- You save for your daughter's wedding   An average wedding costs £8800. A bit of a shock if you don't save for it.
- You think about retiring   The state pension is £54.15 for a single person and £86.70 for a married couple. Only 1 person in 100 in a company pension scheme will receive maximum pension benefit. The sooner you think about a personal pension plan the better.
- You're worth more than you think   Without careful planning you could leave an unnecessary tax bill for your dependents to pay. Take out a life assurance policy under trust.

Distinctive needs

The UK alcoholic market segmentation, above, is an example of this form of segmentation. It was based on secondary data. The Levi's example combined both secondary market data with primary qualitative data.

Andreasen & Belk found six market segments in one survey that combined secondary and primary data:

- the passive homebody
- the inner-directed self-sufficient
- the active homebody
- the active sports enthusiast
- the culture patron
- the socially active.

A succession of complex statistical techniques is needed to collect data and process it into information. Clusters of like people are identified by cross-analysis of many factors. Each cluster is then profiled (described) in terms of its attitudes, behaviour, demographics, psychographics (see below) and media consumption habits. The result is specific segments, unique to a purpose, and named appropriately.

- *Lifestyle*. Based on the chosen (desired) lifestyle of individuals it identifies market targets that share an approach to living. e.g. environmentalists have a preferred life style which certain products can help to satisfy and for which others are totally unsuitable; e.g. tuna is, for many, an unacceptable product because the methods used to catch tuna also trap and destroy dolphins.

It is necessary to profile and describe individual subsegments, since not all within the overall segment share exactly the same needs.

- *Psychographic*. Divides buyers into groups on the basis of social class, lifestyle and/or personality characteristics. Individuals are classified by the traits that they exhibit and some brands have been equipped with 'personalities' to match those identified within the target segment. There seems little evidence that personality alone is sufficiently strong to justify this form of segmentation. (Nor can it be measured in sufficient detail and with sufficient accuracy.)

- *Behavioural.* Behavioural segmentation is quite reliable because it is based upon what people are actually observed to be doing. Thus segmentation can be based around orange juice as a breakfast drink, greetings cards segmented by Christmas, Easter, Get Well, etc. Major occasions that mark life's passages are identified to see if they are (or can be made to be) accompanied by certain needs.
- *Benefit.* Buyers are segmented according to the different benefits they seek. Timex watches were created because research found that only 31% of the American watch buying market bought for symbolism. There was a market gap for a lower-priced watch, with durability.

Benefit segmentation usually forces a brand to focus on satisfying one benefit group. Thus a second, third and fourth brand may be needed to cover the market – but each, although perhaps very similar, must be positioned uniquely.

- *Geodemographic segmentation.* The powerful segmentation tool of geodemographic segmentation is made possible by the computer and the system of Postcodes (Zip Codes) which it enabled the Post Office to introduce. There are over 24 million homes and businesses in the UK and every one has a postcode.

The postcode breaks into constituent parts to provide vital information. Let us examine the postcode MK42 8LA.

MK	the outward code, which identifies one of 120 postcode areas. MK is Milton Keynes.
MK42	a District within the area. There are 2900 districts in the UK. MK42 is the Kempson district of Bedford in the Milton Keynes area.
8	the first digit of the inward code which identifies one of 9000 sectors. MK42 8 is a sector within Kempson.
LA	narrows down to units, which may be a handful of houses on a street or a single business. 174 000 'large users' have individual postcodes. MK42 8LA is a group of houses on King's Road, Kempson.

By cross-referencing postcodes with Government Census data it is possible to identify clusters of households that share similar characteristics. Thus geographic and demographic (people data) come together as geodemographic data.

The originators of the technique have marketed it under the acronym ACORN – A Classification of Residential Neighbourhoods. Several competitors have joined them and use the same basic technique, but provide uniquely tailored services. MOSAIC, for example, is 'the standard for packaged goods, grocery retailing, door-to-door distribution, local media and list owners selection services'. FiNPOINT focuses on individuals in relation to the marketing of financial packages. Choosing between rival suppliers is a question of matching your need to their exact provision. We use MOSAIC data to introduce Chapter 13.

The technique depends for its success on the high probability that like peo-

the *acorn. *targetting*

ACORN CATEGORIES		% OF POPULATION	ACORN GROUPS	% OF POPULATION	
A THRIVING	19.8%		1 Wealthy Achievers, Suburban Areas	15.1%	
			2 Affluent Greys, Rural Communities	2.3%	
			3 Prosperous Pensioners, Retirement Areas	2.3%	
B EXPANDING	11.6%		4 Affluent Executives, Family Areas	3.7%	
			5 Well-Off Workers, Family Areas	7.8%	
C RISING	7.5%		6 Affluent Urbanites, Town & City Areas	2.2%	
			7 Prosperous Professionals, Metropolitan Areas	2.1%	
			8 Better-Off Executives, Inner City Areas	3.2%	
D SETTLING	24.1%		9 Comfortable Middle Agers, Mature Home Owning Areas	13.4%	
			10 Skilled Workers, Home Owning Areas	10.7%	
E ASPIRING	13.7%		11 New Home Owners, Mature Communities	9.8%	
			12 White Collar Workers, Better-Off Multi-Ethnic Areas	4.0%	
F STRIVING	22.8%		13 Older People, Less Prosperous Areas	3.6%	
			14 Council Estate Residents, Better-Off Homes	11.6%	
			15 Council Estate Residents, High Unemployment	2.7%	
			16 Council Estate Residents, Greatest Hardship	2.8%	
			17 People in Multi-Ethnic, Low-Income Areas	2.1%	

Fig. 12.1 The ACORN targeting classification – categories, groups and types

Source: Reproduced, with permission, from the ACORN user guide. ACORN is the proprietary product of CACI Limited 1993. All rights reserved.

classification

ACORN TYPES			% OF POPULATION
	1.1	Wealthy Suburbs, Large Detached Houses	2.6%
	1.2	Villages with Wealthy Commuters	3.2%
	1.3	Mature Affluent Home Owning Areas	2.7%
	1.4	Affluent Suburbs, Older Families	3.7%
	1.5	Mature, Well-Off Suburbs	3.0%
	2.6	Agricultural Villages, Home Based Workers	1.6%
	2.7	Holiday Retreats, Older People, Home Based Workers	0.9%
	3.8	Home Owning Areas, Well-Off Older Residents	2.1%
	3.9	Private Flats, Elderly People	0.3%
	4.10	Affluent Working Families with Mortgages	2.6%
	4.11	Affluent Working Couples with Mortgages, New Homes	3.0%
	4.12	Transient Workforces, Living at their Place of Work	2.2%
	5.13	Home Owning Family Areas	1.5%
	5.14	Home Owning Family Areas, Older Children	2.6%
	5.15	Families with Mortgages, Younger Children	1.9%
	6.16	Well-Off Town & City Areas	1.1%
	6.17	Flats & Mortgages, Singles & Young Working Couples	0.8%
	6.18	Furnished Flats & Bedsits, Younger Single People	0.4%
	7.19	Apartments, Young Professional Singles & Couples	1.1%
	7.20	Gentrified Multi-Ethnic Areas	1.0%
	8.21	Prosperous Enclaves, Highly Qualified Executives	0.7%
	8.22	Academic Centres, Students & Young Professionals	0.5%
	8.23	Affluent City Centre Areas, Tenements & Flats	0.4%
	8.24	Partially Gentrified Multi-Ethnic Areas	0.7%
	8.25	Converted Flats & Bedsits, Single People	0.9%
	9.26	Mature Established Home Owning Areas	3.3%
	9.27	Rural Areas, Mixed Occupations	3.4%
	9.28	Established Home Owning Areas	4.0%
	9.29	Home Owning Areas, Council Tenants, Retired People	2.6%
	10.30	Established Home Owning Areas, Skilled Workers	4.5%
	10.31	Home Owners in Older Properties, Younger Workers	3.1%
	10.32	Home Owning Areas with Skilled Workers	3.1%
	11.33	Council Areas, Some New Home Owners	3.8%
	11.34	Mature Home Owning Areas, Skilled Workers	3.1%
	11.35	Low Rise Estates, Older Workers, New Home Owners	2.9%
	12.36	Home Owning Multi-Ethnic Areas, Young Families	1.1%
	12.37	Multi-Occupied Town Centres, Mixed Occupations	1.8%
	12.38	Multi-Ethnic Areas, White Collar Workers	1.1%
	13.39	Home Owners, Small Council Flats, Single Pensioners	1.9%
	13.40	Council Areas, Older People, Health Problems	1.7%
	14.41	Better-Off Council Areas, New Home Owners	2.4%
	14.42	Council Areas, Young Families, Some New Home Owners	3.0%
	14.43	Council Areas, Young Families, Many Lone Parents	1.6%
	14.44	Multi-Occupied Terraces, Multi-Ethnic Areas	0.8%
	14.45	Low Rise Council Housing, Less Well-Off Families	1.8%
	14.46	Council Areas, Residents with Health Problems	2.0%
	15.47	Estates with High Unemployment	1.3%
	15.48	Council Flats, Elderly People, Health Problems	1.1%
	15.49	Council Flats, Very High Unemployment, Singles	1.2%
	16.50	Council Areas, High Unemployment, Lone Parents	1.9%
	16.51	Council Flats, Greater Hardship, Many Lone Parents	0.9%
	17.52	Multi-Ethnic, Large Families, Overcrowding	0.6%
	17.53	Multi-Ethnic, Severe Unemployment, Lone Parents	1.0%
	17.54	Multi-Ethnic, High Unemployment, Overcrowding	0.5%

ple live together, and that like people behave in similar fashion. Thus if a grouping can be identified, labelled, and its behaviour studied, it is probable that a similar grouping elsewhere in the country will share matching behaviour. As we know, the Census is taken every 10 years, with a sample Census every 5. The most recent was taken in 1991 and the new ACORN data became available at the end of 1993.

ACORN take as many as 79 data items from the 9000 items produced by the Census authorities for each of the 150 000 small geographic areas covering Britain. These include significant facts such as sex, age, marital status, economic position, education, home and car ownership. Where the small geographic areas with similar characteristics cluster in the Census data they form the 54 ACORN types which are then used as a means for defining and understanding the people in any given area.

The types are amalgamated into 17 groups and the groups into 6 categories (Figure 12.1).

The basic description that ACORN provides in its promotional literature for each neighbourhood type is revealing in itself. When subscribing to ACORN this is augmented to meet your special needs (Figure 12.2).

ACORN develops to profile a business from the Census questionnaire to detailed customer analysis (Figure 12.3).

Choosing the right geographical area is vital. Different markets need to view their customer base in different ways:

- Retailers are interested in store catchment areas.
- Direct marketers are concerned with postal geographies.
- TV advertisers deal in TV regions.
- Health care marketers are interested in adminsitrative areas.

ACORN can take an individual client's data and include it within the basic ACORN system. It can then be profiled in whichever geographic areas are most appropriate – from postal areas to the abstract (such as a contour line on a map).

Additionally all geodemographic surveys provide easy cross-referencing to two major marketing research databases. The Target Group Index (TGI), see below, and the National Readership Survey (NRS) allow ACORN profiles to be extended to include data on product usage, holidays, readership, etc.

Adding external data to the Census material can skew the classification and add bias to the analysis. For this reason a range of 'family specialist classifications' is available:

- Change*ACORN   tracks different levels of consumer confidence.
- Household*ACORN   targets households for direct mail.
- Investor*ACORN   identifies people most likely to buy high-value products.
- Scottish*ACORN   defines the distinctive demographics of Scotland.
- Financial*ACORN   isolates areas in terms of their financial activity.
- Custom*ACORN   allows individual clients to define their own classification.

Type 15   Families with Mortgages, Younger Children

These young family suburbs are located in the more prosperous industrial areas of the country. The town with the highest concentration in Britain is Tamworth. Apart from Staffordshire, high concentrations are also found in the Northumberland, Cleveland and Central and Strathclyde regions in Scotland.

DEMOGRAPHICS
ACORN Type 15 contains large numbers of families with young children, particularly 0-4 year olds. There are very few singles in these areas, and also very few elderly people. The classic 'married couple with 1 or 2 children', which is becoming relatively rare on a national basis, is very common here.

SOCIO-ECONOMIC PROFILE
Like ACORN Type 14, these neighbourhoods also have above average levels of manufacturing employment. There are above average levels of skilled occupations, both manual and non-manual. Unemployment is only half the national rate, and there are high levels of working women.

HOUSING
Most homes (81%) are being bought by mortgage. The incidence of outright ownership is only half the national average, and there is very little rented housing. Half the homes are semi detached, while the rest are split roughly equally between detached and terraced houses. Compared with the national picture, this is a bias towards semis (73% more than average) and detached homes.

FOOD AND DRINK
The proportion of households doing daily grocery shopping is 36% above average. Freezer ownership is just above average, but consumption of frozen beefburgers and frozen ready meals are very high. Other grocery products which are purchased more heavily than average are dog food, colas and crisps. Consumption of fresh foods is well below average. These are lager drinking areas though consumption of both vodka and vermouth are well above average.

DURABLES
The number of car owning households is above average, though the rate of 3+ car ownership is slightly below average. Cars in these neighbourhoods tend to be new and large. The price profile peaks in the £10-20,000 band. Company car ownership is 30% above average. 50% more people than average buy computer games systems and games, and the proportions of people buying bikes and golf clubs are well above average. Proportions of people buying household durables are generally very close to the national average

except for built-in ovens which are bought by 68% more people than average. 2.7 times more homes than average are installing new central heating and 93% more than average are having new replacement windows installed.

FINANCIAL
The income profile of these neighbourhoods peaks right in the middle, in the £15-25,000 per annum band. The proportion of people still holding non-interest bearing current accounts is 14% higher than average. The rate of new account opening is much higher than average; in particular 71% more people than average opened new savings accounts. Not surprisingly, given the age profile, the ownership of National Savings Certificates is very low as these tend to appeal to older people. Ownership of plastic cards, especially debit cards, is high. Ownership of all forms of pension plan is above average and 51% more people than average have a hire purchase agreement.

MEDIA
94% more homes than average have satellite television, though the penetration of cable

television is 40% below average. Newspapers are not particularly important to these people - most have below average readership levels. The only title with significantly above average readership is The Glasgow Sunday Mail. Levels of both ITV viewing and commercial radio listening are medium.

LEISURE
People in ACORN Type 15 are just as likely as average to go on a typical two week holiday, but long holidays and winter holidays are only half as popular as average. By far the most popular holiday destinations are those in the British Isles. Propensities to visit pubs regularly and to eat out frequently in the evening are slightly above average. Burger bars, steak houses and Indian restaurants are all more popular with people in these neighbourhoods than average. A large number of sporting activities are enjoyed here, in particular running and training, football, cycling, keep fit, weight training and squash. Other favourite activities are dancing, darts, snooker and visiting theme parks and zoos.

ATTITUDES
People in ACORN Type 15 are much more likely than average to enjoy television and radio commercials, to notice advertisements in the press and to respond to direct mail. They are not particularly interested in keeping up with developments in technology but they love new gadgets and appliances. They also prefer to try somewhere new each time they go on holiday. They like to try out new brands when they see them. They are rather more keen on DIY than average.

27

Fig. 12.2 An example of ACORN classification – category B, group 5, type 15

Using geodemographic data one can, for example:

- be given an exact count of the target household to leaflet, an exact number of leaflets to print, and road maps that specify on which houses to drop leaflets;
- match a target segment against media (who show their readership by geodemographic classification);
- select sites for retail shops so that they are close to their target customers. ACORN data helped retailers to prove that customers choose stores by time and simplicity; not by distance criteria. In other words being close to the customer is not enough. If the journey is difficult, or perceived as difficult, the shopper will go elsewhere. Shoppers will travel 25 miles on a motorway by car rather than 3 miles across town, for instance;
- adjust stock range and levels so that the correct goods are in areas of demand.

To develop specific databases that extend a geodemographic database it is necessary to capture the postcode of customers, and to have a good computer. Visa, for example, have developed their database so that a potential purchase coming through for validation can be matched against a prediction of what the owner of the card could be expected to purchase. If a significant variation occurs, they may identify a stolen card.

One simple way to secure information is through the guarantee cards that most manufacturers ask buyers to complete and return. In the UK there is no need to register a purchase with the manufacturer, one's contract is with the retailer. Yet many of the cards are filled in and returned. You will notice that they normally ask for more data than is needed simply to register a purchase. Every card that is returned extends the manufacturer's database, and provides more information about his customers.

Geodemographic data is very easy to obtain on contract. Individual prices are discussed with those who have a serious interest, but the service is proved to be cost-effective. Extracts from the published ACORN price list give an indication of its potential cost-effectiveness.

When using geodemographic data it is possible to identify a target group and select the best media to access the segment. This is possible because the media have ACORN (etc.) profiles of their readership and it is a simple matter to match need against availability.

Target Group Index (TGI)

Run by the British Market Research Bureau (BMRB), the TGI is a long-standing and greatly respected continuous survey of 24 000 adults. Since 1968 it has been continuously in the field and its reputation is well deserved. Published annually (April to March) it also provides six-monthly figures for April to September. The TGI has 34 volumes and provides considerably detailed information on:

- heavy to light usage of over 3000 brands in more than 200 FMCG product fields and for over 450 other brands;
- brands with over a million claimed users (about 1400), broken down demographically and by media;

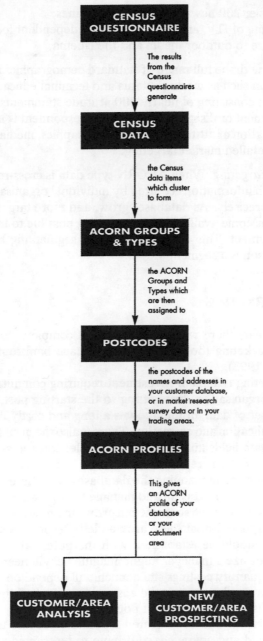

Fig. 12.3 How ACORN helps to profile a business

Source: Reproduced, with permission, from the ACORN user guide. ACORN is the proprietary product of CACI Limited 1993. All rights reserved.

- readership of over 200 newspapers and magazines;
- weight of viewing of ITV, and of listening to independent local radio;
- level of exposure to outdoor media and the cinema.

The TGI works with the full range of standard demographics and offers special breakdowns on such as working status and terminal education age. It has a 'lifestyle' section consisting of nearly 200 attitude statements against which the level of agreement or disagreement, of each respondent is measured. This allows cross-tabulation of attitude against demographics, media and brands to assist with very detailed market targeting.

- *Individualised targeting.* When ACORN type data is cross-referenced with the TGI and with information acquired by individual organisations, it is possible to target precisely. As databases grow, and more targeted media and delivery systems come available, it is becoming possible to target individuals within a segment. This is not the same as segmenting by individuals, where each person is a segment of one.

DATABASE MARKETING

In the next five years there will be two types of company: 'those using the computer as a marketing tool, and those who face bankruptcy' (*Harvard Business Review*, 1993).

Database marketing is a major investment requiring commitment from the top down in the organisation. Just getting to the starting post, by creating a clean and usable set of data, often involves a long and costly process of data extraction, de-duplication and correction. There is also the need to decide upon and validate the data fields knowing that poor selection and set-up has to be tolerated until the system is replaced sooner than is necessary.

Time must be invested in planning the database – and there is no substitute for hiring a specialist team to install and manage the operation. It is important that the database is established so that it can grow, and new fields can be added when it becomes apparent that these are needed. Respective authorities say that the database should be established with the potential to expand to 10 times the maximum size a manager might imagine he will need!

It is difficult to quantify costings since much will depend on the size of the organisation. For a small operation the cost is in the tens of thousands, for a major company it is several millions of pounds.

Maintenance costs have to be budgeted separately because the technology has to be maintained and upgraded, staff have to be trained and kept motivated, and a simple amendment to a customer's address will cost about £1.00.

In 1991 it is estimated that UK companies spent £2.3 billion on information technology. This is expected to grow at a rate of 30% a year. Pioneers of database marketing have been the mail order companies, book clubs, airlines and motor manufacturers such as Honda. Building societies are adapting their customer databases so that they are available as a source for targeted direct mail.

THE ACORN LIST
PRICE BREAKDOWN: JULY 1993

All prices are inclusive of standard geographic and CACI classification selections. We can provide data on tape, label or disk in Postcode, Surname or Mailsort Sortation. All orders are subject to the Terms and Conditions overleaf and a signed List User Warranty along with a copy of the proposed mailing piece is required before any data is released. (NB All mailing pieces must adhere to the DMSSB mailing standards)

The ACORN List SELECTIONS:

Volume:				
	10,000	to	20,000	£70.00 per thousand
	20,000	to	50,000	£65.00 per thousand
	50,000	to	100,000	£60.00 per thousand
	100,000	to	500,000	£50.00 per thousand *
	500,000	to	1,250,000	£47.50 per thousand *
	1,250,000	to	2,500,000	£45.00 per thousand *
Over	2,500,000			£40.00 per thousand *

* Labels charged at an additional £5.00 per '000 on these volumes
Delivery Time 5-7 working days/Fast Turnaround available at extra cost
Minimum order value   £700.00

SPECIAL SELECTIONS

Additional Costs:-

Investor*ACORN	£10.00 per thousand
Change*ACORN	£10.00 per thousand
Scottish*ACORN	£10.00 per thousand
Near Neighbour	£550.00 set up + £10.00 per thousand
Surname or First Name Selection	£300.00 set up + £5.00 per thousand
New Movers	£5.00 per thousand
Mature Families	£300.00 set up + £5.00 per thousand
Attainers	£300.00 set up + £5.00 per thousand
Empty Nesters	£300.00 set up + £5.00 per thousand
Young Persons	£300.00 set up + £5.00 per thousand
Multiple Areas/Batches	Minimum set-up £250

CONTROL LISTING
£5.00 per thousand

DEDUPLICATION

Historical	£5.00 per thousand
Own List	Minimum £250.00 (dependent on volume)

TAPE REFORMATING CHARGES
Prices on request from £250

DELIVERY:
Prices quoted on ordering

TAPE/DISK CHARGES
£25.00 each

All prices are exclusive of VAT which will be charged at current rate.
All prices subject to change without notice.
Discounts available to DMA members.
All data is Mailing Preference Service Cleaned.

Market Analysis • Information Systems • Direct Marketing
CACI LIMITED CACI HOUSE KENSINGTON VILLAGE AVONMORE ROAD LONDON W14 8TS TELEPHONE 071-602 6000 FAX 071-603 5862
(REGISTERED OFFICE) REGISTERED IN ENGLAND & WALES REG. NO. 1649776
DUBLIN • EDINBURGH • LONDON • NEW YORK • WASHINGTON, D.C.

Fig. 12.4 ACORN price list, July 1993

- Key components of a database
  - Basic communication information such as names, addresses and phone numbers.
  - Personal details such as age, gender, occupation, type of house, etc.
  - Transaction data – how frequently does the customer buy? When was the last purchase made? At what cost?
  - Classification data such as a credit-rating or a geodemographic code.

LEGAL REQUIREMENTS

The UK Data Protection Act requires all database users to register and ensure that the information they gather is not excessive for their purposes. The Act also requires that information held should be kept up to date and that individuals should be able to check the details held about themselves. Data may be obtained from questionnaires associated with guarantee cards or prize competitions, but individuals must have the right to exclude their name, so that they are not added to a database for the purpose of the despatch of unsolicited mail.

A marketing database should contain a separate record for each customer and it must have the ability to be indexed and searched according to any of the characteristics included. Lapsed customers must not be wiped from the

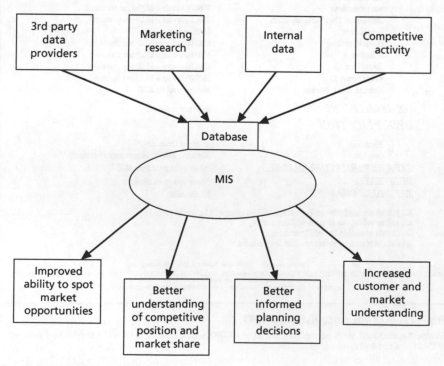

Fig. 12.5 Database and the MIS

Source: Price Waterhouse *Marketing Week* Supplement, June 25, 1993. Reproduced with permission from Centaur Communications.

database without first checking to discover the reason for the lapse and then taking a decision to retain or wipe the record. This is because:

- Managers need to know why customers leave. The reasons may well lead to corrective action – if known.
- Lapsed customers can return – but not if they cease to receive mail because they have been wiped.

Databases are not simply technical information centres. They are active aids to profitability when managers learn how to maximise their potential benefits. They are a vital part of any management information system.

Keeping up to date in this field is important for all managers, and especially those studying to become managers. This is best done through the specialist media since the area is so dynamic that any bound book will be out of date before it is published.

KEY POINT SUMMARY

- Product offerings must offer unique benefits to identified groups of consumers.
- Segmentation is the division of a market into specific groups of consumers/buyers who share common needs.
- Targeting is evaluating and selecting one or more segments to enter.
- Positioning is establishing the package in the minds of the target consumers.
- Segmentation is the foundation of modern marketing.
- The Pareto principle says that 80% of activity will come from 20% of participants.
- Social classification groupings remain valid as 'shorthand'.
- Geodemographic segmentation combines geographic and demographic factors.
- The Target Group Index (TGI) is a long-standing and greatly respected continuous marketing research survey.
- Database management is becoming essential to every organisation.
- A marketing database should have a record for each customer and the ability to be comprehensively indexed and searched.
- Databases are active aids to profitability.
- The provisions of the *Data Protection Act* must be understood and complied with.

WORK-BASED SELF-ASSESSMENT QUESTIONS.

1 How does the segmentation of industrial markets differ from consumer markets? Will consumer segmentation techniques be of value to the industrial marketer?

2 What benefits might a marketing manager derive from a database when planning to market a fashion range to a new segment?

SCHOOL- AND COLLEGE-BASED SELF-ASSESSMENT QUESTIONS.

1 Why has geodemographic segmentation replaced social classifications in many markets?

2 What benefits can Jan Ericson derive from the marketing of the new boot over and above initial sales?

See the end of Chapter 15 for answer guidelines.

CHAPTER 13

Vectoring and positioning

Asian Jewellery is a large retailer originally based in Singapore, but now with subsidiary and associated companies in countries throughout the Asian region. They consider that a British base may be the best way to secure market entry to the European Union. They specialise in hand finished mass-produced costume jewellery which they source from the cheap labour markets of the Far East. Their products are therefore low-bulk and high-price items.

They have called for a feasibility study from a well-known retail consultancy. This is the preliminary report.

THE RETAIL CONSULTANCY
CONFIDENTIAL
To: Cheng Lu,   Date: 15.2.199X
    Managing Director,
    Asian Jewellery,   Ref: JC16/9X
    Singapore.

Subject: Retail store location

1 Executive Summary
  1.1 It is possible to use existing secondary data sources in order to make outline recommendations regarding the potential for you to enter the UK retail market with a high probability of success.

  1.2 Preliminary findings indicate that High Street locations will be preferred sites for your type of merchandise.

  1.3 The tendency has been for UK retailers to move to Retail Parks on the outskirts of towns and cities – but in January 1994 the UK Government made it clear that they are determined to reverse this trend.

  1.4 Whilst preliminary conclusions can be drawn from generalised data it will be necessary to conduct detailed study at the micromarketing level in order to define a precise location strategy.

2 Location Strategy
    Whilst it can be shown (see 4, below) that the High Streets are likely to prove the most viable locations for your stores it is important to determine precise strategy, taking into account the factors which impact on retail success.

  2.1 Catchment – easy access must be possible for customers from areas of suitable demographic mix and spending power.

2.2 Environment – the character and composition of the shopping area must be appropriate to attract your target customers.

2.3 Position – proximity to stores selling associated lines will probably be most appropriate in your case. A solus site is contra-indicated.

2.4 Pedestrian flow – should be generated by associated stores. It is not felt appropriate to recommend location in the less expensive, but less frequented, sectors of the environment:

2.5 Recommendations

    2.5.1 Objective – By 1 May to have completed a detailed profile/environment/position micro-marketing study. This will entail:

    2.5.2 Profiling – customer profiles of your target customer groups should be prepared. (See 3, below.)

    2.5.3 Comparison – a micro-marketing study based on your customer profiles should be carried through on two comparative High Street shopping areas.

    2.5.4 Security – this preliminary study should be conducted entirely within our Retail Network Planning Database using mainly secondary data. Any additional primary data requirement should commissioned by us as part of our known on-going interest in the market.

3 New site location

It is recommended that a sieve approach to be taken. This requires us, in close association with you, to establish a series of requirements which must be satisfied if a site is to be judged suitable for one of your stores. We can draw upon experience of existing retailers, who can be deduced to have a similar market presence – but it will be necessary to generate and validate a model that is unique to your operation. This will require a simulation based on customer and consumer profiling and on-site criteria.

3.1 Profiling

We need to create detailed profiles of typical groups of customers/consumers that we expect to use your stores in the UK. In time we shall be able to define these precisely, but at this initial stage must create 'working profiles' from data on:

    3.1.1 Your existing customers and consumers in other markets.

    3.2.1 Customers/consumers of close competitors already trading in the UK.

    3.1.3 Your assessment of the customer/consumer mix that you wish to target.

3.2 Site criteria

We need to determine as many criteria as possible with these as the minimum:

    3.2.1 Size – the size of store you need to operate effectively.

    3.2.2 Traffic pulls – the need to be close to traders with market pull.

        – or to be on route to or from a trading area with pull.

        – in time we should aim to specify traders who attract customers who profile similarly to your target groupings.

    3.2.3 Catchment – proximity and ease of access for your target customers.

        NB: This may be in travel time rather than distance.

        – ease of access, i.e. car parks, bus routes, etc.

3.2.4 Environment – user-friendliness of the area. e.g. provision for the disabled, refreshment and toilet provision, etc.
– is it a 'nice area' in which to shop?

These need to be cross-referenced against a range of geodemographic data to provide a ranking report. (See Appendix.)

4 High street location

Our suggestion that the high street is the most appropriate location is based on the following generalisations which are validated in our network. It is emphasised that 'high streets' differ, and that some locations within a suitable high street would not be appropriate for your business.

It is necessary, therefore, to move on from this broad finding to the construction of detailed models that directly relate to your business needs. Using these models we shall be able to recommend precise locations, and to rank them in order of priority.

4.1 Convenience and comparison shopping

A UK shopper has objectives that can be classified in various ways. We have found that convenience and comparison provide useful descriptors. Convenience shopping is driven by the need to replenish something that gets used up such as groceries, nappies, batteries or petrol. Comparison purchases are made by comparing the benefits of various brands sold in a variety of outlets. In your case by comparing different jewellery in speciality shops and from departmental store counters.

Time spent in comparison shopping is perceived as leisure activity since typical products offer intrinsic pleasure to the shopper whether buying for personal use or as a gift.

4.2 Portability

The size/value ratio of purchases is a major key to location requirement.

Freezers, video and hi-fi occupy comparatively large and comparatively specialised space in respect to their value. Items such as bulky packs of cushions are light weight, but difficult for customers to carry around. On the other hand items such as jewellery have high value, but require a minimum of space.

4.3 Retail formats and preferred locations

When the convenience/comparison and portability criteria are cross-referenced it becomes possible to determine broadly the different types of location that are most applicable (see Figure 13.1).

4.3.1 Retail parks attract comparison shoppers for such as refrigerators, three piece suites and do it yourself (DIY) goods.

4.3.2 Solus sites are free-standing outlets such as the hypermarkets that feature groceries within a full range of household needs.

4.3.3 Parades are local shopping areas where convenience shoppers buy day-to-day items.

4.3.4 High streets and traditional city centre locations offer attractive ambience and a range of services such as libraries and parks within easy distance. They are attractive locations for comparative shoppers looking for high value/weight items.

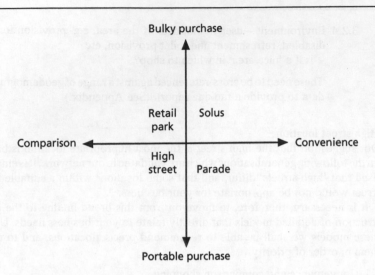

Fig. 13.1 Retail preferred location

Source: Reproduced, with permission, from *Strategies for Retail Network Planning*, CCN Marketing 1993

4.4 Convenience, price, variety and proximity

The benefits offered by a retailer must drive the selection of location. The location must drive the proposition he presents to his customers (see Figure 13.2).

4.4.1 Price is the key advantage offered by the retail park. Lower rents, larger space availability and ease of access for bulk deliveries make it possible to offer keen prices with relatively easy access.

4.4.2 Convenience is the major benefit offered by the solus site. Everything is geared to the convenience of one-stop weekly shopping.

4.4.3 Proximity is the benefit offered by the Parade. Shops there survive because they are the closest to the majority of consumers. It now has a complementary role to play because the one-stop shopper uses it only to top up on essentials such as bread and to replace urgently needed items between the regular major shopping trips.

4.4.4 Variety is the benefit offered by the high street. The sheer number of retailers found on the high street holds the promise that a customer will find exactly what he wants. The treater the pedestrian flow and the larger the number of shops the greater the viability of specialist outlets such as jewellers, stamp and coin shops, vegetarian restaurants and second-hand book shops.

4.5 Retail sales and profitability

Likely factors that drive retail sales and profitability are shown in Table 13.1.

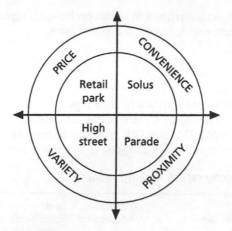

Fig. 13.2 Retail site benefits

Source: Reproduced, with permission, from *Strategies for Retail Network Planning*, CCN Marketing 1993

Table 13.1 Likely drivers of retail sales and profitability

Location	Primary drivers	Secondary drivers
High street	Number of multiples Mix of multiples Population of catchment Pedestrian flow	Geodemographics Neighbour outlets Access from transport links
Retail park	Drive time population Number of competitors Distance to other parks Number of multiples	Geodemographics Conforming values
Solus	Drive time population Traffic flows Visibility Distance to competitors	Competitor floor space Geodemographics
Parade	Walking distance population Geodemographics	Competitor floor space Geodemographics

Source: Reproduced, with permission, from *Strategies for Retail Network Planning*, CCN Marketing 1993.

  5 *Success in the high street – conclusion*
  Obviously there is more to retail site location than merely selecting one of these four areas from which to trade The four types are only the first rather coarse way of grouping a huge number of shopping locations, each of which is slightly different in its own particular way. A key objective must be to discover what the factors are that will apply to your unique requirements.

We have recommended such action in this preliminary report and will be glad to receive your instructions to take the matter further.

Signed:
Kurt Johansen
Appendix
An example only to show a typical ranking report.
This lists the top 10 Shopping Centres in the UK ranked by projected share of households purchasing TV, audio or computer in the last 12 months. Similar reports can be produced for any category of location/products grouping.

Table 13.2 Shopping centre ranking report

Rank	Zone description	Purchasing households	Total households	Penetration of target	Index GB = 100
1	London – Earls Court	1563	6602	0.237	190
2	london – West Hampstead	3250	15 129	0.215	173
3	London – Ladbroke Grove	2963	14 568	0.203	163
4	London – Upper Norwood	1565	7754	0.202	162
5	London – Central	25 523	132 888	0.192	154
6	London – Colliers Wood	976	5116	0.191	153
7	London – Muswell Hill	2509	13 237	0.190	152
8	London – Swiss Cottage	2803	14 794	0.189	152
9	London – North End Road	5375	28 420	0.189	152
10	London – Ealing Broadway	3350	17 729	0.189	152

Note: The index column compares each shopping centre with the average across the UK. It can be read the same as a percentage e.g. London – Earls Court ranks at 190% of the average. It is therefore more attractive than London – West Hampstead, which achieves 173% of the average.

Source: Reproduced, with permission, from *Strategies for Retail Network Planning*, CCN Marketing 1993

(Note: The scenario is based on data supplied by CCN Marketing, who operate the MOSAIC system of marketing planning. MOSAIC operate to the same general principles as ACORN, but their database is selected differently to meet their specialised needs.)

VECTORS

Vectors are segments that have direction as well as size. The 65+ ABC1 female market described in Chapter 12 as 'My Sherry Amour' is an identified segment of people at a moment in time. The make-up of the segment can be identified, and researched in considerable detail. The results will hold good for a time – but for how long?

If we accept that the 65+ female segment is likely to survive for a considerable time we have actually identified a vector.

The vector is the group that makes up the 65+ female market. The 'My

Sherry Armour' segment is a group of ABC1 women within the vector. There are also segments made up of C2s, DEs and, much more significantly, the ACORN types and specialised segments defined by individual marketers.

Today both the vector and the segments within it consist of a certain number of women with an identifiable level of disposable income, plus a range of attitudes, perceptions, values and beliefs. Tomorrow the vector will be much the same. What will it be, say, in five years?

For the sake of simplicity let us assume that this vector is made up of females aged 65–70. Also that each year there is a 20% change, as some women reach 65 and join, whilst others reach 70 and leave. Then in one year 80% of today's women will still be in the vector, and 20% will be newcomers. In two years it will be 60:40, then 40:60, 20:80 and finally all the present occupants will have left.

What will happen to the vector as its occupants change? We are not quite sure, but we can make pretty good estimates if we examine the behaviour of women coming up to 65 and forecast the changes they are likely to take with them as they move across the age border. We can also forecast the number of women in the vector. Is it a growing vector, or in decline?

There is no hard and fast border, of course. In segmentation we cannot be totally precise, but approximations are sufficient provided that they are carefully researched.

> **Until recently our consumers had no idea they were being segmented, and so behaved naturally. There is some evidence now, however, that younger people are very aware of marketing, and are discounting much of what has traditionally been very effective. Branding, in particular, is coming under challenge as attitude is shifting towards a view that competitive brands are likely to be as good as each other.**

If this awareness of marketing continues – as it will, now that marketing is taught in schools – we can now expect some major changes to occur within segmental behaviour.

The concept of vectoring is important because it provides the strategic base and direction for relatively major market areas. Within each vector are several segments, each with identifiable behaviour.

To make matters even more complex we can slot individuals into several segments at once. Only a decade and a half ago marketers segmented by social class. Then a segment was its own vector. It is only with the availability of detailed databases that it has been possible, and necessary, to consider the long-term, strategic aspects – vectoring, and the short-term, tactical aspects – segmentation.

Shotgun or rifle?

Segmentation is often explained by using a shotgun versus rifle example. Without segmentation marketing effort is shotgunned out on a wide front, and only some hits the target. Much effort (budget) is wasted.

'Rifle' fire is far more accurate. In the hands of a good shot a rifle is aimed very carefully and each shot hits a specified target. Today's laser sight technology ensures that it is virtually impossible to miss.

We can thus say that a shotgun may hit the vector, but a laser sighted rifle is needed to hit a segment.

STRATEGIC ALTERNATIVES

A marketing manager has five strategic alternatives:

- *Single segment concentration.* This allows tight focus and concentrated effort. It does, however, involve higher than normal risks since a market change will leave an organisation vulnerable.
- *Multi-segment coverage.* The selection of several segments, which may be very different in character. Risk is spread over the targeted segments.
- *Product specialisation.* Focus is on the production of a single product, which is sold to several segments. Reputation is built on the quality and the range. The risk is that the product itself can be superseded. Hence the focus needs to be on the task, not the product. The classic example is the American railways which focused on product (trains) and not task (travel). Their future lay in transportation, not in railway trains. They could not see that, and so lost their market.
- *Market specialisation.* Full coverage of a single market needs is provided, e.g. 'All you need for your office'.
- *Full market coverage* is possible only for huge organisations since the aim is to supply all consumer groups with all the products they might need, e.g. IBM (computers), Microsoft (software), Ford (vehicles).

The Ansoff matrix

The deceptively simple strategic options matrix developed by Professor Ansoff shows the broad areas in which strategic development is possible. We used this matrix in Chapter 7 (see Figure 13.3).

- *Market penetration.* The aim is to increase the market share of existing products within existing markets. Consumers can be encouraged to use more of the product – men's aftershave in the morning and again when preparing for the evening. Extending its use from an astringic 'wake-up' product to a fragrance.

But you cannot extend beyond a maximum usage point. Once a consumer switches to your brand of motor oil the usage is conditioned by the mileage his car covers, and the age and efficiency of engine. Securing more users is possible – but only up to a maximum level of market penetration.

- *Market development.* Managers look for new markets in which needs can be satisfied with existing products. Automobile manufacturers long ago recog-

	Current products	New products
Current markets	Market penetration strategy	Product development strategy
New markets	Market development strategy	Diversification strategy

Fig. 13.3 Ansoff strategic options matrix

nised the special needs of those who run fleets of cars. Often manufacturers are encouraged to open up new geographic markets because their home market is saturated. This is not an acceptable argument for entering export markets – but one which has underpinned much of the interest in selling overseas.

- *Product development*. Adding features to existing products extends their life, and may open new marketing opportunities. The silicon-based industries are past masters at product development – notably Casio, which dominate the world hand-held calculator market with a bewildering array of ever more complex products, available at affordable prices in the high street.
- *Diversification*. This option requires an organisation to move into a product/market area with which it is unfamiliar. It is a high-risk strategy because each market has unique features that may prove to be extremely subtle. Management has much learning to do here, may often misjudge the time and resources required to diversify.

Extension

It is always best to act from strength. Successful extension to new product or market areas requires a strong base from which to operate. The major alternatives are:

- Brand extension:
  — Mars have very successfully extended their brands into the ice cream market.
  — Levi extended their brand from jeans to skirts, to jackets, to shirts. But they couldn't extend into wool blended suits. The brand, and everything that supported it, was too strongly identified with Levi, who are known for their blue jeans.

- Product extension:
  — Nestlé happily extended their instant coffee into the catering market, and some years later extended the catering packs to the retail shelves.
  — DanAir attempted to extend from a successful charter airline to operate scheduled services. They were unable to shake off their 'Dan Dare' image and when the recession hit they were swallowed by British Airways.
- Skills extension – technical and/or managerial:
  — Apple Centres have extended from the supply and servicing of Macintosh computers to providing classroom and on-site training.
  — Technical College staff have been encouraged to carry out management consultancy, but in many cases they have been unable to deliver because of lack of support, and/or insufficient current practical experience.

Threats

Porter suggests five forces that threaten any marketer in every segment of every vector. His threats are:

- *Intensive segment rivalry*. Segments that already have several active competitors are less attractive. New entrants to a segment threaten those already operating within it.
- *New entrants*. There is constant risk that new entrants will attempt to secure a place. A strong defensive strategy is needed to protect a position.
- *Substitute products*. A major risk is that consumers will switch to substitute products. Fairy Liquid runs a continuing campaign to remind consumers that 'Fairy goes much further than cheapies' for washing dishes.
- *Growth in bargaining power of buyers*. A segment with powerful buyers is less attractive because negotiation is heavily weighted in the buyer's favour. When power switches, as in the UK grocery market, manufacturers can find themselves forced to cut margins and still offer improved service if they want to retain the business.
- *Growth in bargaining power of suppliers*. A segment is unattractive if the organisation's suppliers have too much power over the sources of supply. Too much dependency, on supplier or customer, and the organisation looses its freedom to operate as it would wish.

Segment selection

Managers must identify and define the specific criteria which make a segment attractive – and also those that are unattractive. If each of these criteria is then given a weight on a scale of 10, to indicate its importance, it is possible to assess the likelihood of the criteria being met, and then cross-multiply to secure a weighted average which indicates perceived relative attractiveness. If the results for several segments are then compared the segments can be ranked in order of attractiveness.

Typical criteria include:

- initial market size;

- projected market growth;
- profitability, short-, medium- and long-term;
- effect of entry on competitive position;
- compatibility with corporate objectives and strategies;
- resources needed to effect the desired positioning;
- staff expertise required and available;
- effect upon current segments in which the enterprise operates – overlap? substitution?
- compatibility with existing sales and distribution structures;
- risk of failure – and potential damage to corporate whole.

Likely extra cost areas include:

- product modification;
- administration – initial and on-going;
- inventory increases;
- distribution logistics;
- promotion;
- requirement for new marketing personnel.

A framework for segment ranking is given in Table 13.3

Table 13.3 Ranking

Criteria	Weighting (Importance)	Assessment of occurrence	Weighted Assessment*
Initial market size £5m	10	3	30
Market growth 8% p.a.	8	7	56
Profits, short-term	1	1	1
Profits, mid-term 5%	8	6	48
Profits, long-term 10%	8	8	64
Etc, etc.			
	Weighted total for this segment:		199

*Weighting × Assessment

MARKETING STRATEGIES

When planning a marketing strategy it is vital to be clear in the selection of options.

Undifferentiated marketing

This is a strategy of producing one product and selling this to a market. In undifferentiated marketing an organisation ignores market segment differences in offering this single product to the whole market. Note how even the mighty Coca-Cola have revised their approach by the introduction of targeted versions of their original products.

Undifferentiated marketing is sustainable only in conditions of monopoly or when demand greatly exceeds supply. As competition enters, and when demand slows down, it is no longer a tenable policy.

Differentiated marketing

This marketing strategy requires the design of several products, each tailored to a segmental need. Thus Ford produce up to 18 or 20 versions of each model to cater firstly for the basic needs of a vector and then for individual segment needs, e.g. for a small car to use in the city. Thus the Fiesta is the first choice. Then one can choose from a range of options:

- manual or automatic transmission;
- engine size;
- tuning for performance or economy;
- colour and upholstery options;
- status additions – exclusive models, customisation, etc.;
- one can even mix and match.

Concentrated marketing

The company attempts through concentrated marketing to produce the ideal product for each segment of the market. There are a number of ways in which tangible products and intangible services can be differentiated in the perception of the customer/consumer. Add you own thoughts on customer perceptions to the examples in Table 13.4.

Over and above product and service is the ability to differentiate through personnel and image.

Personnel differentiation

This can be secured by a hiring and retention policy that attracts high-quality staff. High-quality personnel justify their higher cost if managed correctly within a clear corporate policy. High-quality staff will become frustrated and leave unless there is management support from corporate level.

Image differentiation

An image must convey a singular message in a distinctive way with emotional power. An established corporate image gives immediate recognition within the target markets. This is sufficient – it is wasteful to develop an image in markets where there is no intention to trade.

Image is normally expressed in a symbol which conjures up the whole emotional appeal associated with the organisation and/or its products and services. Even a split second's glance at a Happy Eater sign on a busy main road alerts the driver to the upcoming restaurant and provides an immediate and powerful image of exactly what type of food, ambience, service and price are available.

Table 13.4 Product/service

	Product	Service
Branding	A standardised product, or service, can be branded so that the consistency of the offering differentiates, e.g. frozen chicken, high street copier outlets.	
Features Characteristics that add value to a basic offering:	Electric windows on a car. One-touch programming of a video.	Hairdressing in your own home. Call waiting warning from a phone company.
Performance	Faster search and replace software. Safety bags in automobiles.	Happy hour in a bar/restaurant. 24 hour petrol and diesel availability.
Conformance Reliability in extended use	Japanese cars have a reputation for high conformance.	Database of customer's preferences so that they can be satisfied without need for customer to reiterate them.
Durability	Volvo has built an excellent reputation for long-life and high resale value.	The length of time offering the service to a high standard. 'At this site for 100 years!'
Reliability	Sony have built a reputation for long-life products.	The store opens on time. Federal Express answers on the second ring.
Repairability	Standard parts that plug-in and allow speedy repair.	Service Engineer calls on time – and cleans workplace before leaving.
Style	Jaguar's style kept the marque alive even though reliability was poor.	A Harrods plastic bag compared to one from Tesco.
Training	Ensuring that own and dealer's staff are trained initially – and updated so that customer service levels are high. Training users so equipment is used to maximum efficiency.	
Delivery/supply	Speed, accuracy, reliability, care in delivering/supplying to commitment.	
Installation	Clear instructions that are easy to follow. Staff who attend on time and do a neat, complete job.	
Consultancy	Professional advice in advance of purchase with facility to supervise actual installation and also the product/service in use. Hot line back-up to allow quick solutions to user problems.	

TARGET MARKETING

Target marketing, also known as 'niche marketing', is the act of developing products or services to meet the needs of a designated market segment. The car market provides excellent examples of target marketing with models developed to meet vector needs – the Peugeot 106, 205, 306, 406, 606. Each of these models targets a vector, and a range of options allows individual segments to be targeted.

The ultimate target marketing is when products are customised for a single customer.

PACKAGE

'Package' can be used in two discrete ways:

- To describe the protective wrapping of a product. We shall come to this use of the term in Part 6.
- To describe the bundle of benefits that is offered to a particular market target. Any individual product or service may be 'packaged' in different ways to appeal to different market targets.

In promotional planning the marketer packages the proposition, never sells the product or service directly, i.e. package in the promotional sense relates to the symbolic elements that make up a product offering.

Thus one does not sell a refrigerator – one encourages the customer to buy a package of benefits such as ice being always available, milk kept fresh for the morning cup of tea, an attractive addition to the kitchen. Or perhaps, to suit a different customer, one packages and offers reliability, economy in use, convenience of size and interest-free credit.

POSITIONING

'The act of designing an offer so that it occupies a distinct and valued place in the minds of the target customers' (Kotler).

There need be no such thing as a commodity which cannot be targeted. Even simple table salt can be converted into a product which can be targeted. You need to take it in two stages:

- consider it an undifferentiated product;
- identify a way to differentiate. This will come from identification of a target market composed of consumers who have unfulfilled needs.

Developing an overall package of benefits that can be positioned in the minds of the target consumers completes the transformation.

Note that products are not positioned – the term 'product positioning' is incorrect. Positioning refers exclusively to a mental concept. The package that comprises the offer has to be positioned – remember that consumers do not want products, they want what products do for them. They want their needs to be fulfiled.

• *Mars Bar positioning.* Is it a filled bar of chocolate, a piece of confectionery to be found on the sweets counter? No! A Mars, we are told, 'Helps you work, rest and play'. So it is positioned as a nourishing snack that is fun to eat.

Who eats Mars? According to the adverts (the pictures not the words) the eaters are young, healthy, virile, active, fit, and happy.

Where do we find Mars? On the confectionery counters; but also on the biscuits/snacks counters, in vending machines, in cafes – and now we also find 'fun', 'standard' and 'extra large' bars as the Mars brand is extended.

Further brand extension has seen the introduction of Mars ice cream, with similar taste, carrying the same packaging and symbolism as the traditional Mars bar.

Contrast the positioning of Mars with that of other popular chocolate bar products. You should discover that each is trying to establish a unique position for itself.

Positioning maps

By taking two of the key variables influencing consumers it is possible to plot organisations or offerings against one another. This gives a picture of the market in terms of competitive position and helps with the identification of market gaps (otherwise known as niches).

Positioning maps are usually shown in two dimensions for simplicity but it is normal for multidimensional mapping to be used. Several key variables are plotted against each other in order that an identified niche can be accurately defined. The result is a multiscale diagram exactly like the semantic differential scale (Figure 10.3, Bolt Building Products). A multiscale positioning map illustrates a static position and so a series of maps is needed to describe a dynamic situation. Some marketers prefer to use a sequence of simple maps – it is a matter of taste and convenience.

Positioning maps are a very effective tool because not only do they force detailed market study, but they also present information in an easy to understand form.

The Qualcast example

Early in the 1980s there was a battle in the lawn mower market. This battle was between the Hover machines and the more traditional cylinder mowers marketed by the Qualcast company.

Both styles of machine were in the same price brand, but promotion of the Hovers had positioned them in the customers' minds as 'easier to use'.

Qualcast managers, reinforced by consumer trials, were able to prove that the cylinder machines, which could collect the grass they cut, had a significant competitive advantage over the Hovers.

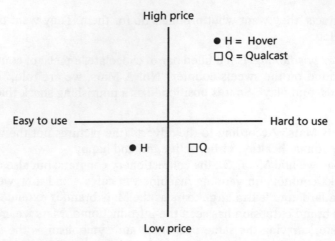

Fig. 13.4 The Qualcast story (i)

Source: Reproduced with kind permission of Angela Hatton, Tactics

Qualcast management set about repositioning their product. The now famous 'A lot less bover than a hover' campaign was launched. By the end of the first year research indicated that customers were aware of the product benefits offered by grass collection.

The second stage of the repositioning strategy took place in the following year. The advertising campaign was continued, but now the Qualcast superiority was reinforced by a substantial price change.

By taking it in two stages Qualcast management successfully repositioned the product over two years from X to Y in Fig 13.6.

Remember:

- In many cases customers will judge product quality by price. Higher prices tend to reinforce the image of 'better' products.
- It is the consumer's perception of the product and its position which is important. Organisations who say that their product is best, but cannot understand why market share does not reflect this, need to look at image and positioning.

Positioning is the key that makes cost-effective promotion possible. A package that attempts to communicate without a clear position will find it hard to generate anything except general statements. You have been asked to look at the positioning of chocolate bars. You will find that some of them are very clearly positioned – others are just 'me too' bars of chocolate, indistinguishable from each other.

A well-positioned package states its position clearly and simply. It has a focus, and everybody associated with it works to the same focus. Thus they achieve synergy, and multiply the effect of their work to the benefit of the sales and profits achieved.

Packages with a clear position can be identified by a simple test. If 'she's a *Guardian* reader' provides a shared concept about the woman, then the product has a position. If not, then no position exists within the mind of the receiv-

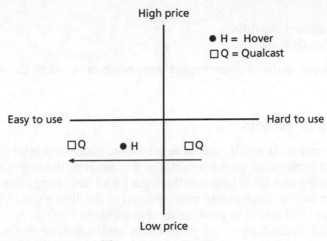

Fig. 13.5 The Qualcast story (ii)
Source: Reproduced with kind permission of Angela Hatton, Tactics

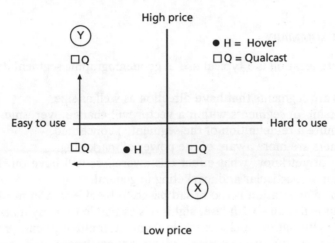

Fig. 13.6 The Qualcast story (iii)
Source: Reproduced with kind permission of Angela Hatton, Tactics

er of the comment. Obviously the person attempting to communicate has a view about the *Guardian*, it has a position for him or for her.

It follows that a package with a unique position has a clearly defined personality, and that consumers within its target market have some form of relationship with it. They are most clearly aware of its existence, and have a formed attitude towards it. Coming from outside the target market you may, of course, be totally unaware of the package.

Positioning is based upon a combination of factors:

- consumer benefits;
- product characteristics;
- price/quality/value/
- use;

- user;
- product class/competition;
- cultural symbolism.

The channels of distribution impact upon position, as do all the support services.

Positioning statements

Very great care and considerable time is taken to produce precise descriptions of the exact positioning of the product in the minds of the target consumers. The positioning statement becomes the focus for all marketing effort and activity, so the creative management time devoted to it will be repaid in long-term benefits. We shall return to positioning statements in Chapter 6.

It is difficult to challenge a competitor who holds a position in a market; usually it is better to define, establish and protect a position which is unique in the market.

KEY POINT SUMMARY

- Retail site location is a typical use of geodemographic segmentation principles.
- Vectors are segments that have direction as well as size.
- Membership of segments within a vector will change over time. This may well require a re-definition of the segment(s) concerned.
- Consumers are more aware of the power of marketing.
- We do not yet know what effect this awareness will have on future segmentation in particular and marketing in general.
- Shotgun segmentation is too broad based to be effective in most markets.
- Rifle segmentation – with laser sights – is available to many marketers.
- Strategic alternatives include: single segment, multi-segment, product specialisation, market specialisation, full market coverage.
- Four strategic options are identified by Ansoff: market penetration, product development, market development, diversification.
- Extension may be of brand, product or skills.
- Porter suggests five threats to take into account.
- Segments must be selected with care using defined criteria.
- Marketing strategies can be undifferentiated, differentiated or concentrated.
- Differentiation must be established in the minds of the target customers and consumers for it to be effective.
- Target marketing is also known as niche marketing. It is the act of developing products to meet the needs of a designated segment.
- The term 'package' can be used to describe the physical packaging and also the promotional packaging of benefits.
- Positioning is the act of designing an offer so that it occupies a distinct and valued place in the minds of the target customers.

- Positioning maps can be two- or multidimensional.
- Repositioning is usually possible, but requires considerable skill and sufficient time.

WORK-BASED SELF-ASSESSMENT QUESTIONS

1 Explain the value to strategic marketing planners of vectors, segmentation, positioning maps.

2 How can the Ansoff strategic options matrix be used dynamically by a marketing planner? (*Note*: This question requires you to think creatively, the answer is not directly to be found in the module but can be deduced from it.)

SCHOOL- OR COLLEGE-BASED SELF-ASSESSMENT QUESTIONS

1 Show how the Ansoff matrix could help focus Asian Jewellery's strategic plans.

2 Use examples to show target marketing in use.

See the end of Chapter 15 for answer guidelines.

CHAPTER 14

Forecasting

Sick as a parrot was exactly how Colin Armitage felt as he avoided looking at the jumbled heap that spilled from his in-tray and across his desk. He flipped open his desk diary and idly glanced to see what words of wisdom were provided for him that day.

These were Fiedler's forecasting rules:

1 It is very difficult to forecast – especially about the future.
2 He who lives by the crystal ball soon learns to live on ground glass.
3 The moment you forecast you know you are going to be wrong – you just don't know when, and in what direction.
4 If you are ever right, never let them forget it!

Ho, ho!, thought Colin bitterly, you don't know the half of it. He decided to list the things that were bugging him to see if there was a common factor – the in-tray could wait!

1 England had lost – again – last evening. The manager ought to be sacked, anyone could have told him his selection was a nonsense. He had cost Colin an evening's frustration, £5.00 in a bet with a Scot, and considerable on-going aggravation from all his Scottish, Welsh and Irish friends.
2 His bank had written. He had overdrawn his account and because he had made no prior arrangement they were charging him the top rate of interest. Would he like to go in and see them? In the meantime, please rectify the situation.
3 He had been late into the office. He couldn't have known a water main was going to burst and disrupt all the traffic, but it had still cost him his 5% punctuality bonus for the month because it was the third late arrival in three weeks.
4 He had been forced to find £350 to get his car through its MOT. That's why he was overdrawn, of course.
5 His girlfriend refused to take his calls, and he was committed to having her with him at the company's annual staff dinner tomorrow evening.
6 The marketing manager wanted to see him. No doubt with a whole list of problems.

   Sales were below budget – but not across the board. Some areas were doing really well, but he didn't expect any credit for that.

   Deliveries had been unreliable because depot stocks were low – but this was because production had failed to produce – surely not his fault?

   Complaints were higher than normal – but with stocks low that was obviously to be expected.

His life seemed full of problems and Mr Fiedler and his flipping rules were not much help. He decided to abandon the heap that was his desk and drop in on Marjorie in the staff coffee shop. She was always good for a laugh.

But not today. Marjorie was in no mood for jollity. 'If you've come here for sympathy you're in the wrong place!' she announced. 'You're obviously in a mess, and you have to sort your thinking out!'

Under considerable pressure Colin produced his list and handed it to Marjorie. She glanced through it and smiled 'Silly man', she said, 'You are just drifting along and letting life take charge. Why don't you make your mind up on the things you really want to do, and then make them happen?' She then went through his list.

1 Football – England were on a losing streak. The facts proved it. They hadn't even drawn a match in the last seven Internationals, and the team selection hadn't changed. If he wanted to take a wild gamble he at least should have got good odds. Betting at less than 20 to 1 was bad tactics.

2 It would have been easy for him to have fixed a temporary overdraft facility at the bank. With his steady salary and good credit record he was the exact type of customer they wanted, if he controlled his finances better. But he would have to know how much to ask for, and then keep a running check on his balance. Until he sorted it out he'd be paying four times as much as he needed to, and his account would be flagged as unreliable. Bad news.

3 Late once in a while is unfortunate – but in modern traffic, unavoidable. Late three times in three weeks showed that he was pushing to get in as near to time as possible. He had no margin for error. The firm did, it was built into their system.

4 He must have known the car needed attention. So a large bill should not have been a shock. Was it a whole series of minor things – a couple of tyres, windscreen wipers, that sort of thing. Or was it one problem such as rust in the door sills? Either way – he could have expected it if he had thought it through.

5 Why wasn't the girlfriend taking calls? Had they fallen out? Did he know positively that she had abandoned him? Perhaps she was sick? Or away for a few days?

6 Why be afraid of the marketing manager? Sales were bound to vary from budget. So was actual production and, following that, depot stocks. Did he know that stocks actually were low? Perhaps they were mis-allocated across depots?

Complaints – were they about delivery problems? All of them? That seemed unlikely. Did he know the facts?

Had he seen Fiedler's Forecasting Rules in the company diary? He ought to sit there, where he was, with a cup of coffee and sort himself out.

Colin felt blasted!

But he did as Marjorie suggested.

• *Rule 1.* It is very difficult to forecast, especially about the future. Yes, of course. But difficulty shouldn't prevent him trying to forecast. Perhaps with practice he would become good at it. And it must be better to have a forecast, then a plan, than to drift along.

- *Rule 2*. He who lives by the crustal ball soon learns to live on ground glass. That was certainly proving to be true. His life was one long series of shattering problems. OK, he didn't literally have to eat glass (!) but he could see the underlying truth.
- *Rule 3*. The moment you forecast, you know you are going to be wrong – you just don't know when, and in what direction. This hadn't occurred to Colin. He had taken forecasts to be the basis for firm plans. He knew that plans had to be changed as one went along, but he hadn't thought that the underlying forecasts have to be checked as well.
- *Rule 4*. If you are ever right, never let them forget it! He wouldn't – but he had to get a forecast right first, and he suspected that might be far more difficult then it appeared.

Suddenly Colin remembered what the England manager had said after last night's game: 'One of my problems is that everyone can pick a football team. Everyone can pick one, but only my selection has to go out there and play. Only my selection can win or lose. Everybody else's selection would have won, of course.'

Perhaps management, perhaps life, was like picking your own football team and then sending it out to play? The only differences were that his 'match' lasted for years rather than 90 minutes and was infinitely more important. At least he would be able to substitute more or less when he wanted to!

FORECASTING

'Forecasting is the act of giving advance warning in time for beneficial action to be taken' (Lancaster and Lomas).

In marketing, forecasting is the basis from which the optimum mix of product, price, place and promotion are determined, so as to achieve the maximum consumer satisfaction at an acceptable return on investment. Without forecasts there can be no management planning because plans are made to achieve forecasted results.

It is normal to forecast over three time periods: short-, medium- and long-term. Exactly what is meant by these terms depends on the organisation, its environment and its markets. e.g.

Table 14.1 Short-, medium- and long-term planning

Industry	Short-term	Medium-term	Long-term
Retail	1–4 weeks	1–2 years	5 years
Consumer durable	6–12 months	3–5 years	8–10 years
Aircraft	3 years	8–10 years	15–20 years

When one is working in an organisation the terms should be clear. But even so, it is good practice to indicate exactly what you mean, e.g. 'short-term (8 week) forecast'.

- *Short-term forecasts.* Normally for tactical and operational use, these provide details of, for example, production planning, short-term cash needs and seasonal sales fluctuations. They can be changed quickly, with minimum effect on medium-term forecasts, but with potentially major effects on current results. For example, ice cream production can be stepped down if the weather is particularly bad. This minimises losses through over-stocks, but cannot replace the loss of profits from the sales that were expected but never happened. Sales of perishable goods such as ice cream and theatre seats can never be made up. Their purchase cannot be postponed.
- *Medium-term forecasts.* Strategic decisions are made over the medium-term, which explains why the more capitalised and therefore inflexible industries need a longer lead time for planning. Serious commitments are entered into on the basis of medium-term forecasts and they are therefore particularly important in business budgeting.
- *Long-term forecasts.* Major strategic decisions are taken long-term. They deal in general rather than specific issues and set the frame within which the organisation is expected to operate. Long-term environmental and social issues are of particular concern, as are attempts to predict the technological advances that will be made by the organisation, and which will become available to it from the marketplace. Companies such as British Petroleum and Esso are thinking strategically into the middle of the next century, and beyond. They have already moved from being oil to energy-centred organisations.

Forecasting guides management

Forecasts can never be accurate – the future is unpredictable in detail. Therefore all forecasting has to be carried through in the knowledge that it is to provide guidance. At first only general direction can be forecast, but as the time for action grows closer, so the accuracy of the forecast can be refined.

In the ice cream industry, for example, long-term forecasting has to do with the size and composition of the demand for ice cream in 10 years time. Medium-term concerns adding new production capacity in time to come on line when needed. Short-term is about responding to weather conditions and forecasts. At the ultimate tactical level short-term forecasting is concerned with the make up of loads on retail ice cream vans, daily.

In the UK demand switches from ice cream to ice lollies at 65°F. Misread the weather at the beginning of the day and sales can be lost. Adding storage capacity to cover demand from all weather conditions is not likely to be cost-effective. There can be no compromise. The ultra short-term weather forecast is critical.

Risk or gamble?

In Chapter 2 risk was defined as 'a hazard of chance where the probability of loss is known' and gamble as 'act in the hope of'.

It can be seen that forecasting is concerned with providing a quantified estimate of future occurrence which management will use to guide decision-making.

You also know that organisational structures should be made of glass for rigidity coupled with the ability to fracture if put under too great a stress. The same principle applies to forecasts. They are never fixed, they must be revised in the light of circumstance.

For example, in his annual budget the Chancellor of the Exchequer increases the rate of VAT. This increases the price in the high street and demand is certain to fall. The wise manager revises the sales forecast and the plans that are based on this. The unwise attempts to achieve the now unreasonable forecast – and fails.

MARKETING PLANNING CYCLE

The sales forecast begins the marketing planning cycle. The marketing concept requires that planning starts from the viewpoint of the consumer. What the consumers need and will buy at given price sets a level of sales expectation. From this procurement, production, distribution, personnel and financial forecasts can be derived.

Only if there is a non-variable within the system may the planning cycle start other than with the sales forecast; e.g. chocolate easter egg production capacity may limit the number that are available for sale. The marketing mix is driven from the maximum that can be sold, rather than from the number that could be sold.

Forecast comparison

It is essential to compare forecasts within context; e.g. a large year-on-year increase may look good, but not if the industry is moving faster, nor if inflation is running at a very high level.

The inflation in Brazil reached 2000% in the first 8 months of 1993 – just to stand still an organisation trading in Brazil would need to show a 2000% increase in annual sales turnover!

For management purposes it is far better to forecast in terms of product than value. The quantity of product sold is the only true, non-inflationary measure. It is a simple matter to relate volume and price to achieve turnover, but far more difficult to derive volume from turnover.

Which is easier to work with, Table 14.2 or Table 14.3?

Table 14.2

Year	Volume	Increase (%)	Price (£)
1988	165 667		10.00
1989	173 950	+5.0	10.50
1990	183 517	+5.5	11.25
1991	190 858	+4.0	11.95
1992	204 218	+8.0	11.95
1993	212 387	+4.0	12.50

Table 14.3

Year	Revenue	Increase (%)	Price (£)	Inflation (%)	Actual £ change (%)
1988	1 656 670		10.00		
1989	1 826 475	+10.25	10.50	+3	+7.25
1990	2 064 566	+13.0	11.25	+5	+8
1991	2 280 753	+10.47	11.95	+9	+1.47
1992	2 440 405	+6.99	11.95	+7	—
1993	2 654 837	+8.34	12.50	+5	−3.34

Obviously it is necessary to understand what is happening in money terms – but historical value is for the accountant. Forecasting is much easier when working with volume, as in Table 14.2.

STRATEGIC PLANNING GAP

A sales forecast is most easily understood when presented as a graph (Fig. 14.1).

Also on the planning graph we can add the sales volume required to meet the corporate objectives. Often (usually?) this will be above what is originally forecast.

To make up the difference it is possible to make tactical (operational) changes and, if these are not sufficient, to reconsider strategy. We therefore can see that there are both strategic and tactical gaps.

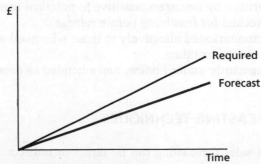

Fig. 14.1 Forecast compared to requirement

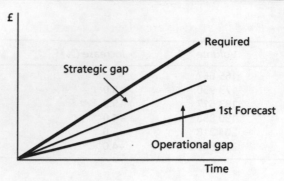

Fig. 14.2 Strategic and operational gaps

If forecasting is approached in a logical manner it becomes a quite straight-forward process. The difficulties occur when:

- Managers have to convert forecasts into plans.
- Plans have to be made to work in practice.

IMPLEMENTATION

It is not surprising that field managers sometimes have little regard for forecasters and planners in Head Office: 'They ought to come out here and see what it's really like.'

There is some underlying truth in this statement because unfortunately those in 'Head Office' can easily become out of touch with those who have to make the plans work. In some cases they have never worked in line management and so have no practical understanding of what is possible.

Working with complex computer models, as management planners routinely do today, can separate the planner even further. Computer models respond mathematically to programmed instructions, and are ideal for evaluating the probable results of proposed plans. They cannot take the human factor into account, however, except as a programming factor.

Almost anybody can write a plan. A prime management responsibility is to ensure that:

- Plans are written by managers sensitive to practical realities.
- They are checked for feasibility before release.
- They are communicated effectively to those who need to know, in time for effective action to be taken.
- They are constantly under review, and amended as necessary.

SALES FORECASTING TECHNIQUES

Techniques of sales forecasting can be direct or indirect. Both are normally used, in combination.

- *Direct prediction.* Past sales are taken into account, and a trend line is established using statistical techniques. This is then compared with the totals of predictions for each sales area.

  A base line of anticipated sales given a 'no change' situation is created.

  Changes are certain, however, and so data from the environment is added into the process as plus or minus factors (see below). The end result is converted into revenue and profit expectation and compared with corporate requirements.
- *Indirect prediction.* Total requirement within the industry or segment is estimated.

Market share strategy is determined.

Market share of a defined market size gives a sales forecast.

i.e. Market size   100 000 units
    Estimated growth   5%
    Estimated market size   105 000 units

Market share:

		Sales forecast
Current	15%	15 750 units (15% of 105 000)
Forecast	18%	18,900 units (18% of 105 000)

This forecast is compared/combined with the direct prediction, converted to revenue and profit expectation and compared with corporate requirements.

Any strategy to increase market share means an increase in sales, but a sales increase may not increase market share. This is because the growth rate of the market may exceed the rate of sales increase, e.g. a market expanding at 10% per year requires a sales increase of 10% just to hold market share. A sales increase of less than 10% results in a smaller share of the market, an increase over 10% gives an increased market share.

Market size	*Sales*	*Market share (%)*
100 000 units	20 000	20.0
110 000 (+10%)	21 800 (+9%)	19.8
	22 000 (+10%)	20.0
	22 400 (+12%)	20.36
	23 000 (+15%)	20.9

Accuracy

- How accurate need forecasts be?

The greater the accuracy, the higher the cost and so the question becomes:

- Does the accuracy justify the cost of achieving it?

There is a serious danger that much effort will be put into trying to produce a forecast that looks accurate and which (on paper) meets the corporate plan. This is not the same as producing a forecast which is sufficiently accurate to meet the profit objectives of the organisation.

Accuracy takes effort and time – and we know that predicting the future is a task that is very difficult since there are so many unexpected things that can happen to blow a great big hole in any forecast.

In general, therefore, unless the value of a project is enormous – launching a space satellite for example – there should be no need for more than adequate forecasting. It is far better to invest in control measures that are fast and efficient.

An example will make the principle clear:

If a cruise liner is setting off from Southampton for the Caribbean it has only two periods of major concern. When leaving harbour and clearing the English Channel, and when approaching its destination. The period in between is cruising in deep waters and although the crew need to be watchful, they will not need to be as active as when manoeuvring near to land.

Accuracy in forecasting is most important when products are at significant points in their life cycle – when they are new to the market, and when they are passing out of the growth and into the maturity stage. In maturity they will have an established market presence and a marketer needs to be watchful, but not as keenly conscious of progress as earlier.

THE SECRET OF FORECASTING

Use the most simple method possible.

There are many complex models that run on computers and impress with their printout. Remember always, however, that computers operate under the GIGO principle:

• GIGO – garbage in, garbage out.

Humans have to input data, humans have to select what to input, humans have to decide on the importance of each piece of data. And humans are fallible.

Knowing that any and every forecast will be inaccurate helps keep the process in perspective, and allows creative time and effort to be devoted to something more useful, such as devising ever more efficient systems of control.

We shall examine control in detail in Chapter 16.

OBJECTIVE TECHNIQUES

These use hard information, which must therefore be historical. A carpet manufacturer may gear up production as house starts increase. His demand lags behind the actions of other variables. Therefore he has a need to anticipate the market, to have products in place as demand comes through. It is fatal for him to be lagging after demand is running strongly.

Marketers have need for research that targets on the key data that impacts upon the products they sell and the markets they trade within.

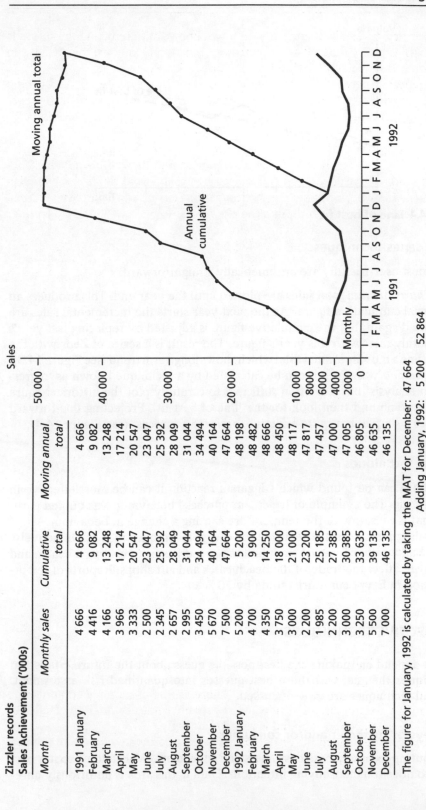

Zizzler records
Sales Achievement ('000s)

Month	Monthly sales	Cumulative total	Moving annual total
1991 January	4 666	4 666	4 666
February	4 416	9 082	9 082
March	4 166	13 248	13 248
April	3 966	17 214	17 214
May	3 333	20 547	20 547
June	2 500	23 047	23 047
July	2 345	25 392	25 392
August	2 657	28 049	28 049
September	2 995	31 044	31 044
October	3 450	34 494	34 494
November	5 670	40 164	40 164
December	7 500	47 664	47 664
1992 January	5 200	5 200	48 198
February	4 700	9 900	48 482
March	4 350	14 250	48 666
April	3 750	18 000	48 450
May	3 000	21 000	48 117
June	2 200	23 200	47 817
July	1 985	25 185	47 457
August	2 200	27 385	47 000
September	3 000	30 385	47 005
October	3 250	33 635	46 805
November	5 500	39 135	46 635
December	7 000	46 135	46 135

The figure for January, 1992 is calculated by taking the MAT for December: 47 664
Adding January, 1992: 5 200   52 864
Deducting January, 1991: 4 666   48 198

Fig. 14.3 Sales Achievement – Zizzler records

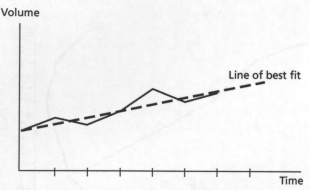

Fig. 14.4 Line of best fit

Time series techniques

The most user-friendly are arithmetically straightforward.

- *Z charts*. Incremental sales are plotted until the year end. This produces an annual cumulative figure. As the next year starts the incremental sales are plotted again, but the cumulative figure is adjusted by replacing last year's monthly sales with this year's figure. The result is a series of Zeds with the top line a moving annual total which shows long-term trend (see Figure 14.3).
- *Trend analysis*. Trends can be calculated by a technique known as 'regression analysis' but it is often sufficient to carefully plot the historical figure on a graph and then look for the 'line of best fit'. Projecting this forward gives a simple, but quite effective, basis for a forecast (see Figure 14.4).

Causal techniques

If a cause can be found which triggers a reaction it can be most effective in forecasting. The example of ice cream purchase behaviour was quoted earlier. That is causal, with the temperature causing a change in behaviour.

Leading indicators are required for causal techniques to work effectively, e.g. a bad weather forecast may discourage tourists from visiting a beach, and therefore affect the trade of the beach cafes and gift shops. Reports of terrorist action in Egypt cut tourist trade by 70%.

SUBJECTIVE TECHNIQUES

These depend on making the best possible guess about the future. Statistical techniques then convert these best guesses into quantified risk assessment. Typical techniques are now discussed.

Surveys of customer and/or consumer

It is routine to survey both customers and consumers. Whilst doing so it is possible to question their buying intentions. Data in this area is notoriously unreliable as people cannot actually predict their behaviour, but it can be helpful to confirm or deny assumptions coming from elsewhere. In matters of detail this kind of survey can be very helpful – on such matters as a range of colours for the new season, for example.

In particular this method is valuable in industrial marketing, where individual professional buyers can be identified. These often know exactly what their needs will be because their own organisation has carried out its sales forecasting and is gearing up its marketing plan.

Prudent manager forecasting

Personnel from the organisation are asked to take the part of buyers in client companies. Their task is to look at the market from the client company's viewpoint, and to determine what each is likely to do. From that assessment they can deduce likely purchase behaviour.

Panels of expert opinion

Also called the jury method, this technique requires specialists to be brought together to share their views and produce a composite forecast. Sometimes this requires compromise because experts may have differing views and so it is important to know just how confident is the group as a whole, and individually. Neither this nor the Delphi method can be of much help with product forecasting. Others are concerned primarily with economic and environmental factors.

Delphi

In the Delphi method experts are again used, but they are kept separate to avoid each influencing the other as can happen in a meeting. Each responds to a questionnaire about market conditions and specific environmental factors. These are reviewed by the project leader and an aggregate forecast produced. This is then passed back to each panel member for review and returned again to the project leader. The process may be repeated up to three times before a clear result is achieved.

SOPHISTICATED FORECASTING

Keep in mind that 'sophisticated' often just means complicated!

If tempted to move away from straightforward techniques run through this checklist first:

- Do you really need the technique?
- Why? What exactly will it do for you?
- Are you sure?

If you go ahead:

- Confirm that you really need it.
- Think the problem through in detail.
- Take advice as to the most basic technique to give what you need.
- Select the variables and leading indicators with care!
- Process the data in the model.

When you receive the results:

- Examine them from a cynical viewpoint. Make them convince you of their reliability.
- Evaluate the accuracy, validity and reliability (as you would for marketing research).
- Use the results with caution, keep them under close control.
- Build confidence in the technique over time – but never trust it completely.
- Continually check for a simpler way to achieve better or the same results.
- Remember that a statistician is a 'number cruncher' – an aid; you are the line manager who makes the decisions.

Remember, also, that it is easily possible to drown in a river of average depth one inch! Never take statistical figures at face value.

KEY POINT SUMMARY

- Forecasting is the act of giving advance warning in time for beneficial action to be taken.
- It is difficult to forecast since the future can never be predicted with certainty.
- Forecasts are guides that you know will be wrong and need amendment.
- With experience the quality of forecasting should improve.
- It is essential to forecast – otherwise there is no direction at all.
- Short-, medium- and long-term must be identified.
- Forecasts help risks to be assessed, and gambles avoided.
- The marketing planning cycle starts from the viewpoint of the customer.
- If a non-variable exists, that will commence the planning cycle.
- Forecast in units rather than currency.
- Forecasts have to be implemented – head office planners can tend to forget this.
- Management should check that plans are feasible, communicated effectively, constantly reviewed.
- Direct and indirect prediction methods can be used.
- Forecasts need only be accurate enough to meet the need.
- Ask 'Does the additional accuracy justify the cost of obtaining it?'
- Control measures are a better investment than highly accurate forecasts.
- GIGO = garbage in, garbage out.
- Objective techniques use hard information which must be historical.
- Subjective techniques use 'best guesses' about the future.
- 'Sophisticated' often means complicated.

- Does a sophisticated technique produce better results in practice than a simpler method?
- Examine forecasts in as critical way as you examine marketing research data – make the figures prove themselves before you accept them.
- Build confidence over time – but never trust a technique completely.
- Check always for simpler ways of achieving better or the same results.
- Statisticians 'crunch' the numbers – managers take the decisions.

WORK-BASED SELF-ASSESSMENT QUESTIONS

1 What forecasts might a marketing manager require when planning the introduction of a new line alongside an existing range?

2 How would you argue for a move to a less complex system of forecasting?

SCHOOL- OR COLLEGE-BASED SELF-ASSESSMENT QUESTIONS

1 Explain how forecasting and planning would benefit Colin Armitage.

2 How might an inaccurate sales forecast adversely affect the strategic operations of an organisation?

See the end of Chapter 15 for answer guidelines.

CHAPTER 15

Scenario and 'What if?' planning

The phone clamoured for attention in the darkened bedroom and Philip Cardrella came out of a dark brown sleep rather reluctantly. The phone wouldn't give up – and so he was forced to reach across and hook it towards him.

'Cardrella.'

'This is Jack Thomson of the *Daily Express*. Can you give me a quote on the coach crash?'

'Crash? What crash?'

'Is this Philip Cardrella, Press Officer of SunShine Tours Incorporated?'

'It is.'

'Then obviously I'm the first to tell you – one of your coaches has gone over the side and into Candlestick Bay. It seems that nobody survived.'

'My God! When did this happen?'

'About an hour ago: that's about 1.30 our time. Look, I've got a deadline to catch, can you give me a quote?'

Cardrella thought for a moment. 'No comment' was worse than no quote. On the other hand he had no facts. What could he say? He decided to buy some time.

'When, exactly, is your deadline?'

'In 45 minutes.'

'Give me a number and I'll get back to you inside 30.'

Cardrella cleared the line and dialled his office in the same movement. The duty officer answered.

'Harry, this is Philip, what can you tell me about the coach crash?'

'Good morning Philip: coach crash, what coach crash?'

Philip rang the *Daily Express* from his car. 'There is no hard news as yet,' he said, 'but you can quote us as saying that we deeply regret any loss of life and any injury. Our local representative is on his way to the scene and we will be able to comment further when we have some hard facts. In the meantime we shall not let anything get in the way of giving every support to those involved. We shall be making urgent arrangements to contact the relatives of everybody who was on the coach, and we will ensure that those who want to visit the island are flown there later today.'

It later became clear that the coach was hired by SunTours of Jamaica and not SunShine Tours of the UK. SunShine Tours had no holidaymakers within 100 miles of Candlestick Bay! That didn't prevent the British tabloid press from carrying splash news of the crash in their early editions, nor from linking the crash to SunShine Tours. The story carried in the earlier editions quickly changed to reflect the true situation, but SunShine Tours remained linked with the crash as the press carried the story through . . . 'earlier it was reported that the coach belonged to SunShine Tours. This is not the case. . .'

Bookings with SunShine Tours fell away markedly in the days following the incident. Although the situation picked up again in a couple of weeks it was estimated that some 500 bookings had been lost – enough to make a significant difference to the profitability figures, because in travel the load factor is critical and once a coach has left there is no way the passenger numbers can be increased. Five coaches were despatched with less than a break-even number of passengers, seventeen ran at just above break-even and a further fifteen had around 10% less than their expected numbers.

A special board meeting was convened to determine what had happened, and to identify the lessons that should be learned. An experienced public relations consultant was asked to attend and give his views.

'I believe that what happened was totally predictable. If anything can go wrong, it will. If anything can go badly wrong, it will. The only questions are When? and To whom? Coach operators are especially vulnerable because you have to deal with the mechanical problems of your vehicles, the human failings of your crews, the uncertainty of road conditions and Acts of God.

'Every month a certain number of coaches are going to have problems with all of these issues. Most are going to be minor – a motorway hold-up causes a delay, a driver takes the wrong route, a passenger is taken ill. Some are going to be serious – a collision involving minor injury, passengers in a fight at a restaurant. A few are going to be major – like this incident where 37 people died because the coach was forced off the road by an out-of-control oil tanker.

'Ladies and gentlemen, we are talking about incidents that can be predicted. And, if they can be predicted they can be anticipated. The aim must be prevention – but the reality is that they cannot all be prevented. So there must be plans to deal with the incidents that are definitely going to happen.'

The board listened, argued amongst themselves, and decided to convene again the next day. Overnight, individual directors thought the matter through, and when they were together again became of one mind. The facts had to be faced: there would be other incidents. They might not affect SunShine Tours – but just one bad one like Candlestick Bay could wipe out a whole year's profit. Perhaps even the company itself. They decided to commission the PR consultant to work with Philip to prepare recommendations for action.

As the Chairman said, 'We have had a serious warning: we were lucky this time, we may not be so lucky again. We have to have contingency plans in place and rehearsed.'

CONTINGENCY PLANNING

Contingency: a future event or circumstance regarded as likely to occur.
(*Concise Oxford Dictionary*)

Contingency planning, therefore, is the making of plans to deal with future events or circumstances that are regarded as likely to happen.

When a situation occurs there is usually too little time to think through the range of possible responses, to select one, assemble the needed resources, ensure that they all work, and set about dealing with the problem.

- *Car drivers*. Many people who have crashed their cars on a slippery road are quoted as saying, 'There was nothing I could do.' In many cases there is a lot that they could have done, but nothing that they did do.

  They couldn't do anything because they:

  – Didn't know what to do?
  – Didn't know how to do it?
  – Hadn't practised skid control?

  If a driver thinks forward he will appreciate that at sometime in his driving career he will have to drive on a slippery road surface. Knowing that he has two choices:

  – Shrug, and deal with it when it happens – I couldn't do anything!
  – Take lessons in skid control, and keep in practice – others were in trouble, but I was OK!

- *Sailors*. When a small boat sailor goes to sea he can assume that the lovely clear weather will last all day, and that everything on his boat will work fine. Or he can assume that bad weather may blow up, that something will fray, and break: that another sailor may have problems he could help with.

  The one will go out in shorts and T-shirt with a can of coke and some sandwiches. The other will have bad weather clothes in a waterproof bag, a flask of hot coffee, flares and distress rockets, a first aid kit, including a thermal blanket, a knife, a compass and, possibly, a radio.

  Both may sail for months before the second has to go to the aid of the first.

- *Managers*. Some managers believe that their staff should be grateful and patient. That they are content to continue working in the knowledge that they are being looked after. That they should be loyal to the manager no matter what. These managers are upset when staff resign and typically react selfishly, 'After all I did for him, this is how I am repaid!'

  Other managers realise that their staff have personal priorities as well as work loyalties. They realise that the most motivated and most valuable staff will be hungry to move into better jobs. Where can they provide the slots to allow the needed movement? The better ones make it clear that the best way is to have a deputy qualified and hungry to take over.

  The one is constantly filling posts that have unexpectedly come vacant. He is 'fire-fighting' and constantly carrying too much responsibility.

The other is motivating and helping subordinates to improve whilst, at the same time, providing successors to the posts that he knows will come vacant.

THE CONTINGENCY PLAN

A contingency plan is a fully worked-through plan available for immediate use. If three possible situations have been identified there will have to be three contingency plans to deal with them.

An outline contingency plan for SunShine Tours Incorporated would have to include:

- Objectives covering:
  — passengers and staff;
  — public image of the company;
  — priorities and speed of response.
- Responsibilities allocated for:
  — central co-ordination;
  — head-office management;
  — on-site management;
  — relatives and next-of-kin contact;
  — media contact.
- Provisional arrangements including:
  — emergency telephone numbers arranged with British Telecom;
  — draft press releases;
  — provisional agreement with airline(s) to fly relatives out and survivors back;
  — reference files for every country/region/area in which coaches run. These to include such items as:
  — official contacts: police, fire brigade, ambulance services;
  — motoring organisations such as EuroAssist and the Automobile Association;
  — the British Embassy and/or Consul;
  — professionals on call: especially a lawyer and perhaps an accountant;
  — media contacts, especially the wire services, e.g. Reuters.

The aim would be to have a complete dossier with every eventuality catered for and a plan in which everyone knew their role. With regular rehearsals the plan would be kept up to date and staff would have its support when (if) needed.

The cost of contingency planning must be set against the loss expected if no such plans exist. It is, as so often in management, a question of balancing probabilities and of assessing risk.

SCENARIOS

Scenario: a postulated sequence of future events.
(*Concise Oxford Dictionary*)

When one thinks through what is likely to happen, one creates a scenario – a description of a possible future. If this scenario is thought through very carefully it can 'come alive' and be planned for as though it were really happening. There is obviously more than one possibility for the way the future will develop. Therefore the manager's task is to identify each of the major potential futures. This is called creating scenarios.

It is strategically important for managers to identify where the organisation should be directed. Scenarios can be used to show the future that the organisation will potentially have to face and, therefore, they allow pre-planning. The intention is to:

- maximise the probability of achieving the most desired future;
- minimise the probability of achieving a least desired future;
- prepare specific contingency plans for the most likely probable futures.

To be successful managers must:

- identify where the organisation could go;
- quantify and evaluate each alternative;
- make the appropriate plans.

Identification – from any point there are several ways into the future. Each is dependent upon an initial decision and then is affected by subsequent events. As one looks further and further into the future the number of alternatives increases until there are too many possibilities for detailed planning. That is why the difference between short-, medium- and long-term planning is so critical.

In the long-term a manager can only deal with generalities. As time passes the number of alternatives decreases until eventually one is planning for tomorrow, even for a couple of hours from now.

Identification requires forward-thinking managers with both intuition and the confidence to use it. Imagination alone is not sufficient, there has also to be the flair of intuitive understanding of what is possible and what is most likely to be possible.

We all have the necessary traits as children, but we are conditioned by many adults as we 'grow up'. Coping with value-loaded terms such as 'childish'; 'grown up' and 'playing games' is difficult for many – but the intuitive manager cultivates the 'childish' virtues of a free-flowing imagination. He lives in a world where everything is possible.

BRAINSTORMING

Brainstorming sessions are of great value in scenario planning. In a brainstorming session the intention is that every possible idea is thrown out by members of the group and captured on a board or series of flip charts for later eval-uation. The board is needed so that ideas can be seen as well as heard.

As individuals we all have patterns of thought which are natural to us, but alien to others. In brainstorming we all benefit because our thoughts spark off thoughts in others that take ideas and twist them into new directions. Those new directions, in turn, spark back into our thinking and the cycle of fresh and developed thoughts continues.

The keys to effective brainstorming are:

- Select a group from a wide range of backgrounds.
- Brief them positively. (We intend to enter a new market, but are not sure which. What shall we do?
- Do not precondition them. (Keep the brief to the minimum possible and do not allow your thoughts to be known.)
- Have one or two neutral 'scribes' to capture and write up every thought, however silly it may seem. (Good ideas are sparked by silly ones) – one mar-keting plan was developed from a brainstorm session in which somebody said 'let's have an airship drift over the desert and throw cigarettes down to the Bedouins'.
- Allow no critical or negative comments.
- Stop the session just as it begins to run down.
- Only evaluate ideas after the group has dispersed.
- Always thank individuals for their help.
- When possible tell individuals what action came from the session.

MIND MAPPING

Mind maps allow an individual to generate far more original thought than our logical systems of lists.

A mind map is created around a central focus, and spreads out in all direc-tion as ideas are sparked. As our minds tend to work best when allowed to jump around, this technique is an excellent way to brainstorm alone.

With practice you will find that mind maps are an excellent way to organ-ise your thoughts, and many people use them routinely. A considerable num-ber take notes in class in mind map form because they allow ideas to be associated, which helps memory.

The mind map example was constructed in 20 minutes as first thoughts for a talk on management. You will see that working from the mind map it would be very easy to prepare detailed notes, and to structure them in a logical order. Working logically it is doubtful if all the points could have been identified in so short a time.

The only way to develop a belief in the power of creative thought is through experiment. An excellent way in is to take a topic and prepare notes in the traditional way. Then try again, but this time use a mind map. Then take a fresh subject and mind map it. Afterwards be honest and check off the points you would have put into a traditional list.

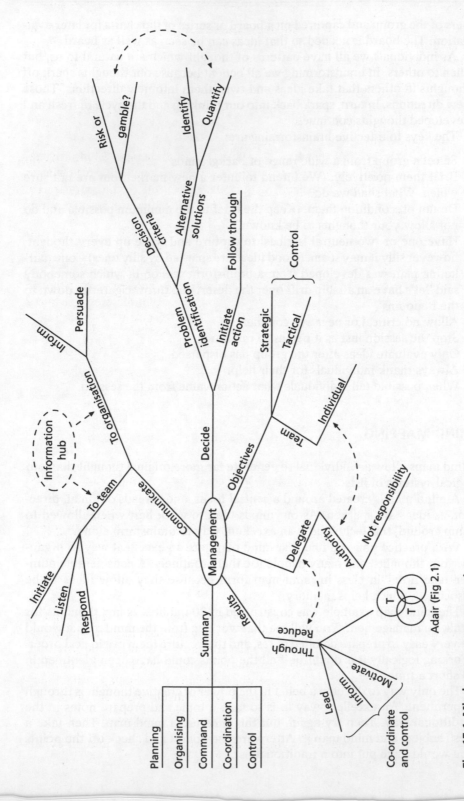

Fig. 15.1 Mind map – management

Speed comes only with confidence and that comes from practice. The benefits of mind mapping and brainstorming are so considerable, however, that the effort is not wasted.

WHAT IF?

What if we did this? What if they did that?

The ability to ask and answer What if? questions is crucial to long-term success. It doesn't matter how far-fetched the question may be – Edward DeBono invented lateral thinking, which is about taking What-if? to the extreme. He says that he goes around always asking What-if? questions, and getting unusual answers.

One example deBono cites is of a flute picked up in Woolworth's. What if it had no holes? Most would say 'then it isn't a flute'. But deBono went on to say 'then the air would come out the end – what if the end was sealed? Then the pressure would build up . . .'. This sequence led to the invention of a device to accurately measure the pressure in the lungs of asthmatics and became a commercial success story.

QUANTIFICATION

Each scenario must be quantified so that:

1 The potential profit or loss is understood.
2 The probability of its occurring is determined.

Obviously low-risk situations with a low probability require little management time. High-risk, high-probability situations require urgent and detailed attention.

The table shows how a manager may allocate priorities for action. The actual split between the four alternatives must be made by individual managers in the light of their own needs. This must be done with care since everything designated high probability/high risk must be planned for in considerable detail. Yet again we have the need for managers to assess risk against cost of protection.

- *Potential profit or loss*. The potential profit or loss of each scenario must be calculated. This is most valuable when an effective and efficient control system exists, since estimates must be based on the best available information. A marketer's natural inclination towards optimism can lead to over-confident estimates. Therefore it can be wise to team the marketer with a financial manager and a production manager when calculating profit or loss.

It is good discipline to insist on three evaluations from the team:

- *Best case*. The results if everything was to work perfectly, and all events were favourable.

	Probability	
	High	Low
Risk assessment · High	50	25
Risk assessment · Low	20	5

Fig. 15.2 Management action priorities (out of 100)

- *Worst case*. The results if everything went wrong, and all events were unfavourable.
- *Expectation*. The results that are expected taking into account the internal factors and external events that can reasonably be expected.

It is not good to work directly from either the best or worst case scenarios – but both are essential to put the expected scenario into focus.

- *Probability of occurrence*. Nothing is ever certain, and so estimates have to be made of the probability of the expected scenario actually happening. Again one works from a total of 100, and allocates a percentage to each of three possibilities.

The aim of all these estimations is to produce, in numbers, an assessment of the most likely future.

Evaluation

The alternatives can now be evaluated, and management action allocated to the scenarios that show the greatest probability of occurrence.

PLANNING

The master plan will occupy most of management's attention since it is expected that it will most closely indicate the actions that need to be taken.

In support will be contingency plans – one each for the most likely alternative scenarios. Obviously most contingency plans are not required, but all are needed, and must be continuously updated against the probability that one will be wanted in a hurry.

The key is to prepare against the certainty that situations will change. As all changes cannot be foreseen and built in to the master plan they must be provided for as alternatives. Change can be beneficial as well as damaging – but only if one is prepared to take advantage.

KEY POINT SUMMARY

- Contingency – a future event or circumstance regarded as likely to occur.
- Contingency planning is the making of plans to deal with future events.
- The choices are: shrug and deal with it when it happens: prepare so you are ready.
- Better managers prepare successors for posts that must, in time, become vacant.
- A contingency plan is a fully worked-through plan available for immediate use.
- Contingency plans must be rehearsed, and kept relevant.
- The cost of contingency planning must be set against the loss in the event of the contingency occurring.
- Scenarios are a postulated series of future events.
- Scenarios can 'come alive' and be planned for as if it is really happening.
- The manager's task is to identify scenarios and prepare to deal with them.
- Brainstorming is a very powerful way to spark ideas in individuals so that they spark ideas in others.
- The keys to effective brainstorming are: have a group with a range of backgrounds, brief positively, do not precondition, have neutral scribes to capture the ideas, allow no negative comments, stop as the session is about to run down, devaluate ideas later, always thank individuals, inform them of results if possible.
- Mind maps allow an individual to brainstorm – and to organise thoughts.
- Working logically to produce a list is not as effective as mind mapping.
- Speed in mind mapping comes only with confidence, and that with practice.
- What-if? thinking opens possibilities that otherwise might remain closed.
- Quantify each scenario . . . in terms of potential profit or loss and assess the probability of its occurring.
- Managers should allocate priorities for action.
- Three evaluations are best: best case, worst case, expectation.

- Evaluate alternatives and allocate management action to scenarios with the highest probability of occurrence.
- Plan thoroughly for each contingency.

WORK-BASED SELF-ASSESSMENT QUESTIONS

1 Explain the role of contingency planning. Show how it affects short-term marketing planning and long-term corporate planning.

2 Some well-researched innovative products fail in the market. Explain why this may be so.

SCHOOL- AND COLLEGE-BASED SELF-ASSESSMENT QUESTION

1 What contingency plans could you put into place to help you deal with crises that may happen in the next two years?

This is a major exercise – you will be surprised how many good and bad things may happen even in such a short time period. Categorising and ranking them is a big task – and then there is the need to plan for the most likely.

SUGGESTED ASSISTANCE TO SELF-ASSESSMENT QUESTIONS FOR CHAPTERS 12–15

WORK-BASED QUESTIONS

Chapter 12

1 Industrial markets have far fewer buyers, each with greater responsibility. They are relatively easy to identify and to target individually. Consumer market segmentation is based on grouping individuals with known characteristics. The techniques developed in consumer marketing, especially the database, will enable even industrial buyers to be classified by type but, more importantly, a greater depth of detail will be maintained on each. Geodemographic data may well be of value when identifying the more complex DMUs found in industrial marketing.

2 The database will carry considerable detail about members of the potential segments. Their preferred lifestyle will be shown, as will the type of products they tend to buy, the shops they frequent, their working and social activities and the people with whom they mix. From this vast range of secondary data a marketing manager will be able to deduce the type of fashion that will be most appreciated and then to refine the range through detailed marketing research based on sketches first and then trial garments later. Access to the segment will be indicated in the database, in terms of the shops used and the media seen.

Chapter 13

1 Vectors have direction as well as presence. They contain one or more segments which tend to be more statistically defined. Understanding vectors allows predictions to be made about the future size, potential and character of the identified market.

   Segmentation allows precise targeting. Database marketing makes extremely precise and unique segmentation available to the marketer.

   Positioning maps allow visual comparison of a market situation and assist in the identification of niches. It is possible to use them to track movements of products within identified vectors.

2 The Ansoff matrix can be used dynamically because a marketer can plot intentions, and set a target time for achievement. Used in this way the matrix becomes a very powerful tool to communicate intention. Figure 13.7 shows a dynamic Ansoff matrix.

Chapter 14

1 He would need, as a minimum, forecasts covering:

- volume sales, stock levels, stock turnover;
- revenue forecasts.

These would be set within forecasts of:

- channel developments;
- seasonal customer demand fluctuations;
- competitive activity, including pricing and promotion in particular.

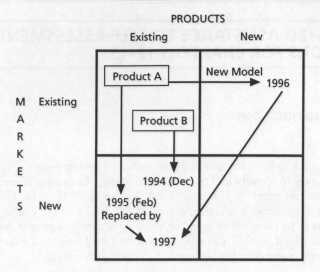

Fig. 13.7 Dynamic Ansoff matrix

2 You would need to show that the same or better results could be obtained without the 'sophisticated' techniques. This would have to take cost-effectiveness into account. It is unlikely that you would win this argument without great effort even if you could prove beyond doubt that a simple graph was as effective as a computer model. The investment has been made, and the equipment will be used! When you get to be a senior manager, remember that glitz and glitter are not necessary to working tools.

Chapter 15

1 Contingency plans are prepared well in advance so that an organisation is prepared to deal with the most likely futures that are not provided for within normal corporate planning.

Short-term marketing plans are for a maximum of a year – perhaps much less – and are highly targeted on tactical issues. Contingencies must be provided for, but these would normally be of a relatively minor nature. Major catastrophes such as a coach crash or sabotage of a firm's products are of corporate concern.

Long-term corporate planning is ranged so far ahead that it is virtually a major contingency plan in its own right. The organisations looking forward to 2050 are doubtless concerned with issues such as the likelihood of global peace, or war; the location of new sources of energy, population changes, changes in the balance of power across the nation states and federation of states.

2 Forecasting is based on marketing research and it is impossible to be certain about the future. When the product was being developed the researchers may have been given totally honest answers by all respondents. But they were answers based on an expectation of a situation. When the actual situation occurred it was not as expected, and so there was a different result than predicted.

SCHOOL- AND COLLEGE-BASED QUESTIONS

Chapter 12

1 The SC groupings are too large to be of practical value. They are dependent upon the occupation of the head of household – with all household members classified as the head. Within each SC grouping is a range of subgroups which can be identified. Geodemographic segmentation allows subgroups to be identified, and for the individual members to be targeted. A database is required, which brings major secondary benefits with it.

2 Jan Ericson can expect to collect very useful data from the guarantee cards packed with every pair of boots – especially if he offers an inducement for the card's return. (Perhaps autographed photos of selected football stars?) This data will enable him to refine his marketing, and also to discover what additional products might be developed to sell to the newly identified segment. He will also have a growing list of known football players to which he can send mail shots about subsequent developments. If he has asked for the data he will also have the names and addresses of football club secretaries to whom he may offer a special discount on the purchase of any products in the Sports Shoe plc range.

Chapter 13

1 The company is new into the UK and so must first of all penetrate a market where it feels there are sufficient consumers of the type they can best supply. Their present range may need adaption, but they will be anxious to match their present range of products and personnel skills to target customers if they possibly can.

In time, once established, they will have to choose – to extend into a wider range of products, perhaps an extension to jewellery; or to move into new markets – perhaps into different forms of retail. It would be dangerous to try both at once!

The option for diversification is just that – new products into new markets – usually a high-risk strategy.

2 Examples of target marketing are everywhere – you should have found dozens of good ones to quote. The need is to be able to draw upon a bank of examples to show an examiner that you do understand how marketing theories really work in the marketplace.

Chapter 14

1 Forecasting is pointless without planning and so the first need is to convince him to plan. He has plenty of evidence of what happens without planning – but it seems that he is a pretty disorganised sort of person. There is need to show him how his life at work and at home will improve, and to persuade him to make a start and to evaluate the results. He has to prove the worth to himself.

When he is planning (or trying to) it would be time to introduce simple forecasting, i.e. getting him to think ahead. Again he will need to be persuaded to make his best guesses, and then review progress so that the forecasts can be refined and his skills improved.

2 Forecasting can be inaccurate by being too high or too low. If too high the production will proceed even though sales are below forecast. The result will be an overstocked position, with extra costs incurred; warehouses filling up and perhaps additional storage needed; stock may deteriorate and have to be sold off or destroyed; prof-

itability and morale will suffer. Under-forecasting means that customers will be disappointed the sales force will feel let down; short-term sales and profits will suffer; overtime may have to be worked, putting costs up; sales lost may never be recovered; long-term confidence may suffer; customers may switch to a competitor and not return.

The need is clearly to monitor carefully, and to adjust the forecast in the light of events. Never stick rigidly to a pre-formed plan.

Chapter 15

1 You need to mind map as many good and bad things that could happen in your life. Then put them into a list. Examine each and assign it a ranking based on importance and probability. Take each very seriously and think through very carefully exactly what your options would be, and what you can do to maximise your chances of successfully dealing with the situation. Then work out detailed plans to achieve the successful outcomes (or perhaps the least damaging ones). For example, if you are just learning to drive will you take the minimum training to get your licence, or target to achieve advanced driver status within 5 years? If that is what you decide . . . how will you fund the training? What priority will you give to it? How will you evaluate and control your progress? How will you discipline yourself not to get side-tracked?

PART 5

Strategic direction and control –
the framework of success

Strategic direction is set by marketing management within corporate policies and strategies. It is, however, of limited value (at best) unless it is expressed in an effective and efficient system of budgetary control

Budgetary control provides a framework into which strategic and tactical plans can be neatly fitted. A budgeting system allows all the activities of an organisation to be integrated, and for predicted results to be calculated. Control ensures that managers receive prompt feedback on results in a form that allows effective response.

The two elements together underpin effective and efficient management at strategic and tactical levels.

Management by exception is provided for by budgetary control and both are dependent on acceptance of the need for *management by objectives.*

Budgets are produced for each operational and staff unit, and combined into budgets for departments, divisions and, finally, for the whole organisation.

The *product portfolio* is the range of offerings made by the organisation within its markets. Portfolio management has developed from the original concept of the *product life cycle* and allows managers to use quantification techniques to aid the difficult task of providing a range of product offerings to meet both current and future demand.

Multifactor and *directional policy matrices* have taken the basic product life cycle concept and developed it into an effective management tool.

Distinctiveness and *differential* are recognised as key elements in product planning – with products having distinctiveness for only a relatively short time. Thus the majority of marketers are concerned with the creation of differential as a way to distinguish and position their products.

Strategic plans have to be communicated if they are to be implemented. Excellent communication, and especially excellent internal marketing, are necessary if strategic intention is to become reality.

CHAPTER 16

Budgetary control

Bill Jessop was the Northern Regional Manager for Associated Copy Services (ACS). With 20 high street copying shops to supervise he was supposed to spend a considerable amount of time 'on the road' visiting the managers. Unfortunately he felt that he was drowning in a sea of paper and was unable to get free of the office for more than two days a week.

Without doubt his region was suffering. Sales were down on forecast, and costs were higher than planned. Profitability was suffering, and with it his bonus – perhaps even his continued employment! If only he could get out he could help the managers to tighten up their operations and become more effective and more efficient.

Bill came south for a quarterly review meeting with the marketing director and the other three regional managers. He knew that his figures were the worst, and they had also been bad the previous quarter. He was not looking forward to the meeting.

He was right to be concerned. The marketing director pulled no punches in the meeting, and was very direct in private. Unless Bill showed immediate signs of improvement there would, reluctantly, be no place for him in the organisation.

Suzanne Wilmshurst, the Southern Regional Manager, was a good friend. She had joined ACS at the same time as Bill, but had moved up to the top manager slot while Bill was slipping into last place. Over a cup of tea Bill told her of the director's ultimatum. What could he do? Why was she so successful? How much time did she spend in the office?

Suzanne's answer was a body blow. She was out working her territory for at least four days a week! Only a single day in the office! It proved what Bill had long known – there is no substitute for personal contact. Management is to people and not through paper!

It was obviously possible to cope with the ocean of paper, and still get out into the field. The question was how? Suzanne laughed – 'Ignore most of it', she said. 'Most of it simply says there is no problem. Why check through data when there is no need? Concentrate on the problems, and on the successes, leave the rest to look after itself.'

To show Bill how she handled the data Suzanne showed him one of the many reports that hit her desk each week (Table 16.1 shows one table extracted from the report for illustration purposes). The report showed the reported revenue and the operating costs of each copying shop. The two sets of figures should correlate since consumables ought to be in proportion to revenue. A discrepancy could mean that a manager is being extra efficient, that he is under-declaring revenue or buying consumables locally and not through ACS. The reports took Bill at least half a day to analyse.

Table 16.1 Southern Region – Week 35

Franchise	Revenue			Costs		
	Target	Achieved	%	Target	Incurred	%
Arundel	5400	5292	98	4050	3645	90
Bagshot	5700	6156	108	4275	4788	112
Croydon	5400	5508	102	4050	4131	102
Dartford	6100	5612	92	4575	4941	108
East Grinstead	5600	5544	99	4200	4242	101
Farnham	5900	5841	99	4425	4381	99
Guildford	7500	6975	93	5625	5288	94
Hassocks	6600	6732	102	4950	4356	88
Kingston	6600	6468	98	4950	4752	96
Larkfield	7350	7718	105	5513	5237	95
Manston	6900	7728	112	5175	5020	97
Newhaven	6000	6300	105	4500	4050	90
Petersfield	6700	6030	90	5025	5226	104
Ramsgate	5900	5959	101	4425	4337	98
Sevenoaks	6420	6805	106	4815	4622	96
Tonbridge	6300	6174	98	4725	5009	106
Uckfield	6200	6324	102	4650	4464	96
West Wickham	6210	5589	90	4658	4564	98

Suzanne explained that she had got the finance manager to present the figures so that they showed exceptions to targets. She also explained that she had set limits within which each manager could vary without it being specifically brought to her attention. The weekly report still arrived each Tuesday morning,but attached to the front was a summary sheet (Table 16.2).

Suzanne could thus see immediately the managers whose results fell outside her limits. The ones doing worst were identified, but so were those doing particularly well. It was then easy for her to schedule her time. Immediate visits to those at the top of the list, phone calls of congratulation to those doing really well, second priority visits to those in the middle of the list and the ones doing well, routine visits to those who were close enough to targets.

Of course the report was valuable, but could be taken item by item when with each manager. There was no need to struggle to extract the information she needed when some pre-thinking, a co-operative finance manager and a computer could short-circuit the process.

Suzanne explained that she applied exactly the same principles to each of the budget factors with the result that her time was released from data analysis to management action.

Bill postponed his return to the north and set up a meeting with the finance manager for 0900 the next morning . . . three months later he was third in the country, and in six months had climbed to second place.

Table 16.2 Southern Region – Week 35 – Exception Report
(showing those branches outside both criteria.)

Priorities	Revenue Target	Achieved	%	Costs Target	Incurred	%
R under, C over						
Dartford	6100	5612	92	4575	4941	108
Petersfield	6700	6030	90	5025	5226	104
R under, C under						
Guildford	7500	6975	93	5625	5288	94
R & C over						
Bagshot	5700	6156	108	4275	4788	112
R over, C under						
Newhaven	6000	6300	105	4500	4050	90
Larkfield	7350	7718	105	5513	5237	95

TERMINOLOGY

- *Management by objectives.* A system of establishing objectives under which each manager agrees to achieve objectives they have helped to establish.
- *Management by exception.* A system of management control under which managers are given reports on variances from expectation.
- *Budget.* A quantified plan of action that aids in the co-ordination and control of an organisation. Building a budget involves integration of the varied interests that constitute the organisation's programme as a whole, which all agree is workable and will lead to the attainment of established objectives.

MANAGEMENT BY OBJECTIVES (MBO)

Managers in any organisation exist to take decisions. These decisions should be to further the attainment of objectives. Under MBO it is recognised that managers who have commitment to the objectives are more likely to achieve them. Hence, under MBO each manager contributes to the setting of the objectives for which he will be responsible.

It is normal for each manager to consider what are reasonable objectives for the unit under his control, and for these to be submitted to his line manager. Managers with several subordinates combine the agreed objectives, and consider what is reasonable for the whole department for which they are responsible. Always there is need for discussion between top management and each individual manager.

Departmental objectives are recommended up the line, and discussed with the next senior manager. In time, therefore, each individual objective has been incorporated into an organisation-wide proposal.

At corporate level the proposed objectives are compared with corporate objectives. If they match corporate need they are accepted. Usually, however, there is need to refer them back down the chain of command for revision.

After further discussion and/or negotiation up and down the management line firm objectives are agreed and established.

The key issue is that objectives are agreed with those who have the responsibility to achieve them. Under MBO individual objectives should not be imposed on managers. In practice, regrettably, they often are imposed, because top management requires more from the organisation than line managers feel is possible. In principle this top management need should be explained, understood and accepted by the junior managers but in reality top management often simply impose their demands.

The terms commonly used to express imposed objectives are target and quota:

- Target. There is no commitment to achieve a target – it is a focus, something to be aimed for, but it is imposed. The most common use of the term is in the context of selling, where sales targets are set for sales areas and individual salespeople.

  Note that the actual target will be what management show they expect. Thus imposing an artificially high target to motivate salespeople can actually demotivate. If a reward is paid for achieving a percentage of target, then the level at which the bonus is paid becomes the actual target in the perception of the sales team.
- Quota. Commonly used in place of target by some sales managers. The terms is also used in the sense of rationing, as when an important quota is established by a government.

MANAGEMENT BY EXCEPTION (MBE)

MBE is often linked with MBO, but does not require objectives to be agreed. MBE can operate effectively providing objectives exist, and are communicated to, and known by the managers.

Information must reach managers in time for effective action to be taken, yet is often contained within a mass of data. MBE takes a range of data and pre-sorts it to indicate where action is needed. The manager is not told when things are running to plan. Only exceptions to expected results are reported.

- The principles of MBE apply to every car driver, every day. If all is well the warning lights in the instrument panel remain dark. If water temperature rises above a safe limit, if a stop lamp burns out or if oil pressure falls, the appropriate warning light will come on. Some cars display a STOP light where the driver cannot fail to see it if matters are really serious.
- Marks & Spencer reduced their paperwork by 90% when they moved to MBE. Previously every store had to stock-take fortnightly and report the progress of each item. M & S discovered that the majority of lines sold as expected. Therefore head office managers were checking weekly through several tonnes of paper, detailed figures, looking for problems. Obviously they missed some.

  When they changed to a system that reported only exceptions to plan, top management were directed to the areas where their expertise was needed, and the volume of paperwork fell by 90%.

The information contained in an MBE report will be targeted on the needs of the manager it is sent to. To take sales as an example:

- A sales director needs information on:
  — total sales;
  — regional achievement.
- Regional managers need information on:
  — regional sales;
  — district achievement.
- District managers need information on:
  — district sales;
  — territory achievement.
- Territory salesmen need information on:
  — territory sales;
  — key customer results.

Detailed tactical information is provided only at the level where it is of immediate use. For all senior levels the information can be consolidated. A region may be meeting its objectives, and so the sales director is not immediately concerned. One district within the region may be well below expectation,with the shortfall covered by the results of the other districts.

The regional manager will be directed immediately to the offending district and, at the same time, the district manager will be directed to the individual territory salesmen who are not meeting the objectives. The salesmen will know which particular areas are causing the problem(s). Thus each level is directed to the key problem areas, and immediate action can be taken.

Note that detailed information is always available to each level of management. MBE simply highlights areas of concern to save managers having to sort through data.

Criteria

MBE criteria must be established for each objective. Once that is done by management the computer software simply compares result with objective and produces an itemised report for each concerned manager. An example of a written MBE report is in Table 16.2.

In graphical form the same data for ASC's Southern Region can be presented as in Figs. 16.1 and 16.2.

It will be seen that Suzanne allows her managers a 4% variation in cost achievement if above revenue expectation, but only 3% below. She expects them to achieve their revenue objective with a 4% plus or minus variation.

These criteria are entirely for the manager to set. In some cases wider cost variation can be allowed if revenue is exceeded – but never if revenue falls short. On occasion (e.g. Easter eggs) when supplies are finite there can be no variation above the revenue target. (*Note:* In this case units would replace revenue as the objective measure.)

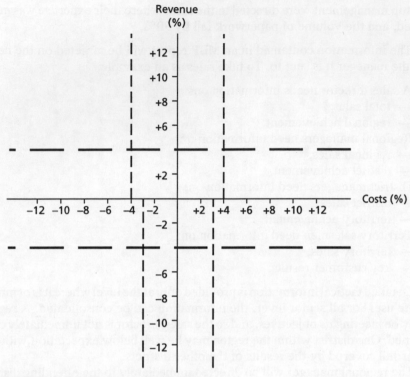

Fig. 16.1 Revenue/costs variance criteria

The keys to the successful use of MBE are:

- Tailor the reporting requirement to need. Ensure that managers decide what they need, and then provide it. It is wasteful and counter-productive to supply more than a manager actually needs to operate effectively.
- Monitor and amend criteria as needed. New staff may not be expected to achieve the same tight controls as more experienced staff – but as their experience grows the MBE criteria should tighten, i.e. on appointment a salesman may be allowed a 10% variance on revenue, after three months 8%, and only after six months be required to fall within a 5% variance.

Once objectives are being set as a matter of course, and the need for a system of MBE recognised, it is a short step to full budgetary control.

BUDGETARY CONTROL

When all units within an organisation produce individual objectives, and they can be consolidated into a set of major objectives to match corporate strategic objectives, it becomes possible to move from MBO to budgetary control.

Budgets are made up of fully quantified objectives which integrate the entire effort of the organisation. Once a budget is established every person in the organisation is committed to achievement of their exact objectives. The inten-

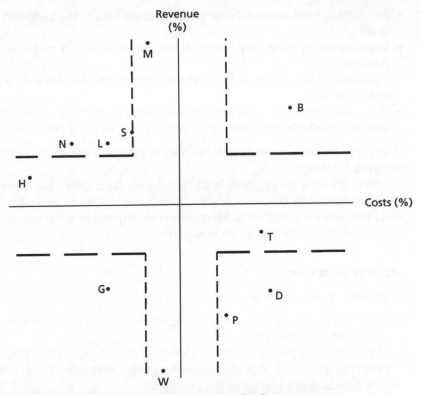

Fig. 16.2 Variances from both costs and revenue criteria

tion is to hit each budget – exactly. Variation over budget is equally as bad as failure to achieve budget.

In budgetary control the term 'target' is never used. 'Quota' is reserved for specific situations where a form of rationing dictates the volume available. This may be a shortage of raw materials, limited production capacity – perhaps following a fire – or any other situation where an absolute maximum has to be set.

The corporate budget is composed of individual budgets for each functional area. The achievement of budget by each function will ensure that the corporate budget, and therefore corporate objectives, are met. Equally, failure to meet budget by any function will affect all other functions since the organisation is a system in which each function plays a vital part.

In a manufacturing organisation, for example, it is necessary to purchase raw materials before production can begin. Production must build up stocks before distribution can move them out to the depots. Only when the organisation is fully committed can the sales effort begin. If any one of the key functions fails to reach its budget the customers are disappointed:

- Finance must reserve funds to pay for the raw materials, the production, distribution and sales expenses before any cash inflow can arrive.
- Procurement must negotiate and sign contracts for raw materials to meet the needs of production.

- Production must allocate factory and machine time to the budgeted requirement.
- Distribution must reserve transport and depot time and space to store the finished goods.
- Sales must take orders at the budgeted prices and for delivery within the specified time.
- Personnel must ensure that the right number of properly qualified and trained staff are available when they are needed to make all of the above possible.

If any one function exceeds or falls short of budget it means that every other function is affected.

Obviously it is never possible to forecast so accurately that every budget objective is met to 100% accuracy. Therefore a system of budgetary control must respond very quickly to variations from expectation. Management must be alerted, and remedial action initiated.

Management need

A manager needs to know:

- *What has happened.* The feedback of results against budget inform a manager what has taken place.
- *Why it has happened.* Budgetary control cannot normally show why an event has happened. This is for the manager to determine. The system exists to tell managers when there is a problem.
- *What to do about it.* Again, the system cannot tell a manager what to do. Having found out why, a manager must decide what to do.

The key benefits that budgetary control bring to management are in:

- the forecasting and planning stages where managers are encouraged to consider what is likely to happen rather than be caught unawares and have to resort to 'fire-fighting' management;
- fast and accurate reports of results against budget. Thus a manager is informed quickly so that he can decide on and initiate the appropriate action.

If a fire causes distribution to lose a depot full of stock, the knock-on effects can be far reaching:

- Sales must be warned to hold back on sales: to take orders only after clearly telling the customer that delivery may be delayed.
- Additional warehouse space must be located, and paid for.
- Production will have to step up – perhaps going to an extra shift at overtime rates. If this is not possible then the stock lost cannot be replaced.
- Procurement may be able to obtain additional raw materials, even substitute product in some cases – but probably at additional cost.

Every budget will have to be amended and re-issued. This will have an effect that reaches right through to the year end, and possibly beyond. Decisions will have to be made about such things as bonus payments to staff and contracts

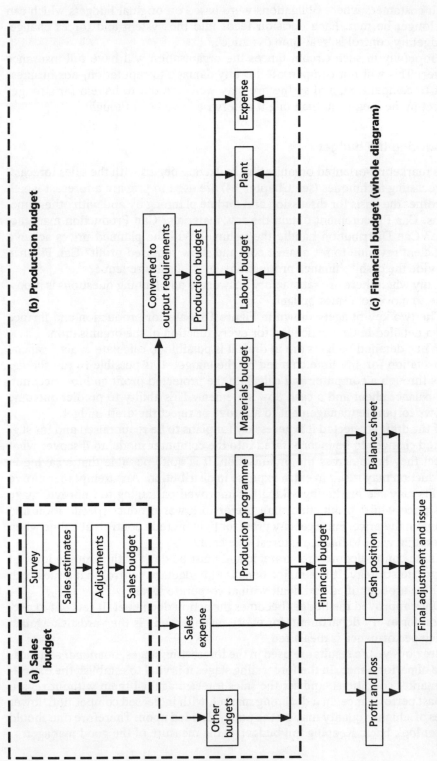

Fig. 16.3 Budgets

(a) Sales budget

Survey → Sales estimates → Adjustments → Sales budget

(b) Production budget

Converted to output requirements → Production budget

Materials budget

Labour budget

Plant

Expense

Production programme

(c) Financial budget (whole diagram)

Sales expense

Other budgets

Financial budget

Profit and loss

Cash position

Balance sheet

Final adjustment and issue

with customers where obligations were based on original budgets which can no longer be met. Each decision feeds into the system and forces change. Budgetary control is 'real-time dynamic'.

Hopefully in such circumstances the organisation will have full insurance cover. This will not compensate for any damage to reputation, nor business lost to competition, and so the fire may well turn out to have a far stronger effect in the long-term than might otherwise have been thought.

Producing the budget

In a marketing-oriented organisation budgeting begins with the sales forecast. Forecasting techniques (see Chapter 14) are used to prepare a forecast which becomes the basis for discussion and outline planning by and with other functions. Can Procurement obtain the raw materials? Can Production manufacture? Can Distribution handle the volume? Will the planned prices achieve sufficient revenue to set against cost and show required profit? Can Finance provide the cash to finance production ahead of sales revenue?

Only when there are satisfactory answers to all planning questions is it possible to move to a sales budget.

The two key budgets shown in Figure 16.3 are for production and finance but a detailed budget is needed for every function of the organisation.

When detailed budgets are in draft it is possible to calculate exact financial expectation for any time covered by the budget. It is possible to run the figures through a computer and calculate the projected profit and loss account, the balance sheet and a cash flow statement. This ability to predict outcome allows corporate management to approve or reject the draft budget.

If the draft is rejected it is necessary for plans to be reappraised and for suggested changes to be incorporated into the computer model to discover what effect they have across the organisation. It is quite possible that a saving in production may result in extra expense in distribution. An attempt to improve profits may see marketing asking for improved packaging to improve image and price whilst production may prefer to lower product specification and maintain the price. Finance may press for tighter credit controls at a time when marketing want to finance interest-free credit.

These contradictions are strategic and must be dealt with from the level of corporate strategy. It is a major benefit of budgetary control that issues such as these are identified and dealt with at corporate level.

Once approved the budget becomes the action document. It sets out expectation for every department, for every manager, and is the yardstick against which performance is measured.

Previous year's results are used in the forecasting stages, but *never* as a measure of performance. In the forecasting stages it is vital to establish the expected market conditions, and set the sales forecast against them without regard to past performance. In a declining market, with increased competition, lower sales of a higher quality may be the policy decided upon. Therefore one should never look back. Keeping 'on budget' is the measure of the good manager.

Financial and management accounts

Financial accounts are concerned with the historical achievement of the organisation. They take what has actually happened in a period and consolidate the information into a form which is acceptable under the terms of corporate legislation.

Management accounts are concerned with everyday achievement against budget. They will be far more detailed than the financial accounts and contain information that is not required to be itemised in financial records. Management accounts are highly confidential documents that are used for day-to-day management.

Budget officer

A budget officer is needed in all but the smallest organisations. With three budgets to handle, it is more likely that there will be a budget department in even medium-sized organisations. The three budgets cover:

- *Last period*. The budget for the period just completed will need to be finalised since numerous activities can only be completed after the period is finished. Selling continues to the last day of the period, and deliveries, settlements from customers and payments to suppliers will carry forward some considerable time into the new budget period. The budget team will want to hand over to Finance, who will deal with all the accountancy matters, but this cannot happen until all the details of achievement and performance criteria against each objective have been agreed.

    There will also be a review of the success of the budget process, and improvements suggested for incorporation into the process for future budgets.
- *Existing period*. The existing budget needs day-to-day management to ensure that data is captured effectively and the flow of reports to management is maintained. Contingency plans need to be in place, and rehearsed, to minimise the potential risks that can be identified. Revised budgets will constantly be produced and issued as results come in and management decisions are taken.
- *Next period*. The planning process for an annual budget must begin early. Line managers must be involved in plenty of time for them to produce forecasts, then draft budgets, and for the drafts to be discussed, negotiated, revised and finalised. For major organisations the budgeting planning starts about 18 months ahead of the budget year. Line managers are involved as many as 10 months ahead.

KEY POINT SUMMARY

- Management should be of people, not of paper.
- MBO establishes objectives which each manager agrees to achieve.

- MBE provides reports on variances from expectation.
- A budget is a quantified plan of action.
- It is equally bad to be over as under budget.
- MBO starts with individual managers drafting objectives.
- Consolidated objectives are compared with corporate objectives and amendments made through discussion and negotiation.
- Targets are focuses – something to aim for.
- Quota indicates a fixed amount. Sometimes used in place of target.
- MBE is often linked with MBO, but doesn't require the objectives to be agreed.
- MBE takes a range of data and pre-sorts it to indicate where action is needed.
- MBE reports are targeted on the needs of individual managers.
- Detailed information is always available – but under MBE most does not have to be actually reviewed in detail.
- MBE criteria are set by management according to need. New staff are often given wiser criteria that narrow as experience is gained.
- Budgetary control establishes a budget for each manager.
- Under budgetary control 'target' is never used since the aim is to achieve budget.
- The corporate budget consists of budgets for each functional area.
- If any one function exceeds or falls short of budget there are knock-on effects throughout the organisation.
- Budgets are produced from drafts, usually starting with the sales budget.
- Draft budgets can be used to predict outcomes so the key financial figures can be forecast and verified as acceptable.
- Only when the key figures and corporate objectives have been matched can the final budgets be authorised.
- Financial accounts are concerned with historical achievement.
- Management accounts deal with day-to-day achievement.
- Management accounts are highly confidential documents.
- Three budget periods exist: last period, existing period and next period.
- For major organisations the budgeting process can start 18 months ahead of the period.

WORK-BASED SELF-ASSESSMENT QUESTIONS

1 Prepare notes for a presentation you are to make to six new salespeople. Subject: budgets, targets and quotas.

2 As the customer relations manager of a large organisation what MBE criteria would be of concern to you?

SCHOOL- OR COLLEGE-BASED SELF-ASSESSMENT QUESTIONS

1 What factors, apart from his new MBE reports, helped Bill Jessop to become the second most successful manager in the country?

2 How could MBE be used by the management in a school or college?

See the end of Chapter 19 for answer guidelines.

CHAPTER 17

Portfolio planning

The Management Training Centre was set in its own tranquil gardens which ran down to the banks of the river. Delegates came from across the EU to attend courses and seminars on all aspects of management. The shortest course ran for three days, the longest – for strategic management – for three weeks.

Senior managers and top academics were invited to present papers on matters of special significance. Hans Dichter felt privileged to have been asked to show why the product life cycle (PLC) is of no practical benefit to a line manager.

These are the notes that he prepared:

1 The PLC is well known throughout all management education and training. In its most common form it has four stages: introduction, growth, maturity and decline. There is also a period of development, which surely is part of a product's life and should be added to the model. Finally there are seven points at which strategic decisions must be taken.

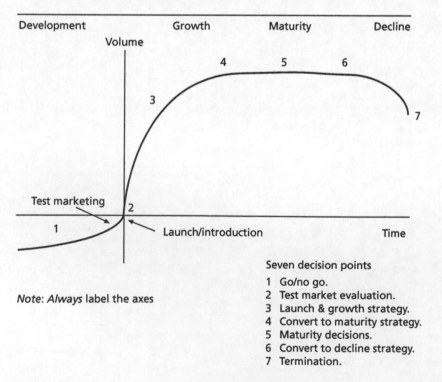

Seven decision points
1 Go/no go.
2 Test market evaluation.
3 Launch & growth strategy.
4 Convert to maturity strategy.
5 Maturity decisions.
6 Convert to decline strategy.
7 Termination.

Note: *Always* label the axes

Fig. 17.1 Product life cycle – decision points

2 There are many different PLC curves. Among the best known are the standard, the leapfrog, the rejuvenated, the staircase, the continuous.

3 The PLC curve within any of these overall descriptions varies in shape, dependent upon the type of product, type of industry and the degree of marketing success. Thus one product may complete its life cycle within a few months, and another may take time to become established, but then remain on the market for a long time. Either of these PLC curves is acceptable, provided it is anticipated. It would be disastrous to expect the curve in Figure 17.3 and achieve that in figure 17.2!

4 The classic PLC is often shown as an upside down U, but this is confusing because it implies that products once launched run all the way from zero sales, up through growth into maturity and then down again to zero.

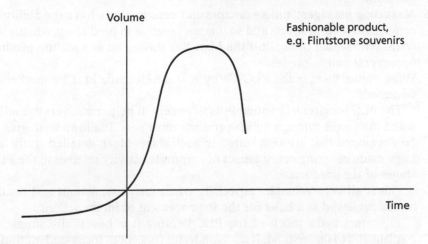

Fig. 17.2 Product life cycle – fashionable product e.g. Flintstone souvenirs

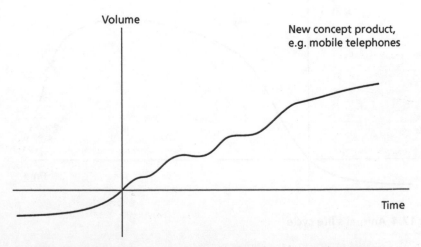

Fig. 17.3 Product life cycle – new concept product e.g. mobile phones

Certainly the end result is death – zero sales. But management often terminates a product before it dies a natural death.

The PLC is frequently compared to an animal's life cycle. To a limited extent this is true. Animal life spans, given regular medical check ups, can be predicted with considerable accuracy. In a developed country a human male can expect to reach 72, a female has about 6 years more.* A large dog is doing well to get past 11, but a smaller dog may make 13 or 14. Illness and accident can terminate the curve early, but this does not invalidate the basic shape of the curve.

5 If the curve terminates early (at the X on the model) it can be seen to be more like an S than a U. Thus managers are usually working with S curves because they practice euthanasia on products that can no longer sustain a profitable life.

6 Marketing managers, unlike doctors and veterinarians, have the ability to rejuvenate their products and so it is not possible to predict a product's life span. Who would bet against the Mars Bar staying on as a mature product for several more decades?

7 What value, then, is the PLC? Why is so much made of it by marketing educators?

The PLC is extremely valuable as a concept. It helps managers to understand the stages through which products must pass. It allows strategies to be developed that are best suited to each stage. Much detailed study has been made covering every aspect of corporate activity relative to the PLC stages of the products.

This is all very valuable, especially when forecasts, actions and results can be reviewed as a basis for the improvement of future actions.

Educators make much of the PLC because it is beautifully simple to explain and to understand. It is a wonderful concept to focus student think-

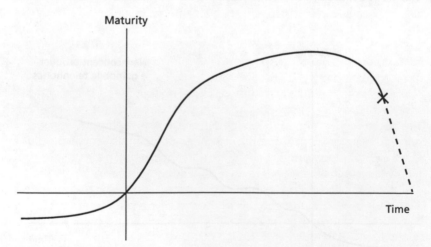

Fig. 17.4 Animal's life cycle

*In the UK the life expectancy at birth of males is 72.7 and for females 78.3.

ing. It allows the need for different strategies and tactics to be explained. It helps to identify the key decision points where strategies and/or tactics must change.

8 The traditional PLC is therefore a historical record. One can always draw the curve given the achieved sales data. One cannot predict the shape of the curve other than to say that it will go into decline unless action is taken. But what action? And when?

Has decision point 4 on the PLC (see Fig. 17.1) been reached? Is it time to convert from a growth to a maturity strategy? Convert too soon and the market will go on expanding while you lose market share. Too late and you waste resources in fighting for market share against competitors who are well established.

There is no way that any of the decision points an be predicted with accuracy – it is for each manager to use his best judgement. The PLC warns that a decision will have to be made, but is of no help in showing when, nor what type of decision it should be.

9 *The S curve concept.* When the PLC is seen as an S curve it becomes more useful to management. Remembering that the PLC is a concept, what happens if we apply it to a technology?

The maximum speed of transport clearly shows an underlying S curve. Within each of the forms of transport there is also an S curve that runs from their development to their level of maximum efficiency. Thus the maximum speed of the pioneer aircraft is slower than the take-off speed of later propeller-driven aircraft. Modern jet fighters cannot fly as slowly as the early aircraft.

S curves are therefore especially useful in new product development. Again the PLC is a concept, but the S curve application shows that every product will run out of impetus and be replaced. S curves tend to run in pairs, with a discontinuity between them. Apple Computers made effective use of the S curve in their pre-launch promotion for the PowerMac in March, 1994. Comparing the CISC (Complex Instruction Set Computing) chips that power the IBM 486 range with the new RISC (Reduced Instruction Set Computing) chips that power the Apple PowerMac they clearly show the advantages of RISC technology.

10 *S curves in the tyre market.* In the US tyre market in the 1950s and 1960s a major battle raged between the makers of tyre-cord for cross-ply tyres. Cotton was the original tyre-cord fibre but it was replaced by rayon. The first $60m investment brought an 800% gain in performance, the next $15m a 25% improvement and the final $25m brought only a 5% improvements as rayon technology reached the end of its S curve.

Nylon replaced rayon, as a paired S curve, but was not entirely satisfactory. Research funds were invested, but nylon was closer to the end of its S curve than had been realised. Huge amounts of money went into research and development (R & D), with only marginal gains. Polyester, on a paired S curve, had a 5 to 1 advantage over nylon technology. Investment in R & D on polyester could be a fifth of that for nylon and produce the same benefit. The same budget brought five times the advantage!

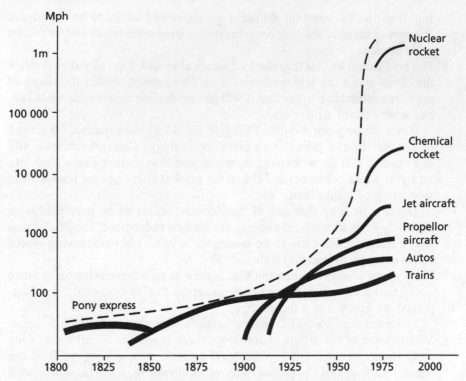

Fig. 17.5 Envelope S curve fitted to maximum speed of transport
Source: Ayres R. V. (1969), *Technological Forecasting & Long Range Planning*

As the search went on for ever more efficient fibres the cross-ply tyre itself was at the end of its S curve. Michelin had abandoned the cross-ply in favour of the radial tyre. Despite the best efforts of the US tyre manufacturers the consumers switched to the superior tyre. Thus the R & D funds that went into improving the cross-ply tyre were misdirected. An understanding that the S curve concept applies to generic products as well as technologies would have encouraged the US manufacturers to search for *replacement* technology as well as *improved* technology.

The research into fibre was not entirely wasted, however. Kevlar was developed, and put to use but in radial not cross-ply tyres.

11 *Management commitment.* DuPont were the leading producers of nylon tyre-cord and had a tyre research centre devoted to improvements in nylon. When polyester cord became available it seemed sense to test it in the research centre. The nylon-focused researchers said it was pretty good, and polyester's developers went away to make improvements. When they came back with a product far superior to nylon they found that DuPont had committed a huge new investment into a nylon tyre-cord factory. Polyester would have to wait until the investment was recovered!

This bad decision, as it turned out to be, shows how management can be blinded by a focus on existing technology. Currently Michelin feel that the new plastic tyres will not be successful – but Michelin are committed

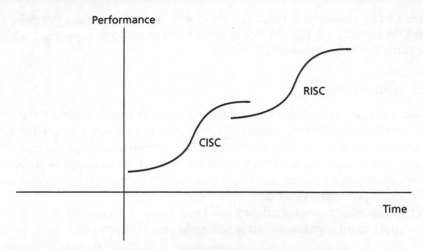

Fig. 17.6 Paired S curves – RISC v CISC performance evaluation
Source: IBM

to rubber. Are we seeing the start of a paired S alongside rubber tyres?

12 *Summary*. The PLC concept is excellent to show what has happened to a product or market. It helps marketing managers to understand the strategies and tactics best suited to each stage. It encourages managers to look for the major decision points.

Unfortunately it cannot be used as a tool of prediction. Therefore it is of limited benefit to a line manager who has to make key decisions without the benefit of hindsight.

The PLC concept is of fundamental importance, not least because it has provided the basis for quantified techniques of life cycle and portfolio management.

STRATEGIC PLANNING

'There is need to develop and maintain a viable fit between an organisation's objectives, its resources and its changing market opportunities. The aim of strategic planning is to shape and reshape the organisation's business and products so that they combine to product satisfactory profits and growth' (Kotler.)

Operational planning is concerned with the tactical matters of achieving strategic objectives. In times of fast growth organisations can get away with operational planning alone, simply because there are so many opportunities. This is not to say that the best choices are made, but when an organisation is making a healthy profit many managers feel no need to plan strategically to achieve more.

Strategic planning is always needed, but this need is emphasised when market conditions tighten, there are fewer opportunities and competition increases.

Strategic planning is based on a 'portfolio' approach. An organisation's businesses can be managed in much the same way as one manages a portfolio of shares on a stock exchange. Which opportunities ought to be supported, which maintained, which abandoned?

Organisational focus

It soon became evident that the concept of organisation or business was too wide for effective planning . . . especially as organisations became larger through acquisition and merger. 'The adoption of the marketing concept changes the focus from a business-centred to a market or customer-centred approach. Levitt made it clear that a business must be seen as a customer-satisfying process and not a goods-producing process.

When this major conceptual step has been taken it is possible to re-define the purpose of an organisation. It is selling benefit, not product.

Product orientation	Market (benefit) orientation
We run an airline	We help people to travel
We sell groceries	We help housewives to nourish their families
We supply telephones	We help people to communicate

When the focus becomes consumer-centred the opportunities for development immediately become far clearer. Rather than being confined to supplying telephones an organisation is free to explore all forms of communication. This immediately presents a problem because 'all forms of communication' is an extremely wide brief!

Detailed definition of the exact benefit orientation provides a more realistic goal. A telephone company may want to focus on voice communication (to include radio, but exclude fax?). Or perhaps to focus on communication down telephone cable (including fax, but excluding portable telephones?). It is very difficult to pin down exactly what an organisation exists to do so that its mission is clear and the opportunities in its range are linked but not too wide.

STRATEGIC BUSINESS UNIT (SBU)

As organisations struggled to come to terms with the need for a market focus the old concept of the organisation changed. No longer could it be seen as one unit operating from one type of business. 'We make cars' was not a precise enough definition.

The process of business identification showed that within organisations there are units that can operate alone, but within the main organisation. From the market's viewpoint they are separate businesses. They are termed strategic business units (SBUs).

An SBU has three characteristics:

- It can be planned separately from the remainder of the organisation because it is a single business, or a collection of related businesses.
- It has its own competitors.

- It is run by a manager who is responsible for strategic planning and profit performance and has control over most of the factors affecting profit.

General Electric in the US were among the pioneers of the SBU approach. They found that they had 49 SBUs within their organisation. They were, in effect, working in 49 different markets, each of which required its own strategic and tactical approach.

Hanson plc in the UK has become one of the world's most successful groups through a policy of acquisition which reorganises each company around the SBU concept. Thus managers of Hanson's subsidiaries are responsible for success, and have control of their businesses subject to achievement of corporate objectives that are agreed at Hanson's main board level.

A manager of an SBU can take strategic decisions without interference from corporate planners. Yet he is supported by a corporate planning team who want to ensure that his return on investment is at an acceptable level. It is a very effective way to run a business.

Wall's Ice Cream

Wall's Ice Cream were well established in static sites across the UK and decided to expand into the mobile sale of ice cream. The mobile ice cream business is made up of many small operators, who work as franchisees. In many cases they are self-employed people running a single ice cream van.

Instead of treating this new venture as an SBU they incorporated it within their overall business and applied their normal terms of trade. Unfortunately this included a monthly account for all retailers.

They found out, too late, that the franchisees expected to pay cash for their product each day. They were not used to dealing on a monthly basis. All went reasonably well through the summer when each month's income was higher than the month before (although even then some mobilers had problems meeting their monthly bills). As trade fell away at the end of the summer the monthly income fell, but last month's stock had still to be paid for. Many simply did not have the money in the bank. Others just abandoned the business and walked away from their bills.

It was a very expensive lesson to learn, but by the next summer Wall's were operating in line with their customer's expectations. They treated mobiling as an SBU, put in a manager with mobile experience and left it to him to run the business. They have since been very successful.

THE PRODUCT PORTFOLIO

Most organisations have more than one product and each will be positioned on its own PLC. Management therefore has the problem of managing the portfolio of products as well as each product itself. Judgements have to be made about which products to support, which to capitalise on, which to run down and terminate. In particular there must be decisions about the areas of R & D from which new products should come.

None of these decisions is helped, except in a general way, by the standard PLC.

The Boston matrix

A leading management consultancy transformed the classic PLC into a quantified form in 1977. The Boston matrix has the major advantages that it is both visual and dynamic. It can be used to map an organisation's products, or the product's market place(s). It is particularly useful to indicate strategic strengths and weaknesses. It is helpful to cash-flow management. It is therefore extremely useful at strategic level.

- *Product location.* Each product is represented by a circle that is proportionate in size to the product's volume. The centre of each circle indicates the product's position relative to the growth rate of the market and the major competitor.

  Thus a new product enters in the top right-hand question mark quadrant to gain the benefits of a growing market and because it will be very small to begin with. As it grows in size it will move across to the top left-hand star quadrant and continue to expand. As market growth slows down the product will move downwards to the cash-cow quadrant. It will then be in the maturity stage of its PLC. In due course it will be superseded and lose ground to competitive products. It will then move across into the dog quadrant.

- *Market growth rate.* The matrix is designed to be of major benefit in growing markets, and it is for management to decide on the rate of growth which they feel is needed if they are to invest in new product development. In many markets the growth rate is negligible – in FMCG it is around 1% – and for these the Boston Matrix is not an appropriate tool.

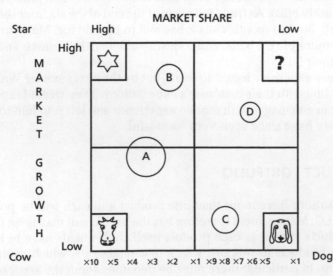

Fig. 17.7 Boston Consulting Group matrix

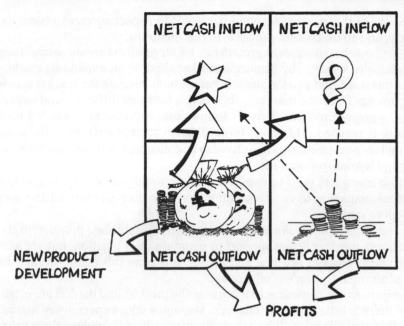

Fig. 17.8 Cash flow

- *Relative Market Share.* The strength of a product has much to do with market share (i.e. size), and with market dominance. If product A has 60% of the market and B has 20%, the relative market share is 3:1. If A had 40% it would be 2:1, and if both were equal the ratio would be 1:1.

  Relative market share indicates the power held by each product in the market relative to the major competitor. This power usually translates into profits and cash flow.
- *Cash flow.* There are only three sources of cash available to an organisation: from the shareholders, reserves and profit. Shareholder require a return on their investment, which can only be paid from profits, and reserves have been generated from profits. Therefore the only valid source of long-term cash is profit.

  Management are concerned with cash flow above all considerations. Without cash a business must fold. Even a business that is trading profitably will close if customers do not settle their accounts. This is quite hard for young managers to understand, but it is extremely important. 'Paper profits' have to be turned into cash flow if they are to have meaning. The importance of efficient and effective control on cash cannot be stressed highly enough.

The quadrants

- *Question mark (low market share, high market growth rate).* Products entering the market need full support. They cannot generate enough to pay their own way and so risk capital is invested in them until they succeed or are forced out of the market. A common error is to expect success to come too quickly, and to underfund products in this quadrant.

- *Star (high market share, high growth rate).* Star products are successes. They are gaining in volume, by acquiring market share in an expanding market. It is at this stage that market share is easiest built because the market is new and growing. Once the market stabilises it is far more difficult – and expensive – to acquire market share. It follows that investment is needed until maturity is reached. This short-term investment pays back over the long-term and so investment decisions have to be concerned with volume achievement and market/product life.

  British managers tend to expect a product to pay its way quite quickly. Japanese managers have a reputation for extensive support all the way through to maturity.

- *Cash cow (high market share, low growth rate).* Established products in stable markets need sufficient support to maintain their position, but are substantial generators of revenue and profits. It is from this quadrant that the bulk of an organisation's profits come.

  A major error is to assume that because the product and market are established there is little cause for concern. Managers who expect every market to be under challenge will be taking positive action to replace their products before a competitor does so.

  It follows that a proportion of profit should be devoted to R & D as well as to the support of products that in time will become cash generators.

  There are two forms of cash cow product. The product which is expected to generate funds over a substantial period and the 'Milch cow'.

  The cash cow is normally of major importance, and holds a substantial market share. It follows that it will have to continually fight off competition, and that funds must be allocated to its long-term healthy survival. It is a major error to drain away too much of the profits earned to support projects that have yet to prove themselves.

  Milch cow products are those which are in the process of replacement, but which are still generating substantial funds. Cross-ply tyres were not replaced by radials overnight – but once their demise was certain they ceased to have long-term value and so could be milked heavily with no investment to sustain their life. Milch cow products are on their way into the dog quadrant.

- *Dogs (low market share, low growth rate).* In the 'dog kennel' are all the products that have either passed through the cash-cow stage or fallen straight into the kennel from the quadrant above. They need not be making a loss, but they are no longer of long-term value in themselves.

  Dog products can supply limited funds for quite a time before being eliminated. They can be useful in support of established products. Finally, it is possible that competitors have similar products and it may be possible to either sell the product to a competitor or to buy from a competitor. Thus two or three 'dogs' may be brought together and between them make up a sufficient force in the market to survive profitability for far longer than any one could do alone.

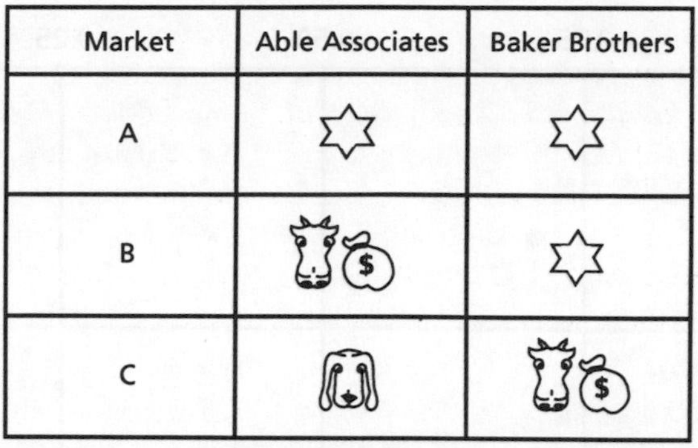

Market	Able Associates	Baker Brothers
A	☆	☆
B	🐄💰	☆
C	🐕	🐄💰

Fig. 17.9 Strategic options matrix

When used in support of an established product they can act as 'loss leaders' and be sold below a competitor's price; they can be promoted heavily in areas of competitive strength; they can be used in sales promotion activity. They can even be used to distract a competitor by aggressive marketing in a market where he is vulnerable and so prevent him acting in another market. For example, if two organisations are active in three markets their product portfolios may be as shown in Figure 17.9.

If Able Associates use their 'dog' product to attack Baker Brothers' 'cash cow' it will cost them very little in comparison to the aggravation caused. Baker Brothers may be forced to divert some resources from one or other of their star products, both of which are challenges to Able Associates.

Dynamic use

The Boston matrix is ideal for dynamically plotting market development. Think of each matrix as a single frame in a cine film. When there are sufficient frames they can be run through a projector and an illusion of movement is created. Several matrices run through a computer generate a similar form of moving picture.

As we know, management is concerned with the future and here the matrix is of major help. Coupled with What-if? planning it is possible to generate as many potential futures as are needed to assist in strategic planning. Results can be matched against expectation and so the basic PLC concept has been translated into a tool of practical benefit.

QUANTIFIED PLANNING

Following the lead set by the Ansoff and Boston matrices management planners and senior academics set about producing more reliable matrices to assist in specific areas of management planning. GEC worked with McKinsey to develop their Multifactor matrix which uses niche cells and makes a serious attempt at the quantification of strategic opportunity. It compares an organisation's business strengths against industry attractiveness.

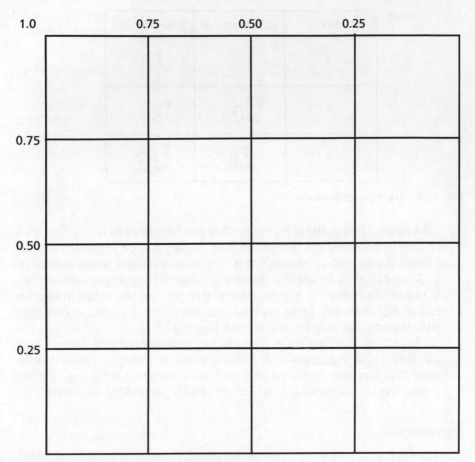

Fig. 17.10 Typical directional policy matrix

The Shell Directional Policy matrix also has nine cells but compares company competitive capabilities against business sector prospects. Ward's 16-cell matrix contrasts market and product newness, and is an extension from Ansoff's original four-cell matrix.

Directional policy matrices need to be adapted for specific need. Typically they look like the one shown in Figure 17.10.

Each of the axes of the matrix is quantified from 0 to 1.0 (or 0 to 100). The most useful criteria are set along each axis. Finally each opportunity is evaluated out of 1.0 (or 100) and plotted onto the matrix.

Note that the scoring is reversed on the X axis. This means that the most favourable cell is in the upper left of the matrix with each succeeding line of cells indicating a less favourable position. The cell scoring least is in the bottom right-hand corner.

Typical criteria that are used by management include:

- *Market attractiveness.* Market size, size of key segments, growth rate, diversity, demand seasonality, price sensitivity, opportunities, competitive structure, entry and exit barriers.

- *Competitive position (business strength)*. Market share, organisation growth rate, depth of product line, distributive/sales/price/promotional effectiveness.

Directional policy matrices are used dynamically, in the same way as the Boston matrix. Because they are tailored to the specific needs of individual organisations they are a most valuable management tool. In the example, the circles represent markets and the segments the size of the market held by an SBU. Thus a whole organisation's portfolio can be shown on one matrix, and broad strategic direction planned. Naturally there is need for each SBU to operate its own detailed planning within the broad parameters established for the SBU as a whole.

ECONOMIES OF SCALE

The key assumption that underpins the striving for the market share is that the more is sold, the more will be produced. The more produced the lower the unit cost.

To an extent this is true, but it is true in a way that is perhaps surprising. Economies of scale rely more on accumulated volume than on short-term volume. The longer a product is on the market, the more that are produced, the more the unit cost is likely to fall.

This is because there is an 'experience curve effect' in addition to the volume discounts that can be negotiated.

- Volume discounts are easy to understand, and to negotiate. The purchaser's negotiating strength grows as his orders become larger and more regular. Within limits he can press for lower prices than his competitor. He can also negotiate continuity of supply so that he has priority in times of shortage.
- The experience curve effect comes from the production experience and expertise that is developed over time. When accumulated volume over time is plotted against unit price an experience curve is revealed. Typically costs may fall between 20 and 30% every time experience (volume) is *doubled*.

    Thus the unit cost at 2000 units will fall by 20% at 4000 units. The next 20% reduction comes at 8000 units, then at 16 000, then 32 000 . . . and so

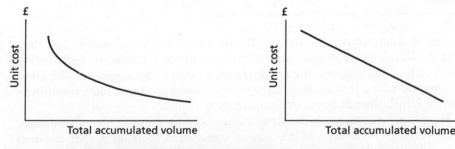

Note: This is the same curve – but plotted on log-log paper

Fig. 17.11 The learning or experience curve

on. In time the volume reaches into the millions and 4 million has to double to 8 million, and then 16 million for the cost benefit to be gained.

Once a product has started down the experience curve it will always have a cost advantage over competitors provided that it remains in front in terms of cumulative volume. Thus a market leader should always have a cost advantage over his competitors. It is easy to see why it is so crucial to make the right decisions in the early stages of market entry – one has major long-term benefits to gain.

- The Japanese have long understood the value of market share. Matsushita captured around two thirds of the world VCR market through a combination strategy of product quality and market share. As soon as cost savings were made they were passed on to customers via reduced prices and the increased sales generated further economies – which were passed on. In a comparatively short time the company had established barriers of entry based on quality and price and even major organisations like Sony, who invented video recording, were dominated.
- Britten-Norman made the Islander aircraft in the Isle of Wight off the south coast of England. They became successful and opened a second factory a few hundred yards from their first. They found, to their great surprise, that the same personnel, using identical equipment, could not make the identical aircraft as cheaply in the new factory as the old! But costs fell as volume in the new site increased.

PLANNING HORIZON

Remember to set planning horizons that meet the needs of the organisation. Different industries have to work within different time frames (see Table 17.1).

Table 17.1 Corporate time horizons

| | Corporate time horizons | | |
	Short	Medium	Long
Retail	3/6 months	1/2 years	5/7 years
Consumer durable	1 year	3/5 years	8/10 years
Aircraft	5 years	10 years	25/30 years
Energy	5/7 years	10/15 years	25/50 years

The planning principles are exactly the same across industries. The time frame differs because of the length of investment commitment needed to bring plans to fruition, e.g. locating and bringing a new energy source on line takes considerably longer than designing a new kitchen appliance, and a retail store can be refurbished in days, weeks or months at most.

Note that *operationally* the time frames become shorter. A retail manager is concerned with today and the coming weekend as short-term, with the next sales period as medium-term, and with next year as long-term. The retail corporate time horizon has to be longer than that, of course.

KEY POINT SUMMARY

- The PLC is an excellent concept that helps understanding, but it is not a practical management tool.
- The PLC is an S curve.
- There are seven major decision points: go/no go; test market; launch and growth; convert to maturity; maturity; convert to decline; termination.
- S curves tend to run in pairs with a discontinuity between them.
- It is important to search for replacement technology as well as for improved technology.
- Strategic planning shapes and reshapes an organisation's business.
- Operational planning deals with tactical matters.
- In times of success it is still important to plan strategically as well as operationally.
- Strategic planning uses a portfolio approach.
- An organisation or a business is often too wide for effective planning.
- Organisations sell benefits, not products.
- A market (benefit) orientation opens opportunities for development that would otherwise be closed.
- SBUs have three characteristics:
  — they can be planned separately;
  — they have their own competitors;
  — the manager has control over most profit influencing factors.
- The Boston matrix is the first product portfolio – it is visual and dynamic.
- Relative market share compares a product's share with that of the major competitor.
- Cash-flow management is helped by an understanding of the Boston matrix.
- Profits are the only long-term source of cash.
- The Boston quadrants are: question mark; star; cash cow; dog.
- Question mark and star products need start-up and development cash.
- Cow products can be either cash cow, with a long-life expectation, or milch cow, with no long-term future.
- Dog products can produce cash for some time before they are sold off or otherwise terminated.
- The SBU and Boston approaches allow management to exploit cross-market opportunities.
- Dynamic planning is made possible by the matrix approach.
- Quantified planning has been made possible by the matrices that have followed the lead given by the Boston.
- Directional policy matrices can be developed to meet individual management need.
- The experience curve effect shows that long-term volume is significant in gaining cost advantage.
- The planning horizon varies by industry, but the planning principles are exactly the same.
- Operationally time frames become shorter.

WORK-BASED AND SCHOOL- AND COLLEGE-BASED SELF-ASSESSMENT QUESTIONS

1 Use the matrix in Figure 17.12 to compare the strengths and weaknesses of the product life cycle and portfolio planning.

	PLC	Portfolio planning
Planning strengths		
Planning weaknesses		
Control strengths		
Control weaknesses		

Fig. 17.12 Question 1 – matrix

2 Summarise the 12 points in Hans Dichter's notes in your own words. Add examples drawn from your knowledge of your organisation (of whatever kind) and your market. You will also find examples in the better press . . . use your initiative to work out why certain changes have been made to products or services. You will also find excellent references in the marketing trade press. Always look for good examples because you need to be able to explain with examples – not simply repeat what you have read in a textbook.

See the end of Chapter 19 for answer guidelines.

CHAPTER 18

Diffusion and adoption

Connie Jones was worried. She was sure that her neighbours were passing derogatory remarks about her. She could just image the conversation in the street and across the garden fences:

'That Mrs Jones – her sheets are so grey.'
'Yes, and her coloureds are not bright are they?'
'Have you been in her kitchen? The floor tiles are a disgrace!'
'And there's a ring around the bath!'
'When I went for coffee the other day it was so bitter!'
'I don't like to go in, it never smells fresh in there.'
'Talking about freshness – have you seen her teeth?'
'Her youngest seems so tetchy – she must be uncomfortable in those nappies.'
'My child borrowed a towel, and it scratched him!'
'Her kids tell mine that her gravy is awful.'
'Yet she says she never has five minutes to relax!'

What could Connie do? She thought about it, and then made some revisions to her shopping list. That very afternoon she would put things right. She would buy:

- Persil   to make her whites whiter and her colours brighter;
- Flash   to put a shine on her floors and save her time;
- Mr Clean   to easily put a sparkle in to the bathroom;
- Mellow Birds   to be rid of bitter coffee and get her friends back;
- Haze   to awaken Spring throughout the house;
- Signal   so she could smile again – with flashing teeth;
- Pampers   so baby would have a dry bottom;
- Comfort   to soften her towels with no effort;
- Bisto   aaah! . . . that gravy granule trick;
- KitKat   so, at last, she could enjoy a break.

She would get right into her car, top up at the Shell station (and not the Esso), go past Tesco to Sainsburys and then stop for a snack at Burger King rather than McDonald's. All would then be well, she would be loved, valued, cherished . . . and then she woke up!

Connie found herself in her chair in front of the television which was whistling away to itself . . . it was two in the morning, so she took herself off to bed. In the morning she remembered her dream and mentally ticked off the items: yes she used every one. But why? Why was Persil so superior to Ariel or Daz? Was Mr Clean really better than Flash? How were Pampers nappies different from Kleenex? Why did she avoid Esso? What was superior about Sainsbury's and Burger King? Could she really tell the difference?

And what about shops' own brands? There was a lot of advertising about own brands, but she had ignored it? Why? Perhaps she ought to give Sainsbury's coffee a chance – the car seemed to run perfectly well wherever she bought petrol, so perhaps the same principle applied to other products?

She resolved to experiment with her shopping – but was far from sure that she would feel comfortable with the changes.

DISTINCTIVENESS

A distinctive product is one which is separate and individual. It is unique. An innovative product enjoys a time when it is distinctive because there is no direct competition. Success comes from persuading customers to divert resources to its purchase. It has to deliver something special, something to which the market responds

Distinctive alone is not enough. A product can be offered to the market too soon, and be rejected. The first launch of Nestea in the UK in the 1960s was a failure, partly because the market was still dominated by traditional tea drinkers. By the 1980s the market had changed (and the product improved). It was launched successfully – and immediately matched on the shelves by other instant teas.

How long a product remains distinctive depends on circumstances. Patent protection can be effective in some circumstances, but similar products may be produced that do not breach patent rights, yet compete fiercely. Sony's Betamax format was the original, the distinctive video cassette system, yet the VHS system, launched later, has become the household standard. (Sony still dominate the professional market.)

Brother say that in the office equipment market a new electronic device has a maximum of three months' distinctiveness.

DIFFERENTIATION

The creation of a difference *in the perception of the potential customers/ consumers* is the key to long-term success. We know that a product has three major characteristics: physical presence, functional purpose, and psychological (symbolic) appeal. Differences can exist in both of the first two categories, but the main impact of differentiation comes from the symbolic area.

Organisations make products, consumers choose benefits. Therefore it is to the area of consumer benefit that management must look to establish differentiation. There is wide potential for differentiation:

Consumer need: To satisfy thirst.
Obvious solution: Drink.
Necessary action: Choose a drink from the range available.

Determine the selection criteria, e.g. urgency, afford-
ability, need for warmth or coolness, still or fizzy, etc.
Select from the range available.

Table 18.1 Differential table

Generic solution	Product class	Product type	Brand examples	Major benefit
Water	Tap water	Still		Free, functional
	Bottled water		Evian	Pure, refreshing
		Gaseous	Perrier	Pure, digestive
			Badiot	Added minerals
Cold beverages:				
Non-alcoholic	Sodas	Colas	Coca-Cola	Taste & image
		Fruit	Orangina	
	Still	Squashes	Robinson	Taste, price
		Syrups	Delrosa	Taste, long life
Alcoholic	Beer			
	Lager	Many different brands across a wide range, all		
	Stout	attempting to offer a differential advantage		
	Wines	(*Note:* Champagne works very hard to		
	Spirits	maintain a distinct advantage)		
Hot beverages:				
Non-alcoholic	Tea	Leaf	Typhoo	Tradition
		Bags	Lyons	Convenience
		Instant	Nestlé	Speed
		Instant,	Brooke	Convenience and
		complete	Bond	speed
	Coffee ⎫			
	Chocolate ⎬	Many brands across a wide range all		
	Malted ⎭	attempting to offer a differential advantage		
Alcoholic	Punch ⎫	Home made from proprietary products		
	Mulled ⎭			

The table shows the major options, and breaks some down into types and
brands. You will see that the consumer faces a major array of choice! A range
of choice similar to this exists for every human need, and so we are constantly faced with a series of formidable decisions. Consumers short-circuit the full
decision process, which would require a detailed market analysis, because they
apply criteria which reduce the search to target areas. They also tend to remain
loyal to products which have proved themselves.

Both of these facts of customers and consumer behaviour work for and
against the manager of marketing. When established as the product in use, the
purchase routine works for the marketer. When trying to introduce a new
product he is faced with the two problems:

- How to break through the perceptual barrier erected by the customer who 'knows what he wants'.
- How, then, to persuade him to try a new product which may be no better – perhaps may be worse – than the one he knows, uses and trusts.

We shall return to this issue in Part 7.

SOURCES OF DIFFERENTIATION

Uniqueness is a key requirement for which every marketing manager should strive. Only if target customers perceive a product to be unique can it be positioned. The perception of uniqueness – of individuality – is crucial to positioning, it is the foundation upon which all else rests.

When products are faced with competition that is of high quality and virtually identical performance it is only possible to establish differential through non-direct means.

Non-direct differentiation

The FMCG market is the originator of non-direct differentiation. Why should Connie buy Persil? Is it truly better than Ariel, Daz, or any of the other leading brands? Is it better than a shop brand such as Sainsbury's? If Connie believes it is better, then effectively it is better – to her.

Image differentiation

Whilst products may look similar, even perform similarly – even actually be identical – they can be differentiated by image. A famous example is that of the Mini. In 1959 it was launched simultaneously by both Austin and Morris, and then quickly followed by Riley and Wolseley. All four car marques were within the British Motor Corporation (BMC). The Austin and Morris versions were identical, except for the range of colour choice, and the badges on the bonnet, tail and steering wheel. The Riley and Wolseley versions were more expensive and 'up-market'. They had identical styling features to differentiate them from the Austin and Morris versions, the only differences between the two were the badges used.

Why, then, did BMC launch four essentially identical cars under four marques?

At that time they were still operating four dealer networks, set up before the companies were merged into the BMC. There was customer loyalty to each marque, because each company had worked hard to establish a unique image and position over more than 50 years. Over the next 20 years BMC sold 4.5 million minis, and reduced the number of marques to one – Austin.

Image differentiation must deliver an emotional message, tailored to the needs of the target customer. Housewife tailoring features recognition for a job well done – gratitude from the family, approval (envy) from other women, pride in achievement. Now that more men are buying 'housewife' products, the imagery is beginning to change. Promotion is now tailored to show men being effective in the home, whilst women look on approvingly. In the UK this can be achieved with a wry sense of humour, hard to achieve in other cultures. This works well during what is probably a transitory stage. As the sex ratio of purchasers and users continues to change we must expect revisions to the emotional content of the promotion.

Confusion must be avoided – an advertisement can easily sell the product, but not the brand. In confusion, customers might set out to buy an 'Electrolux Hoover', or a jar of 'Maxwell House Nescafé.

Alternatively a message can be so powerful that it transcends the brand – Heineken's famous promotion produced a lot of sales, but women, who buy much of the alcohol consumed in the home,* went out to buy the 'beer that reaches the parts that other beers don't reach'. Does it matter that they didn't know the brand? Of course it does, since without a constant promotional reminder, they would be unable to identify one brand from another.

Logos and symbols

Well-designed logos and symbols are very powerful ways of capturing and communicating a complete message in the blink of an eye. Design is far more than the creation of a pretty shape. The logo or symbol must be capable of carrying exactly the same message to a range of targets. It must operate on the subconscious, as well as the conscious level, and every tiny element has its unique part to play.

Logos and symbols take time and resources to establish and should only be adopted if there is commitment to the necessary investment. Once in place their power is considerable. Even an exposure below the level of conscious perception triggers associated messages and emotions attached to the logo.

Stand in a modern high street and look round at the logos displayed. It will be very easy to identify most outlets, and certainly to locate the one(s) that you prefer to deal with.

Association

Image is greatly affected by association. Sponsorships must be arranged so that both the sponsored organisation and the sponsor benefit. Obviously major events such as the Olympic Games offer considerable exposure, but are of value only to mass market products enjoying a global presence. The major sponsors of the Winter Olympics in Norway in 1994 were IBM, Ricoh and Volvo.

Targeted sponsorship takes the product via the sponsored activity into

---

*They don't necessarily drink it. They buy it in 6 packs in the supermarket and keep it in the fridge for their husbands.

the minds of those who watch the activity. Thus the potential sponsor must match the profile of his target audience with that of sponsorship opportunities. There is a considerable difference between the audience for a darts championship, a ladies' hockey final and the Tour de France. Consequently the sponsors are also considerably different.

- *Personnel.* Only a small proportion of any organisation's staff come into contact with customers. These front line people are expected to represent the organisation – and they will be seen in that role by their customers. They must be supported by an organisation that is clear on the need for a customer focus, and which actively ensures that the marketing concept is understood, accepted and acted upon by everybody.

A regular feature of a senior management training course is to ask them to phone their organisation and try to make contact with a specific individual in middle management. Most report that they were treated badly by the telephone operators, and then were delayed – or lost – in the internal system. Some are so horrified that they immediately leave the course and go back to the office to rectify matters!

We shall return to this issue in Chapter 19.

Direct differentiation

Both products and services can be differentiated – but there is some degree of overlap since products must also have a degree of service differentiation. Kotler lists the areas where differentiation is possible.

Product	*Service*
Features	Delivery
Performance	Installation
Conformance	Customer Training
Durability	Consulting Service
Reliability	Repair
Repairability	Miscellaneous
Style	
Design	

Personnel	*Image*
Competence	Symbols
Courtesy	Media
Credibility	Atmosphere
Reliability	Events
Responsiveness	
Communication	

Product differentiation

- Physically some products appear hard to differentiate – salt, steel, eggs for example. Yet salt has been differentiated by its content – added or reduced minerals, and by its packaging – in shakers designed for table use. Steel has a whole range of variations to offer the expert buyer, and can also differentiate on source – for years Sheffield steel set the world's standards. Eggs are differentiated by size, and by colour. In the US white eggs carry a premium, in the UK brown eggs are preferred.

Manufactured products have an infinite variety of differentiation possibilities – especially when they are designed into the product from the very beginning.

- Features can add to the basic function. Japanese car manufacturers led the way in offering fully featured vehicles. Whilst their rivals were charging extra for features such as electric windows the Japanese provided them as standard. Obviously there were manufacturing advantages to be gained from standardisation which helped reduce the real cost of the extras, but the major benefit was in customer satisfaction. Considerable resentment can be caused by the addition of charges at point of sale. This resentment can be deep felt and long lasting. It may be illogical, but no sales person ever got very far by challenging a customer's logic!
- Performance adds differentiation value provided that it is sufficient to impress the target customers without adding too much to the cost. There is a limit to what customers perceive as value. It is important to discover what performance factors are important, and to build them in so that overall profitability is enhanced. (Overall profitability is the measure of profit on volume. It is better to sell 100 units at a net profit of £50 each than 50 units at a net profit of £70, £80 or even £90 each.)

If adding £20 per unit in factory cost increases revenue by a factor of more than £20 unit profit, it is worth doing.

There is always a need to balance quality against price and to believe that customers are driven by quality rather than by price. We shall return to this point in Chapter 29.

- Conformance is the degree to which a product's performance comes close to the operating standard. Customers who buy expect the products to perform to specification. Those which do establish a reputation, such as Champagne, guard it carefully.
- Durability is important in some product areas, but not where technology is changing so fast that a long life is of no benefit. Many computers are scrapped because they are obsolete, not because they no longer function to specification.
- Reliability is an absolute requirement for most products since they are bought for a purpose and when needed are expected to work. A camera which fails at a child's fifth birthday party, or a photo shop which loses the film, are going to be mistrusted in future. Neither are likely to generate repeat business.
- Repairability is important because everyone knows that products will fail at some time. The ones that have the easiest and most cost-effective repair systems provide a psychological safety blanket. On-line help is

becoming a very important part of product support in some areas – it is extremely comforting to know that if the computer goes down, qualified help is only a phone call away.

Counter-productive aspects of repairability include the need to take the product into a service point, and the packaging of spare parts in pairs even though the parts fail singly. Ideal back-up provides easy do-it-yourself repair, or on-site maintenance.

- Style has everything to do with impression – the impression made on the potential buyer, and the impression he wants to make on his contacts. The Apple Macintosh has established itself as the computer of style and Mac users regard the IBM as 'clunky'. This is almost entirely a perception rather than fact, but it is a key factor in the on-going success of the Macintosh range. Mac users feel themselves to be just that bit special.
- Design integrates all of the differing elements. It is essential that the designer is briefed very carefully about the target market so that the product has the necessary features and qualities built in. It is sometimes possible to add differentiation to a product, but it usually shows as the afterthought that it is.

It is for management, therefore, to identify the target market and its needs, wants, preferences and dislikes, before a designer is commissioned. Even a product that is functionally superior will fail if it is not differentiated in a way that satisfies the members of the target market.

Service differentiation

Services can be stand-alone . . . the equivalent of products but without physical presence. They can also be supportive of actual products or stand-alone services.

- Delivery includes the speed, accuracy and care with which the service is provided. ParcelForce in the UK have 0800 (free) numbers, quote prices based on the customers assessment of weight, pick-up within the hour, deliver as promised and are reasonably priced. These are all major customer benefits that together differentiate ParcelForce from the other couriers.

  Product delivery should be to time and by courteous staff who expect to deliver to the point of use and not simply the front door.
- Installation gives purpose to a product. Until then it is simply a useless package that is getting in the way. The longer it sits waiting for installation the more resentful the customer will become. Installation should therefore be easy for the customer – with clear and easy to follow instructions, or it should be co-ordinated with the delivery so that the product is put into use as quickly as possible.

Customer training

If the product or service is not used correctly it will be evaluated as inefficient despite that fact that it is the usage that is at fault. It is in a supplier's self-interests to provide not only training, but also back-up to help develop customer loyalty. Training also has the added benefits of developing an association between customer and supplier – a set of shared values that provide an on-going link.

Consultancy services

A supplier has the major advantages of knowing exactly what levels of achievement can be expected, and also has detailed knowledge of how the product is used elsewhere. Often a usage developed in one industry can be adapted for use within another. Consultancy, therefore, is offered to help customers set up a new operation and also to improve an operation that is up and running. To be effective consultancy must assist customer profitability – only if this is achieved will supplier benefits be derived.

Repair

The quality of the repair service is key to its success. A customer is dependent for profits on its efficient operation and resents any 'down time'. Suppliers who understand this and make provision to minimise the down time are of more value than those who sell a similar product cheaper, but do not supply an effective back-up.

When cars are off the road for service some garages offer service cars to keep their customers mobile. These replacement vehicles can come from the used car stock, and need not incur a heavy cost. Alternatively they can be demonstration vehicles, which may induce customers to trade up from their existing vehicle. A courtesy coach to take customers home and collect them in the evening often induces a customer to take the car for regular servicing.

- Miscellaneous services include all other ways of differentiation that can be devised to meet a specific industry, market or customer need. Better warranties, free insurance with new automobiles, on-site maintenance, hot line contact numbers, frequent flyer programmes – all are effective forms of differentiation.

BRANDING

Doyle defines a successful brand as:

A name, symbol, design or some combination, which identifies the 'product' of a particular organisation as having a sustainable differential advantage.

The key to this definition lies in the phrase 'sustainable differential advantage'. If a product does not have a differential advantage that can be sustained over time then it won't matter how much effort goes into the labelling, the logo, the clever advertising. Brands must deliver to their promise if they are to become established.

Many famous brands have histories that go back a century or more. Many of today's household names were known to our great-great-grandparents, and the values they represented then have not changed much over time. That reliability factor is the hallmark of a successful brand.

Brands can be of the company name, of a family of products, or of single products. Ford is a brand, so is the Ford Fiesta, and so is the Fiesta GTi. In this case notice how the major brand, Ford, acts as an umbrella, and how family brands, Fiesta, Escort, Mondeo, etc., carry the Ford image down to individual models. Also how descriptive brands such as GTi are used across the families: Escort and Fiesta both have GTi versions.

The family brand principle has been adopted by large retailers, and they now challenge the national brands. Only 10 years ago it was being argued that the days of the big brand were over because the retailers were becoming so powerful. It has transpired that the new big brands are at retail level. Safeway, Tesco, Sainsbury, and Marks & Spencer all have brands that cover very wide ranges of products. Building societies and banks are heavily branded, and the principles are extending into other sectors. . . Universities are attempting to brand what they offer, and so are some government agencies.

The demand for branded goods is now extending to include all brands of a particular good. Today the younger customer believes that all branded goods can be trusted. Thus instead of insisting on a Philips TV, for example, a typical customer will now happily accept any of up to a dozen alternative brands: Ferranti, Sanyo, Mitsubishi are all perceived to provide equal value. Only Sony and JVC have managed – so far – to preserve their unique identity in the TV marketplace.

In the supermarkets a major battle is raging with the retail big brands, especially Sainsbury, taking on the established brands. Sainsbury's Cola was packaged so similarly to Coke when it was introduced that Coca-Cola took them to court and secured an injunction forcing them to change the packaging. Sainsbury also were forced to change their labels on Full Roast coffee following pressure from Nestlé. Tesco are challenging Van der Bergh Foods by introducing Unbelievable, a low fat spread closely resembling Van den Burgh's I Can't Believe It's Not Butter brand.

The British Producers and Brand Owners Group was formed in March, 1994, by Nestlé, Unilever, Mars, Proctor & Gamble and Guinness to defend their brands against what they regard as 'passing off' by retailer own-label products.

With Nestlé and Unilever between them accounting for 11 of the UK's top 50 selling brands it can be seen that the situation is serious. Billions of pounds have been invested in the established brands – if these are to lose their unique identity the loss to the owners of the brand identities is literally incalculable.

The big brand

Only 10 years ago there was much debate about the future of the big brand. It was held that the costs of creating a brand were now so huge that no organisation could afford to create and sustain a new brand in a highly competitive marketplace.

Those who argued against the big brand missed two important points: the importance of the retailer and the globalisation of markets.

The importance of the retailer

Power in the distribution channel is now firmly in the hands of the big retailers, each of whom is gathering in strength as the one-stop shopping concept extends even further.

Retailers do not hang their brand on a single product as the manufacturers have tended to. Instead they use their brands as umbrellas over sub-brands – e.g. Sainsbury's range of teas, of wines, etc. Similarly the big retailers throughout the EU are big brands in their own right – with products carrying their brand accepted as of the highest quality.

Globalisation of markets

Brand owners are realising the need to have a common branding across national boundaries. This need is created by the transnational communication channels that have and are opening via satellite, radio, cable and electronic communications. There is also need to ensure that regular customers can continue to buy their favourite products in as many different markets as possible.

The SWATCH is about to outsell the whole Japanese watch production and the Swiss consortium that was set up to rescue their watch industry has shown that highly profitable new global brands are still possible.

The state of the brand market

A survey commissioned by *Marketing Week* in the Autumn of 1993 solicited the views of 150 top marketers about the future of the brand. The key results are:

- 80% think brand loyalty will remain where consumers lack confidence and need reassurance about their ability to buy well.
- 80% agreed that 'the only brands at real risk are those whose makers have lost touch with the marketplace.'
- 88% feel that concentration of the retail trade has provided credibility and a mass market for own-label goods.
- 26% think discounted brands will fade because they do not innovate.
- 27% believe deeply discounted brands will fade because they do not innovate.
- 27% believe deeply discounted goods presented in a stark, no-frills

manner will be shunned for fear of degrading their own image (*Note*: Tesco is moving into a value range and Sainsbury into a price-based ad strategy.)

Two key questions were asked:

— On balance, do you believe that an enduring decline is, or is not, taking place in consumer's brand loyalty?
  In decline: 43%; not in decline; 53%; no answer: 4%.
— Database marketing, allowing more goods and services to be tailored to suit customer needs and preferences, is the real revolution in marketing, *not* changing brand values.
  Agree: 50%; disagree: 35%; neither: 15%.

Branding benefits

A customer buying a branded product is confident that the product will perform as specified, that the quality will be at a known and accepted level and that back-up services will be in place. The brand will not only have been differentiated . . . it will have been successfully differentiated.

Successful differentiation comes from:

- clear definition of the target market;
- identification of target market needs;
- provision of a range of differentiation factors that respond to identified need;
- product design so all factors contribute to the differentiation;
- thorough testing to ensure that design is effective;
- commitment to long-term delivery of the differentiation features;
- commitment to long-term promotion that completes the differentiation;
- concern to develop long-term customer relationships;
- on-going research to ensure the brand is up-to-date in all respects.

Contents and packaging

Brands do not appear to change – nor does the overall style of presentation. In reality there is a constant series of modest changes to keep the brand fresh and current.

Old labels and advertisements show that brand presentation has changed radically – but yesterday's brands are still clearly recognisable today. The changes are brought about for two major reasons:

- *Content*. Product quality is generally higher today, and this is reflected in brand performance. Users will notice the improved performance – especially as it will have been introduced with a 'new and improved' promotion. Note that the function of the brand will not have changed – Persil's promise is still to help produce clean clothes. The composition of the powder in the Persil packet is of concern only to Persil, its competitors and trading standards officers.
  For a long-term established brand content changes provide a promo-

tional message of substance. In their absence the promotional message has to be created – it is amazing how many ways there are to say that a brand performs better – 'washes whitest', 'washes whiter', 'washes brighter', etc.
- *Packaging.* Packaging changes come from:
  — new technology – plastic for board;
  — shopping habits – weekly shops by car allow larger packs;
  — differential need – refill packs of soap powders offer economy, and a free tin with the first pack encourages brand loyalty;
  — promotional need – pack design has been simplified to match the speed with which a modern consumer can accept a promotional message.

Changes to packaging are brought in steadily, normally with one feature changing at a time so that continuity is maintained. A child's growth is noticed by a visitor, but often comes as a surprise to the parents. A brand's development should similarly not be noticed by its users.

It took HP Sauce ten years and four stages to change their label from traditional (old fashioned) to a modern style. They removed most of the descriptive language that was essential in the 1930s, and picked up and enhanced the key symbols so that they dominated the new label and made the product instantly recognisable on the supermarket shelf.

Brand extension

A successful brand has a presence that can be extended into other markets. Mars have very successfully extended their brands into ice cream. Levi were able to extend from jeans into jackets and shirts, but not into wool blended suits (as we saw in Chapter 12).

There is a limit to how far customers can accept a brand extension – it has to make sense to them. It has to match the original positioning that the brand established over the years.

Where brand extension is possible it provides major benefits. It:

- is known and trusted
- has an existing body of users;
- has a presence within the channel of distribution

On the other hand it has to:

- comply with the brand positioning, which may be limiting for a new concept;
- be established at a similar price level, which may be lower than its worth;
- follow promotional policy established for the brand overall.

Brand extension works only when adding product(s) to existing markets, because that is where the brand has presence. In a new market the brand has to start from scratch to build both awareness and positive action before sales action can happen.

In some cases it would be counter-productive to attempt brand extension. It is difficult to see how Chanel No 5 (a perfume brand) could extend to aftershave, although Chanel itself would carry over an image that may be of advantage to a new range in the male market.

We shall return to branding and naming in Chapter 21.

DIFFUSION

New products do not enter a market in a single bound! There is always a progression as new customers find the product, try it, and become regular users. Products are therefore said to 'diffuse' their way into markets. Diffusion is a progressive process and so the key questions for the new product manager are 'how fast will the product be adopted, and by how many?'

Findus made a major (but understandable) error when they introduced the frozen savoury pancake to the UK market. They expected the diffusion process to be relatively slow, and so geared up for a steady production increase. To their amazement they found that demand far exceeded supply, and they had to withdraw the product. Whilst they were commissioning extra production capacity, Bird's Eye rushed ahead with their version of the pancake and got it onto the market in volume, ahead of the Findus relaunch. Bird's Eye became market leaders, and many believe that they invented the product.

Adopter categories

Rogers established five adopter categories (Table 18.2) which have become the standard for measuring diffusion into a market. Over a period of time the product will be taken up by a succession of types of buyer. Generally there is a slow start followed by an increasing rapidity of take-up until the slow down occurs and the 'laggards' find their need for the product. If the adopter categories (and therefore the rate of adoption in volume terms) can be forecast it is of considerable benefit to management. But each product/market opportunity is different, and each must be the subject of separate investigation.

Note: Many make the understandable error of assuming that Rogers' categories extend to the whole potential market. They don't! The adopter categories cover those within the potential market who eventually adopt the product. If the potential market is 1 000 000 users and over time 200 000 adopt the product the adopter categories apply to the 200 000 and not the million.

Also note that Rogers' percentages are typical across markets. As Findus found out, there need not be a steady progression. Finally note that the time taken for laggards to adopt the product may extend over decades or, for such as fashion products the whole cycle may be completed in three or four months.

Table 18.2 Rogers' adopter categories

Category	%	Comment
Innovators	2.5	Venturesome individuals who like to be the first with new innovations. Risk takers.
Early adopters	13.5	Opinion leaders who adopt new ideas readily, but only after careful consideration.
Early majority	34	Deliberate people who will not rush into a decision but prefer to follow along quickly as the product gains market share.
Late majority	34	Sceptical people who take their time before commitment to a new idea.
Laggards	16	Tradition-bound people who are slow to change from what they know even when the alternative is well established.

The diffusion/adoption process refers to products that have been *adopted* as regular purchase needs. Good promotion can sell virtually any product once – marketing is concerned with profits from repeat purchases. It may take a considerable time to establish a product in a market – Rogers' work helps in the management planning by encouraging management to make realistic forecasts of the time needed to secure a loyal customer base.

KEY POINT SUMMARY

- A distinctive product is separate and individual.
- Distinctiveness is not enough – there also has to be consumer need satisfaction.
- Distinctiveness exists for a limited time only.
- Differentiation is the creation of a difference in the perception of the customers/consumers.
- Organisations make products, customers and consumers choose benefits.
- There is need to break through a perceptual barrier, and to persuade a consumer to try a new product.
- Differentiation can come from: image, product, service, personnel.
- Features adds differentiation, as does performance.
- Additional performance may be counter-productive if it is more than the consumer needs.
- Quality must be balanced against price.
- Delivery adds differentiation – if it is by courteous staff, to time, and to the point of use.
- Installation gives purpose to a product.
- Customer training helps the product or service to be used and evaluated properly. It also develops an association between supplier and customer.

- Consultancy and repair services help ensure that the product is used effectively, with a minimum of down time.
- Branding gives an identity to a product or service.
- Umbrella and family brands can carry the branding principle down to individual products.
- Branded products are trusted to perform as specified.
- Younger consumers are beginning to accept branded products as equals.
- Today's big brands are retailer brands.
- Branding is essential to support global marketing.
- The British Producers and Brand Owners Group has been formed to protect the interests of brand owners.
- Branded products have been successfully differentiated.
- Successful differentiation comes from: clear target market definition, identification of needs, provision of a range to meet those needs, design, testing, commitment, concern, on-going research.
- Contents and packaging change routinely, but are not normally noticed by the user.
- An improved formula, etc., can be used as a promotional feature.
- Packaging changes come about because of technology changes, shopping habit changes, differential need, promotional need.
- Brands can be extended into other markets.
- There is a limit to consumer's willingness to accept a brand extension.
- Branded products have to comply with the brand positioning, price levels and promotional policies.
- Diffusion is the process of entry to a market.
- Diffusion is progressive – key questions are 'how fast will the product be adopted, and by how many?'
- Adopter categories have been established by Rogers as: innovators, early adopters, early majority, late majority, laggards.
- Adopter theory applies to those in the target market who eventually adopt the product – not to the whole market.
- Rogers' work encourages management to make realistic forecasts of the time needed to secure a loyal customer base.

WORK-BASED SELF-ASSESSMENT QUESTIONS

1 As a product manager of a non-differentiated product how would you set about establishing it as a brand?

2 Visit a shopping centre and identify the width of brand extension that has been achieved for specified brands. Select two that have achieved a wide extension and identify other areas into which they could and couldn't extend. Underpin your thinking with clear reasoning.

SCHOOL- OR COLLEGE-BASED SELF-ASSESSMENT QUESTIONS

1 Determine how far your school or college is differentiated in its market. What evidence can you find to show that any differentiation is deliberate and managed by the school or college? If it is not differentiated, what actions could (should) it take?

2 Carry out the same assignment as given in the work-based assessment above.

See the end of Chapter 19 for answer guidelines.

CHAPTER 19

Effective communication

Jane Smith is a brand manager working for a GloFoods of Memphis, in the USA. Global Foods Incorporated is a major manufacturer of non-alcoholic foods and drinks. They were founded by a French family in St Louis in 1775 as importers of delicacies from France, but they were forced to restructure when the British navy blockaded France at the time of Napoleon. They never lost their interest in trading outside the continental United States, and built a healthy import/export business in speciality foodstuffs.

After the American Civil War they followed the settlers west, and set up a major production facility in California. By this time they were canning fruits and vegetables, providing a range of coffee beans and beginning to take an interest in the market for sodas.

By the turn of the century they were the third biggest US food processor, with security of supply ensured through long-term leaseholds on agricultural land in the USA, Central America, the Caribbean, Africa, India and, of course, Europe.

After the First World War they decided to extend through acquisition and were one of the first truly global organisations with wholly owned subsidiaries in each of their major markets. So successful was this policy that they continued to expand by acquisition and now have a presence in every country where they can gain access. Currently they are negotiating for permission to set up in China.

They have extended their brand across from canning to frozen and freeze dried products. From coffee to all non-alcoholic beverages; from snacks to full frozen meals; from tinned peas to the fashionable mange-touts; from apples to star fruit. They operate in all relevant markets, from grocery to hotels and restaurants to hospitals and schools.

Jane works for what used to be the Anglo Indian Tea Importing company. Integrated as GloFoods UK Limited since 1935 it still features the traditional AIT imagery on its tea labels, and retains the well-established brand names for its many varieties of tea. The full GloFoods range is managed from the London Head Office from which the entire marketing division operates.

Factories and depots are located across the whole of Great Britain, and many famous British brands have been incorporated into GloFoods as their owning companies have been acquired.

Corporate policy is set in Memphis, and the European HQ is in Paris. (Hardly surprising given the origins of the corporation.) Each national company operates independently, subject to global corporate policies, and each operating division is an SBU. Jane is brand manager of HG Tea, which is the second biggest tea brand in the UK. She answers to the group brand manager (teas) who reports to the marketing manager (beverages).

She is briefed on policies: global, UK corporate and UK marketing. She knows the marketing strategies for her group of products and for her brand. It is her job to create and manage the tactics necessary to achieve strategy. She has established tactical policies to guide her assistant brand manager in every-day matters. From daily contact, and a very tightly focused mission, she has intimate knowledge of her marketplace.

She has very close contacts with her opposite numbers in production, distribution and finance, and has earned a reputation for decisiveness and reliability. Her only contact within the European head office is with the European brand manager for her product. She has no contacts within the US head office where global policies are formed.

The planning cycle is based on the calendar year and she will start work on the next year's marketing plan for her brand at latest in April. With her assistant she will take a very close look at her market, and gather all the relevant information she can to assist her thinking. Part of her information bank will be provided by the European brand manager who has responsibility for implementation of global policies and strategies across Europe. Jane will check the costings of her plan with the help of finance, and check the feasibility of her thinking with colleagues in production and distribution. She will then share her thinking with her group brand manager (GBM) to whom she and three others report.

After negotiation, rethinking and revision her plan will be accepted by the GBM and combined with the plans from the other BMs in the team. The GBM will go through an exactly similar process with the marketing manager. They will also be guided by European managers. Probably there will be some reference back to Jane as the negotiation process continues, but by June the combined draft plan will be ready for submission to the marketing director.

The marketing director, after the routine negotiation, rethinking and revision, will prepare a marketing plan for the company ready for presentation to the board in August. At all levels there will have been continuing close contact with the other operating divisions along the lines of 'If I recommend so-and-so will you be able to schedule it, how best shall we do it?' All operational managers will be producing their plans and this constant, but informal, contact between divisions and departments is very helpful to all the planners. by the time the plans reach director level their contents will be quite well known across the company and there will be no embarrassing surprises.

Whilst tactical management across the company work on their plans there will be activity at corporate level. Exact details of corporate requirement will be confidential to top management, perhaps to board members. Certainly managers at Jane's level could not take them into account; she will work to achieve an 'operational profit' that will be based on ex-factory price or some other measure that does not reveal the full costings nor the full profit.

Corporate planning will be concerned with corporate strategy, and with special focus on the financial requirements for the next year. The views and requirements of the corporate strategic planners will be added to the planning process at marketing manager/director interface. Thus there will be bottom-up and top-down planning.

When the proposals of the operating managers in all the departments have been taken into account and merged there will usually be need for further negotiation, rethinking and revision. There will usually have been some trading off across departments in the fight for limited resources – some things will have been shelved, others included but with a reduced budget. If the overall plan does not reach the required profit level there will be need for further rethinking which will extend back down the company – probably to GBM level.

It can be seen that Jane's destiny is totally out of her hands!

Finally an agreed overall corporate plan, which has the support of the European managers, will be agreed by the board. This will be composed of detailed plans for each operating department, and will form the budget once head office approval is given.

As this is a global company the corporate plan will be submitted to corporate headquarters for incorporation within the global planning process. There will be parallel posts to Jane and her colleagues at European and global level and each national plan will be split into its constituent parts to produce European and global plans for each brand, product group, etc. Each national country will submit its plans in much the same way that BMs submit plans to GBMs who check to see they are feasible, follow policy and do not clash with other activities.

Only when corporate approval has been given can a national plan be broken back down into a budget which includes plans for each division, department and section.

Jane and her colleagues will be given their budget in November if all goes well. It is unlikely that very much of Jane's original thinking will have survived – too many others will have imposed their views – but her job is to implement the approved budget.

At tactical level Jane's task is to see that target customers are identified and then satisfied. This requires highly developed skills of communication. Jane has to manage the external communications through the promotional tools, but she also has to communicate internally.

Key extracts from her diary for a week indicate the width of her range of prime contacts. In addition she has to be concerned with secondary contacts because it is very important that everybody in the company understands and supports her products.

When 'outsiders' contact the company they do not distinguish between marketing, sales, production, distribution and finance. They expect all to be equally helpful. They expect to be transferred smoothly to someone who can help them, or to have a fast response if there is need to call back. Jane knows only too well that a rude or careless remark can do serious damage to a relationship and so works very hard to encourage a positive and helpful attitude within the company. Above all she is concerned to do her part to develop and maintain a strong sense of loyalty that is based on pride in the company and its products.

Table 19.1 Key extracts from Jane's diary

Monday	0930	Finance – check costing of proposals for next period's Sales Promotional campaign.
	1100	Agency – planning meeting re seasonal campaign.
	1400	Sales manager – negotiate sales force incentive.
Tuesday	0930	Factory visit – part of team hosting visit by buyers from major customer.
	1400	Distribution – potential problem with stock cover – sales moving faster than planned . . . Production – can they amend schedule to meet the increased sales? Sales manager – warning of possible stock shortfall. Can he warn team to hold off on absolute delivery promises?
	1600	Review summary of complaints received in week. Prepare for weekly review meeting.
Wednesday	0930	Quality control – tasting of samples from week's production. Review meeting with GBM and team.
	1100	Training – product knowledge session for new employees.
	1500	Train leaves for Edinburgh.
	1800	
Thursday	0900	Fact-finding day working with field salesman.
	1900	Train leaves for London.
Friday	0930	R & D – discuss progress on recipes for new product. Has the packaging problem been resolved?
	1130	Marketing research agency – receive report on research into proposed campaign.
	1430	Exhibition organisers – agree space requirements and put in contact with agency for detailed proposals re stand design and promotional support.

MARKETING COMMUNICATION

Marketers are persuasive communicators above all else. They achieve their results through presenting information to people in such a way that planned action follows. All managers have to communicate, of course, but for marketing managers the need to communicate is central to their success.

The same basic principles apply whether communicating externally or internally. Externally the task is to help customers move from unawareness of a product's existence to becoming loyal users. Internally the need is to convince people of the value of the marketing plan and to secure their assistance in achieving the intended results. In both cases the marketer is not in a position of power. Externally he needs to persuade people of the benefits he offers. Internally he has to persuade people to co-operate willingly and cheerfully.

If senior enough a manager can issue orders, but orders can be obeyed to the letter and not in spirit. It is always far better better to show why an action is necessary, and to have it accepted, than to impose it.

Operational managers such as Jane Smith are actually low on the management hierarchy. They have little authority of their own and depend on authority derived from their line managers. Consequently when dealing with other managers they can be at a severe disadvantage if they try to give instructions. They must develop relationships of mutual trust so that they can secure the required actions from a basis of common understanding of need.

Their communication tools are within the four Ps of the marketing mix – and especially the P of Promotion. The same tools can be used internally as are used externally. Their effective use depends on a thorough understanding of the communications process.

Communications

The simplest model of communication shows a sender in contact with a receiver (Figure 19.1). This is one way contact – not communication – we cannot know that the receiver is even listening to us! If we add a feedback channel we have a basic level model of communication (Figure 19.2).

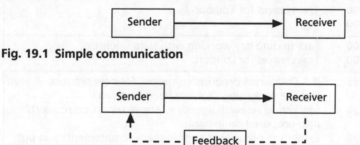

Fig. 19.1 Simple communication

Fig. 19.2 Communication with feedback

When there is feedback we are able to adjust our message. To go faster if it is obviously being understood and accepted, to repeat or rephrase if the receiver is having difficulty. Perhaps to change language from English to French or from verbal to visual. Effective communication is the responsibility of the sender. If the receiver hasn't understood, the sender has not communicated. Compare the difference between:

'I told you to do that an hour ago,' and
'You agreed to do that an hour ago.'

The quality of the feedback determines whether the message has simply been received, or if it has been understood, accepted, will be acted upon.

To understand what is actually happening in effective communication it is necessary to develop the simple model. In the more advanced model of Figure 19.3 it will be seen that the sender is concerned to:

• *Select* – The message must be applicable.
  The receiver must perceive it to relate to his needs or it will probably be ignored.

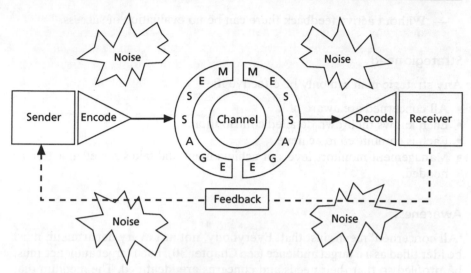

Fig. 19.3 Developed communication

- *Encode* – The receiver must be able to decode it.
  Messages are composed mentally. As we do not have telepathic abilities we have to express the message in some form of code. This may be in speech, in writing, in pictures. It is very important to choose a code that the receiver understands – and to transmit at a speed he is capable of receiving:
  — Use basic English, in short sentences, for non-native speakers of the language.
  — Use (or avoid) jargon depending on the training and experience of the receiver.
  — Support verbal messages with visuals wherever possible.
- *Channel* – Select an appropriate channel.
  Place the message where it will be seen by the receiver.
  Marketing vacancies are well placed in *Marketing Week* magazine, out of place in *Home & Family*. Select the channel that has the strongest protection against the 'noise' that must affect any communication.
- *Noise* – The physical problems and psychological distractions that can affect the quality of the received message. For example, a dirty telephone line can scramble a data link; a stressed manager can misread a memo; a long report must have an executive summary (which is probably all that will be read).
- *Feedback* – Has to be active.
  — 'Do you understand?' almost always produces the answer 'Yes.' – which does *not* prove anything. If the receiver summarises the key points it will show understanding.
  — The receiver acting on the message conveys both understanding and acceptance.
  — The actual actions taken show the accuracy of the understanding and/or the perceived value of the message. The old adage is an excellent guide: 'Believe what he does, not what he says'.

— Without active feedback there can be no evaluation of success.

Strategic need

Any strategic plan can only be effective if:

- All concerned are aware of it.
- Each knows their own detailed contribution.
- Each is committed to achieve.
- Management monitors levels of achievement and takes remedial action as needed.

Awareness

'All concerned' means just that. Everybody, not just every department, must be identified as a a target audience (see Chapter 30). Each target audience must be profiled so that their needs and concerns are identified. The medium that most effectively reaches each target audience must be identified and, if necessary, created.

Having an in-house newspaper does not mean:

1 That it reaches the employees.
2 That it is read if it does.
3 That it is believed if it is read.
4 That it is remembered if it is believed.
5 That it is acted upon if it is remembered.

Effective awareness is achieved only at Step 5 . . . whatever the form(s) of communication used.

'I didn't know we made that!' is replaced by 'Our new product is great – this is why!'.

Three keys to successful communication.

Clarity, brevity and completeness are the three keys to successful communication.

- The message has to be clear in the perception of the receiver. We all know what we mean when we pass on a message, but does the receiver understand? Does he share the same frames of reference? We draw our examples from our own life experience, and we often fail to realise that they are not understood – they are crystal clear to *us*!

  For example, the Americans use a 'tea cup' as their standard measure in recipes. The British use 'tablespoon'. Do the British know the size of an American tea cup? It would be unwise to assume they do. If publishing American recipes internationally it would be best to translate quantities to match the reference frames of the new markets.

- Brevity means compactness – not shortness. Naturally when an item is compacted it becomes shorter, but all the features remain. Brevity in commu-

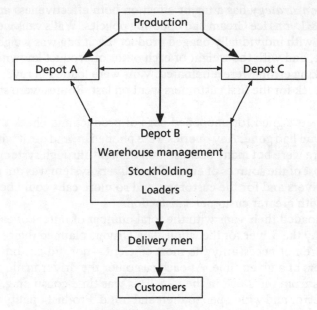

Fig. 19.4 Stockholding and delivery model

nication means stripping out all the unnecessary words. Business English is brief, to the point and easy to understand. Victorian novels are lengthy, with detailed descriptions included for the enjoyment of the reader – they are ideal for their purpose, which is to entertain rather than communicate.

- Completeness is essential. Careful thought must be given to a communication so that no key issue is omitted. It is best to have material checked by a third party because an author can very easily omit something which seems obvious to him, but is not to others. Instruction manuals in particular should be checked, rechecked, and treble checked for completeness and clarity. When they are translated they should be treble checked by native speakers of the new language who are currently living in the target market. Remember that subtle differences exist in language between regions of a country as well as the major differences between countries. The French spoken in Canada is different from the versions spoken in Paris and in Corsica.

TACTICAL CONTRIBUTION

As the strategic plan is diffused throughout an organisation it is broken down into ever smaller elements, each becoming ever more specific and short-term. Thus the efficiency of a delivery driver is conditioned by the loaders, and loading by stockholding and the warehouse management. Stockholding is conditioned by stock control, and by the efficient switching of stocks from depot to depot and by the efficient movement of stocks forward from production.

- *Distribution strategy* has a major effect on both effectiveness and efficiency. Walls & Lyons Ice Cream had opposing policies. Walls vans were stocked overnight with individually bagged product. Each bag was weighed against its invoice, and with the weight of each outer of product known the majority of packing errors were eliminated. Vans were loaded in reverse order so that the stock for the first customers went on last. Routes were specified for the drivers.

  Customers signed for unopened bags of product and check the delivery after the van had gone. Any queries were phoned in, and dealt with by office staff. There were not many because well thought-through systems had eliminated most of the sources of error. The delivery system was quick and easy for the drivers and for the customers and so more calls could be scheduled per van with greater customer satisfaction.

  Lyons loaded their vans with the total number of outers of each product required by the driver for the whole day. Drivers planned their own routes, which were not necessarily the most efficient – nor did customers receive their orders at a given time. At each customer the driver made up individual orders from the stock in the van. This was time-consuming, extremely prone to error and wide open to theft and fraud. Product quality was affected as the day passed and the temperature in the van rose because the door was open so often. Drivers' health was affected through constant changes from the heat of a summer day to the cold of chilled delivery vehicle.

  Walls distribution was evidence of a marketing philosophy, Lyons distribution caused much dissatisfaction at customer and consumer levels.

Commitment

It is not necessary, nor desirable, for all employees to have details of the corporate strategy. It is sufficient to know that it exists, and to have confidence in it. It is essential to know that one's individual participation is planned, monitored and valued.

Managers who keep praise to themselves but hand on criticism are destructive. Marketers who take credit for the achievements of colleagues in other departments are long-term foolish because they depend on others for their success and stealing or withholding credit is counter-productive. It is better by far to seek opportunities for praise, and to very carefully consider how (if) to be critical.

INTERNAL MARKETING

It is just as important to 'sell' marketing plans internally as it is to sell product to customers. The identical techniques can be used within an organisation, and will pay off in handsome benefits.

All communications that originate in marketing are marketing communications. All, therefore, should be targeted, and designed to be persuasive.

The concept of *total quality management*, which is concerned to ensure that every employee actively helps to install, maintain and deliver at the highest levels of quality can be developed to the *inner market*.

Inner marketing fixes quality in terms of the marketing concept and applies to each and every activity, however apparently insignificant. Every employee is encouraged to think of his job in terms of what it means to the customer – what can be done to improve customer service.

This is far more significant than imposed courses in 'customer care' which seek to instil the principles of courtesy, care and consideration. Vital as these are they are only truly effective when supported by a genuine concern with and for the customer. There must be an appreciation that the organisation exists to serve customers and that profits – and employment – come only from a loyal customer base.

The base for inner marketing is – as always in marketing – research. Top management have to audit the present position before planning to make the changes necessary to reach the desired position. Research is needed into such areas as:

- Are customers seen as friends or foes?
- Does a genuine concern to offer service exist?
- Is a customer problem seen as an organisational problem?
- Do employees want to offer good service?
- What will motivate them to adopt a marketing approach?

The culture of the organisation is crucial to the marketing approach. Peters and Waterman, in *In Search of Excellence*, stress the need for 'shared values'. A customer is influenced by promotion, but believes what he experiences when in contact with an organisation. (Believe what they do, not what they say.)

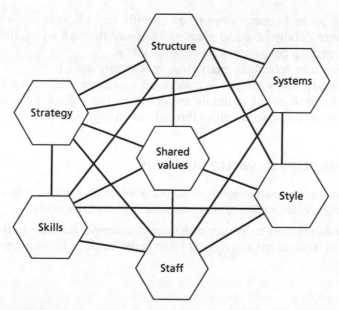

Fig. 19.5 The seven Ss

An organisation can be seen in terms of seven Ss. Unless these all interlink there can be no shared values to underpin the culture, and no culture of concern for the customer.

Throughout Parts 6 and 7 remember that all marketing principles apply internally as well as externally. The difference is in the scale of the operation, not the principle.

KEY POINT SUMMARY

- There are many level of management in a global company.
- Top down and bottom up planning will be used.
- There will be need to match global, regional and national policies and objectives.
- A brand manager has a wide range of prime contacts.
- Low-level operational managers, such as Jane Smith, derive their authority from their line managers.
- Marketers are persuasive communicators.
- Marketing communications flow externally and internally.
- The communication tools are within the four Ps – especially within the P of Promotion.
- Models of communication show that the sender – receiver contact can be complex.
- Messages must be selected as applicable, perceived as relevant, encoded so that they can be decoded, sent in appropriate channels, must cope with anticipated noise and be monitored through feedback.
- Three keys to effective communication are: clarity, brevity and completeness.
- Strategic plans become ever more specific and short-term as they are broken into detailed tactical plans and diffused through an organisation.
- Commitment to corporate strategy is essential.
- Plans should be internally marketed – not simply issued.
- Total Quality Management is concerned to ensure that every employee actively helps to install, maintain and deliver at the highest levels of quality.
- There is need for shared values throughout an organisation.

WORK-BASED SELF-ASSESSMENT QUESTIONS

1 How does your management communicate internally? Is it effective? Write a short report recommending improvements that could be made.

2 What measures exist to inform managers of customer reaction to the organisation and its products or services? What could be done to improve the situation?

SCHOOL- OR COLLEGE-BASED SELF-ASSESSMENT QUESTIONS

1 How does the management of your school or college communicate internally? Is it effective? Write a short report recommending improvements that could be made.

2 How does the management of your school or college communicate externally? Is it effective? What could be done to improve the situation?

See the end of the Chapter for answer guidelines.

SUGGESTED ASSISTANCE TO SELF-ASSESSMENT QUESTIONS FOR CHAPTERS 16–19

WORK-BASED QUESTIONS

Chapter 16

1 1 Welcome. Self-introduction.
  2 Budgets are essential – you will work to budgets when you start selling.
  3 Budgets are expectations. They are to be achieved.
   Budgets are realistic – not optimistic, nor pessimistic.
  4 Everyone in the company works to budget. Therefore production is making, expecting you to sell. You are selling, expecting them to make.
   What happens if either of your exceeds or falls short of budget?
   Either too much or too little stock. Perhaps very unhappy customers. In either case it costs money – and perhaps reputation.
   It will certainly be unpleasant for whoever fails to meet budget!
  5 Targets are not used because they suggest something to be aimed at – but may be missed.
  6 We do *sometimes* use quotas – but only when there is a fixed quantity that must not be exceeded. We use it to give emphasis to the priority not to exceed.
  7 You will find that working to budget is best. You are not forever stretching to achieve ever more. We never look back to last year. And budgets are flexible, so if necessary we can and do make adjustments.
  8 You will find that your life is so much easier under budgetary control.
  9 Questions?

2 As a customer relations manager you would be especially concerned with the feedback received from customers and consumers. You would want MBE reports on such issues as: the number of complaints received; the speed with which they are responded to; the type of complaint; the size/importance of complaint; the number that have to be extracted for special treatment – and why; the performance of each member of your team measured against their individual criteria, and against the average for the team as a whole; any outstanding performance, good or bad.

Chapter 17

1 Your matrix should look something like Figure 17.13.

2 Hans Dichter's points are clearly set out, but as you have transferred them to your own words you will have helped yourself to remember them. It is worth going through them again, and then coming back to your notes in a day or so to refresh your understanding. You will also find that as you develop a habit of reading for examples you will find it easier and more enjoyable to locate and understand them.

	PLC	Portfolio Planning
Planning Strengths	Five stage view: Development Introduction, Growth, Maturity, Decline. Easy to understand as concept.	Focus on SBU portfolio. Allows varity of planning approaches: product, SBU, Organisation, etc. Can be quantified. Allows prediction.
Planning Weaknesses	Historical only. No predictive capability. Often taught as the way to really understand what is happening. Not quantifiable.	Circle sizes may not reflect true benefits. Likely to distort true picture through simplistic visuals. Movement between quadrants dependent on management definition – not necessarily agreed by competition.
Control Strengths	Can suggest the possibility of the need for action. Guides an intuitive manager. Is a useful visual shorthand.	Relative market share indicated. Accurately reflects the current position. Encourages scenario and what -if? planning.
Control Weaknesses	Totally useless: Imprecise and inaccurate. Not quantifiable.	Little value in stable markets – but has been developed into models which are useful.

Fig. 17.13 PLC and portfolio planning compared

Chapter 18

1 Requirements is to identify the needs of the existing and potential users of the products, then to ensure that the product meets the identified needs. A distinct image must be created for the product so that it can be perceived clearly as a differential products. The techniques for establishing the differentiation will vary dependent upon the product/market, but they must be selected with care since there will be need to commit to them for a considerable time. Finally the new brand must be heavily promoted to ensure that it becomes established in the minds of the target customers and consumers.

2 You will easily identify products that have extended across into a second market – but there are others that have extended into several markets. Mars brands are in confectionery, ice cream and cold drinks. They could also go into hot drinks, cakes, biscuits. It is hard to see them moving into vacuum flasks (even though the link is there from drinks). They may introduce cool boxes to carry their ice cream – perhaps as a special promotion, which may become a permanent feature. Note how many cigarette brands have extended into such as clothing and holidays. It is hard to understand how this has been achieved, time will tell if it is long-term successful.

Chapter 19

1 In many cases there will be little attempt to communicate because a majority of managers have yet to appreciate the benefits of effective internal communication. In such cases there is likely to be a strong 'grapevine' through which rumours and half-truths will circulate. Even where newsletters and notice boards are used they are likely to be ineffective since they are unlikely to be targeted on the needs of the employees, i.e. they are likely to be centred on the management or on the organisation. Improvements that could be suggested include: matching the needs of the staff, getting hard information out quickly, not relying on word-of-mouth down the management hierarchy, removing the need for the grapevine through effective and timely communication.

2 Possibly you will find that individual departments have information which is important to others – but are not sharing it. This is usually simply because they don't appreciate the other department's need, and because there is no mechanism to transfer the information. The only long-term solution is one of constant vigilance supported by an effective MIS (or MkIS). There is vital need for shared values if full support is to be given and received.

COLLEGE-BASED QUESTIONS

Chapter 16

1 His personal qualities were of major importance. He had sufficient confidence to ask for help when he needed it, and to listen and take note of the responses. He was prepared to take action, and to take it quickly. If he had not been self-confident he would have failed through nervousness. If arrogant he would have failed through an inability to recognise his need.

2 A school or college is no different, in principle, to many other organisations. Any problem in introducing MBE is likely to come from the reluctance of managers – both academic and administrative – to submit themselves to the discipline of setting clear objectives. This is a perfectly normal reaction which was common in industry twenty years ago. It is first necessary for senior management to decide that budgetary control is needed, and then to plan its introduction over quite a long period of time. There will inevitably be resistance – there always is to change – but in this case the academics have to accept their their performance can be measured – something which many believe is impossible.

Chapter 17

The same questions were given to all (see under work-based questions).

Chapter 18

1 Differentiation is established when an organisation has a distinct presence in the market. Most schools and colleges are differentiated simply because of geographic position, but also have a reputation (an image) as a good school, or a place to avoid if possible.

You should be looking for evidence that the management is aware of the needs of the community the organisation serves, and that positive action has been taken to mount the courses to meet the identified needs and that the offerings have been promoted effectively.

Do not take the existence of a logo, or any such device as evidence of differentiation. Many amateurs in marketing are good at designing headed notepaper – where they fail is in delivering the product to the quality implied by their promotional techniques.

2 See the answer given above.

Chapter 19

1 School and college management has to communicate both with staff and with students. You may not be able to discover very much hard information about staff communication, but you will know a lot about the communication targeted upon yourself. Is it effective? Does it tell you what you need to know, when you need to know it? Is it transmitted in user-friendly form? Is there a 'grapevine' through which rumours and half-truths circulate? Are newsletters and notice boards used effectively i.e. is their content up-to-date and are all old notices removed? Is the information centred on the students or on the organisation? Improvements that could be suggested include: matching the needs of the students, getting hard information out quickly, not relying on word-of-mouth through the tutors, removing the need for the grapevine through effective and timely communication.

2 Does the organisation have a clear identity? One to which all the departments and faculties, etc., wholeheartedly subscribe? If so, is there a clear position on which to base the communication? i.e. Does the organisation clearly know what it is offering and to whom? Are the chosen external communication methods appropriate? Do they target the right audiences? At the appropriate time? With messages that are clear, brief and complete? Are arrangements for signing on to courses made to help would-be students, or do they fit the convenience of the organisation? What could be done comes directly from the answers to these questions – but remember that the target market is limited in size, and the budget is likely to be small.

PART 6

Marketing planning –
the bedrock of success

Once the corporate plan is finalised each operating division can proceed with its planning. Obviously divisional plans will have been developed in draft as part of the planning and budgetary processes but each functional plan can be completed only when the corporate plan is agreed.

In marketing-centred organisations the lead will have been given by marketing – from the sales forecast. In others the lead may have come from another function – most usually production. Once the corporate plan is in place it is the budget which provides guidance and so a marketing plan is needed in every organisation.

The role of the marketing plan is to convert corporate objectives to marketing objectives, and to set out very clearly how those objectives are to be achieved. Four questions explain the marketing planning process:

- What business are we in?
- Where are we going?
- How will we get there?
- How will we know when we've arrived?

The acronym MOST is an aid to remembering the key stages that have to be included in any plan:

M	Mission	What business are we in?
O	Objectives	What do we want to achieve?
S	Strategies	Which direction shall we take?
T	Tactics	How will we get there?

It is not efficient to check only our destination on arrival. If we are on a train journey we automatically check stations as we pass, to confirm firstly that we are on the right train (!) and then to monitor our progress. In marketing we have feedback on results through budgetary control and this allows progress to be continuously monitored.

The marketing plan combines a range of individual plans. There will certainly be strategies for each element within the marketing mix, and a promotional plan is essential. Tactical planning will derive from the strategic plans, and provide for every product and market.

The marketing planning process follows a clearly defined path, but the marketing plan itself can have no fixed format. This is because organisations must plan for their individual mix of products and markets, and the priorities and opportunities for synergy will determine how the plan is constructed.

General principles are common to all marketing plans, but the successful plan is judged on ability to communicate, not on its formal structure.

As we have seen, subsidiary plans must be consistent with established strategies and tactics if overall success is to be achieved. All marketing planning documents are therefore subservient to the overall marketing plan. Research and promotional agencies are briefed on a need-to-know basis, and product, brand and market plans are extracted. Tactical planning is concerned with ever more detailed issues, because the success of the whole depends on very many small individual achievements.

CHAPTER 20

The marketing planning process

Jane Smith (who we met in Chapter 19) was a typically positive and self-confident young brand manager within GloFoods. She had moved up to her present post after a year as assistant brand manager. Before that she had spent two successful years running a sales territory. Twice she had won the top salesman award.

She had proved her training abilities through regular slots in induction and updating programmes and had kept in close touch with developments in the field. She now felt it was time for a career move. She wanted to become a field sales trainer as a major step towards a sales management post.

Experience had taught her that it would be hard to move unless there was someone to take over her present job. A far-sighted young woman she had selected her assistant with care, and now believed that he was ready to take over from her. There was likely to be a suitable vacancy in the field in three months, and she had put out feelers to discover if she might have a chance of getting it. The vibes were good, and she intended to make a strong application for the post.

She couldn't tell Nasser Houssain of her plans, but she could help him to develop the confidence he needed to take over from her. He was already technically qualified, but he hadn't had the external experience. Jane decided that over the next month Nasser would 'shadow' her as much as possible. Where she went, he would also come. To set the scene she decided to take him through her diary for a typical week to show him a brand manager's range of responsibilities. She arranged to meet him one evening after work and over coffee they went through her diary. This is her explanation of the key spots in her week. (Refer to the diary in Chapter 19.)

Monday

Finance are very helpful if you approach them correctly. I don't work out detailed figures when they have everything at their fingertips. Anything I did would have to be checked by them, anyway, so it is better to get things straight from the start.

What I needed was hard information I could use when discussing the next sales promotion campaign with the sales manager. Field sales support is essential, and you know how much each brand manager wants to get salespeople to feature their products. We all have to take our turn because they can't feature everything on every call! I wanted an incentive package that would be attractive to the sales team, within my budget, but not outside reasonable limits, so that we don't set a precedent.

There are too many variables for me to work the figures alone – the cost accountants have the models on their computers, and they know exactly what has been achieved in similar campaigns. I came away with detailed figures for five scenarios and was very strongly placed when I saw the *sales manager* later in the day.

As you know, we agreed on a sales incentive package – you have been working on the details since Tuesday. What you didn't know was that the agreed package had already effectively cleared the finance hurdle so I could confidently start you off on the tactical planning.

Agency meetings are always exciting. The atmosphere in a big agency can be electric at times, and they work to such tight deadlines that it really keeps them on their toes. How they manage to work so hard and keep sane I don't know – their new business manager had five working lunches and four dinners last week! Apparently that is quite normal. He plays squash every day, but has still put on 25 pounds in under a year!

We are meeting to short-list suggestions for the new seasonal campaign. You must come to the presentation and planning meeting next Tuesday. The marketing manager runs the show, and all the GBMs and BMs will be there together with the top brass from the agency. The agency will present the two alternative campaign themes that we agreed on when we met. I've asked for the one I think the MM will like best to be presented second. You have to stage manage these things!

Tuesday

Factory visits get very boring very quickly. The first time it is quite exciting, but after the 10th time around it is all a repetition. But factory visits are a major opportunity to meet with the people who make the product, the ones you will rely on for quality. Also the ones you sometimes have to ask to reschedule their plans. It can't be easy to switch production – especially when machinery has to be stripped and cleaned – but so far they have always done it when I've asked. Mind you I am very careful to only ask when there is no alternative – and I always ask, never tell!

Acting as a host is of great importance. You get to talk with buyers, users, people from head office, journalists. Use your time right and you come away with valuable information a researcher would never get.

Distribution can really screw up if they manage by the book and let the budgetary control system pick up under-stocks. Our system is fast, but cannot always prevent some out-of-stock positions, which let our customers down, constitute a nuisance to our sales force and a pain to marketing. Good relationships mean that I get to hear when distribution feel there is going to be a shortfall, before it actually happens. Then I can do something about it. This time I checked with production and they were able to increase output with no trouble. So I gave the sales manager a ring and alerted him, and then checked back with distribution.

The big problems are always with our lower selling lines. Stocks have to be spread so thin that even a small sales variation can cause a stock-out. Normally stock can be transferred from other depots, but if you are not careful you have stocks moving all over the country. Very expensive! In this case we had stock problems across the UK but production could increase by 50% without trouble because this volume is so small.

Formal meetings are all very well, but I find every excuse I can to ring depot managers and be nice to them. I never go past a depot without calling in, and I always support distribution when they come under fire in a review meeting.

Complaints are a major source of information. I don't see all of them because by far the most are routine queries. Most are not really 'complaints' since there is nothing wrong with the product. But the customer thinks there is, so we take them very seriously. Quite often it is simply a case of not reading the instructions. Last year we had a series of complaints from one lady – she kept finding boiled sweets inside our packs! We checked everything – even down to questioning everybody on the production line. It turned out that her little boy was storing partly used boiled sweets to come back and eat later! Fortunately she wrote to tell us about it – quality control were going frantic!

Each week I get a summary of the complaints received, classified by type and by action taken. We always respond quickly, and follow up later if there is need. We always refund postage, and take the chance to send a sample product as a way of thanking them for writing to us. It all helps to build awareness and to reinforce attitude.

If a serious complaint comes in then everything is dropped until it is dealt with. We want to move fast for our own reputation, but in these days of deliberate sabotage we have a greater incentive to identify, isolate and correct any problem.

Wednesday

Quality control is a favourite of mine. We examine samples from our current production, and compare ours to the competition. Tests are always 'blind' so we never know until afterwards which sample is ours and which from outside. It is a bit scary to know that similar sessions are held in Paris for all European production and in Memphis for global production! We can't release product until it is cleared at the factory, here, and also in Paris and Memphis.

New products are sampled at special closed door sessions with a carefully invited panel.

Training is an excellent way of staying on top of the job. You have to be current and interesting. Presentation is such a big part of BM's job that I welcome every opportunity to sharpen my skills.

Thursday

Field trips are, for me, a vital part of the job. Not all BMs agree, but I believe that I need to talk direct to the customers. Once a month I schedule a day out with a salesman, and I spend the time asking questions and listening. So far I have been able to take over a sales territory for a week each year whilst the salesman was on holiday. This gets me into the front line, refreshes my selling skills, provides lots of useful information, and gives me a break from the office. I recommend this activity very strongly to you.

Friday

R & D is essential, as you know. We have to keep our products competitive, and that means constantly trying to find ways of improvement. We currently have a sealing problem on the new packs. Obviously they were not field tested thoroughly enough, and we shall learn from that. But it is difficult to field test adequately and not tip our hand to the competition.

Marketing research is on-going and I would hate to be without it. Our budget is not very substantial, but I can live with a response that is 60:40, or better. If it is any nearer 50:50 it becomes data, because the sampling error is too high for me to treat it as information.

Exhibitions are exciting at first – as you will find. But the combination of the artificial atmosphere, the need to stand all day, talking and constantly being 'on show' is very tiring. Take at least two pairs of shoes with you, and be sure that both are worn in first.

Stand space is dictated by budget and need – I have settled for less space than we could afford. Stand quality is affected by the imagination, and the budget, that goes into it. I have given a detailed brief to the agency, and they know the promotional policy that the stand must support. I'll be seeing preliminary sketches early next week and I want you to come along with me.

The exhibition is in 6 months time, so you will have plenty of time to work the stand up from scratch. I am going to recommend you as the exhibition manager, so you can take full responsibility almost from day one, and accept full praise when our objectives are met.

Other things

During the week there is much more to do, of course. A whole raft of mail arrives – most of which I pass on to you. The phone never stops ringing with minor queries and requests which can usually be dealt with easily. The GBM needs to be updated regularly – and especially when anything happens that is out of the ordinary.

He is a good boss, but he does want to be kept in the picture. He thrives on being told more than he says he wants, so I keep a note of the main things that happen each day. Then when I see him I can bring him up to date in what appears to be casual conversation. In return he passes on snippets of information, and these are a great help to the way I approach each situation.

A brand manager is a focal point. Not much direct authority, but an incredible amount of derived authority. I never, ever, give an order – I always ask for assistance. Everyone knows that I am backed up by the marketing director, but I know that if I overstep the mark, he will support me but put a black mark against my name. A BM is supposed to get things done, without fuss.

MARKETING PLANS

Managing all of the marketing processes and formulating a sound marketing plan are major tasks for the marketing department. The total operation is dedicated to researching, structuring and actioning a marketing plan.

McDonald makes it clear that where an organisation has a planning team – probably engaged in constructing and managing the budget – the planners have three basic functions: directive, supportive and administrative. They do not exist to write the plan – that is marketing's role. The planners' functions are to:

- *Direct*. On behalf of top management the planner has to ensure that the planning process proceeds, and proceeds to time. Line managers have much to do every day, and a plan can easily be put off because short-term problems seem to be more important.
- *Support*. Planners are more effective when they are supportive and helpful, but they need to get tough on occasion because the plan must be constructed to a deadline.
- *Administrate*. Schedules have to be followed, communications must be accurate and rapid. Records of progress must be kept. This staff management role is highly supportive of line management. As the planning cycle is virtually continuous in a large organisation the need for a strongly supportive planning team is obvious. Line management are focused on external results – they have to be encouraged, persuaded, guided and supported if they are to make effective plans.

THE PLANNING CYCLE

The planning cycle has thirteen stages.

- The mission statement provides the focus. Without that focus individual managers will find it difficult to co-ordinate.
- Corporate objectives are concerned to ensure long-term financial health. Financial dimensions determine the size and scope of the organisation. However brilliant the ideas, however wonderful the products, there must be sufficient finance to put them on the market and support them through to maturity.
- A market overview is needed so that opportunities and threats can be evaluated and planned for.
- SWOT analyses both internal and external factors in terms of strengths to be developed, weaknesses to be repaired, opportunities to be exploited and threats to be faced.
- STEEPLE factors focus analysis of the external environment.
- Portfolio analysis helps identify both strategic need and opportunity and focuses tactical actions.
- Assumptions describe the prevailing conditions under which the marketing plan is constructed.

Table 20.1 The marketing planning cycle

Stage	Planning activities	Marketing techniques & tools
1	Mission statement	Corporate objectives
		Marketing audits: markets
		customers
		competitors
2	Corporate objectives	Forecasts and budgets
3	Marketing overview	Corporate plans
		Marketing research
		Market analysis – structure/trends
4	SWOT analysis	SW – internal analysis
		OT – external analysis
5	STEEPLE analysis	Environmental analysis
6	Portfolio analysis	Product analysis
		PLC – BCG – diffusion – adoption
7	Assumptions	Planning horizons
		Risk assessment
		Scenario planning – What if?
8	Strategic marketing	Strategic focus and selection
	objectives	Ansoff risk/strategic choice
9	Marketing tactics	Four Ps
		Segmental research, ACORN, mosaic
		segmentation, targeting, positioning
10	Marketing programmes	Communication plans, sales plans,
		pricing policies, distribution plans,
		financial plans, budgets
11	Measurement of results	Budgetary control
12	Feedback and control systems	MBE, budgetary control, results
13	Review of programme	MkIS system
		Management reports, meetings
		Change, modification

Source: Adapted from an article by Professor McDonald in the *Quarterly Review of Marketing*, Summer 1990. Reproduced with permission from The Chartered Institute of Marketing.

- Marketing strategic objectives provide a direction for tactical planning.
- Marketing tactics focus on short-term programmes for each of the four Ps.
- Marketing programmes are selected mixes* for specific products and/or markets.
- Measurement is the management function of checking that plans are effective, and ensuring that adjustments are made where and when necessary.
- Feedback of results is critical throughout. It must be fast, relevant, and reach the appropriate managers in time for action to be taken.
- Review is the process of analysing programmes and results with top management, and of maintaining co-ordination within the organisation.

    At the end of each programme feedback and review should combine so that lessons are learned that will improve future performance.

*See following Section.

Mixes

'Mix' is a term used throughout marketing to describe any situation where a programme is a blend of factors from several areas. Thus the marketing mix blends the four Ps. Within the marketing mix, the promotional mix blends the promotional elements and the product mix blends the range of products on offer.

Strategy to tactics

Strategies are objectives – complete with both quantity and time criteria. They indicate the direction that should be taken, but they do not say how results should be achieved.

Tactical objectives are concerned with how to achieve strategy.

It is obviously foolish to write a strategic objective without a clear idea of the tactics needed and an awareness that they are available. Anyone can create a wonderful strategic plan – on paper. Making it work is entirely another matter!

Military strategies and tactics

The conversion of strategy to tactics can be made clear with a military example.

In the armed forces the responsibility for strategy lies with the senior commander. A typical strategic objective for a Brigadier may be:

- To take and hold the farm on the crest of Hill 190 by 07.00 hours on 29th May.

The Lieutenant-Colonel commanding the unit in the attack – the 3rd Battalion of the Parachute Regiment – is given this strategic objective to fulfil. He will decide how best to use this three Companies. He will meet with this three Company Commanders and explain his plan of attack using maps, diagrams, a model if one is available. His strategies may be:

- To take the objective by a pincer attack from the north and south.
- B Company to attack from the north.
- C Company to attack from the south.
- A Company to lay down mortar fire and then hold their position as reserve.
- Attack to commence at 03.00 and final assault to be made at 04.00.
- Attack to be completed by 07.00 hours.

The officers will work out several scenarios within this overall strategy, and say 'but what if . . .' quite often.

When the details of the Colonel's tactics are clear each Company Commander knows what has to be done. Each has a clear strategic objective.

Company Commanders meet with their junior officers and senor NCOs to determine tactics for the Company. When the best tactical plan has been devised it will be written up as a series of tactical objectives.

C Company will:

- Move out at 01.00 and take up a position 100 metres south of the main road by 01.30.
- Launch an infantry attack under cover of mortar fire at 03.00.
- Secure the western end of the farm complex by 04.00.
- Hold the western end of the complex until relieved.

Similar plans will be made in the other Companies so that the actions of all three are co-ordinated and the attack is mutually supportive.

Platoon Commanders can then be briefed on the detailed tactics required of each. In turn they will brief the men in their platoons so that every individual knows the overall objective, his Company's task, and what he has to achieve himself.

If each individual achieves his objective then each platoon will, each company will, the battalion will and the Brigadier will take the farm. He will not know the details of the tactical planning, but he must train and have confidence in the units under his command because without them he cannot succeed.

Table 20.2 Strategy-to-tactics matrix

Person responsible	Strategy – what has to be done	Tactics – how to do it
Brigadier	Take and hold the farm by 07.00	Order the Paras in.
Battalion commander	Take and hold the farm by 07.00	Deploy the Companies Attack at 03.00 Assault at 04.00
C Company Commander	Attack the western complex at 03.00 Assault, secure and hold at 04.00	Deploy platoons Detailed assignment for each
A Platoon Commander	> Attack the south western corner at 03.00 > Draw defenders fire until signalled to assault > Assault, secure and hold the central barn	Detailed assignments for each squad
Squad NCOs	Detailed assignment	Detailed assignment to each man

Marketing strategies and tactics

Marketing strategies do not have the force of military law behind them, but they carry the same degree of urgency and need for clarity. Once a marketing director has determined strategy it is for the marketing manager to take the first steps in achievement. He splits the task tactically, and then delegates. Each subsequent manager accepts a strategic decision, and applies his level of tactical thinking to it. Finally the whole strategy is broken down into a series of tactical actions each the responsibility of a designated person.

Managers devise tactics from strategic direction. Each level of management receives strategy and tactics. To avoid confusion, remember to indicate the type of objective – 'The marketing strategic objective is to . . .. The promotional tactical objectives are . . .'.

Conversion of marketing strategy to tactics results in the creation of detailed and workable marketing plans. Tactical decisions allocate priorities, time schedules, personnel roles and responsibilities, pricing, promotion, stock levels and so on. Tactical management must be flexible to meet the changing situations in the market, but must remain within the agreed and defined strategies. Unless there is a clear determination to achieve the strategic objectives, the tactics will lose focus and become less effective.

THE MARKETING PLAN

A marketing plan is a major document that is fundamental to marketing success. A typical marketing plan has the following sections.

1 *Executive summary*. A brief overview of the proposed plan. This contains the key issues so that senior managers can gain a fast appreciation of the plan's intentions.
2 *Opportunity and issue analysis*. Identification of the main opportunities and threats, strengths and weaknesses, and issues facing the organisation. These must tie back to the corporate objectives, which may be briefly included for reference if necessary.
3 *Current marketing situation*. Relevant background information will assess the market, product(s), competition, distribution and macro-environment.
4 *Marketing objectives*. The marketing goals are selected and the plan is then to achieve these in the areas of sales volume, market share and profit targets, or whatever is decided.
5 *Marketing strategy*. The broad marketing approach to be used to meet the plan's objectives – always feature segmentation, positioning and targeting.
6 *Action programmes*. What will be done? Who will do it? When will it be done? Resources to be used? How much will it cost?
7 *Projected marketing budget*. How much will it all cost? What will be the return in terms of sales volume and/or revenue. The projected cash flow, trading account and balance sheet are part of the corporate plan.
8 *Controls*. Indicate how the plan will be scheduled, monitored and evaluated.

There is no set form because each marketing plan must meet the needs and policies of the organisation at a moment in time. The views of eminent academics are included at the end of this module.

Operational plans

Tactical achievement has to be planned at operational level. The marketing toolbox is an excellent basis for an operational plan:

1 *Research.*   An outline of the key facts, including audits, SWOT, STEEPLE, secondary and primary research, as needed.

2 *Planning.*   Strategic objectives at tactical level, i.e. an overview of the way in which the research has been interpreted and the action it precipitates.
To include quantified objectives.

3 *Product.*   Product related features to include formula/recipe, volume sales, market share, segmentation, etc.

4 *Place.*   Channels of distribution, distributive methods, etc.

5 *Price.*   Recommended price to channel members, discounts, deals, etc.

6 *Promotion.*   Promotional plan, to include each element of the promotional mix.

7 *Evaluation.*   Plans for evaluating achievement against objectives.

NB: This element is often easier written within each of the five action sections above. It must *never* be omitted.

Tactical planning formats

As the planning process becomes more concerned with day-to-day issues, so each plan requires to be more detailed. There is less need to know corporate and marketing strategy, because tactical managers are guided by product, pricing, place and promotional strategies. These come, of course, from the marketing strategies.

The principal operational plans are covered within the appropriate modules.

ACADEMICS' VIEWS ON THE MARKETING PLAN

Kotler

Kotler gives the contents of a full marketing plan (for a single product) as:

1 *Executive summary.*   A brief overview of the proposed plan for management to skim.

2 *Current marketing situation.*   Relevant background data on the market, product, competition, distribution, and macro-environment.

3 *Opportunity and issue analysis.*   Identification of the main opportunities/threats, strengths/weaknesses, and issues facing the product/organisation.

4 *Objectives.*   The goals the plan wants to reach in the areas of sales volume, market share and profit.

5 *Marketing strategy.*   The broad marketing approach that will be used to meet the plan's objectives.

6 *Action programmes.*   *What* will be done? *Who* will do it? *When* will it be done? *How much* will it cost?

7 *Projected P&L statement.*	Forecasts the expected financial outcomes from the plan.
8 *Controls.*	Indicates how the plan will be monitored (evaluated).

Mercer

Mercer agrees with Kotler's approach, but shortens the process to:

1 *Executive summary.*	A short summary of the proposed plan, partly to provide perspective and partly as a quick reference.
2 *Marketing audit summary.*	A very brief summary of the detailed audits that will have taken place.
3 *Audit (SWOT) analysis.*	Again brief and concentrating on the few critical issues.
4 *Marketing objectives.*	In as much detail as is needed.
5 *Marketing strategy.*	Again, in as much detail as is needed.
6 *Action programmes.*	*What* will be done? *Who* will do it? *When* will it be done? *How much* will it cost?

McDonald

McDonald suggests a more specific layout, with a clear distinction between a three-year strategic plan and a one-year operational plan.

Baker

Baker says that it is not meaningful to distinguish between strategic and non-strategic plans. A plan is no more and no less than 'the way it is intended to carry out some proceeding'. If the proceeding is strategic, then so is the plan. He quotes Goddard as saying that 'the Kernel of a strategic plan is the rule that it chooses to break, the orthodoxy that the firm is choosing to challenge . . . There has to be a jump of imagination . . . Without such a jump a plan is a fraud (because) a strategy cannot be fully rationalised. It has to be an act of faith. . . . a theory can be proved by experiment but no path leads from experiment to theory.'

KEY POINT SUMMARY

- Marketing plans convert corporate objectives to marketing objectives.
- The acronym MOST is a helpful aid to remembering the key stages: Mission; Objectives; Strategies; Tactics.
- Jane Smith realised that she needed to plan her career path, and to make it possible for her bosses to promote her.
- Don't work out complex numbers if there is a specialist department available.

- Stage manage presentations and proposals.
- Factory visits are a major opportunity to meet people.
- Contacts and trust are vitally important to a junior manager.
- Complaints are 'genuine' to the complainant.
- Quality control is always important. To a global company it is vital.
- Training others keeps one on top of the job.
- Meeting customers is essential for marketers.
- R & D is essential to keep ahead.
- Marketing research is on-going.
- Exhibitions are exciting – but demand careful planning over a long period.
- A brand manager is a focal point.
- Marketing plans are written by the marketers – often with help from corporate planners.
- The planning cycle has 13 stages, and each must be completed thoroughly.
- Mixes are a blend of factors from several areas.
- Strategies break down into tactics.
- If all the tactics are achieved, then strategies are automatically achieved also.
- Marketing plans have no agreed structure. They should follow general guidelines, but be constructed to meet the needs of a particular organisation at a moment in time.

WORK-BASED SELF-ASSESSMENT QUESTIONS

1 Explain how the marketer contributes to corporate success through effective use of the marketing plan.

2 Illustrate the main differences between strategic, tactical and contingency planning.

SCHOOL- OR COLLEGE-BASED SELF-ASSESSMENT QUESTIONS

1 Explain how a school or college management can use the MOST acronym to guide their marketing.

2 Prepare a strategy to tactics matrix (Table 20.2) for an activity you are associated with. A sports event, perhaps, or a student's union function.

See the end of Chapter 22 for answer guidelines.

CHAPTER 21

Marketing mix strategy

Nasser Houssain was excited at the prospect of taking on more responsibility. He couldn't read Jane's mind, but for her to suddenly open opportunities for him must surely mean that she was either due to take on a wider role, or perhaps to move out of her job altogether! Either way he now had access to Jane's contacts and he intended to maximise the benefits.

HG tea was the second largest brand in the UK. It was very well established, and was holding volume even through the overall tea market was declining. HG tea bags were the third largest sellers by volume, and showing a slight but steady sales increase year on year.

The catering trade was specially provided for with bulk packs of HG tea and tea bags on a string for hotel rooms and Continental style cafes. The HG brand was only for high quality products and so a lower quality tea was sold under the LQ brand into the catering trade. This was available only in bulk. GloFoods packed 'own label' teas and tea bags for two major supermarket chains in the UK.

HG teas were exported to most of the old British Commonwealth countries, and the tea bags were enjoying healthy and increasing sales throughout the EU.

Alongside the range of teas was an impressive range of coffees. HG coffee was supplemented by HG Continental and HG Decaffeinated. Instant coffees with the same branding sold alongside the ground coffees. Bulk packs were sold to hotels and restaurants, and sachets of instant coffee were specially packed for hotels.

To complete the service to hotels Nasser Houssain discovered that his firm supplied sugar and sweetener sachets, individual packs of UHT milk, packets of biscuits and wrapped slices of fruit cake. The catering trade was so important that it justified a brand manager and two assistants, who concentrated on devising special packs of GloFood products already available elsewhere. It was the catering BM that introduced the idea for tea bags on a string which were now selling throughout the EU.

Nasser understood that his job was to sell tea through retailers. He was doing that very well. But he couldn't see how the whole effort was co-ordinated. Why were there no clashes of style in promotion? No variations in package design? How could the same name be used in different markets?

When he widened his mind to the whole of GloFoods range it all became too much to cope with. He decided to concentrate on his own part of the business.

Jane had a training file – he would borrow that and see if he could research some answers for himself.

He discovered that products can be fitted into a simple matrix to show the width and the depth of what an organisation offers. He was quickly able to start a GloFoods matrix (Figure 21.1).

Product line width			
Teas	Coffees	Catering	Etc.

	Teas	Coffees	Catering	Etc.
Product line depth	HG leaf	HG ground	HG tea bulk	
	HG bags	HG continental	HG tea bags on string	
	HG bag on string	HG decaffeinated	LQ tea	
	LQ catering tea	HG instant	HG coffees in bulk	
	Own label tea	HG instant continental	Coffee sachets	
	Own label tea bag	HG instant decaffeinated	UHT milk Sugar sachets	

Fig. 21.1 GloFoods matrix

Yes, he could see the principle. When there was a successful brand it could be extended in width, by adding a product of similar quality alongside. So HG coffee naturally followed HG tea. Caterers and their customers would know the HG brand so both HG tea and HG coffee could extend from the retail to the catering market.

A product or brand could also extend in depth. HG leaf tea was the base from which tea bags and bags on a string had come. Tea as a product had depth potential as well. Caterers did not need nor want to pay for a premier brand and so LQ tea was developed specially for them. GloFoods's tea buying, blending, packaging, etc., skills were in place – but a lower quality could not be marketed as HG. Once the LQ brand is firmly established it could extend to coffees and other GloFoods products and markets. Extension by width and by depth was a policy of continual expansion from a position of strength.

Obviously there were limits to how far one could extend – that would help explain why GloFoods concentrated on non-alcoholic food and drinks. There had to be consistency in what they did, in what they offered.

Yes, within a *policy of consistency* it was possible to manage a product range that had *depth* – several products competing in the same market – and *width* – similar products competing in different markets.

Nasser Houssain then came across a diagram that really clarified the situation for him (Figure 21.2).

Global Foods were divided into a number of SBUs, each based on a product type. This provided both for consistency and for concentration of effort around specialised skills. Within each SBU the product types were broken down into a width and depth of offer mixes to meed the needs of identified target customer groups.

Pricing policy had to be applied across the whole of GloFoods operations because the brand offerings had to have synergy in the marketplace. Consumers had to be able to trust each GloFoods brand to be of a certain quality, and

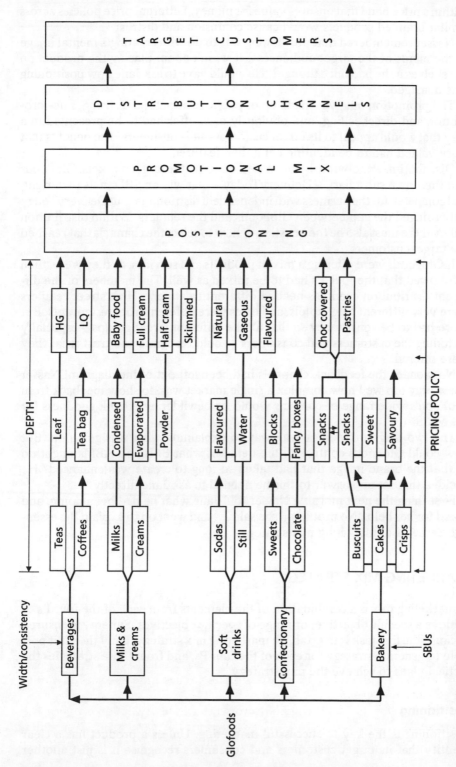

Fig. 21.2 Marketing mix strategy

within a price band that ensures value for money. Different price policies across similar branded products would cause confusion and distrust.

Nasser remembered that positioning was to do with creating a mental image in the minds of the target audiences – it wasn't about placing the product on the shelves as he had once thought! He would have to ask Jane how positioning was managed.

The promotion mix was made up of public relations, advertising, sales promotion and direct selling, and obviously each offer had to be presented in a way that would appeal to its target customers and consumers. The benefits that were valued had to be identified and then featured.

Distribution was obviously the route through to the target markets. GloFoods had their own subsidiary – DeliveryToday – that was an SBU in its own right, and competed for the business with independent distributors. But DeliveryToday only bridged the gap between GloFoods and the retailers. Within distribution policy there must also be the question of how to select the channels that reached the target customers.

If GloFoods were offering a mix of products and services, as they were, then it followed that the four Ps had to be mixed as well. The members of the different distribution channels needed different treatment. High street retailers were very different from hotels, and cafes were different from restaurants. But there had to be consistency so that all the different target groups – especially including the customers and consumers – could recognise and trust what they were offered.

No wonder the feedback channels had been left out of the diagram! Nasser knew only too well how complex a single market was, to show feedback from GloFood's wide range of contacts would be bewildering. Thank goodness for the MkIS!

The two diagrams went a long way to explaining what was going on. But how could GloFoods control all the detail of what BMs and ABMs might do so that the brand image that had taken so long to create was enhanced? He decided that for an answer to this he needed to ask Jane directly.

First thing the next morning Nasser told Jane what he had been doing, and asked for her help. 'No problem,' she said . . . and went on to explain the essential elements of marketing mix strategy.

MARKETING MIX STRATEGY

A marketing mix is a combination of the elements from each of the four Ps to achieve a specific objective, or range of specific objectives. Synergy is ensured because the first task is to establish marketing mix strategy. Only then is it possible to generate strategy for each of the four Ps, and from those strategies the tactical plans to achieve the mix strategy.

Positioning

Positioning is the key to successful marketing. Unless a product has a clear identity that its target customers and consumers recognise it is just another

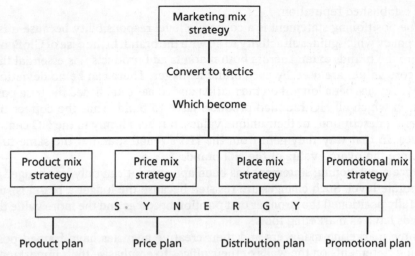

Fig. 21.3 Marketing mix strategy to tactics

product. One of many.

Positioning depends upon clarity of thought, which is tightly focused to produce an exact description of the central core values of the product. It is expressed in a positioning statement.

Positioning statements

These are established at corporate level. They are statements that clearly and unambiguously define the central concept of the product. They focus tightly upon the core values which make the product what it is:

HG Tea is a blend of the finest Indian teas and provides a refreshing drink at any time of the day. HG Tea is the only tea that every generation since 1875 has trusted to provide the perfect cup of tea. Whether in leaf or tea bag, HG tea quality is second to none.

This statement brings together HG tea's core values:

- Finest   quality is implied, and linked to Indian.
- Indian   believed in the UK to be home of the finest tea.
- Refreshing not simply thirst quenching.
- Any time   no limits on time of use.
- Uniqueness the only tea trusted by every generation.
- Reputation established in the UK since 1875.
- Quality   HG equals quality.

These core values guide everything the brand manager does. Product, pricing, packaging, distribution and promotion must all be guided by the positioning statement. The HG brand could never, for instance, be extended to a lower quality product. A rival tea – PG Tips – use chimpanzees to promote their tea. Such a down-market association would never do for the HG brand! The HG approach is more dignified, as is warranted by its high quality image, and established reputation.

The positioning statement is a corporate level responsibility because it is a key policy which guides all activity to do with the brand. In the case of GloFoods where the brands extend across both markets and products it is essential that the core values are used by each brand manager. There can be no deviation!

HG Tea has been longest on the market and so has established the base position on which all HG branded products have to build. Thus the coffees use different descriptions of their unique values, but hold firmly to the HG central values. In that way they gain from the HG strengths, and at the same time enhance the overall value of the HG brand.

Once a positioning statement has been approved it can only be changed at corporate level. Such changes are resisted because the longer a brand is successfully positioned the stronger that position becomes and the more value the brands have as marketing tools.

Some marketing managers and their creative agencies have framed positioning statements on the walls of their offices to emphasise their importance. Key meetings commence with the positioning statement being read aloud to reinforce its importance and to provide a focus for the meeting.

If a product is well positioned it has shared meaning within its target market. If 'She watches the *News at Ten* but he prefers *PM*' has any meaning it can only be because *News at Ten* is known to be the ITV main evening news broadcast, whilst *PM* is known to be the 5 pm news hour on BBC Radio. Both are branded, both are positioned, and an understanding of their core values is shared by their viewers and listeners.

Note: News at Ten came under threat in 1992 and again in 1993, but survived. It was felt by some programme planners that there was greater audience potential if evening programmes were not broken up by a news broadcast at peak time. They argued that the value of running a film continuously rather than in two parts with a 40 minute break was higher than holding the ten o'clock slot for the news. It could run earlier, they argued, before people settled down for an evening of entertainment. The planners lost the argument on both occasions. *News at Ten*, it was felt, was too strongly positioned to be moved.

Repositioning is always occurring, of course. We saw in Chapter 13 how Qualcast repositioned their product – but it took time, cost a considerable amount and was only done to outflank a strong competitor who had secured its own market position.

How to write a good positioning statement

David Boll sets out the stages:

1 Start by looking at the position in the market you want to occupy in relation to competition.
2 Think about how your brand will answer the main consumer questions:
— What will it do for me that others won't?
— Why should I believe you?

3 Use the best people to work on the statement.

4 Let individuals draft their own versions; discuss and modify the alternatives to clarify everyone's thoughts, then pick the best one.

5 Keep it short. Make every word count and be as specific as possible. Vagueness opens the way to confused executions.

6 Search for ways of making it competitive. Try to find some way to use the word 'only'.

7 Indicate clearly the weight of each element.

8 If emotional values, e.g. social conscience, mother care, are important to a brand they should influence the way the statement is written.

9 Encourage the contribution of the technical people where possible.

10 Get wholehearted commitment at all levels in the organisation. Don't be afraid to talk it through; the best statements come after very hard discussion.

11 Don't publish it (internally) until you are reasonably confident you have it right, and are prepared to defend it. Then listen to the comments, and your defence, and adjust as necessary.

12 Keep it up to date. Give as careful consideration to change as you did to the drafting of the original . . . ensure any change is proved to be needed.

BRANDING IN THE MARKETPLACE

As we saw in Chapter 18, branding provides a product or a service with an identity which allows it to be recognised. The tangible aspect of the brand can be a name, a logo or an associated image, but it must be consistent. The intangible aspects are within the perception of the customer and consumer. Unless the product delivers what is promised, no tangible branding features have value. Indeed they may acquire a negative value: 'Don't buy that product, it's awful!'.

Brand identity is critically important, and brand names and brand positioning are of vital significance. The brand must reflect the attributes of the product, and is integral to all communication.

Naming

A named product is not necessarily a branded product – although branded products are named. Much care has to be taken in the naming of products, especially as once committed to a name it is very expensive in time and resources to make a change. It is also likely to cost market share through the loss of recognition from existing customers.

Very many of the more attractive and appropriate names have long since either been used, or registered for later use. Registration of names is essential, and must be carried through in each country where there is even a remote chance that the product will one day need to be sold. If a name is registered by a local firm it can be most expensive to buy it when you suddenly discover that you are prohibited from using your product's name in their country!

Most organisations do not have anyone on the staff with the necessary world-wide experience to ensure that names are properly selected, and correctly registered. It makes sense to use a specialist naming agency.

Product names must:

- *Carry a message.* They will say something about the product because every name carries a subconscious message – it is necessary, therefore, to ensure that it says something good! Something, of course, which matches the positioning. It is silly when it either translates badly – the Vauxhall Nova translates in Spanish as Vauxhall no go! – or when the letters of the name spell a rude word in another language.
- *Be memorable and distinctive.* The distinctiveness will help the memorability of the name. You do not want the customer to be convinced by your promotion, but then to buy the wrong product because he couldn't remember the name! Cross-your-heart bras are very memorable because they always deliver the name with a crossing motion to supplement it visually . . . and they carry the cross through to the packaging and PoS.
- *Be easy to pronounce.* A name doesn't have to logical, nor grammatically correct. Qantas has no u, although it should have. Toys 'Я Us has the R backwards. Both are easy to pronounce, both work well in different languages, and both are memorable.
- *Should suggest what the product does.* Some such as Mr Clean manage it directly, but for most it is a question of long-term association. Butterkist is popcorn to most people, Odeon is a cinema.

Positioning and location

There is a very close tie between positioning and location. An exclusive brand should not be sold through mass market channels. The major perfume houses fought a battle with the Monopolies and Mergers Commission in 1993 to prevent their exclusive brands being sold through Superdrug, a discount high street drug store.

Synergy and added value

Branding is a focus to allow all elements of the marketing mix to combine to exceed the total of the individual contributions. Branding thus adds value to a package. (*See below*).

Consistency in performance

Consumers are now educated to expect a consistency of performance. This means that if they have an Acme toaster, and are satisfied with it, they are more likely to buy an Acme fridge, and then an Acme kettle, and so on. The repeat purchase behaviour, from which come marketing profits, has widened to *brand* repeat rather than *product* repeat. Any Acme product added to the range has to match the quality of those already on offer. If it doesn't there are two alternatives:

- Market it under a premier name, e.g. Acme Elite, if it is markedly superior in performance.
- Market it under a secondary name if it is below standard.

The first alternative extends the Acme brand upwards and could be beneficial. The second alternative would require a different brand.

A consumer must not encounter a disappointing product under a trusted brand, and so a secondary brand makes sense. Equally one must be sure that those consumers who enter the branded range via the superior product are not disappointed when they buy a second product. Thus differentiation within a brand is sometimes necessary.

A branded product is expected to work, and work well, for the normal lifetime of the product. If appropriate, an efficient and effective system of after-sales care must be in place. It is well known that a consumer who complains and is well treated is more likely to become even more loyal, and to tell others.

HELIX – The first truly EU branded product

Shell are the first company to introduce a product designed to be marketed across the whole of the EU under one brand. 'Helix' is an oil the specification for which has been agreed by all car manufacturers, and will not vary by country. There are minor variations in price, which are dictated in part by duty and taxes; in packaging, because the UK cannot fill the same shape of bottle that the other countries are equipped for; and in promotion where a corporate positioning statement can be supplemented (but not changed) to meet cultural need.

ADDED VALUE

High disposable incomes have opened the way for a wide variety of choice. Consumers use value as an aid to selection.

Value can be added to product offerings in many ways . . . simply bringing a commodity such as potatoes, from the fields into the village added a value for which the villagers were willing to pay. Thus potatoes in the field might be five pence a pound; in the village they could sell for sixpence. The potatoes are the same, it is the added value of not having to go out to the fields that justifies the extra penny a pound. It is from this basic understanding that the modern concept of value added has developed.

Given that customers and consumers are willing to pay for value, organisations need to consider what values they are adding, and what values they could and should be adding. Value is within the perception of the customer and consumer and only within the control of the organisation in so far as it matches market need. It follows that detailed marketing research is required to discover which attributes are considered to have value.

Even commodities can have value added:

- Salt – the most basic of commodities – can have value added by purification, fine grading and specialised packaging, e.g.

- Bulk packs of easy pour design to facilitate the filling of salt shakers.
- Ready-to-use and disposable packs for the table:
  - attractive packages for the home;
  - printed with a caterer's logo and promotional message.
- Insertion packs for potato crisp manufacturers, and for airline catering, etc.
- In tablet form to replace salt loss in hot countries.
- Petrol has value added partly by the brand, but mostly through created differential, e.g.
  - additives to help engines run cleaner and smoother;
  - support services.
- Filling stations are becoming one-stop shopping areas. Originally these shopping services offered only motoring and travel essentials, but they are now extending to the provision of groceries, books, cassettes, video hire, etc.

Note that whilst these added value services are designed to enhance the value of the service stations, and therefore to sell more petrol, there is a danger that they may overtake the petrol sales in terms of profitability and energy suppliers could find themselves turning into general retailers. Certainly to properly develop these added value services it has been necessary to engage specialist managers from retail as opposed to energy.

Value may be added in many ways. The key is to understand what customers and consumers will consider to be of value to them – what they will pay a premium for, or what will induce them to purchase your product in place of a functionally equivalent alternative.

THE PROFIT IMPACT OF MARKET STRATEGY (PIMS)

Profits are the measure of success for any commercial organisation, but it is difficult to determine which strategies are the most likely to return an acceptable level of profit. It is possible, of course, to be wise in hindsight – but never to know whether a different choice of strategy would have had better results.

In an attempt to produce hard evidence of success factors the PIMS project was established in the United States in 1972. Harvard Business School faculty members and research assistants worked alongside planning specialists from industry to investigate four major areas of strategic planning:

- *Forecasting profits*. Often forecasts are simply projections of local experience. But when market conditions are expected to change, or when a change in strategy is contemplated, how reliable is the past as a guide to the future?
- *Allocating resources*. Often resource requests from divisions add up to more than can be provided. The problem then, is one of emphasis: which products and markets promise the greatest returns?
- *Measuring management performance*. Corporate management would like some way of determining what level of profit is reasonable or 'normal' for different operating units under given circumstances.
- *Appraising new business proposals*. When considering a prospective new

business development, or acquisition, corporate management would like some method of estimating return on investment (ROI).

The common thread running through the above types of corporate strategic planning situations is the need for some means of estimating ROI in a given business, under given industry and market conditions, following a given strategy.

Initially data was supplied on 350 businesses by 36 corporations. In 1980 data came from 800 businesses owned by 100 corporations. In 1990 the database had grown to over 2800 businesses.

The aim of the PIMS programme is to identify the most significant profit factors, and to provide guidelines for successful strategic management. The main findings are:

1 Profitability is influenced strongly by:
   — competitive position   relative market share;
                                        relative profitability;
   — capital structure   intensity of investment;
   — production process structure   vertical integration;
   — company characteristics   corporate size;
                                        corporate diversity;
   — market environment   customer concentration;
                                        stage in life cycle.
2 When pre-testing a specific business plan never assume that your forecasts are correct. The technology of profit and cash forecasting is too weak to overcome human error. A database that is based on experience is neither emotional nor political.
3 Strategic guide rules for growth businesses:
   — Go for market position early.
   — Push capacity ahead of market.
   — Translate product leadership into market share.
   — Develop a comparative advantage early.
   — Avoid premature vertical integration.
   — Use working capital as an instrument of market strategy.
   — Get the right people, and enough of them, almost regardless of pay.
4 Strategic guide rules for mature businesses:
   — Go for profitability rather than market position.
   — Keep capacity as low as possible.
   — Translate product leadership into profit margin.
   — Differentiate the product and segment the market.
   — Minimise the risk of corporate disaster.
   — Keep investment intensity down.
   — Use modern equipment and methods.
   — Seek comparative advantage in variable costs.
   — Push marketing effort – even if apparently expensive.

PIMS reports are specific . . . 'The average ROI for businesses with under 10% market share was about 9% . . . on average a difference of 10% in market share is accompanied by a difference of about 5% in pretax ROI.'

Significance to marketing

PIMS reports deal with *market* and not *marketing* strategies and so are of key importance at corporate level. Only a marketing oriented organisation would be able to put them to effective use, however, and so the marketing director would be a main user of the data. It would, in fact, have a major impact on the marketing planning process within the corporate planning process that leads to the budget.

BLENDING THE MIX

The marketing mix is a strategic choice from options that are available to the organisation. It is blended from the constituent parts that make up the mix. We have used the four Ps as a useful shorthand to describe the mix, but we must now extend each of the Ps into reasonable detail. Full detail is only needed at tactical level, as we shall see.

Management tools

The strategic options can only be accessed and controlled with the appropriate tools. The key tools that apply across the whole mix are:

- *Marketing research.* In all its forms marketing research is a fundamental tool that no marketing manager can ever ignore. The width of research extends from the discovery of new product concepts to the evaluation of promotional success.

  Often marketing research will extend across the whole mix – as in test marketing, where the marketer is concerned with every aspect of the test. It is wrong to assume that research can test individual elements in isolation. The elements are so interrelated that it is necessary to monitor those not being formally researched to be sure that any unexpected changes that impact on the research are noted and taken into account.
- *MkIS.* The MkIS carries the information to appropriate managers in time for any necessary action. It is used throughout marketing on a regular and routine basis.
- *Market segmentation.* Segmentation is of such fundamental importance that it cannot be included under any one of the four Ps. Segmentation decisions are concerned with the actions needed to achieve desired behaviour. The two most important may seem to be product and promotion – but what good are they if the price is wrong and/or distribution is ineffective?
- *Portfolio and directional policy planning (including the PLC).* Again, this management tool must be concerned with the totality of the effort. It cannot be classified within any one of the four Ps.
- *Risk assessment and decisions.* All actions carry some degree of risk. It is necessary to evaluate the degree of risk in each of a range of options, and then to take clear, unambiguous, firm decisions that are practical, appropriate and which lead to action.

Product strategy

The major elements that allow product strategy to be formed are:

Chapter

- Product offering:
  - — innovation/invention of new;
  - — modification of existing;   23
  - — retention of existing;
  - — strengthening of existing.
- Image:
  - — naming;   21
  - — branding;   18, 21
  - — packaging.   28
- Product mix:
  - — consistency;
  - — width;   21
  - — depth.

Price strategy

The major elements that allow product strategy to be formed are:
- demand and supply;
- costs and volume;   29
- revenue and profit.

Place strategy

The major elements that allow place strategy to be formed are:
- push, pull or push/pull need;
- availability of channels;
- access to channels;   25
- channel logistics;
- integration.

Promotion strategy

The major elements that allow promotion strategy to be formed are:

- management:
  - — behavioural insight;   30
  - — communication skills.   19

The major tools are:

- public relations;
- advertising;   30
- sales promotion;
- direct selling.

Budgeting and evaluation   31

KEY POINT SUMMARY

- Brands can be extended in width and/or in depth.
- Consistency is essential.
- Effort should be concentrated.
- Extension should be from strength.
- The promotion mix is made up of public relations, advertising, sales promotion and direct selling.
- Positioning is the key to successful marketing.
- Core values guide a brand manager's tactics.
- Positioning statements are essential and are approved at board level.
- Positioning statements should be changed – but only after the most careful consideration.
- A named product is not necessarily branded.
- Naming is an applied skill.
- Names should be suitable, translate well, and be registered in every country where they may be needed.
- Product names should: carry a message; be memorable and distinctive; be easy to pronounce.
- Synergy and added value are focused by banding.
- Repeat purchase behaviour is beginning to be repeat brand purchase.
- Helix is the first truly EU branded product.
- Added value can be added in many ways.
- The PIMS studies show the crucial areas to be: competitive position; structure; size and diversity; customer concentration and life cycle stage.
- PIMS suggests that an organisation should: go for growth early; avoid premature vertical integration; use working capital effectively; hire good people.
- The major management tools are: marketing research; MkIS; market segmentation; portfolio management; risk assessment and decisions.
- Strategies are needed for each of the four Ps.

WORK-BASED SELF-ASSESSMENT QUESTIONS.

Consider how value may be added to:

1 A localised network of bus services.

2 The five local stations of a rail service to a city centre.

SCHOOL- OR COLLEGE-BASED SELF-ASSESSMENT ASSIGNMENT

Take a walk around a supermarket, down a high street, or go carefully through a day's supply of newspapers. Note five brands with different market targets and analyse for each:

- how long it has been a brand;
- how long you have been conscious of it as a brand;

- how long you have been conscious of the product it brands;
- whether it has been extended . . . if so to where . . . with what degree of success?
- whether it can be extended . . . if so to where?
- where it should not be extended . . . and why?

See the end of Chapter 22 for answer guidelines.

CHAPTER 22

Blending the mix

Jane Smith was delighted with the dedication that Nasser Houssain was showing. Obviously he was as ambitious as she had thought – and every bit as good as she had hoped. Her concern now was – had she left it too late?

She was helping Nasser to improve so that she could apply for promotion in the knowledge that she had a replacement ready to take over from her. It occurred to her that perhaps she had misjudged the situation. She was a senior brand manager with responsibility for a flagship brand. Nasser Houssain was good, but inexperienced. He could never move straight into a senior brand manager's post. What had she been thinking of!

In a somewhat pensive mood Jane arrived early at her desk and was deeply immersed in drafting proposals for a summer iced tea promotion when her telephone rang. It was the marketing manager's secretary. 'Mr McIlvoy would like to see you in his office at ten o'clock.'

Jane had an hour to ponder why she was being summoned to the marketing manager – she reviewed everything she had done recently – there was surely nothing to warrant a reprimand from the big boss! No – he must want an update before an important meeting, or perhaps he was flying off somewhere and needed to be briefed on the current market situation. Jane busied herself putting together a file of key information that she might need.

At ten minutes to ten she was freshening up and five minutes before 10.00 was in the 5th floor corridor, with its teak panelling, deep pile carpet and general air of quality and exclusivity.

Mr McIlvoy saw her punctually at ten, and immediately destroyed her carefully made plans. 'I don't want to talk about HG Tea,' he said. 'Let's talk about you.'

'You have been with us for five years, and have been very successful in the field. You came into Head Office and have made an extremely good impression. You are seen as good at your job, helpful, decisive and friendly. Congratulations. Have you considered how your career might progress from here?'

Jane had, of course. She was planning to return to the field as a sales trainer ... but she thought it better not to reveal her hand. Something was happening, and she would do better to stay neutral for a time. Let the boss carry the ball for a few yards.

'Obviously I want to progress,' she said. 'But I'm very happy where I am. Running HG Tea is a prestige post and I'd not want to move unless a really challenging opportunity were available.'

Mr McIlvoy smiled. 'Tell me about your assistant. Nasser Houssain, isn't it?'

'Nasser is a very bright person, Mr McIlvoy. He clearly sees that he needs to learn, and is not afraid to ask questions. As importantly, he learns from experience and it is rare to find him making the same error twice. Just at the moment he is working to gain an understanding of strategic marketing – he's already pretty good at the tactical level. I certainly trust him to make tactical decisions, and he works well with the agency people. He's a hard worker – never watches the clock, and seems to get things done without fuss.

'On the down side, he tends to worry that he will make mistakes, and is a little too anxious to receive praise for what he has done. Both, I believe, are temporary phases that he will get over with a little more experience.'

Jane paused, and took breath. Now was the time to jump in with both feet, to voluntarily put her reputation on the line.

'I think he is now ready for promotion,' she said. 'He is ready to take responsibility, and I believe that responsibility will be the making of him.'

The marketing manager leaned back in his chair and contemplated Jane. She fought to keep calm – at least to show a calm exterior. Then he leaned forward, and smiled warmly.

'OK. Jane, let's get down to brass tacks. I've said that we are very pleased with you. Your appraisals have been excellent. Your draft plans reach me with only minor modifications by your immediate boss. You are ready to move on.'

'As you will know, each year GloFoods run a strategic management course in association with INSEAD, Fontainebleau, the European business school near Paris. This year the UK have been given one place . . . and we want you to take it. It will mean three months intensive work. You will travel this weekend. The course starts on Monday. What do you say?'

What should she say? What could she say? She stumbled . . .

'But what about HG Tea?'

'Don't worry. We are having a bit of a reorganisation in the marketing team. You'll hear about it in detail when everything is in place, but I am moving Bill from Coffee to take over from you – and I think Nasser will do rather well as brand manager for canned milks. What do you think?'

'That sounds good to me,' replied Jane. 'But where do I go when I return from INSEAD?' Oh, gosh! That might be a slip! She had accepted without a second's thought!

'Don't worry about that, Jane. We are not going to waste your talent – nor a valuable place at INSEAD. When you finish your course you will probably stay on in Paris for a further three months. You'll be in our European Marketing Department, probably helping to develop HG Tea across Europe. After that . . . well the world's a pretty small place these days. There will be a worthwhile place for you.

'I don't want to talk about this move until it is made official tomorrow because I have to see several other people and it is right that they hear about changes from me. In the meantime why not take Nasser on one side and complete his education. You can't begin to hand over to Bill until the moves are confirmed, and I don't want you to progress anything unless it is genuinely urgent. I don't think you've anything that can't wait a day?'

Jane hadn't anything that couldn't wait. Suddenly her perspective on the world changed. HG Tea was still important, but in half-an-hour had been downgraded from a central present focus to important past history. She decided that the best thing was to do as had been suggested. She would take Nasser Houssain to lunch, and then spend the afternoon showing him how marketing tactics were derived from strategy. She only hoped that she would be able to concentrate!

BLENDING THE MIX

To recap:

- Marketing strategy determines the broad overall direction as a guide to tactical decision making.
- Marketing mix strategy determines the contribution of each element in the mix – how they blend together to achieve marketing strategy.
- Marketing tactics can only be planned once strategy is determined because each tool in each part of the mix has a specific purpose and must be selected with care.

Blending the tools to optimise the return from product offerings requires timing and market intelligence. The mix of tools will vary with the needs of the product and market. Every product is, of course, different, but as a general principle the likely stages and their associated activities can be analysed against the background of the product life cycle concept.

Introductory stage

New product development costs will have been incurred against the expectation that long-term profits will be made. On launch the new product will require an appropriate blend of public relations, heavy advertising, trade and sales promotion, introductory pricing and dedicated personal selling. There must be commitment to see the product through the launch and growth stages.

There is high potential for product failure if:

- The mix elements are poorly blended.
- Insufficient commitment is given to the product.
- Sales forecasting is too pessimistic and stocks run out.

Competitors may:

- wait and monitor the launch:
  — being second in the market, a 'follower', can be a good, low cost/low risk strategy;
- Attack aggressively:
  — to deny access to the market;
  — to secure a share of the market.

Customers may:

- Restrict distribution
  — Trade customers may resist stocking until consumer demand has been

generated. This may lead to consumer disappointment, and destroy the effects of otherwise excellent promotion.
- Wait for a modified/improved version:
  — computer software is notorious for having 'bugs' in new versions, even after extensive testing of 'beta' versions in the development phase;
- wait for price reduction:
  — New models often are highly priced to 'skim' the market. Then they fall to a more generally affordable level.
  — Wait until they see the product in use, and are confident of its value.

Management may:

- take profits out of revenue and deny the financial support needed;
- lose confidence and either/or;
  — pull back on funding – which cripples the product;
  — withdraw the product – and cut their losses.

Growth stage

The product will be acquiring volume and market share. Strong advertising and sales promotion will be needed, with the emphasis beginning to shift towards encouragement of repeat purchase as well as driving to acquire new consumers. Sales pressure must be maintained to ensure that increased stocks are in the channel of distribution ahead of consumer need. Prices are likely to begin to fall as focus switches to obtaining sales from early adopters rather than innovators.

There is potential for product failure if:

- the mix elements are not changed to accommodate the new needs;
- management withdraw support too soon;
- competitors are extremely aggressive.

Competitors may:

- enter the market; this may:
  — speed up the growth of the market overall because of the extra promotional activity;
  — force undesired tactics, e.g. price cuts earlier than had been planned;
- introduce a superior product:
  — and force an early launch of version II;
  — or kill the product.

Customers may develop positively:

- open wider distribution channels as confidence in demand grows;
- become regular users;
- recommend the product by word of mouth.

Or negatively:

- abandon the product as novelty wear off;
- forget the product as promotion is reduced.

Management may:

- Withdraw support before maximum market share has been obtained, thus restricting the product long-term.
- Continue funding for growth past the maximum market share point, thus making a short-term loss, but consolidating a solid base for a long-term market presence.

Maturity stage

The product will be established in the market, with a share likely to remain stable, because there will be entrenched competitors who will protect their own shares. Advertising and sales promotion will be targeted at areas of special interest, e.g. seasonal campaigns. Reinforcement of customer loyalty will be enhanced by the need to attract new consumers. Pricing will be geared to achievement of profits through volume. Sales effort will be directed to maintaining sufficient stocks at PoS, and to the maintenance of trade goodwill. New versions will be actively sought so that the life cycle can be regenerated.

There is potential for product failure if:

- complacency sets in;
- insufficient funds are provided for market maintenance;
- competitors develop new versions that are substantially better;
- the end of productive life is not recognised and acted upon.

Competitors may:

- secure advantage through new product development and/or through differentiation;
- reduce prices:
  — if they are market leaders, to make it difficult for their competitors;
  — if they are losing market, in desperation;
- smaller producers will leave the market.

Customers may:

- demand a series of 'developments' which may force unnecessary differentiation;
- move to generic products as the market becomes swamped with providers.

Management may:

- take the continuance of the product for granted – and lose out to competition;
- fail to recognise that the product is nearing the end of its productive life – and pour resources in to try to rejuvenate.

Decline stage

The product will lose volume. Promotional effort and price reductions will have a marginal effect at best. For a time there will be a declining demand from long-time users and those who are committed to the product and/or its technology. Price cutting may attract a few laggards – but not in significant numbers. Eventually it will no longer be cost-effective to maintain the product and it will be discontinued.

Competitors may:

- abandon the market, and thus allow a temporary upsurge in sales;
- retain their products, and use them as 'fighting brands' to assist new products in other sectors;
- offer to take over the product and possibly its production facilities, and thus consolidate the market;
- be willing to allow acquisition of their product, etc., and allow the market to be consolidated without them.

Customers will:

- Abandon the product in favour of its successor(s).

Management may:

- not recognise the reality of the situation and attempt to resurrect the product;
- decide too early that the product is in terminal decline and abandon it whilst there is still useful business to be done.

The PLC model is ideal to show the changes that are required in a range of activities as a typical product goes through its life cycle.

Note that the profits curve is quite different to the sales curve. You will remember that the Boston matrix shows that only cow products are high cash generators. Question mark and star products (the introduction and growth

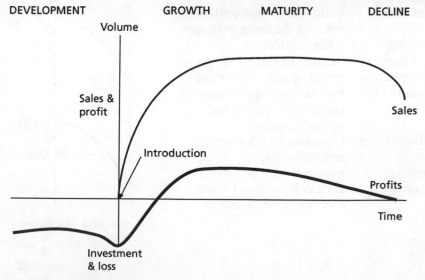

Fig. 22.1 The product life cycle

elements of the PLC) are cash absorbers, i.e. not profit generators. Also remember that each product is unique and so travels along a unique life cycle curve. Generalisations can, of course, be made as aids to management decisions.

Introduction – an investment

Characteristics:

- product   distinctive or differentiated;
- pricing   either skimming for limited distribution, or penetration for fast growth;
- promotion   high profile, high cost;
- distribution   limited at first;
- failure rate   high;
- competition   little, because introduction should be into market gap;
- profits   negative – still investing;
- strategy   commit to support.

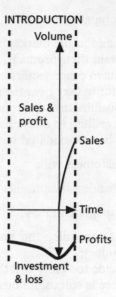

Fig. 22.2 The PLC – introduction

Growth – building market share

Characteristics:

- product   distinctive or differentiated, but edge declining with time;
- pricing   differentiated;
- promotion   medium profile, medium cost;
- distribution   widening and establishing;
- failure rate   low, but long-term potential can be damaged by bad strategic decisions;
- competition   increasing – both directly and indirectly;
- profits   negative – still investing;
- strategy   commit if meeting budget. Pull out fast if necessary.

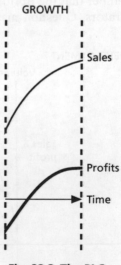

Fig. 22.3 The PLC – growth

Maturity – holding market share

Characteristics:

- product — brand extension;
- pricing — multi-pricing;
- promotion — brand loyalty and reinforce-ment, medium cost;
- distribution — maximum penetration achieved;
- failure rate — low;
- competition — strong – both direct and indirect;
- profits — high;
- strategy — protect position and market share.

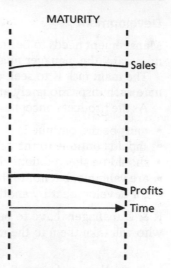

Fig. 22.4 The PLC – maturity

Decline – cash in the remaining benefits

Characteristics:

- product — superseded, either technically or emotionally;
- pricing — cutting, perhaps a competitive weapon;
- promotion — just sufficient to maintain awareness;
- distribution — decreasing;
- competition — fierce;
- profits — modest;
- strategy — dispose – by closing or selling.

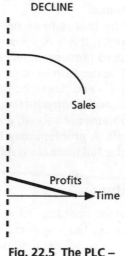

Fig. 22.5 The PLC – decline

MANAGEMENT STYLE

To maximise effectiveness there is need for a different management style at different stages of the life cycle. It is unlikely that any one person can combine the skills needed to carry a product through from conception to termination – even for products which automatically have short lives. For long-lived products there will, of course, be a need for a succession of managers. In this case each new manager should be selected to meet the style of management required.

Development

Management needs to be analytical, careful, thorough. Skilled in research and numerate, the manager must also have an above average creative ability.

The main task is to seek out and recognise opportunities, but then to evaluate each dispassionately and without bias.

As the product concept is developed there is need to recognise those which:

- must be discontinued;
- should continue to the next stage;
- should be shelved until circumstances are more favourable;
- are valuable, but not to the organisation. These may profitability be offered for development by another organisation.

R & D managers have to be able to hand over their 'babies' to the manager, who will take them to the market.

Introduction and growth

Management needs to be entrepreneurial, dedicated, tight focused, active and alert and with fast responses. There is need for determination – to attack the market, and to fight if necessary for the funds to secure the market share potential.

The task is to secure market placement at an acceptable level of market share. If this is not possible, to have the courage to recommend withdrawal in time to prevent unnecessary waste of funds.

The decision to change to a growth strategy is probably the most important of all – and has to be taken firmly and dispassionately. The type of manager needed for introduction and growth is likely to become less interested as the problems are solved, and will happily give the product up as new challenges await. A problem may be to keep him actively involved all the way through to the full market establishment.

Maturity

Management needs to be able to sustain interest in the product and the market over the long-term. Nothing exciting is likely to happen, but there will be many critical detailed decisions regarding both strategy and tactics.

Strategic decisions will have to do with product modification and replacement, tactical with maintenance of freshness in the visible product and its image. In many cases the mark of success will be an unchanged market share over the whole time a manager has charge of the product.

A serious problem can be encountered with senior management who have known the product for years. They may want to force their views onto the younger manager – and those views may be coloured by what was right when they were brand managers twenty years ago!

It can be very difficult for a senior manager to agree that a product he has always known should be regarded as in decline. For that reason the better young manager may be given an old product to save . . . a new product with high potential may be given to a less able manager!

Decline

Management needs to extract every penny of profit from the product without investing any more than the absolute minimum in maintenance. Every opportunity should be taken to be creative with the product – especially the ability to use it to foster other products (as a free gift perhaps) or to block a competitor (by selling at cost in his market).

The manager must be able to be ruthless – to decide when it is necessary to withdraw the product and to be able to do so.

ALTERNATIVE MIXES

The issues which will typically concern management at each stage of the PLC have been identified (above). Management's problem is to relate the reality of each unique situation to the range of alternatives that are available.

Much of tactical marketing is to do with developing the mix that is right for each stage – and making subtle changes to it in the light of experience. We shall examine each of the elements of the mix in the next chapter. For now, let us briefly summarise the options.

Product

Define the product class, its form or range, its name and/or brand, and its target users. The required mix will differ for up-, mid-, and down-market products and must be appropriate to the perceived needs of the target customers.

A high-quality perfume will not sell

- in a down-market package, nor
- from a mid-market outlet, nor
- at a low price, nor
- if it is promoted in media that the target audience do not see, hear, or read.

In the introductory stage unit costs may be close to trade price. This must be accepted as a necessary requirement if long-term profitability is to be achieved.

Packaging

The type of product and stage of the PLC will dictate the packaging need. Possibly more costly technology will be needed in the introduction and growth stages, but it will become routine, and cheaper, as experience grows. As the product becomes more widely accepted the packaging may become less significant (except for protection and legal requirements). It may then be possible to make economies, especially as maturity progresses and there is need to strip costs to the minimum.

Place

Distribution may be hard to secure during the introduction stage where it is needed – fast! Coverage must extend throughout growth. By maturity, we may fight for continuing shelf-space as new competing products are moved into their introduction and growth stages. In the decline stage there may be need to extract the product from the channels so that there is a clean termination. One does not want consumer complaints coming in years after the product has been discontinued.

Pricing

It is normal to charge a relatively high initial price to capitalise on the distinctiveness (or differential) of the new product. It can also act as a restriction in demand if there are good reasons for doing so. Prices will fall as volume grows and competition enters the market. Then prices tend to stabilise at an equitable return. Price competition increases as the product reaches the end of the maturity stage.

Promotion

This is a most complex and subtle area. Promotional objectives change markedly over time. Awareness is created at high cost in the introductory stage. In growth the objectives of 'push' change to 'pull' as customers become more aware. In maturity the campaign is limited, but focuses on reinforcement. In decline the promotional element is virtually removed and focused on the new class of products to follow.

The complexity becomes obvious when one realises there is need to communicate when an ever-changing market. People continuously enter and leave each segment and so at any one time there are:

- new prospects who have never heard of the product;
- those going through an introduction/adoption phase;
- others who are established as regular users;
- some who have tried and disliked the product – but may be attracted back;
- others who have no interest in, nor use for the product.

Marketing managers require the analytical and problem-solving abilities shared by all managers. They must take clear decisions, and implement them. A major difference is that marketing decisions are always to do with the actions and reactions of people in a future that can never be certain.

Marketers need a strong intuitive flair, and the willingness to take decisions without hard information. They also must have management who understand the nature of marketing, and who do not insist on guaranteed results. Unfortunately, however careful a marketing manager may be, he cannot predict the future, and some very unexpected things can either help or hinder.

Marketers are a little like experienced cooks who have to work with unstable and unpredictable ingredients. They blend their mixes, put them in the oven, and monitor results. Most of the time – through experience – they get what they expect. On occasion, however, they get something very much better, or very much worse. There is no certainty in marketing, nor in the kitchen!

KEY POINT SUMMARY

- Jane Smith received a wonderful opportunity as a result of good work, and because she did not jump in with an answer too soon.
- Marketing strategy determines the broad overall direction.
- Marketing tactics can only be planned when the strategy is in place.
- Blending the tools requires timing and market intelligence.
- At each stage of the PLC there is a range of options to choose from.
- Choice is restricted/conditioned by environmental factors.
- Introduction and growth require commitment and heavy promotion.
- Maturity requires a steady management so that position and market share are protected.
- Decline needs clear decisions re the strategic and tactical value of the product before and until it is terminated.
- Different management styles are needed at each stage.
- Do not divert the best managers to try to resurrect an ageing product.
- The marketing mixes must be blended appropriately for each stage of the PLC.
- Each product will follow its own unique life cycle, and must be managed accordingly.

WORK-BASED SELF-ASSESSMENT QUESTIONS

1 In your organisation how does the PLC concept assist in the marketing planning process?

2 Your marketing manager has asked for advice concerning which junior manager should bring a new product to the market. Produce a list of the positive and negative factors which would help him to decide between candidates.

SCHOOL- OR COLLEGE-BASED SELF-ASSESSMENT QUESTIONS

1 If you were Nasser Hussain hoping to take over from Jane Smith you would expect to be interviewed by the group brand manager. What polices would you recommend for HG tea?

2 If you were head of faculty with the opportunity to develop a new course with potential to attract a high level of interest from a new market segment which of these three academics would you appoint as course director – and why?

Mr A   33 years old. Married. 2 children. Master's degree in the subject. Teaching for 7 years. Been with the college for 3 years. Currently an assistant course director for a major course.

Mr B   45 years old. Married. No children. Bachelor's degree in the subject. Teaching for 23 years. Been with the college for 18 years. Senior tutor on a range of courses. Teacher's union representative for the college.

Mr C   52 years old. Married. 5 children. Master's degree in education. Teaching for 5 years. Been with the college for 4 years. An assistant course director on a new course which is proving very successful.

SUGGESTED ASSISTANCE TO SELF-ASSESSMENT QUESTIONS FOR CHAPTERS 20–22

WORK-BASED QUESTIONS

Chapter 20

1 The marketing plan is constructed after bottom-up and top-down negotiation have established strategies. It is a developmental process that starts with drafts and, through negotiation, firms up into a formal document. Corporate success can only be achieved through the individual successes of employees at all levels. The marketing plan (in common with the financial plan, the personnel plan, etc.) allows marketing strategy to be broken down into detailed tactical objectives that interlink across the organisation with the objectives of other functions.

2 All share the need for mission, objectives, strategies and tactics (MOST). The key differences are that strategic planning directs the main thrust of the organisation, division, department, etc. . Tactical planning is concerned with the details of how to achieve strategies. It will be focused on the short-term. Contingency planning provides for probabilities. Detailed plans, including strategies and tactics, are required for eventualities which might occur. Contingencies must also be allowed for within tactical planning since the only certainty is that things are likely to go wrong.

Chapter 21

The services in Questions 1 and 2 are similar, yet very different. The bus service is flexible, in its routing, it can go to passengers. The rail service has to bring customers to its stations.

1 A localised network of bus services can break away from the concept of fixed routes, and set stops. A flexible service that picks up on demand, and adjusts the basic route to assist passengers, can be introduced if mini-buses are used instead of coaches or double decker buses. Bus shelters can be made more comfortable, and it is possible that by the use of radio and telecommunications a bus of the near future will be redirected to where passengers are known to be waiting.

   Bus comfort increases in importance with the length of journey. For short trips the prime requirement is minimum waiting time and reasonable price. Indicator boards could therefore be added at stops to show when the next bus is due.

   Note: This development is happening now, and offers a serious threat to the traditional taxi service since it usurps their flexibility and specialised service for which they have charged a premium.

2 A rail network must make it easier for the customer than the alternatives. Therefore train timings must fit the needs of the commuters and shoppers and, importantly, the car must be competed with. It will be necessary to consider user needs which will involve issues such as: adding car parks with close access to the stations, at reasonable fees; comfortable waiting and/or rest rooms on platforms; special price deals for regular users; catering for refreshment and reading needs. The whole image will need to be shown to be exciting, clean, fast, modern, environmentally friendly.

Chapter 22

1 Where is no need to draw a PLC diagram to answer this question unless you have used it to focus an answer that is totally based on your organisation. Much as the PLC models in this module have been used to itemise the key issues related to each PLC stage.

You should have been able to determine if management works to a planned strategy, supported by tactics, which follows the PLC stages. How far does management plan forward in the realisation that certain actions are probably indicated? Is there evidence that management is aware that product lives can be planned, and that certain situations should be anticipated?

2 A new product requires firm and committed support and so a manager will be more likely to succeed if he is confident, experienced, willing to take risks, not over-awed by management. He must be determined, willing to commit himself, and not frightened by responsibility. Perhaps not best suited would be a manager who is experienced, steady and reliable, desiring to be popular, inclined to accept orders without query.

SCHOOL- AND COLLEGE-BASED QUESTIONS

Chapter 20

1 MOST = mission, objectives, strategies, tactics

A school or college without a mission is without a focus, without a sense of purpose and direction. Missions have to be shared by all staff. They can be imposed – but are not then likely to be effective. Without a clear sense of purpose, of direction, how can corporate objectives be set? And without them there is no way to establish strategies to ensure that the whole organisation is moving in the same direction, with the same sense of purpose. Quite obviously if individuals do not have strategic guidelines their management of individual faculties, courses, teaching programmes will not comply with a central position and the organisation is likely to project a confused and even contradictory image. It follows that management should ensure that they follow through the MOST headings, and that their staff are communicated with effectively so that they acquire a sense of shared values.

2 Clear thinking is needed so that you follow through logically:

1 Determine precisely who is in charge and what he must achieve.
2 Break down the overall task into sections that a single person can be responsible for.
3 Select one of these tasks, and subdivide it.
4 Continue subdivisions until you reach a single individual.

You should then be able to trace the achievements of the individual back up the matrix to see how important the contribution is to overall success.

Chapter 21

Assignment

This is a self-awareness assignment designed to help you become more closely in touch with what is actually happening – now – in the marketplace. You will need to do some research – get your tutor or librarian to help – because the questions cannot be answered simply by observation. You can, however, make some informed assessment – do your parents remember the brand when they were young? Do your grandparents remember it too? What did it cover when first introduced (or when you first noticed it)? How has it been extended? In all investigations of this kind the key question is Why? Keep asking it of yourself until you penetrate all the way through to a satisfactory and complete answer.

Chapter 22

1 Consistency would be the major requirement. HG Tea is well established and holds a high position and high market share. It would be counter-productive, dangerous even, to recommend change. The need is to consolidate, to steal the odd percentage point of market share if possible, to move very fast and heavily to shut out any threat from existing or new competitors. You would need to blend a series of mixes using product, price, place and promotional tools to achieve the overall strategy.

2 Full marks if you said that you don't have enough evidence to make a recommendation! Some of the information is irrelevant (the number of children) and much is missing (what type of people are they?). Perhaps you think that Mr B is a bit fuddy-duddy and not suitable? How do you know? Always beware of judging on second-hand evidence – especially when it is incomplete!

PART 7

Marketing mix –
product and place

The classic four Ps describe the marketing mix sufficiently for everyday under-standing. They are a useful form of short description allowing a broad under-standing to be communicated within marketing.

They are of little use in tactical marketing, however, because each of the Ps is comprised of a variety of tactical alternatives. It is the management of these alternatives – the blend of mix of each P – that allows tactical management to achieve the strategic objectives.

The division into product, place, price and promotion was made in 1952. In the 1980s the importance of packaging was generally recognised as of individual importance, and so in reality we have five Ps today.

We also have a market that is very unlike the one in which the four Ps were cre-ated. Possible the areas of greatest tactical concern have been in the five Cs of:

- customer and consumer expectation;
- channels of distribution;
- competition;
- communications;
- change.

Customers and consumers have successfully pressured for ever more environ-ment- and user-friendly products and services. They have forced governments to take action that has forced manufacturers to amend their policies, and to supply in accordance with a consensus view of what is acceptable. The 'consumer lobby' is very powerful, and its influence is spreading from the developed countries to influence the world.

Channels of distribution have changed beyond all recognition. Rather than large numbers of relatively small middlemen we now have a small number of huge ones. The whole concept of shopping has changed – from daily shopping to weekly or less. One-stop shopping has increased to the point where it is routine. Those who control the channels have taken power from the manufac-turers, who used to exercise control through supply. Now the manufacturers have to provide services such as stock control which traditionally were provided by the middlemen.

Competition has increased in virtually all markets as the high disposable incomes of the 1960s and 1970s encouraged new enterprise. It has continued, in different form, as those in the market strive to hold on through a period of recession which has even reached into the affluent Japanese home market. An incredible rate of technological development has fuelled competition in the marketplace. Ever newer, ever better products are being created faster than ever before, fasten than customers and consumers can effectively cope with change.

Communications have changed beyond recognition, and at an ever increasing pace. Technological development and the market penetration of electronic equipment for radio, TV, telephone, fax and data transfer have increased the media availability. Understanding of human behaviour has greatly increased the effectiveness of the message content travelling through the media. Ever more focused access has allowed tighter segmentation, opening access to niche markets that were previously inaccessible – possibly non-existent.

Change is the byword of the 1990s. It is a very unsettling time for all – probably not even the very young are immune from its effects. We have a society that:

- expects products and services to be readily available;
- requires high standards of performance;
- has a low span of attention;
- is not long-term committed in work nor personal relationships.

Against this background marketers have to make continual amendments to the blending of the mixes of each of the five Ps within the overall marketing mix.

CHAPTER 23

Product and new product development

Sue Thomas was a very experienced nurse. Her husband, Peter, now aged 37, was confined to a wheelchair, having been forced to leave the Army on medical grounds. Sue travelled the local area as a District Nurse, caring mainly for children and the elderly, and working with a large suburban doctors practice. The couple depended on her salary to meet normal household expenditure. Peter had only a small pension.

Whilst nursing a quite heavy patient Sue sprained her back muscles and injured her spine. After hospital treatment she realised that her nursing career had ended. The practice reluctantly retired her, after 15 years, on a small pension.

The problem of meeting expenses for herself, and her invalid husband, whilst continuing to live a fulfilled life seemed insoluble. The only way of attempting to meet their joint living expenses was to develop Peter's hobby.

Peter, having been a Transport Sergeant, was interested in vehicles and transport – and he had more than ample spare time. So he began to paint: pictures of trucks, buses, old steam engines and railway scenes.

He painted for his own satisfaction and as a means of passing time. However, friends had been impressed by the colour and vigour of his painting style. Often they visited, had a long chat, and departed with a small scene on a folding card to send for a birthday, or for special anniversaries for those interested in old transport memorabilia. Could this be the basis of their survival?

Sue discussed with Peter the possibility of making a business plan to sell his paintings as folding, postcard sized reproductions. She needed to know if it was financially viable and so approached a local printer and costed quantities printed in several colours and in quantities of 10, 50 and 100.

This is how Sue and Peter started their new business. By following through a clear discipline Sue and Peter were able to show their bank manager that they had a viable plan – that they were very serious and prepared to work hard to make the project a success. They were also able to see what each element of the marketing mix had to achieve, and how they each locked together.

Their new product development was relatively straightforward because they had only one source of production – Peter. The question became – could they market what he could produce?

As time passed they found that demand was stabilising and they had to decide whether to remain in their niche markets or expand. They decided to

Table 23.1

What they did	Why they did it
1 Approached their Bank to discuss financial backing	To begin process of preparing a business plan
2 Marketing research	To identify consumer needs
3 Identified model railway societies, and railway societies as niche markets	To provide similar but alternate niche market opportunities
4 Listed those with 100k	To allow quantification and promotional planning
5 Selected themes for the cards	Identified their product line
6 Set marketing objectives	To enable budgeting
7 Produced quantified business plan	To provide objectives for each area of their business. To secure support from bank
8 Commenced limited production	To allow quality checks and consumer tests
9 Made marketing plans	To ensure price, distribution and promotion ran smoothly alongside production
10 Produced small batches	To avoid over-stocking unpopular lines To minimise investment
11 Visited societies	To talk to secretaries and enthusiasts To sell cards
12 Assessed initial reactions	To revise/improve initial plans
13 Prepared selling fixture	To display and sell cards
14 Secured permission to sell	Official approval necessary
15 Set up test sites	To make final check on marketing mix
16 Assessed test site sales	To identify the fastest/slowest sellers
17 Re-stocked the faster sellers. Cut back/discontinued slow sellers	To concentrate on success
18 Learned from the experience	So they could do better as the range and geographic area expanded.

extend on the basis of their experience to other similar niche markets and identified aircraft, waterways and gardens as opportunities with sufficient potential.

There was need for consistency of quality, but Peter did not have the detailed understanding to produce paintings to a high enough standard in any of these specialised markets. In any case he was very busy handing the production and distribution sides of the business from his wheelchair, while Sue looked after marketing and finance.

They decided to extend their production capacity by locating a suitable artist and found an aircraft buff who could paint to Peter's requirements. That determined their extension, and they targeted model aircraft societies. They were again successful, and the pattern repeated itself.

In their 10th year their revenue topped £1m, and they had a staff of twelve. Their creative needs were satisfied by freelance artists under contract, printing was subcontracted, they handled marketing and despatch themselves. They were beginning to think of widening their market from the speciality niches to the high street, but were aware that they would then face competition from the huge suppliers such as Hallmark. Did they want to take that responsibility? Was the risk justified? Should they not remain content to be a successful small company?

The major problem – Sue and Peter discovered – was not one of getting business if you clearly targeted customers an offered value for money – it was trying to remain stable in a very unstable world. The problems were not in production, not even in marketing – they were all problems of management and the running of a small business.

NEED FOR CHANGE

Few companies can base long-term existence on a single product. The product concept ages, markets become saturated, consumers become bored, competitors offer alternatives. Even niche markets are in a constant state of change. They are growing, or shrinking in size, and changing in composition as new people enter and old ones leave.

Products that meet the needs of the segment now are not likely to meet the needs of the same segment in perhaps only a short time, months, or weeks even. It can be very hard to predict what the demand patterns will be, and extremely hard to influence them.

Toys are designed a year in advance of the peak selling pre-Christmas period. They are sold to the trade buyers at International Toy Fairs in January or February for delivery in September and October. Consumer buying must be stimulated by an intensive promotional drive leading to a four or five weeks peak sales period. If possible links with current fashion and/or fads must be set up in advance.Thus the TV schedules for pre-Christmas help determine the toys that will be in demand.

Each year manufacturers attempt to develop new toy concepts, new additional lines, extensions to existing products. Most years something happens to throw the careful forecasting off course. In 1993 it was a styrene model, Mr Blobby, coming from a popular TV programme, Noel's House Party.

Mr Blobby was a pink and yellow man-sized character whose sole conversation was 'Blobby, blobby, blobby'. He was mischievous, violent with adults, but gentle with young children. The nation took him to their hearts; he made a record that went to number one in the charts and stayed there through Christmas. Millions of Blobby toys and licensed products swept into the shops. Money spent on Blobby was, of course, directed away from what the trade had planned and expected. Retailers have to be very fast tactical marketers, generally, but in particular with seasonal lines.

Long-term change is often incremental rather than dramatic.

- Dolls were a girl's product that developed from rag dolls through china to plastic. Moving limbs were added, sleeping eyes also. Clothes and accessories changed.
- An innovation was the extension of dolls to include boys through the invention of Action Man.

- Action Man has extended into soldiers of different types, with different weapons and equipment.
- Dolls for both girls and boys have increased their capabilities. They can speak, they can 'learn' speech, they perform natural functions and can be beautified.
- They have never lost their central core values as companions, comforters and playmates.

PRODUCT EXTENSIONS

Products can be extended by offering additional lines that add value. The concept of value is brought to the product by the consumer, and will vary with individual needs and within current fashion. Some items, such as nodding dogs on the rear shelf of cars, are passing fancies. Others, such as seat covers and mud flaps, are more pragmatic and long-lasting. Safety features such as hazard warning and rear fog lights, and air bags, start as added value, but become adopted as essential equipment. Luxury features such as radios become essential, and then extend to include cassette players. The current luxury is CD stacks in the boot with eight track stereo in the car. Then a full car telephone system is added.

House protection is a growth industry, which is extending with need from the simple deadlock through bars, metal screens, electronic eyes and sirens, lighting systems, infra-red detectors and active monitoring through the telephone line.

Add-on sales

Product planning can provide for add-on sales.

A customer at the point of purchase has taken the decision to spend money on a particular product. At that moment of decision he is most vulnerable to add-on sales. It is the easiest time to achieve extra business.

- product   add-ons;
- freezer   thermometer, scraper, ice packs, wire baskets, freezer bags and ties, plastic boxes, labels, etc;
- computer   printer, modem, mouse mat, floppy disk cases, spare disks, manuals, training videos, etc;
- power boat   radio, compass, satellite navigation, echo sounder, flares and rockets, first aid kit, charts, etc.

The key is to understand human nature. Each add-on provides little in proportion to the cost of the product. £150 for a freezer may as well be £170 for a 'complete' freezer. The £20 on top of the £150 is not significant. Yet as a separate sale it may be very hard to get the customer to part with £20 because it will be seen as a purchase in its own right.

MATCH PRODUCT TO NEED

Positioning tactics can help to increase profits:

- Niche segmentation ensures segment domination.
- Target marketing allows tight focus.
- A range of niches and targets can allow several product specialisations from one base concept.
- Marketing through several channels usually requires product changes if the channels reach consumers with different needs and perceptions.
- Competitive positioning requires differential – not direct competition with an identical offering.

The product mix changes rapidly in today's markets. These changes come not by chance, but as a direct result of marketing mix decisions. Products, however, are becoming less important as customer care, customer services and brand loyalty is more focused and the art of positioning is practiced more professionally.

WHAT IS A PRODUCT?

In Chapter 1 we established that a product has three characteristics. It is now necessary to examine each of these in more depth.

- Physical aspects of a product are those of which it is composed. A cup can be of several different forms of china, or of pottery, metal, glass, or plastic. A 'glass' can be anything from the finest crystal to plastic. In shape a product varies with functional and psychological needs.

  Note very carefully that the physical aspects of a product provide no practical benefit. A product exists without purpose. Just as a computer requires software, electricity, and skill to be useful, so every product requires a functional need and a psychological purpose. A service has no physical presence – it is entirely composed of functional need and psychological purpose.
- Function adds use to a product. A cup for morning coffee is of a different shape to one for afternoon tea. A bone china cup is more suited to delicate teas than to cocoa. A young child has a cup that is hard to break, probably of plastic, a climber carries a metal cup or mug.

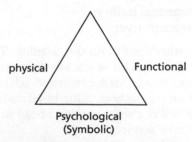

Fig. 23.1 Characteristics of a product

Function is capable of change. When the handle is knocked off a cup it can be used to hold pens and pencils in the kitchen. It can be turned upside down and used to cut circles out of rolled pastry. These secondary functions extend the life of the basic product, and may, of course, be exercised at any time.

A useful exercise is to think of as many uses as you can for a household or well-known product. Paper clips and house bricks, for example, have over 200 potential uses each!

- Psychological (symbolic) value adds worth to the product. A child's photograph will mean much to the grandparents. Much more if it is carefully framed. More still if the photo is of a special occasion, and the framed photo is presented on a birthday.

Psychological values are *intrinsic* to individuals. They can be short-term, such as the appeal of Mr Blobby, or long-lasting, such as a child's attachment to a favourite toy. Long-lasting values can be for life – as when the childhood toy, say a teddy bear, is treasured into old age.

Because they are *intrinsic* to individuals psychological values may not be understandable to, or by, others. They are values that add considerably to the enjoyment, the benefit, and change a functional commodity into a differentiated product (or service).

PRODUCT OR SERVICE?

In marketing terms there is no difference between a product and a service. When viewed from the consumer's viewpoint the requirement is need satisfaction. People do not think in terms of products or services – this is an artificial distinction of use within marketing but of no value in the marketplace!

If the need is for clean clothes the alternatives are:

- throw away the dirty and buy new;
- send dirty clothes to the laundry;
- take dirty clothes to the laundry;
- have them washed at the launderette;
- wash them yourself at the launderette;
- use a fully functional washing machine at home;
- use a washing machine and separate spinner and drier;
- wash by hand at home;
- hand wash in the communal facility;
- hand wash in the stream or river.

The need is 'clean clothes', not to do the cleaning. The three requirements of cleanliness, cost and time, will be balanced with what can/must be achieved, set against what can/must be afforded, and how much time is/can be available. The alternative which offers the best value in terms of cleanliness, cost and time, will be chosen. It will not enter anyone's head to think of whether they are considering products or services.

No one is ever concerned or interested in buying a product. People buy what a product will do for them. The product is simply a means to fulfil a needed function in a psychologically satisfying manner.

'Package'

People buy bundles of benefits – what a product or service will do for them. The range of benefits potentially offered by a product or service must be identified by the marketer. Only then is it possible to 'package' them into psychologically satisfying bundles that have functional purposes.

Marketers sell 'packages' of benefits. There must be physical support, of course, but it is the 'package' that is promoted, the 'package' that is priced. The 'package' that the designer must have in mind as the very first concepts of a new product or service are beginning to emerge. It is far easier to build in benefits than to add them later.

Product development

Product development is the on-going changes made to existing products, so that they are kept fresh in the perception of customers in target market(s). Development may be:

- Intrinsic – physical properties:
  - Fibreglass replacement of wood in the boat industry to add life, improve appearance and reduce costs of maintenance and repair.
  - Modular electronic components to facilitate reliable usage and increase production efficiency even though costs of repair may exceed price of new product (made possible by the cultural shift to a 'disposable' society).
- Extrinsic – symbolism properties:
  - Lucozade changed its image from an invalid's drink to an energy-giving drink for sportsmen.
  - Opera houses are moving from exclusive venues for the socially privileged to musical theatres for discerning music lovers.

CORPORATE PRODUCT POLICY

Long-term corporate objectives impact on the type and number of products that any organisation will support in its portfolio. Sony have a policy of an ever-increasing number of models, all at high quality. Toshiba have a similar quality objective, but concentrate on a limited range. Casio have dominated the hand-held calculator market through an aggressive policy of a profusion of models, each better (even marginally) than the last, but with no intention of maintaining any one model over time.

The underpinning requirements for growth, stability or short-term profits affect all corporate policies, but especially product policy, since that is potentially the longest lasting and with the most impact on long-term success, i.e.

packaging, price, place and promotion can all be changed relatively quickly. Product change time is determined by capital and/or emotional investment.

INNOVATION

'Innovate or die!' – is this a sound company motto, or a meaningful mission statement? The work done by the PIMS researchers in America show clearly that there is need to innovate to stay successful. Examples of firms that thought otherwise provide dramatic evidence:

- Britain dominated the world's cotton and wool industries from the late 19th century until the invention of cheaper processes around the turn of the century. By 1910 competitors, notably in America, were producing both wool and cotton materials at well below the price possible using traditional (old-fashioned) methods. British management fell back on the argument that their product was superior, and people wanted only the best. Unfortunately people proved that they were happy to change. Even when this should have been obvious to all, British managers refused to change, and many of the cotton and wool mills of Lancashire and Yorkshire closed. By 1930 both trades were virtually extinct in the UK, but if strategies had changed, they need not have been so.
- In May 1971 National Cash Register had to write off newly designed cash registers worth $140 million! They were electromechanical, and electronic machines were then available. NCR were locked into traditional technology and failed to notice that it was becoming old-fashioned. To their credit they survived, but only after a decade of struggle. They have never recovered the market dominance that they had for the century before 1971.

Peter Drucker, in *Innovation and Entrepreneurship*, says of Leonardo da Vinci that there is a breathtaking idea – submarine or helicopter or automatic forge – on every single page of his notebooks. But not one of these could have been converted into an innovation with the technology and the materials of his year, 1500. Indeed, for none of them would there have been any receptivity in society, nor in the economy of the time.

Professor Dorf, of the University of Southern California, makes it clear that it isn't the better mousetrap that sells – first there is need of mice that can't be caught in existing traps.

INVENTION OR INNOVATION?

Innovation is invention plus need (Dorf).

Inventions abound, perhaps not as dramatically as in the da Vinci example, but inventors are almost commonplace. The problem comes when trying to make innovations from an invention. Typical problem areas are:

- technical   the processes are not yet capable of manufacture;

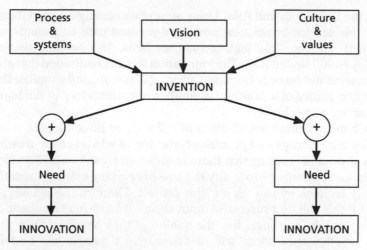

Fig. 23.2 Invention or innovation?

- behavioural   consumers are not able to appreciate the benefits;
- managerial   managers are unable, or unwilling, to leave what they know;
- financial   investment capital is not available, and/or it is decided that
                 investment sunk in existing technology must be recovered
                 first.

> Innovation is far more than just staying ahead of the competition. It is the adoption
> and diffusion of new ideas, products, or processes potentially useful to the customer.

Product extension

Totally new products are rare and so most 'new' products are developments of existing technologies. This does *not* negate nor detract from their 'newness' in the marketplace. Although to a scientist or an engineer they may appear to be no more than tinkering with what is known, to a consumer they offer solutions to identified need. That is all they have to do!

KEY POINTS

- Innovation is the aim of all new product development.
- The creation of differential is innovation if it locks on to need.

Examples of successful adaption of existing technologies to create new products are:

- Air-bag safety technology for front seat drivers and passengers. The innovation is in tying together electronic speed with inflatable raft technology to meet the desire not to have to wear seat belts.
- A new hospital complex (Health Care International) costing £180 million is located in Glasgow to serve severely ill patients form the UK, but mostly

from the EU, Africa and Asia. Using air ambulances flying into Glasgow airport, this service brings new advanced medical care to patients who can afford it. HCI has 260 high-technology beds, 16 operating theatres and employs 4000 skilled staff. The innovation is in the realisation that air ambulances need not be only for emergency repatriation, and coupling this to an identified ability of a substantial number of patients to pay the high prices the service must charge.

- The Channel Tunnel has 93 miles of rail rack, in three tunnels. It connects the UK with Europe and promises faster travel whatever the weather. The innovation is in realising that there is sufficient cross-Channel traffic – both freight and passenger – to justify the cost of applying existing tunnelling and railway technology to such a major project. There is, incidentally, serious doubt if this will be a successful innovation – it has strong competition from the ferries who are upgrading the quality of their services; there are questions whether the service will be faster, and if people will be willing to travel such a distance in a tunnel under the sea.

Marketers encourage and support innovation as a process. Consumers who are classified as innovators and early adopters support new products by pulling them through the marketing system. But an innovation is only successful when it becomes established in the marketplace. Invention is therefore useless unless it fulfils a need.

New product development

The traditional view of NPD is of up to 100 new ideas funnelling into the process, with only 1 or perhaps 2 making it through and on to the market. If we remember that 'traditional' often means 'old-fashioned', it helps us to challenge this view. Why should so many ideas produce so few marketable products? Just because they 'always have' does not make it right, nor sensible!

In fact, with a better understanding of the process, and with better control systems and clear objectives, the conversion rate can be improved considerably.

Compare the two approaches shown in Figures 23.3 and 23.4.

- *The traditional approach.* Booz, Allen and Hamilton's approach to the NPD process has been the standard for many years. It is the process which underpins the traditional view of NPD. When comparing it with Dorf's approach it can be seen that the business analysis comes *after* idea generation initial screening, concept development and testing and marketing strategy development, i.e. resources are committed in a product-centred approach before evaluation of market potential.
- *Today's effective approach.* Professor Dorf proposes a series of sieves – he calls them screens – which require management to be far more specific in the early stages, and then to quantify more rigorously as the process develops. Ideas only become acceptable after they have passed the screens. Thus many ideas are rejected far earlier – before there has been serious investment in them. Those that remain have a far higher probability of market success.

Statement of the NPD
development strategy

↓

Idea generation

↓

Initial screening

↓

Concept development
& testing

↓

Marketing strategy
development

↓

Business analysis

↓

Product development

↓

Market testing

↓

Commercialisation

Fig. 23.3 The traditional view of new product development
Source: Adapted from a model by Booz, Allen and Hamilton

- *Screen 1*. Management policy and strategies have to be proactive (see below). They have to be forward looking and open to creative solutions. The three Ms encourage 'moonlighting' from their technical staff by including a 10% surplus into R & D budgets. Thus researchers can go off on tangents with permission and funding! The famous and highly profitable notelet came from a researcher who was trying for an unbreakable glue but found a way to get a reusable glue instead.
- *Screen 2*. Market auditing must be active. It should not only record what is present in the market, but what is potentially available, and what is potentially needed. Thus the evaluation process is greatly assisted.
- *Screen 3*. Monitor and evaluate existing and future technology. Be aware of the danger of being trapped in existing technology when competitors are working on new.
- *Screen 4*. Expected return must be calculated very carefully, and realistically. A classic example is EuroDisney, which struggled to cope with interest repayments on investment capital despite achieving a surplus on revenue. The major problem facing many new products is management's

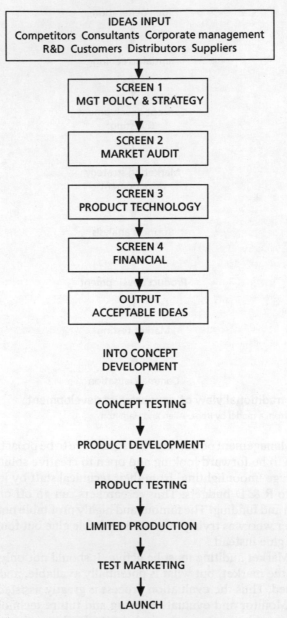

IDEAS INPUT
Competitors Consultants Corporate management
R&D Customers Distributors Suppliers

SCREEN 1
MGT POLICY & STRATEGY

SCREEN 2
MARKET AUDIT

SCREEN 3
PRODUCT TECHNOLOGY

SCREEN 4
FINANCIAL

OUTPUT
ACCEPTABLE IDEAS

INTO CONCEPT
DEVELOPMENT

CONCEPT TESTING

PRODUCT DEVELOPMENT

PRODUCT TESTING

LIMITED PRODUCTION

TEST MARKETING

LAUNCH

Fig. 23.4 An innovative view of NPD – a series of sieves

expectation of payback in too short a time. Products in the BCG's question mark and star quadrants need support if they are to get to cash cow status.

- *Acceptable ideas*. Only if an idea passes the preliminary screens is it regarded as a serious contender for the marketplace. Only then does it pass into the concept development and testing, and then product development and testing stages.
- *Concept and product development*. The extended first stage, with its four screens, insists that potentials are quantified. There should then be no spending on physical development before the concept is tested. By testing to check the acceptability of the concept an immediate feedback that links to consumer perceptions and needs can be incorporated into the actual design of the product. As we know, the earlier that benefits can be incorporated, the more powerful they are likely to be.
- *Limited production and test marketing*. These stages still have to be passed successfully, but if they are there is every confidence that the launch should be successful.
- *Launch*. Products that are launched have passed every test that can be devised short of actual exposure to the market. Circumstances outside the control of the marketer always have an effect on any new product. Sometimes they are forced off the market, sometimes they receive a tremendous boost. Threats and opportunities in the launch and growth stages require a special management style, not appropriate to later stages of a product's life cycle (see Chapter 22.)

There can be no doubt that the Dorf approach, using modelling, scenario/what-if? planning and technological forecasting enables more commercially valid decisions to be taken – earlier.

IDEA ENCOURAGEMENT

It is better to see the process of securing NPD ideas as 'encouragement' rather than 'generation'. The implication of encouragement is of a management that is actively seeking NPD, and wants to develop a positive attitude to newness, to change. Generation is a term that suggests a mechanical process.

New product ideas can be encouraged in many ways:

- A corporate strategy for NPD is essential.
- Understand customers needs. Foxall notes that in food innovation, marketers 'strive to meet buyer's expectations more closely than their rivals do'. This also entails the identification of the innovators and early adopters.
- Search for 'not quite totally new' products: e.g. Virgin launched a new service using the A340 European Airbus rather than Boeing and gained an edge in the European market.
- Encourage and reward those who make useful suggestions. Kotler lists sources of new ideas as: customers, scientists, competitors, company sales representatives, management. Other sources include: inventors, patent lawyers, university and government laboratories, industrial consultants, advertising

agencies, market research firms and magazines and industrial publications. To this list must be added the very important source of internal staff. Those working with the product often know how to make improvement, and have innovative ideas. The Japanese have successfully exploited this source of information, and boosted morale, through their quality circles approach. Reward should be of genuine value in comparison to the commercial return. A £100 reward for an idea will will generate millions will have a demotivating effect and ideas are likely to dry up! Ideas that are suggested and apparently ignored also cause the flow to stop.

Characteristics of the innovators in the marketplace

In a study of diffusion and innovation by Lancaster and Taylor stress is put on the perceptions of the innovators and early adopters because it is they who will determine the rate at which a new product is accepted by society. Studies of farm machinery sales in Australia and America suggest that high rates of adoption depend on:

- ease of communication;
- demonstrable benefits from usage;
- no adverse effects on personal or social lifestyle.

The five important innovative characteristics observed were:

- relative advantage;
- compatibility;
- complexity;
- divisibility;
- communicability.

Lancaster and Taylor conclude that theories relating innovation models to understanding of customer adoption are still some way off. More research is required to develop understanding of the complex interrelationships.

MANAGEMENT STYLE

Management is said to be *proactive* if the structure of the marketing plan and the strategies of the four Ps lead and encourage innovation. This is the true sense of management 'making the future happen'.

Management is *reactive* if it follows trends and reacts only when customers demand new products, or if it follows where competitors lead.

Restrictions on marketing budgets may force the follower role, but the McKinsey *Quarterly Report* of Summer 1993 reported that many chief executives are questioning whether the marketing department is 'able to deliver'. They question whether marketers are . . . 'too averse to risk, unimaginative, and generate too few new ideas . . . with very few examples of new marketing frameworks, or fresh approaches'. Mark Todd, ex-director of Toshiba, points out that 'In Japan, they don't have marketing departments at all.'

The Midland Bank feel that the marketing activities 'should be subsumed into a new customer department run by the chief executive'.

These are not arguments against the concept of marketing, more a pointer to the many opportunities marketing now has within its grasp and how these should be structured and internally organised.

Reactive marketers argue that, by following trends, very great cost savings may be made in research, testing and pre-launch promotion. Many food innovations are trend-following, rather than trend-leading. The advent of electronic multimedia technology tends to encourage more targeting, experimentation and risk taking, particularly in FMCG marketing. Ease of using electronic systems tends to develop market-driven companies to respond more quickly to small segments of consumer demand.

MANAGEMENT SUCCESS

Management success depends on leadership, innovation, creativity and the use of electronic systems. Survival depends not so much on a steady but gradual progression; rather, it requires a redefining of structures, resources and staff training to project the whole management team's thinking forward imaginatively into the future. From a future viewpoint the requirements of the marketing and management systems should be more clearly seen.

The internal struggle for resources show that the present is out of gear with the future. Across the whole of management, targets for change, evaluation and performance and new standards of efficiency are being set. Wilson, Gilligan with Pearson concentrate on the control aspects of management performance and identify potentially dangerous areas that must be tackled:

- *Behavioural.* Management controls should focus on 'what managers should be doing'.
- *Gamesmanship.* Managers can tend to 'play the system' to improve personal achievement without any real effect on results – even to the point of fraudulently manipulating company data.
- *Negative attitudes.* Job tension, conflict, resistance can arise from imposed control.
- *Short-term viewpoint.* Short-term financial reports and accounting practices can divert management attention from creative longer-term activities.
- *Focus.* As management teams focus attention on group team projects, the four Ps and customers may be ignored as the project concentrates internally on schedules and costs. Customer care would be a far more effective focus for managers.

Institute of Management conclusions

In November 1993 a survey of 1000 UK managers by the Institute of Management, with Personal Performance Consultants UK Ltd, revealed that British managers were worried by incompetence in the managerial hierarchy, by office politics, time pressures and poor communications. Of those surveyed, 94% worked longer hours than contractually agreed, 41% regularly worked more than 50 hours per week, 35% had seen work-load increases in the past year and only 6% had experienced a decrease in work-load.

Organisations have a corporate responsibility for preparing managers for change through a restructuring of the organisation, with more training and career guidance. Self-directed work teams and the redesign of business processes tend to reduce the present hierarchical structures. Supervisors and line-managers are disappearing and making way for flatter organisations. Flexible work patterns will reduce cost and put many active managers to work from home, on contract. Customer-driven companies will be more proactive, with more sensitive managers across the spectrum and in closer harmony with markets, competitors, suppliers, shareholders and their public.

KEY POINT SUMMARY

- The five Cs are customer and consumer expectation, channels of distribution, competition, communications, change . . . all external to the organisation.
- Packaging is virtually a fifth P to be added to the four Ps.
- New business start-ups must follow a planned sequence of research, validation, testing, investment, success, expansion.
- There is constant need for change in today's markets.
- Long-term change is often incremental rather than dramatic.
- Add-on sales should be part of the product planning process.
- Add-on sales increase the value of a purchase decision and prevent a second sale having to be attempted.
- Products must be matched to needs.
- A product has physical, functional and symbolic characteristics.
- A service has functional and symbolic characteristics.
- In marketing terms there is no difference between a product and a service.
- People do not buy a product – they buy what the product will do for them.
- People buy bundles of benefits, which are 'packaged' by the marketer.
- Product development can be intrinsic or extrinsic.
- Innovation is essential to survival.
- Innovations are inventions plus need.
- Many new products are extensions of existing technology.
- The creation of differential is innovation if it locks on to need.
- New product development requires management to plan ahead and carefully screen new ideas before commitment to physical development.
- A corporate NPD strategy is essential.
- Ideas must be actively encouraged.
- High rates of adoption depend on: ease of communication, demonstrable benefits, no adverse effects.
- Innovative chacteristic are: relative advantage, compatibility, complexity, divisibility, communicability.

- Management style is proactive if it leads and reactive if it follows.
- Marketing is being seen as an organisation-wide concern.
- management success depends on: leadership, innovation, creativity and the use of electronic systems.
- Potentially dangerous areas that must be tackled are: behavioural, gamesmanship, negative attitudes, short-term viewpoints, focus.

WORK-, SCHOOL- AND COLLEGE-BASED SELF-ASSESSMENT QUESTIONS

1 Paper clips are usually seen as functional items for use in the office. How could their value be extended through innovation?

2 You have a new product idea for a student note-taking pack that contains everything a student requires in class. It has passed all the NPD screens and you are ready to develop and test the concept. Outline your thinking before commissioning marketing research. (*Hint*: Refer back to Chapter 3.)

See the end of Chapter 27 for answer guidelines.

CHAPTER 24

Test marketing

Three minutes to ten on a Monday morning . . . R.O. Bot looked up from his work. Soon the office door would open and the morning refreshments trolley would appear. He was looking forward to a break . . . it was a long time since breakfast and he needed his coffee and a snack to get him through to lunch.

Sharp at 10 the door opened and Molly pushed the laden trolley into the general office. Everybody crowded round, and there was much light-hearted banter as the clerks lined up. R.O. Bot was slightly taller than most and could stretch above their heads to see what was on offer. Hello, a new biscuit – FudgeBar. Bright red packaging, looked attractive, he'd pass his usual KitKat and try the new one.

On Tuesday he had another FudgeBar, but on Wednesday returned to KitKat.

Three minutes to ten on a Monday morning . . . R.O. Bot looked up from his work. Soon the office door would open and the morning refreshments trolley would appear. He was looking forward to a break . . . it was a long time since breakfast and he needed his coffee and a snack to get him through to lunch.

Sharp at 10 the door opened and Molly pushed the laden trolley into the general office. Everybody crowded round, and there was much light-hearted banter as the clerks lined up. R.O. Bot was slightly taller than most and could stretch above their heads to see what was on offer. Hello, a new biscuit – Bar O Fudge. Bright red packaging, but he would stay with his usual KitKat and not try the new one.

On Tuesday Bar O Fudge was still on the trolley, but he remained loyal to KitKat.

Three minutes to ten on a Monday morning . . . R.O. Bot looked up from his work. Soon the office door would open and the morning refreshments trolley would appear. He was looking forward to a break . . . it was a long time since breakfast and he needed his coffee and a snack to get him through to lunch.

Sharp at 10 the door opened and Molly pushed the laden trolley into the general office. Everybody crowded round, and there was much light-hearted banter as the clerks lined up. R.O. Bot was slightly taller than most and could stretch above their heads to see what was on offer. Hello, a new biscuit – FudgeBar. Light green packaging, quite attractive, he would try it.

By the end of the week he had decided that FudgeBar was quite good. He would have one every so often to make a change.

Salim Malik looked up from his screen in some satisfaction. We have the results, he announced. FudgeBar in green is picking up repeat purchase indications throughout the test. In red it makes an impact, but for long-term sales it seems that we need the less dramatic packaging. I'm going to recommend that we go to a full-scale market test in the green packs, and the FudgeBar name. Bar O Fudge just doesn't work, no matter what packaging we use.

Salim worked for the Virtual Reality Research Corporation – the year was 2020, and long gone were the days when products had to be put into the shops for preliminary testing. No longer could competitors pick up new product ideas while still in the pilot stage. When a manufacturer was ready for a market test it was a full-scale test quite unlike the limited tests of the late 20th century.

Virtual Reality identified the complex layers and levels of behaviour present in the average member of a target market. From this research they developed detailed personality and behavioural profiles. Coupling this information to target market information they were able to simulate market conditions within a computer program. Their computers were as far advanced beyond the Cray computers of the 1990s as the Crays had been beyond the IBM mainframes of the 1970s. Within them was a series of markets, populated by totally programmable 'robots'. Through these they could run the same simulation as many times a they wished with only the most minor changes to the product under test.

At the end of each test the parameters could be reset and so each test was measured against identical criteria. Everything could be changed, from ambient temperature to altitude, from disposable income level to taste. The programs were highly sophisticated – and Salim wondered how clients had ever been able to put products successfully on to the market when they had to chance the mood of the target customers, and try to prevent competitors from picking up samples for as long as possible. They obviously had managed – but how?

TEST MARKETING

In Chapter 23 we saw how the new product development process concludes with market testing, launch and commercialisation. It is every manufacturer's dream to be able to test products in complete secrecy so that they can be launched with a very high probability of success. Unfortunately, however, the days of virtual reality testing are not yet with us.

What is test marketing?

Test marketing is a detailed and complex form of marketing research that is conducted to determine if and how a new product concept shall be launched into an identified market.

It helps to establish a reliable estimate for future sales and allows the pretesting of alternative marketing plans.

Why develop new products?

Wilson, Gilligan with Pearson suggest the main reasons for developing new products are to:

- overcome product obsolescence with new products that match new or changing environmental conditions;
- create new market segments as markets tend to fragment;
- spread risk over a wider market, or over new segments;
- match competitor moves into new products;
- beat competitors to opportunity;
- avoid patent protection;
- soak up surplus capacity;
- fulfil long-term growth and/or profit targets.

Note: Remember that 'new products' means a new product offering. Thus a redesigned product is 'new' and a repositioning requires 'new product' treatment.

Why test the market?

Throughout the NPD process a product idea is developed from a concept until it achieves the status of a product that can be offered to the market with a high probability of success:

- The concept is tested for acceptability.
- The business screens test for potential profit.
- The prototype is developed and tested – new pharmaceutical products and/or medicines are clinically tested and approved before general release. Cars are taken to remote locations and tested rigorously before going into production. Foods are tasted by 'blind tasting' panels (tasters are blindfolded), before a recipe is accepted and a shelf-life established.
- The packaging is designed to be not only functional, but protective, legal, attractive and user-friendly.
- Distribution channels are tested to be sure the product will survive in good condition all the way through to the consumer.
- User instructions are drafted, checked, translated, checked, back-translated, checked.
- Promotional campaigns are developed.

Kotler identifies four reasons for test marketing:

- To determine the rate of trial; of first repeat; of adoption and of purchase frequency.

But even after the most careful test the ultimate challenge awaits. Will the target market welcome the product? Will they adopt it as an on-going purchase, or will they buy it as a novelty while the promotion is running and then revert to what they use now?

There are only two ways to find out what the target audience's reactions will be:

- a national launch of the product;
- a test launch

Tables 24.1 and 24.2 show the advantages and disadvantages of the two options.

National launch

Table 24.1 Advantages and disadvantages of a national launch

Advantages	Disadvantages
Full market coverage quickly	High investment.
Lead over competitors	High risk.
Major distributors can come on board at once	Distributors may insist on waiting for customer demand before stocking.
National media can be used	Very high research costs.
The national campaign can be run effectively	Results may not be uniform across the country, making evaluation difficult. The sales and distributive effort may be too much for the supplier to handle.

A national launch secures market presence very quickly, but at high cost. The cost comes partly from the high investment in production equipment and in stock, but also from the need to convince distributors to handle the line. An untested new product, even from a major manufacturer, will not secure shelf space as a right. Retailers have the power within their channels of distribution and manufacturers will probably have to buy their way on to the shelves.

Fast distribution can be ensured if 'commando' sales teams and specialist distributors are used – but the investment in resources, both cash and management time, are extensive. (A commando sales team is one that is for hire from an agency. It is composed of experienced salespeople who work on behalf of the client for a limited period.)

The major area of high risk centres on distributors who may not be willing to handle the line – Levi's Tailored Classics were killed by lack of distributor interest (as we saw in Chapter 12). The secondary high-risk area centres on potential customers who may not respond to the promotion, may not try the product even if they buy it and may not adopt it if they try it. (Some buy on impulse, but then never actually try the product once they get it home.)

It follows that most new products go through extensive market testing to minimise the areas of risk. In many cases it is worth allowing a competitor a little advance warning because this is a far lower risk than going into the market blind.

A test launch

In a test launch one or more selected areas are chosen that are similar to the national profile. In each area the product is launched using local media and local distributors. If several areas are used it is possible to vary the total pack-

Table 24.2 Advantages and disadvantages of a test launch

Advantages	Disadvantages
Minimum investment	Competitors have time to copy
Each element can be tested	Production volume may be low and success may not be able to be capitalised upon
Own sales team can concentrate	National promotional campaign has to be simulated using local media.
Commando support limited	No guarantees that local reaction predicts national reaction
Limited area to research	Test areas population is conditioned to testing – is their response typical?
Each element of the test can be researched in depth	
Local media are set up to assist	

age and then to cross-evaluate to discover the most effective mix of product, price, place and promotion.

Normally a test is supported by limited manufacture, and this can lead to problems if the product is extremely successful and production capacity is exceeded.

Competitors, will, of course, be monitoring the test very carefully. They will be able to secure samples, strip them down and replicate them very quickly. There is always the risk that a competitor will get into a full market launch before the originator. Many organisations have a policy of being a 'me-too' follower, rather than an innovator. Their innovation is in opportunity recognition and their ability to get 'cover versions' on to the market very quickly.

MARKET TESTING

A market test is a controlled launch under reliable conditions. This enables test results to be accurately researched and fed back into the NPD process so that the full launch has a much higher probability of success. To be reliable the whole test marketing plan must be statistically sound but, unfortunately, this is extremely difficult (impossible?) to achieve.

The problems of selecting a test marketing area are:

- Size of the test area needs to be related to the budget.
  Thus the size may be smaller than would give reliable and valid results.
- The selected area should reflect national characteristics.
  — The target audience must be represented in sufficient numbers, and the channels of distribution must be in place.
  — Climate, population and consumption patterns must be representative.

- Media and distribution coverage must be similar to national coverage.
  - It is important to test like with like. If TV is in the promotional campaign it cannot be replaced with cinema – nor can a TV campaign spread out of the test area.
  - It is difficult to translate national plans into local equivalents.
- The areas must be isolated as measurable segments so that the test can be confined.
- Outside factors such as the economy or the weather may affect the test – positively or negatively
- Detailed research is needed on sales, customer reaction, retail and/or distributor results, pricing tests, communications tests, etc.
- It is difficult to base national sales estimates on the results of a localised test.

Test marketing decisions

The point of test marketing is to assist management to take decisions – it is an extended and very detailed form of research with one aim – to reduce the risks inherent in launching new products onto the market. Typical decisions that are assisted by test marketing are:

- If tests are positive, when should the product be released, and to which segment(s) of the market?
- Where should it be launched? Should it go out regionally, nationally, or globally?
- To which precise groups should the new product be targeted?
- What combination of marketing tools should support the launch?

Test market areas

The need for a test market area to have national characteristics and yet be isolated means that only a few areas can be used. The media in those areas have set up a full structure of commando sales forces to get fast distribution and marketing researchers with a full modelling of the area to carry through detailed research. Newspapers make provision for testing, with such as split run copy tests, and TV and radio offer special packages that target the geographic area of the test.

Note: Split-run copy testing evaluates two ads. They are printed in alternate copies of a newspaper or magazine so that results can be evaluated (see Chapter 31).

Well-known test areas centre on York, Derby, Norwich, Cardiff, Exeter and Southampton.

- The Meridian ITV transmitter is situated on the Isle of Wight which is just off the south coast of England. It is limited in its coverage to the north by the range of hills that run up to 10 miles inland, to the south is the open sea. Its power limits transmission range to the east and west. The result is a compact area that runs along the coast from Eastbourne to Bournemouth and centres on Southampton.

Test syndrome

Unfortunately there are insufficient test areas to meet the need and so they are over-used. The result is that people became aware of the research procedures and became conditioned responders. This is difficult if not impossible to provide for when analysing results.

Retailers can use selected test stores, but this option is normally not open to manufacturers.

ROLL-OUT MARKETING

As an alternative to full test marketing a target area can be selected for a full-scale launch. Once the product is successful in the limited area it can be 'rolled out' to adjoining areas . . . become established . . . and roll out again. This has the major benefits of first establishing a solid base which is protected against competitors, and only then extending across the available market in a carefully controlled development. It also allows for limited production in the early stages if there is doubt about the sales levels which will be achieved.

Note: Beware that competitors do not go to a national launch whilst you are committed to roll-out!

To test or not to test?

How to test a new product is one of the most difficult, and most significant decisions that management has to make. It is helpful to construct checklists to assist with the decision process. The following examples can be used as a basis from which to develop checklists that are exactly applicable to your needs.

Checklist 1   TEST MARKET STRATEGIES

Validity & security | Yes | No
| 1 | Must I test? | ☐ | ☐
| 2 | Is a suitable test area available? | ☐ | ☐
| 3 | Have I sufficient budget – men and money? | ☐ | ☐
| 4 | Will it take time to copy the product? | ☐ | ☐
| 5 | Can I handle competitors' attempts to disrupt? | ☐ | ☐
| 6 | Am I confident in the proposed research methodology? | ☐ | ☐

When competitors test
| 1 | Can we disrupt? | ☐ | ☐
| 2 | Shall we gain from disrupting their test? | ☐ | ☐
| 3 | Can we mount a research study to benefit from their test? | ☐ | ☐
| 4 | Have we time to react effectively? To do more than observe? | ☐ | ☐

Benefits

		Yes	No
1	Can we benefit from a test?	☐	☐
2	Sufficiently to justify the effort?	☐	☐
3	Sufficiently to justify the risk of product exposure?	☐	☐
4	Is it better, overall, to test them to launch?	☐	☐

Positive answers open the way to test market action

Checklist 2   SETTING UP A TEST MARKET

		Yes	No
1	Clear strategic objectives set?	☐	☐
2	Are these objectives:		
	• actionable?	☐	☐
	• quantifiable?	☐	☐
	• internally consistent?	☐	☐
3	Have I produced a test marketing plan?	☐	☐
4	Has the plan met with senior management approval?	☐	☐
5	Have go/no go decision criteria been set?	☐	☐
6	Have clear tactical objectives been set?		
	• product/service?	☐	☐
	• price?	☐	☐
	• PR?	☐	☐
	• advertising?	☐	☐
	• sales promotion?	☐	☐
	• place?	☐	☐
	• sales force?	☐	☐
	• support?	☐	☐
7	Is a marketing research proposal ready to be commissioned?	☐	☐
8	Does my planning contain controls to ensure:		
	• true replicability nationally?	☐	☐
	• maximum objectively?	☐	☐
	• ease of measuring results?	☐	☐
	• flexibility to respond to competitors and/or environmental changes?	☐	☐
9	Am I confident that the test is needed?	☐	☐
10	Do I have all planning in place, and all needed authority?	☐	☐

Positive answers indicate a test market 'go' decision

COMPETITIVE ACTION

Test marketing requires a product to be placed on public sale. This means that every competitor will quickly have a sample to strip down and examine in detail. The need is to discover if the new product is likely to prove serious competition and if it should be matched in the marketplace.

It is no accident that Proctor & Gamble and Lever match each other so quickly. Both are working to achieve the same ends and have huge R&D budgets. It only makes sense, however, to launch a new product when there is need either to stimulate sluggish demand or to match the competition.

- The Flymo Garden Vac – best product of 1993 – is a vacuum cleaner for the garden. It is extremely functional, having a shoulder strap and a collecting bag, and picks up all manner of small garden rubbish very efficiently. It is particular effective on dead leaves and was launched in late summer – in time to get full distribution ahead of the autumn. It uses no new technology. The innovation is the translation of domestic vacuum cleaner technology to the garden.

    No competitor followed them to the market and so it seems that their security was good. The product has been so successful, however, and the technology is to simple, that they must be gearing up to meet serious competition sooner rather than later.

ACTIONS FOLLOWING A TEST MARKET

There are four decision choices that management can make during and/or following a test market:

- continue to full launch;
- redesign the product;
- amend the mix of promotion, price and/or place and then go to full launch (it is possible, but unusual, to go to a second test);
- discontinue the product.

When faced with the need to make this crucial decision a manager will be aware of the problems that hopefully have been overcome, and the pitfalls that await.

Technical problems in the design of the test market

- Test objectives prove to have been badly drafted.
- Research facilities and/or competence is inadequate.
- Test area is not representative of the larger market.
- Testing is held at the wrong time, e.g. Spring for an Autumn product.
- External and uncontrollable conditions affect the test, e.g. economic crises, strikes, natural disasters.

Problems of market projection

- Test sales forecasts and results are too inaccurate to be relied upon.
- The risk of wrongly estimating sales potential is too high.

- Costs of the test market may have caused short cuts to save costs, but also reduced the validity of the test.
- Estimates may be unreliable for such as: repeat purchase rate and speed of market expansion.

Problems of managerial decision making

- Data may be misinterpreted or misunderstood. Over-pessimistic or over-optimistic plans may result.
- Scrutiny of test data may not be sufficiently rigorous.
- The launch decision may be taken outside the marketing department – perhaps for non-marketing reasons.
- Managerial decisions may be taken in a climate of internal uncertainty, e.g. internal politics may intervene.
- Local test area results may be too limited to allow marketing planning on a national basis.

Problems due to product selection

- Inadequate product screening may have allowed an unsuitable product to go through to test.
- Manager's uncertainty may have confused the test market purpose.
- Managers may fail to agree on which products should have been tested.
- Insufficient attention and consideration may have been paid to:
  — marketability;
  — durability;
  — product characteristics;
  — growth potential.

It is essential to examine test results carefully before making decisions on which products to launch, where and when. Oliver suggests that knowledge of penetration levels and repeat purchase rates are essential if new product sales are to be forecast accurately. He sees a link between penetration and repeat sales and the length of the trial period in weeks . . . 'the average repurchase frequency is becoming shorter as buyers move to deeper trials'.

The correlation between the trial and repurchase rates is shown in Table 24.3.

Table 24.3 Management decision choices

Trial rate	Repurchase rate	Management decision
High	High	Go for launch
High	Low	Redesign the product
Low	High	Amend promotions mix
Low	Low	Kill the product

NEW PRODUCT SUCCESS

Studies into the reasons for product success list technological innovation as the prime factor. There must be:

- a clear market need for the product;
- acceptance of the product's benefits;
- available resources sufficient to support the new product through the growth stage of the PLC;
- efficient and effective management.

Success is not certain, however well the test is conducted. Even when the results are highly positive there is no certainty that a national launch will succeed. Equally failure is not guaranteed if test results are negative. Poor management can cause new products to fail, but good management cannot guarantee success.

A good example of the need for effective test marketing is the Sinclair three-wheel electric car. This was a technical success, but a marketing disaster. It was ecologically sound, cheap to run, and reliable. Unfortunately it was tiny and looked fragile, especially when seen alongside a London double-decker bus. Its testing was carried out, we are told, inside a village hall as a security precaution!

Test marketing would have helped Sir Clive, as it has helped countless others, to at least identify the major benefits and drawbacks that customers and consumers perceive – may of which cannot be anticipated. Test marketing, therefore, can aid management in avoiding costly product failures, and thus contribute to long-term success.

INDUSTRIAL-GOODS MARKET TESTING

Fewer, larger, products are manufactured for industry and the problems of testing are different from those that apply to consumer goods. Testing is, nevertheless, a very important part of the NPD process.

Objectives and research

As for all forms of testing, clear objectives must be set and thorough research commissioned to measure results against expectation.

Industrial new product testing includes:

- *Product-use testing*. A prototype is supplied to a customer with whom there is an on-going relationship. In conjunction with the customer's team the product is put through its paces, the results evaluated and amendments made as necessary.

  The customer is asked to express purchase intention and to provide a testimonial which can be used in promotion . . . 'New product as used by . . .'.

- *Trade shows*. Only of value at point of launch, the trade show allows a range of views to be quickly collected, at the same time as sales leads are established and, perhaps, orders are taken. Competitors will obviously visit the stand and have a full run down of the product and so an immediate launch is necessary if the competitive edge is to be maintained.
- *Dealer display rooms*. The product can be displayed in selected dealer display rooms and trade opinion obtained. This is of limited value because it exposes the product to inspection but not to use. It also makes it available to the competitors. Finally it may (should) stimulate orders, which the manufacturer will possibly not be ready to satisfy.
- *Pilot manufacture*. A limited production run can be initiated with the products being sold on quota to selected customers. The product in use is then monitored by the service engineers as part of their normal back-up – although these can be supplemented by technical researchers. As lessons are learned from version I it is possible to modify and extend so that the bugs are eliminated from version II, which goes into full production.
- *Joint development*. Where long-term relationships exist it is possible for a new product to be a joint effort between the R&D teams of the customer and the manufacturer. This is especially applicable where the manufacturer is supplying a product to contribute to the end product that is sold by the customer. For example, paint spraying equipment for a car manufacturer may be developed jointly by the R&D teams of the car maker, the paint supplier and the spraying equipment manufacturer.

Disruption

In all test marketing it is important to remember that it is in the competitor's interests to learn from and to disrupt the test. Thus a marketer must expect the product to be stripped and examined in detail. He must also expect heavier competitive action than is likely in the main market.

Competitors may be trying to close the test market to him – by attractive stocking offers to the dealers, by getting a rival product into the market first or by running very attractive offers within the test area only. Extra heavy promotion may be mounted in the test area, and key media slots he needs may be booked by the competition as a spoiling action. Any of these actions will, of course, distort the results of the test.

Obviously it makes sense to monitor competitive action, to identify their market tests, and to do all one can to learn from them. At the same time it is in your interests to load up the dealers and to mount promotional activity to distort their research. You do not want a competitor having a clear run at a test, but you do want to learn all you can from their test.

It is not surprising that people in the limited number of test areas are conditioned respondents – they are so used to tests and to counter actions that it must be difficult for them to distinguish and be loyal to an on-going product.

KEY POINT SUMMARY

- Test marketing is a detailed and complex form of marketing research.
- It helps to determine if and how a new product should be introduced to the market.
- It is an aid to management decision taking.
- It would be ideal, but not practical, to test products in full secrecy.
- New products are developed for a variety of reasons, from overcoming obsolescence to soaking up surplus production capacity.
- Kotler's four reasons for test marketing are to determine the rate of trial, of first repeat, of adoption and of purchase frequency.
- Target audience reaction can only be judged through either a national launch or a test market launch.
- A national launch has advantages such as: full market coverage, lead over competitors and the ability to use national campaign tactics.
- A national launch has disadvantages such as: high investment, high risk and possibly too many demands on the sales and distributive efforts.
- A test launch has advantages such as: minimum investment, sales team concentration and depth of research.
- A test launch has disadvantages such as: competitors are alerted, local media cannot simulate national media and the population is conditioned to testing.
- Problems of selecting a test area are such as: budget, reflection of national characteristics, and isolation.
- Roll-out marketing is where launch is in a selected area – consolidation is achieved – the product is 'rolled out' into an adjacent area.
- Roll--out marketing allows concentration of effort, development from strength and limited production.
- Roll-out marketing does not prevent a competitor going straight to a national launch after absorbing the lessons learned from observing the results of your marketing plan.
- Four decision choices are available after a test market: launch redesign the product, amend the mix, discontinue.
- Problem areas that a manager may face include: technical design of the test market; market projection; management decision making; product selection.
- New product success appears to come from: a clear market need, product benefit acceptance, support through the growth stage, efficient and effective management.
- Industrial goods can be tested more individually.
- Industrial testing includes: product-use; trade shows; dealer display rooms; pilot manufacture; joint development.
- Disruption must be expected, and allowed for.
- A competitor's test should (usually) be disrupted if possible.

WORK-BASED SELF-ASSESSMENT QUESTIONS

1 Suggest the criteria that a marketer may use in the screening processes before an idea goes into a concept development (see Figure 23.4).

2 Explain the differences between concept testing and test marketing.

SCHOOL- OR COLLEGE-BASED SELF-ASSESSMENT QUESTIONS

1 Show how a school or college can use NPD techniques to help it decide between three potential new courses when there is only sufficient budget to launch one.

2 If your new course proposal was accepted how would you set about developing the concept and market testing the product?

See the end of Chapter 27 for answer guidelines.

CHAPTER 25

Place

The Head of the Loamshire County Ambulance Service, Charley Pound, had to prepare for what was likely to be a stormy meeting with the Loamshire County Council's Health Committee.

It was not going to matter that he had submitted report after report, recommendation after recommendation. It would not matter that he had warned of the consequences. Political will had not been strong enough to provide the additional funds that the ambulance service needed. Year after year, budget after budget, higher priorities had deprived Charley of vital funds.

The result was that his budget had allowed for essential maintenance, but not for replacement. Certainly not the extension of his fleet. They had got by, of course they had. His team were all dedicated and conscientious people who were motivated by their role in saving lives and relieving suffering. But getting by was not enough. It never had been, and it certainly wasn't now that young Leon was on the critical list.

Leon Platel was just 14. He was by all accounts a bright and cheerful teenager, and with promise of becoming a fine rugby fly half. He had already represented the county at schoolboy level, an those in the know reckoned he could make the England team if he kept working at his game.

It had been a normal game, between two schools with no aggravation. Leon had taken the ball cleanly, but the flank forward was faster than he had thought and he went down under a perfectly fair tackle. Tragically he fell badly, and suffered a compound fracture to his right leg. He also, although nobody knew at the time, suffered a severe internal injury. It was later diagnosed that his liver had ruptured. Not immediately fatal, but a severe injury needing fast attention.

A spectator had dialled 999 on his portable telephone and an ambulance was despatched. The log was clear.

14.35 Incident occurred (approximate timing).
14.43 Emergency call received.
14.44 Ambulance Baker One despatched.
15.13 Baker One on scene.
15.25 Baker One on route to Maychester Hospital.
15.28 Maychester Hospital alerted to emergency.
15.33 Baker One reports breakdown (later identified as a blown head gasket).
15.34 Charlie Three despatched.
16.12 Charlie Three takes patient from Baker One.
16.25 Charlie Three arrives at Maychester Hospital.

The breakdown had added 39 minutes to the journey. Long enough for Leon's condition to worsen – particularly as the internal injury had not been diagnosed.

But that wasn't the worst of it. It took Baker One 29 minutes to reach the scene – and the target response time was 7 minutes! So Leon's arrival at hospital was delayed by a total of 61 minutes! Enough time for him to lapse into a critical state, from which he may not recover.

Putting aside the emotional problems Charley considered what was now needed and what he would almost certainly get now that public opinion was so outraged.

- Obviously his ambulance fleet needed to be increased, with the older vehicles pensioned off.

  But he needed more vehicles on the road at any one time. The delays in getting to the sports field and then to Baker One had occurred because the fleet was spread too thinly for today's traffic. Charlie Three had come in 20 miles by motorway because although Baker Two was only 3 miles away it was 3 miles of cross-town traffic, and the longer run was the quicker.
- His team needed specialised training. He had wanted at least one qualified paramedic on each ambulance but there were training costs to cover, and then the higher wages earned by paramedics.
- If there had been a paramedic in Baker One the lad's condition would have been checked and an air ambulance called in.
- If there were an air ambulance, that is! People had been incredulous when he put forward a case for a helicopter ambulance. But Loamshire was a big county with rugged country that attracted climbers like bees to a honey pot. Volunteer mountain rescue teams had dealt with the situation for many years, and there was always the RAF to call on. But it just wasn't good enough.
- Finally, equipment – it hadn't mattered in this case, but the ambulances needed the most modern equipment for emergency treatment – and also to guarantee effective communication.

A lot of money needed to be spent, but Charley was convinced that the investment – for that is what it was – an investment in health – would be worth while. He hoped that, this time, he could carry the day. That this time he would get the support and the budget.

What has this tragic scenario got to do with marketing? Well, not a lot! But it has everything to do with the P of place, and everything to do with distribution.

DISTRIBUTION

The role and purpose of distribution is to transport goods and services in the most cost-effective and efficient way, from where they are, to where they need to be. Charley Pound could be the general manager of any major distribution company. How different is his job to that of the Federal Express regional manager? Couriers have to respond quickly to calls for their services. They have to transport things against deadlines from where they are to where they are needed. They have to do it cost-effectively.

Any distribution manager is faced with the dilemma of balancing availability against need. Depots can only hold limited levels of stock, yet stock has to be available against need. Consequently stock is moved forward from production in anticipation that depot space will have cleared by the time it arrives. In a similar way airline managers oversell aircraft seats in the expectation that not all passengers will show up for departure. It is better to oversell and have to compensate one or two who are 'bumped' from a flight than to sell 100% and see the flight depart with empty seats.

Whatever the form of distribution – it is always a delicate balance of space, transport, time and budget. It is a highly skilled form of management, and it needs dedicated and skillful managers to operate to maximum effect. distribution is not necessarily within every marketing management's range of skills – but the skilful use of distribution is of major importance to marketing.

PHYSICAL DISTRIBUTION MANAGEMENT

When is a refrigerator not a refrigerator? When it is in Bristol at the time it is desired in York.

It is a merchandising management cliché to say that the right goods of the right quality have to be in the right place at the right time. Of course they do! The problem comes when trying to turn the cliché into reality, for it cannot always be done.

No physical distribution system can simultaneously maximise customer service and minimise distribution cost. Maximum service implies large inventories held close to the customers, with very flexible transportation available. Minimum cost implies low stocks in few depots, with slow and cheap transportation. Somewhere between these two extremes a balance has to be struck.

Kotler suggests eight areas that must be taken into consideration:

* the speed of filling normal orders;
* the supplier's willingness to meet emergency merchandise needs of the customers;
* the care with which merchandise is delivered;
* the supplier's readiness to take back defective goods and re-supply quickly;
* the availability installation, repair services and parts from the supplier;
* the number of options on shipment loads and carriers;
* the supplier's willingness to carry inventory for the customer;
* the service charges – are services included in the cost or separately priced?

It is essential to research the relative importance of these various customer services to the target customers. Also to discover what the competitors are offering, and what they are actually managing to provide and achieve.

Then it is necessary for management to decide upon a competitively viable mix of customer services. Only after that has been done can distribution specialists design a physical distribution system.

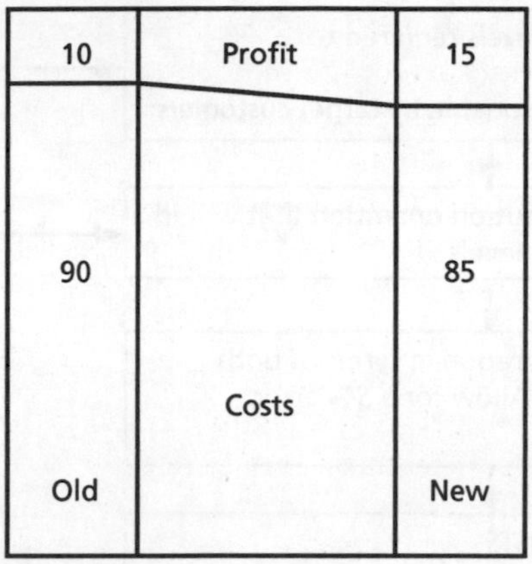

10	Profit	15
90		85
	Costs	
Old		New

Fig. 25.1 Profit leverage through cost reduction

The importance of physical distribution management (PDM)

Cost-effectiveness is crucial in PDM. With distribution costs running at around 20% of sales even a small saving shows a marked effect. Figure 25.1 shows how a 5% cost saving adds 50% to profit. To achieve the same return from increased sales would require a 50% sales increase!

The cost reduction from 90% to 85% produced a 50% profit increase. This 5 to 50 ratio of cause and effect is called a *gearing effect*.

Own network, or specialist

It is a corporate decision whether to distribute or subcontract distribution to a specialist. A thorough evaluation of the cost-effectiveness of the operation is needed, but the first, essential, step is to determine the exact level of service provision required. Only when this has been done can the cost-effectiveness of the alternatives be evaluated.

Specialist distributors

PDM is a highly skilled process involving a range of skills from logistical route planning through to vehicle maintenance. It is now well recognised that there are considerable benefits in contracting out distribution:

- no capital costs;
- no property to maintain;
- no specialist management, nor equipment required;
- no responsibility for ensuring the operation meets legal requirements;
- revenue costs can be directly associated to sales;
- no long-term commitment;
- benefit from shared costs with others to whom the distributor is contracted.

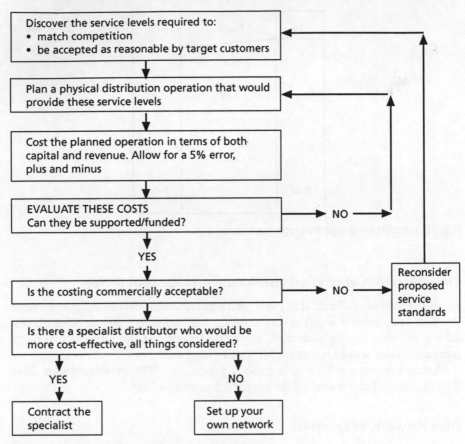

Fig. 25.2 Determining the form of distribution

PDM strategy

Whether or not it is contracted out the PDM function is a specialism. It exists to satisfy the distribution objectives established by marketing management, and so it is for distributive management to decide:

- how many depots are needed;
- if stock should be held in all depots (if not, which should be the tranship-ment centres);
- what form the inventory control system should take;
- if stocks of all items are to be held in all stockholding depots;
- if existing depots are still suitable – by location, function and operation;
- how depot investment relates to consideration of fuel pricing and availabil-ity – now and in the future;
- the action needed to satisfy EU and British Regulations on such as drivers' hours and vehicle safety;
- how to adapt to changing techniques of materials handling and new vehicle designs;

- how to exploit advances in data handling and IT.

DISTRIBUTION CHANNELS

The channels of distribution are the routes through which products flow to reach the final customer. This involves two distinct activities:

- channel logistics;
- channel selection.

Channel logistics

The physical movement of goods through channels of distribution may be by truck, plane, container, barge, or by a combination of several means of transport. Channel logistics are concerned with the costs and effectiveness of alternative methods of delivery. Stocks may be held in depots on manufacturer's premises, near the main markets, adjacent to motorways, near seaports, in central or decentralised locations.

The following factors are vital to the decisions:

- *Costs of holding stock.* Stock represents committed finance, and finance has to earn its keep. Thus, in addition to the physical costs of running depots, etc., there is a finance charge to be paid – interest on the capital invested in the stock.

  If stocks can be moved down the channel the costs can be shared with middlemen.
- *Cost of protection and delivery.* Stock must have sufficient protection to survive in the selected channel. Specialist equipment may be needed. The total costs of the channel must be calculated and set against the benefits.
- *Routing.* Major savings can be made by efficient routing. This can be fully exploited only by making it the focus to which the whole system is targeted. Thus items on delivery notes are printed in a determined order that allows warehouse staff to 'pick' stock efficiently. Warehouses are designed to make their picking process as quick, easy and foolproof as possible. Drivers are trained to follow their routes, and are instructed how to handle orders that cannot be delivered.
- *Stock control.* Warehouse management must maintain the strictest control to ensure that the first goods in are the first goods out (FIFO), or that last in is last out (LILO).

Channel selection

The range of channel alternatives must be identified before an appropriate selection can be made.

The produce (or supplier) has to consider the requirements that must be met if the product is to reach the consumer in good condition. For example:

- Frozen foods and ice cream require a distribution network that can guar-

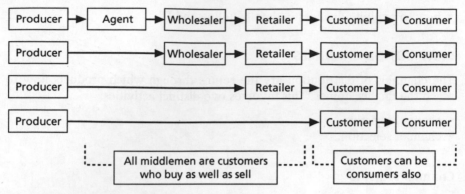

Fig. 25.3 Alternative channels of distribution

antee that the products will be kept at a temperature of no more than –8°C (18°F).
- Roofing tiles need no protection from the elements, and are robust whilst in their bulk packs.
- Fresh foods need swift processing from being picked at dawn; through cleaning, grading and packaging; transport to retail stores and availability on-shelf as the stores open.
- Carnations are flown from Columbia to London each day. Specialist dealers take their consignments at Heathrow and rush them either to Covent Garden or direct to florist shops.

Minimum total transactions

The principle of minimum total transactions determines if one or more middlemen add value to a channel.

If 10 retailers are being served by 2 suppliers there are 20 deliveries to be made. At a cost of £20 per delivery the total channel cost of distribution is £400. (10 retailers × 2 suppliers × £20.) A middleman is viable only if he reduces the total distribution costs.

With a middleman involved in the channel, the suppliers make one deliver each, at £50 = £100. The middleman makes 10 deliveries, at £10 = £100.

Middleman profit = £100.

Total channel cost = £300.

In this simplified example there is a total cost saving of £100 whilst the middleman is effective, and each party in the channel gains benefit:

- Suppliers save the costs of direct deliveries, and need a smaller distribution operation.
- Middlemen break the bulk deliveries, and charge a fair profit for their services.
- Retailers have one delivery rather than two, and from a supplier who is closer, smaller and more able to react quickly if necessary.

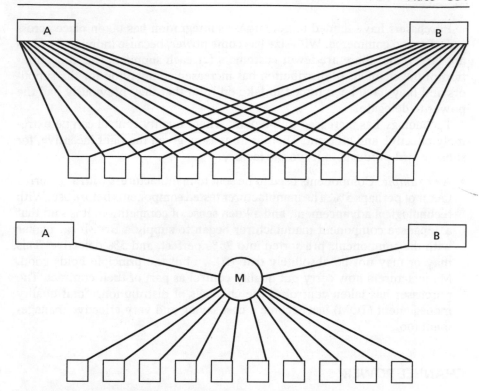

Fig. 25.4 The principle of minimum total transactions

Channels of distribution are not fixed for all time. They adapt to changing circumstances, but are governed by their cost-effectiveness. Thus the grocery wholesalers in the UK have been forced out of business by the supermarket chains who have taken over the role of breaking bulk, and have made it an internal function. This makes complete sense when such an extremely wide range of merchandise is being carried. Within a bulk order it is possible to deliver even small quantities of an individual item.

Major retailers have been able to reduce their stockholding at store level because of the fast back-up from their own depots and direct from manufacturers. They have more flexible control on their stocks, have reduced stockholding overall and because of the sheer power of their negotiating position, have been able to pressure suppliers for just in time (JIT) deliveries.

Just in time management (JIT)

JIT stock control relies on the supplier to provide a guaranteed delivery of quality controlled products just as they are needed. It has been made possible by three key factors:

- purchasing power;
- competition;
- technology.

Purchasers have tended to get larger as integration has taken place across industry and commerce. With size has come power, because individual orders are larger, and there are fewer customers for each supplier. This concentration of the channels of distribution has increased competition for the suppliers and they have been forced to take on roles that they previously had the power to delegate.

Technology has increased to the point where quality control can be extremely effective and efficient. There is no reason, given the right incentive, for substandard products to leave the factory.

- *An example.* Components used to be sent to manufacturers with a +/– error factor of perhaps 5%. The manufacturer tested components before use. With technological advancement, and a keen sense of competition, it is said that a Japanese component manufacturer began to supply a British car maker with the components pre-sorted into 95% perfect, and 5% defective! This may or may not be absolutely true (!) . . . but the principle holds good. Manufacturers now carry out quality control as part of their contract. The purchaser has taken control of the channels of distribution. Total quality management (TQM) has become a cost saving and very effective management tool.

CHANNEL POWER

Power in the channel is critical to profitability, even survival, of those within the channel. The middlemen in UK grocery have lost out to the more efficient supermarkets, and FMCG suppliers can no longer dictate terms to their customers. Sir Alistair Grant, chief executive of the Argyll group and vice-president of the CIM stated in November 1992 that at Safeway 'I focus entirely on things that grow the business and make it more competitive and profitable.'

Power is gained through size, sales volume, competitiveness, profitability and efficiency.

In 1992 Sainsbury's sales were £10 billion, with 8 million people weekly passing through their 350 supermarkets. Sainsbury use an IBM mainframe placing 90% of their orders with UK suppliers electronically; 65% of its invoices are returned via the computer. The payment of suppliers, 'closing the loop,' has not yet been set up on the computer, nor is it a priority at present.

INTEGRATION

Integration of operations can be horizontal or vertical, or both.

When integrating horizontally, organisations move sideways to acquire, or merge with, other organisations. Much of the UK grocery power has come from horizontal integration. In fact the big five chains, Sainsbury, Tesco, Gateway, Asda and Safeway, account in 1994 for over 60% of all UK grocery sales. The take-over of the small corner shop is, however, not solely due to

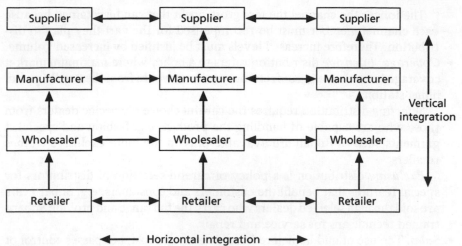

Fig. 25.5 Vertical and horizontal integration

horizontal expansion of the big five and their followers. Massive rises in the rental values of city, town and village shops has also contributed to the decimation of many of these businesses, contrary to the trends in French villages, where a range of family shops and boutiques continue to survive.

Vertical integration is when an organisation acquires others who operate before, or after it, in the channel. It is done to secure the source(s) of supply, and/or to protect market access. For example, Marks and Spencer have very successfully integrated vertically to secure control over many of their suppliers and operate a policy of supplier support.

Channel decisions

Channel decisions tend to be long-term and tactically difficult to adjust. They have major effects on every other aspect of marketing and therefore are of considerable strategic concern.

Strategic decisions are concerned with:

- *Power*. Power in the channel is crucial. Once lost it is difficult, if not impossible to regain. Thus long-term strategy must be concerned with opportunities and threats relating to channel power.

Control

Associated with power, control refers to the maintenance of the desired degree of legal control over the channel members, but crucially over the product.

- *Levels*. The greater the number of levels in the channel the less actual control is possible. Even if contracts are watertight they have to be enforced through intermediaries and the process is not likely to be effective in practice. Thus if control over product quality, price, etc. is required the channel has to be shorter rather than longer.

The longer the channel the less gross profit that can be retained because each channel member must be recompensed for the part they play in distribution. Therefore increased levels must be justified by increased volume.

- *Coverage*. *Intensive* distribution refers to a policy where maximum market coverage is needed, e.g. confectionary is everywhere from theatres to petrol filling stations.

  Selective distribution requires the careful choice of specific dealers from those who are capable of handling the product, e.g. fashion and specialist garments such as Rohan are available only in the more exclusive clothes retailers.

  Exclusive distribution is a policy of careful selection of distributors for special features that benefit the customers and consumers, e.g. Subaru cars are sold through selected dealers who carry the full range and provide Subaru trained technicians for service and repair.

- *Sales*. The use of middlemen reduces direct sales cost, but passes control of the sales effort to a third party who may be handling other products. Achieving the needed degree of priority can then become a serious problem.

- *Title*. Legal title to the goods can pass on to the middlemen and, officially or otherwise, pricing negotiations can move as well. Once title has passed the goods belong to the middleman whether he pays his accounts or not. The remedy is through the courts, which can be a long drawn out, expensive, time-consuming, and frustrating business.

Location

Sales outlets can be crucial to product success. The product offering must be accessible in the place and at the time it is needed by the target market. Financial products create special problems because customers cannot easily get to them in work hours, and yet their own staff need lunch breaks, and not to work anti-social hours. Restaurants increase staff levels over the midday peak, but this brings with it the need for shift working, and for temporary staffing.

Services, in particular, need to be where consumers want them . . . or where they can find them easily. Exclusive and specialist services tend to group, e.g. electronic stores re in Tottenham Court Road, bookshops in the Charing Cross Road. Cafes and restaurants are usually found grouped closely together.

- *Time*. Distance is often less important than time. Twenty minutes on a motorway is infinitely preferable to 20, 15 or even 10 in heavy traffic. Parking must be provided for convenience and to save the consumer's time. Out-of-town shopping malls have developed to meet the demand for one-stop shopping, convenience and easy parking.

- *Promotion*. There must be encouragement for the target audience to visit the location. The benefits of the location need to be marketed equally as the benefits of the products available there. It must be possible for people to find the location, so road signs are needed. There must be a welcoming ambience, and high stock levels are essential.

Technology

New technology is constantly coming on line to improve the quality of distribution decisions. The bar code, in particular, has enabled management to have instant updates on sales and on stockholding.

- *Electronic point of sale (EPOS)* has been made possible by the bar code and the computer. With EPOS managements can monitor sales in extreme detail. Not just what is selling, but when, and in what combinations. It is possible to set up special offers in the computer so that 'Two for the price of one' (and similar deals) are triggered automatically as the second item passes over the bar code reader. It is also possible to make price changes instantly, from head office, so that all cash points in the country register the change instantaneously.
- *Electronic funds transfer at point of sale (EFTPOS)* allows customers to pay for their goods by a variety of methods, not least by the SWITCH card which acts as an electronic cheque and simultaneously debits their account and credits the retailer.
- *Electronic data interchange (EDI)* is the transfer of information between computers in a structured message format that improves the standard of communication and minimises the possibility of errors.
- *Intermodal services* are those in which more than one type of transport is used in the course of a single contract, e.g. rail/sea/rail or road/sea/rail. The contract with the buyer of the service, consignor or consignee, is with a single supplier who puts the end package together.

Jim White, Director General of the British International Freight Association is quoted as saying 'The establishment of the Single European Market is having a profound effect. Distribution channels are being totally revised as organisations are coming to terms with the requirements of a single domestic market of 320m persons.'

Control

It is essential to monitor the effectiveness of the distribution channels and to be aware of opportunities for improvement. Management should especially monitor what is happening overseas because the need for distribution exists everywhere but the process of distribution varies from country to country, from organisation to organisation.

- *Supply chain management (SCM)* has become a most important discipline with Proctor and Gamble claiming stockturn* increases of up to 400% whilst cutting staff costs by 50%! As the number of product lines increases with ever tighter targeting the need to manage proactively is being fully recognised. Coca-Cola now has a logistics director. SmithKline Beecham, a leading exponent of SCM, has one vice-president responsible for production,

*Stockturn = total sales divided by average stocks held. The higher the figure the more effective the stock management. (See Chapter 29.)

distribution and purchasing whilst a second is in charge of sales, marketing and planning.

KEY POINT SUMMARY

- Distributions role is to transport goods and services in the most cost-effective and efficient way.
- Distribution managers have to balance availability against need.
- The balancing factors are: space, transport, time and budget.
- Skilful distribution is of major importance to marketing.
- No physical distribution system can simultaneously maximise service and minimise cost.
- The importance of the various potential customer services must be determined so that a distribution strategy can be decided upon.
- There can be a considerable gearing effect with relatively small savings in distribution, increasing profit levels dramatically.
- It is usually advisable to set distribution up as a separate function – or to hire the services of a specialist organisation.
- PDM strategy is a matter for the distribution director.
- Channels of distribution are the routes through which products pass to reach the final customer.
- Channel logistics are concerned with the physical movement of goods through channels of distribution.
- Logistical decisions are concerned with: costs of holding stock, costs of protection and delivery, routing, stock control.
- Channel selection is concerned with choosing the most suitable channel from those available.
- The principle of minimum total transactions shows that middlemen can only justify their place whilst they show a cost saving to the channel as a whole.
- Channels of distribution are constantly evolving.
- Just in time management relies on the supplier to guarantee delivery of quality controlled products just as they are needed.
- JIT is made possible by three factors: purchasing power, competition and technology.
- Channel power is gained through: size, volume, competitiveness, profitability and efficiency.
- Integration can be horizontal (sideways) or vertical (up and down).
- Channel decisions tend to be long-term and tactically difficult to adjust
- Control over the channel members and over the product is desired, but hard to achieve.
- The longer the channel length the lower the control.
- Intensive distribution aims for maximum market coverage.
- Selective distribution aims to use specific dealers who are capable of handling the product.
- Exclusive distribution is a policy of careful selection of dealers for the special benefits they can offer customers and consumers.

- Location can be crucial to success.
- Services, in particular, need to be where the consumers want them.
- Time is often more important than distance.
- Location must be promoted, so customers are aware and can visit.
- Electronic point of sale (EPOS) provides a wealth of management information and facilitates tactical actions.
- Electronic funds transfer at point of sale (EFTPOS) allows payment by a variety of methods.
- Electronic data interchange (EDI) is the transfer of information between computers in a structured message format.
- Intermodal services are those in which more than one type of transport is used in the course of a single contract.
- It is essential to monitor the effectiveness of the distribution channels and to be aware of opportunities for improvement.
- Supply chain management (SCM) has become a most important discipline.

WORK-, SCHOOL- AND COLLEGE-BASED SELF-ASSESSMENT QUESTIONS

Background
In the UK newspapers are distributed through wholesalers to established newsagents, some large, but many very small independent traders. The smaller newsagents are spread throughout the community and carry a wide range of other goods of immediate use to their near at hand customers. Often known as confectioners, tobacconists and newsagents (CTNs), they have widened their ranges to include groceries, soft drinks, greetings cards. Some are sub-post offices, some have a small video hire section. Many in the UK regard them as essential to community welfare.

Large supermarkets, often in out-of-town locations, are insisting on a strategy of intensive distribution. Some are already selling newspapers and magazines, and a few have sub-post offices, but this is because they have negotiated special deals in individual circumstances. For the moment the policy of selective distribution remains in place.

QUESTIONS

1 As a newsagent:
  (a) Analyse the main reason(s) why newsagents are against intensive distribution.
  (b) Itemise the arguments they can use to support their case.

2 As an assistant marketing manager for a major newspaper:
  (a) Determine the issues facing your organisation.
  (b) Itemise the arguments for and against moving to a policy of intensive distribution.

See the end of Chapter 27 for answer guidelines.

CHAPTER 26

The after market

Four large brown cardboard boxes were waiting in Brian McMurphy's office when he returned from a visit to an important customer. He wasn't feeling very pleased – it had been a bad day – and to find his new computer system delivered but not assembled was almost too much!

He put thoughts of the computer on one side whilst he reviewed the events of his day over a cup of tea.

First thing had been the phone call from Pettifer's. The delivery they had been promised for yesterday had not arrived and they were short on stock. If it wasn't there today production would stop! They would be in real trouble, and so, of course, would Brian. The contract was for JIT delivery and this was the third late shipment in only eight weeks. Brian had chased the order with Despatch and they had promised that it was on the way. So he had phoned back to Pettifer's, and the van was in the receiving dock, so that was all right.

Except that it wasn't all right. Two hours later he received a fax telling him of five omissions from the order and putting him and his firm on notice that they were in breach of the contract terms. Brian had saved the day, at the cost of a previous commitment, by driving up and delivering the missing items himself.

In the meantime he had dealt with three queries on incorrect invoicing, two on non-delivery and four on demands for payment from firms which were not in debt!

After lunch he had been able to get out to see his regular customers, and had taken four big orders. He had been forced to make promises about delivery that he hoped the factory could meet – they were pretty good at squeezing in last minute orders, so he felt reasonably confident.

He had helped one plant engineer with the guidance notes on the laser control mechanism – it was a shame that they were badly translated from Korean, they confused everybody.

Three service engineers worked from Brian's office and he had reviewed their reports for the previous week. Situation normal: 17 complaints of late delivery; 3 machines down for 48 hours because of delays in the supply of spare parts; 14 calls to machines that were in perfect condition but with operators who were not trained properly.

Oh well – Brian turned to his pile of boxes.

To his surprise the computer went together extremely easily. A packing list let him check that he had all he needed and simple diagrams showed how the components fitted together. There were written instructions, but Brian had met computers before and he was able to work solely from the schematics.

With the unit fully assembled he switched on the power and was pleased to hear a satisfying Bing! followed by a fully working system. He was much relieved when he found that although the software disks had been provided their contents had already been pre-loaded. His supplier had even loaded the additional software he had ordered.

In under half an hour he had a fully operational system – all he needed to do was transfer his working data from the old machine – and they had even supplied a dedicated cable so that copying across was made as simple as possible.

He did have a couple of queries, but found the manuals to be clear, written in perfect English, and with a detailed index. There was a UK hot line support for voice calls 10 hours a day, and for fax contact at any time. If he wanted he could get 24 hour support for the cost of a transatlantic call because the US hot line operated 365 days a year.

It was a joy to experience such consideration and just for a moment he wondered how they could do it whilst his firm could not?

THE AFTER MARKET

'The after-market consists of all post-sales efforts to satisfy customers and, if possible, secure regular or repeat purchases' (Jefkins).

Marketing is making the future happen. The main functions of marketing are to identify and satisfy customer need(s) . . . and to make a profit whilst doing so. Regular and repeat sales will lead to on-going profits and so interest in the sale should not cease when the order is delivered, nor when it is paid for.

Management of the after-market is crucial to on-going success. Everything that can be done to make it easier for the customer to derive maximum satisfaction from the purchase should be done. Provision for after-market support must be designed into the product from the very beginning, and monitoring of the product in use is crucial to exact understanding of customer and consumer needs.

The requirements of the after-market affect all levels of management:

After-market rationale

The after-market makes good marketing sense because profits:

- Come from repeat business.
  It is important to help buyers maximise the benefits they obtain from their purchases.
- Customer satisfaction is needed.
  Without satisfied customers there will only be repeat business in a monopoly of essential goods.

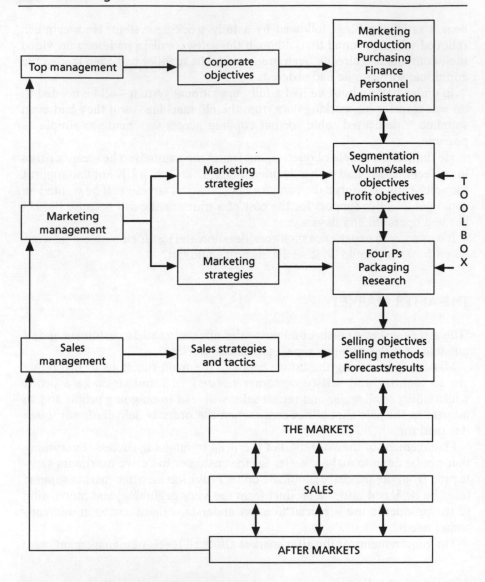

Fig. 26.1 The importance of the after market

After-market involvement

Marketing should be deeply involved with the after-market. Effective management of the after-market does much to reassure customers and retain loyal users. (See Cognitive Dissonance, Chapter 30.)

There are five strategic areas of concern:

- The product should be seen to be easy and safe to use.
- It should deliver value for money.
- It should be installed, or otherwise put into use, fast and with little trouble.
- It should do exactly what it is claimed to do.

- The supplier must build and protect a reputation for concern for the customers.

Typical after-market management concerns are discussed under the following headings.

Market education

An informed customer can locate the product, select it and then use it to maximum effect. Insurers, bankers and the building societies have explanatory leaflets but also branch officials who specialise in helping customers with their problems.

- Little Chef restaurants have road maps that identify all other locations in the chain.
- Gardening products give planting instructions and gardening tips.
- The new Garden Vac from Flymo comes with a short video as well as an instruction manual.
- Apple Macintosh computers come with a user familiarisation program ready installed.

  Exhibitions provide a stimulus for new product purchase and reinforcement of the product values for existing customers.

Deliveries

Should not be promised unless the promise will be kept. Customers are dependent on the supply of their purchases and goodwill comes only from regular and reliable deliveries.

Easy use of product

Customers and consumers must be able to put their purchase to practical use with the minimum of effort. Careful consideration is needed, therefore, to such issues as packaging and instruction manuals – and also on routine servicing required from the user. So far as possible a product should be foolproof and fail-safe.

Fast repair

A defective product is a constant negative reminder that will make it more difficult to repeat sell. Depending on the product a hot line support with service engineers in the field may be appropriate. Perhaps a range of service depots, or special arrangements with dealers to carry out 'factory trained' servicing (as in the motor industry).

Guarantees and warranties should be generous, and not exclude common faults within the small print.

Refunds and exchanges should err on the side of generosity. The damage done by a poorly handled complaint far outweighs the cost of a generous settlement in most circumstances.

Spare parts should be readily available for the lifetime of the product. Customers should be supported until they have exhausted the value of their purchases.

Continuing customer interest

Customer interest should be stimulated after the sale. The aim should be to increase the involvement the customer has with the product and/or supplier.

- The product seen in prominant use is the most powerful reinforcement. Thus IBM heavily featured the use of their products and staff in the management of the 1994 Winter Olympics. There are two major reactions:
  — Gosh! I use one of those!
  — If it can handle a problem that size, it will deal with mine OK.
- Sales promotion schemes encourage customers to remain loyal – film processors offer free film and post paid envelopes, so tying customers to their system.
- Customer clubs add value to the package – from airline executive clubs and frequent flyer programmes to information on and spares for vintage cars.

Product recall

When a fault is detected, perhaps through after-sales service calls, a recall will reassure customers provided that it is backed up with sound PR. It is essential to put minds at ease, and to have the experience add to feelings of confidence rather than detract from them.

Codes of practice

Voluntary measures of customer protection currently cover such areas as motor cars, mail-order, electrical goods, package holidays and footwear.

Customer and consumer satisfaction

After-sales service has increased in importance as products have become more complex and this trend is likely to continue. The need is to ensure customer satisfaction even though the product has moved through a channel of distribution and is several stages away from the manufacturer. Hence the organisations most directly concerned with customer satisfaction are the retailers. Behind the retailers are the manufacturers – it is their product, and they will ultimately carry the blame even if the error is within the channel. They, after all, selected the channel.

The realisation that customer satisfaction is a vital part of corporate marketing strategy has brought about the introduction of customer charters (see Chapter 6). Concern for customers is a positive reflection of sensitivity to customer feelings. Concern for customer satisfaction must stem from top management, and must extend to every member of staff within the organisation if a customer-driven business is to be created and maintained.

KEY POINT SUMMARY

- The after market consists of all post-sale efforts to satisfy customers and, if possible, to secure regular or repeat orders.
- Marketing is making the future happen.
- Management of the after market is crucial to on-going success.
- Provision for the after market should be designed into products.
- Profits come from repeat business.
- Customer satisfaction is needed.
- The five strategic areas of concern are: ease and safety in use, delivery of value, easy installation, performance to specification, supplier's reputation.
- Market education informs customers and allows them to locate and use the product.
- Delivery promises must be kept.
- Customer's needs for ease and speed of use must be met.
- Repairs should be fast.
- Refunds and exchanges should err on the side of generosity.
- Spare parts should be available throughout the product's lifetime.
- Continuing customer interest should be stimulated.
- Sales promotion schemes can help to keep customers loyal.
- Faulty products must be recalled quickly, and customers reassured.
- Codes of practice should be developed, and followed.
- Customer charters are visible evidence of top management concern.

WORK-, SCHOOL- AND COLLEGE-BASED SELF-ASSESSMENT QUESTIONS.

1 From your own experience, and from careful questioning of others, locate 10 examples of good and 10 examples of bad after-sales care.

2 Select the worst three of the bad examples and for each pretend that you are a customer. Write a letter to the marketing director of each supplier suggesting what should be done to rectify the situation.

See the end of Chapter 27 for course guidelines.

CHAPTER 27

Franchising

It was a routine day for Maria Serrano. She had left her Hertz car at the airport, caught the flight booked for her by Exchange Travel and taken the train into London. On her way through Victoria Station she'd bought a scarf from Tie Rack, picked up some evening socks for her husband at the Sock Shop, and been tempted by the French bread sandwiches at the Jardin de Paris. Fortunately her Weightguard pledge prevented her from indulging in a second continental breakfast.

At the office she found a note that her car was off the road for service, but that it had been replaced by a vehicle from Budget. 'Why not Avis' she mused, 'or Practical?' Her secretary had gone out to pick up some copying from Prontaprint and her new business cards from Kall-Quik. She would bring back the usual sandwich lunch from Subway and go to Belina for some Belgian chocolates for her to take to friends that evening.

Calling home, Maria found that British Damp Proofing had finished on schedule and that her son was taking his driving test that afternoon. His instructor at the UK School of Motoring had secured a test slot at short notice. There was a message. Her sister would spend some time at the Body and Face Place and would await her at the Holiday Inn, where they were to dine. She was going round to get her husband's suit from Safeclean – did Maria want anything collected?

Maria picked up her phone again – she had just a few moments to ring Alfred Marks about a temporary replacement for her secretary and then the engineer from Computerland was due. It would be good to have her printer operating again!

What else had she to do? Oh yes, call Home Tune and arrange an appointment for the weekend; talk to the Great Adventure Game about a day's team development for her staff; ring her daughter to confirm they were meeting on Friday at Pronuptia de Paris for a wedding dress fitting.

Just a normal day in 1994 – nothing unusual, except that it couldn't have happened that way 20, even 10 years before – 23 franchises unknowingly used, and mainly in the service sector.

BACKGROUND

We all use franchises every day without being conscious of the fact. Every business that Maria used is a franchise. One of the keys to franchise success is that each appears to be an individual branch of one company – a company that is trusted, and that has strong brand recognition.

In the United States in 1992 the franchises accounted for sales of over $1 trillion – or 25% of GNP. This from a sales figure of over $175 billion in 1988! The growth of US franchise business outstrips the growth in the economy, which signals a significant shift from centrally owned firms.

Franchising is big business because it works.

Franchisor or franchisee?

A franchi*sor* is the owner of a concept, a product, a process, a service – or even a celebrity name. A franchi*see* is someone licensed to make or use something in return for a fee and/or a royalty. A franchisor gets into the market much faster, and for much less cost. A franchisee secures the use of a proven package, and a protected location in which to operate. The franchisor uses the franchisee's capital and, in return, helps the franchisor to succeed. It is in both their interests for a good contract to be established – and for its terms to be honoured fully. Cheating on a franchise is bad business policy.

Forms of franchising

Some of the earliest in the franchise business were the brewers – in the eighteenth century. Their 'franchise' operation has only recently been judged against the public interest by the Monopolies and Mergers Commission, and the 'tied' landlords and tenants have had to be released from their restrictive contracts.

A car manufacturer with supply dealerships operates a franchise system. These 'supply dealerships' used to dominate the UK franchise marketplace, until the high street 'business format franchising' became established within the last 10 years.

Under 'business format' franchising a detailed and clearly defined trading style is established, and the franchisor takes an active part in the control of each individual operation. The most successful franchisors insist that their business plans are followed absolutely, and have very detailed manuals supported by efficient training to ensure that standards are maintained across all franchisees.

The best known example is probably McDonald's, who have very tight controls upon their operation and who have established a Hamburger University which they take very seriously indeed. Taking up a McDonald's franchise costs a minimum of £400 000 (and a lot more in a city) – so they are talking serious business and behaving accordingly. So confident are they in their control, and so important is it to them, that even in Moscow they are guaranteeing that the product will be identical to all other McDonald's outlets across the world.

McDonald's and Kentucky Fried Chicken between them have more outlets than the entire UK franchise community. It is probable that the 20 or so largest franchisers have between them more outlets than the whole of the EU. It seems obvious that the shift to franchising is likely to continue, especially in areas such as financial counselling, home repair, insurance, legal service centres, accounting service centres, dental clinics, weight reduction clinics, exercise studios.

Franchising has reversed the statistics covering new business start-ups. It is reckoned by the British Franchise Association (BFA) that 90% of new franchisees succeed. An exact reversal of the expectation that 90% of new franchisees succeed. An exact reversal of the expectation that 90% of new business ventures fail! Evidence of the belief in this stark statistic comes from the major high street banks. Barclays, for example, have set up a special franchise unit, with its own hot line, and offer tailored finance to aid franchisees get started. The National Westminster Bank have taken a strongly supportive position too. Not only do they have a special unit exclusively for franchise operations, they commissioned the Power Report in 1987 to provide authoritative data on the UK franchise market.

Franchising in the UK

A survey sponsored by the NatWest Bank and the BFA in 1992 showed that about 370 business format franchise systems were on offer in the UK (down from 430 in 1991). Unfortunately only comparatively few of these franchisors are judged to have viable offers that franchisees could take up with confidence.

The average number of units per franchisor is 36, with some 18 000 outlets in total. Franchising employed some 184 000 people in 1992.

Franchising has grown quite dramatically, assisted by changes in the UK's economic and political conditions. The recession of the 1980s provided large redundancy payments to a substantial number of people – which became, for many, the capital needed to start their own businesses. Franchising offers the independence of self-employment with the security of a business format, and that this combination is both attractive and effective is proved by the very few business failures and the large percentage who sign-up again when their contract expires.

Table 27.1 How franchising has grown

Year	Annual Sales (£bn)	Number of units	Jobs created
1984	0.8	7 900	72 000
1985	1.3	9 000	93 000
1986	1.9	10 900	126 000
1987	3.1	15 000	169 000
1988	3.8	16 000	181 500
1989	4.7	16 600	185 000
1990	5.2	18 260	184 000
1991	4.8	18 600	189 500
1992	4.5	18 100	184 000

Source: Barrow and Golzen, *Taking up a Franchise*, 10th edn, The Daily Telegraph Guide, Kogan Page Ltd, London.

Code of Practice

The British Franchise Association first published their *Ethics of Franchising* in 1987. This guide lays down ethical standards for BFA members (who are all franchisors), and gives a lead that should be followed by non-members as well. The BFA will act as arbiters in any dispute between members and their franchisees, which is an important element to provide for in any franchise agreement.

The UK prefers to trade within voluntary codes of practice rather than statutory regulations and this helps to put the importance of the BFA ethical code into correct perspective. It is certainly used by the finance houses when evaluating proposals from prospective franchisees, and without full evidence of compliance it is unlikely that a loan will be made.

Financial support

All the major financial houses who finance franchises have their own checklist for evaluating proposals. The National Westminster Bank has one of 9 sections and 40 major headings. Better franchisors will have made a deal with banks on behalf of their potential franchisees. There is then no need for a franchisee to prove the viability of the franchise. But he does have to show that he is capable of making it work in his chosen area.

Franchises are branded packages

Making it work is fundamental to the success of the franchise overall. Franchising is a highly branded package. It follows that brand identity must not be compromised by a bad franchisee. Therefore the franchisor must monitor performance and take prompt action to prevent slippage.

The franchisee owes it to himself, the other franchisees, the franchisor and the public to get it right. There is no sense, and no long-term profit, in cutting corners or reducing standards.

The franchisor must work hard to maintain and develop the brand identity. This means an effective central marketing team that operates with the franchise as with any other branded product. There has been much debate throughout the last decade as to whether there is room for the 'big brand' in modern marketing. Perhaps there isn't for a new single product. Perhaps we shall not see the launch of another Bovril or Bisto. But there is certainly need for big branding tactics in franchising. The difference is one of degree. A single product cannot support the costs of big brand marketing, but a franchise often involves a mixture of product and service, with a high sales revenue. Holiday Inn is a big brand, so are Kentucky Fried Chicken and Berni Inns, so too are the big car rental franchises.

Franchising in Europe

Franchising in the UK has come a long way in a very short time. The route is now open in Europe as a whole. Franchising is formally recognised by the European Commission as an employer of considerable significance. In 1986, throughout Europe as a whole, it is estimated that some 85 000 franchise outlets were in operation. Major strengths of American business have always been the common language, open frontiers, and excellent communications.

The EU won't have a common language – but with big brand marketing it is not needed. Ariel were one of the first to advertise, by satellite, in German to all within the satellite's footprint. The formula for detergent advertising is so universal that the spoken language is unimportant, the message comes home. So it will for big branded franchises. Coco-Cola is one of the world's topmost brands. Coke is universal, and is a franchisor. Others will follow where Coke has led.

There was concern that anti-cartel laws would prevent franchising, but the Commission in 1987 released the distribution of goods and services from those constraints. An attempt has been made to regularise franchising. Specific backing has been given to the restriction of franchises to specified locations; franchisors have been given legal redress to former franchisees who attempt to launch look-alike operations; franchisees have been given flexibility in pricing and allowed to buy from each other.

These last points are intended to encourage the standardisation of pricing across national frontiers since a franchisee will be able to buy where his specific product is cheapest. It should not be in a franchisors interests to allow price differential by geographic area. Of course this may have the effect of hoisting prices. Market forces, it is felt, will take care of this eventuality.

FRANCHISING

Franchising is defined as:

- A particular form of licensing in which the franchisor makes a total marketing programme available, including brand name, product, method of operation and management advice (Chee and Harris).
- A franchise is a contractual relationship between the franchisor and the franchisee, in which the franchisor offers, or is obligated to maintain, a continuing interest in the business of the franchisee in such areas as knowhow and training, wherein the franchisee operates under a common trade name, format or procedure owned or controlled by the franchisor, and in which the franchisee had, or will make, a substantial capital investment in business from his own resources – The International Franchise Association (IFA).

John Frain sees franchising as an increasingly important industry in any country, providing employment and encouraging new businesses in such as management and consultancy services, secretarial services, damp-proofing, house drive paving, printing, wedding attire, and cleaning services.

Common factors

A contractual agreement forms the basis of a licence to franchise and will include these common basic factors:

- The franchisor owns a name, idea, manufacturing process, piece of equipment, or service.
- The franchisor grants a licence, called a franchise, to the franchisee permitting the use of the name, idea, equipment, or service.
- The franchise agreement contains conditions relating to the operation of the business through which the franchisee exploits commercial opportunities.
- The franchisee pays the franchisor for the rights obtained in the franchise agreement.

Key benefits to the franchisee

- Business training:
  - The Hamburger University;
  - Happy Eater Restaurants have a residential training centre;
  - mechanics are factory trained by car manufacturers.
- Independence as his or her own boss with their own business, yet backed up by an established brand name and proven operation.
- The franchisor's name, reputation, logo, and decor which save the time and investment otherwise required to build a business from start-up.
- Lower capital requirement than operating independently.
- Business planning, finding a suitable site and setting up an operational system of sales, stock control and ordering are provided for within the agreement.
- Direct benefits from regional and national advertising and sales promotion carried out by the franchisor.
- Reduced business risk – and the support of a head office organisation to give confidence.
- Bulk purchasing advantages.
- Unique selling points (USPs) based on the use of patents, trade marks, secret processes (e.g. Coco-Cola), logos (McDonald's is contracted to be the first to advertise from space).
- Regular progress checks with practical help available as needed from the franchisor.

Disadvantages to the franchisee

- The franchisee pays an initial fee and also pays a percentage of sales, or an annual fee, or both, to the franchisor.
- An initial fee has to be paid, (from £5000 to over £400 000 depending on the franchise.)
- Royalties, and/or regular payments, are a drain on the franchisee's profits.

Key benefits to the franchisor

- The franchisor can concentrate on operating a small core business. All the problems of expansion and the day-to-day problems of a large business are delegated to the franchisees.
- A specialist management centre can control a sizeable empire of small businesses.
- The need for large injections of investment capital is offset by the fees paid by franchisees. This enables extra financial support for the four Ps generally and the communication mix in particular.
- Small operators expand rapidly and the growth rates of the franchisors is therefore comparatively very high.
- Expansion into international markets is eased through contracting to local franchisees who have no language nor cultural problems in their own market.
- Franchising attracts personnel at all levels who are motivated and keen to succeed. Organisational conflict is reduced because of the type of staff and of the organisational structure.

Disadvantages for the franchisor

- The franchisor becomes a manager of a network of small businesses, but does not enjoy the advantages of full ownership.
- If the marketing back-up operation (four Ps support) is not seen to operate on a fair and equal basis, the franchisees can become critical and disgruntled.
- The 80–20 Pareto effect applies – 80% of time and effort can be spent on supporting the weakest 20% of franchisees.
- Complexity of control procedures, training courses and monitoring can easily take more resources than planned. Control procedures, therefore, are critical to success.
- Franchisees can falsely declare their takings and/or buy local stocks so that they pay less to the franchisor. Effective personal control is required to ensure this is prevented.

Franchisor/franchisee synergy

Franchising is an important element in creating long-term success for the franchisor and the franchisees. All are dependent upon every other member of the franchise. If one franchisee is below standard it will reflect on the trade, and profits, of others. It is for the franchisor to insist on standards being maintained, and to take firm action if they are not. Franchisees look to the franchisor to set and maintain standards because only if an acceptable level is set will the whole operation be able to continue as a profit-making venture. It follows that the franchisor has to have an efficient and effective system of management and control which is targeted on the actual needs of the entire operation.

SETTING UP A FRANCHISE

The purchase agreement is a short document which simply states that, subject to the franchisor finding a suitable site, the franchisee will enter into the contract set out in the franchise agreement (which he will have read). A sum is paid to the franchisor's solicitors as part of the initial fee, and the franchisee can then proceed with a search for a suitable property.

This search will focus not only on commercial viability, but also on confirming that the necessary planning permissions and consents would be available for its intended use. If no suitable site is found in a reasonable time then the initial fee is refundable. If the prospective franchisee changes his mind, however, the fee is forfeit.

The franchise agreement

This covers:

- the nature and name of the activity being franchised;
- the franchise territory;
- the term of the franchise (how long it is granted for);
- the franchise fee and the royalty on trade;
- what the franchisor agrees to do;
- what the franchisee undertakes to do;
- the conditions under which the franchisee may sell or assign the business;
- the conditions under which the franchisee may terminate the franchise and what his obligations are in that case;
- the terms and obligations of the franchisor in similar circumstances.

It is essential that documents be read in draft, and that legal advice is taken before signing. Whilst a reputable franchisor will provide a fair contract it will inevitably be biased slightly in their favour. Any negotiations to change this must be completed before signature – it is too late afterwards!

FRANCHISEE PERSONAL CHARACTERISTICS

Professor Russell M. Knight of the University of Western Ontario researched the qualities needed for success as a franchisee. He reports that franchisors and franchisees disagreed only in their ratings of management ability and creativity – a point that may provide some clues as to what franchisors are really looking for in a franchisee (see Table 27.2).

Table 27.2 Personal franchisee characteristics required for success

	Franchisee (%)			Franchisor (%)		
	Very Important	Important	Not Important	Very Important	Important	Not Important
Previous management experience in same industry	0	20	80	2	14	84
Previous own business experience	12	46	42	16	47	37
Management ability	84	15	1	66	31	3
Desire to succeed	90	10	0	93	7	0
Willingness to work hard	92	8	0	93	6	1
Creativity	26	56	18	12	44	44
Strong people skills	63	32	5	64	34	2
Financial backing	71	27	2	67	27	6
Support from family	52	28	20	46	32	22

Source: Barrow and Golzen, Taking up a Franchise, 5th edn, The Daily Telegraph Guide, Kogan Page Ltd, London.

OTHER FORMS OF MARKET PENETRATION

Whilst franchising is an extremely important method of achieving market penetration, it is particularly suited to the service industry. Other forms of market penetration are available, and are in wide use.

Management contracting

Joint ventures and management contracting are both key elements in entering and penetrating overseas markets (see Chapter 34).

Licensing

Licensing is a long-term extension of management contracting. The licensee takes a licence for the sale of a patent (product or process) and receives technical assistance, the use of a trade mark, or a trade name on a contractual basis. This is a method of gaining access to overseas markets, using the management contract to forge long-term links. Technical expertise is provided and opportunities created to develop business in tandem with other companies.

Advantages of licensing

- The operation of licence agreements is a major contribution to world sales – contracts are negotiated on the basis of an initial payment, an annual fee, or specific payments for components, design, or technical assistance.
- Licensing requires comparatively little capital outlay, which is of advantage

to the small firm.
- Access to local overseas markets is immediate, with distribution and 4Ps support.
- Licensing may:
  - Avoid tariff barriers.
  - Remove the need for high setting up costs.
  - Relieve low production capacity and/or limitation of factory space.
  - Do away with expensive freight charges, and problems of currency exchange movements.
- Government support for licensing arrangements is strong, hence Coco-Cola gained access to the Russian and Chinese markets.

Disadvantages of licensing

- Disagreements between the various parties to the licence may occur – often during changes in market conditions. Distance may aggravate the problem and solutions are more difficult when language, cultural and/or structural differences exist between the parties.
- When the licence ends the licenser and licensee have gained experience which may now be unusable.
- Control of production quality may be difficult.
- Sales, profits, return on investment may be restricted by government action.
- As technology advances the partnership may tend to break down with the parent company moving on rapidly and the licensing company left in the older technologies. Russia and East Germany are in this position.

Licensing has more advantages than disadvantages. It encourages technological partnerships, the use of total quality management, the training of personnel and higher investment in research and development.

JOINT VENTURES

Joint ventures are projects agreed by two or more parties in which an agreement is made to invest (see also Chapter 34).

As businesses become larger and more powerful there are less opportunities for the small businessman to make a start. Larger competitors are quite capable of forcing a small business to quit through opening close by and undercutting his prices. The cost to them is minor, the working capital of a small business is limited. This is ruthless, but business is, at base, a jungle in which the tough and the lucky survive. It certainly helps to be part of a powerful organisation.

KEY POINT SUMMARY

- Franchising is a long-established form of doing business.
- We all use franchises every day, without being aware of it.

- The franchisor owns the franchise.
- The franchisee licenses use of the franchise.
- Business format franchising works under a detailed and clearly defined trading style.
- The US is about 10 years ahead of the UK in franchising.
- About 90% of new franchisees succeed in the UK.
- In Britain the BFA *Ethics of Franchising* is the code of practice.
- Major finance houses have special franchisee departments.
- Many franchisors are big brands.
- Franchising is recognised by the European Commission as an employer of considerable significance.
- Common factors include: the franchisor owns the franchise, he grants a licence to the franchisee, the agreement sets out the conditions, the franchisee pays for the rights obtained.
- Benefits to the franchisee range from business training to reduced business risk.
- Disadvantages to the franchisee include on-going royalties.
- Benefits to the franchisor range from concentration on a small, core business to above average growth.
- Disadvantages to the franchisor include management without ownership, the need to personally monitor and control.
- Synergy is very important throughout the whole franchise operation.
- Setting-up is in two stages: the purchase and the franchise agreement.
- Read legal documents carefully. Understand them before you sign.
- Successful franchisee characteristics include management ability, desire to succeed and the willingness to work hard.
- Franchising is only one form of market penetration, widely used in the service industries

WORK-, SCHOOL- AND COLLEGE-BASED SELF-ASSESSMENT QUESTION

1 This question is in three parts:

A Which of these could not be a franchise:
   (a) a snack bar in a football ground;
   (b) a sailing school on a Greek island;
   (c) a historical monument such as the Coliseum in Rome;
   (d) an aerospace manufacturer;
   (e) a pet's hospital?
B Which of these would suggest that an applicant is not suitable as a franchisee:
   (a) man, retired company director, aged 57;
   (b) woman, just left university, aged 24;
   (c) apprentice plumber, aged 21;
   (d) unmarried couple, out of work 3 years, aged 35 and 31;
   (e) single parent with two young children, aged 34, 3 and 1?
C What would be the key information you would put together before visiting your bank to discuss their supporting you in a franchise contract?

WORK-BASED SELF-ASSESSMENT QUESTION

2 A friend has said she is thinking about taking up a franchise in your town. Write her a letter explaining the benefits and disadvantages she might encounter and in your own words express what it is like to be the owner of a franchise business.

SCHOOL- AND COLLEGE-BASED SELF-ASSESSMENT QUESTION

2 Write a report to senior manager in your school or college suggesting an area of the institution that could be franchised.

SUGGESTED ASSISTANCE TO SELF-ASSESSMENT QUESTIONS FOR CHAPTERS 23–27

WORK-, SCHOOL- AND COLLEGE-BASED QUESTIONS

Chapter 23

1 This is an excellent opportunity to use a mind map to identify the many different approaches that çan be taken: value can be added to the basic product by colourful plastic coating, they can be packed in jars, in dispensers, made part of a desk tidy that has room for pens, pencils, etc. The desk tidy idea may open the door to a whole new range of office and desk top aids. The paper clip concept can be widened to allow larger versions: 5, 10, even 50 cm to cope with different retaining needs. They can have flat writing surfaces added to allow contents to be labelled . . . they can be developed into attractive hair ornaments.

The basic concept has so many potential extensions . . . once you have understood that a paper clip need not just be a twisted piece of wire some 3 cm long!

Note: Remember that innovation must match to need. It may be necessary to show through promotion just how your new idea works in practice so that potential customers understand what you are offering. Never allow a new idea to drift out on the assumption that people will understand how to use it.

2 Your need is to get active feedback from potential consumers. You need to know?

1 How welcome is the pack? Does it meet needs that can be identified?
2 What changes are required to make it more marketable?
3 What market segments exist?
4 What is the likely price that would be paid?
5 How can the consumer be accessed in terms of product and promotion?

Your research objectives will, therefore, be something like this:
Within 12 weeks, research typical student users to:

1 identify needs for the pack as perceived by typical students;
2 identify modifications/improvements that would add value;
3 determine the market segmentation;
4 gain an indication of the price that would be paid;
5 determine where the pack would be bought from (the channel(s) of distribution);
6 discover the media that accesses the target segments(s).

You would need to commission panel research in addition to individual interviews because of the subjective nature of the process and to benefit from the interplay of several individuals approaching a common problem from a range of backgrounds and interests.

There is a need for confidentiality, since you would not want a competitor beating you to the market, nor following quickly with an improved version.

Chapter 25

1 (a) The main reason is survival. It is more than simply a fall in profits. Without a near monopoly on newspapers and magazines the regular flow of customers

each day would fall, and with it would go the additional business they transact whilst buying their newspaper. Falling revenues would mean reduced staff and lower levels of service. Opening extra hours to make up the shortfall would incur additional costs – and add severe strain to the proprietors.

(b) Arguments are likely to be:

- We provide a valuable service because we are close to our (and your) customers.
- We are efficient, proven, established, in place.
- Many customers are too far from a supermarket to switch purchases there – but we shall not be able to survive if even a percentage of our trade is taken away. Margins are already very slim!
- If we go out of business your overall sales will fall.
- Your costs will rise, and so will your cover prices . . . therefore your sales will fall still further.
- With lower sales your advertising revenue will fall, and your profits will suffer.
- In summary – you need us, we need you.

Note: Note that the argument turns to the effect that change will have *on the supplier.* Organisations are self-motivated!

2 (a) The issues facing the newspaper are:
- An established channel of distribution is in place and working well. General principle: don't touch something that is working fine.
- The supermarkets are huge, and very powerful.
- Supermarkets advertise in our paper, and have strong influence with their suppliers, who are major advertisers. It would be possible for them to reduce their advertising, even switch all funds for a time to other media. How long could we hold up in profit terms if that happened?
- Other newspapers may be tempted to switch to intensive distribution. If they do we shall be left behind while they sign the special deals.
- How powerful is the consumer lobby in comparison to the supermarkets?
- Will our sales rally fall as badly as the newsagents predict? If so, will our profits fall even if circulation is reduced – costs may come down too with fewer delivery points.
- Can we find a compromise position?

(b) The arguments for staying with selective distribution are:

- It is established, in place.
- It is costed and budgeted.
- It is close to our customers.
- Channel members individually are weak, we are in control;
- If we change the supermarkets may secure power over the channel.

For moving to intensive distribution:

- Much larger volume to fewer delivery points.
- More powerful PoS tactics.
- Guaranteed payment of our accounts.
- Larger advertising revenue through higher volume.
- Lower costs through fewer accounts, larger and fewer deliveries, etc.
- The CTNs have a range to rely on, the newspaper element is not as crucial as they say.

Chapter 26

1 Your selection will be highly subjective because satisfaction is judged from the perspective of the customer and is coloured by their biases, attitudes and beliefs. Nevertheless that is the reality with which suppliers have to cope.

Typical good examples are:

- The phone call from the salesman the day after delivery to check that all is fine.
- Immediate acceptance of a request for the return of goods wrongly ordered, or just not liked.
- Discrete checking that requests for return are not because the product has been copied (software) or worn (a ball gown).
- Filling stations that provide free water and air, and who have paper towels available at the pumps.
- Software houses that send news on updates as a priority to all registered users.

Typical bad examples are:

- The flower shop which supplies potted plants in sealed pots together with guidance notes which say 'Do not overwater – keep in a drained pot.'
- Counter clerks who suddenly go off duty whilst there is still a queue.
- Technical back-up that tells you the problem can't be happening . . . when it is!
- Manuals which contain trouble-shooting guides that don't cover the trouble you are in.
- Textbooks that set end of chapter questions, but give no answering guidance.

2 You should not need help with your letters . . . but remember that you are setting the tone of the communication exchange. It is generally unwise to commence strongly. Give the director the chance to respond. If there is no response, or if it is negative in some way, that is the time to become stronger. Getting a situation sorted out can take extreme determination – there is need to keep pursuing the matter, if you are certain you are in the right, until action is taken.

Chapter 27

1 A (c) It is unique.
   (d) Too large, complex and capital intensive.
  B None are unsuitable on the limited evidence. (If you excluded any remember that you must decide on relevant facts, not general background.)
  C The bank would want to see that you are dedicated, capable of working hard, know fully what you would be getting into. Evidence would be needed, not simple oral assurances. Therefore some track record information about you life and career would be needed.

The nature of the franchise and its location is important.

Details of the franchisor would be crucial . . . there are good, very good, not so good and downright dishonest people offering 'franchises'. A bank official should be able to help you ensure that your contact is genuine.

Usually a bank will want you to put up some of the money. You should have thought through what you can, and are prepared to offer before you visit.

WORK-BASED QUESTIONS

Chapter 24

1 Typical criteria include:
1 *Management policy and strategy.* Corporate mission, corporate objectives, marketing strategic objectives.
2 *Market audit.* SWOT analyses using STEEPLE factors to isolate, quantify and rank potential market niches for exploitation.

   Feedback on performance and acceptability of existing products (ours and competitors) to determine if there is need for improvement or replacement.
3 *Product technology.* Audits to determine the limits of present technology and – importantly – the new technology which is available, or coming soon.

   What opportunities are opening due to technology for redesigning existing products, creating new products, defining new market needs that are perhaps not yet open?
4 *Financial.* Only after the needed information is to hand should financial considerations be dealt with in detail. There is need to evaluate risk. The risks of going forward *with this idea* against the risks of dropping or postponing it. If the idea cannot be progressed because of lack of capital can it be licensed (or sold) to a richer organisation?

   Financial issues involve such as: capital needed to fund the R&D, and then to carry the product through to the maturity stage. Without this all-the-way commitment there is little point in passing the idea into concept development.

2 Concept testing is the preliminary research, usually conducted qualitatively, which determines whether the underlying concept is acceptable. From this preliminary research comes the ability to identify target audiences and to match their needs with product benefits. Concept testing guides the designer so that needed benefits are designed in, not added as an afterthought.

   Test marketing is the exposure of the finished product to the marketplace to determine not only its acceptability, but also how best to blend the marketing mix.

Chapter 27

2 The benefits and disadvantages are listed in the chapter, so they should have given you no trouble. You will have had to use your imagination regarding the second part of your answer, but that part of your letter may read something like this:

> Now that we have dealt with the benefits and disadvantages you might like to think about the day-to-day issues. You are going to be the owner of your own business! That means you will have to be in charge – recruit and select staff, manage the finances, set up the marketing, deal with customers, buy stocks, manage the admin – it will all centre on you!
>
> Now you can't do it alone, so I suggest that you very carefully select a senior assistant – someone who has management potential that you can train to be your right-hand person. Perhaps you will divide responsibilities – in which case you keep finance and personnel! Money and people, that's what business is about!
>
> You are going to be in before your staff, and leave after them. You will work 6 days a week – at least – until you are fully up and running. But if you are determined you will, in a couple of years, have a thriving business and be able to cut back to only 5½ days each week!
>
> I wish you well.
> Sincerely,

SCHOOL- AND COLLEGE-BASED QUESTIONS

Chapter 24

1 There is no marketing difference between a product and a service, and so NPD techniques work equally well in education as in industry.

Use Figure 23.4 as the basis for your answer. Each of the three course directors would have to make a case to senior management that showed why his course (product) provided the best long-term opportunity to the institution. He would have to show evidence that he had examined the areas covered in each of the four screens, and come up with a quantified end result. Do not believe anyone who says this cannot be done – it is routine practice in industry. It is difficult, but possible.

(For further guidance see the answer to Work-based Question 1.)

2 You would know the needs of your identified target audiences – who would be the authorities who have to approve your new course, the employers who may sponsor students, the students, the tutors who will teach on it, the administrators who will have to support it.

Blending these conflicting needs would be done from the perspective of the student and employer – the user of the course.

Outlines would be written and concepts tested with respondents selected for their affinity to the target audience(s). Individual models could be worked up and tested in other courses that are already running. Short courses could be mounted – at a discount, perhaps – to test the material in use.

A pilot course could be mounted, with entry restricted to a manageable size. Finally, if all was well, the total package (after all reworking) could be offered to the market.

Note: This process is lengthy, but competitors would have to follow the same path. They could not beat you to the market unless you lost time through unnecessary delays.

Chapter 27

2 You will have had to think hard. What areas of the school or college have unique benefits? Perhaps one area is a leader in its field – for research, in examination results, in student recruitment? Perhaps the head of security has devised a unique control system to monitor the entry and exit points?

Many opportunities exist to sell through consultancy, or license through franchising, but many are missed because those who have the specialist expertise do not realise how valuable it is to others. To them it seems routine – but after all they invented it. To them it *is* routine.

PART 8

Marketing mix –
packaging, pricing and promotion

As can easily be seen, the marketing mix is the home ground of the marketer. Two chapters have been needed to do it justice in this, a management book.

It is sometimes tempting to believe that one understands another's specialist area – costing is not very difficult at all, and employing people is just recruitment and selection – Wrroonnnngg!

Obviously a person can get snarled up in the detail of their subject, looking always for more theories and regulations and principles – often simply to give the impression of super efficiency. Remember always to cut through your own unnecessary detail just as you expect others to. It is also necessary to stick your heels in when an issue is genuinely important, and not be afraid that action will offend . . .

A junior marketing manager, who is now writing this book, learned this non-interference lesson the hard way. The firm were producing a new product – tartare sauce – in bulk packs for caterers. All had gone very well – the product had passed all screens and been welcomed by the caterers who tested it. Approval had been given for the initial production run, the sales force had samples, they were beginning to take orders. As a matter of routine a couple of 2 litre jars were sent on to marketing, and the junior marketer opened up one to taste it. It was sour! Too much vinegar! But the production people were efficient, products were tested rigorously – and the button had been pressed, orders were coming in. The junior decided he was wrong. He wasn't wrong, and fortunately for the company, his boss also decided to check. He immediately rang the production director and alerted him to the problem. All stocks were withdrawn, a fresh batch was made, the situation was saved – and everyone was grateful to the boss. (We shall draw a veil over the interview with the junior.) But the junior learned that if it is wrong, it is wrong – no matter who has made the error. It takes courage, but it is surely better to fail safe than to fail.

David Ogilvy, probably the most famous self-made advertising man, says that his career was built on always taking on the tough accounts, the difficult clients. They gave him the opportunity to shine. A safe client, a 'bread and butter' account, only needs nursing, and it is hard to stand out.

Finally – in this general appreciation of what a young marketer ought to know – always take credit and responsibility for your own work. It is tempting, sometimes to join a pool – to share the responsibilities. But that means that you share the credit too. If you believe in yourself, avoid pools of responsibility. Grow broad and strong shoulders – you can't get to the top without them.

CHAPTER 28

Packaging

Matilda Merriman was upset and extremely frustrated. It was too much . . . milk had gushed out of the litre pack like a fire hose . . . all over her clean kitchen floor . . . she felt she would explode!

Fortunately her good friend Salina was at home – she would go round for a coffee and unburden herself.

Salina made her welcome and as the kettle was boiling so Matilda's frustration came to the boil as well. 'Why do we put up with it?' she cried. 'They say it's for our own good, but my life is being made unbearable by the stupid things they do with wrappers and packaging! Some you can't unfasten, others open much too easily!'

The two women settled at the table with their coffee and over the next hour went through all their frustrations in simply trying to gain access to things they routinely needed.

- Vacuum packs with lids that are too shiny to get a grip, and so large that the handles of a jar opener are too wide apart for single-handed use.
- Foil packs that are too strong to tear, and have no easy opening provision.
- Boil-in-the-bag and microwave packs that have to be cut open while scalding hot.
- Salad cream that has a hidden inner foil seal that has first to be found and then can only be opened with a very sharp and pointed knife.
- Face cream with an inner foil seal that also has to be pierced and cut open.
- Ointment tubes that need the cap reversed and screwed back on to make a hole – very clever once you know how!
- Trying to find the start of a toilet roll – and of Sellotape and of Klingfilm.
- Snap-off tops and tear-off strips on cleansers.
- Treble packs on chilled foods. Why the need for sealed packs to go into plastic bags and then into carrier bags? What a waste!
- Shirts in cardboard boxes that can't be re-used, and then have 12 pins, four clips and a complicated piece of cardboard to get rid of.
- Chocolates individually wrapped, in a pre-formed tray, underneath a corrugated board and a saturated paper liner all inside a fancy box which is covered in transparent film.
- Birthday cards that are individually bagged in film
- Bar-coded price tickets that are security glued and put prominently on products so they can't be removed without spoiling the appearance – but spoil it anyway if they are not removed!
- Press-out tablets that pop everywhere and have to be hunted for on hands and knees before the dog gets to them.

- Child-proof bottles that only a seven-year-old can access easily.
- Newer child-proof packs with double lid arrangements that need both downwards and sideways pressure whilst twisting.
- Aspirin tablets in bottles of maximum size 50.
- Wrapped portions of butter and jam that are a fraction too small!
- PIN numbers from Access and Visa, and salary details from employers that are so securely packed that the contents are invariably torn.
- 13 amp fuses that are packed in fours when only one is needed.
- Airline cutlery and condiments, individually wrapped inside heat-sealed bags.
- Snack products that only half fill a large box but are legal because their weight is shown on the label.
- And the final rub, price stickers that remain so firm on products, even soap and water fail to remove them!

Matilda suddenly stopped – in mid sentence – as Salina jumped to her feet. 'Sorry' she exclaimed, 'but I have ten minutes to get all the labels out of the clothes that I got back from the cleaners this morning. I do wish they wouldn't use those plastic tags.'

Back in her kitchen Matilda started to clean up the mess – it wasn't so bad after all. Perhaps the packaging problem wasn't so bad either? Perhaps it had just been a focus for her general frustration? After all she was old enough to remember when milk had to be put in a wet earthenware pot under muslin to be kept cool on a large stone slab in the pantry – and how it was never quite fresh. How vegetables were sold off the counter and the retailer cleared old stocks before putting the new forward. How disappointed she had been with a lovely box of chocolates, only to find they were discoloured and over a year old! How people had been killed by criminal idiots who sabotaged products in stores!

Perhaps the minor frustrations of coping with modern packaging were worth while after all!

PACKAGING

No longer seen as simply a container or wrapper, packaging is sufficiently important to be treated as a fifth P in the marketing mix. Today packaging has five roles, all of which it must meet within the ever-tightening legal requirements established by governments. Packaging's roles are as shown in Figure 28.1

Legal

Legal requirements cover all aspects of packaging.

- *Protection*. Dependent upon the contents, legislation may require a minimum quality and type of packaging, e.g. in the UK petrol may only be dispensed into metal containers that are clearly labelled; drugs must be

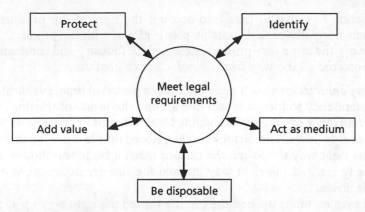

Fig. 28.1 Packaging's roles

dispensed into childproof packs by qualified pharmacists.
- *Labelling.* The weight or contents of a pack must be shown, as must a description of its contents, the detailed ingredients if appropriate and the country of origin. Usage instructions are required by law for some products. Use-by dates are mandatory on food products. Warnings are sometimes mandatory – as with health warnings on tobacco products. Minimum typeface, style and proportion of the package or label is specified for some products. Publisher information is required on publications.

Protection

The prime purpose of packaging is to protect the contents so that they retain their freshness until they are finally consumed. Thus resealable packs are needed for all products which are not intended to be used immediately upon opening.

Protection must take into account everything that might reasonably happen to the product from the time it is packed until it is finally discarded. For example:

- Individual jars may be packed into dozens, with lattice protection between each jar. The outers of 12 jars may be packed into cases of four dozen (four boxes of 12 jars). These, in turn, may be made up into pallet loads and moved by forklift truck through automated warehouses and delivery vans, until the cases are opened in the store and the jars put on the shelf – perhaps in their outer, which may be designed for shelf display.
- Individual jars have to fit onto typical shelving, and resist the effects of casual handling by shop staff and customers.
- Protection against sabotage must be designed into packaging at all stages, but particularly for in-store PoS.
- Jars have to travel in badly packed shopping baskets to domestic homes.
- When opened the contents have to be fresh, and they have to stay fresh until the jar is empty.

Protection has also to take into account the user of the product – hair colourants normally pack disposable plastic gloves with the product.

In exactly the same way products designed for industry and commerce have to be protected all the way from manufacture to final use.

- *Quality enhancement – an example.* Over a period of time, evaporated milk has a tendency to form a cream line around the inside of the tin. To delay this occurrence for as long as possible Ideal Milk tins are packed 48 to a carton – upside down. The cartons are then stored upside down, so that the tins are the right way up. When the cartons reach a trade warehouse they are naturally stacked the right way up, and the tins are automatically turned upside down.

  As each carton is opened the tins are turned the right way up as they go on the shelf. Thus, through innovative thinking, every can of Ideal Milk is turned four times between production and retail sale, and the in-can quality is maximised.

Identification

The packaging identifies the product. A white powder in a transparent bag may be anything from detergent to sugar to salt. Conventions have developed in many markets to help the task of product identification. We expect sugar to be in 2 lb paper bags – but these can be confused with flour if not careful. Detergents are packed in waxed boxes – now in refill bags and waxed cartons as well. Instant coffee is packed in glass, but ground coffee is in vacuum packed foil, or tins.

Many aspects of identification can be subconscious. Guinness found that their product 'disappeared' from view when their oval labels were replaced with round ones in a pilot test of a new design.

Research shows that a product on a supermarket shelf has one fifth of a second to identify itself to a customer as the shopper's glance sweeps down the shelves.

Added value

Typical features which add value:

- an attractive appearance which enhances the environment where it is used;
- secondary use:
  — as a storage container or a children's toy
  — special packs – leaf tea packed in a tea caddie;
- user-friendly features:
  — ring pulls on cans
  — salad cream and toothpaste packs designed to stand upside down when open;
  — swan-necked toilet cleaners.

Most of the time the added value feature is obvious to the manufacturer – but it may not seem obvious to the customer or consumer. As with Matilda and Salina the short-term inconvenience may hide considerable long-term values.

It is necessary not only to add value, but also to make it a communications feature.

Media

In direct contact with customers and consumers alike, a package is a major opportunity to communicate.

A package has the potential to carry the main promotional message through to PoS and Point of Usage (PoU). It can, of course, also carry sales promotional messages through to PoU. Repeat purchases are commonly stimulated by on-pack offers that require several proofs of purchase (bottle tops, labels, etc.).

Note carefully that the product and the packaging are in continuous communication with customers and consumers. If the packaging is difficult to open or unwrap the results can be negative. If the product is not fresh when opened the response is also negative. A balance has to be struck, with safety and freshness always paramount.

Direct and indirect communication must be planned for each package design. The benefits of the packaging add value to the product and should be featured in the promotion.

Disposal

Empty packaging has to be disposed of safely. Environmentally friendly packaging may be biodegradable, but some packaging can be toxic unless disposed of with care.

MANAGEMENT CONCERNS

- That the packaging is effective in all five roles.
- That it conforms to legal regulations and codes of practice.
- That it is efficient – i.e. that minimum weight/cost materials are used to achieve the desired result.
- That synergy applies:
- The *primary* package reflects all the values, above, it is intrinsic to the product and stays with it to PoU.
- The *secondary* package carries one or more primary packages and is discarded as its contents are used. It should carry the same messages as the primary package, especially if designed to go on a sales shelf or to be taken by the consumer as a bulk pack. It provides additional protection, and allows middle men to break bulk down – 48 (4 × 12) – to units of 12 each.
- The *shipping* package ensures that the primary and secondary packages are protected, and that the case or outer allows easy identification, and provides handling instructions in visual as well as verbal terms.

For example, a wine glass silhouette is used to indicate fragility, an arrow to denote 'this way up'. The total strength of all three levels provides the synergy. It is wasteful to make the shipping package too robust.

Innovation in packaging

An example

Maggi soup mixes were sold to the catering trade in bulk. Each tin was individually packed in a fibre carton that was attractively printed in Maggi red and yellow and measured 25 cm × 20 cm × 20 cm (10 in × 8 in × 8 in). There were 18 varieties, and the Maggi depots and the wholesale trade routinely made up orders from across the range for individual hotels, restaurants and cafes.

Individual packaging was maintained since the users of the product – the chefs – did not want several cans of each flavour. Better to have one or two of the most popular and one each of the others. Each individual carton was handled in the factory, on the distribution vehicle to the depot, at the depot, on a vehicle to a wholesaler, at the wholesaler, on a vehicle to the caterer, and by the caterer himself.

The brand manager, on a field visit, noticed the amount of labour involved in handling each outer individually – and the solution was an excellent example of innovation in use. A simple cardboard tray measuring 60 cm × 40 cm × 5 cms (24 ins × 16 in × 2 in) – just large enough to hold 6 outers – was provided, and outers were packed in sixes in the factory. The six-packs could be palleted and moved by forklift.

The six-packs retained their integrity until they were broken down to make up individual orders . . . but then the trays could still be used since outers were of a common size, and caterers normally ordered more than six flavours at a time.

Package testing showed that the weight of board used in individual outers could be reduced considerably when outers were packed in sixes – and the whole of the new packaging system showed a substantial cost saving, even when taking the new trays into account.

TESTING

The most comprehensive testing trials are needed to ensure that a package delivers adequately under all six headings. Test under worse than expected conditions; test to destruction; follow through and take the product from the PoS and test it, test from the user's workplace.

Give a product to the most stringent critics to test: e.g. children make excellent testers – especially of 'child-proof' packages.

In all testing trials remember that a product can be over-protected. The aim is to provide sufficient packaging under all six areas of concern. Over-protection adds considerably to cost, and annoys consumers. Under-protection must, of course, be avoided – hence the need for the most meticulous and on-going testing and evaluation.

The number and type of complaints can indicate packaging efficiency. If a fragile product is over-protected there may be no breakage claims. If under-protected the claims may rise to extreme heights. Perhaps it is better to plan for a reasonable number of complaints because the cost of replacement is less than the cost of full protection? This, of course, is a financially centred argument. The customer viewpoint would be that having to return any broken product is less than satisfactory.

COMMUNICATION

Packaging is a major communicator. The communication potentials must be recognised and used effectively, otherwise the package is simply a protective device. This appreciation of the role of packaging as a communicator has spread into industrial and business-to-business marketing, where functional packaging might be expected to be sufficient.

It is insufficient because orders are placed by people, and people naturally prefer to deal with attractive rather than boring things. If all else is equal the attractive package will swing the sale.

In communication terms a package has to:

- Secure attention   in conditions of extreme 'noise'.
- Persuade   the potential buyer that it is value for money.
- Link   with the potential buyer to build and develop brand loyalty.
- Be memorable   so it will be easily recognised, and sought next time.
- Instruct   in how to open, and how to use.
- Inform   about mandatory factors such as size, weight, origin, etc.

Silent selling

A package is a part of the sales team. It cannot speak in the accepted sense, yet it communicates with words and pictures. It must therefore sell itself, first off the shelf, or out of the catalogue, then out of the storage cupboard. (A surprising number of new products are bought, but never used.) It then has to repeat sell when next the customer is purchasing.

PACKAGE DESIGN

The package designer has six variables with which to work:

- shape
- size
- colour
- graphics
- materials
- smell

It is the effective blend of these factors that makes a successful package.

Good design is never noticed, nor remarked on by consumers. Just as a good referee is not noticed in a football match, so good package design remains 'unseen'. It is, of course, 'seen'. It is just not noticed.

The detailed issues of packaging design are highly technical in nature, and of concern to tactical management. The tiniest details can make a considerable difference to a package and it is for a specialist designer to take these into account when complying with the design brief. An example of the effect on Guinness of a label change has been given above. Other examples are:

* Wines from the regions of France can be distinguished by the shapes and colours of their bottles.
* Many bottles carry identification in Braille which is moulded into the glass or plastic during manufacture.
* Jif Lemons are known instantly from their shape and colour.
* The Coca-Cola swirl visually identifies the product no matter what language is used on the label.
* Red tends to suggest richness and strength (in the UK). Blue is associated with coolness. Green was an unlucky colour, but its image has changed dramatically within the last decade.

Design briefing

Strategic considerations of package design must be thought through and used as the basis for a detailed design brief.

A design brief is structured:

* Background
  — details of the organisation, its product range, its current packaging;
  — general statement of why the package is needed.
* Market details
  — objective facts: Size, growth, location, etc.;
  — subjective opinions: Customer and consumer expectations and needs, etc.;
  — communication objectives for the organisation at corporate and strategic levels;
  — the positioning statement;
  — specific objectives written against time to indicate exactly what the package is required to achieve and who are the targets.
* Contacts
  — creative and production contacts (to allow direct communication during the creative process);
* Budget
  — an indication of the budget available, or a requirement that a detailed budget be prepared;
* Time scale
  — when the job should be completed;
  — requirement for a schedule showing target times for the achievement of each stage.

- Evaluation
  - either: an indication of the researchers available to evaluate the design as it passes through the stages of development;
  - or: a requirement that the research to be undertaken be specified;
- Other considerations:
  - any other pertinent facts, opinions or requirements.

PACKAGING DESIGN PROCESS

Design briefs require as much care as any other management briefing. Without a specific set of instructions and clear guidance a designer cannot be effective.

Note: The term 'package' can be used to describe the full range of benefits – including physical packaging – which are offered to customers and consumers. Do not confuse the usage of the terms (see Chapter 23).

Services packaging

Packaging is normally thought of in connection with a physical product, and not with a service. Most services are not exclusively intangible, however.

- Hairdressing is a service that requires the ambience of a salon, and a range of product options in the form of shampoos, etc.
- At-home car maintenance is a service but requires good presentation – van, equipment, overalls. The communications system must be efficient and give exactly the right impression to customers.
- High street copier shops provide a service, but need to be located close to need, to supply a range of papers and support services. They, too, must be well presented.

It follows that a service needs to be well packaged, in the sense of professional presentation, as any physical product.

In Figure 28.2 the package designer is shown as working to produce a bottle and a label – but the brief could as easily have been for the complete presentation of a service.

It is for the marketing manager to know clearly what he wishes the presentation to convey, and to have the communication skills to transmit this concept to the designer. It is for the designer to use his skills to translate the concept into reality, and to continuously check (research) each stage of the progress.

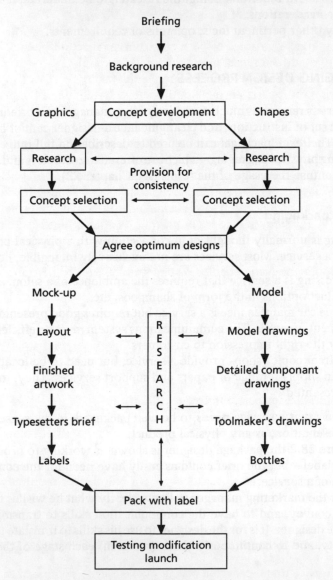

Fig. 28.2 A typical packaging design process

Source: Developed from Smith P R (1993), *Marketing Communications: An Integrated Approach*, Kogan Page Ltd.

KEY POINT SUMMARY

- Packaging can over-protect – and be very annoying.
- Minor frustrations are worth while given today's expression of product quality – and the risk of sabotage.
- Packaging is a fifth P in the marketing mix.
- Packaging has five roles to be met within legal requirements. To protect, identify, add value, act as medium, be disposable.
- Legal requirements cover: protection and labelling
- Protection must carry through until the end of the life of the product.
- Protection must also take the user's needs into account.
- Identification is by shape as much as by label.
- Value is added by: appearance, secondary uses, user-friendly features.
- As a medium, packaging is in direct contact with customers and consumers.
- Direct and indirect communication must be planned for each package.
- Disposability is very important, given today's environmental concerns.
- Management is concerned that: packaging is effective in all roles, conforms to legal regulations and codes of practice, is efficient, enhances synergy.
- The primary package is intrinsic and stays with the product to the PoU.
- The secondary package carries the primary packages.
- The shipping package enables secondary packages to be transported cost-effectively and efficiently.
- All packaging acts as a medium.
- Testing is essential – on a continuing basis.
- Aim not to over- nor under-protect.
- The number and type of complaints can be a guide to packaging effectiveness and efficiency.
- In communication terms a package has to secure attention, persuade, link, be memorable, instruct, inform.
- Packages are silent salesmen.
- Package designers work with six variables: shape, size, colour, graphics, materials, smell.
- A design brief requires as much care as any other management briefing.
- Services are packaged physically – e.g. a hairdresser requires a salon, an ambience, and a range of product options such as shampoos.

WORK-, SCHOOL- AND COLLEGE-BASED SELF-ASSESSMENT QUESTIONS

1 Select a service that is provided in your marketplace – not one of those quoted as examples in this chapter. Analyse it to determine the elements that make up the product and the service features. How important are the product features to the success of the service?

WORK-BASED SELF-ASSESSMENT QUESTIONS

2 Examine the output of your organisation – product(s) or service(s). Use the following matrix to help you assess their effectiveness and what can/should be done as improvements – or to make them legal!

Table 28.1 Packaging matrix

ROLE	GOOD POINTS	AREAS FOR IMPROVEMENT
Legal: • law • codes of practice		
Protection: • primary • secondary • shipping		
Identification • conscious • subconscious		
Add value • features • secondary use • user-friendly		
Media • direct communication • indirect communication		
Disposability • biodegradability • instructions		

SCHOOL- OR COLLEGE-BASED SELF-ASSESSMENT QUESTION

2 Examine the activities of your school or college. Use the matrix given (Table 28.1) to help you assess their effectiveness and what can/should be done as improvements – or to make them legal!

Hint: You will probably have to restrict your task to an identified area of the organisation since so many products and services are offered. Either take a general view, by focusing on departments as a whole, or penetrate to individual courses offered within a department or faculty.

See the end of Chapter 31 for answer guidelines

CHAPTER 29

Pricing

Ian was a most unhappy young man. He couldn't go to work, and he only hoped that the boss would understand. Surely he would – this was an emergency after all!

All had been fine when Janice and he had gone to bed, but they had been startled out of their sleep by a terrible crash. The ceiling in their lounge had collapsed under the weight of water that had accumulated from a leaking pipe in the bathroom!

They didn't know that at first, of course. The immediate reaction was of horror at the destruction. Virtually the whole lounge was affected. If it had just been water it might not have been so bad, but they lived in an old house and the ceiling was made of plaster and horsehair. It was a revoltingly sticky mixture that covered three parts of the floor area! Their three-piece suite was ruined, the dining table and chairs were as well. The carpet had had no chance.

Obviously the first thing was to turn off the water at the main, but there was still 40 gallons in the roof tank. Ian had found a ladder and got into the loft to tie off the stopcock, but not before a further 20 gallons had poured into the lounge.

At 6.30 Janice started to ring the plumber who had installed their new bathroom six months before. She kept ringing every ten minutes until at 8.40 she was answered. To her horror she was told that the plumber had left the area three months ago! No, there was no forwarding address and, yes, there were lots of people trying to contact him.

In despair they wondered what they could do. Were they even covered on their insurance?

The insurance broker answered the phone at 9.05. Yes, they were covered for the damage to the house, and for the plumbing repairs. For their furniture they would get an allowance of about 50% of original cost, not replacement value. They would remember that they could have taken the additional protection, it was an optional extra, but they had decided not to.

Ian went into his house file and took out the estimates he had received when they were planning the new bathroom. They had taken the cheapest quote, and the job had been done quite well. The bath had turned out to be lightweight plastic, and a bit shorter and narrower than they had expected; they had replaced the plastic toilet seat with a polished wooden one from Texas Homecare, but on the whole they hadn't been too unhappy.

The second quote had been 30% higher, but it was from a firm who had been in business since 1922. Surely they would answer their phone?

By 11.30 emergency repairs had been completed, and the water was back on. The general manager had visited and recommended that the bath be either changed, or that its mounting should be strengthened. He explained that as it was lightweight plastic it would flex and separate from the walls. Then water from the shower would run straight down the lounge wall! He also recommended that a tap be fitted in the airing cupboard so that the roof tank could be isolated. At the same time, perhaps isolation taps for the central heating? That had potential to cause real problems.

Ian and Janice sat in their kitchen with mugs of soup. The worst was cleared, the carpet thrown away, fan heaters were going full blast to dry the room, and a builder was coming round to quote for replacing the ceiling. He had been recommended by the plumber that morning so, hopefully, would arrive on time an then be free to do the job quickly. The insurance claim form was in the post to them.

'Janice' said Ian, 'there is one lesson to be learned from all this – never take the cheapest quote without knowing what you are buying!'

PRICE OR VALUE?

Value: The intangible package of benefits that the decision-making unit believe attaches to the product.
Price: Money or other consideration for which a thing is bought or sold.

Value is always subjective in nature and the term is completely misunderstood by the average purchaser.'I buy at the lowest price' usually means 'I buy at the lowest price when I have taken all my needs over a period into account.' In other words 'I buy the best value that I can afford'.

Value includes:

- benefits offered;
- after-sales service;
- status attached to the brand;
- ease of installation and/or of use;
- useful lifetime of the product;
- reputation of the supplier;
- price asked, gross and net;
- guarantee/warranty period.

Marketing is an exchange of value. Price is simply a convenient method for indicating a major part of the value package. The objective of any transaction should be mutual satisfaction. If both sides are happy with a deal it is a marketing transaction.

When establishing a value package it is essential to examine the product offering from the viewpoint of the customer. Terms such as 'cheap' and 'expensive' only have meaning in a particular context. It is for the customer to judge if something is worth buying, and not for the supplier to pass judgement.

Appreciation of value changes with disposable income, experience and circumstances:

- Over time customers' tastes change, and so does their disposable income. Shoe shop assistants know that some people do not think £100 shoes are 'expensive'. For the average 17-year-old it is, of course, a ridiculous sum to pay for shoes.
- Tickets to see Manchester United play football for 90 minutes at Old Trafford cost less than if they play the same team in the FA Cup Final.

PRICING

Price is related to volume of sales and the quality of the product offered over a time period. It must be co-ordinated with corporate and marketing objectives. It must relate to the other elements of the offering mix.

As a basic principle pricing should always aim to achieve the maximum possible return consistent with long-term repeat business.

Pricing is a strong tool of the marketing mix to reinforce:

- selection of market segments and targets;
- selection and loyalty through brand image;
- the formulation of the marketing mix as a tactical tool;
- the linkage of strategic with tactical pricing to meet irregular market conditions and/or special events.

Selection of specific price strategies and tactics can be related to:

- resources
- cash flow
- advertising
- promotions
- distribution
- target markets
- niche markets and market segments.

Return

The return should be measured in profit on sales revenue – never on profit per unit. This is because volume sold makes a very considerable difference to total profit. It is not the % profit per unit that counts – it is how many times you make that percentage. To illustrate:

> Should a shopkeeper invest £100 in bread, with a daily stock turn and a gross profit of 5%; or in canned fruit with a monthly stock turn and a gross profit of 30%?

We must work out the return over a period. Let us take a year.

The stock turn for bread is daily. All the bread will sell each day, make £5 profit, and the £100 will be reinvested in fresh bread tomorrow. That is 6 days a week for 52 weeks in the year . . . = £5 × (52 × 6 days) = £1560 gross profit (GP) p.a.

Canned fruit will sell out each month, make £30, and the £100 will be reinvested 12 times . . . = £30 × 12 (months) = £360 GP p.a.

So the higher profit line returns less cash profit over the same period.

To achieve the same profit as on bread the canned fruit would have to be sold and replaced 52 times a year, i.e. once a week, i.e. a stock turn of 52 . . . = £30 × 52 = £1560.

Notes
- Stock turn   the number of times a product sells out completely in a period.
- p.a.   per annum (each year).

PROFIT

Profit is the difference between revenue and cost. Because there are several kinds of cost there are several types of profit. A trading account shows the different profit (see Table 29.1).

Table 29.1

	£	%
Sales revenue	1 000 000	100
Less: cost of good sold	650 000	65
Gross profit (GP)	350 000	35
Less:		
Fixed costs	150 000	15
Variable costs	70 000	7
Net profit before tax (PBT)	130 000	13
Tax	60 000	6
Net profit after tax (PAT)	70 000	7

It is from profit after tax that dividends can be paid, and so profit after tax is the measure of judgement for return on capital employed (or return on investment). Unless the organisation can earn more than is available as interest on a safe investment in a bank deposit account it will not attract shareholders' funds. In this case 7% net profit after tax is too low.

Where can the organisation look to make improvement? Higher profits can come from:

- Revenue increase:
  - with fixed costs remaining unchanged;
  - with volume discounts reducing the cost of goods sold.
- Cost of goods sold:
  - Tougher negotiation reduces the purchase price of goods and/or raw materials.
  - Volume discounts obtained from suppliers through increased sales.
  - Consolidation of purchases onto fewer suppliers to achieve volume.
- Fixed costs reduction:
  - Costs such as rent and rates which remain unchanged whatever the level of activity. The percentage of revenue will change as volume changes, but the actual cash needed to pay them doesn't change.
  - Generally changes to fixed costs are not a short-term option.

- The lower the fixed costs the less GP has to be generated to cover them.
- Variable costs reduction:
  - Costs that vary with the cost of production, such as raw materials, electricity and overtime payments. These costs will increase or fall as volume changes. But increased sales do not necessarily bring about reductions! If an extra shift has to work, at double time, the net profit may fall despite the additional business going through. In times of recession a priority target is productivity – more achievement per head at the same or lower costs. (*Note:* Productivity should *always* be of prime concern, it should not take a recession to make management aware of the need to maximise productivity.)

COSTING

In principle, costing is extremely simple. In practice, it is extremely complex. How costs are allocated can make a major difference to profitability. As an example, should the fixed costs of a factory be charged out pro rata per unit produced, or pro rata to space occupied?

If costs are charged to each unit then high- and low-priced units will carry the same fixed cost. This is surely unfair? But if they are charged on space occupied they may still be charged to the lower priced unit! Then again the lower priced unit may have by far the highest stock turn!

There are 'overhead' costs which are incurred, such as central administration. How should they be allocated? Pro rata per unit? As a proportion of gross profit earned by each item, each line, each product mix?

How should the costs of a new product be allocated? Perhaps it is being sold deliberately low to secure market share. If so, where should the shortfall be charged?

Costing can become extremely complex, and lead to many arguments as costs are apportioned across products. Naturally each marketer wants his product to carry as low a cost as possible, and each is likely to argue strongly for a form of costing that is advantageous to himself.

Cost accountants specialise in this complex subject – and they generally have the final word. It is for senior management to ensure that most apportionment is realistic, and related to the long-term good of the organisation. It is short-term madness to show high paper profits on one product, and high paper losses on others, if this is simply the result of an internal wrangle between managers.

The key issue guiding all managers is that organisations survive and thrive on a positive difference between costs and revenue. The more positive the difference, the more the organisation thrives.

Never confuse a percentage move with a cash result. Always translate percentages into cash. 'OK, so we have a 5% sales increase – what does that mean in cash terms?' Too often you are likely to find that a sales increase has been purchased with discount or special deal. The cash made on the new sales level may even be lower than previously earned! If this is expected – fine. If not, the manager who authorised the deal has some serious questions to answer.

PRICING STRATEGIES

Corporate objectives guide the pricing strategies. The cardinal principles that guide strategic price planning are:

- Ensure that the market price covers all costs, and provides at least the minimum return on investment needed to achieve corporate objectives.
- Always set price against anticipated volume, and always calculate on the basis of overall actual cash profit. Never work to percentage figures alone.
- Always cost on the basis that the agreed settlement terms will be exceeded, i.e. that debts incurred will not be cleared in 30 days – perhaps 45 is more accurate.
- Market share is not secured long-term by price. The only long-term security comes from offering value.

Pricing strategies can be selected with various objectives in mind, as discussed under the following headings.

Survival

If survival is paramount the pricing must be competitive, even cutthroat. Conditions that create a survival situation may be:

- stock levels too high;
- production capacity under-utilised;
- extreme competition;
- recession – may well be the cause of any or all of the above.

Survival policies are not for the long-term – but the long-term must wait. The effect in the market is damaging since extremely low prices force down the competition. There is a short-term benefit to buyers, but not long-term if the suppliers are reduced in number.

Maximising current profits

The unit profit/stock turn equation that maximises return is selected. This often will not be the highest volume that could be achieved and so market share may fall. There is little point having a high market share at the expense of long-term profitability. On the other hand, long-term returns may be more valuable – in which case this would be the wrong policy.

Maximising current revenue

Sales revenue and demand must be balanced to achieve the maximum return. Management needs to forecast what will happen to volume as price changes. In some cases volume will increase with a price increase! i.e. if the benchmark price (see below) is above current price many potential customers may be deterred from buying.

Benchmark: A level of price which guides purchasers regarding the value of a product offering. It indicates what one would expect to pay for a product that would work effectively. Higher perceived value allows pricing above the benchmark level.

Maximising sales growth (also market share acquisition)

Higher unit sales leads to higher market share and lower unit costs, greater security in the marketplace and higher long-term profit. Therefore it can be beneficial to price low to secure market entry, even if this means taking a loss in the short-term. New products often come into the market with deliberately low prices. (See Price wars and Penetration pricing, below.)

Product quality leadership

Higher than average prices may be charged for quality products. This tactic needs strong advertising backing to create demand in the market. Designer label suits, quality perfumes and sports cars all price to suggest quality leadership. Chee and Harris suggest that price provides a guide to consumers 'through benefits gained by owning and using the product for which they have to make a (monetary) exchange'. It is the benefits of ownership that are valued.

Price can also enhance uniqueness:

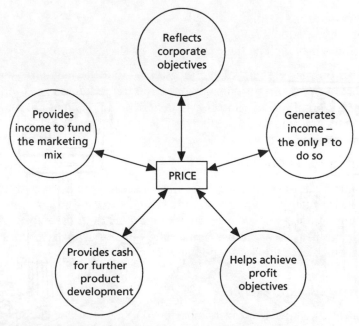

Fig. 29.1 The uniqueness of price

PRICE WARS

Price wars are started when one organisation lowers price, a competitor follows and the first cuts again. The second may cut again, and the first follows. In this way prices can be slashed in a bid to gain supremacy, but the end result is that neither have secured a price advantage. They are still in the same price positions relative to each other. All that has happened is that both have cut into their profit margins – possibly wiped them out altogether.

The buyers will have benefited substantially in the short-term – and possibly long-term as well – because the end may well be a new market price below the original level. If the average price is £10.00 and eventually it stabilises at £8.50 there is £1.50 less profit per unit available to members of the distributive channel. Volume may increase, and if so the tactic may be justified, but only if this was the original objective.

A far better way to achieve a short-term price advantage is by special offers which are limited by time. These are common in petrol marketing where filling stations have short-term price offers which the others do not feel the need to match. Often several filling stations will have offers in sequence – one after the other. Motorists may switch brands for a time, but the overall interest generated justifies the tactic.

Fig. 29.2 Price war

KEY STRATEGIC DETERMINANTS

Pricing is not an inside-looking-out activity. Prices may be asked by an organisation, but they are set by the market. (If the asking price is too high there will be no takers.) Three key factors which impact on pricing policy are:

Demand

Pricing policy is dependent upon accurately estimating demand. This is not simply a factor of customer and consumer willingness to buy and to use. It is an estimate of the ability to buy *at this time*.

Never assume that because an order is taken the goods are sold! Title may change because legally the goods are sold, but in practical terms nothing is sold until it is paid for. This can be a very difficult lesson for the sales force to learn . . . but anyone can take orders from those who have no ability to pay!

Economists approach pricing from the viewpoint of elasticity of demand and this is a very useful concept for marketing to master. A demand curve can be plotted to show how sales volume changes in line with price.

Figure 29.3 shows that although the price has fallen quite significantly there has been little change in demand. A 25% price fall has generated only a 5% sales increase. Customers are not greatly affected by price – their demand is *price inelastic*.

The same price decrease in a different market may bring about the result in Figure 29.4. Here there is a 40% sales increase – demand is *price elastic*.

Price changes may alter the relative value of a product, and either make it available (through a price decrease) or prohibitive (through a price increase). Perhaps an alternative will be substituted, perhaps the product will be reclassified as 'luxury' and purchases rationed, or postponed. Essentials such as water, heating and lighting are price inelastic because they have to be obtained at

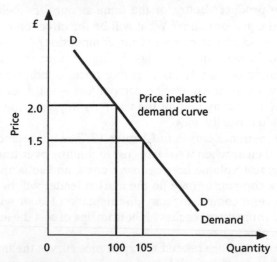

Fig. 29.3 Price inelasticity

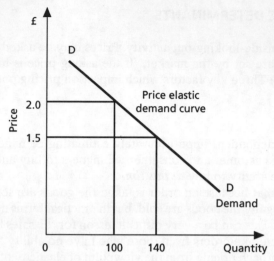

Fig. 29.4 Price elasticity

whatever cost. Holidays are price elastic because they are not absolutely necessary.

Prices must reflect the levels of demand within a market. In seasons and situations of strong demand prices tend to rise. When demand is low prices tend to fall. Short-term price variation can encourage demand, e.g. diners in Country House Restaurants eat at a 33% discount if they order before 6 p.m.

Competitors

Competitive action can have major impact. Do they meet or beat prices? Are their products comparable in the perception of the target market? Will they also launch a new product? Better or the same as ours? Is their promotion and/or distribution equal or better? What will be the effect on our customers – will they switch purchases to or away from competition?

What image should we project? A slightly higher price to indicate higher quality, or a matching or slightly undercutting price to indicate value? How powerful, and how determined are the competitors – will they match price competition penny for penny and all the way? As in poker, the cooler head and the thicker wallet usually wins.

We examined experience curves in Chapter 17. The importance of market leadership becomes clear when we relate cost to volume over time. The competitor with the largest volume has the lower costs, and so is able to dictate prices. Whatever a competitor may do the market leader will be able to dictate prices. Whatever a competitor may do the market leader will be able to match, and when a competitor reaches his bottom line of cost the market leader will still have a surplus in hand.

When pricing strategies are related to experience curves the importance of judging the transition from growth to maturity becomes even more clear.

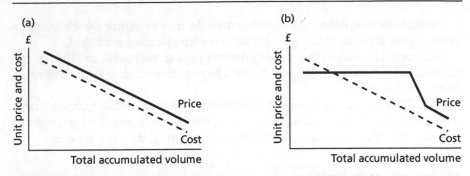

Fig. 29.5 Pricing – alternative strategies (Figure 17.11 put to practical use)
(a) Cost plus pricing
(b) Penetration pricing – initially price is kept as low as possible to establish
market dominance. As cost reductions are achieved through economies of scale,
price can be further reduced. Eventually it will be too expensive for new
entrants to establish themselves in the market.

Positioning and life cycle

- Pricing affects customer demand within a market segment and therefore
  decisions on positioning.
- Pricing changes during the product life cycle.
  — Introduction   High promotion costs.
                     Prices tend to be high.
  — Growth   High promotion costs.
                     High sales growth.
                     Prices start to show signs of coming down, of being
                     competitive.
  — Maturity   Lower promotion costs.
                     Sales growth slows down, profit is taken.
                     Prices stabilise at a level determined by the market
                     share/volume/cost relationships.
  — Decline   Minimal promotion costs.
                     Sales volume declines.
                     Prices remain stable

Debtors and creditors

If those who buy do not pay as agreed it will mean that the debtor's ledger
will be higher than expected. More capital will be tied up than planned for,
and higher interest charges will have to be paid. Thus overall costs will increase.
If these are not passed back to the market in higher prices it means that profits must suffer.

In times of recession it is common for a 30-day credit period to extend to
60, even 90 days. In many cases this lack of ability to get money in from debtors
has forced companies out of business. Profits are only realised when the cash
comes into the organisation.

Control over the debtors' ledger – getting the money in quickly whilst maintaining a good relationship with clients – is a key management skill.

Note carefully that in may cases firms are paying their debts in 30 days, but allowing 45, 60 and more days of credit. They are thus funding their customers. Not a good policy!

Note: This practice is regarded as immoral by many trading nations, and is illegal in some. There is strong pressure in the UK to secure the legal right to charge interest on accounts owing beyond the agreed date for payment.

The price floor and ceiling

Hatton and Oldroyd show that there is a price floor and a price ceiling within which the marketer has to establish price (see Figure 29.6).

In between the floor and the ceiling lies the band of *price point options* that are available.

Fig. 29.6 Price floor and price ceiling
Source: Hatton and Oldroyd (1992), *Economic Theory & Marketing Practice,* Butterworth-Heinemann.

PRICING AND POWER

Distribution channel members want products that are in demand, and which show a good profit. But they are, essentially, only boxes on a shelf. If boxes 'A' are not justifying their place they will be dropped in favour of boxes 'B'.

Retailers, in particular, are now very efficient in controlling the amount of profit they expect each cubic metre of space to generate, and each area of the shop has its budgeted performance to meet. Thus Marks & Spencer only sell gloves in the gift buying time before Christmas. They are profit-earning gifts to M&S, not a garment to be stocked throughout the year. Gloves cannot justify their space other than in the period before Christmas.

The pricing tactics that M&S apply to gloves is based on their gift policy, not their policy covering basic clothing. One would expect them to earn less on underwear than on gloves . . . but to sell far more, the year around.

For glove manufacturers the highly seasonal M&S policy must be extremely frustrating!

PRICING TACTICS

Pricing is a highly effective tactical weapon to secure short-term gains and/or to counter competition. It is possibly the most volatile element of the marketing mix and so there is usually a need for a variety of pricing tactics, and for the tactical mix to vary more often than the mixes of the other Ps.

Profit, of course, is always a prime consideration – but the first essential is to at least recover enough revenue to cover all costs.

- Skimming pricing is the deliberate setting of a high price on the introduction of a product to the market. Thus one 'skims' off the business from the innovators and some of the early adopters whilst restricting demand to allow evaluation of the true market potential.
- Penetration pricing is establishing price levels which ensure that the market will be thoroughly penetrated – that as many as possible will buy and use the product.

   The Americans have a reputation for going quickly to penetration pricing, whilst the British are said to traditionally have favoured a higher profit, but lower volume 'skimming' policy.

It is often better to set the penetration aspect as a form of discount. Then the actual price is indicated, but innovators and early adopters can buy at the 'introductory discount' price. If necessary the discount period can always be extended . . . but there will never by any doubt of the list price. The alternative is to open at a lower price, and then to introduce a price increase just as the product is beginning to become established. This can have a serious effect as price increases are always noticed, and usually resisted.

- Psychological pricing is the establishment of a price level which appeals psychologically. Thus prices are set around *price points*. Typical psychological price levels are:
   — £49.99   appears much lower than £50.00
   — £145.00   seems well below £150.00 and yet not much above £125.

Points to avoid are:

- Round pounds e.g. £1.00 – because once the £1 barrier is breached customers relate to a price band that stretches from £1.00 up to, perhaps, £1.20. Therefore demand will not be very much different at £1.00 and £1.19.
- Points immediately above a price point. If you are going to break through a price point it is better go go right through into a different pricing zone. An increase from £95 to £105 may just as well be to £109, or even higher, dependent on market circumstances.

The above examples are from retail, but the principles of psychological pricing extend throughout all industries, markets and organisations.

Psychological pricing also extends to the setting of deliberately high prices for luxury goods, so that those able to afford them are enabled to demonstrate their status and power.

- *Imitative pricing* follows competitors and so matches their tactics. Often this is the only course open since the dominant competitor, the one with the largest market share, is usually the price leader.
- *Marginal cost* pricing is based on the marginal cost of producing one more unit. In any production process there are fixed costs which cannot be changed, and variable costs which are directly related to the cost of production.

  Thus the manager of a high street photo processing laboratory will know just how much it costs in chemicals, paper, electricity and time to develop and print a roll of film. That *marginal cost of production* is the minimum he can charge without making a definite loss on the transaction. It is possible, therefore, to make special offers based on marginal costings, or to accept a large volume job to fill an otherwise slack period.

  Marginal pricing only covers variable costs, however, and the fixed costs of the shop, equipment, staff, rates, standing charges for electricity, etc. all still have to be paid.

  If the price is set above marginal cost but below full cost there is no profit – simply a 'contribution' to fixed costs. Profit is made only when both variable and fixed costs have been recovered.

Determining price

The more popular approaches are:

- *Cost plus pricing.* Prices are fixed in relation to cost. When costs have been determined a fixed percentage is added to ensure that the targeted return is achieved. This allows a fixed percentage profit, but takes no account of market conditions. It is virtually certain to result in a price that is either too high for the market, or too low. In the one case sales will suffer, in the other the whole marketplace will suffer as competitors are forced to match prices.

The argument that this competition is good for the buyer takes no account of the need for organisations to provide for the future. Cost plus pricing probably will not include anything for R&D. Therefore there will be no new products coming forward and in the long-term the buyers will suffer.

To calculate a price the purchase cost is taken as 100% and a set percentage is simply added as a 'mark-up' (Table 29.2).

Table 29.2

Supplier price	= 100%	Mark-up	Selling price	Rounded	Psychological price
£10.00	= 100%	15%	£11.50	£11.50	£11.49
£27.00	= 100%	15%	£31.05	£31.00	£30.99
£42.47	= 100%	15%	£48.85	£49.00	£48.99*

*This may very well be marked up to £49.99.

- *Target pricing,* or price lining, is the levelling out of a range of items bought at different prices so that they can be sold on at recognised price points. Thus the objective may be to price at £4.95, £5.95, £6,95, and so on. In establishing price the most suitable price point will be chosen – provided that it affords an acceptable level of profit.

- *Buyer-based pricing* (what the market will bear). This starts with a detailed analysis of the target market and aims to determine the price that the target customers are prepared or willing to pay – what they regard as a fair price for the value bundle you are to offer. If you can meet that price, well and good. If not there is need to re-examine strategy.

  The term is often used to indicate unfair pricing made possible through real or artificial shortage of supply. This is immoral practice, and should never be considered by an organisation that is marketing oriented.

- *Competitor-based pricing.* Competition may vary from light to severe, merchandise may differ – especially in quality. There must be a decision whether to take the competition on head-to-head or whether it is possible to differentiate the product offering and so establish an independent price. One will, naturally, always be conditioned to some extent by the prices that competition charge.

- *Going-rate pricing.* When demand is elastic and competitive products are available the prices are likely to fall to a level that meets general market demand. The world's stock markets are governed by going-rate pricing since share values change in line with demand.

- *Sealed-bid pricing.* This is used for large contracts with the intention of preventing cross-negotiation and ensuring that the lowest possible prices are quoted. After detailed discussion that centre on a specification prepared by the customer each potential supplier calculates its price and submits its bid in a sealed envelope.

  All are opened at the same time and the one offering the best terms secures the contract.

BREAK-EVEN ANALYSIS

The *break-even point* is the sales level at which total revenue equals total costs.

It is very helpful to be able to determine in advance the needed sales volume at a given price in order to break even, and then to make an overall profit. If differing price levels are likely to result in differing sales volume (a price elastic market), then the break-even graph can be used to help determine the optimum price/volume/profit relationship.

A break-even graph is very easy to construct, once the cost elements have been allocated. Identifying each and every element of coast is vital, and so is their allocation as fixed or variable.

Constructing a break-even graph

1 Total all fixed and all variable costs.
2 Choose a scale for the basic graph.
  Draw the axes and label them as volume (X) and revenue (Y).
3 Draw a horizontal line at the level of the total fixed costs.
  Fixed costs do not change and so the line must be horizontal.

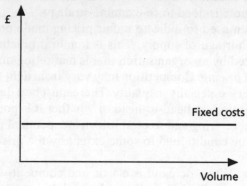

Fig. 29.7 Constructing a break-even graph – fixed costs

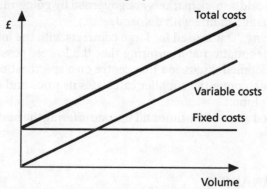

Fig. 29.8 Constructing a break-even graph – variable costs and total costs

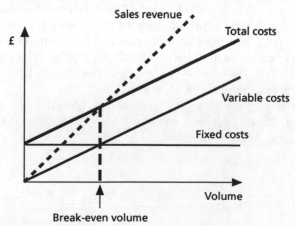

Fig. 29.9 Break-even volume

4 Multiply the total variable costs by a production volume.
  If VC = £4.00 and volume is estimated at 50 000 then the total variable cost
  for 50 000 will be £200 000.
5 Locate the volume/revenue point on the graph.
  Draw a line from it to the intersection of the axes.
  Draw another line parallel to it from the intersection of the Y axis and the
  fixed cost line.
  The result is a line which indicates total costs at levels of sales volume.
6 Estimate sales volume at given prices and multiply the two to give you estimated sales revenue, as in Table 29.3.
7 Draw each of these lines in turn onto the break-even chart.
  From where each sales line crosses the total cost line run a vertical line downwards. The point where this line crosses the volume (X) axis tells you the
  exact sales needed to fully cover all costs to break even.

Table 29.3

Estimated sales	Price (£)	Revenue (£)
40 000	5.00	200 000
45 000	5.00	225 000
55 000	4.45	244 750

PRICING NEGOTIATION

When negotiating prices at a tactical level the following techniques may be
used *if carefully costed and approved by management*. (*Note:* A list price is
the price given in the price list – the top price that the end-purchaser sees – it
is the price on which discounts and deals are based.)

- *Bonus*. A bonus is paid as a reward for some action. A first purchase, achievement of a level of sales volume. Carefully costed into the pricing calculation
  they act as an incentive to continued use or resale, and therefore further
  purchases.

  Introductory bonuses are common, to induce stockists to handle the
  product.
- *Discount*. A sum allowed off the list price in consideration for some action.
  For example, a discount for prompt settlement, or for cash, or for quantity
  purchases. Discounts should give benefit to both the buyer and the seller.
- *Sale or return*. An agreement that allows a stockist to have goods on account
  with the guarantee that if they do not sell they will be taken back by the
  supplier. Often the only way into a channel (see Pricing and power,
  above), but give no incentive to the stockist to put pressure behind selling
  the product.

  It is often better used in limited fashion e.g. 50% will be taken back if it
  doesn't sell. (*Note:* Dealers will hold out for the full 100%!)

- *Special offer*. A special offer differs from a discount because it is a sales promotional tool that is limited by time. Offers are made to achieve specific marketing objectives and are usually in addition to agreed discounts. They are funded from the promotional budget, and are not part of the regular pricing calculation.

  The product itself is often the subject and reward in a special offer, e.g. two for the price of one yields double value to the buyer, but it costs only the production cost to the seller. Thus there is a gearing effect
- *Wholesale prices*. Are discounted from retail, either as a straight allowance given for recognition as a wholesaler or, more commonly today, on the basis of actual volume.

KEY POINT SUMMARY

- Buying the cheapest is not usually the best policy.
- Buy the best value one can afford.
- Value is an intangible package of benefits.
- Price is money or some other consideration for which a thing is bought or sold.
- Value includes: benefits, useful lifetime, after-sales service, supplier reputation, status, price, installation, use, guarantee/warranty.
- Marketing is an exchange of value.
- Avoid terms such as 'cheap' and 'expensive'.
- Pricing must be co-ordinated with corporate and marketing objectives.
- Pricing should aim to secure the maximum possible return consistent with long-term repeat business.
- Return should be measured in profit on sales revenue, not in percentage terms.
- Profit is the difference between revenue and cost.
- There are several kinds of profit because there are several levels of cost.
- Higher profits can come from: revenue increase, reduction in cost of goods sold, fixed cost reduction, variable costs reduction.
- Costing is complex.
- Never allow cost apportionment to become an internal wrangle between managers.
- Corporate objectives guide the pricing strategies.
- Market price must cover all costs and provide the targeted profit return.
- Price is set against anticipated volume.
- Assume that agreed payment terms will be exceeded.
- Market share is not secured long-term by price.
- Pricing strategies can be for: survival, to maximise current profits, to maximise current revenue, to maximise sales growth, to establish product quality leadership.
- Price can enhance uniqueness.
- Price wars are to be avoided.
- Use special offers as the weapon of price attack.

- Pricing is not an inside-looking-out activity.
- Elastic demand is when volume changes with price.
- Inelastic demand is when volume remains static with price changes.
- Competitors have a major impact on pricing strategies and tactics.
- Pricing affects customer demand within a segment, and therefore decisions on positioning.
- Pricing must change as the life cycle progresses.
- Manage the debtors' and creditors' ledgers effectively.
- Pricing must move around price points between a price floor and a price ceiling.
- Pricing is a highly effective tactical weapon.
- Skimming pricing takes the cream from the market.
- Penetration pricing aims to achieve wide coverage.
- Psychological pricing is based on price points that have psychological power and/or appeal.
- Imitative pricing follows competitors.
- Marginal cost pricing is based on the marginal cost of producing one more unit.
- Marginal pricing covers variable costs only.
- Cost plus pricing adds on a fixed percentage to the cost of goods offered for sale.
- Target pricing, or price lining, evens out the prices of a range of items.
- Buyer-based pricing – what the market will bear – aims to price according to the target customers' willingness to pay.
- Competitor-based pricing sets a price policy for dealing with competitive action.
- Going-rate pricing works where demand is elastic and supply is plentiful.
- Sealed-bid pricing attempts to secure the lowest prices through requiring prices to be set against specification, and allowing no further negotiation.
- Break-even analysis allows the required sales volume needed to cover all costs to be forecast.
- Bonuses are paid as a reward for some action.
- Discounts are sums allowed off list prices in consideration for some action.
- Sale or return allows a stockist to have goods for sale with the guarantee that they will be taken back if not sold.
- Special offers are sales promotional tools that run for a limited time.
- Wholesale prices are discounted from retail on the basis either of wholesale status or volume purchases.

WORK-, SCHOOL- AND COLLEGE-BASED SELF-ASSESSMENT QUESTIONS

These questions are designed to help you understand the complex nature of pricing decisions.

1 What are the major benefits of marginal pricing?

2 What would happen if: (a) 40%, (b) 60%, (c) 80%, (d) 100% of contracts were agreed at marginal level?

3 You are the managing director of a supermarket group and Christmas is 8 weeks away. The toy manufacturers are desperate to do business. Will you:
   (a) Cut toy prices deeply, advertise the cuts widely, squeeze additional discounts from your suppliers to cover the costs?
   (b) Hold the toy prices and cut back on advertising because the customers are coming anyway?
   (c) Take normal margins, hold existing policy?
   (d) Take normal margins, advertise, and also squeeze your suppliers?

4 You run a fleet of chauffeur-driven limousines. Fixed cost per car is £500 per week. Variable costs are £120 a day. Assume each car is forecast to work a 5-day week and that each day it covers 200 miles.
   (a) What would your minimum daily charge be?
   (b) How many days each week does each car have to work to break even:
     • at minimum charge plus 100%?
     • at minimum charge plus 150%?

5 Your college has the opportunity to run a series of short courses. What would you recommend as the pricing strategies for courses targeted upon:
   (a) local businesses;
   (b) national businesses;
   (c) businesses already sending students to the college on part- and full-time courses;
   (d) local schools?

See the end of Chapter 31 for suggested assistance.

CHAPTER 30

Promotion

Elaine Kong was trying very hard to spend some money – quite a lot of money. She had saved hard, and now had enough to buy a fully functional computer. She had thought deeply about why she wanted a computer and how she could justify the outlay. Finally she had taken the plunge because she had been asked to be publicity officer for her active amateur drama group.

She had clear ideas of her needs. She needed to produce correspondence and also visuals. Perhaps she could produce a newsletter? And if her press releases were attractively presented they would surely stand a better chance of being printed.

Confidently expecting to return home and start computing she had shot off in high spirits. Unfortunately her confidence quickly proved to be unfounded.

She thought she would start in a major retailer and at least get the feel of what was available. It looked good. There was a row of machines, all working, and all priced. Excellent. Then she discovered that they were running exhibition programs, which she couldn't access. A salesman passed by and she called him over. He didn't know about computers, but he would send someone over.

Ten minutes passed, and Elaine was about to leave when a young man appeared. 'Can I help you?' he enquired.

Elaine explained – but he didn't seem to be listening. 'How much do you want to spend?' he asked. 'I don't know? Which will be best for me?' They are all good', he replied. 'Yes but there must be some difference . . .?'

'Well, of course, some have 2 meg of RAM and others have 4, but you can always upgrade and with the Performa you can switch in virtual memory, but that slows down performance. . . '

'Hold on', interjected Elaine. 'Which one will do what I want?'

'They all will.'

'So what are the differences?'

'It depends on taste, I suppose.'

'Doesn't it depend on memory and speed? Haven't I read about a 68040 processor, on an Intel at the heart of the machine?'

The sales assistant picked up the card describing the nearest machine. 'This is 486 compatible, and has the Intel chip if that's what you want.'

Elaine could see that he knew very little, and cared less. How could he spend all day in the store and not know about his products! She left.

In the computer specialist stores she received a little more help, but found herself struggling beneath a welter of technical terms: RAM and ROM; CISC or RISC; printer interface; ink jet or laser; modem and communications software; dedicated cables; QuarkXpress or PageMaker; Word or WordPerfect;

Claris Works or Microsoft Office.

She moved on . . . and on . . . and on . . . and gave up.

All she wanted was someone to show her how to achieve what she wanted to do. She didn't want to be a technician, she didn't care how the machines worked – didn't even mind what badge they had on the front. If only someone would treat her the way she treated her customers.

Elaine was a manager of a TV rental store and had been top salesperson in the region every month for the last seven. Her method, she thought, was very simple.

Everyone who came in, she reasoned, had come for a purpose. They wanted to rent or buy a TV or video, or to buy blank video tapes, or to settle their account. They didn't come in for a chat, and they did feel that they were important.

Elaine also thought they were important. If they stopped coming in her salary would cease! So she made a point of smiling at everyone who came in, and at least speaking briefly to them . . . even if she was with another customer she managed a quick smile and a 'Hello'.

Her sales success was based on asking questions. First she needed to find out exactly what the customer wanted – not in technical terms because most didn't understand the technology. So she didn't ask what size screen they wanted . . . she asked how large the room was. She didn't ask if they wanted Teletext, she asked if they wanted fast updates on news, sports and programme information. She didn't ask 'Can I help you?' because obviously she could.

Only when she was sure she knew what the customer wanted in terms of entertainment, information and ease of use did she begin to show the range she had to offer. Armed with the key information she could suggest the model most likely to be accepted, and also the one above it. She never used technical terms except in answering a query that the customer expressed technically.

She found that many of her customers said that they were 'only looking'. At first she had accepted this and said 'Fine, do come back when you have decided.' But she changed her tactics when she discovered that only a few did come back.

The real secret of her success was that she truly believed no other company could beat her offer. There was no point in a customer spending time visiting several firms – the differences were in the make of equipment offered, not in the performance. With modern TVs and videos the on-screen quality was so similar as not to be worth comparison, so why not help customers to save time? Why not go for the contract on first contact?

Customers, she found, responded well to her new approach. They obviously appreciated it because she saw them regularly as they came in each month to settle their accounts. This gave her a series of excellent opportunities to keep track of how the equipment was performing, to monitor the effectiveness of the service back-up, and to sell replacement video tapes.

She was looking forward to a new range of opportunity when the company added Hi-fi and then computers to their range. Both were on market test, and by all accounts proving very successful.

She suddenly realised that she was missing something – she had computer experts in her company now. Why hadn't she made contact with them and worked out a specification of her equipment needs? She would now!

She would also remember how ineffective the computer sales approach had been. If this was typical she wouldn't have much of a problem renting or selling computers herself . . . especially with a firm base of loyal customers all ready to be approached.

STRATEGIC PROMOTION

This is concerned with:

* bridging the information gap between suppliers and customers and consumers;
* developing and retaining loyal consumers.

Strategic need

This is to bring potential customers and consumers who are unaware of a product offering to a status as regular and repeat users.

Strategic management

This is concerned to select and direct the promotional tools to their maximum effect. Promotional tactics is the detailed selection of specific tools to achieve strategy.

Promotional objectives

Strategic and tactical objectives, with a supporting budget, are required in promotion exactly as in any form of management. They are far harder to create and evaluate because of the subjective nature of the task – but they are needed. We shall examine objectives and evaluation in Chapter 31.

Promotional tools

The promotional tools are:

* public relations;
* advertising;
* sales promotion;
* personal selling.

Each tool has a role to play, and each works in association with the others.

Note:
* Personal selling is also known as 'sales force' or 'direct selling'.
* Packaging has a role within promotion – as a medium (see Chapter 28).

- Direct marketing is a channel of distribution. It is not a promotional tool (see below).

MANAGEMENT OF PROMOTION

Promotion is the one area of marketing where marketers have almost total control. In the other three Ps they are recommending actions to production, R&D, accountants, distribution managers, etc. The P of promotion is the marketer's own territory.

Strategically there is need to set objectives that conform to corporate and marketing strategies. Tactically there is need to manage the detailed elements of the promotional mix.

This book is focused on marketing in management, and so the detailed study of marketing's own specialism has to be left to specialist books. In this and the following chapter we shall outline the principal characteristics of the promotional P – you will find recommendations for books that provide a detailed cover of promotion in Appendix F.

Promotion

- Communication undertaken to persuade others to accept ideas, concepts or things (Engel, Warshaw, Kinear).

The literal meaning of 'promotion' is to *move forward*. As we shall see, the prime purpose of promotion in marketing is to move prospective customers 'forward' so that they become loyal and regular users.

There is always a reason for communication. The most effective communicators seek out the reasons why they need to communicate, and match these to the interests of their audience. Tailoring communication to meet identified need(s) makes it more likely that the message will be accepted.

Communication

The marketer must be guided by the communication model that we met in Chapter 19 (Figure 19.3).

- Sender   the marketer;
- Encoding   in a form that can most easily be understood;
- Message   to meet the identified need(s) of the target audience;
- Channel   the medium that most cost-effectively reaches the target audience;
- Decoding   by the receiver – hopefully in the exact form intended;
- Receiver   the individual members of the target audience;
- Noise   all the other messages that are scrambling for attention:
    - literacy, language, cultural, racial barriers;
    - lack of interest, negative experience with product, brand or organisation.

MARKETING COMMUNICATIONS

This term is often confused with promotion . . . but there are clear differences between the two terms:

- Promotion is a part of the marketing mix, with a prime focus on developing the market for the goods or services offered by the organisation.
- Marketing communications includes all of the communications originated within and by marketing.

Thus promotion fits within the overall concept of marketing communications in the same way that market research is a part of marketing research.

Marketing communications – defined

Marketing communication is persuasive communication originated by and within marketing and directed at specific targets both internal and external to the organisation with the intention of achieving one or more predetermined objectives.

This presumes that feedback is an essential part of communication and requires no specific mention.

PERCEPTION

The process of recognising or identifying something (Dictionary of Psychology).

Perception is far more than seeing because it involves all human senses in a detailed study to determine exactly what one is sensing. We have five physical senses: sight, sound, touch, taste and smell. We also have a very important ability to co-ordinate present with past experiences. It is easiest to think of this as a 'sixth sense' providing we remember that it is an extremely complex factor which is deep-seated in our mental processes.

The 'sixth sense' is our ability to combine memory, experience and the input from a range of senses to come up with what appears to us to be the right answer.

When any of our senses is exposed to a stimulus – a flash of light, a sound, a touch – we immediately and automatically attempt to fit it into a frame of reference. We have to know what it is – it might be dangerous, it might be profitable. Most of our perception is entirely automatic. If it were not we would have to consciously process every signal from every sense receptor on our entire body every split second. Fortunately, although we do monitor continuously, we have learned which signals to discount and which need conscious attention.

Members of a target audience constantly monitor the signals they decode. Are they appropriate? Are they of interest? Shall I look at them consciously?

Research shows that we are exposed to a minimum of 5000 advertisements each day, not counting the brand labels on clothes, such as the Levis patch on their jeans, nor the logos we carry on the front of sweat shirts, etc. We have learned that most of them are not for us. We perceive them to have a focus. If it is not one in which we are interested we let it go by.

The key to promotional success is understanding that perception is a relationship of every sense of each individual in a target audience. We must then consider what happens when we try to promote something. What process do we have to manage in the individuals who make up our target audience? How do customers and consumers behave?

Perception examples

Critically examine each of these two examples. Do you recognise the situations? Can you relate to what is happening? Do you see the importance of monitoring feedback to determine what individuals are perceiving? How they are interpreting your messages?

The cafe

At the beginning of the summer a husband said to his wife 'Look the beach cafe is just opening up.' 'I'm never going there again', she answered. 'Last year they overcharged me, and the meal was not very good.' The wife's learned experience was not to trust that cafe: she didn't check if it had a new owner.

The advertisement

Dunlop ran an advertisement featuring the extreme safety of a new tyre. It showed the amount of rubber that is in contact with the road – about as much as on the sole of a man's shoe. The result was unexpected – people were horrified, not reassured. Their attention was drawn to the limited contact between car and road, and the intended safety message was perceived as a danger warning.

CUSTOMER AND CONSUMER BEHAVIOUR

We have established that marketers are in the business of persuasive communication. Also that we must know what we want to achieve *before* setting out to communicate. We have seen the importance of understanding perception if we are to promote effectively.

Are we sold to, or do we buy from?

A good marketer never 'sells' anything. Instead he encourages the potential buyer to move through three stages:

- awareness where the product or service comes to the potential buyer's notice;
- attitude where a favourable attitude develops within the prospect;

- action   where the purchase is made.

It is not possible to make a sale (or a purchase) without passing through these three stages . . .

You are going home after a tiring day in town. As you enter the bus or train station you see a vending machine 20 metres in front of you, between you and your bus or train . . . you may react something like this:

- You suddenly fancy a bar of chocolate, you quickly check your small change . . . OK, you have enough.
  Awareness of your need has been achieved.

- You approach the machine. Do you really want the chocolate? Should you pass it by? Yes, you should, but on the other hand you deserve a treat, and one of the bars on sale is your particular favourite. You will buy one.
  Favourable attitude to purchase has been achieved.

- You reach the machine, bring out your small change, put it in the slot, take the bar, board your transport and reward yourself.
  Positive action has resulted.

Note that this whole transaction has taken place within about 20 seconds, and that there has been no communication with any salesperson. It is a self-motivated purchase. Or is it?

- The machine has been carefully sited where you will see it in time to decide. It is clean, hygienic, stocked, and gives change. The product is known to you, and well promoted on the machine.
- Next time you visit the same bus or train station you may have your money ready. In time you may come to rely on the machine for a bar of chocolate after work.
- Next time you see a chocolate vending machine you will be favourably inclined towards it. The more times you buy from the machines the more you will learn to trust them.
- If a machine lets you down once you may forgive it. Twice and you will be annoyed. Three times and you may be so angry that you say you will never use a machine again!

The higher level response set (HLRS)

Also known as the 'continuum of behaviour' the HLRS is a term imported from psychology. It is easier for most marketers to think of behaviour as a *continuous* series of activities. These can be drawn in a model, which is called a continuum because it shows a process which is continuous, not broken. We shall examine an actual continuum of behaviour in a moment.

Research has identified the steps that potential customers pass through on their way to a decision. The awareness, attitude, action stages result from this research.

In the early 1920s Daniel Starch, a pioneer of advertising measurement, established that an advertisement to be successful:

- must be seen;
- must be read;
- must be believed;
- must be remembered;
- must be acted upon.

Starch outlined the 'behaviour' of advertising as:

- calling attention to and informing people about products and services through mass-communication media;
- establishing a favourable link between a need and a brand name so that when the need arises the brand name will come to mind with a favourable image established;
- leading to buying action because of the existing favourable image, the attention-getting and reminding process and the persuasive–activating power of the message.

Starch identified two sets of forces which constantly influence the effect of advertising. One set tends to weaken the effect:

- forgetting;
- fading memory;
- competitors' counter-advertising strategies.

The other set may strengthen the effect through:

- the power of repetitive advertising;
- continued satisfaction with the product in use.

In 1963 Colley produced his DAGMAR model, which he described as 'applied common sense'. DAGMAR – defining advertising goals for measured advertising results – shows that a prospect must be carried through four levels of understanding:

- From unawareness to awareness;
  - awareness to comprehension;
    - comprehension to conviction;
      - conviction to action.

The long-established sales model AIDA is based on the same understanding:

Attention must be secured before . . .
    Interest can be aroused and only then can . . .
        Desire be generated so that . . .
            Action follows.

Lavidge and Steiner, in 1961, developed previous thinking by relating the process to a three-phase psychological model:

- cognitive   refers to the intellectual mental or 'rational' states;
- affective   refers to attitude, to feelings and emotions;
- conative   refers to an action state.

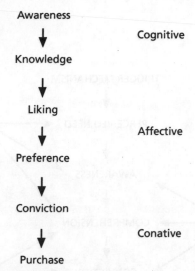

Fig. 30.1 Three-phase psychological model
Adapted from Lavidge and Steiner's model (1961)

The HLRS is a development from the six-step sequence of Lavidge and Steiner. The purchase situation differs across markets and so a continuum must be developed for each market. The continuum shown works well for FMCG and allows us to introduce, broadly, where each promotional 'tool' has major effect.

Note that a *trigger* is needed to start the process. A promotional trigger may be as simple as an empty packet in the larder – which causes the product to go on the shopping list. It may be carefully planned, as in the location, timing, size and content of vending machines. It may be a range of ads to launch a new product. Every purchase has to be triggered – whether the trigger is planned or spontaneous a purchase cannot happen without it.

Note: Word-of-mouth recommendation is always important. If I am unhappy with a service I am likely to warn my friends and so damage the provider of the defective service. If I am happy I am likely to recommend. But I am more likely to criticise than praise.

Consumer behaviour is important enough to justify detailed study of each market situation. For general purposes, however, you will find that the three stages of awareness, attitude and action allow a planned campaign to be constructed and its results to be evaluated against clear objectives.

Note: All customers and potential customers are mentally somewhere on your continuum. It is very important to start marketing communications activity from where they are! Therefore it is necessary to carefully monitor the progress of target audiences as a routine part of promotional research. (See Chapter 31.)

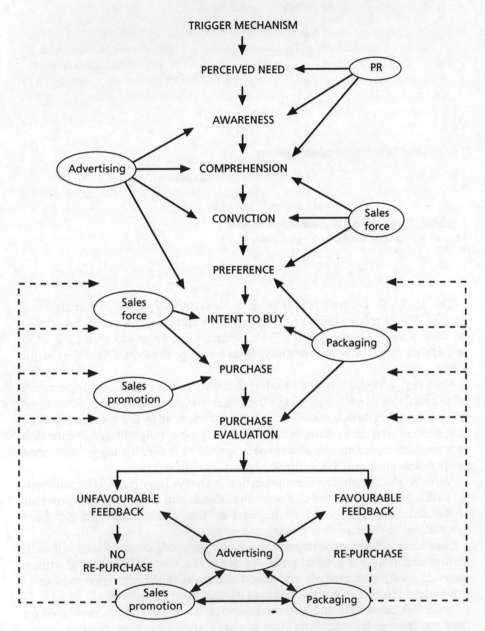

Fig. 30.2 Continuum of behaviour (showing likely target for promotional tools)

THE PROMOTION MIX

Each of the four promotional tools has several strategic uses and a range of tactical purposes. It is essential to remember that:

- Every communication has a spin-off effect. It will be seen by some who are not in its target audience. Thus the core value messages must always be the same. This is the main purpose of the positioning statement, of course.
- Tools used to achieve one objective with one audience may also have an effect on a second. Treat this as a bonus, but don't lose sight of the prime objective in an attempt to achieve too much.

Long- and short-term strategies

Every promotional tool, and each promotional activity, must be a part of a long-term strategy. Some tools are excellent at achieving immediate tactical results, but this tactical use must be within long-term strategy.

Typical promotional strategies include:

- Building and reinforcing brand image   long-term
- Strengthening user loyalty   long-term
- Securing and retaining new users   medium-term
- Securing and retaining a stated level of distribution   medium-term
- Repositioning a product offering   short-term
- Securing leads for sales force follow-up   short-term.

We shall show how promotional objectives are set in Chapter 31.

Personal and non-personal

The only personal contact with members of a target audience is made by members of the sales force. All other communication is non-personal. Many retail products cannot have personal representation at PoS. This helps to account for the development of sales promotion, as we shall see.

Techniques of non-personal communication have improved vastly from what was recognised as state-of-the-art only a decade ago. This is partly because new technology is opening new opportunities, but mainly because marketers are developing better ways to match tools to needs.

Non-personal tools are *stand alone* unless feedback is specifically obtained through marketing research. They are out of the marketer's control because they allow of no immediate amendment in the light of customer reaction.

Personal contact allows for immediate adjustments to be made as a result of feedback. Therefore the more significant the transaction the more likely a need for personal contact.

Public relations

- This is defined as non-personal stimulation of demand for a product, service or business unit by planting commercially significant news about it in a published medium or obtaining favourable presentation of it on radio, television or stage that is not paid for by your sponsor (Kotler).

PR also has an important role in keeping bad news away from the media, and in the management of any crisis so that damage is minimised.

PR does not pay for space in the media, but is not without cost. A budget is needed to cover the PR staff and their support, the costs of setting up PR opportunities, of preparing news releases and photographs, etc.

Publicity is generated by PR and can be extremely powerful since it runs in the editorial columns of the media and is not seen to be paid-for advertisement.

Publicity

Note carefully the distinction between PR and publicity . . . they are *not* the same. Publicity happens: e.g. if a builder's crane is blown down by high winds there may be headline coverage in the media. This is not generated by PR, but by events. It is then the role of PR to minimise the damage done by the unfavourable publicity. (We saw in Chapter 15 how SunShine Tours suffered through publicity, even though they were blameless.)

PR therefore has two major roles:

- the securing of favourable publicity, and
- the prevention (or minimisation) of unfavourable publicity.

Jefkins includes market education as a PR objective and gives the examples of non-drip paints, computers and dairy spreads as requiring customer education as a preliminary to advertising.

In times of national or company disaster a mix of advertising and public relations is used. The AIDS awareness campaign of the 1980s is an example of raising public awareness by a joint PR and advertising campaign.

Access

The media must have access to informed sources. Therefore individuals have to be selected, trained, and designated as media contacts. Careful selection and training are vital – it takes great skill and confidence to face a journalist who wants a story.

Robert Townsend of Avis makes the situation crystal clear in *Up the Organisation:*

One day Ford Motor Company announced they were going directly into the rent a car business through any Ford dealer that wanted to. The *Wall Street Journal* phoned and was put through to the general manager of our rent a car division. Next day the front left-hand column was heavily salted with quotes from their conversation.

Far down the page our competitor's V.P. of Public Relations had pulled off this coup: 'A spokesman for the Hertz Corporation said they were studying the matter.' Hertz was older and twice our size, but who looked like the industry leader that morning?

Avis had 10 managers designated as media contacts. They were given a framework within which they could be themselves and talk freely:

- Be honest. If you don't know, say so. If you know but won't tell, say so.
- Pretend your ablest competitor is listening. If he already knows your latest marketing plan, you use the call to announce it; if not, shut up.
- Don't forecast earnings. If asked why not, tell them we don't do in public anything we can't do consistently well – and nobody can forecast earnings consistently well.

ADVERTISING

- Any paid for non-personal presentation and promotion of ideas, goods or services by an identified person (Kotler).

Advertising is paid for an advertisements will be clearly identified within the media. Thus they will be expected to flatter the product offering. Most people expect most adverts to over-state their case. A degree of 'puff', of over-statement, is allowed for by UK law but adverts still have to remain legal, decent and honest.

The range of media that carries advertising is bewildering and selecting the right mix is a highly specialist task. It can only be carried through effectively if there is a specific brief from the marketer. Since the invention of geodemographic segmentation (Chapter 12) each medium has been able to determine the segmentation of its readership. It is therefore possible to match target audience profiles against media profiles and come up with the most cost-effective media schedule.

How advertising works

Much work has been done, and is being done, to answer this question. We shall examine the progress that has been made in Chapter 31.

SALES PROMOTION

Short-term incentives to encourage purchase or sale of a product or service. *(Kotler)*

The emergence of self-service retailing meant that 'push' policies of distribution had to be replaced with 'pull' policies. The products had to sell themselves off the shelves and it was discovered that a PoS incentive was needed to trigger the purchase, *now*.

Sales promotion (SP) was invented to generate action at PoS. The advertising agencies who discovered the need found that they had to charge a fee for their work since there was no established media to pay them a commission. Therefore a convention developed that spending where a commission was paid would be 'above the line'; where a fee was charged would be 'below the line'.

There is, of course, no actual line, but the convention provides a shorthand

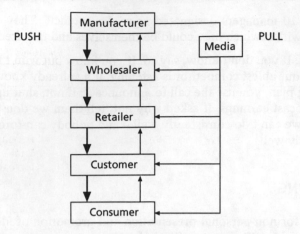

Fig. 30.3 The push and pull model of distribution

way of describing how a budget is allocated . . . '40% above and 60% below.' Campaigns are designed to run *through the line* so that a common theme extends all the way from unawareness to repeat sales.

Above and below the line

Promotional budgets are divided into above and below the line. Above the line is advertising in media which pay commission. All other non-personal communication is below the line. The sales force has its own budget.

Through the line means that a campaign is planned using above-the-line media linked to below-the-line activity. Thus a PR and advertising campaign will link, the PoS activity will pick up the same theme, and personal selling will be geared to the same objectives and use sales aids, etc., that draw their imagery from the campaign theme.

It is the positioning statement which makes this high level of integration possible.

It is simple to distinguish SP from other activity . . . any device which is targeted upon achieving sales *now,* is SP. Advertisements sometimes carry SP content, salespeople use SP to nail down an order. The exception to the general rule is special discounts which may be offered by salespeople in direct contact with customers, these are part of the price negotiation. Once a price is agreed it may still be necessary to get the order today – now – in which case an SP offer may be made.

SP techniques have been extended from retail into every other sector, both profit and not-for-profit; retail and industrial; product and service; and can be an extremely effective way of turning intention into purchase.

Examples of SP are shown in Table 30.1

Table 30.1 Examples of sales promotion

	Objectives	
	Prime	*Other*
Free samples	Trial	Added value
Frequent flyer programmes	Repeat purchase	Loyalty
		Database
Price-off-labels	Value	Repeat purchase
		Trial
Two-for-one	Value	Increase usage
		Block competition
Personality promotions	Endorsement	Status
		Involvement
Premium gifts with proof of purchase	Purchase and repeat purchase	
Trading stamps	Repeat purchase	Loyalty

SALES FORCE

- Direct selling is an oral presentation in a conversation with one or more prospective purchasers for the purpose of making sales (Kotler).
- 'Purchase' and 'buy' apply to products and services – but equally to the acceptance of a concept. You are 'buying' the material in this book if you put what you read into use. A tutor is a salesman, using many of the same techniques as a sales representative in the field. The terms actually mean that a person has agreed to a course of action, or accepted a change suggested by an external source.

Selling is as old as time, and remains of vital importance since there is almost always need for a salesperson to secure the business. The only exception is in such as off-the-page, or off-the-screen, buying where the purchaser orders in writing. A 'tele-order' establishes an oral link and is a sales, not simply an order-taking contact.

In areas such as retail the selling role has changed from direct sales of product to the selling of whole promotional campaigns.

Five buyers control over 50% of the UK retail grocery market and a failure to sell to any one of them prevents access to all the stores that they control. Thus they are 'key accounts' meriting senior salespeople of considerable experience. Once a buyer has committed to a campaign an instruction will be issued to all branches. This will itemise the actions needed in-store to fulfil the retailer's side of the bargain. At the same time the supplier's sales team will be notified of the agreement.

Retail field salespeople no longer sell product to retailers. Today they:

- 'sell' store managers on giving the best coverage their instructions allow;
- ensure that stocks are on the shelf and in the stock rooms in sufficient depth;
- arrange and manage in-store promotion to the retail customers.

It follows that *merchandising* and *display* have developed in technique because customers need information at PoS (merchandising) and must be able to easily locate the products they need (display).

In business-to-business and industrial selling the traditional role of the salesperson continues, but direct response marketing – which includes a heavy element of direct sales – is showing signs of replacing face-to-face selling for many of the smaller customers.

OTHER PROMOTIONAL ACTIVITIES

These activities are not promotion or communication tools. They actually exist to provide opportunities for *the use of the tools of the promotional mix*. Because they provide major opportunities for communication with target audiences they are of special concern to the marketer.

Direct response marketing

This includes direct mail, from which it has developed. A range of channels of distribution have opened – and continue to open – as technology expands opportunity. There is now greater penetration of electronic technology together with greater understanding of its use: the combination of television, the telephone and credit card ownership make immediate purchase possible. This can be encouraged by the use of 0500, 0800 and Freefone numbers. Interactive TV is on its way, and cable TV will make contact with individuals possible on both a direct and indirect basis. It will even be possible to advertise to the neighbour of a person who has recently taken some action . . . promotion of chain link fencing to the neighbour of a person who has just acquired a new Doberman Pinscher perhaps!

Sponsorship

This is of major importance, especially as advertising is closed off to certain types of product. It is a form of medium that can carry advertising and sales promotion and greatly enhance corporate and/or brand image.

Exhibitions

A very powerful channel of contact – part medium, part sales – which is of great importance in many markets. Exhibitions are very effective for product demonstrations, building corporate image and, most importantly, for building sales contacts and securing orders.

Corporate identity

PR plays a major role in creating and maintaining corporate identity. Once established the corporate identity has a branding effect that can extend across all brands: e.g. Nestlé are adding their corporate brand to their subsidiary company brands, so that Rowntrees famous brands are now claimed by Nestlé and we have Nestlé KitKat, Nestlé Smarties, Nestlé Quality Street, and so on.

Packaging

As we have established in Chapter 28, packaging has a major role as a medium and influencer.

COGNITIVE DISSONANCE

The work of behavioural scientists has been of major benefit to marketers but, unfortunately, some of the terms appear difficult at first. Fortunately what they describe is not difficult to understand.

Cognitive dissonance was first put forward as a theory by Leon Festinger in 1957.

'Dissonance' refers to mental unease. Festinger showed that an individual always tries to achieve 'consonance', or harmony.

The best-known marketing example of cognitive dissonance comes from the new car market. A new car purchase is of major importance – both financially and psychologically – and a buyer wants reassurance that his decision was wise.

Dealers can contribute to cognitive dissonance if they do not carry the sale right through into the period of regular use. It has been shown that for a sale to be truly effective it must be continued into the after-market (see Chapter 26).

Dissonance can also be created after the purchase, through advertising, because individuals tend to continue to be very aware of car advertising *after* the purchase:

- Competitors' advertising may look especially good – particularly if the customer is having trouble with his new purchase.
- Your advertising may create dissonance, especially if a new model is announced soon after the purchase is completed.

A good dealer will ensure that customers are satisfied . . .

- A car salesman has taken a prospective customer through from first enquiry to purchase. The vehicle is paid for and is coming out of the pre-delivery service tomorrow morning at 10.00. The customer is due to collect the car at 11.00.

The salesman will reduce cognitive dissonance by:

- Clarifying the objective:
  To cement the customer's loyalty so that they will be satisfied with their purchase and return when next they change their car.

To achieve this he will:

- check with service that the car will be ready on time in all respects;
- fill the tank with petrol and ensure the car is washed and valeted;
- check that the road fund licence is straight on the windscreen;
- park the car where it is easy for the customer to drive away, and lock it;
- have all the documents, and the keys, at his desk;
- tell the receptionist to expect the customer, and reinforce the customer's name;
- greet the customer with a smile and a reassurance . . . 'Your new car is all ready, she looks superb, you're going to be very proud of her';
- Hand over the documents and show the customer where the phone number is to be found 'In case you want to ask anything' (actually so that they are reassured they are not being thrown out with no support);
- hand over the keys and lead the customer to the car;
- encourage the customer to walk round the car and be impressed;
- let the customer unlock the door;
- when the customer is settled offer to run through the controls;
- leave the customer on a positive note . . . 'You will be very happy with your decision, enjoy your new car';
- watch the customer drive away, wave if necessary;
- follow through:
  - with service to say 'well done and thanks' (thus setting up good service for your next sale);
  - with the customer, on the telephone next day ('Just confirming that the car is everything you expected.' If it isn't he can initiate action before the customer is forced to complain. If it is he reinforces that fact. Either way he demonstrates concern with the customer's well being);
- update the customer records so the details are to hand when next in contact with the customer.

SUPPORT

Promotion's role is to help potential customers move from unawareness to regular user status. This is a continuous process, with new potential customers coming into the target segments and existing consumers moving out.

The promotional mix must be blended so that the optimum value is obtained from the budget . . . a very detailed and specialised series of activities.

The marketer must have specialised and technical support since it is not reasonable to expect any one person to be an expert in the very diverse activities that come together to make a promotional campaign successful. The marketer's role is to manage – to achieve results through people.

In many cases the people that a marketer uses will come from specialist agencies who are outside the organisation. Each will contribute their own special expertise – but under the leadership and control of the marketer.

The promotional mix must be blended so that the optimum value is obtained from the budget . . . a very detailed and specialised series of activities.

The marketer must have specialised and technical support since it is not reasonable to expect any one person to be an expert in the very diverse activities that come together to make a promotional campaign successful. The marketer's role is to manage – to achieve results through people.

In many cases the people that a marketer uses will come from specialist agencies who are outside the organisation. Each will contribute his own special expertise – but under the leadership and control of the marketer.

KEY POINT SUMMARY

- Salespeople should listen to the customers.
- Salespeople should know their product range.
- Help people buy – do not 'sell' to them.
- Believe in your products.
- Strategic promotion bridges the gap between the suppliers and customers and consumers – and develops and retains customers.
- Strategic need is to bring customers to the status of regular and repeat users.
- Strategic management selects and directs.
- The promotional tools are: PR, advertising, SP and personal selling.
- Packaging has a role as a medium.
- Direct marketing is a channel not a promotional tool.
- Promotion means 'to move forward'.
- Promoters are communicators.
- Promotions is part of marketing communications.
- Perception is the process of recognising or identifying something.
- Perception, to a marketer, means awareness that perception is a relationship of every sense of every individual in a target audience.
- The 3As are: awareness, attitude and action.
- The continuum of behaviour (the HLRS) maps the progression from unawareness to committed user.
- A trigger is needed to start the move to awareness.
- Every promotional tool has a spin-off effect.
- Tools used for one objective can benefit others.
- Each promotional activity must be part of long-term strategy.
- The positioning statement is crucial in ensuring consistency of approach and purpose.
- The only personal contact is through personal selling – the sales force.
- PR secures unpaid-for space, but is not without cost.
- Publicity happens, and often requires PR to magnify the effect or limit the damage.
- Advertising is the use of paid-for space.
- Sales promotion adds inducement to buy – now!
- Above the line refers to budget spent in commission-paying media.
- Below the line is budget spent where a fee is payable.
- Through the line refers to integrated promotion.
- Merchandising provides information at PoS.
- Display enables goods to be found at PoS.

- Sponsorship is now of major importance.
- Exhibitions are part media, part sales.
- Cognitive dissonance is a mental unease experienced by customers.
- Good planning ensures consonance, or harmony.
- The marketer's role is to achieve results through people.
- Specialists exist to provide expertise.
- Leadership and control are called for from the marketer.

WORK-, SCHOOL- AND COLLEGE-BASED SELF-ASSESSMENT QUESTIONS

1 List up to five products or services where repeat purchasing is not immediately seen to be a marketing goal.

For each item identify why repeat purchasing is, in fact, of vital concern.

2 Allow an hour spread over a week.

Select three current promotional campaigns for products and/or services targeted upon different markets. For each:

- Deduce the target customers.
- Identify the base of their appeal in terms of the work done by Maslow.
- Consider if their targeting is so tight that it excludes those not in the target group.

Note: A promotional campaign involves a range of media such as TV, radio, press, in-store. You need to check how effectively the whole campaign holds to its targeting, which is why you need to spread this assignment over time.

See the end of Chapter 31 for answer guidelines.

CHAPTER 31

Promotion – budgeting and evaluation

The alarm clock beside the bed went off first, at 6.30. Its high pitched buzzer was designed to rouse even the deepest sleeper but Gareth Williams merely tucked further into his duvet. Next was the clock cassette radio. It was timed for three minutes later, and a heavy metal band blasted into the bedroom. Finally the sound he really hated, an old fashioned double belled clockwork alarm standing on a tin tray in the sink. When that let off there was no way anybody could stay in bed!

Fortunately there were no neighbours, thought Gareth, as he always did five mornings a week. Hooray, tomorrow was Saturday.

By ten to seven Gareth had finished in the bathroom and was running the electric shaver over his chin while waiting for the kettle and the toast. He managed half a cup of coffee, before having to run for the bus – with a piece of toast in his teeth.

He finished the toast at the bus stop, where he had to hang around for a frustrating 5 minutes – why was there a delay today of all days? The bus lost more time on the way down the valley to the main line station. If he hadn't a season ticket he would not have caught the train.

Twenty minutes later he was in the city, and at 7.59 clocked into work. Made it, but with only a minute to spare. One lousy minute later and he would have lost his bonus! A whole 10% of salary for the month if he was ever late. It applied to everyone – he had overheard the managing director complaining of a traffic jam only three days ago that had blown his bonus away for the month!

There was a large post to be sorted, but by 8.45 Gareth was on his way round the building. He always took the lift to the top and walked down – any sensible person would. It conserved effort, and enabled him to work faster.

Back in the basement by 9.30 and it was time for a cup of coffee and an update on the sports pages. Cardiff City were still being ripped to shreds following their midweek disaster against Lyon. How could they have thrown away a two-goal away lead from the first leg? No doubt the team manager had them looking through the match video – if were left to Gareth they would have to watch it every morning for the rest of the season. He thought he might as well go to the match tomorrow – see if they had learned their lesson.

At twelve sharp he was out of the door – a free man. Friday was not the normal day for college, but his results were due and in the afternoon there was a Board of Studies on which he was course representative. His firm had approved his extra half-day off per term, and it was certainly an interesting experience.

College wasn't as good as he had expected. Results were borderline, and his tutor took him to task very strongly. Yes, he knew that his results had been marginal right through – but he had passed everything (with just that one slip that needed a re-sit in the first year). He had passed this time, but the tutor said he had used up every ounce of generosity and the examiners were not going to be lenient in the final exams in only three months.

If he had taken any notice of his results – and that is why the course was graded on continuous assessment – he should have worked harder, sooner. Now it was necessary to concentrate hard, and to put the hours in.

That evening he went, as always, round to his Aunt Gwyneth and Uncle Morgan. His aunt was a super cook, and she invariably had the meal ready bang on time. He walked in the door at five to and the meal was on the table at seven.

After the meal he and his uncle walked down to the canal and sat on the bank watching the fishermen. Their conversation was a little different this evening. Normally they chatted about football and rugby, about Gareth's parents and uncle's racing pigeons – but not this evening.

Uncle Morgan was very serious for a hard-hitting five minutes. It was about time that Gareth took notice of what was happening – there were enough clues. His aunt was most annoyed – did he think he could just breeze in and sit down week after week? He was too old for that, it was not the behaviour of a young adult!

And his college results should have warned him – what was he going to do about those? Work wasn't easy to get in South Wales, and he needed his certificate. If he expected the Cardiff City manager to monitor his players, and to have them learn from experience, then the same thing applied to Gareth.

On Monday he was to see his own manager for his annual appraisal – what plans had he made? Was he going to get his hair cut tomorrow, take his suit to the cleaners and polish his shoes? He was being evaluated all the time – didn't he know that? He obviously did, more's the pity, because he could get things done just in time – but there was no margin for error.

If he wanted to move into management, he had to learn to manage himself, and that meant to set objectives, and then to evaluate his progress against them.

PROMOTION – HOW DOES IT WORK?

Promotion has traditionally been regarded as advertising and sales: advertising to spread the message and to generate demand, sales to nail the demand down into orders and to secure on-going business with customers. We shall use the term 'advertising' rather than 'promotion' in the early part of this module because it was from the problems of dealing with 'advertising and sales' that the concept of promotion developed. We know, of course, that we also need public relations and sales promotion to move a prospect through the three stages of awareness – attitude – action.

The ad/sales approach encourages a manager to use factual measures of success:

- How much business is generated for each unit of spend in advertising?
- How much from the overall spend on advertising and sales?
- How many orders are secured from how many sales calls?
- How many repeat orders are secured?
- Etc., etc., etc.

This *numeric* approach is not effective because the individual achievements needed to ensue overall success are often non-numeric. Prove this to yourself by trying to answer these two questions:

1 Does an additional 20% in advertising budget increase sales by a predictable amount?
2 How does advertising work?

1 Increasing an advertising budget does not automatically increase sales. If it did the whole issue would be straightforward. Unfortunately something else is working for and/or against advertising.

It is obvious that some advertising works better than others. Some campaigns pull business, others flop, although they have the same potential. Logical approaches have been taken to identify the factors that can have an effect on advertising success.

- Media selection   Was the spend wisely split between the media?
- Content   How did advertisement content affect sales?
- Market   What did the customers and consumers actually need and want?
- Competitors   What were the competitors offering?
  What advertising were they doing:
  What special offers were they making?
- Environment   What factors such as unemployment, inflation, social changes, Act of God, etc., needed to be taken into account?

The need for detailed information led to the beginnings of marketing research. Even with research figures coming forward to confirm circulation and readership it was clear that something was happening that had not been identified. This led to the second question: How does advertising work?

2 It seems that there are at least five levels at which advertising impacts upon the customer.

Once it is understood that the advertising message is being used for a variety of purposes it is possible to consider such questions as Who? Why? Where? When? How?

In 1967 the British Market Research Bureau and J. Walter Thompson published a joint study into how advertising may work. Note that we still do not *know* how it works, but we do have the ability to make it more effective.

It is believed that advertising has an effect on both attitudes and purchase behaviour. Attention can be secured by creative work that takes into account the perceptions and biases of target audiences. Attitude change can be initiated, assisted, accelerated, reinforced – but attitudes take time to change. It is

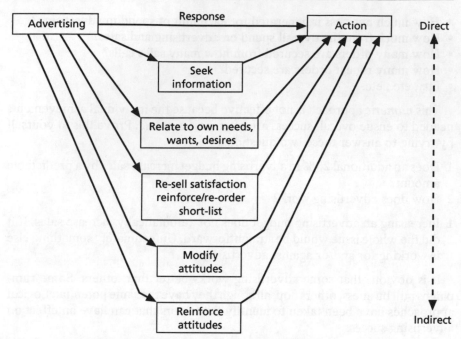

Fig. 31.1 Scale of direct/indirect responses to advertising
Source: British Market Research Bureau and J W Thompson (1967)

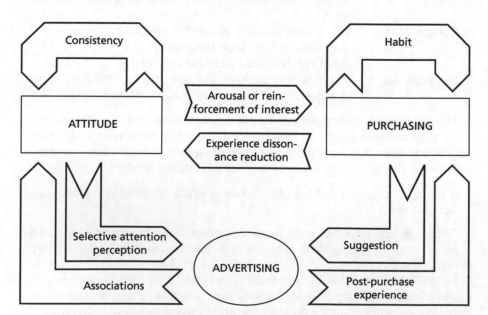

Fig. 31.2 How advertising may work
Source: British Market Research Bureau and J W Thompson (1967)

hardly surprising that attitude change is usually slow because so many conflicting messages are received from the environment (of which advertising is only a part).

Purchasing – a learned experience

Purchasing is a habit that we learn from experience. Once we have accepted a product we tend to continue to use it.

- We are unhappy when a supermarket rearranges it shelves. We have to relearn stock positioning and have better things to do.
- We don't like to change brands because we know just how to get the best out of the one we currently use.

Advertising has a powerful role in suggesting a course of action, but has also to cope with post-purchase experience which may or may not be favourable.

The link between attitudes and purchasing is most important because attitude has much to do with learning. Personal experience of the product is important. It is normal for a new purchaser to take advice from those with experience – those who have learned something about the products on offer – before making a purchase.

Word-of-mouth advice is a very important element in promotion – something the marketer wants to be working for his product. Advice can be asked for – often it is given anyway. In particular it is given when a person is unhappy with a product, or the service that supports it.

PROMOTIONAL BUDGETING

There are four methods of setting a promotional budget.

Percentage of sales

Relying on past experience it allows the sales results to determine how much is spent on promotion! In a bad year promotion will fall, and when things are good promotion will rise! A well established brand will have more spent upon it than a new brand which needs support desperately!

All you can afford

A firm may allocate all it can afford. If this is sufficient to do the job, fine – if not it is money wasted.

To determine how much can be afforded on promotion it is only necessary to charge the required profit against the product, as a cost, and allow the balance to become the surplus that is available (Table 31.1).

Table 31.1 Budgeting for promotion

	£	£
Revenue	100 000	
Cost of goods sold	40 000	
Gross profit		60 000
Fixed and variable costs of manufacture	20 000	
Fixed and variable costs of distribution, admin.,	10 000	
etc.	10 000	
Required profit (10% ROI)	10 000	
		50 000
Maximum available for promotion		10 000

Remember that if the balance is not sufficient to achieve the needed task(s) it is wasteful to spend it. Either set new objectives or locate a source of additional funding.

Competitive parity

This assumes that the competition is getting it right, and that what is right for them is right for you! Sometimes this method is used because of insecurity. Sometimes because salespeople need to see advertising as evidence of support.

Objective and task

This is by far the best, but the most difficult to introduce and to manage.

Clear promotional objectives must be set and specific plans made to meet those objectives. Effective controls are essential, to ensure that the effectiveness of the spend is known. Thus a firm may decide it will increase awareness of Brand A from 40 to 50% at latest by 1 July next. It follows that it has to know the level of awareness now, and to be able to monitor change. It has to have an effective research operation.

Objective and task is difficult to introduce because:

- It requires data initially. This must be obtained, and budgets must be experimented with to acquire information. Once the database is established the budgeting becomes effective.
- Management must be:
  — willing to accept control;
  — capable of using control effectively;
  — willing to invest in promotional research;
  — prepared to take the time to establish the database.

PROMOTIONAL OBJECTIVES

Underpinning all promotional objectives are certain key understandings:

- We know that prospective customers have to be made aware – that without awareness (or attention) they will take no interest in any promotion.
- Once awareness has been secured we have to generate and maintain a positive attitude.
- Only after there is a positive attitude can we hope to induce the action we require – purchase.
- When the purchase is complete the customer and consumer will evaluate the product in use.
- This evaluation in use feeds back as a positive or negative influence on attitude and further action.
- True marketing success comes from keeping customers and consumers in the *loyal user loop* of:
  purchase . . .
    use and like . . .
      purchase again . . .
        use and like again . . .
          purchase again . . .
            use and like again . . .

It is always better to move in short steps rather than in huge jumps – therefore we can use the attention – attitude – action stages for strategic planning, but for tactical planning we need a continuum of behaviour that shows the detailed stages that have to be passed through. The more detailed our understanding, the more precise our tactical planning can be (see Chapter 30).

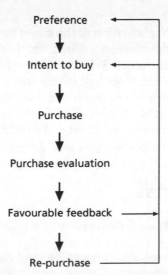

Fig. 31.3 Loyal user loop

Target audience identification

It is essential to identify our target audience(s) in as much detail as possible. Segmentation and vectoring are crucial to effective promotion (Chapters 12 and 13).

Remember that there is a constant movement of people into and out of each segment. We have to constantly make new entrants aware, and start them down the continuum, while at the same time moving others, stage by stage, through attitude and action and into the loyal user loop.

Strategic objectives

For each identified target audience strategic objectives can be written in terms of each of the three As:

- In the quarter to 31 March we shall, within our identified target audience increase:
  — awareness   from 45% to 50%
  — positive attitude   from 32% to 36%
  — purchase action   from 15% to 20%.

Note: There are always more aware of the product offering than have a positive attitude towards it, and more who have a positive attitude than take positive action.

It is not reasonable to expect all those who know of the offering to feel positive towards it. Not all of those who do will actually make a purchase. Not all who buy will like the product, however good it is!

Tactical objectives

These are written for each subdivision of the target audience across the whole width and depth of the promotional area. Individual salespeople will set objectives for each call on each customer. Sales promotion, advertising and PR objectives will be similarly detailed. Note that PR objectives will not be set in terms of the space obtained. Space is less important than that the PR objectives are met – awareness is attained, attitude is reinforced, etc.

Unless detailed tactical objectives are set and evaluated there will be a waste of resources, and strategic objectives are not likely to be attained.

EVALUATION OF SUCCESS

This can only be against promotional objectives which are written for each target audience.

Once objectives have been set they can be used as a basis for evaluation. The MkIS will provide information, and there are many sources of external research.

The results of promotional activity must be evaluated within an understanding of both controllable (internal) and uncontrollable (external) factors. Perhaps a promotion was successful only because competitors failed to respond – if so, could it be relied on to have the same result if used again? The key factors which impact on the success of promotion include:

- Controllable:
  - product, price and pack changes;
  - distribution efficiency;
  - trade margins and attitudes;
  - stock shortages;
  - production problems;
  - the campaign itself:
    - its quality and suitability for the target audience;
    - how efficiently it is managed.
- Uncontrollable:
  - competitive activity;
  - longer-term trends affecting the market, e.g. healthier eating;
  - short-term effects, e.g. a health scare;
  - the economic situation, climate, etc.

Objective and subjective evaluation

Research breaks down conveniently into primary and secondary, quantitative and qualitative.

In order of ease of access they are:

- quantitative, secondary;
- qualitative, secondary;
- quantitative, primary;
- qualitative, primary.

Secondary data is always researched before primary, and is carefully validated before use. Given that understanding it is not necessary to subdivide the remainder of this section into secondary and primary. It will be obvious when secondary sources are quoted, as will the need for additional primary data to be commissioned to fill in the gaps left after the secondary data search.

To avoid confusion over terminology we shall use objective and subjective to distinguish the two main areas of research concern.

Objective research

The first information gathered by 'advertisers' – they were not yet marketing communicators – was factual: advertising spend, media circulation, sales calls, etc.

Media

The need for information led to evaluation of readership as compared to circulation.

- readership   the number and kind of people who read publications;
- circulation   the average number of copies sold.

The *Financial Times* has a readership far in excess of circulation because office copies are circulated internally, it is made available as a service in clubs, waiting rooms, etc. Similarly the readership of *Woman* is higher than its circulation, but here it is the doctors' and dentists' waiting rooms coupled with long life that have high significance.

What should the media charge for? Circulation or readership? Readership, obviously. Better if the readership can be identified – the beginnings of targeting as a science go back to the first readership survey in 1936.

Thresholds

A threshold or 'trigger' level must be reached before targeted individuals respond. Colin McDonald, in the UK, has produced a survey showing that two exposures were necessary to shift purchase behaviour patterns, three or more exposures had no further effect on the sales response. Michael Naples, in the USA, showed that two or three exposures were necessary, more added no further benefit.

But it must be remembered that heavy users of the media will receive more exposure than needed . . .
If 80 million advertising messages are directed to the 20 million UK housewives they will, on average, receive 4 each, but the distribution will vary. Typically 20% will have seen no advertisement at all; 16% will have seen one; 13% two; 10% three; 9% four; 32% five or more. Thus there will have been wastage, and inefficiency.

PROMOTIONAL RESEARCH

Promotional research is a major subsection of marketing research. A wide range of sources of information and research techniques is routinely used. Those concerned with depth, motivational and attitude research throw up subjective responses and are usually primary research. (An exception might be the use of a continuing survey to track attitude, but if it was originally specially commissioned it remains primary research throughout its life.)

Above the line

Research into above-the-line media is concerned with:

- quantitative measures of readership and circulation. Media statistics are highly detailed and routinely available.
- qualitative studies into the effect of the contents of the messages carried in the media.

Below the line

The availability of reliable research is increasing with technological advances and demand for marketers. Objective information is being produced that is growing in value as experience is gained.

- Quantitative research is concerned with physical counts of the results of specific activities: the number of coupons redeemed, the number of enquiries generated.
- Qualitative research is concerned with discovering reaction to various appeals, and identification of customer and consumer response to given scenarios.

Three critical areas of change which have led to increased information on below-the-line activity are:

- Consumer   Greater individuality demands a sharper focus and tight targeting of promotions.
- Retailing   Greater concentration of shopping and the sophistication of operation have created new opportunities for in-store marketing and in-store research.
- Technology   Scanning databases that are linked directly to the checkouts are capable of producing highly detailed figures that can be relied upon.

Information

Information is the key to meeting the challenges and opportunities opening through retail and consumer change. The impact of electronic data capture has been enormous and scanning databases are fundamental to the changes that are taking place.

Bar-coded lines have become the basis for objective research data. It is estimated that in 1995 some 80% of all packaged groceries will pass over scanners (from 65% in 1993). At the same time the concentration of grocery retail power will further increase from the 52% that the top four retailers had in 1993. FMCG has traditionally been the developmental area, with its experience spreading into other sectors. Therefore marketers can expect more accurate information, more quickly, in all sectors before too long.

Scanning-based information provides the tools to control niche marketing and marketers are able to move at a new and much faster pace. Below-the-line activity can now be piloted and the results fed back in days rather than weeks – and with more reliability and accuracy.

Daily and weekly scans reveal short-term fluctuations and with monthly tracking these are smoothed out. Therefore a greater understanding of the dynamics of a market can be achieved, and appropriate action initiated. There is a powerful learning curve effect because results can now so quickly be related to action, with environmental forces taken into account.

- *A C Nielsen* are the biggest and best-known retail auditing researchers with offices throughout the world. In Europe they are in 18 countries, including each EU country, but are co-ordinated into a single pan-European operation. They have moved rapidly ahead from their days of simple stock checks to the provision of a range of information that has a startling depth of precision and measurement.

An example. Nielsen figures show that at Christmas instant coffee sales are brought forward from January so that overall trend is not disturbed. Ground coffee sales, however, show a marked increase ahead of Christmas thus revealing their Christmas seasonality.

- *Harris International* provide a shopping and intelligence service that is based on 50 000 interviews with grocery shoppers each year. It is unique in that as part of the service it compares actual with intended purchase.
- *Nielsen Safeway Information Partnership* – this began in January 1993 and exists to market specific Safeway information to manufacturer and supplier. Safeway intend that their sharing of information will enhance management's effectiveness by allowing them to work more closely and productively with suppliers. It will also generate revenue.
- *Information Resources Inc, (of Chicago)* – launched in 1987 and claimed to be the US grocery industry's leading scanner with an annual revenue of more than $140 million. They are now active in the UK and have announced a deal with ASDA to market their scanned data in the same way as the Nielsen Safeway Information Partnership.

Many other sources of objective secondary data exist – the European Market Share Reporter from Gale Research is typical. Their promotion explains the rationale behind the product:

So much information, so little time . . .

There is a wealth of European business info available – but it's almost impossible to track down *all* the data in hundreds of different publications.

For the first time, find *in one source* tables of market shares of thousands of companies, products and commodities. . . . 2,600 companies, 1,400 products/services, 260 countries/regions.

As always with marketing research data there is need to be extremely careful that it is providing you with information that is of true value. It is extremely easy to become swamped by data which appears to be helpful but actually is either off target, or not reliable for some reason.

Always check accuracy, reliability, validity and applicability.

Cost-effective research

Research must pay its way. If it is not targeted it is wasteful of resources and will probably result in data that is late and/or confusing. In promotion the requirement is to attempt to either predict how a new launch will be accepted, or how well a campaign met its objectives. Primary research is therefore mostly concentrated on obtaining subjective rather than objective data.

Omnibus surveys, where a range of sponsors come together to provide questions, are in common use. The number of competitors means that it is cost-effective to join an omnibus survey, and this is a useful halfway house to commissioning a primary research survey. NOP, Gallup, BMRB and Taylor Nelson AGB – all blue chip names – all conduct keenly priced weekly surveys of up to 4 000 adults. MORI runs monthly surveys, and is increasing the frequency to fortnightly.

Cost or value?

Nigel Spackman of BJM Research said at the 1992 AMSO Conference that clients tend to look at cost instead of value.

Value, in research, Spackman argued, comes from an evaluation of the usefulness of the obtained information to the client. That means to evaluate the quality and validity of the decisions that are taken from it. Cost must be related alongside the more significant issues of survey design, execution and interpretation. Only in that way can the true value of a research commission be judged.

Subjective

What do people buy? Do they buy physical product? function? symbolism? It is generally agreed that the symbolic/psychological area is by far the most important. Thus campaigns feature the emotional appeals as they sell the packages of benefits that research has suggested individuals in the target audience will respond to.

Despite the fact that the campaigns have a high subjective content, marketers must condition themselves to always check objective responses to their plans.

- People may like the proposition . . . but not respond to it.
- They may hate the proposition . . . but sales may improve.

Marketers must know *why*? Why will people respond? Why will they not? What do they actually want, as compared to what they say they want? Why are they disguising their true feelings?

For example, why do so many people claim to want to slim, yet so very few actually commit to a regime that will make them slimmer? It may be because they are too lazy, or because they lack determination, yet both conditions can be changed given sufficient motivation. It has taken over 20 years in the UK to shift smokers to an awareness that they can give up. Previously they were, like slimmers, constantly claiming they wanted to stop – but didn't.

If you are not by now convinced that people's behaviour is more important than any other aspect of marketing communications consider:

- More than 40% of respondents who refused kippers 'because they didn't like them' did not know what a kipper was.
- A group were individually asked if they ever had taken a loan. All said no. Some even became violent. Yet all had been selected from a list of borrowers!
- Soap manufacturers used to sell cleanliness . . . now they sell the promise of health and beauty.

- Early solid state radios were regarded as inferior because of their lack of weight.

Marketing communicators are influencers of behaviour. Marketers have to discover need and what triggers a motivation. Then they have to supply not only the trigger and motivation, but a series of reinforcements to encourage buyers down the continuum of behaviour.

CAMPAIGN PLANNING

All forms of promotion share the common purpose of moving target customers down the three As and into the loyal user loop. They are concerned to appeal to specific individuals, and their success must be measured against results from the specified targets.

The basic techniques are described from the viewpoint of advertising, but the techniques are also used in planning and evaluating the other forms of promotion.

Concept testing

Research into the effectiveness of advertisements is carried out by independent bodies, normally commissioned either by the advertiser or the advertising agency. Pre-testing is concerned to find out which themes, slogans, prices, brands and company names make impact on the target segment of the market. A selected audience is invited to rate several advertisements. There may be many changes before the most effective copy, theme, or format for each advertisement is determined.

All regions are tested for differences, so enabling the advertisers to make alterations in copy, imagery or format.

The effectiveness of every advertisement should be measured for:

- reaching maximum targets in the defined segment;
- reinforcement potential;
- persuasive impact.

Content research

This is concerned with the ability of an advertisement to achieve impact and to project the desired message to the target audience. An advertisement must be judged only from the perspective of its target because that is the sole reason for its creation. The purpose is to confirm that the *creative* and *copy platforms,* the general theme, and presentation of the advertisement achieve the desired results.

- *Pre-testing* is ahead of publication to confirm that the advertisement should work as intended.
- *Post-testing* is after publication to test the actual achievement.

- *Focus groups* are discussion groups formed around experienced researchers so that a proposal for a new advertisement, a new product, a below-the-line scheme, etc., can be discussed by typical members of the target audience. Focus groups can be very powerful, but great care must be taken not to bias or in other ways influence the results.

Effectiveness research

Post-testing is an important part of evaluation since it is important to know what happened, and why.

- *Recall and recognition testing.* This can be oral and/or pictorial.
  - Recall is 'unaided' and respondents are asked if they have seen a particular advertisement, and if so, what they remember about it.
  - Recognition is 'aided' – also called 'aided recall'. Respondents are shown a series of advertisements, usually mounted on cards, and asked how much about each they can remember.
  Recall and recognition may be 'same day' or 'day after'.
- *Split run testing.* Two different advertisements can be run in alternate copies of the same publication. Post-testing can then determine which was the more effective.
- *Tracking study.* A continuous research which measures awareness, attitude or action before, during and after a campaign. Some major brands have tracking studies that extend for decades.
- *Test marketing.* Market tests and pilot studies take the product and/or promotion into a limited area to check how it stands up within the marketplace. We examined test marketing in Chapter 24.
- *Qualitative.* The appropriate technique must be used to evaluate the level of success, e.g. if the objective is to improve awareness by 5% then recall and recognition testing is appropriate. If attitude shift was the objective then before and after research, or on-going tracking study, is needed. A marketer needs to work with an experienced and reliable researcher to determine the exact form of research best suited to defined need.
- *Quantitative.* Cost-per-response, cost-per-enquiry, cost-per-conversion (sale) are self-explanatory. Each response or enquiry must be tracked to see that it is properly followed through. Too often responses gather dust in the office when they should be routed to the sales force!

SIX KEY PRINCIPLES

1 Plan evaluation procedure well in advance. Learn from previous evaluations.
2 Plan with reference to clearly set objectives. Tailor the evaluation plan to the needs of the specific campaign.
3 The evaluation plan should lay down the evaluation design, information requirements and intended approach to analysis.

4 Evaluation has two main roles:
- Audit – what did we achieve?
- Development – what do we do next?

Both are equally important.
5 A successful evaluation is a combination of business-related physical measures and people-related psychological measures of effect.
6 A complete evaluation should aim to obtain an appreciation (not necessarily a quantification) of how the promotion has contributed to the longer-term future health of the product offering.

KEY POINT SUMMARY

- Monitor results as a guide to action.
- Prepare thoroughly for an expected future.
- A numeric approach is not suitable to a review of advertising effectiveness.
- Response to advertising can be direct or indirect.
- Advertising works at several levels of consciousness to achieve several tasks.
- Purchasing is a learned experience.
- Advertising has a powerful role in suggesting a course of action.
- Word-of-mouth is very important in promotion.
- Promotional budgets may be set as: percentage of sales, all you can afford, competitive parity, objective and task.
- Objective and task is best, but more difficult to introduce and manage.
- Promotional objectives aim to move people into the loyal user loop.
- It is better to move in short steps rather than huge leaps.
- Target audiences must be identified and segmented.
- Strategic objectives can be based on the three As.
- Tactical objectives are needed for each subdivision of the target audience.
- Success can only be evaluated against promotional objectives.
- Key factors that impact on promotional success include controllable and uncontrollable factors.
- Controllable factors are such as product, price and pack changes, distribution efficiency, the campaign.
- Uncontrollable factors include such as competitive activity, the economic situation.
- Secondary data is always researched first, and quantitative before qualitative.
- Media must be evaluated for both readership and circulation.
- A threshold or trigger level must be reached before targeted individuals respond.
- Promotional research is a major subsection of marketing research.
- Three critical areas of change leading to increased information on below-the-line activity are: greater individuality, greater shopping concentration, technology
- Bar-coded lines are a basis for objective research.
- Very many sources of research information exist.

- Value in research comes from the usefulness of the information to the client.
- Subjective values are crucial. They must be researched.
- Marketers must know why.
- Thorough pre-testing and post-research are essential to on-going improvement.
- Plan evaluation well in advance.
- Tailor evaluation to the needs of the specific campaign.
- Plan the design, information requirements and intended approach to analysis.
- Audit and develop . . . What did we achieve? What do we do next?
- Blend business-related physical measures with people-related psychological measures.
- Determine how the promotion has contributed to the long-term health of the product offering.

WORK-BASED SELF-ASSESSMENT QUESTIONS

1 How can an inaccurate sales forecast affect the planning of the promotional mix?

2 Produce an HLRS – a continuum of behaviour – which sets out the stages through which one of your customers must progress.

SCHOOL- AND COLLEGE-BASED SELF-ASSESSMENT QUESTIONS

1 Produce an HLRS – a continuum of behaviour – which sets out the stages through which a would be student must pass.

2 Develop another continuum to define the stages that an employer must pass through if he is to take up places for his staff (or children if you are at school).

SUGGESTED ASSISTANCE TO SELF-ASSESSMENT QUESTIONS FOR CHAPTERS 28–31

WORK-, SCHOOL- AND COLLEGE-BASED QUESTIONS

Chapter 28

1 Using a cafe as an example we would find:

Service features
- quality of the food;
- width of the menu;
- promptness of the service;
- attitude of the staff;
- cleanliness;
- accuracy of the bill;
- range of methods to pay;
- price/value perception.

Product support
- Raw materials – food, drink, etc.;
- Table linen, cutlery, crockery, etc.;
- Staff uniforms;
- Equipment – tables, chairs, kitchen, etc.;
- Menus – cards, typewriter, etc.;
- The building – location, decor, etc.

The products are pulled together to support the synergy package that is created as the service provided by the restaurant.

Chapter 29

1 Marginal cost pricing allows for variable expenses to be recovered – and perhaps to recover a proportion of fixed costs whilst still undercutting a rival. The wise use of marginal pricing allows a business to fill what would otherwise be slack time. It keeps equipment active and so helps to boost morale since people like to be busy. It gives the impression of a very busy and successful organisation – and people like to trade with successful firms. It enables continuing trade with suppliers, and boosts volume so that quantity discounts and other privileges continue. It can also secure prestige clients and so boost the firm's reputation and help them secure other full price customers. No firm will, however, trade at the margin if it doesn't have to. The aim is to have a full workload of full-priced business.

2 Marginal costs cover only variable expenses. Therefore a firm with 40% of its business at the margin would make profits on the other 60%. This may not be unreasonable provided the marginal work fills slack time that otherwise would be unoccupied.

As the ratio moves to 60:40 in favour off marginal pricing so the burden on the full-price work increases. Perhaps a 60% level would be sustainable — for a time. At 80% a firm would not last long – it would be a policy of survival! If 100% of the business were at the margin there would be no income to pay fixed expenses and the firm would soon run out of cash.

3 Option (a) is aggressive and typical supermarket behaviour. Remember, they have the power in the channel. The need is not simply to sell toys. The MD wants customer flow so that all his goods are sold. This gives a wonderful opportunity to use the emotion of Christmas as a basis of promotion that will appeal to the hearts of his customers.

Option (d) is the second choice, but it won't sell as many toys.

The other options are not sustainable in a competitive environment.

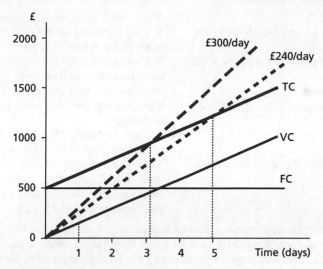

Fig. 29.10 Break-even graph

4 (a) Minimum daily charge must be £120 since this is the variable cost.
  (b) At 100% over marginal cost your daily charge is £240.
      Break-even is 5 days.
      At 150% over marginal cost your daily charge is £300.
      Break-even is 3.1 days.
      See break-even graph (Figure 31.4).

5 (a) Local businesses are important to you as a source of students, and of goodwill.
      Many who work in them will be at the college, have children who are at the col-
      lege or who know people who are at, or will be coming to, the college. The word-
      of-mouth contact is important, and you need to be a good neighbour, anyway.
      Probably you will work to a cost-plus system, but check that you are identifying
      all costs before applying a mark-up of, perhaps 15%.
  (b) National business can be approached using a competitor-based approach. They
      are used to sending staff on courses of all kinds. With commercial organisations
      charging very highly it allows the typical college a substantial 'window of oppor-
      tunity' between what they would charge locally, and what business regards as
      reasonable. There would be an absolute need to deliver at the quality expected,
      however!
  (c) Businesses already sending students to the college are regular customers and, as
      such, entitled to special consideration. Special offers and discount deals would
      be suitable, especially as these need not directly involve cash, since you could
      offer free places and/or consultancy.
  (d) Local schools would be served at the margin, or just over. They are feeders to
      you, and you will have a close affinity with them and, in particular, with their
      staff. They also have quite limited budgets, but are used to fitting into educa-
      tional expediency.

Chapter 30

1 Your list will contain items such as set out overleaf.

Item	Why repeat sales are important
Funerals – we get buried only once.	It is the surviving relatives that buy the services of the funeral director.
Double glazing – we only glaze once.	But we move house – and the office may need replacement windows.
Wedding ring.	Shall we not need other jewellery in time?
Education.	Shall we not perhaps need to return for updating? We are certainly likely to send children and/or employees to school and college.
Referral from doctor to consultant.	The consultant may or may not need to be visited again, but the hospital where he works may be come of vital importance to you, your family and friends.

2 To take one famous campaign as an example:

Babycham is a sparkling perry (a cider made from pears) which is packed in single glass sized bottles and targeted on teenage girls. Its campaigns have been run ahead of holiday periods, notably Christmas and the New Year. The 'Babycham' is an attractive, perky, little animal with a resemblance to Disney's Bambi.

The advertising (TV, national press, general interest magazines) shows a party in full swing. Men are present, but as supporting figures to happy girls. The whole image is clean, fresh, exciting, safe. Men buy Babycham, but are never seen to drink it. It is clear that girls are to be looked after . . . it is 'acceptable' for men to buy what they might regard as a 'cissy' drink.

The girls, who are the end-users, advisers and deciders, are teenage, but with escorts who are in their 20s. Thus the promotion is drawing on the middle levels of Maslow's hierarchy.

The promotions strictly avoids any sexual connotation and there is absolutely nothing which is aggressive, dominant, non-social.

Women's media are avoided because the purchase is made by men, and sufficient contact can be made through broad band media.

In-store the theme of the main promotion is carried through to the counter and the shelf. The product is packed attractively, and the little Babycham is prominent . . . even to the extent of providing plastic models as merchandising aids.

WORK-BASED QUESTIONS

Chapter 28

2 Only you can judge how effective your research has been. By now you should be very experienced in researching your own organisation, but you may have found it difficult to discover just which laws and codes of conduct apply to your product range. The organisation should know! If they do not, then they may be at serious risk.

Chapter 31

1 The inaccuracy can be either forecast high–sales low, or forecast low–sales high. In both cases there is need to identify areas where the variations are occurring.
   • Are they localised?
     If so, by sales region, by salesman, by type of customer, by individual customer?

Only with hard information can you target the optimum response.
If sales are lower than forecast:

- Short-term stimulus possibly needed. Consider:
  — an SP campaign to pull business through the channel;
  — dealer incentives to encourage them not only to stock, but also to promote – e.g. as with Christmas toys from the supermarket (Chapter 26).
- Contingency planning should ensure that a suitable plan can be mounted quickly.

If sales are higher than forecast:

- Can production/procurement/distribution handle the extra business?
- If yes – continue with campaign.
- If no, consider:
  — cancelling the remainder of the campaign;
  — setting sales quotas;
  — restricting sales to certain regions.

In both cases there is need for post-campaign evaluation. What happened? Was it predictable? Was it picked up quickly enough? Could it have been noticed sooner? Was the remedial action sufficient and appropriate? What have we learned for the future?

2 Base your continuum on the models in Chapter 27. Figure 30.1 gives the needed framework. Figure 30.2 shows a continuum developed for the FMCG market.

SCHOOL-AND COLLEGE-BASED QUESTIONS

Chapter 28

2 It is not likely that your organisation will be in breach of the law, but they may be unaware of the potential for synergy that exists within any educational institution. You may have found that individual courses are 'packaged' and sold without central guidance – even that such centrality is resisted as conformity. It is, unfortunately, not likely that you will be able to do anything about it – but remember the lessons for when you are in a position of authority.

Chapter 31

Both questions call for some detailed thinking, and some research to discover exactly what happens within the decision process. Base your continuums on Figure 30.1 and use Figure 30.2 as a model. Your continuums will take time to developed thoroughly, but you will learn a lot about customer behaviour as you work on them.

PART 9

Marketing overseas –
necessary for growth

Marketing overseas can take a variety of forms – from simple exporting of surplus capacity to a full global presence.

Certain issues are critically important to all forms of overseas marketing, and many of these are shared with cross-cultural marketing within a single market. Marketers face many of the same problems when marketing into the ethnic mix that is Birmingham as they do marketing into an overseas country. Probably the only differences of note are the absence of an exchange rate problem, and the simplicity of effecting delivery.

> *International marketing concerns itself with the application of marketing operations across national frontiers (Paliwoda)*

Once this key principle is understood international marketing becomes far easier to understand – it is no more and no less than straightforward marketing, but applied across national frontiers. Thus the issues of language, culture, expectation and behaviour have to be identified and understood within and for each market opportunity. Laws, codes of practice and trade custom and practice must be identified and complied with. A marketing manager does exactly this, of course, for the home market.

There are two major differences when marketing internationally:

- Great care has to be taken to understand the overseas markets – the principles of research, segmentation, vectoring, etc. apply, but within the context of the target market.
- Marketing research data must often be treated with caution since many overseas countries do not yet have reliable research processes.

As the scenarios for Part 9 we are grateful to have detailed information concerning a British company that has built a thriving international business. Paul Lockwood is the Managing Director of Meridian Freight Services Limited who are based at London's Heathrow Airport.

Meridian are a very successful provider of international air, sea and road freight services for companies and individuals requiring the import or export of goods – and recently have added UK distribution to their services. Paul kindly agreed to answer 30 questions on the international freight market and how Meridian became and remains established as a flourishing operation within it.

CHAPTER 32

International marketing

INTERNATIONAL MARKETING – DEFINED

The Chartered Institute of Marketing's definition of marketing can be extended to an international context with a simple addition:

The management process responsible for identifying, anticipating and satisfying customer requirements profitability (across national boundaries).

These terms are sometimes *incorrectly* used to describe international marketing:

- Selling abroad   simply means selling products in a country other than one's own.
  It does *not* include any element of marketing and is sales concept driven.
- Export selling   again refers exclusively to selling and not to marketing.
- Dumping   refers to the practice of getting rid of surplus production – it has nothing to do with a marketing approach.

International marketing is a management activity that operates internationally exactly as domestic marketing operates at home. Customer satisfaction is central to marketing thinking and profits are made from repeat business. These principles apply identically in international marketing. If they don't – then the organisation concerned is selling, but not marketing.

Comparisons between local and overseas markets show that each has a unique set of characteristics. Differences in laws and codes of practice, demand patterns, competition, pricing, methods of distribution and communication mean that managers require mix strategies for each market. Differences in managing 'controllable' and 'uncontrollable' factors are experienced in national and international environments and vary greatly within each of 189 countries that are open to international trade.

Writers wrongly concentrate on multinational and global brands – McDonalds, Coca-Cola, Ford and IBM – seeing them as the only leading exponents of international marketing. Paliwoda defines a multinational enterprise as:

A corporation which owns (in whole or in part), controls and manages income-generating assets in more than one country. In so doing, it engages in international production, sales and distribution of goods and services across national boundaries financed by foreign direct investments.

He then puts powerful arguments for and against the multinational organisation – is it a force for good or for evil?

Self-interest

On 12 December 1993, Michael Heseltine, Present of the Board of Trade, made it clear in a television interview with David Frost that the European Community was made up simply of a group of nations 'pursuing their individual and economic self-interest'.

This 'self-interest' approach may be the more realistic view taken by managers of organisations, including multinationals and governments. Certainly it is realistic in the light of government subsidies paid to support coal, steel, financial institutions, agriculture and shipping. These are opposed by the UK, but are backed by the majority of EU governments. On 1 January 1993 the Single European Market (SEM) became reality and this decade will see long negotiations to rationalise subsidies, trade agreements, tariffs and, in general, to set an economic climate in which the economies of EU countries may enjoy harmonised trading practices. The current term used to describe the effect of such harmonisation is the establishment of a 'level playing field'.

This is a good time to start the interview with Paul Lockwood, managing director of Meridian, freight forwarders at London's Heathrow Airport.

Q. *Paul, Meridian Freight Services Limited is a well-established company, how did you start?*

A. My partner and I formed the company in 1982, and apart from adverse trading in 1983, we have enjoyed steady and controlled growth. Having survived recession, we are well placed to take advantage in any upturn in the economy.

Q. *Could you outline how you operate and explain your mission and objectives?*

A. The mission of Meridian is to continue to be successful in a highly competitive industry. Companies progress or fall back. We have no tangible product, so we market and promote our services by 'packaging' them as a 'product'. When two companies provide road services to Paris, with similar rates and timetables, only the quality of service differentiates the two. So we implemented a quality management system to BS 5750 Part 2 standards, and 'a never ending improvement of quality of service we provide to our customers' is the one long-standing objective of the company. The company provides international air, sea, and road services for companies and individuals requiring to import or export goods and, more recently we have added UK distribution. These services are provided by working with international airline operators, steamship lines, road hauliers and in partnership with similar minded overseas forwarders.

Q. *Paul, what is your role in the company?*

A. I deal with all aspects of sales, marketing, the appointment of overseas business partners, pricing, administration, financial year-end accounts, and quality policy decisions through internal quality audits.

Q. *Was it easy to start a freight forwarding business in overseas markets?*

A. In 1982 there were no restrictions to access to the industry and so it was easy to start the business. We survived when others failed by sound financial and operational skills, operating on large company practices, but as a 'two-man band'. Our main advantage was the recognition that overseas business partners were essential – you need a good overseas agent to complement the business. Other firms without agents are limited to UK-controlled business. If they target exports to Hong Kong and imports from New York, for example, they are working on a limited UK customer base.

We found that a UK forwarder must have reliable overseas partners, but the search for a good agent can be a long and tedious one.

ENVIRONMENTAL FACTORS

The key environmental factors to be considered when forming opinions about a foreign market are covered by the STEEPLE acronym (see Chapters 5 and 6).

S Social/cultural environment

The social/cultural environment that underpins markets is a patterned way of thinking, feeling and reacting to complex values, ideas, attitudes and other meaningful symbols created by man to shape human knowledge, experience, or sets of behaviour patterns. Included are:

- material culture   technology, tools and machinery;
- language   interpreting world events and experiences;
- aesthetics   colour, design, folklore and fashion;
- education   human goals and aspirations;
- religion   beliefs and values, practices and behaviour;
- attitudes and values   working practices, risk taking, change, time and acquisitions;
- social organisation   family, status, class, power.

T Technological environment

Nations are developed to differing technological levels. These are often reflected in the levels of manpower skills. Therefore a product may be right for several markets, but wholly inappropriate for others. Home heating is an example: fully developed in Norway, Finland and Sweden; of concern to northern countries such as Holland, Belgium and the UK; of little interest to southern European countries such as Italy and Greece and of no interest at all to countries in central Africa.

Within the EU there is a range of electrical regulations, and electrical fittings which vary around a common theme. At present one country's plugs will not fit another's sockets. Moves are in hand to standardise, but to which standard?

E Economic and market competition

The economy of a country is closely tied to its national resources and raw materials; its topography, climate and the skills of the labour force. The population of each nation differs in: numbers, age composition, growth rates and incomes.

Governments impose constraints including import and export controls. Non-tariff barriers regulate trade through such as exchange control or documentation (stockholding, machinery, state of technology).

Competition will be relatively weak where competitors are scarce, or strong where many larger organisations compete. Strong entry barriers may deter competitive activity, with governments discriminating in favour of local suppliers.

The commercial infrastructure will vary dependent on the numbers, types and efficiency of retailers, wholesalers, agents and distributors.

E Education, training and employment

The levels of education and training attained by individuals within countries is of key importance to their value within the economy. Employment, however, is a factor which is often beyond the control of the individual and is a matter for entrepreneurs who are constrained by governmental policies.

P Political

The role of government varies from total state control of business operations and the means of production and/or distribution, to freedom with limited safeguards, e.g. health and safety standards, trading agreements and law enforcement.

Business abroad is vulnerable to expropriation of assets and markets. This suggests that international firms need to prepare to operate in conflicting environments. Therefore research and a sound MkIS system is invaluable to the international marketer.

L Legal

There are differences in home and foreign law. Overseas regulations need to be known and understood by the manager who wishes to trade in any country. Risks vary as ideologies change and national self-interest often works against the development of trade agreements.

The key relationship legally and politically is between the organisation, and legislation of the home government and of the host government abroad.

E Environmental protection

The concept of environmental protection varies widely between countries – as does the belief in the need for it. It is understandable that less educated people who are existing on a subsistence income will be less concerned with the long-term effects of global warming and the destruction of the rain forests.

It is less hard to understand how the USA can claim to support the cause of environmental protection, but refuse to sign the international treaty of environmental control. It is worth noting – in context with several of these headings – that the American politicians have felt unable to introduce effective environmentally friendly legislation. Is it the power industry lobby which prevents them, or selfish public opinion within the United States?

The differences across these seven environmental areas show that the marketing mix elements must be blended specifically for each market . . . but that marketing nationally or internationally is fundamentally similar in principle.

International marketing, therefore, is a 'philosophy' adopted by firms seeking profit opportunities abroad as well as at home. The way into full international marketing is, for most, via exporting from the home base.'

At this point let us return and discuss several points with Paul Lockwood.

Q. *How did you begin to operate in a foreign country, is the business mainly air cargo from London Heathrow, or do you operate from other airports?*

A. Our core business is air freight, handling almost an equal number of air imports and exports. We have also developed ocean traffic, both full and part containers, and European road freight, contributing 15% of sales revenue. This will increase rapidly. In handling ocean traffic we deal in most major UK ports.

Q. *What are your main problems in dealing with freight transport from and to large companies and multinationals?*

A. Increasingly we are handling clients who are 'global players', having worldwide manufacturing and distribution centres. We are able to compete with global forwarders by using our agency network. For example, we have been appointed by our Chicago agent to handle all UK and European consignments for a worldwide fashion house in New York. Meridian is responsible for co-ordinating goods to and from the Far East and USA, without seeing the goods in the UK. It is easy to tender for this business as requirements and responsibilities are clearly defined.

Q. *What difference has the European Union made to your business following the Maastricht Treaty and its operation from 1 January 1994.*

A. The main difference is that now the place at which VAT is accounted for, or the point of entry into the country, has moved away from the agent to the client's premises. So we are no longer responsible to H M Customs for the collection of VAT and in the UK this has resulted in faster transit time as formal customs entry is no longer required. The main impact is a loss of revenue for all EU imports, and some agents at UK ports having large proportions of EU business no longer exist. Whilst the UK views EU traffic as 'goods in free circulation' and imposes few restrictions, this is not the case with some of our European partners. There is some confusion as to exactly where VAT is accounted on freight charges and this is under review. The main impact is that many clients are now buying and selling in Europe and treating this as though it were a domestic UK movement, as was intended by the Treaty.

Q. *Did the end the 'iron curtain' and the political changes in Russia, increase business with Eastern Europe?'*

A. It is difficult to see a pattern emerging – business opportunities are there in the Eastern bloc, but care is required. Tinned foods, clothing, and capital equipment are being transported, but the lack of infrastructure and the uncertainty of political alliances make it a high risk business, when transporting goods across those borders. Consequently many UK companies and freight services are targeting specific individual areas. There is money to be made, but only for the adventurous!

DEVELOPMENT OF INTERNATIONAL ORGANISATION

Decisions by an organisation to go international are well researched. In a recent survey by Piercey of Cardiff Business School the decision is shown to be not necessarily always rational. Often it is a chance decision based on six stages:

1 No interest. Overseas orders are rejected.
2 Some unsolicited orders are met, but there is no active drive to export.
3 Active export is considered.
4 Experimental marketing activity takes place in a 'closed' and friendly country.
5 The organisation becomes established in that export market.
6 Possibility of trading with more distant countries is considered.

From here it is a relatively easy step to the establishment of an international marketing operation.

In a recent survey of 300 leading UK exporting companies Brown and Cook analysed the main reasons for exporting (Table 32.1).

Table 32.1 The main reason for exporting

Reasons given	% of respondents
To gain more sales	77.1
For long-term survival	69.6
To achieve market leadership	60.8
Due to lack of UK opportunities	60.3
Exporting proved to be more profitable	49.9
To absorb overheads	47.1

Source: Chee H and Harris R (1993), *Marketing, A Global Perspective*, Pitman Publishing

The dominant reasons for exporting appear to be growth and profits through increased sales, with survival in mind. Market leadership and the lack of UK opportunities are major, secondary, but important motivations.

Selling overseas brings a need for changes – in particular to the organisation structure and to the way the product is presented. The product life cycle may well be extended, especially if selling into a less developed country. Foreign competition will increase, but firms will plan to stay ahead.

Strategic options

Three distinct strategies are available.

• undifferentiated marketing;
• differentiated marketing;
• concentrated marketing.

Undifferentiated marketing

Through a *geocentric* approach the organisation aims for a world orientation.

The organisation applies 'single market' mix strategies worldwide. This is difficult unless the company has a suitable product and sufficient resources to follow this policy profitability. The new Ford Mondeo, voted car of the year 1993, is an example of a product with true global presence. Coca-Cola, Pepsi Cola, McDonald's and IBM have a geocentric approach, as do the big power companies such as Exxon.

The world's largest multinational corporations are truly huge, with a significant number actually larger than some individual national states!

Table 32.2 The world's top 12 multinationals in 1992

Rank	Multinational corporation	Nationality	Market value ($ billion)
1	Royal Dutch/Shell Group	Netherlands/UK	77.82
2	Nippon Telegraph & Telephone	Japan	77.52
3	Exxon	US	75.30
4	Phillip Morris	US	71.29
5	General Electric	US	66.00
6	Wal-Mart Stores	US	60.82
7	Coca-Cola	US	58.47
8	Merck	US	58.41
9	AT&T	US	55.85
10	IBM	US	51.82
11	Glaxo Holdings	UK	42.64
12	British Telecom	UK	40.45

Source: *Business Week*, July 13, 1992. Copyright © 1992 by McGraw-Hill Inc.

Differential marketing

Using a *polycentric* approach the organisation adopts an orientation which is specific to each host country. A marketing mix is developed for each market across the world. This is a complex and high cost option.

Concentrated marketing

A marketing strategy is established to exploit a limited number of markets. These may be defined geographically, by economic or other region, by nation, by market niche.

INTERNATIONAL AND MULTINATIONAL ORGANISATIONS

Patterns of organisations can be divided into six main types.

Direct functional relationships

The senior staff of the multinational have a direct relationship with the foreign subsidiaries and functional organisation transcends national borders.

Holding company

An organisation with operational divisions controlled through a holding company responsible for corporate strategy. Relationships are negotiated between managers across regional, national and international groupings.

Product organisation

Product group managers have direct control over subsidiaries operating in their product area.

Matrix organisation

Managers of subsidiaries report along product, group, geographical, or occasionally functional lines.

Project type organisation

The company is organised into a series of project groups or teams, e.g. large-scale assembly line operations such as BAe aircraft construction. *Note:* This type of organisation is proving an ideal way to enter into joint ventures. BAe and Aero-Spatiale of France jointly designed, manufacture and sell the successful Airbus range. Neither could single-handedly have managed the operation.

Multidivisional organisation

The international organisation is divided into autonomous divisions, each organised as best meets the needs of the organisation.

Advantages of divisionalisation

- Identification of individual activities tends to centralise specialist skills/expertise.
- Managers can focus on resources, finance, cost centre controls.
- Objective analysis of potential markets can be carried out.
- Communication is eased.
- Expertise is grouped.
- Problems can be identified early.

Disadvantages of divisionalisation

- Separation may not enhance the quality of decision-making – duplication may cause problems.

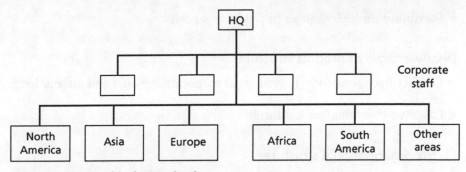

Fig. 32.1 Geographical organisation

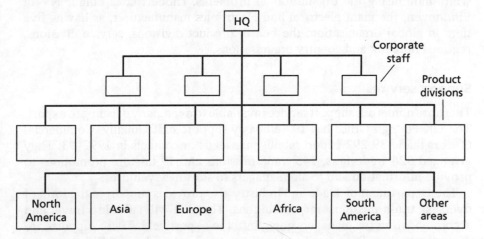

Fig. 32.2 Product division
Source: Adapted from a model by Hibbert

- Dilution of company resources may result in loss of management efficiency.
- Friction between national and international divisions may grow.
- Communication and/or language problems may occur.

Divisional structures divide global marketing into geographic regions and are often a useful approach for stable products and high-technology markets, e.g. pharmaceuticals (Figure 32.1).

Organisation by product structures

Hibbert examines the basic alternative structures available to internationals (Figure 32.2).

Advantages of product structures

- Global responsibility is taken for each product.
- Advantages are positive for companies with diverse and unrelated product groups.

- Flexibility through changes in products is positive.

Disadvantages of product structures

- Conflict between product divisions at corporate, product and international level.
- Effective co-ordination is difficult.

Matrix organisational structures

A matrix organisational structure is a format that best meets corporate goals, while minimising the organisational problems. Hibbert cites Philips NV of Eindhoven, the giant electrical and electronics manufacturer, as having five tiers in global organisation, the board, product divisions, service divisions, regional bureaux and country organisations.

Support services

There are numerous support services available to a company deciding to export. The UK Foreign Office has 197 embassy support staff globally. Commercial officers made 39 292 export intelligence leads or contacts in 1992–93. They arranged 324 trade fairs, 145 trade missions and 19 in-store promotions to provide information and to aid managers to start new ventures.

The Department of Trade and Industry also provides support in the form of overseas trade missions and exhibitions. The DTI will subsidise travel and accommodation for managers going into the export field. These supports are of particular benefit to small and medium-sized enterprises (SMEs).

Chambers of Commerce and Industry provide overseas contacts, trade directories and a vital export documentation service.

Specialists in the banking field have several generations of business experience and contacts within certain product groups. The merchant banks in the City of London specialise in support services and in the estimation of overseas risk.

Agencies

Specialist agencies will be found throughout the world to take responsibility for trade and others exist to provide support in marketing research, advertising, sales promotion, pricing surveys, channel contacts, language services, etc.

Agency support to take trade responsibility may be contracted from:

- *Commission agents.* They do not hold stock, but take orders which they pass through for processing.
- *Stocking agents.* They carry stocks and can make deliveries within a minimum time.
- *Spares and servicing agency.* They carry stocks of spares and have repair facilities which are approved by the manufacturer.

- *Del credere agents.* They work on commission and carry stocks but also accept credit risks and pay the principal if the customer defaults.

Agency search

In searching for an agency abroad the first consideration is to conform to Article 85 of the EC regulations covering competition. Exclusive agency agreements may easily infringe the new directives and rules on competition. Professional legal advice is required before contractual agreements with agencies are signed. The guidelines are simple. No restrictions are permissible on agents, either integrated or non-integrated.

If an agency is integrated then restrictions are illegal if they attempt to:

- prevent competitive goods being handled;
- grant exclusive rights or territory of operation;
- impose restrictions on selling outside that territory;
- contain any non-competitive clause for a period of up to two years after the expiry of the contract or agreement;
- require that at least one third of turnover must be derived from a single client.

If the agency is non-integrated the criteria for competition are:

- Does the agency operate for a number of clients with several products?
- Does the agency operate for a number of other suppliers?

A third party excluded from a territory by an illegal agreement may sue either the contracting company or the agency. Companies risk up to 10% of their global turnover for breaching EC competition rules.

Agency selection checklist

The search for a compatible agency requires planning and contacts. Selection of an agency from a short list of potentials requires careful pre-analysis of need so that individual agencies can be evaluated, in depth, against common criteria. A basic search and selection checklist is:

- Establish the type of agency needed:
  — outline their role and function.
- Key facts checklist:
  — agency profile, histories of owners/managers;
  — other contracts held;
  — geographical area covered;
  — knowledge of markets;
  — levels of competence;
  — qualifications and numbers of staff employed,
  — financial stability.
- The human factors:
  — agency's enthusiasm and interest in the new products/services;
  — ability to work together – do you like each other?

Agency agreement

An agreement must be formalised in writing and contains, as a minimum:

- the laws under which the contract will operate;
- nature and character of the agreement – purpose, products/services, territory to be covered;
- exclusivity (within Article 85 if within EC regulations);
- duties agreed: consignment of stocks, commission rates, etc.;
- duration of contract, termination terms.

Decisions on whether to employ local or expatriate staff depends on the area, language, learning and cultural differences.

Advantages of support from local agencies

Local agencies have detailed local knowledge of customers and of markets. They understand the culture and so can advise on designs, colours, sizes, materials and the most suitable promotional strategies. They can show how to achieve positive impact, help with translations and the avoidance of errors. In addition they often offer a cost advantage over setting up a wholly owned organisation.

These problems of selecting sound and effective overseas agents were emphasised by Paul Lockwood of Meridian. Let us continue to question him on this:

Q. *How do you select a new overseas market?*

A. Without local contacts or specialised knowledge of the local market, it can be very difficult to enter an emerging economy without detailed research, investment, and associated risk. However, for those who do overcome these difficulties, the results can be profitable.

Q. *Do you organise your company on a divisional basis, or on service or product lines?*

A. As our 'product' is a service, we divide our import and export into two divisions. Within each there is a specialised knowledge of various industry sectors, such as pharmaceutical and art-works, for example.

Q. *Do you use agents as support services?*

A. Meridian has a network of overseas business partners. These agents are similar to us in size, business type, and philosophy. We have set and established two-way credit terms with each other, and also an arrangement to jointly share profits derived from various worldwide trade routes. Most arrangements are formalised by signed agreements.

Q. *How does Meridian communicate with your agents and control assignments in transit?*

A. The agreement with agents overseas is for 'sole representation'. Therefore our agents are not specialists in a narrow field of forwarding, they must have a broad range of products and services which we can both promote.

It is the agent's location, in the global sense, that determines his role, e.g. agents in Taiwan and Seoul tend to be export orientated, our agents in Malaysia tend to be import orientated.

We are in constant daily communication with most of our agents, receiving and sending information regarding shipments in transit. Most of this exchange is transmitted by fax.

Q. *A final question at this stage, Paul, how do you initiate a search for a new agent or partner?*

A. Because forwarding is a global business, the best method of locating a new agent is by recommendation from existing agents who already deal with them. For example, our Los Angeles agent could provide details of his agent in Manilla. In this way we all reduce the risk of employing a bad one.

IMPACT OF IT ON MANAGEMENT CONTROLS AND COMMUNICATION

The impact of information technology is immense. Visa, MasterCard and American Express allow goods to be purchased in Kuala Lumpur, the USA or Australia only seconds slower than in one's home city. Electronic data exchange (EDI) via dedicated land lines and satellite has revolutionised the ease and speed of business transactions.

Transfer of commercial and administrative data between governments, trading partners, HQ and divisions, is carried out by computer interchange using either magnetic media or via telecommunications networks.

Data standards have been agreed so that data can be smoothly transferred across the world. In the UK two bodies, the Simpler Trade Procedures Board (SITPRO) and the Article Number Association (ANA) have defined national and international message standards based on the Electronic Data Interchange for Administration and Transport (EDIFACT).

The EC commissioned Trade Electronic Data Interchange System (TEDIS) in 1988–89 and TEDIS 2 for three years 22 July 1991 to 1994 to unify standards with three objectives:

* to integrate the establishment and development of EDI in the EU countries;
* to analyse and increase awareness of users of EDI especially in small firms, including hardware and software manufacturers;
* to analyse the impact of EDI on managements of public and private enterprises and make them aware of the economic and social implications.

EDI problems of compatibility will improve through the activities of SPIRO working with ANA. The legal and security aspects will come clearer with experience. The end result will be a considerable aid to the economic growth prospects of all EU trading nations.

For interpersonal communication by mobile telephones the European Telecommunications Standards Institute (ETSI) are introducing a new Global System for Mobile Communication (GSM). A pan-European mobile phone system led by Orbitel, a Hampshire-based company, will enable the same cellular phone to be used across all EU countries.

THE INTERNATIONAL DECISION

Decisions to trade internationally are not taken lightly, nor in crisis. They should be the result of a carefully planned strategy which reflects a desire in the organisation to go for growth. The international firm needs to develop specialist resources, contacts and systems to successfully pursue export goals and objectives.

There are many ways to approach the international dimension. Two examples must suffice to illustrate:

- *Russia and Eastern Europe.* Russian business systems have differed greatly from the American and West European systems. The former consists mainly of state run operations, the latter mainly non-state private organisations. Moves towards more privatisation will characterise the final decade of this century.

  Shortage of hard currency means that trading into Eastern Europe may depend largely on multilateral barter agreements. Hence many industrial goods and durable consumer goods from the West are exchanged for oil, timber, or raw materials. The intention is to move the eastern economies to a more western approach, but the lack of the necessary cultural background, and the difficulties of enforcing the needed legislation are creating the very real risk that the Russian market, in particular, will be dominated not by business ethics, but by the harsh laws of supply and demand.

- *Licensing.* Fosters and Castlemain XXXX lagers were brought into UK from Australia by two companies each with strong home production and distributive facilities. It was less costly to buy the rights to these products than for the British brewers to design, test and launch new lagers. In the same way Carlsberg and Stella Artois lagers are brewed under licence in Britain.

  Let us give Paul Lockwood the last word in this chapter – he says 'the uncertainty of political alliances makes it a high-risk business when transporting across borders.'

KEY POINT SUMMARY

- International marketing is marketing overseas.
- To the normal marketing issues faced in the home market must be added those which apply to the target overseas market(s).
- Selling abroad, exporting and dumping are not international marketing.
- A multinational enterprise owns, control and manages income-generating assets in more than one country.
- The EU is working towards the achievement of a level playing field for SEM trade.
- STEEPLE provides the base framework for international auditing, just as it does for the home market.
- Decisions to 'go international' are often made in sequential stages.
- The main reasons given for British firms to export are: to gain more sales, long-term survival, to achieve market leadership, due to lack of UK opportunities.

- Three strategic options are: undifferentiated, differentiated and concentrated marketing.
- Multidivisional organisation benefits include: they can focus, be more objective, have group expertise, identify problems early.
- Disadvantages of divisionalisation include: separation and duplication, dilution, friction.
- Product structures have the advantages of: global product responsibility, flexibility. They are most suited to diverse and unrelated product groups.
- Product structures have the disadvantages of difficulty in co-ordination and potential conflict.
- Matrix structures best meet corporate goals whilst minimising organisational problems.
- Numerous support services are available to the exporter.
- Specialist agencies will be found throughout the world.
- Agencies to take trade responsibility include: commission, stocking, spares and servicing, del credere.
- Agencies must be selected with care.
- Agency agreements must be formalised in writing, determine under which laws they will operate and cover all the terms of the agreement.
- Local agencies can provide detailed knowledge and support – and offer cost advantages.
- A major IT impact on management controls and communication is in progress.
- Decisions to trade internationally should be the result of a carefully planned strategy which reflects a desire in the organisation to go for growth.
- Development of specialist resources, contacts and systems is necessary to successfully pursue international goals and objectives.

WORK-, SCHOOL- AND COLLEGE-BASED SELF-ASSESSMENT QUESTION

1 You are expecting a foreign national to join your organisation (company, school, college) and you know that he or she has never been abroad before.

   Prepare a checklist – in outline and then in detail – of the things he or she will need to know, understand and comply with.

Hints:

A You will find a map useful.

B Do not expect to complete this assignment quickly, nor alone and unaided.

C It will help if you put yourself in the shoes of the visitor. What would you need to know if you were going into a foreign country for the first time. (What did you need to know when you actually did go abroad?)

See the end of Chapter 35 for answer guidelines.

CHAPTER 33

Deciding on market entry

By the twenty-first century a truly global system of marketing will be firmly established. Global marketing will face accelerating fragmentation of markets. Marketing managers will require to study the precise detail of customer need in each segment of an overseas market and will rely heavily on virtually instantaneous communication systems and easy travel. Many national frontiers can be expected to have far less significance as the need for international trade between countries and trading areas is seen to be ever more important.

Plans to enter an overseas market can only follow a policy decision on the form of overseas marketing or selling to be adopted. Policy can only be determined in the light of knowledge. Therefore top management needs information. They are not normally interested in tactical issues – but this is because normally they are working in their home market and are generally aware of what is – and is not – possible. For overseas marketing decisions they will need a broad understanding of the tactical issues that apply in the overseas market(s). They will also need to investigate the logistics of distribution, and how they can be sure of being paid.

Once a general background, sufficient to inform a policy decision, has been obtained it will be far easier to see how to establish strategies for actual market entry.

Normal research practices used in the home market must be adjusted and/or replaced by methods that reflect the differences found in the overseas market under study. These differences will be researched as of prime importance within a STEEPLE audit. If that is a Go result then research can move on into channel logistics, customer preference, local distribution and customer service. The results of the research will guide product design or modification, promotion, packaging and pricing. The case for meticulous international marketing research is overwhelming.

The information required before trading decisions can be made must be identified and each element evaluated to determine how necessary it is. Only when the essential information is to hand can even basic decisions be made concerning market entry. Data for the MkIS system must be compatible, comparable, reliable and credible. International research is always more expensive than that for the home market and therefore there is even greater need to manage the process effectively.

The principles of Marketing Research covered in Chapter 3 apply – but the problems of operating research in another country require careful management attention.

- Is there sufficiently accurate basic data?
  Can a census be relied upon? Is there a system of post or zip codes?

- Will respondents' replies be reliable?
  What cultural problems may there be in securing accurate answers?
- Communications may not allow certain forms of research.
  Telephone and postal surveys may not be possible.
- Language difficulties may intervene.
  Concepts vary with culture and language. It is sometimes difficult to be sure one is researching what one intends.
- Local agencies may not be sufficiently skilled.
  High-quality research comes from agencies that are regularly called on for such work. If there is not yet a tradition of research in a country it is unlikely that local agencies will be sharp.
- Research can be too expensive.
  The high cost of gathering data in many developing countries is prohibitive.
- Customs and religions intervene.
  Access is sometimes denied by custom and/or religion.

RESEARCH – ROLE AND TASKS

The role of international marketing research is identical to domestic MR. It is to provide management with the information they have specified in order that they are helped to make decisions. CATS criteria apply exactly as in domestic MR.

The key tasks of international marketing research are shown in Table 33.1

Table 33.1 Key tasks of international marketing research

Market decision	Intelligence needed
1 To go international or remain home/domestic (Policy)	Assessment of global demand and firm's share (or potential share) of the market. Local and international competition. The political and legal framework.
2 Which markets to enter? (Strategy)	Ranking of world markets – potential sales, competition, financial, political stability.
3 How to enter target market? (International tactics)	Size of market, trade barriers, customer demand, distributive channels, media and promotional availability, company experience in each overseas market.
4 How to operate within the target markets? (Tactical marketing)	For each market: buyer behaviour, competitive practice, channels, transport costs, government attitudes.

Secondary data sources

Many sources of secondary data exist, especially since small firms in the UK may find primary research methods too expensive and thus have to rely on secondary data for most of their information. Key sources of data include:

- research services provided by the British Overseas Trade Board (BOTB);
- omnibus industrial surveys with firms researching the same markets;
- entries in trade directories, e.g. Kompass, to solicit overseas enquiries;
- exhibitions and international trade fairs;
- information from Chambers of Commerce and Industry, the Chartered Institute of Marketing, seminars, private contacts, banks and commercial organisations with branches overseas.

The major sources of quantitative data are shown in Table 33.2.

Table 33.2 Some sources of quantitative data

The Department of Trade & Industry	The BOTB
Export Credit Guarantee Dept. (ECGD)	*The International Business Register*
Commerce International (LCCI)	*Directory of European Business*
Information	
Distribution for Exports (CIM)	Euroguide
Europe Year Book – world survey	The Institute of Export
Export Data (Benn Publications)	Export direction
Export Times	*Exporters Handbook*
How to Start Exporting	Jaeger's Europa Register
Shaw's *Export Guide*	Trade directories
Stores of the World	Systematic export documentation

INTERNATIONAL TRADE

The world is changing from a number of nation states, each trading independently, to a series of trading blocks within which the member states can trade freely.

The advantages of large trading blocks, or macro-international groups, are far more than protectionist. The member countries benefit from wider trade agreements giving more choice of goods and services. Countries are able to specialise, some in land-based agricultural and raw material industries, others in high technology. The development of new and advanced industries is aided by the exchange of ideas and technologies. Job opportunities and wealth creation provide more resources for each national infrastructure.

Individual companies benefit from dealing with overseas customers. This not only increases demand, it also yields economies of scale. It may extend the product life cycle and thereby increase profits. Diversification into similar products, services and/or markets will help firms to spread risk and provide against local fluctuations in demand.

The advantages coming to UK firms from the Single European Market are offsetting the manufacturing shift from Europe to Asia and the Far East which adversely affected industrial marketing during the 1980s. The EU is expected to provide firms with competitive advantages that will lead to the saving of industries and a reversal of the trade deficits of the last decade.

We raised these issues with Paul Lockwood of Meridian.

Q. *With new overseas freight organisations, do you draw up a tight legal contract, or work to a loose 'gentleman's agreement'?*

A. Most agreements are detailed, in writing, with both parties signing and exchanging agreements. It is rare for agents to get into contractual disputes. Mutual support leads to success. If one party fails to perform, then the other would quickly find a replacement, and business is too precious to jeopardise.

Q. *What part does information technology play in operating your business?*

A. Within the forwarding industry there has been an explosion of IT during the last five years. It started with simple computerised accounting systems, then specialised programs to detail with specific customer requirements. This was followed by extending computer programs into the operational environment. Software houses saw a previously untapped market for expensive bespoke programs. It was then only a small step to totally integrate the two systems into a fully computerised working environment.

Two other developments were taking place. Firstly, the local network by which agents and airlines communicate with each other for bookings was being revised and secondly, H M Customs and Excise were changing the means of interacting with the agent community.

The solution, not surprisingly, was EDI. Each agent now processes information within its own in-house system, and has the facility to communicate electronically within the agent community and with H M Customs.

The British International Freight Association (BIFA) is now promoting the global network (GEISS) as a means of agents exchanging data on a worldwide basis. Some of the larger forwarders already have global tracking networks. It will be some time before this becomes established practice, but considering the global nature of our business, BIFA are convinced that this is the way forward.

Q. *Do you undertake any marketing research prior to entering a new overseas market?*

A. The forwarding business deals with a whole spectrum of industry and the service sector. We can easily 'tap in' to a product, research it and promote our services to other companies in that particular industry.

We can also promote a specific route and handle many different products, but all to the same destination.

On the other hand, we are faced with the same problems as any other company in developing new markets – except of course, as I said before, we have the help of our overseas partners.

Q. *What advantages will accrue to your company from the freeing of world trade brought about by GATT agreements?*

A. Successful GATT talks are welcome news. Any increase in economic activity generates more international freight movement. However, the USA is imposing mandatory regulations on its own forwarders and their overseas business partners. They have to file tariffs with the Federal Maritime Commission, together with a host of other requirements. These are estimated to cost the forwarder and hence the international trader some $25 million in administration fees annually.

Q. *The European Union has eliminated internal border posts, how has this affected freight services and your own operation in Europe?*

A. The abolition of custom controls within the EU has had a detrimental effect on the forwarding industry in terms of lost revenue, as goods no longer require customs clearance. The recession in Europe makes it difficult to judge, but more companies seem willing to trade and are demanding a door-to-door service, rather than to airport only.

Forwarders can provide this service by air and road, and very soon the distribution of goods within the EU on a door-to-door basis will become established practice. This will be a replacement source of revenue for forwarders who may have lost revenue on European traffic.

The potential threat to us now lies in the very nature of Europe. International companies supplying mainland Europe may choose France and Germany for their European distribution.

GATT

The General Agreement on Tariffs and Trade (GATT) is a multinational initiative to reduce national tariff barriers and expand the volume of international trade. Over 40 years the membership has quadrupled to 115 trading nations which have, in a series of 'rounds', agreed on tariff reductions that range from 5 to 40%. In the same period the volume of international trade has increased twentyfold.

In 1972 the 'Kennedy' round reduced tariffs on 60 000 commodities valued at $40 billion. The Kennedy round aimed to reduce by 50% across the range of industrial products – but exceptions were negotiated for chemicals, steel, aluminium, pulp and paper. The Kennedy round achieved an average reduction in tariffs of 35%.

The 'Tokyo' rounds in 1973 and 1978 aimed at liberalising world trade. An attempt was made to reconcile different styles of government and types of economy. The outcome was disappointing, but some liberalisation did take place.

The 'Uruguay' round ran from 1986 to 1994. The major stumbling blocks were between the US and the EU. The Americans wanted a reduction in European farm subsidies. The French wanted to protect the 5% of their population who are small farmers. There was also concern to protect the European film and video industry.

The invisible goods sector – banking, telecommunications, and computer programming is dominated by US companies and is the fastest growing international trade sector. In 1991 this cross-border trade was valued at $850 billion. America objected to unfair competition in the General Agreement on Trade in Services (GATS) and also to the Most Favoured Nation (MFN) rule, a central policy of GATT, which stipulates that all the 115 member countries must trade with each other, very much as a nation would with an ally.

GATT principles are summarised by Chee & Harris:

- Member nations adhere to the MFN rule, trusting others without discrimination or trade restrictions.
- Members must eliminate tariffs and quotas between nations.
- Preferential treatment must be given to developing nations.

- When disagreements arise, member nations must negotiate a settlement.

The Uruguay round of GATT negotiations was concluded only after aircraft, films and videos and financial services were put aside for further negotiation. It is expected that an increase in world trade of some $150 billion will result in an extra 400 000 jobs created in the EU. This after seven years of hard bargaining is felt to be worth the long hours of negotiation.

European Union

The European Union (EU) was formed from the countries of the European Community on 1 January 1994 following the ratification by the 12 member governments of the Maastricht Treaty. With 320 million inhabitants in 12 advancing economics the EU is a powerful force in world trade.

The Maastricht Treaty amends the Treaty of Rome and establishes the European Union in place of the European Community. The intention of the EU is to form a more politically stable as well as economic community and provisions exist to cover:

- additional powers to legislate through the European Parliament.
- alterations to the balance of power between EU and EC institutions.
  Note: The acronym EC now stands for European Commission – the administrators (civil service) of the EU.
- A new agreement on economic and monetary union.

This gives member states easier access to EU markets, sees the end of internal border controls and does away with much of the documentation needed to transport goods across state lines. Free movements of labour, a single currency and the freeing of contracts, financial transactions and technical transfer will unify in the longer-term much of the earlier fragmentation of European markets.

Maastricht also binds 11 nations to the social policy in the Treaty of Rome. (The UK is allowed to opt out of the wide-ranging social measures which may damage the competitiveness of British industry, costing jobs and deterring foreign inward investment.) The Maastricht Treaty improves vocational training, research and development, and the protection of the environment. New infrastructures were agreed in projects for transport, telecommunications, energy supply, industry and consumer protection. Any distortion of competition will be excluded.

Stage II of the treaty covers the monitoring of convergence and transition of the 12 economies. Stage III, scheduled for completion by December 1996, will allow the UK to opt out of a single currency and member states will comply with norms of economic performance. Responsibility for monetary policy will be transferred to the new European Central Bank located in Frankfurt. The UK may opt to stay out, or join, the single currency – there is, in fact, considerable doubt that European economies will be sufficiently stable to allow the aim of a single currency to be achieved this century. Certainly the Exchange Rate Mechanism (ERM), which provides for a transitional coming together of currencies, has come under major pressure from speculators since 1992. Britain and Italy were forced out of the ERM, and Spain, Portugal, Ireland and Denmark came under extreme pressure.

European Economic Area

The European Economic Area (EEA) is composed of the twelve EU member states, plus the seven countries of the European Free Trade Area (EFTA). In due time the seven will join the twelve within the EU. Austria, Finland, Norway and Sweden are scheduled to join in 1995 (Table 33.3).

Table 33.3

EU States		EFTA States
Belgium	Italy	Austria
Denmark	Luxemburg	Finland
France	Netherlands	Iceland
Germany	Portugal	Liechtenstein
Greece	Spain	Norway
Ireland	United Kingdom	Sweden
		Switzerland

Note: Former Eastern Bloc countries are negotiating for membership of the EU.

Border controls between the EU and EFTA will be maintained. Each group will retain their existing trading policies. EFTA enjoys free trade in fish and fish products. The EU secured improved fishing rights in Norwegian waters in exchange. Specific agreements cover free movement of goods, services, capital and people.

Association of South East Asian countries

The Association of South East Asian countries (ASEAN) includes the thriving economies of Taiwan, Hong Kong and Singapore, known as the 'economic tigers', with 'neo-tigers' Thailand, Malaysia and Indonesia, plus Japan in a state of limbo and China emerging and producing the bulk of UK imported plastic toys.

The growth rate for ASEAN economies, excluding Japan, was 7% in 1992, compared with 0.5% globally. An emerging middle class customer, excellent service industries, hotels, stores and shopping malls have risen through low labour costs, research of customer needs and capital investment. Business air travel in Malaysia, for example, is almost as easy as taking a taxi in London, with regular and easily affordable flights.

United States Free Trade Association

USFTA is an association of Canada, the USA and Mexico, a trading block larger than Europe, mainly English speaking, it is made up of EDI/IT-oriented companies. This vast market is rich in raw materials to the north, production- and marketing-oriented in the centre and has a population surplus – and therefore cheap labour – in the south.

TRADING TERMS

Management of international trade is more complex than domestic business. Partly this is because of the long distances involved, but mainly it is because of the methods which have been forced onto firms by the existence of nation states. The key issues of concern are:

Currency

Research into comparative rates of currency will yield extra profit and reduce loss. Invoices may be paid in host country currency, exporter's currency or that of a third party. American dollars and German marks are commonly used as the currency of trade because of their widespread acceptability. The European Currency Unit (ECU) is a composite currency backed by the central banks of the EU and the member states.

Exchange rate fluctuation can affect every transaction and firms are wise to have a Treasury department to specialise in securing the best rates of exchange. Management of foreign exchange can enhance or destroy profits on trade and the very large multinationals can make more profits on the money markets than from trading in their products!

Consider this example:
An order for cloth is taken at £6000 when the exchange rate is $1.50 to the £1. The differences between contracting the payment in sterling or dollars is easy to see (Table 33.4)

Table 33.4

Invoiced in sterling

	Sales price (£)	Exchange rate ($/£)	Buyer pays ($)
1	6000	1.50	9000
2	6000	1.60	9600
3	6000	1.40	8400

Invoiced in dollars

	Sales price ($)	Exchange rate ($/£)	Seller receives (£)
4	9000	1.50	6000
5	9000	1.60	5625
6	9000	1.40	6429

It is obviously important to decide who carries the foreign exchange risk – and then for him to provide for it by buying currency 'forward' when the rate is favourable.

Credit and legality

Rarely is the exporter able to take cash with an overseas order. Some form of credit is inevitable. Precise delivery quotations and the point at which goods are legally transferred require careful planning and negotiation.

The terms of delivery may be:

Ex-works

The exporter delivers goods at the factory gate and title passes immediately to the importer, who is responsible for all shipment, insurance, etc.

Free on rail (FOR)

The exporter delivers the goods to the railhead, where the title passes to the importer.

Free alongside ship (FAS)

The exporter delivers the goods to the quay alongside the ship, when title passes to the importer. All loading charges, shipping and insurance from that point passes to the importer.

Free on board (FOB)

The term 'free on board' is so frequently used it has passed into the language. We therefore use the phrase 'FOB Liverpool', or 'FOB UK port'. The exporter is obliged to pay dock charges and place goods aboard the ship with the export documentation correctly processed to show that the goods have been either 'received on board' i.e. 'shipped', or have a 'bill of lading' signifying that the goods are 'received for shipping'.

Under an FOB agreement the exporter is responsible for export packing, delivery to the docks, inland insurance only, dock charges, wharfage, lighterage and often port charges. Title changes when the export documentation is handed over.

Cost, insurance and freight (CIF)

The exporter is responsible for goods until delivered at the overseas port, airport, or entry point. Charges include insurance to this point, at which the title to goods passes to the importer.

Franco domicile

The exporter pays all charges to the importer's place of business. This is the favoured method for overseas buyers.

To illustrate the problems of research needed into export price quotation and the legalities involved we will return to the UK cloth exporter and the £6000 of cloth priced ex-works (Table 33.5).

Table 33.5

Cloth exported	Cost (£)	Accumulated cost (£)	Quotation
Price ex-works	6000	6000	Ex-works, unpacked
Cost of packing	300	6300	Ex-works packed
Transport to docks	450	6750	Free alongside ship
Port dues/loading	60	6810	Free on board
Freight by sea	875	7685	
Insurance	75	7760	Cost, insurance, freight (CIF) port
Landing charges	90	7850	
Duty payable	1200	9050	
Transport to buyer	150	9200	
Insurance, all risks	100	9300	Franco domicile

The accumulated cost column shows the increasing costs incurred as the goods move from factory to buyer's warehouse. The risks to be covered and the stages at which invoice prices may be negotiated can clearly be seen.

Payment

Payments are transferred between importer and exporter by means of cheques, letters of credit, bills of exchange or bankers draft. Electronic transfers aid the system of payment and ease the means to transfer credit from buyer to seller.

Tariffs

Tariffs are financial barriers to trade – taxes. Non-tariff restrictions are such as import quotas, restrictive trade agreements, 'buy national' policies, requirements to comply with national standards and restrictions on technical services. Tariffs take several forms:

- ad valorem – a percentage of the value of goods calculated at the port or point of entry;
- specific tariffs – an amount levied per weight, volume, length, or other similar means of calculation;
- alternative duty – measures yielding high revenue;
- component or mixed duties;
- Countervailing or variable import duties to raise imported prices to the level of domestic prices;
- temporary import surcharges to raise prices and protect in the short-term;
- compensatory import taxes – VAT is returned within EU countries, it is not refunded from America. (Value added tax – VAT – is a sales tax.)
- Anti-dumping duties – preventative measures to protect local firms.

Countries may levy a higher tariff on finished goods than on semi-finished goods and raw materials. There may be differences in the nominal, actual and effective rate of duty charged. Research needs to discover the rates of duty, the tariffs charged and normal trade practices in each separate market.

Micro issues

There is need to also examine, in *outline*, the 'micro' aspects of the market. Why do customers need our type of product? What channels are available? What media?

Consumers

Outline research at the initial stages – very detailed research later – is required into such issues as: Where is the market located? Is it accessible? Who are the buyers? Are there segments large enough to identify and reach? What inducements will encourage sales? Will growth be sustained? How can the product benefits be communicated and at what cost? (See Chapter 34.)

Quantity

Quantitative methods of assessing potential overseas markets range from remote statistical to personal visits.

In markets where classic marketing research techniques are not available, or not reliable, it is necessary to carry through the best research possible. Predictions of likely sales and forecasts of events can often be made with the aid of commercial officers from the embassy and by taking guidance from local experts such as local bankers. It is *always* advisable to spend a considerable time in the market – to penetrate below the superficial level which is all that most tourists see.

The support of the local embassy will open doors which are otherwise closed. Contacts may lead to joint ventures, or trials of the product range, thus building up a research data bank of local needs, channels, media methods and pricing structures.

Quality

Commissioning of qualitative research follows the same pattern as for the home market and is subject to the same problems of finding a qualified researcher. Useful comparative studies and in-depth surveys are available from the EC, EFTA, Organisation for Economic Co-operation and Development (OECD), the UN, GATT, and specialised agencies.

Channel research

Channel research concentrates on the question of performance specifications, channel type and which distributor to select for market entry, initial and sustained development. Channel decisions need to be long-term and strategic. Research is important because channel procurement is slow and costly. Future patterns need to be known in order to select the channel(s) with the best potential quality and access.

Research needs to feed back data on the nature, size and geographical location of the customers, their degree of affluence and their lifestyle. Customer preferences and choice of channels need to be known. Only by a full understanding of the customers, market structures and competitive activities can a company break into an overseas market.

KEY POINT SUMMARY

- A true global marketing system is in course of development.
- Virtually instantaneous communication and ease of travel are opening up the globe to the marketer.
- Plans for market entry will be focused on research into customer preference, distribution and customer service.
- Normal research practices from the home market will be adapted and/or replaced as necessary.
- The basic principles of marketing research apply – but the need to verify accuracy, reliability and validity increases considerably.
- The key MR tasks are to help with the decisions: to go international, which markets to enter, how to enter, how to operate within a target market.
- Small firms may have to rely on secondary sources.
- GATT agreements are reducing barriers to trade.
- Trading blocks are being formed as nations come together to facilitate trade.
- The European Union is bringing European states together into a Single European Market.
- The European Economic Area (EEA) is the EU plus the European Free Trade Association (EFTA), 19 states in total.
- Four EFTA states have applied to join the EU from 1995.
- The EU is considering applications from former Eastern Bloc countries.
- ASEAN brings together the thriving South Eastern Asian countries.
- USFTA is an association between the US, Canada and Mexico.
- Trading terms are crucial to success.
- Exchange rates fluctuate.
- The currency of a contract must be specified.
- Buying 'forward' can minimise risk, but experts are needed.
- Credit must be extended in most cases – credit guarantees are often available.
- Terms of delivery may be: Ex-works, FOR, FAS, FOB, CIF, Franco Domicile.
- Payment is made by cheques, letters of credit, bills of exchange or bankers draft.
- Electronic funds transfer is now in use.
- Tariffs are financial barriers to trade.
- Micro issues are crucially important. They include such as: Why do

customers buy? Where? What inducements to offer? What medium is available – and effective?

- Research varies from distant statistical analysis to personal visits.
- A full understanding is needed if an organisation is to be internationally successful.

WORK-, SCHOOL- AND COLLEGE-BASED QUESTIONS

Without looking back into the chapter:

1 How many of these acronyms can you identify?

ASEAN	BIFA	BOTB	CIF
CIM	DTI	EC	ECGD
ECU	EDI	EEA	EFTA
ERM	EU	FAS	FOB
FOR	GATS	GATT	IT
LCCI	MFN	MR	OECD
PR	SEM	STEEPLE	USFTA

2 What do these terms mean?

Ad valorem	Commission agent
Del credere agent	Dumping
Ex-works	Franco domicile
Stocking agent	Tariff

It will help your learning if you try to do as many as possible. Then go and do something else for a while before trying to increase your score. When you have been through the lists a second time fill in the gaps by finding the answers for yourself from the book. Only then turn to the answers, which are given at the end of Chapter 35.

CHAPTER 34

Market entry and consolidation

SELECTING A MARKET ENTRY STRATEGY

There is no universal best entry method. Overseas markets do not necessarily develop gradually from export targets through to full exploitation. Each opportunity and need has to be evaluated on its merits. The key criteria are:

Market potential and attractiveness

Unless the market has sufficient potential in both the short- and long-term it probably will not justify other than export marketing. Research must determine:

- the size of the market;
- trends in purchase behaviour;
- location of customers and potential customers;
- competitors in place and potential;
- similarity to the home market, especially regarding promotional tools needed;
- customer and consumer needs;
- means of purchase and channels used and available.

A mission statement supported by international marketing objectives must be in place, and portfolio assessment may be researched using the Boston Consulting Group approach. This allows potential overseas markets to be prioritised.

Similarity

Psychological proximity of home to foreign markets is often of greater importance than geographical proximity. The 'feeling at home' factor is often rooted in a long-term relationship between the domestic and the overseas market and may encourage customers to prefer to buy products from the home market. The European language of different parts of Africa is conditioned by which nation was the colonial power. In many cases there remains an affinity with the nation of the language – and its products.

It is important never to forget that the overseas market is different from the home market. The differences may be small, but they will be present. Every action, therefore, has to be researched and carefully planned – reactions must *never* be taken for granted.

Accessibility

The logistics of transport availability, delivery time, management communications, exchange control mechanisms, tariffs, etc., will influence decisions to enter a market.

Speed of market entry

The intended speed of entry will determine decisions on whether to gradually build channels, to acquire a foreign subsidiary, to licence local production, or to use agents or distributors, etc.

Costs – direct and indirect

Savings of direct costs may be outweighed by high indirect costs, e.g. insurance, freight, unreliable labour, or irregular supplies of raw materials. Hence the opportunity cost of staying out of the overseas market has to be considered.

Note: Opportunity cost is the cost of taking one action in terms of the other actions that therefore cannot be taken because only a limited budget is available. If we choose a second sandwich instead of a second glass of milk we are giving up the opportunity of milk in favour of a sandwich. Therefore the opportunity cost of the sandwich is the glass of milk. If we decide on Zambia the opportunity cost may be the business we could have done in South Africa.

Flexibility

Markets are protected by domestic legal frameworks. Even if rapid expansion is not planned careful consideration should be given before agents or distributors are granted exclusive and/or wide-ranging territorial dealerships. There is a balance to be struck between securing a loyal agent or distributor, and retaining the initiative within the market.

Risk factors

Risks, both actual and potential, must be identified and provided for. A local joint venture may be justified because it will minimise the risk of political expropriation, or of local competitive activity. A market may be avoided because although it is potentially very lucrative it is difficult to extract the profits.

Investment payback period

Licensing and franchising may provide higher short-term payback. Joint ventures and equity investments take longer to mature.

Long-term profit objectives

Planned sales volume and profit levels may lead to the decision to establish a wholly owned subsidiary as the route into a new market. The subsidiary may act as an exclusive agent, or manufacture and operate fully in its own right.

Control and administration

Direct involvement leads to centralised administration and control by the parent company. On the other hand, less direct involvement requires greater delegation to local managers and the use of local skills. The more local the SBU becomes the more customers are likely to feel involved through purchasing and using a 'local' product.

Let us now see what Paul Lockwood's views are on the global situation.

Q. *Will the trading agreement between the EU and EFTA countries affect your business?*

A. Most UK companies trading with EU and EFTA countries do not distinguish between them. The services we provide as a forwarder transporting goods are the same for both. Because some border controls remain, the shipper still has to produce export documents for customs control and an import customs clearance still has to be made.

Q. *How will ASEAN affect the volume of UK business with Asian nations?*

A. The EU and Far East markets are very important to the UK in terms of importation of finished goods and the export of capital equipment. Many UK companies source their supplies from Taiwan, mainland China, Korea and many others. You have to understand the intense competition and political differences that surround them. Hong Kong, for example, will benefit enormously from growth in southern China and is fast changing from a manufacturing base to service industries.

   The situation is always volatile and complex. Taiwan will soon be in direct competition with Hong Kong as relations with mainland China improve and Taiwan seeks to become a main transhipment point. Relations between Malaysia and Singapore are not really settled. We are therefore conscious that these markets are in a state of constant change.

Q. *Do you receive market information and assistance from the BOTB, Chambers of Commerce and Industry, or others?*

A. Yes we do – from BOTB, Chambers of Commerce, exhibitions and trade fairs and from private companies active in various overseas markets. This information helps us to develop both product and route plans.

Q. *How do currency fluctuations affect freight charges?*

A. It is common practice for the forwarding industry to convert inbound freight charges to UK currency at the prevailing daily bank buying rate. We then add a minimum charge to this conversion, or 2.5%, whichever is the greater. We assume the risk of future fluctuations, and stand to make a profit, or loss, when freight charges are paid to our overseas partners.

The exchange rate also affects the amount of duty and VAT paid. Duty is calculated on the price of the goods, plus the cost of freight in sterling. VAT is calculated on the price of the goods, plus freight, plus the amount of duty.

Q. *How do you quote prices for delivery?*

A. We deal in all the stated terms – ex-works, FOR, FAS, FOB, CIF and franco domicile. For example, UK exporters to the Far East tend to be ex-works, buyers purchasing from the Far East tend to be FOB. Importers buying textiles tend to be franco domicile. If you research this, I am sure you would find the particular 'norm' for various industry sectors.

Q. *Paul, turning to the costing example in Chapter 33 – is the example realistic?*

A. Yes, the only item missing, which could be included in 'landing charges', is the local fee for customs clearance. We are frequently asked to quote 'pre-paid door-to-door', which is in fact franco domicile, but the charges are paid by the exporter instead of the importer.

Q. *How would you list the key criteria for entering an overseas market?*

A. 1 Market potential
    2 Availability of local logistics
    3 Risk factors
    4 Ability to present and sell the total concept.

Selecting a market

Organisations must be selective and avoid entering too many markets in too short a time.

The advantages of this concentration are:

- a shorter span of management control;
- greater accumulation of market intelligence;
- the ability to identify and enter the most appropriate markets.

Concentration also leads to a smaller staff, lower overheads, better understanding of foreign agents and distributors and closer ties with the customers. Products are sold less on price, more on delivery, reliability, brand recognition and image. The marketing mix elements are brought to bear with more force and impact.

An alternative to national concentration is segmentation of world markets according to buying expectations and buying climate. This approach groups culture, social strata and family structures. Kenwood and Sony products have successfully targeted markets where similarities in urban dwellers have been identified.

BRAND NAMES AND TRADE MARKS

A very strong brand name can be sold more easily overseas due to its universal recognition, which is based on the quality of the overall offering (see Chapter 18). It may take time to establish the brand in the local market, but the effort will be as worth while overseas as at home.

Quality recognition transfers very well. Over the past 60 years the 'Kitemark' has been a recognised symbol of quality. It has been granted to manufacturers on quality standards by the British Standards Institute (BSI) and has become trusted to indicate a quality product. The EU has now established the 'CE Mark' which is based on a similar system to that operated by the BSI. The CE Mark will become the quality passport for products passing over borders. The quality standards of performance, durability and reliability confirmed by the CE Mark will be as valid overseas, where there will often be an equivalent quality standard.

Remember that brand names and trademarks must be protected in each country. Registration is essential to secure protection in law. Up to 20% of the product development cost may need to be spent on registration.

PRICING STRATEGIES

Long-term profit rather than short-term tactical gain wins more stable overseas relationships – but price can be used effectively within the context of long-term market presence. The recognised pricing options covered in Chapter 29 apply equally in international marketing.

Discounts

Discounts must not become a routine part of the pricing plan. They should be negotiated with middlemen in return for quantity or for auxiliary services. With customer/consumers they can help ensure accelerated payment. Discounts should *always* be used to achieve specific objectives. They are a tactical weapon, not a strategic one.

International price standardisation

It is difficult, and unnecessary, to charge the same price in every market. The problems arising are currency fluctuations, differing costs of transportation, insurance and standards of product quality. Import duties will differ, price controls and non-tariff barriers will create unique pricing problems in each market. In any case, pricing should be based on customer expectation – in France, for example, toiletries and flowers have a higher benchmark than in Britain. On the other hand ground coffees and cheeses are far cheaper.

Transfer pricing

When goods are shipped from country to country a decision must be made regarding the price to be charged. Whatever prices are charged to the end customers there is the question of how much to charge the distributors.

Where agents or distributors are trading in their own right normal negotiation determines a price that allows a fair profit. Where they are wholly owned, however, there is the opportunity to control the amount of profit they earn. Thus profits can be kept out of a country by simply controlling the prices shown on the invoices that are paid by the trading company.

In some cases trading companies are set up in a tax haven such as the Bahamas and these buy and sell from and to branches of multinational companies. In that way the profits earned by both the manufacturing and trading company can be minimised, and the holding company can extract the profits where they attract little if any tax.

Governments seek to see that transfer prices are fair in order to levy taxes on normal rather than artificial profit levels. They are also anxious to collect VAT on normal rather than on artificially low prices. Governments also find difficulty with barter deals where goods are exchanged but little or no money changes hands. Buy-back deals, clearing arrangements for exchange products and switch deals where raw materials are exchanged for finished goods, also present difficult tax and pricing problems.

Pricing strategy will depend on the degree of discretion the firm has over the final price. The product position on the life cycle curve will affect the prices charged. Flexibility to meet pricing problems is needed day to day and price objectives and benchmarks need to be changeable rather than set and inflexible.

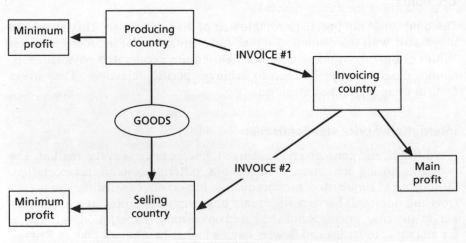

Fig. 34.1 Transfer pricing

CHANNEL CRITERIA

Channel decisions are costly and long-term. A distribution network has three main components:

- the HQ organisation developed by the producer to implement international marketing operations;
- the logistical channels between nations, i.e. the system of sending products overseas;
- the internal channels, i.e. the means by which products reach the consumer.

Market entry and consolidation will depend very much on the distributor, the nature and size of the geographical area, the needs of the consumer, and the level of internal economic development. Product characteristics are important: value, volume, bulk, technological advantage, complexity and perishability all have their impact.

Marketing through channels will be in the hands of middlemen and they differ in experience, honesty and application. Government policy impacts on distribution. Market coverage may be intensive or extensive. The former gives blanket coverage in selected areas, usually urban, the latter gives wide coverage over all the market.

Promotional strategies

Export promotion is the transmission of messages to the target customer to inform and to develop positive attitudes towards the product or service. PR, advertising, sales promotion and personal selling combine to sell products and services in just the same way – in principle – as they do in the home market. There are differences of degree, of course, and these must be taken into account with the aid of local management.

Important adjustments to the message need to be made because of the dynamics of cultural, religious and ethnic differences. Key factors to be considered are as follows:

- Boundaries, zones and specific segments within nations.
  - Catalonia is within Spain but is a separate market. Singapore differs from Malaysia even though they are side by side.
- Cultural factors, language, groups and subgroups.
  - Every country has several versions of its mother tongue. The English spoken in the north east varies in dialect considerably from the midlands and the south west. Local usage does not transfer, and has to be understood.
- Disposable income, discretionary spending power, income distribution.
  - What people choose to regard as disposable income varies by subculture, and what they choose to spend it upon also varies considerably. The Scandinavian countries tend to spend far more on their homes than the southern Europeans, who allow the exterior of their properties to become quite shabby by northern Europe standards.

- Industrialisation, market infrastructure, development of advertising agencies within these structures.
  - Some forms of marketing are more possible in certain societies than others. Without a well-developed infrastructure it is unlikely that advertising agents will have been able to develop to anything like the levels achieved in industrialised nations. Even if they have, their potential actions will be affected by the availability of effective media, and by the sophistication of those in the target segments.
- Political, economic, legal systems and stability factors.
  - Simply because there have been free elections supervised by the United Nations it does not follow that full Western-style democracy has been established.
- Social class structures.
  - Class structures will often link to tribal structures even in well-developed societies. What is actually happening must be evaluated rather than taking matters at face or reported value.
- Market differentiation and development.
  - Market differentiation follows the availability of disposable income and the moving away from commodity-based markets. It may be necessary to wait for a market to develop rather than attempt entry before there is sufficient perceived need.
- Buyer behaviour and attitudes; motivation to purchase.
  - Purchase motivation is always critical. Buyer taste is conditioned by national factors and value judgements can only be applied within a society and from the viewpoint of a society.

Media

The main media problems are legal – restrictions on the freedom of the press need to be checked and national laws complied with. Social conventions may affect the message and standardised advertisements may offend or fail in translation. A local translator is always necessary to be sure that language is used correctly. Nothing can be taken for granted: e.g. Spanish in South America and French in Canada are quite different from the oral and written languages in Spain and in France.

The availability of media may be restricted and local laws and/or taboos may prevent some products from being advertised. In African countries the radio may be the only effective media available. Local taxation may be high on advertising, with increased levies on imported advertising material. Research is best delegated to a local agency, if one exists.

CONSOLIDATING MARKET ENTRY DECISIONS

Entry criteria having been researched and strategies selected, the next stage is to consolidate market entry decisions. Using data returned from agents, distributors, overseas subsidiaries, etc., the next phase is to develop strategies of assembly overseas, contract marketing, licensing, franchising, joint venture, or further alliances with local companies. A portfolio of data for each strategic alternative will focus on success and limit those methods that do not work in any specific overseas location. A flexible policy for each overseas market should be developed.

Centralisation or decentralisation?

Corporate objectives, philosophy of business operation and the efficiency of each unit in individual countries will impact upon the decision.

Centralisation may prove most effective where products are single, homogeneous and standardised. If international agencies can be used, distributive channels shared and HQ has an intelligence system that is well tuned to customers, suppliers and competitors, then centralisation may be the best practical option.

Centralisation may not work if political and/or legal dictates set a minimum stakeholding of at least 51% by nationals of the market, or where products are very different due to local customs and demand. Here standardised products may not yield economies of scale and financial planning may favour local rather than corporate taxation. Decentralisation may work best where fragmentation of markets, product development and corporate policy encourages local initiatives.

Agents

The use of overseas agents may well enable speedy entry into specific segments of the overseas market. Longer-term the agent may not provide research data, customer care and after-sales service to the level the parent company requires. As competition grows the agent may neglect present products – and supervision from a distance is difficult. More effective means of selling may then be devised by using existing contacts and developing joint ventures, contract manufacturing, or franchises with larger local organisations (see Chapter 33).

Levels of control

Chee and Harris suggest the levels of control to be considered when analysing market entry.

Indirect exporting is organised by means of export houses, trading companies, export management companies (EMCs) and piggy-backing along with an existing trader.

Direct exporting is through agents, distributors and wholly owned subsidiaries.

Franchising can be a very effective means of securing market entry (see Chapter 27).

Joint ventures are projects in which two or more parties invest. The investment must be a long-term commitment if it is to be effective in international

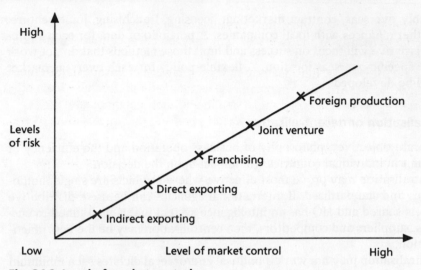

Fig. 34.2 Level of market control
Source: Chee H and Harris R (1993), *Marketing: A Global Perspective*, Pitman Publishing

marketing. The two parties must both have something signifi-cant to contribute, and something significant to gain. Without this double edged need there is the danger that one party will be less committed, and work correspondingly less hard. The result will be disastrous for the committed partner.

Foreign production is, of course, a full commitment to the market – a solid investment with the expectation of long-term presence, and long-term profitability.

Subsidiaries

The home company can set up a branch within the host country. This may be staffed by home or host personnel. The subsidiary may exist to import, or may be developed to assemble under licence, or to provide selling and distribution services. The advantage are a physical presence in the market, closer contacts and close control of stock levels, spares, or servicing facilities. The local staff are in closer contact with customer need and can provide effective customer care.

Note that it is possible to export from the overseas production unit just as though one were exporting from the home market. The benefits can be considerable. They include:

- *Access to markets*. The Japanese are external to the EU. Their solution has been to invest in production plant within the EU itself, and so gain market presence as a local company. Nissan, for example, are making their cars in Britain.

- *Cost savings*. Lengthy logistical channels can be avoided. Production costs in the overseas unit may be cheaper than in the home market.
- *Market awareness*. Europeans are far more aware of European differences than of Asian, African, American or Australian. Similarly those from other market areas have a broad understanding of their neighbours.
- *Earnings and profits*. Can be arranged to best suit the organisation, overall.

International marketing has to be a staged process. It is one with a considerable learning curve effect and it is unwise to rush decisions because they have very long-term consequences. The first crucial decision is at policy level, where top management will take long-term considerations into account, probably looking a minimum of 20 years forward. If policy is a 'Go', then entry and consolidation strategy can be determined. If strategic options are favourable then – and only then – can tactical issues be examined in detail.

When all the pieces are in place, probably down to an outline tactical plan, the commitment decision will be made. Strategy may well call for a staged entry, perhaps through indirect exporting to joint venture and finally to a subsidiary producing in the market. This pattern works well: the Japanese have shown it to be very effective.

KEY POINT SUMMARY

- There is no universal 'best' method to enter a foreign market.
- Research must help management determine the attractiveness of the market.
- A mission statement will be needed.
- Overseas market opportunities can be prioritised using the BCG approach.
- Psychological proximity is often more significant than geographic.
- Other important considerations include: speed of entry, costings, flexibility, risk, payback, long-term profit objectives, control.
- Avoid entering too many markets in too short a time.
- Brand names take time to establish in a new market.
- Quality recognition transfers well.
- The new CE Mark will become a quality passport.
- Price for long-term profit.
- Use discounts to aid negotiation.
- Do not attempt to price standardise across markets.
- Transfer pricing allows profits to be taken where it is is most suitable – providing national governments are satisfied that 'fair' profits are being declared in the home and overseas countries.
- Channel decisions are costly, and long-term.
- A distribution network has three main components: head office organisation, logistics between nations, the internal channels.
- Middlemen differ in experience, honesty and application.

- The promotional mix operates as at home – but with variations to suit the market characteristics.
- Identify:
  — boundaries, zones and segments within nations;
  — cultural, language, groups and subgroup factors;
  — income levels;
  — market infrastructures;
  — political, legal, economic and stability factors;
  — social class structures;
  — market differentiation and development;
  — buyer behaviour;
  — purchase motivation.
- Media may be subject to laws regarding what they may carry.
- Value judgements can only be applied within the society, and from the viewpoint of that society.
- Market entry must be consolidated.
- Centralisation is effective when products are: single, homogeneous and standardised.
- Political and/or legal dictates may require a 51% holding by nationals of the market.
- Agents may enable speedy entry – but are not a long-term option if policy is to establish a subsidiary.
- Foreign production is full commitment to the market.
- Exporting is possible from the overseas market.
- International marketing has to be a staged process.
- The first crucial decision is at policy level.
- Entry and consolidation strategy follows policy.
- Tactical planning follows strategy.
- A commitment decision will be made only when outline strategic and tactical planning show a high probability of success.

WORK-, SCHOOL- AND COLLEGE-BASED SELF-ASSESSMENT QUESTIONS

Opportunity cost

1 Management
   (a) Select a product with which you are familiar. This may come from the worlds of work, school or college.
   (b) Identify strategic options that are available to management.
   (c) Use opportunity costing to identify the option that is most appropriate. Remember that resources are always limited. The need is to select the option(s) that allow the best possible resource use.

2 Personal
   (a) From your social life of your own career opportunities select a 'purchase' which is open to you, i.e. something you can buy with cash – or 'buy' with commitment, work, dedication.
   (b) Identify the options that are open to you.

(c) Use opportunity costing to identify the option that is most appropriate. Remember that your emotional resources are also limited. If you are to commit to one activity it will be at the expense of another – unless you do both badly! Only you can put a value on your subjective feelings. Use non-scaler techniques as in Chapter 10.

Hints:

- For step (b) use What-if? thinking and mind-map techniques.
- For step (c) take each option in turn and decide the advantages and disadvantages of proceeding. Good questions are: 'If I do that, what will happen?' and 'If I do this within option A, what will be the effects on option B?
- Finally sum up the advantages and drawbacks – taking the interrelationships into account. The result should be the options, ranked in order of opportunity cost.

CHAPTER 35

Global developments

Sven Olaffsen was pleased to be back. Even with two crews the B997s were hard work. Still, only 14 hours ago he had been in Sydney, Australia, and now he was driving out of the SAS aircrew parking at Stockholm airport at the beginning of a three-day break.

There had been a lovely message from his family on the car video-ansafone and he was glad that he had found the time to send a quick colour fax while over the South Atlantic. No doubt his wife would have the kids in bed by now, but he would ring her when he had settled in to confirm his time of arrival at their summer cabin tomorrow.

In the meantime he ran through the list of instructions he had sent to his home computer from the crew room as he was changing. He had initiated the central heating, drawn the curtains, overriden the time switch on the lights, told the oven to warm itself up and chosen the CD tracks he wanted to listen to. Was there anything else?

Darn it! He had expected to be back in time for Star Trek, the fifth generation. No problem – but he was glad he had remembered. His Volvo responded immediately to his voice command for second gear and he pulled over to the hard shoulder. It took only a moment with his wrist communicator to program the satellite receiver and set the digital micro-video. He had a permanent override on the advertisements – but had to remember to switch it out if there was an advertisement he really wanted to see. Perhaps the Gold Blend grandchildren were up to something new? He remembered with nostalgia his parents' stories of how the original couple had met back in the late 1980s.

As Sven pulled into his road the house IFF system routinely interrogated the car and, receiving the correct response, switched on the security lights, opened the drive gates and, when he was safely inside the property, closed the gates and rolled up the garage doors. The car's cruise control nudged her gently into place and the computer connected itself to carry out the daily maintenance checks.

The garage door closed and, the activation plate came alight beside the house door. Sven's hand print activated the lock and the door swung open. His music was playing, the house was warm and snug. He was home again.

All of the above, and more, are now technically feasible. The whole package hasn't been put together yet – but it will be, especially as computer chips get even faster and smaller.

INFORMATION TECHNOLOGY

Information technology gives the international company advantages and benefits throughout its entire operation. It is the key to global development. IT affects the production process, enhances channel information, aids what if? and scenario planning, helps establish price structures, improves communication and customer service. Proper use of IT results in all this and overall cost savings as well!

REACTIVE OR PROACTIVE?

The successful GATT Uruguay protocol of 1986–94 eased world trade but potentially will make developed nations more wealthy whilst developing countries may become poorer because subsidies will no longer protect home products. The developing countries may be consigned to a role as supplier of raw materials and cheap labour. If so they are then likely to become reactive to new products and/or technologies.

Reactive

Many reactive customers are quite happy to follow trends and will come along as late adopters and laggards within the Rogers model. Companies will also adopt a reactive policy and, at low cost, will copy or modify existing products and services. The global battle of the giant corporations, multinationals and international leaders will force the smaller organisations to settle for a smaller share of an increasing global market.

Make global – market locally

The emergence of the multinational company (MC) is leading global expansion. Ford and IBM sell globally, but manufacture locally. This, plus personalised marketing (Ford of Britain), provides the customer with feelings of support for a local, regional or national company. Passive receivers of communication filter out international messages. The traditionalists can live quite contentedly and in lifestyles of quality without needing every new product from advancing technology. They are also probably unaware or unconcerned that the product(s) they buy are imported.

Proactive targets

Hibbert maintains that 'Different forms of communication must be used to develop relationships with the major 'publics' involved with the company's operations.' He then lists publics to include customers, suppliers, government, employees, the local community, bankers and creditors, media organisations and shareholders. Of these the key reactive targets must be customers.

To create pull from overseas customers may be more difficult than from home buyers. Cultural values, language and customs may render the innovator and early adopter quite reluctant to buy what may be regarded as 'foreign imports'. This is partly why global companies are anxious to establish a local presence in markets.

The targeting and positioning of niche market offerings overseas is therefore dependent on the contacts with and the reactions of the local publics. If they can be won over as friendly supporters, and loyalty is encouraged by strong promotion, then progress into an overseas market can be achieved. Innovator encouragement should be a key strategy of the international company.

Globalisation has been assisted by improved communications via satellite, cable, terrestrial communications, IT and telecommunications. Video and satellites enable conferences to be held across continents, without participants having to travel. They provide access which is relevant, immediate and proactive. The global brand is truly with us, and can only become stronger as modern communications penetrate deeper into more markets.

The process of marketing brands strongly to innovative customers must be part of corporate policy if an organisation is to compete. More understanding of how customers make decisions at the point of sale; the influence of brand messages; the response to quality, to price and to benefits; all are urgently needed in order for organisations to survive. Global branded giants are taking share from smaller competitors. Only companies seeking to identify the key customers, and who can then communicate with and influence them to create world demand can hope to survive on the international scene.

Microsoft is the world's largest software house. It was created by Bill Gates who is its CEO. His *personal* fortune is estimated at a minimum of $4 billion.

Even such a huge and successful organisation is vulnerable today – Gates was quoted in June 1994: 'In this business, by the time you realise you're in trouble, it's too late to save yourself. Unless you're running all the time, you're gone.'

The reactive innovators within each overseas market have shifted from an acceptance of simple availability to a demand for quality. To meet this change in demand a root and branch alteration to marketing structures is now taking place. Keith Holloway, Commercial Director of Grand Metropolitan, said in 1994 that 'Everyone is trying to create a global structure to migrate ideas around the world as quickly as possible.' The technology is available to do this. The day of the proactive innovator and early adopter is here now. The global giants will use new structures and their powerful resources to take each other over, to merge or make alliances and to acquire the facilities for international expansion.

TRENDS TOWARDS SOPHISTICATED, DEMANDING, MOBILE TARGETS

The GATT protocol of 1994 supports global expansion on the grounds of wealth creation, more employment and the advance of international co-operation. Meanwhile the world markets fragment and it becomes more difficult to satisfy individual customer demand.

As global brands become more sophisticated and the public becomes more demanding and mobile there is constant need for marketing to:

- restructure and/or clarify objectives;
- identify and/or redefine target markets;
- reinforce or reposition product offerings;
- identify and capitalise on technological advances;
- operate through sound and supported marketing strategies with the effective tactical deployment of the four Ps.

In many markets it is no longer possible to remain a large frog in a small pond – to remain simply a national player. The frontiers are opening, and the global perspective is sweeping through national markets. The power of the global brand will pressure any organisation that tries to protect its home base without taking a proactive stance on the world stage. By the first decade of the next century it is forecast that all volume markets will be dominated by global operators. Only limited and specialised markets will be left for the small organisation, markets that are not economic for a global organisation.

THE GLOBAL VILLAGE

Marshall McLuhan, writing in the 1950s and 60s, formulated the concept of the 'global village'. At the time his ideas were received with limited understanding and little acceptance. His insights are now being seen to have been remarkably accurate and much of what he forecast is now reality.

McLuhan's key theories were:

- *The medium is the message.* The medium itself, the whole manner in which it carries and transmits information, is more important than any single message it can contain. We are affected by the totality of what we experience, on the conscious and subconscious levels, not simply by the apparent content of the message.
- *Electronic media will pull people into tribal unity.* The close-knit tribal communities were broken up by the invention of type, and of printing. The oral culture in which history was passed by word of mouth was no longer necessary once history could be written down.

  The 'global village' concept is that all individuals will be (now actually are) able to interact with other individuals within the same 'village'. McLuhan's village is the whole world!
- *There are 'hot' and 'cool' media.* Hot media provide plenty of data – the

radio and cinema are typical. Cool media provide little data by comparison. There is need for the receiver to add to the message. The telephone and television are typical.

For example, on the telephone we are in personal and real-time interactive contact. We deduce what underlies what we hear and test our assumptions by the way in which we respond. We are involved.

McLuhan's thinking can be translated into guides for today's marketers:

- Be alive to the environment. Question assumptions constantly – probe for areas of growth.
- Try to predict environment.
- Try to change environment.
- Use each medium for what it can do best.
- Let the audience participate.
- Make sure a picture tells the real story – be sure that the depth messages are consistent. For example, a man getting out of a BMW should have clean shoes.

Time – not distance

People are divided now by time and not by distance. The jet aircraft has opened up the world so that Concorde crosses the Atlantic in 3.5 hours (faster than the Sun). It is literally possible to pop over to New York for lunch. The benefits have reached ordinary people as well. Holidays are regularly offered in the Spanish islands or Greece for less than £100 for a week from London – and that includes the return flight, a hotel and breakfast each day!

Hong Kong to Paris is 12 hours, London to Australia is only 23. People, and goods, can move quickly:

- Flowers are flown from South America to be fresh each day in London.
- Seafood is flown from Brittany fresh into New York and Los Angeles each day.
- Vegetables are picked at dawn, cleaned and packed, and are on UK supermarket shelves by the time the store opens.
- Nothing need now be out of season – it always can be available, at a price.

A replacement for Concorde is under way. A European consortium is negotiating an agreement for a joint venture. At one time it was thought that the American Boeing company would join – but they have decided to work on their own supersonic aircraft.

Costs of air freight, coupled with a decline in the weight of products through miniaturisation and plastics, is opening up more opportunities for the fast supply of goods – thereby reducing the logistical problems of ships and shipping, and reducing the amount of stock (capital) tied up for weeks on ship.

Let us have a last word with Paul Lockwood and ask him for his views of globalisation.

Q. *How has global communication affected your firm?*

A. We have always operated as global player with worldwide clients and agents.

Q. *How important is pricing – do you price above, or below competitors such as DHL, TNT and UPS?*

A. Competitors DHL, TNT, and UPS are worldwide operators offering integrated services, using their own transport. The product they have in common is an express parcels service, not the heavier consignments we handle. They do not have total control. We can offer a quality service and sell at a higher price. Our service is tailored to the client's needs, which they are not always able to do – smaller means more flexible. The saying 'the moment they have it, it's lost!', does not apply to us, and is partly due to their high volumes moved, but waiting time is a client problem.

   We recently won a contract for UK distribution of small parcels from TNT and UPS, by offering the same service at a lower price.

Q. *Do you operate closely with retail organisations and manufacturers exporting overseas, and do you become involved in selecting channels of distribution abroad?*

A. We do assist companies exporting overseas in export documentation, costings and advice on the most efficient routes and means of transport. Our support stops when the goods reach their destination, and the local agent takes over the handling. As an example, we hit 100 different companies in Hong Kong by means of a single consignment which is then distributed locally by our agent.

Q. *As your business expands, will you retain centralised or decentralised control and will you employ more overseas nationals?*

A. In the UK we operate centralised control systems, but use the knowledge and expertise of our operations on a localised basis, so if we opened an office in Manchester, we would employ local staff, but control would remain in the Heathrow London office.

Q. *Finally, Paul, we thank you for your frank exchanges and the time you have given to answer these questions, but do you think global communication and IT have helped you to become reactive, or proactive in your markets?*

A. We would be unable to operate without our IT system. We are reacting to client needs and are proactive in creating new routes and services. Joint ventures may be a way forward, and for example, we may open a New York office with our partner in Los Angeles. Communication is so easy through IT we can operate from London, or tailor products and services near to the core markets. Our selection in the end comes down to cost considerations!

Containerisation

Containerisation moves goods through docks quicker. From factory to lorry – rail – dock – ship – dock – rail – lorry – warehouse. Containers are sealed by Customs and therefore are faster moving, and offer the economies of standardisation. It is in the interests of individuals across the world to agree common standards. This self-interest leads to regular contacts, which in turn, lead to greater understanding and acceptance of cultural differences.

COMMUNICATION TECHNOLOGY

Information can flow quicker than products thanks to electronics: telex, then fax, now modems and satellites. The move from copper wire to fibre optic cables is fundamental to the IT explosion of the next decade and beyond. Optical signals are virtually instant and extremely clean.

An optical fibre is as thin as a human hair.

It can be as long as the British Isles.

It is fed by a laser which is as small as a grain of salt, and as bright as the sun.

A single optical fibre has the potential to carry all the calls made in the USA at the peak moment of Mothers' Day.

Fibre optics are opening a new vista of communications possibilities.

Today's communication technology is revolutionising the way that business is conducted. Request, tender, agreement and contract can all be processed in a single working day. Salespeople can work out quotes on portable computers and/or link to Head Office through a telephone from anywhere in the world – even from an increasing number of trains, car ferries and aircraft. In-car faxes have long been available, and portable computers have a bewildering range of attachments so that they can be compatible with the world's range of telecommunication sockets and electricity supplies (90–240 volts).

The money market has opened up to ordinary people thanks to instant updates through Teletext on a domestic television. Funds can be transferred instantly through an automated teller machine, or by automated telephone banking. Credit checks from portable credit card machines are made, via satellite, to the master computer in seconds. (AMEX verify all transactions in Arizona.)

Visa maintain a security monitor to compare the proposed purchase with the established travel and buying pattern of the card holder as well as with his credit limit. Thus if a purchase is outside normal expectation it can be queried. All whilst one is finishing the after dinner coffee in the restaurant. Portable telephones are becoming routine equipment. They are not yet standardised across Europe, let alone the world, but industry watchers forecast that within 10 years we shall have our personal communicators and hard wired phones will be a thing of the past, even in offices.

Broadcast communication is now global. Satellite communication accesses vertically and is bringing video and radio to remote areas. CNN were laughed at when they started a decade ago. Now they have the widest coverage of all TV news stations and are the most respected television news programme in the world. They have also added Teletext and a radio service.

Satellites ignore national and cultural boundaries:

• Nation states cannot long-term block reception – no more jamming of unwanted news coverage. (But Iran has made ownership of a satellite dish a serious religious offence.)

- Marketing communicators must cope with cultural differences when promoting a brand:
  — Will the global positioning statement need amendment to take into account national differences?
  — How will the form and content of the promotional plan be changed by the size and wide background of the potential audiences?
  — What changes will there need to be in packaging and to labelling in particular? For example, Esso give vouchers for petrol sales – they used to be nation specific. Now Esso UK honours vouchers issued by Esso across the EU. As more cross-border traffic develops how will country schemes be funded internationally? Will large firms be forced into international promotion with a central clearing house and, perhaps, an international budget?

TV and video products automatically accept three or more broadcast standards. National interests demanded different standards but the electronics have caught up because consumers wanted to access the signals from different broadcasters.

'Narrowcasting' down a cable is opening up the practical segmentation by individual. Cable TV is reckoned to be so powerful a medium that giant telecommunications and entertainment corporations are scrambling to secure the rights to cable vast areas of developed countries.

Narrowcasting services will carry not simply TV. They carry radio, of course, and the newer installations offer telephone and home security. Video-on-demand is planned – and British Telecom is well advanced in the development of its own competing service.

A LAW OF INNOVATION
A law of innovation says that there is always someone out there who doesn't know it is impossible. If you can conceive it today, then you can probably do it tomorrow – or the day after.

Technology in use

An example – Direct Line Insurance

Direct Line Insurance was formed by the Royal Bank of Scotland in the early 1980s to move into the insurance market.

Traditionally underwriters provided the product (the policy), and brokers sold it to the customer, who is also often the consumer. Brokers work on a 15% commission, and carry no risk. Underwriters had no sales operation.

Some of the bigger underwriters set up their own sales departments – but Direct Line's innovation was to realise than even in the insurance market the traditional 'push' methods of distribution could now be replaced with a 'pull' strategy.

Direct Line realised that the motor insurance market was little different in principle to any other retail operation.

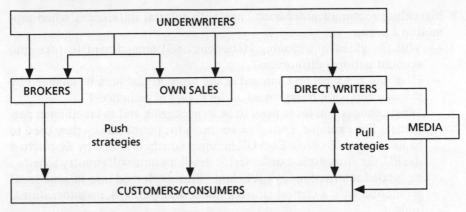

Fig. 35.1 Channels of distribution – motor insurance

Expert system

An expert system is a database which reacts in real time.

The British Airways booking system is expert because all loading information on all aircraft is tracked. As one seat is booked or cargo sold the aircraft status changes instantly. Thus a customer can be offered a seat, check his or her diary, and in that moment find that the seat has been sold elsewhere in the world.

The benefits are obvious, management has an accurate source of reliable information that is always current, and customers can be immediately satisfied. The high cost of design, installation and maintenance is more than offset by the benefits it brings to the organisation.

Direct Line invested in an expert system database and carefully targeted a market segment – individuals aged 35–50 driving a limited number of car models. They used the freephone 0800 service as their only sales contact, invested heavily in direct response promotion and actively sponsored popular but minority sports, particularly tennis.

Traditional insurers felt that products sold down the telephone could not be differentiated – some felt that insurance was a commodity market. Traditionalists felt the buying experience needed to be 'memorable', and that closeness and personal service were vital factors.

The traditional view was wrong. People responded extremely well to the Direct Line approach, and obviously were prepared to deal by telephone – to be their own brokers, as it were.

As Direct Line's experience grew, and as their database expanded, they added to their target market. Moving one step at a time they extended the range of models, and the ages of the drivers, until they offered a wide range of cover. They do not – and will not – cover everybody. They carefully assess the risks they are prepared to underwrite, and the premium to be charged.

Traditional brokers use a standard set of questions to obtain quotes from underwriters. Thus all have to quote from the same generalised information. Direct Line control their own system and so can personalise and alter the questions asked of a potential customer and then provide an instant quote.

With on-line credit card payment they can provide immediate cover – with the formal proposal to follow in the post. Because they can set their own questions and secure management information in real time they are able to *risk manage*, where the traditional underwriters are risk assessing from historical data.

Experience has shown that the more detailed the information the more accurate the quotation. Different risk factors are associated with the same car model, depending on issues such as colour, the number of doors and the fitting of a sunroof – not factors which would have been thought significant a couple of decades ago.

Service is important in the motor insurance market. Direct Line, again through their expert system, have built a reputation for the speed with which they process claims. It is commonplace for the Direct Line notification of a claim to arrive at a brokers in the same post as the initial contact from their client.

Not everybody wants to use a direct writer, of course. But Direct Line, and its competitors, have revolutionised the motor insurance market (Table 35.1)

Table 35.1 The motor insurance market (percentage shares)

	mid 70s	mid 80s	1992	2000 (est.)
Brokers	70	60	45	20
Insurers	30	40	40	45
Direct writers	—	—	15	35

Direct Line's approach minimises the costs of operation because they can site their telesales anywhere they choose – no need for a high street presence. They open longer hours – allowing sales to be made in the evenings and at weekends when their customers are free to get to the telephone. Their system allows them to assess the probability of fraud and so to determine which claims to investigate and which to accept. Their overall cost savings are passed on to the customer in reduced premiums and added benefits. In 1994, for example, they became the first insurer to offer a 70% no-claims discount to older drivers.

The end result is that as their experience grows they have a cost advantage over competition, and it is day by day becoming more difficult to enter their market. It is not likely that the traditional broker will be able to support the high costs and slow response of the traditional system and it may be that the British market will follow the American where the top ten motor insurers are direct writers and control 55% of the market.

Direct Line, incidentally, are extending their services . . . into others forms of insurance and, notably, into credit cards – brand extension into related markets where their unrivalled database will be of the utmost assistance.

KEY USES FOR NEW TECHNOLOGY

This section will be out of date before the book has passed through it's proofing stages! Breakthroughs are everyday occurrences – whilst this paragraph was being written Casio announced their wristwatch and TV/Video remote control unit!

In the management of marketing these are typical of today's key issues:

- The PC and the database are becoming essential parts of a marketer's personal equipment.
- Electronic communications mean that paper-free memos, reports, copy, visuals, can be passed between individuals in different continents, annotated, adapted, agreed and approved for action.
- What-if? forecasting can use highly complex models, but be accessed easily and routinely.
- Video-conferencing – and video phones – can open face-to-face contact.
- Fax and answer machines mean that nobody need be inaccessible.
- We are forecast to have personal phones, and personal phone numbers, and not be tied to wires.
- Database marketing is becoming available to even small organisations.
- Internal data can automatically be interrogated for management information. P.A. Consulting estimate that around half of FMCG companies' lines make about 150% of the profits with 50% then being thrown away in loss-making lines. A database can tell which is which.
- Nielsen has a goal of real-time reporting – which already exists within the major retailer's internal and confidential systems.
- Cable and satellite systems are set to revolutionise targeting, with individuals in households – and neighbours of individuals in households – being 'narrowbanded'.
- Multimedia through the computer, as well as the TV, will affect every link in the marketing chain: salespeople will run video demonstrations; video booths will open direct visual access to staff in organisations; product development groups will interact with research focus groups; digital assistance will prompt marketing research interviewers, who will record data electronically; market analysis software will allow data to be cut, compared, adapted, accessed in ways that are currently impossible.
- Touch screen video will extend into the home to allow fully interactive contact with individuals.
- Fibre optic, laser and ever faster chip technology are the current foundtions of the new communications 'superhighway' that is about to open for traffic.
- IBM have forecast a fall, by the year 2000, of 20% in software, 60% in hardware and a 99% fall in the cost of processing.
- Apple introduced the first personal computer using RISC technology in March, 1994. Previously RISC microprocessors had been used for high-performance systems such as workstations and servers. RISC on the desk top means that PC speed will increase tenfold on the maximum previously possible.

- Hunting for information currently takes time, but within a decade we will be able to have intelligent software 'agents' hunting on our behalf through global communication networks. Foundations of the communications 'superhighway' are already in place. It now only awaits the 'levelling and surfacing' teams.

These changes are happening gradually, and it is easy to miss the developments and to wake up one morning and suddenly discover that something new has happened. The analogy is with a parent and child. The child grows slowly, but the parent doesn't realise until – suddenly – the child can reach something that was previously safe from sticky hands. Grandparents notice, because they see the child at intervals. Many a parent has said 'If only I had taken photos, recorded the changes . . .' As a student of marketing you need to 'take photos and record the changes' so that you are at least with, if not ahead of, the game and can benefit from the opportunities.

Technology in telecommunications

As a second example of the power of technology we have only to look at modern telecommunication. We take it for granted that fast answering is a must for business. Customers will not hold on to a ringing phone.

Automatic call distribution (ACD)

The technology answers the phone, speaks to the caller, sets up a hold (usually with music), keeps in touch with the waiting caller, routes the longest waiting caller to the first available person. Many callers have on-hook dialling, and the 0800 and 0500 numbers are free so the only cost to the caller is in terms of time and patience.

ACD can offer more than simple call waiting. It can:

- tell callers how long the queue is, and the anticipated delay time;
- offer short cuts to different sections via the keypad: 'Press 1 for Service, 2 for Sales';
- allow regular callers to bypass the switchboard and dial straight into the internal system, using their access number;
- speech recognition to allow the system to 'talk' to a caller on routine matters – with supporting literature, confirmation or whatever is needed despatched later.
- ACD management provides real-time, comprehensive, management information which enable staffing levels and opening times to be optimised. Whatever goes through the computer can be extracted, analysed, processed and presented as management information. *Note*: One of the biggest problems for today's, let alone tomorrows's manager is deciding what information is needed – really needed, and what can be done without!

Two examples:

- British Gas have a dedicated ACD line, with no human intervention, that takes gas meter readings from those who were out when the meter reader called (by touch pad, or voice).

- First Direct are the first British Bank to offer 365 days a year banking exclusively over the telephone – using human operators. (Payments in are by post or through a branch of the Midland Bank.)

- *Calling line identification (CLI)*. Available, but not introduced because it will require political approval. With CLI it will be (is) possible to know who is calling before you answer, and to bar calls from certain numbers, e.g. the bank at the end of a month!

- *Direct dial identification* (DDI). New digital exchange lines can handle more than one number per line. If 2000 numbers are routed through 10 lines they will be controlled by digital communication.

- *DDI campaign tracing*. DDI numbers can be used to key advertisements with the computer and are then able to analyse the response without the need to ask the caller where they saw the advertisement.

  Thus a split-run advertisement could carry different DDI numbers. The calls would come in on the same line, but each would be automatically tracked back to the originating advertisement by the computer.

- *DDI product specification*. A call received via a DDI number can be shown on the salesperson's screen so that a direct response can be made: 'Good afternoon, you must be calling about . . .'.

- *Computer integrated voice response (CIVR)*. The British Gas ACD line uses a CIVR system that can ask for meter readings. The system can be used for many other purposes – such as securing a frequent flyer's account number whilst he waits for connection, and then bringing all his details up on the teleperson's screen as soon as he is available. Information can be added in real time and will follow the call from screen to screen if the call is routed onwards within the organisation.

- *Intelligent call routing (ICR)*. An ICR system can make an 'intelligent' decision about where to route a call.

- *Mix and match*. Mix and match the options to meet identified need. You can, for example, issue personal DDI numbers to your best clients. Then when they phone, your system will route them to your terminal, put their details on your screen and you can answer with confidence 'Good afternoon Customer X. How can we help you today?'

INDIVIDUALITY – WILL IT SURVIVE?

There is still a strong cultural need for individuality. Within the EU there is a major problem with inadequate air traffic control equipment and systems. Unfortunately all countries agree there is urgent need for improvement – but all want to upgrade via their system!

Skies over northern Europe are filling with aircraft, the control systems cannot cope, but politicians squabble rather than compromise. There is obvious encouragement, therefore, for electronics companies to agree commonality (as with the Philips audio tape and the VHS video tape), and in time (hopefully) to remove the blocks coming from purely national interests.

Communication technology is opening the world and people are now divided by time rather than by distance.

Within the global village concept is unionism replacing nationalism? Will the EU and ASEAN and NAFTA replace the countries that form them? Or will the countries give way to their constituent regions? There seems clear evidence that the trend is back towards regions. The evidence is the break-up of the USSR, Czechoslovakia and Yugoslavia and the Basque demands for autonomy within Spain. Will such tiny units be more inclined (or less?) to support the trading blocks? Will it be possible for any individual country, let alone region, to survive as an independent unit as the global trend to standardisation and joint ventures gathers speed?

KEY POINT SUMMARY

- IT is the key to global development.
- The GATT protocol may mean a further division of richer from poorer.
- Global giants are likely to force smaller firms to settle for less.
- Market global – make local.
- Target proactively.
- Market brands to innovative customers.
- Unless you're running all the time, you're gone.
- Marketing must: restructure and/or clarify objectives; identify/redefine target markets; reinforce/reposition; identify/capitalise on technology; operate sound marketing strategies and tactics.
- The 'global village' is with us: be alive to the environment; try to predict/change the environment; use media well; let the audience participate; tell the story in depth.
- Division is by time, not distance.
- Containerisation speeds up and simplifies transhipment.
- Information flows faster than products.
- Communication technology is revolutionising business.
- Satellites allow global communication.
- Marketing communicators must cope with cultural differences when promoting a brand.
- Broadcasting is open, general communication.
- Narrowcasting is via cable to individuals in their home, etc.
- Direct Line Insurance have broken the mould of insurance sales through innovation.
- It is essential to get up to date, to keep abreast of developments and to keep ahead of competition.
- There is still a strong cultural need for individuality.
- Is unionism replacing nationalism?
- Will it be possible for any individual to survive as an independent unit?
- The global trend to standardisation and joint ventures is gathering speed.

WORK-, SCHOOL- AND COLLEGE-BASED ASSIGNMENTS

You will enjoy carrying out these assignments . . . they are intended to provide you with the basis of an on-going, regular and routine involvement in the developments that are of such crucial importance.

1 Targeting is vitally important, as we know. What criteria could you use to differentiate between two identical twin girls who achieved the same English degree at the same university, share the same religion, live in identical side by side four bedroom semi-detached houses, are happily married and have twin sons born within a day?

2 Take a walk through a good newsagent, turn the pages on your radio and TV programme guide. Keep your eyes open in the street, in shops and on public transport. Identify the targeted media that you encounter.

3 To set yourself up as a major source on future potential all you have to do is scan the quality press, the marketing trade press and, in particular, the computer magazines to be sure that you are up to date on technology, both in use and planned. It is an exciting area that is well documented, and as it impacts so dynamically on your life, as a marketer and as a private person it is an important and worthwhile on-going activity.

   It is an activity which you need to maintain for as far into the future as you care to plan.

4 Be as imaginative as you possibly can – presume that anything you want can be available. Select at random some activity with which you are not familiar. Not an overall business, some aspect of business or social life.

   Then design the changes that could be possible. How could the activity be made more valuable through the use of technology?

   (The random example used in the suggested assistance is a taxi-cab.)

SUGGESTED ASSISTANCE TO SELF-ASSESSMENT QUESTIONS FOR CHAPTERS 32–35

WORK-, SCHOOL- AND COLLEGE-BASED QUESTIONS

Chapter 32

1 You will have needed help because the viewpoint of the opposite six is crucial. Men and women are placed differently in the culture of each country and can find the expectations and standards of another culture quite bewildering.

You should have a very detailed checklist that covers issues such as:

- Language   Idiomatic English is very different to textbook English.
- Laws and customs   What must be done, what is acceptable behaviour.
- Dress   To meet the needs of varying circumstances.
- Expectations   Of bosses, teachers, colleagues, people in the service industry.
- Money   What it is really worth, where to get the best value.
- Prices   Benchmark indications
- Medical methods   Some like their medicine as tablets, others as injections, some prefer suppositories.
- Medical help   Doctors, dentists, hospitals.
- Emergency services   Medical, fire, police – and what to expect from them.
- Hours   Of work, of shop opening, of social activities, etc.
- etc., etc.

Chapter 33

1 Don't worry if you didn't get many at first. They are complex and confusing! You should have looked up the answers already. . . here they are for those who haven't.

ASEAN	Association of South East Asian countries
BIFA	British International Freight Association
BOTB	British Overseas Trade Board
CIF	Carriage Insurance & Freight
CIM	Chartered Institute of Marketing
DTI	Department of Trade and Industry
EC	European Commission (*not* the European Community)
ECGD	Export Credit Guarantee Department
ECU	European Currency Unit
EDI	Electronic Data Interchange
EEA	European Economic Area
EFTA	European Free Trade Association
ERM	Exchange Rate Mechanism
EU	European Union
FAS	Free Alongside Ship
FOB	Free on Board
FOR	Free on Rail
GATS	General Agreement on Trade in Services
GATT	General Agreement on Tariffs and Trade
IT	Information Technology

LCCI	London Chamber of Commerce and Industry
MFN	Most Favoured Nation
MR	Marketing Research
OECD	Organisation for Economic Co-operation and Development
PR	Public Relations
SEM	Single European Market
STEEPLE	Social/Cultural; Technological; Economic and Market; Education, Training, Employment; Political; Legal; Environmental.
USFTA	United States Free Trade Association

2
Ad valorem	A tariff calculated as a percentage of the value of the goods at port of entry.
Commission agent	Do not hold stock, but take orders which they pass through for processing.
Del credere agent	Works on commission. Carries stocks. Accepts credit risks.
Dumping	Getting rid of surplus production overseas.
Franco domicile	The exporter pays all charges to the importer's place of business. The favoured method for overseas buyers.
Stocking agent	Carries stocks and makes deliveries within a minimum time.
Tariff	Financial barriers to trade – taxes.

Chapter 34

1 As a manager you should have been able to quantify many of the options, but did you remember to take the subjective elements into account? Both scaler and non-scaler techniques are needed to effectively rank the options.

2 Let us assume that you have reduced your holiday choice to two alternatives, sun and beach or sun and snow. Then your thinking may go along lines something like Table 34.1.

Table 34.1

SUN & BEACH		SUN & SNOW	
Advantages	Disadvantages	Advantages	Disadvantages
Good hot sun, get a lovely tan.	Skin cancer?	Good hot sun, get a lovely tan.	Skin cancer. Only on hands and face.
Water sports. Not too expensive. Spending money available.	Friend doesn't swim. Crowded. Air traffic delays?	Friend loves skiing. Top of my budget.	I don't ski. Restricted spending money.
Relatively safe. Insurance costs low.	Less excitement. None.	Thrilling. Insurance available.	Relatively unsafe. Relatively expensive.
Can go almost anytime	But budget may restrict choice.	None.	Limited season to choose from.
Equipment costs low.	None.	Can rent.	Equipment costs high.
Plenty of food.	Basic.	Excellent food.	Pricey. Etc.

When your thinking is complete only you can evaluate the relative values of each aspect of the decision . . . but whatever you decide, it means that another option cannot be taken up.

This, of course, is exactly the process that every customer and consumer passes through – but it takes a professional buyer to recognise it – and a professional marketer to provide for it in terms of built-in customer and consumers benefits.

Chapter 35

1 There are so many differentiation criteria that can be used. Some examples are given in Table 35.2.

Table 35.2

Criteria	Twin 1		Twin 2	
	Herself	*Husband*	*Herself*	*Husband*
Employment	Librarian	Surgeon	Restaurateur	Banker
Car	Fiesta	BMW	Peugeot 505	Rover
Sports	Tennis	Tennis	None	Golf
Hobbies	Cookery	Wines	Gardening	War Games
Holidays	Sun & Sand	Climbing	Winter Sports	
Credit card(s)	Access	Access (Gold)	AMEX	Visa

2 You should have been overwhelmed because all media today are targeted to some degree. But did you notice the way in which broadband media are targeting themselves? The BBC, for example, produce programmes especially for different types of physically handicapped people; they have programmes targeted by race/colour/culture; their Woman's Hour is itself split into segments that appeal to different types of women.

The commercial slots on ITV are themselves targeted, with each profiled so that advertisers can maximise the OTS of their designated target audiences. There are national and regional TV and radio programmes that target local audiences by time of day and listening/viewing preferences.

Advertising is carried inside as well as outside buses. Is it targeted differently? Are the advertisements on the metro targeted differently again? Do the rail or bus tickets carry advertising? Perhaps a special offer at a local store?

Is your milk carton carrying advertising? In the UK eggs are now being used as media with advertisements printed on them at the cleaning, sorting and packing stage. In France a special offer has been 11 fresh eggs and a free chocolate egg packed within the standard box that holds a dozen eggs.

How do shops target their customers whilst they are on the premises? Do they plan their whole image to attract the type of customer they want to serve?

What direct mail do you receive? How were you selected? Why were you targeted? How many of the marketers profiled you correctly? . . . We could go on, but the point is made.

Whilst working on this assignment did you consider the state of mind of the targeted individuals? Would they have been relaxed and particularly receptive? Were they tense, concerned? Rushing through breakfast to catch their train? Driving through heavy traffic? Why is it that flight insurance is sold from machines in airport departure lounges?

Once the target audience is identified the job is just beginning! There is then need to structure the communication so that it attracts attention – the right kind of attention – delivers the message – makes the intended impact.

3 Seeing opportunities for the use of technology ahead of the competition can give you a huge competitive edge.

- A chemist wholesaler introduced ordering by computer and modem two years before it became routine. The effectiveness of the service increased dramatically and the sales team were reduced in number and changed from order takers into sellers.
- A big London advertising agency used their video studios for sales training whilst VTRs were the routine equipment in use, video couldn't be edited, and camcorders had not even been dreamed of, i.e. back in the dark ages of 1964.
- British Airways designed, pioneered and perfected the first airline reservation system using an expert system that has given them not only a competitive edge but also ancillary sales of consultancy and a bookings service for other airlines.

What uses can you foresee for the up-coming new technology?

4 Taking a taxi-cab as the random example we could imagine a cab of the not too distant future having:
For the passenger:

- on board phone, fax, modem socket;
- satellite TV, radio, on-line video;
- commercials narrowcast from in-cab, or broadcast from the cab's HQ;
- frequent user's clubs bringing special benefits;
- VDUs showing routes and showing mileage, waiting time, fare details, etc.;
- credit card slot for automatic payment – no cash ever accepted;
- refreshments;
- climate controls;
- shoe cleaning machine built in under the seat.

For the driver:

- security locks and safety cage (protects passengers too);
- crash prevention override;
- cruise controls;
- video maps that indicate the best route in real time, so avoiding traffic jams;
- video cameras to record passenger, for security;
- a 'black box' and video camera as evidence in the event of accident;
- full video contact with the controller, of course!

PART 10

Qualify in marketing –
the basis for career development

Marketing is a serious profession which is gaining in recognition and status by the day. It used to be regarded as simply advertising and sales, and much of management thinking about marketing has been internally centred – hence the titles product manager and brand manager.

This internal focus is changing rapidly to an understanding that marketing must penetrate and permeate the entire organisation. Hence we are finding qualified professionals from other functions studying for and acquiring a marketing qualification. Accountants, lawyers, health professionals, educationalists – all are appreciating the need to be recognised as professional marketers.

It is obviously good to have this depth of marketing understanding in organisations, but it will put extra pressure on the marketing professionals to become not only highly skilled in marketing strategies and tactics – they must also extend their understanding of the other functions within an organisation.

Both the Chartered Institute of Marketing and the London Chamber of Commerce and Industry have recognised this fact, and both have introduced new syllabi in 1994.

The LCCI
The new LCCI Level 3 marketing syllabus has a strong management content, and 50% of the questions set in each examination require candidates to show a management understanding. The title of this book, *Marketing in Management*, shows how the emphasis has changed from the management of marketing. Marketing is without question a major management activity in any organisation.

Level 3 marketing remains the lead paper in the LCCI Marketing Higher Diploma, which also requires candidates to pass three examinations chosen from (1) advertising, (2) public relations, (3) selling and sales management and (4) purchasing.

The LCCI are introducing a new Level 2 marketing syllabus. This is targeted to help younger and would-be marketers to show they have the necessary understanding to make valuable employees. Question papers, marking schemes and examiner's reports are included in Appendices A–C.

The CIM
Syllabus '94 has totally revised the CIM's examinations. Gone are the traditional knowledge-centred subjects. In their place are action-centred syllabi which lead

to examination papers that require candidates to show they can practise marketing, and that they have much more than simple understanding of principles and theories.

The new CIM structure is:

- Certificate in Marketing:
  - business communications;
  - understanding customers;
  - marketing environment;
  - marketing fundamentals.
- Advanced Certificate in Marketing:
  - promotional practice;
  - management information for marketing and sales;
  - effective management for marketing;
  - marketing operations.
- Advanced Certificate in Sales Management:
  - sales communication practice;
  - management information for marketing and sales;
  - effective management for sales;
  - sales operations.
- Diploma in Marketing:
  - marketing communications strategy;
  - international marketing management strategy;
  - strategic marketing management:
    - planning and control;
    - analysis and decision, the case study.

Registered Marketer

The first Registered Marketers earned the designation in the year 1993/94. Full members of the CIM, they undertook an organised programme of continuing professional development to show that they remain committed leading edge marketers.

All the evidence is that marketing is a major force in organisations of all kinds, and that a qualified marketing professional can look forward to a career full of opportunity.

CHAPTER 36

Passing a marketing examination

Tung Kuo-Feng is seventeen and looking for a job in marketing. He has secured an interview and the manager behind the desk says 'There are two others who are short-listed for this job, what are the main reasons why you should be successful?' Tung answers immediately:

'Because I have a track record of hard work, and I hold the LCCI Level 2 marketing qualification.'

Tung Kuo-Feng is nineteen and looking for a better job in marketing. He has secured an interview and the manager behind the desk says 'There are two others who are short-listed for this job, what are the main reasons why you should be successful?' Tung answers immediately: 'Because I have a track record in marketing, and I hold the LCCI Higher Diploma in Marketing.'.

Tung Kuo-Feng is twenty-one and looking for a better job in marketing. He has secured an interview and the manager behind the desk says 'There are two others who are short-listed for this job, what are the main reasons why you should be successful?' Tung answers immediately: 'Because I have an excellent track record in marketing, and I hold the LCCI Higher Diploma in Marketing and the CIM Certificate in Marketing.'

Tung Kuo-Feng in twenty-two and looking for a junior marketing management post. He has secured an interview and the manager behind the desk says 'There are two others who are short-listed for this job, what are the main reasons why you should be successful?' Tung answers immediately:

'Because I have an excellent track record in marketing, and I hold the CIM Advanced Certificate in Marketing.'.

Tung Kuo-Feng is twenty-three and looking for a brand manager's post. He has secured an interview and the manager behind the desk says 'There are two others who are short-listed for this job, what are the main reasons why you should be successful?' Tung answers immediately: 'Because I have an excellent track record in marketing, and I am an Associate Member of the Chartered Institute of Marketing and I hold their Diploma in Marketing.'.

Tung Kuo-Feng is twenty-six and looking for a senior marketing management post. He has secured an interview and the manager behind the desk says 'There are two others who are short-listed for this job, what are the main reasons why you should be successful?' Tung answers immediately:

'Because of my marketing success at strategic and tactical levels, and because I am a Corporate Member of the Chartered Institute of Marketing and I hold their Diploma in Marketing.'

Tung Kuo-Feng is thirty and looking for a marketing director's post. He has secured an interview and the manager behind the desk says 'There are two others who are short-listed for this job, what are the main reasons why you should be successful?' Tung answers immediately:

'Because of my marketing success at strategic and tactical levels, and because I am a Registered Marketer.'

Tung Kuo-Feng is forty and the managing director of a very successful manufacturing company that brings in valuable foreign exchange as it trades 90% overseas. His wife brings the morning's mail to the breakfast table . . . 'Congratulations', she says, 'you have just been invited to become a Fellow of the Chartered Institute of Marketing. You deserve the accolade!'

QUALIFICATION

Professionals need to be qualified. It is the one certain way to show that one has a professional competence that is based on both theory and practical ability. To start with, of course, competence is based more on theory than on practical experience, but with time the balance shifts.

It is very important indeed to always test theoretical understanding against practical results – and then to redefine the theory if necessary. Theories are guidance, results are reality!

Motivation

Why take a marketing examination? Surely there can be only one reason . . to pass it!

A more useful question is 'Why do you want to pass a marketing examination?' The answer to this question is the key to your success. If you don't have a good reason to pass you will not be motivated to succeed. You are not likely to prepare for the exam, and you are very likely to fail! What a shame!

Underpinning everything else has to be a sense of purpose. Why do you want to pass? What is the benefit to *you*?

For most people a marketing examination is a stepping stone to a better job, to a career. Employers are able to pick from many applicants, and those with qualifications and experience have a better chance of being selected.

Until you are sure that you know why you want to pass . . .why it is worth doing the necessary work to learn the subject . . . why it is worth turning up on the examination day . . . until you are motivated . . there is little point in bothering. Take some time now to write down your objectives. What is it you intend to achieve?

Your objectives might look something like this:

MY OBJECTIVES
Strategic:
To, within six months, have secured a job as a junior marketing manager.

Tactical

Job:

Immediate: To start a job search to determine the type of vacancy that exists and the qualifications and experience asked for.
To begin acquiring the necessary experience through part-time and voluntary work.

3 months: To begin applying for jobs, with confidence.

6 months: To be in suitable employment

Academic:

Immediate: To locate a suitable course of study leading to an examination that meets my needs.

1 month: To have started serious study.

5 months: To start revision ahead of the examination(s).

6 months: To provide the examiner with a paper that meets the examiner's requirements.

8 months: To receive confirmation that I have passed.

It follows that I must:
— Understand what the examiner requires.
— Prepare to provide *exactly* what is needed.
— Practice in answering typical questions.

Understand and use

The examiner sets out to test marketing knowledge and the ability to put knowledge to use. He must be shown that you know and understand marketing principles. That you can use them in context.

Material which is used is kept in the forefront of the mind. Current telephone numbers are automatically remembered . . . but those used only occasionally have to be looked up in the directory. Learning can only be *effective learning* if it remains in the mind.

To 'learn' something and then forget it again quickly is not true learning. It is simply putting something into short-term memory without the motivation to transfer it into long-term memory. Your short-term memory is very useful in everyday life, but not for the amount of material needed to satisfy a marketing examiner. You have to learn to store material in your long-term memory.

You have control over what you remember. Your mind responds to your direction. If you want something in your long-term memory you have to show your mind that it is important. Anything not flagged as important is disregarded – and 'forgotten'.

To flag material as important the mind has to see that you both understand and use the material. Understanding and use come together into the Double U principle.

The Double U

The Double U principle works throughout life. Our minds allocate importance in direct ratio to use. Therefore plan your learning so that you immediately use what you learn. It is wasteful to simply read and memorise material. That can be boring – and certainly does not give your mind any reason to store your 'learning' away long-term. In fact it may not even stay in your mind overnight!

Make your learning fun. Test it against practical examples . . .

* Take a TV advertisement and think through why it is being shown, to whom it is targeted, what positioning statement it comes from, etc.
* In the supermarket check out the different sales promotions that are running. If you were selling into the store what could you do to make your products stand out?
* How would you repackage a product you use regularly to make it easier to open, and/or to use?
* How would you raise money for a local charity? Would this be different to raising money for a national charity, or for one overseas?
* Are the campaigns for a healthier lifestyle effective? If not, why not? What could you do that would be better? Why are the current marketers not doing what you think they could?

Evaluating theories in practical use gives you a powerful insight you will never get from textbooks and academic study. It also gives you examples to enliven your answer papers in the exam room.

Recapitulation

Your learning needs to be kept current. Think of your mind as a store cupboard. You can get long-term memories safely onto the shelf, but they will stay there and gather dust if you don't do some housekeeping regularly.

All you have to do is review your notes every time you begin to study. Tony Buzan has made a major study of learning and has clearly shown that those who review their work can retain eight times as much as those who do not (see Figure 36.1)!

Learn by association

When learning, look for ways to help you remember. Marketing is full of acronyms that are easier to remember than the terms they stand for. It becomes even easier when you can *associate* the acronyms. Visual association works best, but so do rhythm, rhyme, striking examples and fun. The trick is to show your mind that you feel this is worth remembering.

* Each of the four CATS is occupied in the criterion he represents.
* There is a lookout on the STEEPLE to make the illustration come alive.
* Most people can remember SWOT easily because it is such a punchy word – and the audit that comes from it is fun to do.
* MBO and MBE are usually remembered together because they have a kind of rhythm when linked.

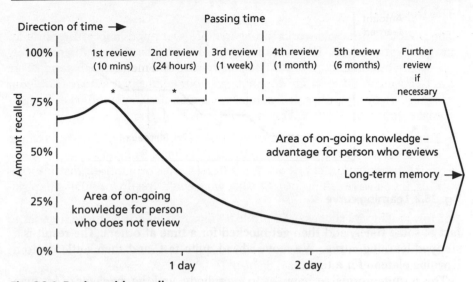

Fig. 36.1 Review aids recall
Source: Buzan T, *Use Your Head*, BBC Books. Reproduced with kind permission.

Take time to create an association for everything you want to remember. Something that makes it really stand out in your mind. The more outrageous the better because our brains respond like little children to bright colours and loud noises. Take a few moments to relate a new theory to your existing knowledge, then deliberately open up your senses to look for examples of it in use. The more you open up to new experiences that more you will notice, and the easier they will be to cope with.

Revision notes

Set up your notes so that they are full of key points that trigger a mental response.

Triggers work best when they are unique to you and therefore link into your learning style. Create them as associative links which your subconscious mind can identify and locate.

With a system of triggers you will find that you suddenly have a better memory! You haven't of course, but you are now beginning to use it effectively.

In an active system of revision you should reduce your notes to their key points, using the triggers as the spur to your memory. You will find that the key point triggers are all you will need. Your mind will automatically run through its index and pull up the information associated with each trigger.

Let the 'penny drop'

Learning is not a steady progression. When the amount learned is plotted against time the result is not a straight line. We each learn at our own speed, and we find some things easier than others. Therefore we move ahead quite

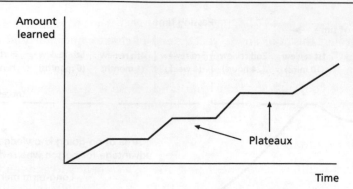

Fig. 36.2 Learning curve

fast at some times, and then get blocked for a time at others. The result is a stepped learning curve. We move ahead quite fast, and then settle on to a learning plateau for a time.

This is quite normal, it happens to everybody, and the manager of his own learning comes to expect the plateaux and does not panic!

It is also normal to suddenly find something come clear. This is called a 'Gestalt' experience and is the result of a whole series of stimuli suddenly being sorted in your brain. You suddenly see how materials interrelate where previously they had only confused you. 'Oh yes! I see now.'

Practice

Sports people train before any event, and they warm up before every training session and before every race. Their bodies work so much more effectively if time is taken to loosen the muscles, to focus the mind and the body on to the task in hand.

In just the same way a person working with their mind should warm it up and help it to focus before putting it under stress. The first few minutes of any session must be devoted to getting a focus, and then working up to speed. If you analyse your own behaviour you will discover that you do this anyway. You have to because your internal systems force a period of adjustment on to you.

Recognise that you have to make an adjustment – it is then easier to see that with a planned adjustment you will be under control, more effectively, and more quickly. You will no longer be confused by trying to do something for which your mind is not yet ready.

Reviewing your notes is a fine way to get into the swing of learning, and has a major synergistic effect because it also boosts your recall and confidence with the subject.

Revise actively

Revision is *not* sitting for hours on end reading and re-reading textbooks. Active revision is putting your skills and knowledge into a practical context.

A very good way to revise is through planning answers to typical questions. Go back through this book and re-visit the end-of-chapter questions and assignments. Work out answers to the questions you didn't tackle before (it doesn't matter if they are work-, school- or college-based – try them).

Then check your answers from your notes. Only if there is need, go back and check from your books. Build trust in yourself.

Student or candidate?

There is a major difference between your role as a student and as a candidate.

A student is concerned to take in knowledge, to acquire new skills and abilities. A candidate has to bring out the appropriate knowledge, and illustrate it with the best examples. A candidate has to work under time pressure knowing that he gets only once chance.

You must practise your role as a candidate? Would you learn to play chess from a book and then enter a tournament and expect to do well? Would you study a street map of a city and expect to find your way round as easily as a city dweller? Of course not.

As a candidate you have to take note of what the examiner is asking, and then to supply answers that go to the heart of each question. This is a skill that can be learned – but it is *not* one that students have naturally. You have to consciously plan to turn yourself from a student into a candidate.

What must a candidate do?

A candidate must:

- arrive at the examination centre in good time;
- be fully equipped;
- impress the examiner with a neatly presented answer book;
- select the most appropriate questions from those offered;
- understand exactly what is required as an answer to each question;
- illustrate theory with practical examples;
- manage time so that each question is answered fully.

To change from a student to a candidate it is therefore necessary to practice the skills of answer planning, time management and presentation. There is no substitute for practice!

Common failings

Time and again, over decades, examiners report the same failings in candidates. Typical comments are:

- A common weakness was when candidates did not answer the question and wandered off into irrelevant answers.
- Some candidates had memorised information which they tried to force into answers no matter how irrelevant it was.

- Many misread or misunderstood the questions and their answers had nothing to do with the questions asked.
- It was difficult to award marks because the standards of presentation were very poor and we cannot mark what we cannot read.
(See Appendix C.)

The examination paper

A marketing examiner is concerned to test a candidate's ability as a marketer. This means that a high standard of presentation will be expected – marketers are communicators above all else.

Candidates may be asked questions from any part of the syllabus, but they do not have to know the whole syllabus in order to pass. Even although the examiner can select any part of the syllabus as a base for his questions it is still necessary to ask a range of questions from across the syllabus.

Often the candidate has a choice of questions. Perhaps question one is compulsory, but there is then a choice of four questions from a further nine offered.

It should be difficult to fail because the candidate can choose his questions, and even then does not have to achieve more than 50% to pass!

50% requirement

Candidates need only secure 50% of the marks from the questions they choose. This is simple for the well-prepared candidate.

The key to success is to analyse each question and identify the key points that must be made. Marks are attached to the key points, and help the examiner to find them easily. Compare these two examples of presentation. Which would you rather mark if you were an examiner? Which would more easily get the higher marks?

Example 1

A promotional budget may be established in several ways. There is the percentage of sales. which is a crude measure. All you can afford. which may be the only choice if resources are limited. Competitive parity. which is also crude. but used frequently – especially by sales dominated companies who feel they 'have to be equal in the marketplace' but without knowing why. Finally there is Objective & Task. which is an ideal solution that is very hard to apply in 'real-life'.

Example 2

> A promotional budget may be established in several ways:
> - *Percentage of sales*   – *a crude measure.*
> - *All you can afford*   – *which may be the only choice if resources are limited.*
> - *Competitive parity*   – *also crude. but used frequently - especially by sales dom-*
>   *inated companies who feel they 'have to be equal in the*
>   *marketplace' but without knowing why.*
> - *Objective & Task*   – *an ideal solution that is very hard to apply in 'real life'.*

Example 1 is a direct quote from a student's assignment. Do you feel that he/she answered adequately if the bad presentation is ignored? The tutor gave 3 out of 5. The explanations of the first two budget types are superficial.

Check your work

As you develop the skills to become a candidate check the quality of your work. Use these checklists (developed by Angela Hatton) to see how far you have met the examiner's needs, and to determine what you need to do to improve the probability of a good pass in the examination.

EXAMINATION CHECKLISTS

Turn the pages on your work:

1. Is it well laid out?	Yes	No
2. Have you used report format?	Yes	No
3. Underlining by ruler?	Yes	No
4. Plenty of white space?	Yes	No
5. No red nor green ink?	Yes	No
6. Does it look professionally credible?	Yes	No
7. Can someone else read it easily?	Yes	No
8. Would you accept it from one of your staff?	Yes	No
9. Would you submit it to your boss?	Yes	No

Now turn back to the question paper and read it again. Check your answers against the questions . . .

1. Does your answer reflect the weighing of marks given to each section?	Yes	No
2. Does each answer *directly* respond to the question asked?	Yes	No
3. Do your answers contain:		
Quantified objectives?	Yes	No
Clarification of assumptions?	Yes	No
Time scales?	Yes	No
Clear decisions?	Yes	No
Recommended actions?	Yes	No
4. Are your decisions practical and realistic?	Yes	No
5. Would a line manager regard the answer as competent?	Yes	No

---

Presentation

It takes practice to write clearly, and to lay out work effectively. But there is little point in submitting excellent work that is difficult to read. If you have bad handwriting, and especially if you spread onto the lines above and below, you must take action. Write on every other line if you have to – but it is better to learn to write more clearly.

Get a second opinion on your written work, see if others can read it. Then practice until you reach an acceptable standard.

Always draw diagrams with a ruler – never use freehand sketches.

Always label the axes of graphs and diagrams. Full marks can only be awarded to complete answers.

Answer choice

It is very important to select the questions that you are going to answer – and to forget those that you are not! The tick, cross and question technique sorts questions for you:

1 With *pencil* in hand read down the questions very quickly. Don't try to analyse them or ponder over them.
2 Against each put either a tick, a cross or a question mark. (A tick means you can do the question, a cross 'no way', a question mark 'maybe'.)
3 Count the ticks. If you have three or more you have a paper, and can pass.
4 Count the question marks – if you have a further two you have a paper with which you can do well.
5 Ignore *totally* the crosses. For you they *don't exist*. They are not a problem, and must not get in your way.

In three minutes you have established how good a pass you can get – and have disposed of all the negative effects of questions that you can't answer.

If you have six ticks you can choose which five to answer. Any combination of two, three or four ticks plus three, two or one question marks focuses you on to your answers. Remember, you can pass with only three tick questions. Here's how:

Each question = 20 marks. Pass = 50% (50 marks).

Ticked questions – you achieve 15 marks each	$3 \times 15 = 45$ marks	
Question marks – you achieve 8 marks each	$2 \times 8 = 16$ marks	
Total	= 61 marks.	
Safety margin	= 11 marks.	

Even on 'cross' questions, if you are forced to tackle one, you will pick up a mark or two. So the worst scenario could be:

Ticked questions	2×15	=	30
Question marks	2×8	=	16
Crosses	1×4	=	4
Total		=	50

But you should do better on question marks than 8 out of 20!

Answer preparation

You will know very quickly which questions you are going to answer. Now you have to maximise the marks for each question. Many people find this hard to do – but the technique pays off so well that it is worth taking the time and effort to build the needed confidence.

Plan all answers together

Do *not* start to answer right away. All around you the other candidates will be writing answers – but you need to plan your answers to all questions before you start to write answers. Why?

- Spread your knowledge across your answers.
  Better to score 14 on all the questions than to have a couple of 18s and then an 8, a 6 and a 2! Don't use all your material in the first two answers!
- Spark better answers.
  In the planning of answer three you will be reminded of something that can go into one or two. If you had already written these answers it would be too late!
- Concentrate.
  Better results come from concentration. Do one thing at a time. Concentrate on answer planning and then on answer writing. The alternative is to keep switching from planning to writing and back again and this prevents you settling into a rhythm.

Use of time

Examinations vary in the time allowed, and the number of questions to be answered. You must know in advance what form your examination takes. Then you can prepare to manage your time. If the examination was 5 questions of 20 marks each, in three hours, a good time plan would be:

0–2 minutes	Tick, cross, question mark.
2–6	Select ticks and question marks.
6–30	Plan answers to all questions on one double page spread in the middle of the answer book.
	Shift material around between questions so that it is used to best advantage.
30–85	Write the two answers that will most impress the examiner. (Good content, right style, well presented.)
85–90	Break. Stretch, relax, have a drink, look round, feel good.
90–170	Write three answers.
170–180	Read through and correct.
	Write the numbers of the questions you have answered in the boxes on the cover of the answer book.

Check that your name and number are on the answer book and on all the sheets, and that any extra sheets are tied into the book.

Answer planning

You need to look for two things:

- What *content* is required.
- The *style* you have to use.

Planning of content must be done in *context*. If you do not take time to identify the context you will very easily go off track when writing the content.

For example, the same material can be used to answer a basic marketing question – but it would need to be used differently if the *context* were a profit-making commercial enterprise, a not-for-profit activity such as a school fete or a public sector organisation such as a hospital.

The style must be as called for. Essays are not usually wanted in professional papers. Read the question carefully. If the examiner asks for a report, a memo, a letter, a letter, that is exactly what you write. Write a report if no style is directly specified.

It follows, of course, that you have to learn how to write in business style, and that you have to practise the various forms of business communication.

Answers should have an introduction, a middle and an end. Content should be in context to the question.

An easy way to plan an answer is to use three columns. For example, for the question 'Write a letter to a friend explaining how they can use direct response marketing to extend their business', a possible answer plan is:

Table 36.1 Answer plan

	Context	*Content*
Introduction	LETTER. Extend business.	Hello. Congratulations. Potential.
Middle	Direct response marketing.	Define DRM. Examples: mail, tele, fax, TV, radio.
	Selling at a distance.	FREEPOST, Freephone, 0500/0800. Payment methods, cheques, credit cards.
End	Offer help.	Cost-effective if managed well.
	LETTER CLOSE.	Detailed help available.

Appendix A contains the syllabus for the LCCIEB's Level 3 marketing examination.* You will see that it calls for candidates to show that they understand marketing at a strategic as well as a tactical level. Marketing is a dynamic subject and so the syllabus reminds candidates of the need to keep up to date through 'planned exposure to appropriate media'. To succeed it is necessary to show that you are alert to what is happening in your home market.

Appendix B is a question paper which is typical of those set at LCCIEB Level 3. Candidates have 3 hours to answer Question 1 and 4 others. Note that Question 1 is always in the same format, and is *compulsory*.

- The same format means that you know you will have to show how marketing strategy and tactics are used. The organisation that candidates are asked to 'work for' changes and so there is a need to understand how management adapts to different environments and to the long-, medium- and short-term requirements of different markets.
- 'Compulsory' means that the question *must* at least be attempted. No attempt means an automatic fail! But knowing the structure of the question in advance should help you to guarantee excellent marks and get you away to a flying start.

You have the opportunity to set up a mock examination for yourself and to evaluate your areas of strengths and weaknesses. Just as fighter pilots spend hours in flight simulators to sharpen their skills so should you take time to practise the skills you need to pass your examination.

Appendix C is typical of the marking scheme that a Chief Examiner provides for the examining team. Use it along with the checklists earlier in this chapter to evaluate how well you understand the subject . . . and how well you have presented your answers. It is good sense to ask an experienced friend or colleague to take the answer plan and rate your work against it – that way you will pick up areas of weakness whilst there is time to correct them.

The day of the examination

The most important thing is to control panic. It is very easy to say, but very hard to do because all candidates are bound to be nervous.

It is good to be nervous – that shows that you are keyed up, sharp, concerned. It is bad to be scared, or in a flap (or a panic) – that shows that you are not ready, that you have not worked as you should have.

If you think about it for a moment it becomes obvious why you are nervous:

- You are putting yourself at risk.
- You are going into the unknown.
- You are going into an atmosphere of stress and tension.
- You badly want to do well.

It is the same for everybody . . . but those who do best understand what is happening to them, and to actively control and focus the nervous energy your

---

*The LCCIEB Level 2 marketing examination is expected to become available in 1995.

body makes available to you. As soon as you settle with the exam paper your nerves will vanish – it is just a question of getting through until then.

The basic rules

- Find out the examination centre's location well in advance. If possible visit it to check it out, and to confirm the journey details.
- Buy your tickets at least the day before.
- Wear comfortable loose clothing, and have several layers so you can regulate your temperature.
- List the equipment you will need well ahead of time and prepare two easy-to-carry bags – one can fit inside the other. You will need to pack under two headings:
  - What you need on the day – basic day-to-day materials; packed lunch; revision notes for the exam, and perhaps for a second exam in the afternoon. This bag will have to be placed at the front of the exam room.
  - What you need in the exam – specialised materials, e.g. pens, pencils, rulers, calculator, etc. You can keep this bag on your desk or table so you should include some sweets and a small and carefully sealed drink or whatever is going to help you through the length of the exam. Do not include anything that might upset other candidates (apples are noisy, oranges smelly and messy).
- Be careful about mascots. Your confidence can be shattered if your forget a mascot!
- Always have a breakfast, even if you normally do not. This is not a normal day and your system needs extra sustenance.
- Leave good time for your journey, better to be one train too early than one train too late!
- Run through your revision notes one last time to occupy yourself on the journey – but everything you are going to know you know already so try to relax.
- Don't hang around with other candidates. They are likely to upset your peace of mind, and that has to be your prime concern.
- Take possession of your part of the exam room. It will be your home for three crucial hours and you want to feel in charge. It is worth physically moving your table and chair – even a couple of inches movement is enough to let you feel they are where you want them to be.
- Write your personal details on the outside of the answer book while there is no pressure before the examination begins. Take considerable trouble to write neatly.

General hints and tips

- Always make an attempt at the required number of questions. Give the examiner the opportunity to allocate even a single mark . . . and you may end up with 50 pass and not 49 fail.

- Make it easy for the examiner. With up to 800 answer books to review an examiner naturally is in a hurry. Those books that are user-friendly generate a feeling of warmth.

  You would visit a customer with a smile on your face – your answer book should make a good impression on the examiner before he or she has read a single word.

  Your aim is to make the examiner feel good about your answer book – the one he is to mark next.
- Never use a red or green pen. These are the examiner's colours.
- Always leave good margins so that the examiner can easily find the marks he has given to your work.
- Lay your work out with plenty of white space. It looks better, and can be marked easier.

Preparation is the overall key to success. The successful candidate plans well forward – he does not try to cram material at the last moment. He goes into an examination with a plan of action, and the confidence that his trigger notes and practical experience of the marketplace will give him the theories and examples he needs to make an excellent impression on the examiner.

KEY POINT SUMMARY

- Professional qualifications are important to a career marketer.
- You have to be motivated to study and to pass.
- Set career and study objectives.
- Understand and use – the Double U principle.
- Keep your knowledge current through recapitulation and review.
- Learn by association.
- Prepare for your revision as you make your notes.
- Set up your notes with trigger points.
- Use a system of active revision.
- Wait for the 'penny to drop' – learning is a process of variable speed.
- Practise
- Warm up before study.
- Make the move from student to candidate as you run in to the exam.
- Do what the examiner requires.
- Aim for a good pass using the tick, cross and question mark technique.
- Don't worry about questions you don't want to answer.
- Check your work.
- Present your work as a professional marketer.
- Always draw with a ruler.
- Always label diagrams and graphs.
- Spread your knowledge across the questions.
- Answer with the right content, in the right context, and using the right style.
- Practice with past examination papers, and with questions from this book.
- Take charge on the day of the exam. Get your nerves working for you.
- Attempt the required number of questions.

- Make it easy for the examiner.
- Aim to make the examiner feel good about your answer book.
- Never use a red or a green pen.
- Always leave good margins.
- Lay your work out with plenty of white space.
- Preparation is the overall key to success.

WORK-, SCHOOL- AND COLLEGE-BASED ASSIGNMENTS

These are focused on helping you to prepare to pass your marketing examination.

1 Style and technique
  (a) List *six* aspects of style and/or technique which you are pleased about, and which you will retain and polish.
  (b) Make a list of *four* things which you will improve in your style and/or technique.
  (c) Set clear objectives for improvement, with time targets.
  (d) Review your achievement against each objective.
  (e) Consider what remains to be achieved and set new objectives.

2 Control
  (a) Prepare a detailed action plan for the run in to the examination.
       Start it four weeks before, and set out what you plan to do each day.
       As the examination comes nearer your plan should become more detailed.
       Check your progress regularly, and amend your plan.
  (b) Research the physical details of the examination.
       Determine the route you will take, the times of transport.
       Discover where the exam will be held – a large hall, or a small room?
       Where are refreshments to be obtained? (Especially if you have morning and afternoon examinations.)
  (c) Produce detailed checklists of your needs on the day.
       Do not leave this until the last moment. Do it early and amend it as you think of additions and improvements.
       Note: Review your final checklists after the examination and keep them for next time.

3 Above all – take charge of your learning – of the examination environment – of your success.

Good luck.